THE ENCYCLOPEDIA OF DRUG ABUSE SECOND EDITION

Robert O'Brien, Sidney Cohen, M.D., Glen Evans and James Fine, M.D.

New York • Oxford

THE ENCYCLOPEDIA OF DRUG ABUSE, SECOND EDITION
Robert O'Brien, Sidney Cohen, M.D., Glen Evans and James Fine, M.D.

Facts On File, Inc.
460 Park Avenue South
New York NY 10016

Library of Congress Cataloging-in-Publication Data

Evans, Glen.
The Encyclopedia of drug abuse / Robert O'Brien, Sidney Cohen, Glen Evans, and James Fine.—2nd ed., Rev. and expanded.
p. cm.
Rev. ed. of: Encyclopedia of drug abuse / Robert O'Brien and Sidney Cohen. c1984.
Includes bibliographical references.
ISBN 0-8160-1956-8
1. Drug abuse—Dictionaries. 2. Drugs—Dictionaries.
I. O'Brien, Robert, 1932– II. Cohen, Sidney, 1910–
III. O'Brien, Robert, 1932– The encyclopedia of drug abuse.
IV. Title.
HV5804.E94 1990
362.29'03—dc20 89-71531

Facts On File books are available at special discounts when purchased in bulk quantities for businesses, associations, institutions or sales promotions. Please call our Special Sales Department in New York at 212/683-2244 (dial 800/322-8755 except in NY, AK or HI).
Composition by the Maple-Vail Book Manufacturing Group
Manufactured by Hamilton Printing Company
Printed in the United States of America

10 9 8 7 6 5 4 3 2 1

This book is printed on acid-free paper.

CONTENTS

Sherlock Holmes took his bottle from the corner of the mantelpiece, and his hypodermic syringe from its neat morocco case. With his long, white, nervous fingers he adjusted the delicate needle and rolled back his left shirt cuff. For some time his eyes rested thoughtfully upon the sinewy forearm and wrist, all dotted and scarred with innumerable puncture marks. Finally, he thrust the sharp point home, pressed down the tiny piston, and sank back into the velvet-lined armchair with a long sigh of satisfaction.

—Arthur Conan Doyle,
The Sign of Four (1889)

PREFACE

It has now been more than five years since the late Robert O'Brien, with 30 years experience as an author-editor of many reference books, and the late Sidney Cohen, M.D., former director of the Division of Narcotic Addiction and Drug Abuse, National Institute of Mental Health, compiled and wrote *The Encyclopedia of Drug Abuse*. The publisher, Facts On File, explained that for the first time, in an easy-to-read A-to-Z format, a reference book covered drug abuse from its earliest recorded history to its current state as a major worldwide problem in the late 20th century.

The two highly regarded co-authors designed and researched an in-depth, concise reference covering virtually every significant aspect of the ever-growing drug abuse phenomenon in the United States, as well as in other countries throughout the world. With more than 500 pertinent entries, the Encyclopedia provided extensive data and information on not only drugs and drug abuse, both licit and illicit, but also on the vast number of social institutions, customs and socio-political-economic interrelations that have an impact on drug abuse and are in turn affected by drug abuse. It also described the physical and psychological manifestations of drug use, misuse and abuse.

O'Brien and Dr. Cohen did their work well; the book was an award-winning text that has since proved of great use to the lay person and the professional alike. For the lay reader, the co-authors described the subject as clearly and concisely as possible, avoiding the encumbering distraction of medical jargon or other unfamiliar language. At the same time, they carefully managed to avoid being medically or academically simplistic. They took great care to define and explain technical terms and concepts with precise meanings that needed to be understood to ensure the readers' accurate comprehension.

For professionals working in the field of drug abuse, whatever the specialized focus, O'Brien and Cohen provided sharp, clear statements of familiar material as well as a comprehensive reference whereby elusive facts, data and statistics could be easily found. They also included valuable reference lists after many entries plus a substantial end-of-book bibliography.

The successful work proved to be the equivalent of a "bible" on the subject of drug abuse—unique to the field and meaningful personal interest to lay persons. In the five-plus years since *The Encyclopedia of Drug Abuse* was first published, it has received critical acclaim as both an outstanding informational source and an academic reference book.

Because of the ongoing explosion of new and changing information within the drug abuse field, this revised, expanded, and updated edition is being issued. This current volume is a necessary and vital continuation in a field of information that concerns a major social problem for which the solution is still nowhere in sight.

As the author-editors of the first *Encyclopedia of Drug Abuse* noted in 1984, "Research into drug abuse and the extent of the problem continues to accelerate and new information becomes available almost daily." *The Encyclopedia of Drug Abuse* is a "work in progress," and, of necessity, this updated and any future editions will strive to keep abreast of this most important and ongoing issue.

Glen Evans
Stamford, Connecticut

ACKNOWLEDGMENTS

Because of the enormity and complexity of research for a volume of this sort, many hands come into play. A detailed listing of all those who assisted in supplying information and material for the book would require more space than is available here. However, mention must be made to the cooperative staffs of several federal agencies, bureaus and organizations: Office of the Director, National Drug Control Policy; National Institute on Drug Abuse; Drug Enforcement Administration; Federal Bureau of Investigation; U.S. Department of Justice; Alcohol, Drug Abuse and Mental Health Administration; U.S. Department of Health and Human Services; Office of the White House Conference for a Drug Free America; Food and Drug Administration; House Select Committee on Narcotics Abuse and Control; National Clearinghouse for Alcohol Information; National Clearinghouse for Drug Abuse Information; National Institute on Alcohol Abuse and Alcoholism; National Association of State Alcohol and Drug Abuse Directors; National Council on Alcoholism; U.S. Department of State's Office of International Narcotics Matters; National Highway Transportation Safety Administration; U.S. Public Health Service; Gallop Poll; Roper Organization; Louis Harris Organization; World Health Organization; Addiction Research Foundation (Canada); League of Red Cross Societies; Alcoholics Anonymous; Al-Anon; National Self-Help Clearinghouse; and Public Citizen Inc. (Health Research Group). Also, the various state and provincial (Canadian) agencies, as well as the embassies and agencies of other nations who responded to requests for information.

Glen Evans would like to thank Joyce O'Brien, the widow of Robert O'Brien, for permission to update and expand upon her late husband's work; also, my wife, Margie, and daughter, Lisa, both extremely supportive and generous in their tolerance and encouragement. Further, my thanks to Christina Padgett, whose transcribing, typing and copy reading drafts and final manuscript are always top notch.

And foremost, to my editor and friend, Kate Kelly, who capably directed the monumental task with able help from project editor Neal Maillet.

The word *acknowledgment* simply fails to describe my debt to the above persons and organizations for their essential advice and assistance.

PREFACE TO THE FIRST EDITION

Since the 1950s, drug abuse has become an increasingly disturbing problem throughout the world. *The Encyclopedia of Drug Abuse* has been designed to give an overall view of the issue, with entries ranging from descriptions of the medical and physical effects of drugs, to psychological factors in drug abuse, to political and legal factors, and, since the problem is international, to how widespread drug abuse is around the world and how it is handled in different countries. Additionally, there are appendixes of tabular material concerning use, treatment and traffic and a substantial glossary of street language and slang synonyms for drugs.

The Encyclopedia of Drug Abuse is intended for both the lay person and the professional. We have tried to keep the language simple without becoming simplistic, so that the volume can be used by counselors, educators, and community leaders, as well as by the individual who thinks that he or someone in his family may be facing a drug problem. Whenever a term cannot be simplified, we have tried to define it as clearly as possible.

Drugs and drug abuse are much wider subjects than many people realize, and we have therefore given information about many drugs, not just the "dangerous drugs," such as heroin and cocaine, but substances such as caffeine, nicotine and over-the-counter preparations that have some potential for abuse and can be damaging either physically or psychologically.

Because of the limitations of our format and space, we obviously cannot provide all the information that we would like to. For this reason we have included an extensive bibliography for the reader who needs more information.

While *The Encyclopedia of Drug Abuse* is not the first A to Z volume to appear in the field, it is, to the best knowledge of the editors, the first "encyclopedic" reference. The others are largely devoted to the drugs themselves, without articles on medical and biological aspects, ethnic groups, geographical areas, organizations, laws, and other topics which make up the breadth of the field of drug abuse.

The Encyclopedia of Drug Abuse has been designed as a companion to *The Encyclopedia of Alcoholism,* edited by Robert O'Brien and Dr. Morris Chafetz. It follows the earlier volume in format, approach and presentation of subject matter. Each volume, however, is designed to stand alone. Since alcohol is a drug, and one that is subject to abuse, alcoholism and alcohol abuse are covered in this volume, although not as extensively or in the same depth as in *The Encyclopedia of Alcoholism.*

Another difference between the two volumes is the larger proportion of space devoted to legal aspects in the present volume. Alcohol, while regulated by a variety of laws, is one of the few major drugs of abuse for which the use, possession or sale outside of proper channels is not a criminal act. With drug abuse, the aspect of criminality not only has a significant impact on the problem, it is often a major part of the problem itself.

Research into drug abuse and the extent of the problem continues to accelerate and new information becomes available almost daily. *The Encyclopedia of Drug Abuse* is a "work in progress." Future editions will keep abreast of this all important and continuing issue.

Robert O'Brien
Sharon, Conn.

Sidney Cohen, M.D.
Los Angeles, Calif.

ACKNOWLEDGMENTS FROM THE FIRST EDITION

Since projects of this kind are necessarily enormous and cumbersome, they involve the work of many hands including those of the staff members whose names appear on the copyright page.

Any detailed listing of other contributions to this volume would require much more space than is available here. However, some mention should be made of the staffs of the following agencies and organizations: the National Institute on Drug Abuse, the Drug Enforcement Administration, the Federal Bureau of Investigation, the United States Department of Justice, the Alcohol, Drug Abuse and Mental Health Administration, the Food and Drug Administration, the United States Department of Health and Human Services, the Gallup Poll, the Roper Organization, the World Health Organization, the Addiction Research Foundation (Canada), the League of Red Cross Societies, the National Institute on Alcohol Abuse and Alcoholism, the National Clearinghouse for Alcohol Information, the National Clearinghouse for Drug Abuse Information, the National Council on Alcoholism, Alcoholics Anonymous, the various state and provincial (Canadian) agencies, as well as the embassies and agencies of other nations who responded to our requests for information.

Robert O'Brien would like to thank those without whose personal help this book would not have been possible: Dr. Robert Schurtman and Joyce O'Brien.

THE HISTORY OF DRUGS AND MAN

"Pharmacology antedated agriculture."
—Aldous Huxley

The language of drugs has changed considerably over the centuries, although the use of drugs, as defined in this volume, predates the use of language itself. Until the 18th century, a drug was any substance used in a medicinal, chemical or even industrial preparation (dyes for fabrics, for example.) We still use the word *drugs* as a catchall: today it means not only medications, potentially addictive or not, that require a prescription, but also over-the-counter drugs, ointments, lotions, even toothpastes and deodorants—anything, in fact, which may be found in a drugstore or drug department. A drug is any substance either organic or manmade that creates a change—a change that is either emotional, mental, physical or psychological.

Addiction, as we use the word today, was also slow to develop its present meaning, although the phenomenon was common enough. Addiction was the delivery or surrender of a person or thing ("Did this addiction make him legally a slave?"). Only later, as the word assumed the meaning of "self-addiction," did it take on its modern meaning in connection with drugs. In many ways, this changing vocabulary of drug use and abuse reflects people's ambivalence toward these substances over the centuries.

The history of non-medical drug use is thousands of years old. Man consumed the juice of opium poppies long before there were narcotics such as morphine and heroin. Man chewed coca leaves long before cocaine was extracted from the South American coca plant. Man dried peyote cactus long before hallucinogens were synthesized. Throughout recorded history, drugs have been used for both medicinal and religious purposes. Both uses—to enhance physical well-being and to heighten religious and metaphysical experiences—are closely related to drug use for its own sake. Drug use has always included recreational intoxication and self-induced relief from psychic pain and emotional malady. Distinctions between these various uses are often difficult, and are often arbitrary ones imposed by a particular culture, religion or social group.

The earliest known records of drug use concern the plants that were discovered to have medicinal effects on the body or mind. This practice is, of course, part of folk medicine even today, and the early history of drug use is inseparable from the early history of medicine.

The Sumerian people of Asia Minor, who created the cuneiform alphabet, included references to a "joy plant" in their earliest written records, which date from about 5000 B.C. Most experts believe the plant was the opium poppy, and its mention in these tracts suggests medicinal use as a sedative.

In China, *ma-huang,* a species of ephedra *(Ephedra sinica),* a shrub containing the alkaloid ephedrine, was in use as an inhalant by 3000 B.C. A Chinese tract from 2737 B.C., attributed to Emperor Shen Nung, documents how the hemp plant *Cannabis sativa* could be brewed into a tea and used for medicinal purposes. Cannabis was introduced into India by about 2000 B.C. and the Indians may have been the first people to dry the plant and smoke it. Thus, even at the earliest stage of drug use several methods of administration quickly evolved. There is such a multitude of vegetable remedies and methods of consumption found in early records that it is often difficult to distinguish not only the substances used but also the reasons for which they were used.

Although some historians are reluctant to attribute drug use to Semitic people, the Old Testament abounds with references to the cultivation and administration of medicinal herbs. There is, for example, a provocative inventory of favored plants in the Old Testament Song of Solomon (4: 13–14):

> Thy plants are an orchard of pomegranates, with pleasant fruits; camphire, with spikenard,
> Spikenard and saffron; calamus and cinnamon, with trees of frankincense.

Centuries after this was written white men would discover spikenard in use as a cough medicine among the Chippewa Indians in America.

Early records also indicate an awareness of the dangers of drug consumption. Alcoholic beverages must have originated in primitive times by accidental fermentation, and the oldest known legal code, the Code of Hammurabi, inscribed in Babylonia in about 1700 B.C., includes strictures against drunkenness. Ancient Egyptian papyri dating from 1500 B.C. document fears of opium elixirs because of the hallucinogenic delusions they produced. The Egyptians were familiar with the fact that certain drugs produce a stuporous effect and they used them as a kind of primitive anesthetic in order to perform the earliest forms of skull surgery on patients. While many of the apparent references to drugs in the Old Testament remain open to question, there is little doubt that an incident recorded in Genesis refers to Noah's drunkenness from alcohol.

In Ancient Greece alcohol and other drugs were used extensively and there are many references to them in classical literature. Homer's epics, the *Iliad* and the *Odyssey,* which date from about 800 B.C., contain several references to wine and occasional suggestions that some heroes, perhaps even Achilles, the hero of the Trojan War, suffered from overindulgence. In the *Iliad* Helen is said to have brought a drug-like substance, nepenthe (which some people believe to be marijuana and others opium), with her to Troy; and in the *Odyssey* the "lotus eaters" encountered by Ulysses suffer from a self-induced lethargy and forgetfulness clearly associated with drugs. At the beginning of the fifth century B.C. the Greek historian Herodotus recorded that the Scythians, nomads who lived in part of what is now Russia, cultivated a hemp plant which they burned as a kind of incense in closed rooms. He noted that they inhaled the fumes of the burning hemp and became as intoxicated as Greeks drunk on wine. Around the same time, about 400 B.C., Hippocrates was experimenting with medicinal preparations and using opium as an ingredient. This was also the era when the Greek cult of Dionysus combined wine-drinking with phallic worship, according to debaucheries described by Euripides in the *Bacchae*.

The Roman Empire preserved such wine festivals in its own bacchanalia, which by 100 A.D. had inspired anti-drunkenness laws. Because the Romans, like the Greeks, were conquerors of other lands, they also came into contact with other drug cultures. It was during the Roman conquest of the eastern Mediterranean in the first century A.D. that they became familiar with opium. Dioscorides, a Greek surgeon who traveled with the Roman army on its campaigns, described in *De Materia Medica,* his authoritative medical text, how liquid opium could be prepared by crushing the pod of the poppy plant. Galen, who was appointed court physician to Marcus Aurelius in 164 A.D., had learned his medical lore from the drug-conscious Egyptians and was an ardent proponent of the benefits of opium eating, among other vegetable therapies. Such was his authority that similar preparations were for centuries known as Galenicals.

In the first millennium A.D. the cultivation of cannabis began to spread and well-defined patterns of consumption developed. The *Susruta,* a treatise produced in India about 400 A.D. documents local use of cannabis at that time and this and other sources provide unusually detailed information of the specific grades of cannabis used by Indians. *Bhang,* the least potent grade, was brewed into a tea by the lowest classes; *ganja,* a stronger grade, was usually smoked by the "middle" classes; and *charas,* the most potent preparation (equivalent to hashish), was made into fancy concoctions with nuts and honey and eaten by the most affluent classes in Indian society.

The word *hashish* dates from 11th century Persia, where drugs first became associated with criminal activities. This drug preparation takes its name from the Persian cult leader Al-Hassan ibn-al Sabbah, "The Old Man of the Mountains." Hassan led a group of the Isma'ili sect of Shi'ite Muslims called *hashishi* ("hemp-eaters"), who allegedly incorporated the use of hashish into their violent reprisals against political rivals. They are said to have consumed hashish in order to induce ecstatic visions of paradise before setting out to face martyrdom, and in this intoxicated state launched suicidal attacks on challengers to their tribal hegemony. The word "assassin" also derives from the cult of Al-Hassan, although in early European usage it meant devotee and only later acquired the meaning of murderer.

The Middle Ages were characterized by increasing contact between Western and Eastern civilizations and the ensuing cultural exchanges included exports from "drug-rich" Asia to "drug-poor" Europe. The Crusades of the 11th and 12th centuries increased European knowledge of Middle Eastern drug preparations, including hashish and distilled alcohol. Marco Polo returned from expeditions to the Orient not only with the spices and silks usually cited in history books, but also with detailed knowledge of opium cultivation and drug cults such as the *hashishis.*

Much of the lore spread in this era was apothecary in nature and little understood until modern times. Belladonna, for example, was first discovered in Europe in late medieval times, although there are references to it in Greek mythology. This preparation was made from the berries of *Solanum nigrum,* a variety of the nightshade plant known as "deadly nightshade." While modern science has revealed the plant's diaphoretic, narcotic and antispasmodic properties, it was actually used by Italian women to dilate their pupils for cosmetic effect, hence its name belladonna ("beautiful lady"). By the late 1400s, however, Cesare Borgia (thought to be the model for Machiavelli's *The Prince*) had made stronger concentrations of belladonna notorious as a deadly poison. It was not until 1833 that P. L. Geiger isolated the active ingredient of belladonna—the alkaloid drug atropine—which is now used as an antispasmodic.

During these early times, the discovery of drug properties varied in different parts of the world according to the local vegetation. The Indian civilizations of the Americas discovered different drugs from those of the Old World and the Orient. In the Americas one favored drug was derived from a mountain shrub now classified as *Erythroxylon coca.* As long ago as 1000 B.C. the Incas, in what is now Bolivia and Peru, were chewing coca leaves for their stimulant effects. The leaves increased energy, suppressed appetite, and produced short-term euphoria—effects that helped the people endure the rigors of their harsh mountain environment. The drug was also used in the Incas' religious ceremonies and was considered more valuable than gold or silver.

Further north, the Aztec Indians of Mexico had built a culture dating to 100 B.C. around the magical properties of the peyote cactus, the psilocybin mushroom, had *ololiuqui*, the seeds of a variety of morning glory containing a hallucinogenic chemical similar to lysergic acid amide. In North America the most common kind of drug consumption was inhaling smoke from burning tobacco leaves. All the drug practices from Indian cultures would fascinate and eventually captivate the earliest European explorers of the New World.

It was through the travels of early explorers that the familiar stimulant, caffeine, came into widespread use. The coffee tree is an evergreen native to Ethiopia. It was cultivated in early times in Arabia and its berries were mixed with liquid to make a stimulating drink. European explorers in the Middle East recorded seeing Mohammedans drinking coffee for energy during long religious pilgrimages and vigils in the 14th century. Coffee was introduced into European countries during the 16th and 17th centuries and the first London coffeehouse was established in about 1652. Frequented by writers and wits, coffeehouses became the rage in late 17th and 18th century London. Coffee's stimulant effect and popularity were ridiculed by Alexander Pope in *The Rape of the Lock* (1714):

> Coffee (which makes the Politican Wise,
> And sees thro' all things with his half-shut Eyes).

It was via England and its global sea trade that coffee cultivation spread to South America, which now produces most of the world supply.

Thus, in their travels to the East, Europeans discovered a variety of drugs that were soon incorporated into their own life-styles. But in their travels to the West, to the Americas, they discovered a veritable treasure trove of drugs ready for export home. The meeting of the Old World with the New stands as the most crucial drug exchange in recorded history. The explorations begun by Columbus discovered, among other resources, cocaine from South America, hallucinogens from Central America and tobacco from North America. These drugs were brought back to European courts and received with as much relish as parrots, gold and furs. The drug exchange became complete when the Europeans introduced into the Americas distilled alcoholic beverages and, in Chile in 1545, cannabis from Asia.

The tobacco revolution of this time was an especially remarkable instance of drug exchange. Indians persuaded to travel to Europe insisted on taking a supply of tobacco with them. They introduced it to European sailors and smoking—with its alternating stimulating and tranquilizing effects—immediately became popular. Ships traveled with supplies of tobacco leaves and seeds, thus insuring the spread of the cultivation of tobacco and the practice of smoking along the world's sea-lanes. Magellan introduced tobacco to Africa, the Dutch carried the plant to the Hottentots, and the Portuguese transported it to Polynesia. In England, which controlled the tobacco-rich region of Virginia, the craze for tobacco reached epidemic proportions, despite its high price. Sir Walter Raleigh brought pipe smoking to England and by 1614 tobacco use had spread even to the very poor, and it had become "a commoditie that is now as vendible in every Taverne, Inne, and Alehouse, as eyther Wine, Ale, or Beare. . . ." (Berthold Laufer, *Introduction of Tobacco into Europe*, Anthropology Leaflet 19, Chicago: Field Museum of Natural History, 1924, p. 16). The addictive nature of nicotine, which was named after Jacques Nicot, who brought it to France in 1560 claiming that it had great medicinal potential, was quickly apparent. In 1623 Sir Francis Bacon described smoking tobacco as "a certain secret pleasure" and wrote: "Those who have once become accustomed thereto can later hardly be restrained therefrom." Earlier, in 1604, James I of England had issued his *Counterblast to Tobacco*. Japan acted to prohibit smoking in 1603, and papal encyclicals against smoking were published in 1642 and 1650. All proved futile and by the late 1600s most European countries had replaced outright prohibitions on smoking with high and very profitable taxes on tobacco. Tobacco became common in every culture to which it was introduced, the last being the tribes of the Arctic regions in the present century. No social practice matches the virtually universal appeal of smoking, which can only be accounted for by the addictive quality of nicotine and the conditioning established after thousands of nicotine "hits" to the brain.

At the same time that the use of tobacco was becoming so widespread, the use of opium in various forms was also increasing. In 1541 the Swiss alchemist Paracelsus introduced laudanum—opium in liquid form—and it quickly gained great popularity throughout Europe as a medical panacea.

The heaviest national use of opium developed in China. Opium had been used in China since early times, but it was not until well after the discovery of America that the practice of *smoking* opium became common. By 1650 opium use was recognized as a serious health problem, but nevertheless an organized commerce in the drug developed. The Manchu dynasty attempted to restrict importation of opium to its people, but it proved powerless against the economic leverage of the English East India Company, which began shipment of opium from its colony India in 1767. Chinese rulers went so far as to make opium smoking a capital offense in 1776, but this first national effort to control drug abuse failed to curb the appetite for opium. In 1839 the Manchu government escalated its battle by prohibiting the importation of opium; to insure compliance it ordered all shipborne imports to be confiscated and all vessels involved to be detained. The result was the Opium War between China and England (1839–1842) in which the Chinese were defeated by an England bent on protecting its trade prerogatives. A second Opium War broke out in 1856 and by the subsequent Treaty of Tientsin in 1858 China was forced to permit importation of opium subject to high tariffs. In a pattern that would be repeated in other nations' attempts to curb drug traffic, the tariffs only succeeded in encouraging smuggling and criminal conspiracies.

England's justification during the Opium Wars was that it was also encouraging shipment of opium to its own shores. The drug was, in fact, a common staple in British medicine throughout the 18th and 19th centuries. James Boswell recorded that on March 23, 1783: "I breakfasted with Dr. Johnson, who seemed much relieved, having taken opium the night before." Johnson, however, protested against the use of the drug as a common remedy and thought it should be given only in cases of extreme necessity and then with the utmost reluctance. Despite such fears, the use of opium and opium derivative preparations spread throughout England, Europe and North America, and they were used for their intoxicating effects as well as medicinally. Some of the English Romantics came to associate the effects of the drug with their aesthetics of the sublime and of the suprarational. Samuel Taylor Coleridge's poem "Kubla Khan," with its vision of a "stately pleasure dome," is said to have originated in an opium vision, and Coleridge did indeed suffer progressive physical and intellectual debilitation from his well-documented addiction to opium in the form of laudanum.

The mythology of the inspirational benefits of opium was given its greatest boost at this time by Thomas De Quincey in his book *Confessions of an English Opium Eater* (1822). It was De Quincey who invented the term "tranquilizer" to describe the effect of the drug. De Quincey began taking opium during his student days at Oxford and drug use by writers, part of a mystique still popular today, was further promulgated by the hashish cult surrounding the French poets Theophile Gautier and Charles Buadelaire in the 1840s. It was symptomatic of the times that in the same decade the Swede Magnus Huss invented the term "alcoholism" to describe another, less elitist, form of drug abuse.

Opium use became epidemic in 19th century Europe, particularly England, and America.

Tragically, the most widespread use of the drug was in children's medicines marketed under names such as Godfrey's Cordial, Munn's Elixir, and Mother Bailey's Quieting Syrup. The most popular household guide of the time, *Beeton's Book of Household Management,* felt compelled in its 1869 edition to warn that certain "preparations, which are constantly given to children by their nurses and mothers, for the purpose of making them sleep, often prove fatal." But for the poor, especially women who did textile work in their own homes, there were few alternatives. An English survey of 1842 called *The Second Report to the Commissioners* addressed the dilemma that drove poor women to "dope" their children with opium.

One outsider who responded with emotion to this form of drug abuse was Frederick Engels. In *The Condition of the Working Class in England in 1844,* he provided a chilling description of increased dosage as infant bodies developed resistance to the drug. Because of the ever-larger doses, "they become pale, stunted and weak, generally dying before they are two years old," he wrote. "The use of this medicine is widespread in all the great cities and industrial towns of the country."

As drug use became more common in the 18th and 19th centuries advances in chemistry and pharmacology were making new and more potent forms of drugs available.

In 1730 the German physician Friedrich Hoffmann introduced anodyne, a liquid form of ether, as an effective medicine for a variety of ailments. It became popular both as a drink and as an inhalant because it was thought to be an intoxicant free of the addictive qualities of alcohol.

In 1776 Joseph Priestly discovered nitrous oxide (N_2O). It was synthesized a year later by the chemist Humphry Davy, who held "laughing gas" parties in his home.

In 1831 chloroform was simultaneously developed by chemists in several countries. By 1847 it was in use as an anesthetic; it was also used for its pleasurable intoxicating effects, despite the acknowledged danger of fatal overdose.

In 1869 chloral hydrate was developed by Oscar Liebreich as the first synthetic sedative hypnotic. In spite of its objectionable odor, it was widely used recreationally to produce intoxication, especially in combination with alcohol—a possibly lethal combination which earned the nicknames "knockout drops" and "Mickey Finn."

In 1896 mescaline was isolated as the active ingredient in peyote. It would be rediscovered as yet another "risk-free" drug during the LSD era of the 20th century.

One of the most important developments in drug use occurred around 1803 when the active ingredient in opium was isolated. This discovery is usually attributed to the German pharmacist F. W. Serturner, who named the substance morphine after Morpheus, the Greek god of dreams and sleep. Morphine soon came into common medical use as a pain killer, with the devastating consequence that hundreds of thousands of individuals became addicted to it. In 1853 the hypodermic needle was introduced and used for injecting morphine during emergency surgery. At the time, physicians mistakenly believed that hypodermic administration of morphine was harmless and non-addictive because the drug bypassed the digestive tract.

American medical reliance on morphine reached its apogee during the Civil War, when hideously injured soldiers littered disease-ridden battlefields and prison camps. In 1868 Dr. Horatio Day wrote that "maimed and shattered survivors from a hundred battlefields, diseased and disabled soldiers released from hostile prisons, anguished and hopeless wives and mothers, made so by the slaughter of those who were dearest to them, have found, many of them, temporary relief from their sufferings in opium." Day's comments were published in a book called *The Opium Habit,* which is significant for its recognition of the danger of addiction and resignation to the necessary use of the drug in desperate circumstances. By most accounts, the Civil War produced about 400,000 morphine addicts in the army alone, who were said to suffer from "the soldier's disease." The lesson was not readily heeded, however, and a large number of morphine addicts were created in Europe during the Franco-Prussian War of 1870–71. By then the results of morphine addiction had been dubbed "morphineomania."

After the Civil War a pattern emerged in American drug consumption of heavy reliance on patent medicines based on opium, often in lieu of professional medical care. The medicines were marketed under names such as Mrs. Winslow's Soothing Syrup, Darby's Carminative and Ayer's Cherry Pectorial. The English import Godfrey's Cordial was also popular. By 1885 a survey of Iowa—a state with a population under two million—documented 3,000 stores that were selling opiate elixirs. Such patent medicines proliferated until the end of the century. There were three reasons for this. First, magazine advertising and mail order sales helped make them known and available in remote parts of the country. Second, self-medication encouraged frequent and increasing dosage. Third, users ran less risk of social criticism than they did if they developed other drug habits, such as alcoholism. As the *Catholic World* observed in September 1881: "The gentleman who would not be seen in a barroom, however respectable, or who would not purchase liquor and use it at home, lest the odor might be detected upon his person, procures his supply of morphia and has it in his pocket ready for instantaneous use. It is odorless and occupies but little space."

Although the use of these "modern" drugs was growing, alcohol was the most abused drug during the 18th and 19th centuries as it continues to be in the 20th century. While alcohol had been used in Europe for centuries, "it was not until improved methods of distilling spirits were discovered in the late 17th century that alcohol abuse became widespread. The results were devastating. The English in particular became very concerned about the dangers of alcoholism among the lower classes. In London during the 18th century, gin was available at low cost and rapidly acquired a vast popularity, especially among impoverished women, so much so that it was given the nickname "mother's ruin" because so many women could be seen lying in the streets drunk on gin. William Hogarth portrayed the evils of alcohol abuse in illustrations such as *Gin Street* and *Beer Street* and the novels of Charles Dickens are full of warnings against intoxication. These two men took different approaches to the problem: Hogarth showed that abuse of alcohol led to poverty and misery, while Dickens felt that poverty and misery led to the abuse of alcohol. Both approaches probably contain some truth.

In 19th century America, the American Indians suffered from alcoholism in extraordinary proportions after westward-moving white men introduced them to whiskey. In the 1870s the Commanches began to use peyote in their religious practices, a drug whose use was spreading northward from Mexico. Peyote is currently the only hallucinogen whose use by certain American Indian tribes is sanctioned by the United States government. In 1964 the California Supreme Court upheld the right of members of the Native American Church to consume peyote during religious ceremonies.

In 1878 cocaine in alkaloid form became readily available as a treatment for morphine addiction among Civil War veterans. It took on another medical use when the pioneering American surgeon William Stewart Halsted began injecting cocaine as a regional anesthetic for surgery in 1886. In that same year, the drug reached the population at large in a surprising form. John Styth Pemberton, a marketer of opiate liver pills from Atlanta, Georgia, mixed coca leaves with wine in what he called French Wine Coca. A year later he added caffeine from the kola nut and called the product Coca-Cola. The company switched to "decocainized" coca leaves in 1906, but it was not until 1982 that it marketed a caffeine-free version of the popular soft drink.

By the 1880s cocaine use was spreading in Europe in the same way, in popular drinks and misguided medical applications. The most notable European cocaine elixir was called Vin Mariani after its Corsican manufacturer Angelo Mariani. Users of the coca leaf and red wine concoction included Pope Leo XIII. In 1883 the German physician Theodor Aschenbrandt began to provide Bavarian soldiers with alkaloid cocaine produced by the pharmaceutical firm of Merck. Aschenbrandt's optimistic publications on the use of cocaine as a stimulant attracted the notice of Sigmund Freud, then a practicing neurologist. Freud began to use cocaine in 1884 as a treatment for depression, and he published his own optimistic accounts of its psychological benefits. Freud appears to have been always able to control his cocaine use, although he would die in 1939 of cancer of the jaw and heart ailments caused by a life-long addiction to cigars.

Freud's cocaine habit was known only to specialists in his own field, but the cocaine addiction of a fictional genius of the same time was the stuff of popular literature. One of the principal characteristics of Sir Arthur Conan Doyle's detective Sherlock Holmes was his use of cocaine injections to counter depression. The first Holmes stories, published in the 1880s, were graphic about this habit: "Quick, Watson, the needle!" But in the later stories in the series, after Holmes was improbably rescued from the Reichenbach Falls to satisfy public demand, he had been cured of his habit.

The resurrection of a "clean" Sherlock Holmes was a significant reflection of changing public attitudes toward drug use. Although the world continued to prize medical pioneering in drug research and to readily accept drugs dispensed by physicians, recreational use of drugs was becoming subject to suspicion, superstition and gross stereotyping.

As we have seen, the Chinese enacted the first drug laws in the modern world in 1796, and the results were unsatisfactory. The Chinese appetite for opium also underlay the first American drug laws. In the 1860s tens of thousands of Chinese immigrated to California to work on railroad gangs; after the tracks had been laid, the laborers drifted back into West Coast cities, where the opium dens to which they were accustomed naturally grew in number. The first U.S. drug law was an 1875 San Francisco city ordinance against "opium houses" which proved unsatisfactory. Nevertheless, the San Francisco law was followed by an identical one in 1876 in Virginia City, Nevada, and by 1914 there were 27 city and state laws against smoking opium. The grade of opium used for smoking, however, was far weaker than the opium that was used in patent medicines, which remained legal.

Governments had already responded to alcohol abuse with heavy taxation, thus retaining legal control over trade, and benefiting from accumulating revenues. For a time the same principle was applied to other drugs subject to widespread abuse. In 1883 the U.S. raised the tariff on imported smoking-opium to $10 per pound. It did not raise taxes on the finer grades of opium consumed in other ways and it did not act against American-grown opium. In 1890 the tariff was raised to $12 per pound and then, in 1897, it was reduced to $6 per pound. The government thus found a level of taxation that discouraged the habit without surrendering control of the drug to criminal elements. Opium smoking was still associated in the popular mind with the Chinese subculture, however, and in 1909 Congress bowed to public pressure and made it a criminal offense. Illegal commerce in smoking-opium continued unabated, though, and in 1930 the Federal Narcotics Commission reported that "opium dens could be found in almost any American city." In effect, the law itself had created a drug underground.

The original Pure Food and Drug Act of 1906 was the first U.S. action to protect the safety of drug consumers. It required that the so-called patent medicines containing opium indicate the fact on their labels. The Harrison Narcotics Act, which followed in 1914, regularized licensing and taxation of people who dispensed "opium or coca leaves, their salts, derivatives, or preparations." The act also specified that drug prescriptions be issued only by registered physicians. Subsequently courts refused to define addiction as a disease and they banned prescriptions of opium to addicts as not being within the parameters of a doctor's "professional practice." Thus the Harrison Act cut off the legal supply of opium to addicted persons and drove them to seek illegal supplies. This precedent of punishment-without-treatment was emulated by later U.S. drug laws.

At the same time the first international efforts were launched to respond to the problem of worldwide drug abuse. In 1907 India and China entered into a 10-year agreement: China would act to limit domestic opium cultivation and India would end exportation to China within the decade. In 1909, at the urging of U.S. President Theodore Roosevelt, the first International Opium Commission met in Shanghai with 13 nations in attendance. This exchange led to meetings in The Hague, Netherlands, from 1912 to 1914 that ratified the first Opium Convention, a treaty to regularize international trade. International discussions on the topic were suspended during World War I, but the Treaty of Versailles, which ended the war in 1919, also empowered the new League of Nations to restrict commerce in opium to countries indicating consent by formal licensing procedures. Six more international agreements culminated in the Geneva Convention for the Suppression of the Illicit Traffic in Dangerous Drugs, signed in 1936. By then the superiority of control over total prohibition had been demonstrated by the failure of U.S. efforts to prohibit alcoholic beverages between 1919 and 1933.

During this time medical researchers increased the kinds of drugs that could be abused or used to support illegal commerce. In 1898 the Bayer company of Germany began commercial production of heroin, which was three times as potent as the morphine from which it was derived. In 1903, also in Germany, barbiturates were introduced, launching a search for profitable variations on barbiturate acid. In 1912 amphetamine, synthesized in 1887, came into use as a substitute for ephedrine in asthma treatment. In 1932 benzedrine inhalers were introduced, also as a treatment for respiratory ailments. A synthesized opioid marketed under the name Demerol was introduced in 1938. The era was rich in new drugs, but there were virtually no significant advances in the as yet ill-defined field of drug treatment.

At the end of World War II, the new United Nations adopted a protocol that brought drug control under the jurisdiction of the World Health Organization (WHO), still the most important international agency in the field. From 1948 to 1964 the agency spearheaded a series of agreements that severely limited international trade in opium, and which restricted legal trade in cocaine and marijuana to supplies necessary for medical and scientific usage. Today WHO continues to collect the most reliable worldwide statistics on drug abuse, including alcoholism.

In the 20th century the governments of the world have played, and continue to play, an increasing role in protecting individual members of society from drug abuse through the control of legal drugs and the elimination of the flow of illegal drugs. In spite of all international efforts, however, the use of illegal drugs (such as marijuana) and legal drugs (such as amphetamines and barbiturates) has become almost commonplace—in some cases even socially acceptable—and, in one way or another, affects almost everyone.

Although it is illegal throughout most of the world, marijuana is the fourth most popular mind-affecting substance used (the first three are caffeine, nicotine and alcohol). The cultivation and use of the hemp plant, from which marijuana is obtained, is documented throughout recorded history. It is perhaps the oldest cultivated nonfood plant and has been valued for its commercial, medical, religious and recreational uses for thousands of years. Marijuana was introduced to the New World in 1545 when the Spanish brought it to Chile. The Jamestown settlers in Virginia began cultivating hemp for its fiber. It was introduced in New England in 1629 and became a major crop in America until well after the Civil War. Its role in colonial economic policy was so important that in 1762, "Virginia awarded bounties for hemp culture and manufacture, and imposed penalties upon those who did not produce it." (Cited by George Andrews and Simon Vinkenoog, eds., *The Book of Grass: An Anthology of Indian Hemp,* New York: Grove Press, 1967, p.34.)

Cultivation of marijuana continued throughout the 19th century on large hemp plantations in Mississippi, Georgia, California, South Carolina, Nebraska and New York, with the bulk of production centered in Kentucky. Commercial production declined with the invention of the cotton gin and other industrial machinery, and with the competition from cheap imported hemp, but as late as 1937 it is estimated that 10,000 acres of marijuana were still being cultivated in the United States. During World War II cultivation was increased for a while to meet the demands for hemp.

Throughout this time the hemp plant was used not only for its fiber but also medicinally for a wide-ranging variety of conditions; fluid extracts of marijuana were marketed by leading pharmaceutical companies and sold as low-priced over-the-counter household remedies. Although its medicinal use declined after 1903 with the discovery of more modern and effective drugs, the therapeutic value of marijuana extract remained valid and many doctors continued to prescribe it until medical use of the plant was prohibited in 1937.

During the second half of the 19th century marijuana was also used recreationally, mostly in the form of hashish. From all written accounts, it would seem that its use was largely limited to two groups: the affluent classes who frequented secret hashish houses in the cities; and black farm workers who would load up their pipes in the fields with the flowering tops of the hemp plants. It was not until the 1920s that marijuana came into general use as a recreational drug—and not until the 1960s that its use "trickled down" and became so widespread that today some consider it epidemic.

During Prohibition the commercial trade in marijuana for recreational use increased but was still relatively limited to the large cities, especially New York, and to local rural areas where it was grown. In the 1930s marijuana use began to be linked to the crime wave sweeping the country, and this resulted first in state legislation banning marijuana and then in the passage of the 1937 Marijuana Tax Act, which outlawed the possession or sale of it.

In spite of its illegality, marijuana use continued to spread. In the 1950s it was popularized by "Beat Generation" author Jack Kerouac. In the 1960s it gained widespread popularity among college and high school students. Since the 1970s the use of marijuana has transcended all social strata and all age groups—the estimated number of *regular* users of marijuana in the United States in the 1980s ranged from 16 million to 30 million. During this time its strength and potency increased dramatically.

Because its use is so widespread and far-ranging in our society, and because of the lack of extensive research, the controversy surrounding marijuana continues: Is it an addictive drug? What are its long-term effects? Why do so many people use it? Should it be legalized? Groups such as the National Organization for the Reform of Marijuana Laws (NORML) continue to work toward the legalization of marijuana. They have been instrumental in decriminalizing possession of a small quantity of marijuana for personal use in 11 states; these states now provide a written citation and charge a small fine rather than charging an individual with a criminal offense. Interestingly, as of November 1991, 34 states have enacted legislation authorizing legal access to marijuana for treatment of victims of glaucoma and cancer. However, the only legal access to marijuana is through the Federal government.

The use of amphetamines began in the 1930s when they were widely prescribed for depression and obesity. During World War II, the U.S., British, German and Japanese armies issued them to their enlisted men for increased energy and alertness. The stimulating effect of amphetamines, along with increased self-confidence and euphoria, was soon sought by housewives, truck drivers on long trips, and students studying for exams, among others. They were also widely prescribed by doctors as an anorectic, and there were few problems in obtaining a prescription. The demand for amphetamines soon exceeded supply, resulting in illicit manufacture and amphetamine lookalikes. Commonly referred to as *speed,* they are now often experimented with by high school students. In the late 1980s, *ice* a smokeable form of amphetamine appeared in Japan and Hawaii, where it was reported to have high addiction and abuse potential. It has not yet caused problems elsewhere.

In 1950 meprobamate was synthesized, introducing the era of minor tranquilizers. Soon members of the benzodiazepine family were in widespread use because their margin of safety was greater than that of the barbiturates. Today benzodiazepines are among the most widely prescribed drugs. When taken in excessive amounts they produce a state of intoxication remarkably similar to that of alcohol. When combined with alcohol, they serve as a means of suicide (a method particularly common among women). In great demand, the source of supply may be no further than the family medicine cabinet and, if not, they are readily available on the illicit market. The fully stocked medicine cabinet and the pattern of use by parents are thought to be two reasons for the recent increase in drug use among young people. Polydrug use, the taking or two or more drugs at once, has also developed in the last decade or so and it is common among some users to take a stimulant in the morning and a depressant at night.

The late 1950s and 1960s saw a rash of fad drugs whose popularity quickly waned. In 1959 there was a craze for glue sniffing among young people, particularly boys in the 13 to 15 age group. It has been suggested that nationwide media attention may have alerted potential users and contributed to the abuse.

LSD, used as an adjunct to psychotherapy in the 1950s, was popularized in the 1960s, particularly as a result of proselytizing by Dr. Timothy Leary. Use of LSD, easily produced by basement chemists, peaked in the late 1960s and then there was a steady decline. Both glue-sniffing and LSD use were fads that concerned a drug with limited addictive qualities, and each was followed by media scares that abruptly ended their popular appeal.

The U.S. has the dubious distinction of being the trend setter in drug abuse patterns around the world. If a drug suddenly becomes popular in the U.S. it is almost a sure thing that it will surface elsewhere in a very short time. A prime example is the use of LSD, which gained great popularity in the 1960s and then rapidly declined. The same pattern is reported by authorities throughout the world. The 1990s have so far shown a slow, yet steady increase in the use of hallucinogenic drugs.

Just as the Civil War produced morphine addicts, and World War II saw extensive use of amphetamines, long-lasting drug problems emerged from U.S. military interventions in Southeast Asia. In Korea, soldiers took advantage of the availability of heroin and often mixed heroin with amphetamines to produce *speedballs.* In Vietnam the military found both heroin and highly potent marijuana readily available and very inexpensive. Alarmed at the extent of the abuse, authorities made a concerted effort to curb the use of marijuana—but their efforts actually had the effect of increasing heroin abuse.

Heroin use in the United States has been extensive since the early 1900s when there were an estimated one-quarter million to one million users, mostly among lower and upper socioeconomic groups in urban centers. Since American involvement in Southeast Asia in the late 1960s and early 1970s, when the flow of heroin into the U.S. increased, the use of heroin has spread from metropolitan areas to the suburbs, and from upper and lower socioeconomic groups to the middle class, especially youth. Recent studies estimate that there are now between 400,000 and 750,000 heroin users in America. When not available from one illicit source, another source materializes: Southeast Asia supplied most of the world's market until the late 1970s, then Southwest Asia emerged as the leading opium producer in the world. It is ironic that when first introduced in 1898 heroin was thought to be a cure for opium and morphine addiction. A 1990s trend is the smoking of heroin and futanyl marketed as heroin, which can be deadly.

Cocaine, which came into use in the late 19th century, was used in combination with heroin and by drug culture individuals but did not have widespread popularity in the U.S. until the 1960s. The popularization of cocaine was dramatic and noticeable among the affluent but not confined to that strata. Perhaps because many people believed that it is not addictive, its popularity was steadily increasing among the young, particularly college students, and in many blue-collar circles as well despite its cost. After several years of increasing use and publicity cocaine consumption seemed to have leveled off. However, during the mid-1980's a new readily marketable form of smokeable cocaine has become increasingly common, especially in depressed urban areas. The use of *crack,* as this drug is called, has become endemic in many parts of the United States and is of tremendous concern. Although crack was initially 90–95% pure, its purity is now 25–40%. It is now cut mainly with crank, a methamphetamine.

In the 1950s scientists began experimenting with a drug called phencyclidine as an anesthetic. In the 1970s this drug, commonly called PCP or Angel Dust, became so popular among adolescents that in 1978 President Jimmy Carter was forced to enact specific legislation against it. A new sedative, called methaqualone, came into general use as a "downer"; it became known as "ludes" after its most common brand name, Quaalude. The last legal source of methaqualone has been withdrawn since the early 1980s. Amyl nitrite has also become popular among those who are seeking an alteration in consciousness.

Amateur athletics was so troubled by drug abuse that in 1976 the Olympic Games authorities required urine analysis of medal winners and other selected entrants. By 1983 more sophisticated tests had been developed and produced mass disqualifications at the Pan American Games in Caracas, Venezuela, for the use of anabolic steroids, a synthesized form of the male hormone testosterone. In the 1988 Olympic games Canadian sprinter Ben Johnson was stripped of a gold medal and world record when he tested positive for steroids after winning the 100 meter dash.

Alcohol and tobacco are the most abused mind-altering substances. In the U.S. alone there are an estimated 50 million smokers and an estimated 100 million who drink alcohol (10 million are classified as alcoholics and an additional 10 million are classified as "problem drinkers"). Since the mid-20th century there has been extensive research on both smoking and drinking and numerous educational campaigns have been initiated to combat the problems. The advertising of distilled spirits and cigarettes is prohibited on both radio and television and in 1966 all cigarette packages were required to carry the statement: "Caution: Cigarette smoking may be hazardous to your health." Studies have shown that these two most abused substances are generally used together: heavy drinkers also tend to be heavy smokers.

Since the mid-1950s treatments for drug abuse have been based on the principles that blanket legislation against drugs is irresponsible and that therapy is essential to the control of dangerously addictive drugs. This philosophy has permitted rationality in response to the popularity of marijuana among all sections of the U.S. population and a general easing of criminal penalties for personal use of the drug. Most important, this philosophy encourages the scientific study of treatment methods for dangerously addictive drugs, especially heroin. The first viable treatment programs were therapeutic communities. One of the first was Synanon. A treatment center founded by Charles Dederich in California in 1958, its aim was total abstinence and it was designed to provide support during withdrawal. Although plagued by relapses, Synanon influenced other organizations in the 1960s such as Daytop Village, Phoenix House and Odyssey House. The same period saw the development of the first clinical programs to counter addiction to heroin. The Methadone Maintenance program, which began in 1964, substitutes methadone, another narcotic, for heroin in the hope of weaning the addict.

Efforts at treatment helped sensitize the U.S. government to the nature of the nation's drug problem and to design more reasonable legislation to counter it. Among the immediate results was the Drug Abuse Control Amendment of 1965, which moved to regulate stimulants, depressants and hallucinogens not previously recognized by law. A year later the Narcotic Addict Rehabilitation Act legalized civil commitment of addicts for treatment. In 1970 the Controlled Substances Act classified all mood-altering drugs into five categories, or schedules, in order to better define each one's proper medical use and to provide reasonable controls against their abuse. At the same time the power of law enforcement agencies to search and seize was altered to concentrate on dealers rather than users of most drugs.

While these actions have managed to improve treatment and control of dangerous drugs, they have not by anyone's estimation managed to end the problem of drug abuse. New drugs continue to appear and continue to sidestep the legal defenses of today's drug-educated public.

The use of intoxicants dates to antiquity and the most used and abused drugs worldwide are caffeine, nicotine, alcohol and cannabis (marijuana, hashish etc.). It is unlikely that new treatment technologies, laws or enforcement methods will eliminate mankind's use of mind-altering substances. However, a better understanding of the complex issues involved may lead to improved education, more effective treatment and more meaningful legislation.

DRUG CLASSIFICATION

ANTIDEPRESSANTS

MAO Inhibitors
- Isocarboxazid (Marplan)
- Phenelzine sulfate (Nardil)
- Tranylcypromine sulfate (Parnate)

Seratonin Uptake Inhibitors
- Trazadone hydrochloride (Desyrel)
- Fluoxetine hydrochloride (Prozac)

Tetracyclics
- Maprotaline hydrochloride (Lydiomil)

Tricyclics
- Amitriptyline hydrochloride (Elavil; Endep)
- Amoxipine (Asendin)
- Clomipramine hydrochloride (Anafranil)
- Desipramine hydrochloride (Norpramin; Pertofrane)
- Doxepin hydrochloride (Adapin; Sinequan)
- Imipramine hydrochloride (Janimine; SK-Pramine; Tofranil)
- Nortriptyline hydrochloride (Aventyl; Pamelor)
- Protriptyline hydrochloride (Vivactil)

ANTIPSYCHOTICS

Butyrophenones
- Droperidol (Inapsine; Innovar)
- Haloperidol (Haldol)

Phenothiazines
Chlorpromazine (Thorazine)
Fluphenazine hydrochloride (Permitil; Proloxin)
Loxapine hydrochloride (Loxitane)
Perphenazine (Trilafon)
Piperacetazine (Quide)
Prochlorperazine (Compazine)
Promethazine hydrochloride (Phenergan; Remsed; Synalgos; ZiPan)
Thioridazine hydrochloride (Mellaril)
Trifluoperazine hydrochloride (Stelazine)

Reserpates (or Rauwolfia alkaloids)
Deserpidine (Harmonyl)
Reserpine (Serpasil)

Thioxanthines
Chlorprothixene (Taractan)
Thiothixene (Navane)

Others
Clozapine (Clozaril)

CANNABIS

Cannabis derivatives (THC)
Hash Oil
Hashish (charas)
Kief
Marijuana
Sinsemilla

COMBINATIONS

Chlordiazepoxide hydrochloride and amitriptyline hydrochloride (Limbitrol)
Perphenazine and amitripyline hydrochloride (Triavil)
Secobarbital sodium and amobarbital sodium (Tuinal)

DISSOCIATIVE ANESTHETICS

Phencyclidine (PCP)
Ketamine

HALLUCINOGENS

Dimethoxymethamphetamine (DOM; STP)
Dimethyltryptamine (DMT)
Ditran (piperidyl benzilate)
Lysergic acid diethylamide-25 (LSD)
Mescaline

Methylenedioxyamphetamine (MDA)
Methylenedioxymethamphetamine (MDMA)
Peyote
Psilocin
Psilocybin

NARCOTIC ANALGESIC AGONISTS

Opiates
- Natural
  - codeine
  - hydrocodone bitartrate (Dicodid)
  - morphine
  - opium
    - laudanum
    - papaverine
    - paregoric
- Semisynthetic
  - heroin (diacetylmorphine)
  - hydromorphone hydrochloride (Dilaudid)
  - oxycodone hydrochloride (Percocet-5; Percodan; Tylox)
  - oxymorphone hydrochloride (Numorphan)

Opioids (synthetic opiates)
- LAAM (levo-alpha-acetylmethadol)
- Levorphanol tartrate (Levo-Dromoran)
- Meperidine hydrochloride (Demerol)
- Methadone hydrochloride (Dolophine)
- Pentazocine hydrochloride (Talwin)
- Propoxyphene hydrochloride (Darvon)
- Fentanyl citrate (Sublimaze)

NARCOTIC ANTAGONISTS

Mixed agonists and antagonists
- Buprenorphine Cyclazocine
- Lavallorphan tartrate (Lorfan)
- Nalbuphine hydrochloride (Nubain)

Pure
- Naloxone hydrochloride (Narcan)
- Naltrexone

NONPRESCRIPTION ANALGESICS

Acetaminophen (Datril, Tylenol)
Aspirin
Phenacetin

SEDATIVE HYPNOTICS

Alcohol
- Beer
- Distilled spirits (liquor)
- Wine

Benzodiazepines
- alprazolam (Xanax)
- chlordiazepoxide hydrochloride (Librium)
- clonazepam (Klonopin)
- clorazepate dipotassium (Tranxene)
- diazepam (Valium)
- flurazepam hydrochloride (Dalmane)
- lorazepam (Ativan)
- oxazepam (Serax)
- temazepam (Restoril)
- triazolam (Halcion)

Diphenylmethanes
- diphenhydramine hydrochloride (Benadryl)
- hydroxyzine hydrochloride (Sedaril)

Meprobamate (Equanil; Miltown)

Tybamate (Tybatran)

Barbiturates

Ultra-short-acting
- methohexital sodium (Brevital)
- thiopental sodium (Pentothal)

Short-acting
- hexobarbital sodium (Sombucaps)
- pentobarbital sodium (Nembutal)
- secobarbital sodium (Seconal)

Intermediate-acting
- amobarbital (Amytal)
- amobarbital sodium (Amytal Sodium)
- aprobarbital (Alurate)
- butabarbital sodium (Buticaps; Butisol Sodium)
- butalbital (Buff-A Comp)

Long-acting
- barbital (Veronal)
- mephobarbital (Mebaral)
- metharbital (Gemonil)
- phenobarbital (Luminal)

Nonbarbiturates
- bromides
- chloral hydrate and other chloral derivatives

ethchlorvynol (Placidyl)
ethinamate (Valmid)
glutethimide (Doriden)
methaqualone
methyprylon (Noludar)
paraldehyde
triclofos sodium (Triclos)

STIMULANTS

Ergot alkaloids (Alkergot; Deapril; Hydergine)

Primary
Amphetamine relatives
benzphetamine hydrochloride (Didrex)
clortermine hydrochloride (Voranil)
diethylpropion hydrochloride (Tenuate; Tepanil)
mazindol (Sanorex)
methylphenidate hydrochloride (Ritalin)
phendimetrazine tartrate (Bacarate; Bontril; Melfiat; Plegine; Prelu-2; Trimtabs; Wehless-35)
phenmetrazine hydrochloride (Preludin)

Amphetamines
amphetamine sulfate (Benzedrine)
dextroamphetamine sulfate (Dexedrine)
methamphetamine hydrochloride (Desoxyn)

Cocaine and coca

Secondary
Arecoline
Caffeine
coffee
tea
Khat
Nicotine

VOLATILE INHALANTS

Amyl nitrite

Anesthetics (general)
Gaseous
nitrous oxide
Vaporous
ether
chloroform

Butyl Nitrite

Hydrocarbons
- chlorinated
  - carbon tetrachloride
- fluorocarbons and other aerosol propellants
- ketones and acetates
  - acetone
- Petroleum based
  - benzene
  - gasoline
  - naphtha
  - toluene

A

absenteeism Absenteeism among drug users is a major problem in industry today. Although absenteeism usually means actually being away from a job, there is another kind of absenteeism, too: on-the-job absenteeism which occurs when a person is physically present but not mentally alert enough to be productive. The cost to industry in lost production due to drug abuse is estimated at about $116 billion in 1990. Absenteeism is often the first indication of a drug problem and allows for early intervention by employers, teachers and union personnel.

absinthe An alcoholic beverage made from the oil of the leaves, stems and bark of the common herb *Artemisia absinthium* (wormwood). Absinthe is habit forming. It also has a harmful effect on the nerves; can produce convulsions and hallucinations; can cause delirium and, sometimes, a permanent mental deterioration known as absinthism. Though banned in most Western countries (in 1912 in the United States) because of these severe health hazards, absinthe can still be legally consumed in some countries, including Spain. Imitations of absinthe, such as the aperitif Pernod, still survive.

absolute alcohol The amount of pure alcohol in a beverage or substance. There is about 1½ ounces of pure alcohol in each of the following, for example: three 1-oz drinks of 100-proof whiskey; a half bottle of wine; four 8-oz glasses of beer. Pure alcohol is obtained by brewing followed by fractional distillation.

absorption The process by which a chemical compound such as a drug or nutrient passes through the body membranes (intestinal lining, etc.) into the bloodstream.

abstainer One who abstains completely from the consumption of a substance. The term's application can depend on the context in which it is used, though. Many agencies reporting on alcohol abuse group abstainers with moderate and social drinkers, for example. Alcoholics Anonymous and Narcotics Anonymous however, insist upon complete abstinence in the strictest sense—meaning no alcohol or drug consumption at all.

abstinence Complete abstention from the use of alcoholic beverages or other abused drugs at all times. The abstinence syndrome is the pattern of withdrawal symptoms that appears when drugs that produce physical dependence are discontinued.

abuse A general term applied to the misuse of a drug. Usually the term applies to the use of drugs to alter consciousness, or to gratify physical needs. But abuse can also mean using drugs in forms and styles that are illegal; using drugs without appropriate and adequate supervision; or using drugs to the point where the taker loses control of his behavior.

Generally abuse is the use of a substance in such a way that both mental and physical health may be impaired. The Food and Drug Administration defines *drug use* as the "taking of a drug for its intended purpose, in the appropriate amount, frequency, strength and manner"; the FDA defines *drug misuse* as "taking a substance for its intended purpose, but not in the appropriate amount, frequency, strength and manner"; and *drug abuse* as "deliberately taking a substance for other than its intended purpose, and in a manner that can result in damage to the person's health or his ability to function."

abuse potential A drug's susceptibility to abuse or abuse patterns.

abuse programs See REHABILITATION and individual programs: AFL-CIO drug-alcohol and safety and health policies and programs; American Medical Association substance abuse programs; DARE; DAYTOP; Department of Housing and Urban Development (HUD) drug-free program; Indian Alcoholism Counseling and Recovery House Program; Indian Health Service (IHS) alcoholism and substance abuse programs; National Association of Broadcasters (NAB) abuse programs; National Basketball Association (NBA) drug policy and abuse program; Navy Drug and Alcohol Abuse Treatment Program; SANE; Sports Drug Awareness Program; Women's Sport Foundation drug use program.

Academy of TV Arts & Sciences anti-drug program The academy has a program designed to educate its members about the danger of media glamorization and tolerance of illicit drug use. In coordination with other media efforts to de-glamorize drugs, this group is committed to ending favorable or tolerant pictures of illicit drug use on television.

accidents A person under the influence of a drug is more accident-prone than someone who is not, and the role of drugs in the occurrence of accidents is receiving increasing attention today. Accidents, whether at home, in public places or on the job, are usually a result of the following factors: inhibited coordination; mental confusion; lengthened reaction time; decreased motor performance; risk-taking behavior; paranoid ideas of grandiosity; and impairment of judgment and sensory skill.

Occupational accidents affect a significant portion of the working population. Although many types of drugs are used during working hours, the ones of principal concern are alcohol, cocaine, amphetamines and marijuana. Experiments have demonstrated that alcohol intoxication can alter a normal person's performance up to 18 hours after ingestion, and the use of alcohol prior to and during the work day is widespread. Skills begin to decline at blood alcohol levels as low as 0.05% (a blood level percentage that is considered to be the mark of intoxication in some European countries). Because of a high rate of absenteeism among those who might otherwise have been involved, drinking-related industrial accidents may be lower than expected. Alcohol-related problems, including accidents, reduced productivity, and lost production due to absenteeism, cost American industry $54.7 billion in 1987. While the role of alcohol in industrial accidents has not been well documented to date, the problem is unquestionable and readily acknowledged. This is demonstrated by the vast number of EMPLOYEE ASSISTANCE PROGRAMS available.

Cocaine has recently become an on-the-job drug; often because of considerable demands and expectations on the part of employers and feelings of stress and insecurity on the part of employees. Although the action of cocaine is brief, many employees use it because they believe it speeds up the thought process and provides a feeling of competence. However, even small amounts of cocaine snorted or smoked can disturb judgment and coordination.

Marijuana-related accidents are apt to occur on the skilled-occupation level. Marijuana intoxication can be as impairing as alcohol intoxication and it particularly affects spatial perception. Ability to judge distances is markedly disturbed and short-term memory is impaired. Serious skill impairment can be measured for hours after a single marijuana cigarette has been consumed. Along with memory and perception difficulties there is also a decline in psychomotor activities, such as hand steadiness, and in reaction time and attentiveness. These effects become particularly significant when an employee is operating a motor vehicle or a complex industrial machine.

Amphetamines are often used by employees who work night shifts and by truck drivers on long cross-country trips. Both of these groups seek the stimulant effects of amphetamines to relieve sleepiness and fatigue. Adverse reactions can result in accidents, however. Even moderate doses of amphetamine can produce tremors of the limbs, blurred vision and impaired coordination.

Between 1975 and 1985, some 50 train accidents were attributed to drug or alcohol-impaired workers. In those accidents, 37 people were killed, 80 were injured and more than $34 million worth of property was destroyed.

A study by the Firestone Tire and Rubber Company suggested that plant accidents were 3.6 times as likely to occur when an employee was under the influence of a drug. The study also revealed that drug users were five times as likely to file a worker's compensation claim and 2.5 times as likely to be absent longer than a week. Drug users also received three times the level of sick benefits as those who did not use drugs, and they tended to be repeatedly involved in grievance procedures. Compared to other employees they were estimated to function at approximately 67% of their work potential.

Drug-related industrial accidents and motor vehicle accidents (see DRUGS AND DRIVING) are the major accident categories. But accidents that occur in the home are also significant. Falls account for the majority of drug-related accidents, both in the home and in public places. A 1983 study of accidental falls found that almost 60% of those who were injured from falls had been drinking. There are no comparable figures for falls related to other drugs but because many drugs alter coordination, it can be assumed that statistics would be just as high.

The use of drugs appears to be strongly involved in fires and burns. Compared to the general population alcoholics have been found to be 10 times more likely to die in a fire. Alcohol lowers oxidation in the cells which also increases an individual's risk of being overcome by smoke inhalation. As alcohol is a sedative drug, it follows that other sedative drugs may have the same effect. The involvement of alcoholics and drug addicts in cigarette-related fires is three times that of fires resulting from other causes.

Drug use is also reported to play a significant role in drownings. Such accidents are probably the result of poor judgment, faulty coordination and confusion. In the case of alcohol and other central nervous system depressants, there may also be a depression of the swallowing and breathing reflexes which can turn a normal situation into a dangerous one. There may also be another complication: "risk taking behavior." A person who has taken a depressant may stay in cold water for too long a time because the depressant has a "warming effect."

Although drug-related accidents are unquestionable, they are also occasionally denied or ignored. Further study is needed to promote public awareness of the costs involved to personal life, property and industry.

acetaldehyde The first step in the metabolism of alcohol results in its conversion to acetaldehyde, which is even more toxic to the body than ethyl alcohol. The second step converts it into acetate, most of which is oxidized to carbon dioxide, but some acetaldehyde still escapes into the bloodstream—particularly with heavy consumption. Acetaldehyde is thought to play a central role in the toxicity of alcohol. Probably because of liver damage, alcoholics metabolize acetaldehyde less effectively than nonalcoholics. The substance has been shown to adversely affect muscles, particularly the heart muscles, and because of its effect on nerve impulses it may be a contributing factor in alcohol addiction. When someone taking Disulfram (ANTABUSE) consumes alcohol it can result in a toxic reaction because the person's blood acetaldehyde concentrations increase five to 10 times higher than normal.

acetone A solvent, commonly found in plastic cements and nail polish removers, which may produce euphoric effects when inhaled. Acetone is a volatile HYDROCARBON.

Ackoff's model A method of determining the assignment of alcoholic patients to treatment facilities which takes into account alternative courses of action. Usually treatment facilities are determined on the basis of vacancies rather than on the basis of where the patient will receive the best treatment ("uncertainty conditions"). When Ackoff's model is used, alternative courses are researched and uncertainty conditions are changed to "risk conditions."

ACLU See AMERICAN CIVIL LIBERTIES UNION.

acne rosacea Frequently caused by excessive drinking over a prolonged period, acne rosacea is a facial skin condition. It is characterized by a flushed appearance and sometimes also by broken capillaries and puffiness. (See also RHINOPHYMA and GROG BLOSSOM.)

Acquired Immune Deficiency Syndrome (AIDS) A condition caused by a virus and characterized by a defect in the body's natural immunity to disease. AIDS victims are vulnerable to severe illnesses that are usually not a threat to anyone whose immune system is intact. Over half of the persons diagnosed with AIDS have died. Fifty percent of all persons with AIDS die within one year of diagnosis.

The virus that causes AIDS, human immunodeficiency virus (HIV), is transmitted through the exchange of body fluids, including blood and semen, from the infected individual to a noninfected one. Casual contact does not spread AIDS. It is not an airborne disease. The belief that AIDS is a disease of gay white men is a myth. As of June 1990, 58% of persons with AIDS in the single-exposure category were homosexual or bisexual men. Intravenous (IV) drug users are the second largest at-risk group for AIDS. Twenty-six percent of all people with AIDS are IV drug abusers; 20% percent are heterosexual IV drug users and another 6% are male homosexual or bisexual IV drug users. Thus 38,857 of the 137,385 diagnosed adult/adolescent AIDS cases (as of June 1990, according to the Centers for Disease Control) involve IV drug use as a risk factor. This is a cumulative figure that excludes 84,164 deaths. The cumulative number of diagnosed cases is expected to increase to 285,000 by 1991, 365,000 by 1992 and 450,000 by 1993. It has been estimated that by 1991 there will be 2,750,000 persons infected with HIV.

The New York City/New Jersey area has reported one-quarter of all diagnosed AIDS cases in the United States including approximately 75% of drug-abusing cases. There are an estimated 1.1 million to 1.3 million IV drug abusers in the United States and of these, 38,857 are people with AIDS. While the New York City area is hardest hit, it is important to realize that at least one IV drug abuser with AIDS has been reported in all 50 states.

Experts estimate that nearly 500,000 IV drug abusers inject heroin regularly, while thousands of others inject cocaine or amphetamines. All of these persons are at increased risk for AIDS. Among IV drug users, transmission of the AIDS virus most often occurs by sharing needles, syringes or other "works." Small amounts of contaminated blood left in the equipment can carry the virus from user to user. IV drug abusers who frequent "shooting galleries"—where paraphernalia is passed among several people—are at especially high risk for AIDS. Because not every IV drug abuser will enter treatment and because some must wait to be treated, IV users in many cities are being taught to flush their "works" with a dilute of one part bleach to ten parts water before they inject. Used correctly, a bleach dilute can destroy virus left in the equipment.

In 1988, then New York City Mayor Edward I. Koch began a controversial needle exchange program for IV drug abusers. This was done over the strong objections of many black and Hispanic officials who compared it to genocide of those particular minority groups. Most support for the program, the first government-sponsored exchange in the nation, came from health professionals and some drug treatment groups. The program remained the only one in the United States until a similar program began in Portland, Oregon in November 1989.

In mid-February 1990, newly elected Mayor David N. Dinkins scrapped New York City's needle exchange program and abandoned the AIDS prevention study that had provoked such bitter debate. Exchange programs nearly identical to New York's were successfully blocked by political opposition in Los Angeles, Boston and Chicago in December 1988. But early research has shown that needle exchange programs in Tacoma, Washington and Amsterdam and London reduced needle sharing and the risk of transmitting AIDS without increasing drug use.

Minorities are over-represented among IV drug users and a disproportionate number of persons with AIDS have been blacks and Hispanics. Although black Americans represent only 12% of the population in the United States, they account for 28% of all people with AIDS. Hispanics account for 6% of the U.S. population and 16% of people with AIDS. Minorities account for 80% of cases among heterosexual IV drug abusers, 81% of heterosexually transmitted AIDS cases and 76% of pediatric AIDS cases. Members of minority groups survive for a shorter period of time after being diagnosed as having AIDS than do whites with the disease.

IV drug-related transmission is especially significant for women. Of women who have AIDS, 52% are IV drug users, while approximately 20% are the sexual partners of IV drug users. And researchers estimate that HIV-infected mothers will infect their infants prior to or at birth about 50% of the time.

In addition, the potential spread of AIDS by prostitutes is of special concern, since a substantial portion of female IV drug users and some male users resort to prostitution to support their drug habits. In one study of prostitutes in seven communities across the United States, about one-half of the prostitutes were intravenous drug abusers. Thus, there is considerable opportunity for the spread of HIV from IV drug users to the nonusing population.

Health care workers who treat intravenous drug abusers are at a very low risk of contracting HIV infection as long as they follow the Centers for Disease Control AIDS precautions when handling body fluids from persons with HIV virus and IV drug users. Special care must be taken in handling used needles.

Sexual relationships with IV drug abusers should be avoided. At a minimum, sexual partners of IV drug abusers should refrain from practices involving exchange of body fluids (such as blood and semen) to reduce the risk of exposure to the AIDS virus.

Condoms should be used when having intimate contact with high risk individuals. It is important to realize that while condoms might make sex with an IV drug user safer, there is no such thing as "safe sex" with a person at high risk for AIDS. Moreover, sexual practices that may cause injury to tissue, such as anal intercourse, should be avoided.

The National Institute of Drug Abuse (NIDA) has funded studies to examine the spread of the AIDS virus among drug abusers, their sexual partners and their children. Research is also being supported to improve the effectiveness of drug abuse treatment and to develop other effective AIDS prevention strategies. NIDA is also studying the immunosuppressive effect of many common drugs of abuse to better understand their relationship to AIDS.

NIDA has established an AIDS outreach and counseling demonstration research program targeted at IV drug abusers and their sexual partners. Comprehensive programs have been started up in 11 cities thus far, and plans are for 12 additional city programs to be initiated in the near future. Targeted programs are being tested at present in 30 community sites.

NIDA has also produced a series of ads, posters and other material concerning drug abuse and AIDS, along with 12 different 30-second radio public service announcements and one 60-second "rap" song addressing the issue. Copies of these print and radio materials may be obtained from: National Clearinghouse for Alcohol and Drug Information (NCADI), P.O. Box 2345, Rockville, MD 20852. Telephone: (301) 468-2600.

Division of HIV/AIDS, Center for Infectious Diseases, Centers for Disease Control, Atlanta, Ga., *HIV/AIDS Surveillance,* issued July 1990.

John Langone, "How to Block a Killer's Path," *Time,* January 30, 1989, 60–62.

National Institute on Drug Abuse, Research Monograph 80, *Needle Sharing Among Intravenous Drug Abusers, 1988,* U.S. Department of Health and Human Services, Washington, DC.

National Institute on Drug Abuse Capsules, *Drug Abuse and AIDS,* revised August 1988.

Todd S. Purdom, "Dinkins to End Needle Plan for Drug Users," *New York Times,* February 14, 1990.

acupuncture Although its origins are lost in antiquity, acupuncture has been a traditional Chinese medical treatment for over 3,000 years. In recent years it has gained popularity in the United States and other countries around the world. Rooted in Eastern philosophy, acupuncture is a complex system of medicine which involves *ch'i,* the vital life source or energy that the Chinese believe flows through specific pathways in the human body. If the flow of *ch'i* is blocked or impeded an imbalance—a surplus or deficit—can occur in an organ or area of the body and result in pain or disease. Once the nature of the imbalance has been identified by a variety of diagnostic techniques, the appropriate acupuncture points on the body are selected. These points are then stimulated by acupuncture (the insertion of fine, solid needles), moxibustion (heating with mugwort, a traditional Chinese herb) or acupressure (massage). Modern technology has contributed some new techniques to the ancient practice of acupuncture, including electrical stimulation of the needles, ultrasound and laser beam stimulation.

No single explanation of the phenomenon of acupuncture is presently accepted, but it is acknowledged that the treatment has been effective in many cases, particularly among patients suffering from chronic pain. Despite overwhelming reports of its effectiveness, however, the Food and Drug Administration and the American Medical Association still consider acupuncture to be an "experimental" form of treatment and little research has yet appeared in the scientific literature.

There has been a recent trend in the United States to treat drug addiction with acupuncture therapy. Acupuncture is currently being used in several major treatment centers in New York City and elsewhere to facilitate withdrawal from stimulants and narcotics and as a longer term treatment for detoxified (drug-free) individuals to help maintain abstinence from all classes of drugs including alcohol. Many patients and many physicians and other health professionals feel it to be an effective treatment and a number of studies are currently underway. It is inexpensive and has thus far demonstrated virtually no dangers.

acute The term used to describe a condition that quickly develops into a crisis, as opposed to a CHRONIC condition or disease which is characterized by slowly progressing symptoms.

acute addiction Because addiction is usually considered a CHRONIC disease this term is seen as ambiguous. It could refer to intoxication, poisoning, or to temporary disturbances caused by excessive short-term drug use.

acute intoxication A term used to refer to severe short-term intoxication, or poisoning, which is the result of a defined episode of intoxication as opposed to a prolonged or chronic state of intoxication.

adaptive cell metabolism Tissue cells may adapt to exposure to drugs by requiring greater amounts for the same effect. This condition is called TOLERANCE. If this adaptation results in the cell requiring the presence of the drug to function normally then PHYSICAL DEPENDENCE has developed. When the drug is no longer supplied the disturbance in normal cell function causes symptoms (illness) called WITHDRAWAL.

Adatuss® (Merchant) A narcotic, opiate cough suppressant containing the codeine derivative HYDROCODONE BITARTRATE. A proprietary drug, it is slightly more potent than codeine.

addict subculture See SUBCULTURE, DRUG.

addiction In the early part of the 20th century the term "drug addiction" simply referred to the illicit use of drugs, and did not distinguish between patterns of drug use and the effects of various drugs. The term "habituation" came into use in the early 1930s. It meant dependence on the effects of a drug was psychological—emotional distress but not psychological illness resulted if the drug was stopped. Drug addiction was then distinguished from habituation and came to mean physical dependence on a drug's effects with illness, or withdrawal, occurring if the intake was stopped completely or severely reduced. Although physical dependence is clearly not the only aspect of addiction, the term addiction is still used to refer to physical dependence.

In 1957 the World Health Organization's Expert Committee on Addiction-Producing Drugs defined drug addiction as:

> a state of periodic or chronic intoxication, detrimental to the individual and society, produced by the repeated consumption of a drug (natural or synthetic). Its characteristics include: (1) An overpowering desire or need (compulsion) to continue taking the drug and to obtain it by any means; (2) A tendency to increase the dose; (3) A psychic (psychological) and generally a physical dependence on the effects of the drug.

They further defined *drug habituation* as:

> a condition resulting from the repeated consumption of a drug. Its characteristics include: (1) A desire (but not a compulsion) to continue taking the drug for the sense of improved well-being which it engenders; (2) Little or no tendency to increase the dose; (3) Some degree of psychic dependence on the effect of the drug, but absence of physical dependence and hence of an abstinence syndrome; (4) Detrimental effects, if any, primarily on the individual.

There was still some confusion surrounding these terms, however, and in 1965 a more neutral term, "drug dependence," was adopted by the World Health Organization, and was defined in the following general way:

> a state, psychic and sometimes also physical, resulting from the interaction between a living organism and a drug, characterized by behavioral and other responses that always include a compulsion to take the drug on a continuous or periodic basis in order to experience its psychic effects, and sometimes to avoid the discomfort of its absence. Tolerance may or may not be present. A person may be dependent on more than one drug.

(See also DEPENDENCE.)

Addiction Research Foundation A nonprofit Canadian organization involved in drug abuse prevention and research. The foundation has made notable contributions in the field and produces numerous publications, journals, newsletters, films and other audiovisual materials.

additive effect The action attained when the combined effect of two drugs taken together is the sum of the two separate effects. Contrast with SYNERGY and POTENTIATION.

Adipex-P® (Lemmon) An anorectic that contains 37.5 mg of phentermine hydrochloride, it is used for weight control. Tolerance can develop within a few weeks and because its activity is similar to that of AMPHETAMINES it has a high potential for abuse. Psychological dependence and social dysfunction can occur. Overdosage can result in restlessness, tremors, rapid respiration, confusion and hallucinations. It is supplied in white oblong tablets with blue specks.

administration There are various methods of administering a drug and each has advantages and disadvantages. Sometimes a drug abuser will have to choose between such factors as: time of onset; maximum potency; and duration of effects. For example, an injected drug will produce the quickest onset and usually give maximum potency, but an orally administered drug will produce longer-lasting effects. The main categories of drug administration are: (1) oral, which includes eating (swallowing), smoking (breathing), and sublingual ingestion (dissolving under the tongue); (2) parenteral or hypodermic injection (intravenously, intramuscularly and subcutaneously); (3) nasal inhalation, which includes spraying and snorting (sniffing); and (4) rectal (suppositories). Other miscellaneous methods are sometimes tried but are generally not effective or produce adverse reactions.

In order to exert effects on the body, a drug must be absorbed into the bloodstream and then carried to the CENTRAL NERVOUS SYSTEM. Absorption points in the body are the lungs, the gastrointestinal tract (stomach and intestines), mucous membranes found at natural openings to the body, and the bloodstream itself.

Oral Administration Oral administration is the most common way of ingesting a drug, whether it involves swallowing a pill, drinking a beverage, placing a drug under the tongue and letting it dissolve (sublingual), or smoking. Drugs that are swallowed are absorbed by the gastrointestinal tract; alcohol is largely absorbed by the stomach, while other drugs are absorbed in the intestines. When a drug is dissolved under the tongue it is absorbed through the mucous membranes and absorption time is unpredictable. When a drug is smoked it is absorbed by the lungs, a method that produces faster effects than a drug absorbed by the gastrointestinal tract or even injected: not all of the drug is inhaled, of course, so a portion of it will be lost through smoke. Smoking a drug is usually associated with the use of tobacco and marijuana, but there are numerous other drugs that can be, and are, smoked, such as opium, heroin, crack cocaine, "ice" (street name for crystalized methamphetamine), DMT, DET, hashish and various herbs. Some drugs, particularly DMT and DET, are sprinkled on tobacco or marijuana in very small quantities and then smoked. Smoking can be done with the substance rolled in cigarette paper or through the use of a water pipe which cools the smoke and makes it less harsh. Some drugs, such as LSD, cannot be smoked because heat breaks them down chemically before they enter the system.

Drugs administered orally will generally produce longer-lasting effects than injected or smoked drugs but have less potency and a longer onset time. There are drugs which cannot be taken orally, such as cocaine, because they are not soluble in stomach fluids or they are partially metabolized by digestive juices. Oral administration can produce adverse reactions such as vomiting, but this reaction can also be beneficial if it rids the body of a toxic overdose.

Parenteral Administration This method is used for relatively quick onset of effects and more complete delivery than possible by smoking. The effects, however, will not last as long as a drug administered orally and there are complications and dangers involved in parenteral administration.

The three methods for parenterally administering a drug are: intravenous injection into a vein; intramuscular injection into a muscle (usually the upper arm or buttocks); and subcutaneous injection (also known as SKIN POPPING) under the skin. Injecting a drug into an artery can be particularly dangerous and should never be attempted because it may cause severe damage to the area. This is because a drug injected into a vein is delivered from the tissue to the heart, a drug injected into an artery delivers the blood from the heart to an individual tissue mass—a foot, a hand, and so on—where there is the possibility of centralized damage which can result in gangrene, abcesses or visible tissue poisoning.

The greatest danger of hypodermic administration is infection from germs that may be present on the skin, on the needle, or in the drug itself. TETANUS is generally associated with subcutaneous injection because the anaerobic bacteria have a low oxygen tissue—the fat cells—to grow in. AIDS and HEPATITIS are most often associated with intravenous injection of the virus from a contaminated needle. There is a tendency among addicts to share needles and in some cases needles are rented out to provide income. Addicts are usually so preoccupied with "getting their fix" that little time or thought is given to sterilizing their equipment.

Heroin is the most common drug injected by addicts, although cocaine and some psychedelics are also administered hypodermically. An addict can never be sure what additives have been put in his purchased heroin, as the drug is rarely in pure form and has usually been diluted many times and handled by several people (see CUTTING). Bacteria and viruses found in diluted heroin, which might easily be destroyed by stomach enzymes if the administration is oral, become dangerous when injected into the bloodstream. Heroin is often diluted with quinine or with various sugars, such as lactose. Quinine can, in large amounts, cause blindness and can also affect the central nervous system, the heart and kidneys. Certain tablets (Ritalin, for example) have a talcum powder base that is insoluble in water. It can block small blood vessels in the lungs and cause fibrosis.

The various methods of injection produce varied effects. Intravenous injection produces the quickest onset of effects using the least amount of the drug because it is injected directly into the vein. Cocaine, amphetamines and heroin are poorly absorbed from intramuscular injections and can cause painful abscesses. Cocaine and amphetamines have poor subcutaneous absorption. Heroin can be absorbed subcutaneously but the rapid onset (RUSH) prized by many addicts will be lost and more heroin will be required than if intravenous injection were used.

Some addicts are addicted as much to the act of injecting as they are to the drug they are using. For this reason a person may administer a drug in several small injections just for the joy of injecting. This type of NEEDLE FREAK may even resort to injecting plain water, sugar water or any liquid available.

Other dangers of frequent parenteral administration include collapsed, infected veins (phlebitis), endocarditis and other infections. Abscesses are common in subcutaneous injection.

Nasal Administration Snorting a drug through the nostrils is an effective way of getting the substance into the bloodstream.

The drug is absorbed by the small blood vessels located in the mucous membranes of the nose. Cocaine, heroine, PCP and many hallucinogens can be snorted. Frequent snorting, which is the most common method of using cocaine, can result in irritation of the membranes; heavy use can result in a need for nasal surgery because of eroded membranes and, ultimately, deterioration of the nasal cartilage of the septum. Because cocaine acts as an anesthetic, a chronic user may not even be aware of damage being done. The effects of cocaine by snorting are felt within five minutes and the duration can be from 10 to 30 minutes. The drug is usually snorted from a cokespoon (similar to a small saltspoon) or from a rolled paper or matchbook. One nostril is held closed and the cocaine is sniffed strongly through the open nostril. The process is then repeated with the other nostril.

Volatile drugs are also administered nasally by inhalation. The absorption point in such cases is the lungs rather than the nasal membranes. Among the volatile substances which are inhaled for their intoxicating effects are organic solvents (petroleum derivatives) and vaporous anesthetics such as chloroform, ether and nitrous oxide. Deaths have occurred from the practice of placing a plastic bag over the head to enhance the effects; often death is caused by suffocation rather than the effects of the drug (see INHALANTS). Effects produced by inhalation usually have a duration of approximately five minutes. There are warnings that frequent inhaling of volatile solvents causes brain, heart and kidney damage.

Rectal Administration Rectal administration is the method used for inserting suppositories, semi-solid substances that contain a drug, and in the case of enemas. The drug is absorbed by the mucous membranes of the anus. Drug abusers rarely administer a drug in this way; it is a method used by doctors when a person is unconscious or cannot swallow.

Topical Administration Drugs administered topically (placed on or rubbed into the skin) are rare and usually ineffective. People who handle LSD have encountered accidental absorption, however. Blue stars, which are LSD-laced tatoos, often marketed to children, are administered topically.

Effect on Abuse Potential Some experts believe that the more acceptable (less deviant) the route of administration, the more likely it may be for a person to initiate use of a substance. Smoking (tobacco) and oral administration (alcohol, medications) are common culturally accepted modes of administration while snorting and, finally, injecting represent progressively more deviant modes. While this idea is not yet proven, the increase in cocaine use when smokable "crack" became available and the fact that heroin users almost, invariably begin by snorting and progress to injecting offers some support.

adrenochrome A red (pink adrenaline) derivative of epinephrine that produces hallucinogenic effects.

adulteration The process by which a drug is made impure or inferior by the addition of an improper substance. Heroin is often cut to dilute its potency and increase the initial amount (see CUTTING). Other drugs are often adulterated with active substances in order to increase the desired effects or to make users think they are getting a more potent drug.

adverse drug reaction A negative psychological or somatic reaction to drug taking. There has been controversy over what actually constitutes an adverse reaction, just as there has over what constitutes ACUTE versus CHRONIC (long-term) adverse reactions. It has been theorized that "normal well-adjusted" individuals are least likely to experience adverse reactions. Adverse psychological reactions are associated with hallucinogens, cocaine, amphetamines, barbiturates, alcohol and all other categories of drugs.

advertising Drug consumption, for both medical and recreational purposes, is influenced both directly and indirectly by the same advertising techniques used to market consumer items such as cars and toilet paper—but with more far-reaching and serious consequences. Drug advertising raises ethical considerations that are difficult to resolve in light of the dual nature of the product in question: manufacturers are obliged by free enterprise to maintain and increase the profit margin on the product they sell, but drugs have the capacity to prolong life (in which instance they are more than a luxury item), or to endanger it (in the case of alcohol and cigarettes and in overdose). Applying the profit motive and powerful, persuasive advertising techniques to chemical substances seems unethical, if not downright dangerous, argue those who oppose such advertising. Their tenacious opposition has resulted in the abolition of TV advertising for cigarettes and distilled spirits but has not affected the equally dubious areas of nonprescription drugs and pharmaceuticals. (At an estimated $2.8 billion a year, cigarettes are arguably the most heavily and promoted consumer product in the United States today.)

Beer and wine ads still appear on television, and advertising for cigarettes and liquor continues in other media, apparently quite effectively. Both advertising and sales of alcoholic beverages have increased steadily since 1950. In 1977 the industry spent $492 million on advertising, employing the slickest, most successful agencies to develop glossy and persuasive and campaigns. By 1982 that figure had gone up to $1,108.7 billion spent on ads for wine, beer and distilled spirits. Ads for alcohol typically appeal to people's fantasies about sex, money, sophistication and youthfulness. In 1988 alone, brewers spent $170 million on sports sponsorship, according to *Special Events Report* newsletter, which tracks sponsorships. Although trade associations maintain advertising codes, their guidelines do not go so far as to limit effectiveness. Rich, beautiful and healthy young people frequently appear on the screen, billboard or magazine page, smilingly and seductively grasping a glass or bottle, creating associations the manufacturer of the product hopes will influence the consumer's behavior at the checkout counter. Sports heroes and (increasingly) ethnic groups figure prominently in alcohol and cigarette advertising. Brewers and beer distributors spend $15 million to $20 million a year marketing their products on college campuses. In the last decade or so, manufacturers of these products have recognized women as an important market and have made changes in their product lines as well as in advertising to accommodate and attract the new market. More and more "light" beers and wines and "feminine" cigarettes appear every year and advertising in women's magazines has increased dramatically.

One of the problematical issues most frequently raised is whether such advertising serves to promote a particular brand effectively or the actual acts of drinking and smoking. It is clearly in the manufacturers' interest to increase consumption, but is it in the public interest? This concern has led to counteradvertising by various health groups and sometimes by the manufacturers themselves. Ads warning against smoking, which have decreased since TV and radio cigarette commercials were banned in 1971, have probably contributed to a decrease in cigarette consumption in recent years and to the increasing popularity of low tar cigarettes over more toxic blends. Television and print media spots encouraging moderation in drinking, and warning especially of the dangers of drinking and driving have been stepped up, with as yet unmeasured results.

Advertisements for nonprescription "over-the-counter" (OTC) medications flood the media. Manufacturers spend $350 million to $400 million annually to promote their products and as a group comprise one of the biggest television advertisers. Most of their television efforts are concentrated on the daytime market and are therefore directed mostly at women. As well as being the largest group of television viewers during that time slot, women are also the biggest buyers of OTC preparations.

Ads for nonprescription drugs often illustrate the worst aspects of advertising technique. For example, they try to convince consumers that they need something they really don't. Despite their advertisers' claims, most OTC preparations are relatively ineffective; at best they treat symptoms not an illness itself. Too often the packaging becomes the real product. There was a case recently, for instance, where one manufacturer's larger dose of asprin was being touted as more effective than its lower dose rival. Careful wording, such as "medically proven effective"—which implies much but reveals little real information—is created to prey upon the consumer's ignorance and fears.

Recently, more stringent controls with regard to honesty in advertising have compelled manufacturers to be more forthright in warning about possible side effects and unsafe ingredients. (These controls do not compel manufacturers to justify all their claims, however. The makers of Anacin, for example, do not have to admit that their "more effective" product contains nothing more than an aspirin preparation and caffeine.) Moreover, it may be too late to correct the basic dishonesty that is implicit in manufacturers' attempts to persuade the American people that they should never suffer a moment's discomfort of any kind, and that they need OTC products to ensure that they won't. Encouraging this kind of mentality has helped produce a drug dependent society in which during any 24–36 hour period, 50–80% of the adult population takes at least one medical drug. The casual way in which Americans swallow 50 million aspirin daily doubtless influences young people and contributes to our casual recreational drug habits.

Another group of drugs whose sales depend on advertising and other promotion is pharmaceuticals—prescription drugs that manufacturers market to physicians for eventual use by their patients. The pharmaceutical industry has grown dramatically in the last 40 years, and expenditures for prescription drugs have tripled in the last decade. Clearly, pharmaceutical sales constitute big business and the industry has developed an extensive network through which to promote its products. A key component are sales representatives called "detailmen" who, usually without the benefit of medical, or scientific training, visit doctors on a commission basis to convince them of their products' merits. Studies have shown that what detailmen say, and the order in which they describe drugs, definitely influences physicians' ideas about the medicine and, therefore, their prescription practices. Often the only information doctors receive about a drug is what they hear directly from the manufacturer.

Medical journals, which doctors receive free, depend entirely on advertising dollars from drug companies. Accordingly, about 45% of their content is pharmaceutical advertising. Physicians may rely heavily on such advertisements to educate themselves about available medications. Necessarily, they are relying on biased presentations of information, and medical journal advertising is clearly at least partially responsible for the misuse and overuse of prescription drugs in this country. Benzodiazipines are heavily advertised and heavily prescribed. Ads devised to promote them encourage doctors to prescribe them for use in the most mundane anxiety-provoking situations, such as spending an evening with the in-laws. The use of sedatives is also recommended to ease patient management—that is, for the staff's benefit—in nursing homes and other institutions. Repeated implications, if not assertions, that certain groups, such as women or the elderly, for instance, need psychoactive drug X fosters stereotypes that clearly affect doctors' prescription practices. Manufacturers who are reticent in advertising a drug's side effects can doubly harm a patient.

Pharmaceutical advertising is perhaps the most problematical area of drug advertising. Manufacturers incur great losses whenever they introduce new drugs; profits from the existing product line must compensate, therefore. But prescription drugs are not subject to such economic forces as supply and demand that govern the sales of most products. Patients generally have no choice but to trust their doctor's medical expertise to determine what they need to be healthy, and buy the drugs their doctor prescribes for them. Doctors, however, are largely at the mercy of the pharmaceutical companies' inherently biased advertising. Some modification of advertising practices seems called for, whereby the drug manufacturers accept responsibility for providing clear, complete information about their products and—most important—agree not to promote in any way the unnecessary prescription of chemical substances.

Another controversy in advertising is brand-name vs. generic drugs. When the generic-drug industry took off in the mid-1980s, brand-name pharmaceutical companies attacked with a massive campaign to raise doubts about the cheaper substitutes. Nonetheless, the number of prescriptions filled with generics has climbed from less than 10% to more than 30% in five years. In late 1989, the Food and Drug Administration placed 11 generic drug companies under investigation and took more than 100 generic drugs off the market because of doubts about the adequacy of product tests. As a result, the major brand-name companies mounted a fresh advertising and promotional offensive against the use of generic drugs.

AEDS See ALCOHOL EPIDEMIOLOGIC DATA SYSTEM.

aerosol sprays See INHALANTS.

aftercare The package of services that are provided for an individual after he or she has been successfully discharged from a drug abuse treatment program. Aftercare activities include involvement in self-help groups, supported work programs, and staff follow-up contacts and interventions. Aftercare is the first line of defense against a return to drug use. (See also REHABILITATION.)

aging See ELDERLY.

agitation Frequent symptom of intoxication or withdrawal. It is characterized by irritability, excessive restlessness, pacing, hand wringing, fidgeting and other forms of constant motor activity.

agonist A drug that produces a pharmacological action at a receptor site of a cell. A drug that nullifies or prevents that action is an antagonist. Some drugs have mixed agonist-antagonist actions. Morphine is a narcotic agonist. Naloxone is a narcotic antagonist. Talwin (pentazacine) is a narcotic agonist-antagonist.

AIDS See ACQUIRED IMMUNE DEFICIENCY SYNDROME.

airplane glue See INHALANTS.

Al-Anon An organization designed to provide help for the relatives and friends of the chemically dependent. It is officially known as the Al-Anon Family Groups. Although the two operate independently, Al-Anon's philosophy, program and structure correspond to the related organizations ALCOHOLICS ANONYMOUS (AA) and NARCOTICS ANONYMOUS (NA). The only requirement for membership in Al-Anon is to have a relative or friend who is chemically dependent. Members are taught that they are not responsible for the actions of the addict; they are responsible only for their own reactions and responses to the addict and to what he or she does. The primary purpose of Al-Anon is not to stop the addict from using, but to help his or her family and friends. Members are taught neither to interfere actively with the addicts use nor to protect him from the consequences of use. The assumption is that the addict will be forced to a point where the effects of using have become so severe that he will be motivated to stop voluntarily.

Alateen Patterned after AL-ANON, Alateen is an organization designed to help teenagers from 12 to 20 who have been affected by someone, usually a parent, with a drinking or drug problem. The person who is drinking or "drugging" does not have to be a member of ALCOHOLICS ANONYMOUS (AA) or NARCOTICS ANONYMOUS (NA). The organization was started in 1957 by a boy in California whose father was an alcoholic in AA and whose mother was a member of Al-Anon.

alcohol For the past 300 years the term "alcohol" has been synonomous with spirituous liquids as well as referring specifically to the drug they contain. There are four major types of alcohol and they have one distinct chemical feature in common: the presence of an oxygen atom and a hydrogen atom bonded together to form a single unit (this single unit is known as a hydroxyl group). A hydroxyl group is more precisely classified by the number of hydrocarbon units that occur in it: methyl alcohol is the drug used to make alcoholic beverages and therefore the one that is most abused. The others are poisonous.

Methyl alcohol (methanol): Commonly referred to as "wood alcohol," it is used commercially in the production of formaldehyde and other organic chemicals, such as antifreeze and industrial solvents. It is now manufactured synthetically because distillation processes can produce only limited amounts of varying purity.

Isopropyl alcohol (propanol): Commonly referred to as "rubbing alcohol," it is now manufactured mostly from a petroleum by-product. It is used commercially in hand and shaving lotions, as an additive in shellac, lacquer and antifreeze, and as a rubbing compound.

Butyl alcohol (butanol): Produced both by fermentation and by synthesizing the petroleum by-product butene, it has perhaps the broadest range of commercial uses. It is used, in various forms, to produce photographic film, dye, plastic, artificial leather and safety glass.

Ethyl alcohol (ethanol): Produced commercially by fermentation, it is commonly called "grain alcohol" and is used to make alcoholic beverages. Because potable alcohol is heavily taxed, when ethyl alcohol is intended for another purpose, such as an industrial solvent, it is "denatured" and rendered unfit for consumption. Denaturing is accomplished by adding a variety of toxic or nauseous chemicals that cannot be removed.

There are also a variety of high-carbon alcohols that extend beyond these four basic types. They are produced in limited quantities for more specialized uses such as jet fuels, nitroglycerin explosives, etc.

There is no period in recorded history that lacks references to the production and consumption of ethanol. The history of alcohol consumption is inseparable from the history of alcohol abuse, and codes limiting its consumption date back to 1700 B.C. Over the years a pattern of increasing availability of alcoholic beverages has led to concern about resulting alcohol-related problems. After the failure of Prohibition in the United States, the *moral* approach to the problem gave way to a more scientific approach and the *disease* concept of alcoholism was increasingly acknowledged. Since World War II particularly, the scope and depth of research studies have provided a wealth of information about alcohol abuse.

While ethanol is not nearly as poisonous as the other forms of alcohol described here, it is a toxin that in sufficient doses can damage virtually every organ system in the body. The degree of damage, if any, is determined by the quantity and length of exposure, the nutritional state of the user, coexisting medical conditions and probably genetic factors.

alcohol amblyopia A rare eye disease that usually occurs in alcoholics who have a lengthy history of severe drinking problems. It is also associated with nutritional deficiency. The disorder begins slowly with a slight vision impairment, then becomes progressively worse. It is believed to be due to a toxic reaction in the orbital portion of the optic nerve, and if not treated adequately may be followed by optic nerve degeneration. The disease is most common in male alcoholics who are also smokers.

alcohol concentration The proportion of alcohol in a tissue or fluid expressed as volume or weight of alcohol per volume or weight of fluid or tissue. (See also BLOOD ALCOHOL-CONCENTRATION.)

alcohol discharge rate To get this rate the number of alcohol-related discharges for a given hospital subpopulation or category is divided by the total number of discharges then multiplied by 100,000. The term "discharge" means the formal release of a patient from a hospital. The National Center for Health Statistics defines "alcohol discharge" as a discharge given to a person who has at least one of the following diseases: alcoholic psychosis (delirium tremens, Korsakoff's psychosis, or other alcoholic hallucinosis); alcoholic paranoia; cirrhosis of the liver; alcoholism manifested by habitual excessive drinking or addiction or other unspecified alcoholism; toxic effects of ethyl alcohol; and acute or chronic pancreatis. The alcohol discharge rate can be used to determine the approximate alcoholic population at any given time and is a significant index of alcoholism and alcohol abuse. There are limitations, however, as only those who have actually sought treatment are counted and there are occasions when a patient may go for more than one treatment. It is estimated that the majority of alcoholics are never identified since they are not in treatment.

Alcohol, Drug Abuse and Mental Health Association (ADAMHA) An umbrella agency that in addition to its own administration staff, includes the National Institute of Mental Health, the National Institute on Drug Abuse, and the National Institute on Alcohol and Alcohol Abuse. ADAMHA is part of the Public Health Service of the U.S. Department of Health and Human Services.

Alcohol Epidemiologic Data System (AEDS) The National Institute on Alcohol Abuse and Alcoholism established in 1977 an Alcohol Epidemiologic Data System that is the centralized, national repository of alcohol-related data sets, including mortality, morbidity, transportation-related, treatment-related and health/alcohol population surveys. The mandate of AEDS is to identify, locate, acquire and analyze appropriate alcohol-related epidemiologic data under the direction of NIAAA's Division of Biometry and Epidemiology. AEDS research analysis also provide epidemiologic data, reports, referrals and/or copies of machine-readable research data sets upon request. People who usually make AEDS requests include NIAAA staff, researchers and alcohol program planners.

AEDS operates an electronic bulletin board system that provides current data on alcohol topics. The data can be accessed by an individual using a terminal or personal computer and modem to communicate with the AEDS system. In addition, AEDS publishes annual surveillance reports, data references manuals and other special research reports.

alcohol pathology A general term that refers to any morbid physical damage or individual harm caused by the direct or indirect effects of alcohol consumption and abuse.

alcohol poisoning. See ALCOHOLIC POISONING.

alcoholic Used as a noun, the term refers to a person who manifests signs of ALCOHOLISM. Used as an adjective, the term pertains to the use or presence of alcohol, as in ALCOHOLIC BEVERAGE CONTROL LAWS and ALCOHOLIC TREATMENT CENTER.

alcoholic beverage control laws (ABC laws) The purpose of ABC laws has always been to prevent the fraudulent sale of alcohol, to assure availability and to secure revenue for the state. ABC laws date back to the Code of Hammurabi almost 4,000 years ago.

After the repeal of PROHIBITION in the United States, emphasis was placed on the promotion of temperance and the prevention of abuse. This concern gradually changed and the primary emphasis of the ABC laws became to maintain an orderly market and collect revenue for government agencies. With an increase in alcohol consumption per capita over the last 30 years, attention is again being given to prevention. There has recently been debate between those who suggest that the control laws are not very effective anyway and ignore cultural, biological, social, and psychological forces involved in problem drinking. Opponents of stricter laws suggest that they will work in opposition to prevention programs based on the promotion of responsible use by individuals. They further suggest that increased control will lead to resentment of the system; increased use of toxic substances; and the growth of illicit alcohol trade.

ABC laws vary a great deal from state to state and a large number of federal, state and local level agencies are responsible for making and enforcing regulations. There are two major types of control systems: the monopoly system and the license system. The individual state operates all or part of the wholesale and retail sale of alcohol under the monopoly system. Under the license system the state creates a partial monopoly for private enterprise by restricting competition. Significant conclusions about the comparative effects of the two systems have not been found.

Regulatory controls are exercised through outlets, age restrictions, pricing and taxation regulations, and through miscellaneous controls such as laws concerning PUBLIC DRUNKENNESS and DRIVING WHILE INTOXICATED. Restrictions on outlets—both those where alcohol can be sold and those where it may be consumed—is the most frequent method employed for controlling availability. The age at which alcoholic beverages may be purchased is 21. Regulation through pricing and taxation is unpopular with both the public and the liquor industry, but while their impact is inconclusive, there seems to be evidence that they do have some effect. Some states support a doubling of the U.S. government export tax on liquor ($10.50 per gallon in 1980) and use the additional funds for the treatment and prevention of alcoholism. Federal, state and local taxes on alcohol vary around the country. Before his retirement in September 1989, U.S. Surgeon General C. Everett Koop recommended dramatically higher federal excise taxes on beer and wine. The tax on a six-pack of beer would rise from 16 cents to 65 cents. It would increase from 3 cents to 59 cents on a bottle of wine. In many states a "sin" tax was assessed in 1990 against the sale of alcohol and tobacco.

alcoholic hepatitis See LIVER.

alcoholic muscle disease See ALCOHOLIC MYOPATHY.

alcoholic myopathy A disease that occurs in several forms and which is associated with changes in muscle tissue. Its cause is unknown but alcohol is a primary factor in its development. The condition has only been recognized in the past 25 years. Even in severe cases the prognosis is good and improvement occurs if the patient stops drinking.

Subclinical Myopathy A disease indicated by increased levels of the enzyme creatine phosphokinase, considered to be of muscle cell origin, in the blood. Frequently there is also a rise in lactic acid. The condition affects more than one-third of the alcoholic population and is difficult to detect because patients may not complain of muscular symptoms. It may progress to more severe forms of myopathy.

Acute Alcoholic Myopathy Characterized by severe muscle cramps, particularly in the arms and legs, it generally appears abruptly in chronic alcoholics. If the patient abstains from alcohol recovery is possible.

Chronic Alcoholic Myopathy A slowly progressive disease, it is characterized by weakness and muscle atrophy, particularly in the legs. This form of myopathy is associated with heavy drinking over an extended period of time but, as with other forms of myopathy, it can be alleviated if the patient abstains from alcohol.

Alcoholic Cardiomyopathy Progressive and often fatal condition characterized by loss of contractile strength of heart muscle fibers (cells). It can be arrested in early stages by abstaining. No other treatment is available.

alcoholic poisoning This condition differs only in degree from a state of extreme alcohol intoxication. Dr. Mark Keller of the Rutgers Center of Alcoholic Studies suggests that a BLOOD ALCOHOL CONCENTRATION (BAC) above 0.4% indicates the occurrence of this condition.

alcoholic polyneuropathy While the origin of this disease has still not been determined, it is thought to be caused by a thiamine deficiency. Characterized by numbness and pain in the lower legs, which sometimes progresses to the upper extremities as well, the condition develops slowly over a number of years. While partial recovery is possible some permanent impairment is frequent.

alcoholic psychosis Vague and outdated term for severe mental disorder caused by the effects of alcohol consumption, generally referable to KORSAKOFF'S PSYCHOSIS and WERNICKE'S ENCEPHALOPATHY syndromes as well as D.T.'s.

Alcoholic Treatment Center (ATC) Funded by the National Institute on Alcohol Abuse and Alcoholism, these centers offer treatment for alcoholism in three major settings: hospital, intermediate and outpatient. These different modes of treatment enable a center to fit the particular needs of a client. Most ATC clients receive a combination of treatments, hospital care being quite short and intermediate and outpatient extending over a much longer period.

Hospital Setting Three kinds of care are offered: inpatient, 24-hour service; partial hospitalization, the patient being allowed to go home or to work at appropriate times; and detoxification, which provides a short "drying out" period to handle serious symptoms.

Intermediate Setting This setting also offers three kinds of programs: halfway houses, living quarters along with job counseling, psychotherapy, and other services, for patients who do not require hospitalization but need extensive care; quarterway houses, more intensive care than halfway houses, and often offering physical care; and residential care, living quarters with little or no therapy.

Outpatient Setting This setting offers four kinds of therapy: individual counseling, sessions given by a paraprofessional; individual therapy sessions given by a professional (someone with a degree in social work, psychology, medicine, etc.); group counseling sessions given by a paraprofessional; and group therapy sessions given by a professional.

Alcoholics Anonymous (AA) Founded in the United States in 1935, Alcoholics Anonymous is a nonprofessional organization of alcoholics which is international in scope. Its purpose is to maintain the sobriety of its members through self-help and mutual support. The only requirement for membership is the desire to stop drinking. Incorporated as a non-profit organization, AA is supported by the contributions of its members, although there are no dues or fees for membership and contributions from any individual may never exceed $1000.

Alcoholics Anonymous was founded by Bill Wilson (or as he came to be known, Bill W.), an alcoholic who decided to dry out after attending a meeting of the OXFORD GROUP. This nondenominational group, headed by an Episcopal clergyman, stressed the importance of taking stock of oneself, confessing one's defects, and being willing to make up for past wrongs. These principles form the basis of AA. Wilson believed strongly in the disease concept of alcoholism; as a member of the Oxford Group he tried preaching his theories to other alcoholics but had no appreciable results. Then, during a business trip to Akron, Ohio, Wilson met another member of the group, Dr. Robert Holbrook Smith, an alcoholic who was still drinking. Wilson told his story, this time without preaching, and stressed the disease aspect. Smith sobered up and Wilson started a group, although not formally under the name of Alcoholics Anonymous, in Akron. AA dates its "birth" as June 10, 1935, the first day of Smith's "permanent sobriety." When Wilson returned to New York, where he had once worked on Wall Street, he developed a second group. In 1939 a third group was formed in Cleveland, Ohio, and membership numbered around 100.

In 1938 and 1939 Wilson put together a collection of articles which formed the basis of the growing organization. Entitled *Alcoholics Anonymous,* the volume was published by AA and has become commonly known as "the Big Book." Although it did not do well at first, the Big Book gradually gained in popularity and by the end of 1988 had sold well over four million copies.

Included in the Big Book are the 12 STEPS which form the basis of A.A.'s program of recovery. Developed on a practical and empirical basis by the early member-founders of AA, the steps are a progressive series of suggestions stressing the need for peer group support and a spiritual reliance on a "higher power." The first step entails a clear acceptance of the individual's despair and inability to control alcohol. The second step is the hopeful assumption that a return to health is possible. The third step involves the individual's expressed willingness to rely on powers outside themselves for guidance. Specifically a higher power is mentioned which is variously interpreted as God or frequently a collective spiritual presence of the group. These three steps are consistent with the clinically accepted disease model of addiction which holds that 1) addicted individuals are powerless to control mind altering chemicals; 2) that treatment and improved health are clearly possible; 3) that the illness is characterized by a social isolation and changes in personal thinking (Denial) that render the individual unable to clearly see the nature of their illness and plan their treatment alone. The remaining steps involve seeing and admitting negative behaviors, making amends, developing strategies for coping, improving relationships, helping others with similar difficulties and achieving a sense of acceptance. Helping others work this program is called 12 Stepping.

Headquarters for AA were set up in New York City and the organization began publishing an international monthly magazine, *The Grapevine,* as well as books dealing with alcoholism. AA is run by two operating bodies: AA World Services, Inc. and the AA Grapevine, Inc. both responsible to a board of trustees.

Because different conflicts were breaking out among AA groups on such questions as organization, religious status and anonymity, tenets known as the Twelve Traditions were formalized in 1946. They specify that the unity of AA is paramount; that leaders serve but do not govern; that all who desire help will be accepted; and that groups are autonomous. They further specify that while the AA message is to be spread, other enterprises are not to be endorsed and no sides are to be taken in controversies; groups are nonprofessional and self-supporting, with as little formal organization as possible; personal ambition is discouraged and anonymity is protected.

Group organization, on the local level, is kept to a minimum. A few officers arrange meeting programs and maintain contact with the General Service Office, and responsibility for leading groups is rotated. New groups are usually started by an experienced member in an area where there is a demand. Group meetings are open to all alcoholics whether or not they have ever attended a previous meeting. Meetings are classified as "open" or "closed." Open meetings are open to everyone, alcoholics and nonalcoholics. Closed meetings are limited to alcoholics only so that members will feel more free to discuss particularly difficult or intimate problems.

The desire to stop drinking is the only requirement for membership in AA. A new member is urged to come to 90 meetings in 90 days, a crash program designed to provide maximum support during what is considered a dangerous time. He or she is also urged to select a "sponsor," an experienced AA member in whom they can confide on an individual and continuing basis. The length of a member's sobriety is often mentioned in a positive way in AA and anniversaries are celebrated. The risk of relapse, resumption of use, is always felt to be present. Individuals who relapse after extended abstinence consider their abstinence as dating only from their last relapse. This is consistent with the chronic nature of addiction and the program's approach to attempting abstinence one day at a time. There are no guarantees and all addicts share the same risk.

Members of AA are not asked to promise to stop drinking for all time but are encouraged to keep their problems as simple as possible, to "stay away from just one drink for just one day at a time." New members are encouraged to focus their social activity on AA and are urged not to make any major and possibly stressful changes in their life, such as career changes or new romantic relationships, for the first year of membership. Regular attendance at meetings is stressed, as is a relationship with a "higher power." In the early days of AA this higher power was identified as God, but as AA has grown to include people with many different religious beliefs, the concept of a higher power has been broadened.

In 1958 there were 6,000 AA groups with approximately 150,000 members. By 1990 the worldwide membership had grown to over two million in 93,914 groups. In 1990, AA membership in the U.S. alone was 676,000. At its 50th anniversary convention in Montreal, approximately 30,000 members attended. Members are primarily middle class, middle aged, married, white and male. However, the percentage of women is rising: from 22% in 1968 to 31% in 1980 to 35% in 1989. From 1977 to 1989, the number of new members 30 years and younger increased from 11.3% to 21%. As of 1989, 42% of AA members report dual addiction, indicating a continuing rise in the number of people addicted to a drug besides alcohol.

Because AA views alcoholism as a permanent state that cannot be cured, only treated, it encourages and increases its members' reliance on the organization. This has been criticized by some who feel that such reliance strips members of their identity leaving them with only the label alcoholic addict.

Critics of AA recognize, however, that the organization has helped to sustain large numbers of alcoholics who would otherwise be without hope or support. Also, despite some peer pressure, members are always free to choose exactly how they will, individually, "work the program." Although achievements and failures of AA cannot be proven because there are no membership records to document them, the organization claims a success rate of 75%; 50% on the first approach to AA and half of the first-time failures who later return. Some studies corroborate AA's success claims for 50–60% of the alcoholics who use the organization. Estimates show that 5–10% of the alcoholics in the United States are members of Alcoholics Anonymous.

The overwhelming majority of treatment experts feel the 12 Step organizations (AA, see also NA and CA) to be tremendously valuable and successful. They provide a support network more extensive, more easily accessed and at less cost than any other treatment modality. The majority of treatment programs in the U.S. today utilize 12 Step literature and when possible direct links through the institutional meetings and speakers that the Fellowships provide.

alcoholism There are a variety of definitions of the term alcoholism but it is generally considered a chronic disorder associated with excessive consumption of alcohol over a period of time. Alcoholism is recognized by most authorities as a "disease," but this position is disputed in some medical circles on the basis of the belief that it is self-inflicted and cannot properly be termed a disease. The disease concept has been around for a long time, however. References to it have been found in the works of the Roman philosopher Seneca, the English medieval poet Geoffrey Chaucer, and the 18th century American physician Benjamin Rush.

In 1956 the American Medical Association recognized alcoholism as a disease and was followed shortly by the American Bar Association. A landmark resolution, it has had tremendous impact on laws, insurance coverage, program financing (both state and federal) and the legal status of alcoholics.

Certain religious groups, particularly fundamentalist Protestants, continue to oppose the disease concept. They view alcoholism as simple drunkenness and therefore a "sin." Some social scientists view alcoholism as a social dysfunction. They suggest that terming it a disease is to do no more than give it a medical-psychiatric label and that the medical approach is not only constricted but ineffective. These groups tend to have the same approach to people who are dependent on other drugs.

Among the arguments raised against using the disease concept are the belief that diseases must name a specific structural abnormality and the fear that irresponsibile individuals will abuse both legal and medical benefits if they are labeled "sick," and that the disease concept excuses and dignifies drunkenness.

The World Health Organization considers the disease of alcoholism or physical dependence on alcohol to consist of the development of tolerance, a withdrawal syndrome (delirium tremens) if the substance is suddenly stopped, and a psychological desire to continue drinking.

In 1990 the American Society of Addiction Medicine (ASAM) and the National Council on Alcoholism and Drug Dependence (NCAAD), formerly AMSAODD and NCA respectively, developed the following definition of alcoholism as a result of a two-year committee process by recognized experts.

> Alcoholism is a disease characterized by continuous or periodic: impaired control over drinking, preoccupation with the drug alcohol, use of alcohol despite adverse consequences, and distortions in thinking, most notably denial.

alcoholist In Scandinavian countries this term is frequently used to refer to a person whose drinking results in the abuse of alcohol. The definition varies; it is also used to describe a person who uses alcoholic beverages heavily but is not an alcoholic.

alcoolisation The French use this term to describe a pattern of large daily consumption of alcohol, particularly wine, which has harmful effects on health and contributes to a shortened life span, but which does not result in either physical or psychological dependence.

alcoolist A person who follows the pattern of ALCOOLISATION.

alienation An individual's feeling of dissociation or estrangement from the surrounding society. It is a state characterized by feelings of powerlessness, depersonalization, isolation and meaninglessness.

alkaloid A diverse group of some 5000 bitter compounds of plant origin that contain nitrogen in their molecule, as well as carbon, oxygen and hydrogen. They are usually physiologically or pharmacologically active (that is, producing mind-altering or toxic effects). Examples include morphine, nicotine, caffeine, strychnine, atropine and mescaline. The word is often a synomyn for *active ingredient*.

alkyl nitrites Organic nitrites, usually amyl, butyl or isobuytl nitrite. Originally used as coronary vasodilators for angina, the substances were prepared for ampules covered with mesh, and were crushed in the hand and inhaled for anginal chest pains. When inhaled before orgasm, they appear to slow the passage of time and prolong climax. More recently these volatile nitrites have been sold in small, dark bottles and used either for sexual enhancement or to produce a "high." They are said to be favored by male homosexuals because a relaxation of the anal sphincter occurs.

The street term "poppers" comes from the popping sound made when an ampule is crushed.

allergy It has been suggested that an allergy to alcohol may be the cause of alcoholism. The theory, which was published in Alcoholics Anonymous literature, was first presented in 1937 by William D. Silkworth of the Charles R. Towns Hospital, New York. There is no medical evidence to support the theory, however, and the American Medical Association states: "There is no similarity between the signs and symptoms of alcoholism and those of known allergies." There is the possibility that a person may be allergic to some constituent of an alcohol beverage, though, such as a CONGENER. A hypersensitivity to alcohol, known as pathological intoxication, exists in a small number of individuals. It consists of intoxication and sometimes aggressiveness following ingestion of minute quantities of alcohol.

allobarbital An intermediate-acting BARBITURATE.

allopathy The main system of Western medical practice, based on the concept of treating an illness by counteracting its symptoms and pathology. It is contrasted with the homeopathic approach, which seeks to induce increases in the body's natural resistance.

allyl isothiocyanate Oil of mustard. Following the rash of glue sniffing in the 1960s, the largest manufacturer of plastic cement, the Testor Corporation, announced the addition of allyl isothiocyanate to its basic formula as a method of controlling the problem. When oil of mustard is sniffed, it produces severe irritation in the nostrils.

alpha-chloralose An alcohol form of a chloral derivative. It is converted in the body to CHLORAL HYDRATE.

alphaprodine A synthetic analgesic which produces morphine-like effects but is neither as potent as morphine nor as long-lasting in effect. It is a Schedule II drug.

altered state of consciousness (ASC) A broad term that covers a variety of states induced by a variety of drugs and autosuggestive techniques, including intoxication, delirium, meditative and visionary states and the phases of sleep and dreaming. During such psychological states a person's perception of time and space is somehow influenced and altered.

Alurate® (Roche) A sedative hypnotic, intermediate-acting depressant containing the BARBITURATE aprobarbital. It is used for insomnia and daytime sedation and may be habit-forming. It is available in red and green elixirs with a 20% alcohol content.

American Civil Liberties Union (ACLU) The organization has criticized the concept of using drug testing to "diagnose" drug use and opposes those who would "permit urine searches to creep into our schools on the coattails of forced medical examinations." ACLU insists that drug use is not an illness but "plain old criminal conduct." Trying to combat it with "forced medical exams," it contends, "is a great intrusion on the individual's privacy." (Note: In August 1985, a high school in Becton, N.J. tried to make drug testing part of the complete medical examination required of all its students. Five students challenged the policy in the courts and on December 9, 1985 the New Jersey State Superior Court ruled against Becton's school board.)

The ACLU's Executive Director, Ira Glasser says that sports employers who demand general searches of their athletes are wrong, and that people have a right to protect their privacy and their interest against accusations stemming from a mistake.

Gilda Berger, *Drug Testing* (New York: Franklin Watts, 1987), 49, 67.

American Council for Drug Education (CDE) Formerly the American Council on Marijuana and other Psychoactive Drugs (ACM). The name was changed in 1983 to better reflect the council's aim—that of educating the public about the health hazards associated with the use of psychoactive drugs. Established in 1977, the council believes an educated public is the best defense against drug abuse; consequently, it promotes scientific findings, organizes conferences and seminars, provides media resources and publishes educational materials.

American Council on Alcohol Problems (ACAP) A non-profit organization that provides a medium through which individuals, churches and social agencies can cooperate to find a moral and scientific solution to the alcohol problem in the United States and promote abstinence. It has been in operation since 1895 under different names: the Anti-Saloon League of America, the Temperance League of America and the National Temperance League.

American Indians Drug abuse is a relatively new phenomenon among American Indians, though the use of mind-altering substances dates back to antiquity in their culture. As early as 100 B.C. hallucinogenic psilocybin mushrooms figured prominently in religious observances of the Aztecs and other Mexican Indians, who called them "flesh of the gods." Use of peyote as a spiritual agent which enabled the user to experience transcendental visions also originated in Mexico. It was administered only under the supervision of the tribe's shaman. Religious practices involving peyote spread further north as a result of 19th century raids into Mexico by Indians of the American Midwest.

Peyote is currently the only hallucinogen whose use is sanctioned by the United States government: in 1969 the case of *California v. Woody* established the constitutional right of the 250,000 members of the Native American Church to consume peyote during religious ceremonies. On April 17, 1990 the Supreme Court in *Oregon v. Smith* upheld an Oregon law making it illegal for peyote use even in Indian religious ceremonies.

Because use of psychedelic mushrooms, peyote and other natural drugs (tobacco, morning glory seeds and some substances unknown outside Indian cultures) had always been subject to strict cultural controls that were unquestioningly respected, excessive consumption of intoxicating substances was unknown until European colonists introduced the Indians to "firewater." Until this time, they had used fermented corn and cactus preparations very sparingly in religious ceremonies and did not otherwise consume alcoholic beverages. The Europeans took advantage of this unfamiliarity with alcohol to get the Indians drunk and then cheat them of land and goods. This was done with such unscrupulous regularity that dismayed tribal chiefs finally requested laws which would prohibit the sale of alcohol to Indians. Enacted in 1832, these laws, which also banned public drinking, remained in effect until 1953. The damage had already been done, however, and the laws simply forced the Indians to drink in secret. Because of the laws and the way they were introduced to alcohol, Indians never developed a pattern of moderate social drinking in their culture; in some tribes no word exists for any drinking pattern except quick, heavy consumption intended to get one extremely drunk.

Today the American Indian nation consists of 482 federally recognized tribes totaling one and a half million members who live in cities, in rural areas, and on reservations. Alcoholism is the single biggest health problem facing Native Americans. It has been estimated that at least 60% of the adult population are excessive drinkers, and that 30% of the male population and 15% of the female population are alcoholics. American Indian adolescents have high rates of consumption, with 42% of male drinkers and 31% of female drinkers reporting alcohol problems, compared with 34% of white male and 25% of white female adolescent drinkers with alcohol problems. Indians are five times more likely to develop alcoholic cirrhosis than the general population, and cirrhosis, followed by suicide and homicide, is the leading cause of death among them. Alcohol abuse is also reflected in the extremely high rate of arrest among Indians for drunkenness and alcohol-related violence.

Abuse of such drugs as barbiturates, amphetamines and hallucinogens also occurs in the American Indian population, but not extensively. Cocaine and inhalant abuse (the latter especially among adolescents) seem to be fairly widespread. More significantly, a recent study performed at schools on eight reservations showed that marijuana use among Indian youths has reached epidemic proportions and is far more prevalent than among non-Indian youths, particularly in the younger age brackets. Of Indian youths in grades 10–12, 89.3% had tried marijuana at least once as opposed to 52.8% of their non-Indian peers. Among those in grades 7–9, 64.4% had tried it as compared to 24.3% of non-Indian youth; and in grades 4–6, 22.7% had tried it as opposed to 6.6% of non-Indian children. Among eighth graders, 46% classified themselves as users of marijuana, a figure that compares to non-Indian high school seniors.

The investigation found that Indian children are exposed equally to marijuana and alcohol, indicating comparable acceptance of the two drugs in their culture. In non-Indian society alcohol is clearly more widely condoned than marijuana. The alarmingly young age at which Indian children were found to begin smoking marijuana (grades 4–6) may have serious consequences on their development, since THC—the active principle in marijuana—affects testosterone and estrogen levels. Further problems are posed by the likely combination of marijuana and alcohol, which amplify each other's effects (see SYNERGY).

Numerous explanations for the particularly high incidence of alcoholism and, now, abuse of other drugs have been proffered, many of them fairly obvious. As members of a racial and cultural minority, American Indians suffer from social prejudice as well as poverty, unemployment and poor health. Many justifiably feel unrightfully deprived of both territory and tradition. Oppressed and uncomfortable in white America culture, they combat low self-esteem with mind-altering substances. Parental influence and peer pressure seem to be operative. Prohibition laws directed at Indians may also have lead them to fulfill perceived expectations of alcohol abuse. Inherited (genetic) risk factors, demonstrated to exist for alcoholism, may also be increased in certain ethnic groups including American Indians.

Rehabilitation programs for drug abusers have not proved particularly helpful because Indians generally resent treatment programs originating in white middle-class society. More successful approaches, like the one employed at the Lincoln (Nebraska) Indian Center, have combined mainstream programs such as Alcoholics Anonymous with holistic principles consistent with Indian tradition and belief in the interrelationship of physical, mental, emotional and spiritual existence. Indian women, who in 1975 accounted for almost 50% of Indian deaths from cirrhosis, are especially difficult to help since traditional family and sex roles demand that they remain at home with the children.

Epidemiological research indicates high incidence of fetal alcohol syndrome (FAS) in some Indian populations. Although incidence varies, certain Plains culture groups showed 9.8 FAS infants per 1,000 births—the highest incidence yet recorded. Pueblo women showed a prevalence of 2 cases per 1,000 births, Navaho women 1.4 cases per 1,000 births.

American Medical Association (AMA) substance abuse programs In 1974, the AMA adopted guidelines—which have the force of policy—affirming that physicians have a responsibility to meet the needs of alcohol and other drug abuse patients by providing care at one of three levels: (1) diagnosis and referral (designated as the minimum acceptable level of care), (2) acceptance of limited responsibility for treatment (i.e., restoration of the patient to a point of being capable of participating in a long-term treatment program) or (3) acceptance of responsibility for long-term treatment and follow-up care.

Physicians are expected to have knowledge of and skills in the care of substance-abusing patients, including common terminology and diagnostic criteria; epidemiology and natural history; familial, sociocultural, genetic and biologic risk factors; basic pharmacology and pathophysiology; patient evaluation techniques; referral and appropriate referral resources; long-term care needs; and legal and regulatory requirements about prescribing to and/or treatments of alcohol and drug-abusing patients; release of information; and consent to care.

The AMA also encourages all physicians to consider the degree to which they are personally at risk of developing alcohol and other drug-related problems, together with their ethical obligation to intervene with a colleague who gives evidence of such impairment (Council on Mental Health [1973]; McAuliffe and Rohman [1984], "Since these guidelines were issued, many of the barriers to physician involvement in the prevention, early identification, and treatment of alcohol and other drug abuse have been recognized," according to Bonnie B. Wilford, Director, Department of Substance Abuse, American Medical Association. But Wilford adds, "Eliminating them, however, remains a formidable task."

Bonnie B. Wilford, "Stopping Silent Losses," *Alcohol Health & Research World,* 13:1 (1989), p. 69.

American Medical Students Association (AMSA) An independent professional organization representing the concerns and interests of some 30,000 physicians-in-training. Since the 1970s, AMSA has conducted programs aimed at enhancing medical curricula on alcohol and drug abuse and at protecting the health of its members, their future patients, and their physician colleagues. The association has 140 allopathic and osteopathic medical schools throughout the United States.

AMSA publishes a monthly journal, *The New Physician,* which has a 50,000-plus circulation, and in 1987, in collaboration with National Institute of Alcoholics Anonymous Association and four primary care specialty societies, it published the *Directory of Training Sites for Medical Student Education in Chemical Dependency.*

A major initiative in the area of student well-being has been the development of Aid to Impaired Medical Students (AIMS) programs, which are designed to help identify, refer for treatment and prevent fellow medical students' maladaptive behaviors, including impairment by drugs and alcohol. AMSA estimates that about 25% of the nation's medical schools have established AIMS programs. In addition, in 1988, with support from the Office for Substance Abuse Prevention (OSAP), AMSA launched a project that uses medical students to teach alcohol and other drug abuse prevention to adolescents in communities surrounding their medical schools. Joan Hedgecock, M.S.P.H., is associate director. Contact: The American Medical Student Association Foundation, 1890 Preston White Drive, Reston, Virginia 22091.

American military Conditions of military life have traditionally been such that soldiers have often resorted to mind-altering substances, primarily alcohol, to relieve homesickness, loneliness, frustration, boredom, fear, and even hunger and cold. Drinking is also socially conditioned fraternal behavior. Since the American Revolution alcohol abuse has been a problem among enlisted men, though not the only example of drug abuse. Drug problems have not resulted solely from enlistees' efforts to intoxicate themselves. The American Civil War broke out shortly after the invention in 1853 of the hypodermic syringe. Many of the physicians serving both Union and Confederate troops mistakenly believed, along with the rest of the medical profession, that intravenous administration of morphine circumvented the danger of addiction to the drug since it bypassed the stomach. Consequently, they administered morphine freely to wounded soldiers and often provided them with their own personal drug supplies and syringes. Doctors also routinely distributed other opium preparations to relieve dysentery and diarrhea. In the years following the war, their error in judgment became apparent. Some 400,000 ex-soldiers showed evidence of morphine addiction: it came to be known, in fact, as "the army disease."

In the early 20th century, when American military forces occupied the Panama Canal Zone, government authorities became concerned about heavy and widespread marijuana smoking among military personnel stationed there. Up to 20% of enlisted men admitted a marijuana habit consisting of an average of five cigarettes a day over the previous 14 months. A military investigation into the matter concluded that such individuals were "constitutional psychopaths and morons." Later studies confirmed there were underlying personality deficiencies involved but found they had little effect on military performance.

Marijuana use in the ranks persisted during World War II, by which time it had also gained significant popularity among civilians, but it received little attention and was not considered a serious problem. During the Korean conflict, military personnel in the Far East took advantage of local availability to experiment with heroin and other narcotics, but few addictions or other problems developed.

Recent history has shown that drug trends in American society are reflected in even the strictest military environments and may be exacerbated by factors unique to wartime circumstances. Drug offenses at the military and naval academies (West Point and Annapolis) have increased markedly in the last few years, as have court-martial and dishonorable discharges for such infractions. Moreover, during the unpopular war in Vietnam the scope of military drug abuse and addiction enlarged dramatically, shocking authorities (after their rather late recognition of the problem) into establishing educational, treatment and rehabilitation programs. These programs, which included surprise urinalysis to test for drugs, met with some success.

American soldiers stationed in Vietnam, particularly those involved in heavy combat, found themselves in an ambivalent situation which made them especially prone to develop drug habits. They fought in a dubious war, which their civilian peers outspokenly opposed, and many undoubtedly questioned their own participation. Combat duty naturally increased their stress. Many of those men who enlisted late in the war had already developed patterns of drug use in civilian society, where drug popularity continued to spread. Finally, these men were stationed in a place where extremely potent marijuana and pure heroin were available very inexpensively. Abuse of these drugs was less obvious than alcohol intoxication, which was subject to severe penalties. In light of these factors, the development of heavy drug consumption among enlisted men is not surprising.

Alcohol, marijuana and heroin were the drugs most commonly used by servicemen in Vietnam combat zones, and most men who indulged in drugs used a combination of several. On their return home, almost all veterans said they drank while in Vietnam, and about 11% admitted drinking problems; 69% said they had smoked marijuana during their tours of duty and most consumed very large doses. One-third of these men quit smoking marijuana after their return. Many complained that they were unaffected by the marijuana available in the United States because the THC content of the marijuana available in Vietnam reached 10 to 14%, making it even stronger than hashish.

The years following 1970 saw a dramatic increase in heroin use. In a study of soldiers returning to the United States in September, 1971, 34% admitted heroin use during their stay in Vietnam. Since easy availability made economic considerations (the usual impetus for injecting) unnecessary, most smoked or sniffed the heroin. It was 92–94% pure. Although reported average daily consumption exceeded an astounding 1000 mg, the method of administration and the relatively short duration of regular use (most men were in Vietnam for only a year) limited the development of heroin addictions. Upon their return home over two-thirds of the narcotic users quickly discontinued their habits. Changes in personal environment (returning home), lack of parenteral use by many and relatively short duration of use (approximately one year) have been suggested as factors facilitating this discontinuance.

Despite the severity of the drug problem in Vietnam, a higher percentage of nonveterans than veterans currently use drugs. The armed forces tend to reflect drug use in American society at large, and soldiers generally exhibit no more tendency than the rest of the American people to abuse drugs, except perhaps under extraordinary conditions such as those found in Vietnam. Nevertheless, drug abuse in the military, especially in combat situations, presents a more serious problem than in the general population. Combat fighting demands that soldiers, who represent and defend an entire nation's interests, be alert, attentive and fully responsive in order to achieve full mission effectiveness.

Since 1981, regulations include irregular urine testing and Breathometer tests for alcohol. The military currently gives about 3 million drug tests a year to its 2.14 million soldiers, sailors, and marines. According to the Defense Department, the military drug program costs over $47 million a year. The presence of marijuana and other drugs, including alcohol in intoxicating amounts, can lead to discharge if rehabilitation fails. During the Persian Gulf conflict illegal drugs and alcohol were difficult to obtain and Pentagon officials noted fewer disciplinary problems among the troops than had occurred during the Vietnam war.

American Nurses Association Founded in 1896, ANA's 188,000 members have, over the years, made important contributions to the diagnosis, treatment and rehabilitation of persons dependent on alcohol and other drugs. Frequent contact with individual patients, together with the holistic approach to patient health embodied in professional nursing, enhances the potential of nurses to provide services at all stages of alcohol misuse and dependence. The ANA takes the position that, ideally, all nurses should have the knowledge and skills to enable them to support intervention throughout the continuum of alcohol abuse and alcoholism treatment. The organization, along with other nurses' groups of addiction specialists, works to better serve clients and patients through an improved understanding of actual and potential nursing roles in prevention, treatment and rehabilitation activities and through ongoing programs that strengthen and increase the presence and visibility of nurses.

The ANA has recently completed, with the National Nurses Society on Addictions (NNSA), *Standards of Addictions Nursing Practice with Selected Diagnoses and Criteria.* The document establishes 12 standards for the specialty of addiction nursing. For a copy contact: Judith Ryan, Ph.D., R.N., Executive Director, 2420 Pershing Avenue, Kansas City, MO 64108. Telephone: (816) 474-5720

M. Edith Heismemann and Agnes L. Hoffman, "Nurse Educators Look at Alcohol Education for the Profession," *Alcohol Health & Research World,* 13:1 (1989), 48–51.

Madeline A. Naegle, "Targets for Change in Alcohol and Drug Education for Nursing Roles," *Alcohol Health & Research World,* 13:1 (1989), 52–55.

American Society of Addiction Medicine (ASAM) The organization's principal founder was the late Dr. Ruth Fox. In the beginning it was called the New York City Medical Society on Alcoholism, which later became the American Medical Society on Alcoholism and other Drug Dependencies (AMSAODD). The national/international group has more than 3,500 physician members, who are interested in the disease of alcoholism and other drug dependencies and in other problems associated with psychoactive drug use as they affect the public health. The society extends and disseminates knowledge in these fields, enlightens and informs medical and public opinion regarding these problems and encourages research, teaching and the delivery of better care to chemically dependent persons and their families. The society offers a certification examination for members so that they may ascertain the extent of their knowledge of alcoholism and drug dependence and the care and management of patients. The society's executive director is James F. Callahan D.P.A., administrator director Claire Osman. Its headquarters are at 12 West 21st Street, New York, NY 10010. Telephone: (212) 206-6770.

AMERSA See ASSOCIATION FOR MEDICAL EDUCATION & RESEARCH IN SUBSTANCE ABUSE.

AMSA See AMERICAN MEDICAL STUDENTS ASSOCIATION.

amethystic A descriptive term for a treatment method or substance that can offset the effects of alcohol on the body or accelerate the normal sobering process. Researchers have for some time been looking for an agent to counteract the effects of alcohol on the central nervous system but, unfortunately, there are no antidotes at present. Of primary concern to researchers are the potential possibilities of such an agent in treating medical emergencies caused by overdose.

ammonium chloride The administration of ammonium chloride in a 1 or 2% solution is a method of treatment for PCP overdose. PCP is readily excreted in acid fluids, and ammonium chloride increases the acidity of the urine.

amnesia A loss of memory. It may be temporary or permanent, may affect only recent memory as in Korsalcoff's (alcoholic) Amnestic Syndrome, all memory as in Alzheimer's disease or just distinct episodes as in BLACKOUTS.

amobarbital An intermediate-acting BARBITURATE which is commonly sought by drug abusers. (See AMYTAL.)

amotivational syndrome A term used to describe a condition associated with heavy regular marijuana use. Poorly defined and vague, it was based on a study of unemployed men, using tremendous quantities of marijuana in a West Indian drug subculture. It has yet to be defined by other investigations. It is characterized by loss of effectiveness and apathy; and by a reduced capacity to carry out long-term plans, endure frustrations, follow routines or concentrate for long periods.

amphetamines Amphetamines are central nervous system STIMULANTS with actions that resemble those of the naturally-occurring substance, adrenaline. Up until recent years amphetamines were widely prescribed by physicians for conditions such as obesity, depression, certain types of hyperactivity in minimal brain damaged children, and narcolepsy (uncontrolled fits of sleep). Amphetamines have also been widely used nonmedically—by students studying for examinations, for instance, and truck drivers on long trips. Others have used amphetamines for purely hedonistic reasons, enjoying the euphoria and sense of self-confidence the drugs produce. In the United States during the 1960s some users began to inject massive doses of amphetamine (usually methamphetamine). Such chronic abusers are known as "speed freaks." This abuse pattern was common in Japan and Scandinavia following World War II, when doses of amphetamine supplied to service personnel were dumped onto the civilian market.

Amphetamine was first synthesized in 1887. Over the past 40 years it has been manufactured in two chemical forms. Its clinical use as a decongestant under the trade name of Benzedrine began in the early 1930s. Soon after, the drug's central nervous system stimulating properties became widely known and by the end of the decade it was used primarily as an analeptic or stimulating drug. Later, dextro-amphetamine (DEXEDRINE) was marketed as a more potent form (on a weight basis) of amphetamine. The pharmacological effects of both are identical.

Methamphetamine, commonly called "speed," "crystal," and "ice," is an amphetamine derivative. Manufactured under the trade name Desoxyn, it is more potent as a central nervous system stimulator. Amphetamine appears in a variety of forms; tablets and capsules are the most common. Methamphetamine usually appears in powder or crystal form and is usually illicitly made. Pharmacologically similar drugs with different chemical structures include benzphetamine (DIDREX), phenmetrazine (PRELUDIN), phendimetrazine (PHENAZINE, PLEGINE), methylphenidate (RITALIN), diethylpropion (TENUATE), and chlorphentermine (PRE-SATE).

Effects: When taken orally at low doses (usually those prescribed therapeutically), physical effects include increased breathing and heart rate, rise in blood pressure, reduction of appetite, and dilation of pupils. Reflexes are brisk and fine tremors of the limbs may be exhibited. At higher doses, dry mouth, fever, sweating, blurred vision and dizziness may occur. There may be teeth-grinding movements. Very high doses may cause flushing, pallor, very rapid or irregular heartbeat, tremors, loss of coordination, and collapse. Although few deaths have been reported as a direct result of amphetamine use, those which have occurred were the consequence of burst blood vessels in the brain, heart failure, or very high fever.

Psychological effects of short-term use typically include feelings of euphoria, enhanced self-confidence, heightened alertness, greater energy, and an increased capacity for concentration. Users become more talkative and sometimes more irritable. They are restless and move about frequently. Although the reason is not yet fully understood, in hyperactive children these drugs often produce a calming effect.

As the drug effects wane, feelings of fatigue, "let down" and drowsiness occur and some users may be depressed emotionally. Most users than fall asleep for a relatively normal length of time. With mild amphetamine use there is generally no hangover on awakening; however, if there is a pattern of oral abuse, hangovers do occur and often grow more severe as use continues.

Injection of amphetamine, usually methamphetamine, results in higher drug concentration in the blood and often a different pattern of abuse. For most who use the drug intravenously the sensations experienced almost instantly on injection (the "rush" or "flash") are the effects most sought after. Most users compare this initial sensation to a sexual orgasm or to an electrical shock. Often there is a very short interval between injections, less than two hours in some cases, because users are eager to reexperience the initial sensations. After shooting up users feel energetic and self-confident and are generally sociable. They may have feelings of enhanced sexuality; orgasm is delayed in both men and women, prolonging and intensifying sexual intercourse. Dry mouth and difficulty eating and urinating are also experienced.

One pattern of abuse is known as a "run"; a period of continuous amphetamine use for from three to five days. On the first day of a run a user is generally euphoric, with typical feelings of sociability and enhanced self-confidence. By the second day, concentration on one particular thing is difficult and abrupt changes in mood occur. The user may experience frightening visions or feel that bugs are crawling on his skin. Paranoid symptoms invariably follow prolonged heavy injection of methamphetamine. A combination of this suspicious, anxious state with feelings of great energy may lead to outbursts of violence. Speed freaks have a persistent desire to be sociable, but as they are known for their aggressive behavior they are often only tolerated by other speed freaks.

As the run progresses the user is less and less able to cope with the outside world. Behavior may become repetitive and useless. Eventually the run ends and the user sinks into an exhausted sleep (crash). The period of sleep may last several days and is said to be proportional to the duration of the run. The crash may occur because the user runs out of drugs or because they no longer produce the desired effect. On awakening after crashing the user generally experiences great psychic discomfort including anxiety, emotional depression, and irritability. He or she usually has a large appetite and feels lethargic and fatigued.

Fatalities due to an overdose of amphetamine are fairly rare. The symptoms are convulsions, coma and cerebral hemorrhage. The size of a lethal dose varies from individual to individual; a habitual user can ingest much more than a nonuser. Death may also result from infectious diseases caused by non-sterile needles.

A chronic speed user may have a number of symptoms. Weight loss of 20 to 30 pounds or more is a common finding. Nonhealing ulcers and brittle fingernails may develop, possibly due to malnutrition. Teeth grinding occurs frequently during runs. Violent behavior and the onset of a psychotic state are two of the most common negative symptoms that can occur.

The speed user typically has paranoid suspicions and an essentially clear state of consciousness. He or she is more likely to act successfully on violent impulses than someone who may be uncoordinated and more easily distracted, such as a drunkard or someone on LSD.

Amphetamine psychosis is a paranoid psychotic state that may develop after the ingestion or injection of large doses of amphetamine. After drug usage is stopped the psychosis usually subsides within a week; however, 5 to 15% of patients fail to recover completely and continue to exhibit disturbances for months or years after the last episode of drug abuse. Other psychological changes have been observed in speed users, including greatly increased suspicion (toward everyone), reduced ability to concentrate, and an impairment of memory. Upon cessation the "crash" previously described may include significant depressive symptoms including suicide (successful or attempted), sleep and appetite disturbance and delusions. Such states may be brief or prolonged for months and may require psychiatric hospitalization.

According to the National Institute of Drug Abuse, 3% of Americans over the age of 14 surveyed in one study reported having used stimulants within the previous six months. According to a recent government survey (1986), nearly 37 million Americans have used one or more illegal drugs at some time. Americans now consume 60% of the world's illegal drugs. A 1988 survey by the National Institute on Drug Abuse (NIDA) showed that by their mid-twenties, some 59% of today's young adults have tried an illicit drug. In 1980 the Institute for Social Research reported that 26% of high school seniors had used stimulants at some time and 12% considered themselves current users. In early 1989, however, the Department of Health and Human Services released results of a national survey that showed drug use among the high school senior class of 1988 at its lowest level since 1975. From 1987 to 1988, the proportion of seniors who used cocaine, for example, at least once dropped by one-fifth, from 15% in 1987 to 12% in 1988. "Current use" of cocaine (at least once in the last 30 days) also declined from 4.3% in 1987 to 3.4% in 1988. Amphetamines, often marijuana and cocaine, are the third most widely used class of illicit drugs. Although no hard data on use is available, some 32% of high school seniors say they have been around someone using them to get high (1987). Five percent say they are "often" around people doing this.

Addictive aspects: Amphetamines are profoundly habituating and frequently result in addictive behavior and symptoms. While it is generally believed that no physical DEPENDENCE on the effects of amphetamines develops regardless of the pattern of usage, there are a number of investigators who believe that the amphetamine hangover and depression are actually symptoms of WITHDRAWAL. Psychological dependence on amphetamines does occur. Experiments with animals have shown that those addicted to amphetamines and then withdrawn will work very hard to get more of the drug, and will keep trying approximately twice as long as similar animals who are addicted to heroin and then withdrawn.

Tolerance: Tolerance appears to develop to the euphoric effects of amphetamines. Users increase dose size considerably as a run progresses and there is a tendency to increase the amount of the drug used over a period of weeks or months. Tolerance to the cardiovascular effects of amphetamines is suggested by the fact that habitual users can survive single intravenous doses of 1000 mg or more with only occasional negative physiological effects, while a non-user would be at considerable risk at this dose. No tolerance seems to develop to the awakening or anti-sleep action of these drugs.

Amphetamines with alcohol: Amphetamine users have been known to use alcohol as an aid to induce sleep or to counter the wired-up feeling produced by a large amount of amphetamines. On the other hand, alcohol users have been known to take amphetamines to counter the depressant effects of alcohol. Although there is possible antagonism of the depressant effects of alcohol on the central nervous system, there is no improvement of impaired motor coordination. Not only can the combination of alcohol and amphetamines produce gastrointestinal upset, there is also the danger of producing a false sense of security which can lead to carelessness and accidents. Amphetamines can be dangerous when combined with alcohol because the safeguard against overdosing with alcohol—unconsciousness—is evaded. Some alcoholic beverages, Chianti wine for example, contain tyramime, a white crystalline base derived from the amino acid tyrpsine. The combination of tyramime and amphetamine can cause an excessive rise in blood pressure. The belief that amphetamines will increase the brief high produced by alcohol is false.

Sources: Amphetamines are commercially produced, but are limited by the CONTROLLED SUBSTANCES ACT as of 1972. Amphetamines are also smuggled in from Colombia and Mexico and sold on the black market. They are also illicitly manufactured in this country. Demand greatly exceeds supply and a large number of amphetamine look-alikes have appeared on the market. Currently available without prescription, and called "legal speed," are preparations of Phenolpropylenolamine (PPA's). Weaker than the amphetamines, when taken in large quantities mimics all the effects of amphetamines. These pills are advertised in magazines often aimed at youth. A new smokable form of methamphetamine has recently (late 1980's) emerged in the Orient and Hawaii (See ICE).

Traffic and control: Amphetamines and amphetamine-BARBITURATE preparations are Schedule II drugs under the Controlled Substances Act.

Synonyms: speed, crystal, meth, bennies, dexies, uppers, pep pills, diet pills, hearts, footballs, cranks, splash, and many others.

amyl alcohol The chief constituent of fusel oil, amyl alcohol is used as a source of amyl compounds, such as AMYL NITRITE. It is a colorless liquid with a burning taste. The term should not be confused with ETHANOL which is the principal chemical in alcoholic beverages.

amyl nitrite An inhalant used for vasodilation and to lower blood pressure, and occasionally in the treatment of asthma and

History of Amphetamines

1887 Amphetamines first synthesized.

1927 First medical use of amphetamines as a stimulant and as a nasal decongestant.

1932 Marketed as Benzedrine tablets and inhalers.

1937 First used medically to calm hyperactive children.

1940s American, British, German and Japanese governments issue amphetamines to soldiers to counteract fatigue, elevate mood and increase endurance.

Use of amphetamines by athletes and businessmen reported as early as 1940s.

Black market begins—"pep pills" used by students and truck drivers.

1949 Manufacture of Benzedrine inhalers discontinued because of danger of overdose.

1950s First wave of abuse. American soldiers in Korea and Japan mix amphetamines with heroin to create the first "speedballs" and use intravenously.

Amphetamines prescribed for narcolepsy, chronic fatigue and as an anorectic. American housewives begin abuse of "diet pills."

Amphetamines combined with barbiturates or tranquilizers (Dexamyl) and prescribed for depression.

1960s Widespread abuse begins. "Speedfreaks" inject massive doses of methamphetamine (Methedrine). FDA begins antispeed campaign with slogan "Speed Kills." Methedrine withdrawn from distribution through retail pharmacies (remains in distribution to hospitals) and black market manufacture booms.

1970s–1980s Widespread abuse continues and increases in the U.S. Studies show 12% of youth (aged 18–25) in 1972 used amphetamines; in 1982 this figure had risen to 18%. By 1988 use by this age group was estimated at 11.4%.

convulsions. Discovered in 1857, it was first used to treat angina pectoris. Amyl nitrite causes a sudden lowering of the blood pressure by dilating blood vessels; the lowering of blood pressure causes the heart to pump rapidly. The substance is supplied in glass vials (ampules) which are broken open and inhaled; amyl nitrite is only active when inhaled. A very quick-acting drug, it takes effect in 15 to 30 seconds and its duration is approximately three minutes. It is prized among drug abusers for its purported sexual stimulation and ability to intensify orgasm. It is also used to produce an intense brief euphoric high. Tolerance can occur but dependency is rare. It can have unpleasant side effects—vomiting and nausea—and can be dangerous for anyone with a heart problem.

Synonyms: pearls, poppers, snappers. (See also ALKYL NITRITES.)

Amytal® (Lilly) A sedative hypnotic DEPRESSANT containing the moderately rapid-acting BARBITURATE amobarbital. It is used for insomnia, daytime sedation and as a preanesthetic medication. Overdosage can cause central nervous system depression: symptoms are respiratory depression, reduction in reflexes, pupil dilation or constriction, decreased urine formation, reduced body temperature and coma. When used with alcohol or other CNS depressants it can have a potentiating effect. It is occasionally used non-medically. It is available as an elixir containing 34% alcohol and is also available in tablet form: 15 mg are light green;

30 mg yellow; 50 mg orange; and 100 mg pink.

Amytal Sodium® (Lilly) A sedative hypnotic DEPRESSANT containing the short-acting BARBITURATE amobarbital, which is used for the control of convulsions and as a diagnostic aid in schizophrenia. It can be administered intravenously or intramuscularly but administration should be closely supervised. It is occasionally used non-medically. Amytal Sodium is available in ampules to be mixed with sterile water before injection, and in 65 mg and 200 mg blue capsules.

anal administration See ADMINISTRATION.

analeptics A class of drugs that act as stimulants on the central nervous system, such as caffeine and amphetamines.

analgesic A drug used for the relief of varying degrees of pain without the loss of consciousness. Some analgesics will produce sedation.

anesthetics Substances, usually gases, which are used to produce anesthesia (coma) for surgical procedures. Along with their use in medicine, anesthetics have a long history of abuse. (See NITROUS OXIDE, ETHER, CHLOROFORM and INHALANTS.)

Anexsia-D® (Beecham Lab) A narcotic opiate containing the CODEINE derivative hydrocodone bitartrate, which is used as an analgesic. Its habit-forming potential is greater than codeine and less than morphine. It also contains aspirin, caffeine and phenacetin. A Schedule III drug, it is available in white uncoated compressed tablets.

angiitis, necrotizing A disease characterized by inflammation of small and medium sized arteries and segmental necrosis (death of living tissue in a localized area). It has been associated with viral infections such as hepatitis and the intravenous use of such drugs as methamphetamines and heroin. The disease usually terminates in the failure of vital organs and is generally fatal.

anileridine A synthetic NARCOTIC whose activity is similar to meperidine and which produces morphine-like effects. It is a Schedule II drug.

anorectics Drugs used as appetite suppressants in cases of obesity and for weight control. In recent years a number of anorectics have come on the market to replace AMPHETAMINES, and though they are less potent they produce many of the effects of amphetamines and have a very high potential for abuse. Some of the more common anorectics are benzphetamine, chlorphentermine, diethylpropion, fenfluramine, mazindol, phenmetrazine, phendimetrazine and phentermine.

Anstie's Law Sir Francis Anstie made public Anstie's Law of Safe Drinking in 1862: the law stated that 1½ ounces of absolute alcohol per day was the upper limit of safe drinking. Anstie was a British psychiatrist who established the first women's medical school in England. Even today after years of research, his law is viewed as a good general guideline for the average drinker. One and a half ounces of absolute alcohol is equivalent to four 8-oz glasses of beer, a half bottle of wine, or three 1-oz drinks of 100 proof liquor. It must be remembered, of course, that some individuals cannot tolerate any alcohol so the law does not apply to everyone.

Antabuse® (Ayerst) A drug used to stop people from drinking while they are being treated for alcoholism. Antabuse alone has little effect on the body, but if a patient combines it with alcohol he will have severe reactions, including headache, flushing, vomiting, breathing difficulty, and sometimes collapse and coma. Reaction begins 5 to 10 minutes after ingesting alcohol and may last from 30 minutes to several hours, depending on the amount drunk. The reaction occurs because Antabuse interferes with the metabolism of alcohol in the liver by causing a toxic buildup of acetaldehyde by inactivating aldehyde dehydrogenose. Its real value is in the knowledge of what will occur if a drink is taken, and though far from a complete answer, it can be a major aid in the treatment of alcoholics. The brand name of the generic drug disulfiram, it is supplied in white scored tablets of 250 and 500 mg. It should never be administered to a patient in a state of alcohol intoxication or without the full knowledge of the patient.

anticholinergic A drug that blocks cholinergic (or parasympathetic) nerve transmission. Therefore anticholinergics will dilate the pupils, cause dry mouth, cause the gastrointestinal tract to stop its movements, and sometimes produce delirium. Many drugs used in medicine have anticholinergic properties: examples are anti-Parkinsonian agents, antispasmodics, some antihistamines, antidepressants and antipsychotic drugs. Atropine is a classic example of an anticholicnergic drug. Abused for the side effect of delirium. Belladona is a toxic potent naturally occurring anticholinergic.

antidepressant A major classification of drugs developed in recent times to medically relieve depression in severely depressed patients. Antidepressant drugs are rarely used recreationally because although they seem to have a stimulant effect in cases of pathologic depression, they appear to have little immediate pleasurable effect on normal mood states. In fact, amitriptyline (Elavil) is occasionally abused for its sedative effect. Antidepressants are subdivided into cyclic antidepressants (TCA) and monoamine oxidase (MAO) inhibitors, and others.

Anti-Drug Abuse Act of 1986 (P.L. 99–570) In 1986, the Congress passed and President Ronald Reagan signed the Anti-Drug Abuse Act of 1986 (P.L. 99-570). One requirement of that legislation was the establishment of a White House Conference for a Drug Free America. The president appointed 127 citizens as conferees on the basis of their experience and commitment to a drug-free society. Chairman of the conference was Lois Haight Hessington, a former Deputy Attorney General of the United States. The Conference held six regional meetings in 1987. A national meeting took place in Washington, D.C. from February 28 to March 3, 1988. A final report was issued in June 1988 and included findings and recommendations, as well as proposals for certain legislative action necessary to implement such recommendations. The conference's final report is available from the U.S. Government Printing Office, Washington, D.C. 20402.

antihistamines Drugs used as histamine antagonists. They are usually prescribed for allergies, runny nose, sneezing, and motion sickness. They have central nervous system DEPRESSANT properties and when used with alcohol or other CNS depressants (narcotics, barbituates, tranquilizers) they can have an additive effect. Some antihistamines are combined with codeine or pentazocine (Talwin) and are sought after by drug abusers for their sedative effects. This combination is called T's & Blues (Talwin & pyrobenzamine). Alcohol, found in some antihistamines, produces a synergistic effect which increases the sedative properties of both the alcohol and antihistamine.

Antilirium® (O'Neal, Jones & Feldman) A drug containing physostigmine, a salicylic acid derivative of an alkaloid extracted from the seeds of the calabar bean (Physostigma venenosum). It is used to reverse toxic effects on the central nervous system (hallucination, delirium, disorientation, coma, and so on) caused by drugs which produced anticholinergic poisoning. It is supplied in 2 ml ampules for injection.

antipsychotics Also referred to as neuroleptics and previously as major tranquilizers, drugs in this category are rarely used nonmedically because they do not produce euphoria and can produce unpleasant side effects.

antitussive A drug used to relieve or prevent coughing, such as codeine or dextromethorphan. Many are narcotics.

anxiety A state of overwhelming and abnormal apprehension or fear often characterized by tension, increased pulse and sweating. Anxiety is a primary symptom of drug dependence and may at times be a factor in developing addiction. When someone learns that a drug can have an immediate effect in the management of these disturbing feelings, a pattern of drug abuse can be quickly established. But abuse and heavy consumption are often the cause of anxiety.

anxiolytic A minor tranquilizer that reduces anxiety.

aphrodisiac A substance that enhances or heightens sexual arousal or activity. (See SEX.)

apomorphine A chemical derivative of morphine that is used to induce vomiting. Unlike morphine it does not produce dependency and has no euphoric effects. It is also used in AVERSION THERAPY, in the treatment of alcoholism.

approval See PEER PRESSURE.

aprobarbital An intermediate-acting barbiturate generally used for sedation and to produce sleep. (See ALURATE.)

arecoline An alkaloid found in the nut of the betal palm, *Areca catechu,* native to Malaya. It has mild stimulant effects when chewed or sucked.

ASAM See AMERICAN SOCIETY ON ADDICTION MEDICINE.

asarone A drug found in the roots of the marsh herb sweet flag which grows wild in the United States. It is purported to have hallucinogenic effects similar to MESCALINE.

Ascriptin with Codeine® (Rorer) A narcotic opiate containing CODEINE and aspirin. An analgesic used for moderate to severe pain, Ascriptin also contains Maalox, an antacid medication, which keeps aspirin-induced gastric distress at a minimum. It is often used for arthritic conditions and can be habit-forming. It is also available without codeine.

Asian drug trade In the drug-trafficking countries of Burma, Laos and Thailand, the so-called Golden Triangle in Southeast Asia, political turmoil and favorable climate have provided conditions for increased narcotics production and trafficking. In April 1989, David L. Westrate, assistant administrator of the Drug Enforcement Administration, reported to a congressional subcommittee that "in addition to Burma being a major source country for narcotics transiting Thailand, it is expected that there will be an increase in opiate products from Burma transiting China, India, Laos, and Bangladesh." In Thailand, according to Westlake, "opium poppy planting during 1988 was estimated to increase slightly over the 4,000–5,000 hectares planted in 1987." Cannabis is being cultivated and smuggled out of Cambodia, the Philippines continues to serve as a transit/transshipment point for Southeast Asia marijuana and heroin destined for the United States, and Hong Kong—the third leading financial center in the world—continues to be a safe haven for narcotic-generated funds because of bank secrecy and weak currency control laws.

Opium poppy cultivation in 1987 in Pakistan's Northwest Frontier Province was approximately 205 metric tons, and the same in 1988. In September 1988, the United States and Pakistan signed the Tribal Areas Agreement, which provides for the gradual enforcement of an opium production ban. The five-year program is designed to eliminate all poppy production in the Mohmand and Bajaur agencies of the Northwest Frontier Province. India, on the other hand, continues to be concerned about its role as a transit country for narcotics produced in neighboring countries, particularly Pakistan and Afghanistan. India is the world's largest traditional supplier of legal raw opium. However, illegal poppy production and diversion of opium from legal production exist in India.

Afghanistan is a major producer of opium and hashish, with 1987 opium estimates ranging from 400 to 800 metric tons. Turkey continues to play a major role in the trafficking and transshipments of opiates from South Asia. From there opiates are smuggled westward through Bulgaria and Yugoslavia into Western Europe and/or the United States.

The U.S. Department of State reported in March 1989 that global production of coca, marijuana, opium poppies and hashish increased sharply in the last year, partly because of political and economic instability in drug-producing countries.

Elaine Sciolino, "Drug Production Rising Worldwide," *New York Times*, March 2, 1989.

U.S. Department of Justice, *Drug Enforcement Administration (DEA) Briefing Book*, 1989.

aspergillosis A number of samples of marijuana are contaminated by the fungus aspergillus. Only a very few instances of pulmonary aspergillosis have resulted from smoking marijuana, however, because heat destroys most or all of the fungus, and the healthy human is unlikely to become ill from a minor invasion of aspergillus fungi.

Association for Medical Education & Research in Substance Abuse (AMERSA) Organized in 1976 by the Career Teachers in Alcohol and Drug Abuse, AMERSA has been in the forefront of national organizations that address the unique interests and concerns of medical educators in the area of alcohol and drug abuse. The group has concentrated recently on training issues relating to primary care and has formed working alliances with the national leadership in psychiatry, pediatrics, family medicine, internal medicine, emergency medicine and obstetrics and gynecology.

AMERSA hosts an annual national conference, usually held in November in the Washington, D.C. area. In 1982, the organization held its first international conference on medical education in Berkeley, California. Cosponsors of the conference were the World Health Organization (WHO), the National Institute on Alcohol Abuse and Alcoholism (NIAAA) and the National Institute on Drug Abuse (NIPA).

AMERSA publishes the quarterly journal *Substance Abuse,* which is distributed to more than 400 members (all faculty members of U.S. medical schools) and to some 350 subscribers. The association maintains both a speakers' and a consultants' bureau available to organizations and institutions involved in or interested in advancing medical education in alcohol and other drug abuse. Recently, AMERSA joined with other national groups to define the availability of standards for fellowship training in the addictions.

Asthmador A cigarette containing stramonium and atropine and once used by asthma suffers. It is now obsolete. Along with relieving bronchial spasms, in large doses it also produced hallucinogenic effects.

ataraxic drugs Drugs used as TRANQUILIZERS. Also called ataractics.

at-risk populations Among the general population subgroups that have been identified as being particularly susceptible to drug abuse because of some risk factor such as age, environment, being a child of an alcoholic or drug abuser, etc. At-risk populations include adolescents, the elderly, and certain minority groups such as blacks and Puerto Ricans. Such subgroups have been targeted by drug misuse and prevention organizations.

Atropa belladonna See BELLADONNA.

atropine A belladonna (deadly nightshade) alkaloid that has also been synthesized. While generally used as an antispasmodic because it relaxes smooth muscle, it is also used as an antidote to certain poisons. In large doses it is toxic and since ancient times has been used as a sedative and poison. There have been fatalities among children who have eaten deadly nightshade.

attack therapy A group therapy in which individuals are verbally (never physically) attacked in the expectation that their defensiveness, rationalizations and denials will be broken down. They are vigorously confronted with their inappropriate or "junkie" thinking and behavior, so that they are compelled to examine themselves stripped of their defensive armor. Some therapeutic communities place the person under attack on a "hot seat" at the center of the group for greater focus.

Following the attack the individual is given considerable group support and understanding so that he can reconstitute his shattered psychological defenses into something more honest, realistic and resilient.

Australia Aside from excessive drinking which is the major drug problem in Australia, government surveys clearly show that marijuana is the illegal drug most often used in the country's various states. Not only is its use widespread, it is also increasing. Heroin use is also on the increase but in comparison to marijuana it is small in volume. There has been an increase in the use of methaqualone, too, particularly Mandrax (a British trade name). These trends are also clearly illustrated in statistics on drug charges prepared by the Australian Federal Police. Although barbiturates and amphetamines were popular in the late 1960s and were much abused, their use has declined. LSD, also popular in the 1960s, now enjoys minimal abuse. A survey in the late 1970s showed relatively minor use of cocaine, though if overseas trends affect Australia this could become a major problem.

Evidence presented to the Royal Commission of Inquiry into Drugs in the early 1970s showed illegal drug use was confined to certain community groups; by 1979, surveys showed a spread to almost every social, economic, cultural and age group, with the exception of the state of Tasmania. The latter was probably due to Tasmania's small population and its isolation from the mainland. The Royal Commission of Inquiry into Drugs is sponsored by the federal government. In Australia the responsibility for drug prevention is shared by the federal and state governments; the federal government acts privarily as a coordinator and adviser while the state governments are responsible for implementing policies and programs in their areas.

Government surveys carried out during the 1970s indicate certain trends among drug abusers in Australia. The majority are between the ages of 16 and 35 and within this range the 18–24 age group predominates. The predominance of young users is particularly noticeable in relation to heroin. It was found that use was far more prevalent among persons who had left school than those still attending, however. The same is true of marijuana use, though there has been a recent increase in use among older high school students. Although the 18–24 age group predominates, surveys showed that use of marijuana by well-educated people over the age of 30 is not uncommon. Regardless of whether the surveys investigated illegal use of drugs in general or specific drugs, the results showed that more males than females are abusers. The male to female ratio was, generally, three to two and two to one. It should be noted, however, that more males were involved in answering the surveys than females.

Few surveys have attempted to determine a connection between drug use and socio-economic background and the few that have are generally inconclusive. Inconclusive as they are, though, findings did indicate a higher rate of drug use among middle class children than working class children. One survey (Melbourne, 1973) found that the percentage of middle class fathers decreased in proportion to the intensity of drug use. Children of unskilled workers were more likely to become intravenous users than their middle class counterparts. There was also a trend of drug abuse among the unemployed.

Although few surveys have considered ethnic background and nationality, a 1972 study showed that the highest rates of abuse were among those who came to Australia from the British Isles and western Europe. Immigrants from southern and eastern Europe and Asia reported using drugs nearly three times less frequently. Midway between the two groups were those born in Australia. It should be noted, however, that the survey did not discriminate between tourists, newly-arrived settlers, and people who had lived in Australia for a number of years.

Although there was an indication that illegal drug use is more common among those who profess no religion than among those of a particular faith, again the surveys are inconclusive.

In recent years Australia has approached the drug situation with greater emphasis on abuse as a medical problem. Government programs now focus on education, treatment and rehabilitation along with continued law enforcement. Drug abuse treatment is provided, in one form or another, at all public hospitals. There are also voluntary community organizations in all states and territories which give additional help that the more rigid federal government is unable to provide.

In 1969 the government established a nationally coordinated approach to drug abuse control; the National Standing Control Committee on Drug Dependence, comprised of federal and state members. In 1970 the Drug Education Sub-Committee was established. It is made up of state and territorial health members with expertise in education, law enforcement and management fields, and has developed a National Drug Education Program aimed at incorporating drug education into the wider concept of health education in the community.

Federal hospital and treatment services are funded on a cost-shared basis with state governments. Many private organizations and hospitals also receive financial support from the government. As no single form of treatment is appropriate to all forms of drug dependence, a variety of programs and treatments are offered by the various institutions: (1) counseling and consultation; (2) detoxification with both chemical and psychological support; (3) controlled maintenance through methadone with the support of therapy; (4) psychiatric treatment; (5) participation in therapeutic communities; and (6) attendance at "drop-in" centers with advisory service. There is also continuing rehabilitation in the form of vocational guidance and counseling.

Law enforcement with respect to drugs in Australia is handled mainly by the following three bodies: the Australian Federal Police who police Commonwealth laws; state and territory police who work in conjunction with Commonwealth authorities; and the Bureau of Customs which has the responsibility of enforcing regulations in the importing and exporting of drugs. All state governments have agreed to a uniform code of penalties based on those applicable under Commonwealth government legislation. The Australian Federal Police serve as the national agency for the systematic collection, collation, evaluation and dissemination of information concerning illicit drug traffic and use in the country. The 1980 chart included in this article is an extract from the detailed statistics published in their annual report, *Drug Abuse in Australia.*

Drug and Drug-Related Offenses: Number of Charges* Involving Specific Drug Types: Australia 1978 to 1980

Year	Possess	Import	Use/ Administer	Traffic	Steal	False Pretenses	Forged Scripts	Other	Total
Narcotics									
1978	1,394	30	1,469	483	222	89	257	318	4,262
1979	1,068	73	1,009	414	137	73	379	367	3,520
1980	877	36	783	352	85	114	136	228	2,611
Cannabis									
1978	8,589	126	3,263	780	15	–	–	1,476	14,249
1979	10,688	102	3,472	862	23	2	–	2,352	17,501
1980	12,269	95	4,027	1,266	37	–	–	2,584	20,278
Amphetamines									
1978	46	–	46	5	–	5	18	3	123
1979	94	1	57	12	12	20	37	12	245
1980	85	–	49	25	–	22	14	6	201
Barbiturates, hypnotics									
1978	200	–	156	46	12	8	51	30	503
1979	359	–	263	53	45	32	104	51	907
1980	224	–	197	59	11	30	65	44	630
Tranquilizers									
1978	54	–	50	10	29	10	32	8	193
1979	79	–	40	29	34	12	36	18	248
1980	64	1	66	30	11	19	12	17	220
Hallucinogens									
1978	191	–	46	45	1	–	–	3	286
1979	186	–	40	33	–	–	1	18	278
1980	183	3	32	58	–	–	2	12	290
Other									
1978	53	–	14	10	32	2	212	9	332
1979	46	–	12	48	30	8	14	14	172
1980	50	–	23	51	24	74	41	22	285
Total									
1978	10,527	156	5,044	1,379	311	114	570	1,847	19,948
1979	12,520	176	4,893	1,451	281	147	571	2,832	22,871
1980	13,752	135	5,177	1,841	168	259	270	2,913	24,515

*Charges arising from offenses involving a number of different drug types have been counted under each drug type involved.

SOURCE: *Drug Abuse in Australia, 1980.* Australian Federal Police.

Excessive drinking is the major substance abuse problem in Australia. This was acknowledged in the country's Alcohol and Drug Addicts Treatment Act of 1961. According to several government studies, the most important cause of the alcohol problem is that excessive consumption—usually of beer—is not only accepted by most of the population but is actually expected and encouraged. Though there is some variation in the drinking pattern in urban and rural areas, the country as a whole is prone to associate heavy drinking with civil liberty, a pioneer identity, and other images of pride and freedom embedded in the Australian concept of "mateship." Between 1962 and 1972 there was a 25% increase in per capita consumption of beer. Extrapolations from limited surveys suggest that 5% of the male population (215,000) and 1% of the female population (43,000) are alcoholics. Surveys in Perth indicate that 11.4% of the aboriginal population suffer from "chronic" drinking problems and another 29% suffer indirectly from "environmental" problems associated with alcoholism. Adolescents are a particularly vulnerable group in Australia. A 1974 survey by the Department of Education and Health reported that by age 11 nearly half the boys and a third of the girls in the survey had been introduced to alcohol, usually by their parents.

By 1984, Australia ranked eighth in the world in beer consumption—153.3 liters per person ages 15 years and over—14th in wine consumption (28.4 liters per person age 15 and older), and 28th in spirits (pure alcohol) consumption (1.6 liters per person age 15 and over). (Note: 1 liter equals 1.06 quarts.) Total alcohol consumption—12.5 liters per person age 15 and over—placed the nation 14th in the international survey conducted by the Brewers Association of Canada in 1986.

The cost of alcoholism to the country is shown in traffic fatalities and injuries; hospitalization costs; and productivity losses by the labor force. Treatment is complicated by the difficulty of operating a centralized program in a country of continental proportions. One major detoxification unit, three clinics, and various social work centers are operated by the Alcohol and Drug Addicts Treatment Board. The board also coordinates the work of various volunteer organizations. Beyond these efforts, establishment of treatment centers is the responsibility of individual states, and it should be noted that facilities and treatment philosophies vary considerably throughout the country.

aversion therapy Based on experiments by the Russian scientist Ivan Pavlov (1849–1936), it is a behavior therapy based on conditioned reflexes and is used in the treatment of alcoholism. In aversion therapy a patient is detoxified and given a nausea-producing drug, such as APOMORPHINE, and then a shot of liquor. The nausea produced by the apomorphine subsequently becomes associated with the alcohol. Electric shock and verbally induced aversion are variations of this therapy. It has been stressed that alcoholics in such aversion programs must be provided with alternative ways of securing gratification while sober.

Disagreements have occurred as to whether aversion therapy provides a long-lasting cure and many patients drop out of this type of treatment because of its unpleasant effects. Previously popular in some Eastern European countries, it is not a type of therapy that is widely used in the United States.

aversive conditioning See AVERSION THERAPY.

ayahuasca A psychedelic beverage brewed by the Chama Indians of Peru. It is prepared from the vine and sometimes the leaves of *Banisteriopsis caapi*. The active alkaloid is HARMALINE.

Synonyms: caapi, natema, yage.

B

babies, drug-addicted and -exposed The rise of cocaine use, especially crack, has led to a higher proportion of pregnant women addicts. Consequently, reports of infants born with evidence of drug exposure have increased across the country. Moreover, cocaine-exposed babies are more likely to die before birth or to be born prematurely. They tend to be abnormally small for their age at birth and have smaller-than-normal heads and brains and an increased risk of deformities. Cocaine-exposed babies also may be at an increased risk of crib death, or sudden infant death syndrome (SIDS).

A 1988 survey of women having babies at 36 hospitals around the country found that on average, 11% were exposing their unborn babies to illegal drugs, with cocaine the most common. Rates varied among hospitals from less than 1% to 27%; hospitals in the study included those in urban as well as rural areas, with some serving the poor and others serving higher income groups.

According to reports, infants born in New York City alone with drug exposure or withdrawal symptoms nearly doubled during the 1987 fiscal year and were increasing by an additional 50% during the first four months of fiscal year 1988. Babies with exposure or withdrawal symptoms for the fiscal year that ended in June 1987 totaled 2,521.

Best estimates nationally are that more than 1 in 10 women, and 1 in 5 in inner-city hospitals, are giving birth to babies affected by drugs. In fact, the problem has prompted a loose confederation of fetal-protection advocates made up of physicians, social workers, prosecutors and even some prospective fathers dedicated to protecting unborn children against dangerous actions such as drug use or abuse by their pregnant mother. Some advocates are using the civil laws in an attempt to expand their efforts beyond cases of drug abuse. Women's rights advocates protest that the rush to protect the fetus will backfire and could deter women from coming forward for treatment. The American Civil Liberties Union (ACLU) agrees. A U.S. Supreme Court decision that grants legal status to fetuses could unleash a torrent of fetal protection cases.

Meanwhile, health authorities face an epidemic of drug-affected infants. Emerging medical findings indicate that effects on drug-exposed babies can include retarded growth, stiff limbs, hyper-irritability, tendency to stop breathing with higher risk of crib death, strokes and seizures, malformed or missing organs, facial deformities and mental retardation.

Jane Brody, "Cocaine: Litany of Fetal Risks Grows," *New York Times*, September 6, 1988.
Ted Gest, "The Pregnancy Police, on Patrol," *U.S. News & World Report*, February 6, 1989.

BAC See BLOOD ALCOHOL CONCENTRATION.

Bacarate® (Tutag) A brand of phendimetrazine tartrate which is used as an anorectic for weight control. The drug elevates blood pressure and stimulates the central nervous system. Its activity is similar to that of AMPHETAMINES and tolerance to its effects can build up within a few weeks. Overdosage results in rapid respiration, restlessness, tremors and hallucinations. It is available in 35 mg pink tablets.

BAL Blood alcohol level. (See BLOOD ALCOHOL CONCENTRATION.)

balloon effect A term which refers to the substitution of one type of drug for another when authorities clamp down on the original drug of choice: the crackdown on Mexican marijuana in southern California, for instance, resulted in an increase in heroin use. The phenomenon is likened to the squeezing of a balloon which, when squeezed in one direction, will expand in another.

banana smoking In the mid-1960s there was a widespread rumor that smoking the scrapings of the inside of a dried banana peel would produce a marijuana-like high. It was a hoax played on narcotics authorities, who would have found it impossible to prohibit the sale of bananas. Banana smoking not only produces no high but can actually be poisonous.

Bancap® (O'Neal, Jones & Feldman) A narcotic opiate containing CODEINE which is used as an analgesic for minor pain. It may be habit-forming, and overdosage can cause excitability.

Banisteriopsis caapi See AYAHUASCA.

bar drinker A person with a pronounced habitual tendency to consume alcoholic beverages in bars, saloons and other public establishments rather than at home or at social functions. A tendency to drink in bars can be caused by several reasons: because the person wants to hide a drinking problem; because of parental disapproval (particularly if the drinker is a minor); because drinking at home or at social functions is discouraged or disapproved of for religious reasons; or for other reasons. Convivial anonymity is characteristic of bar drinking, of course. There is little peer pressure; transient relationships are conducted in an atmosphere of at least mild intoxication; and alcohol is central to all involved. Alcoholics Anonymous, which stresses anonymity, group support and a desire to stop drinking, suggests that recovering alcoholics with past patterns of bar drinking are most receptive to their type of self-help group.

barbital A long-acting BARBITURATE with an onset time of up to one hour and a duration of up to 16 hours.

barbiturates Sedative (calming), hypnotic (sleep inducing) drugs that act as central nervous system (CNS) depressants. They slow down or decrease the activity of the nerves that control the emotions, breathing, heart action and a number of other body functions.

The first barbiturate was synthesized in 1864 from barbituric acid (malonylurea). It was first manufactured and used in medicine in 1882 as barbital and released under the trade name Veronal in 1903. Initially, barbiturates were used to induce sleep, replacing such aids as alcohol, bromides and opiates such as laudanum. Since the appearance of Luminal (a phenobarbital) in 1912, several thousand barbituric acid derivatives have been synthesized. Each of the 80-or-so brand names manufactured come in a variety of forms: tablets, capsules, suppositories, liquids for injection, and in combination with many other drugs. However, the medical profession considers five or six types sufficient for clinical use.

Classification: Barbiturates are metabolized (broken down chemically) in the liver and eliminated by the kidneys at varying speeds according to their types: slow- or long-acting (mostly phenobarbital and barbital); intermediate and short-acting (mostly secobarbital and pentobarbital); and ultrafast (thiopental).

Slow- or long-acting barbiturates take one to two hours to reach the brain through the bloodstream. Their effects last six to 24 hours with a half-life of 48 hours for phenobarbital and 24 hours for barbital brands. They are used medically to induce sleep, to provide day-long sedation in the treatment of tension and anxiety problems, and in combination with other drugs in the treatment of epilepsy and other convulsive and neurological conditions. They are also used in withdrawal treatment for alcoholism and addiction to other sedatives. Long-acting barbiturates are metabolized slowly and pass through the liver unchanged, leaving most of the work of detoxification to the kidneys.

They are the preferred type for patients with liver problems. Because barbiturate users want quick action they are seldom attracted to slow- or long-acting brands and this group of drugs rarely makes its way into the black market.

Intermediate and short-acting barbiturates take effect in 20 to 45 minutes and are very much alike. They are metabolized rapidly by the liver, placing much less strain on the kidneys and are consequently preferred for patients with kidney problems. Short-acting barbiturates are the type commonly known as "sleeping pills." Their effects last only five or six hours and they produce little or no hangover when not abused. They are used medically as sedatives in obstetrics, in the treatment of insomnia, anxiety neuroses, high blood pressure and coronary artery disease and for various diagnostic procedures. Because of the speed with which they take effect, short-acting barbiturates are invariably the choice of abusers and are most likely to produce dependence. The four most in demand, according to the Drug Enforcement Agency, are Nembutal (pentobarbital), Amytal (amobarbital), Seconal (secobarbital), and Tuinal (secobarbital and amobarbital combined). They are most like alcohol in the speed with which they take effect, in the kind of intoxication produced by their abuse, and in the addiction which can result. These are the sleeping pills most in demand by would-be suicides.

Ultra-fast-acting barbiturates produce unconsciousness in a very few minutes. The best known type is sodium pentothal (thiopental). It is used almost exclusively in hospitals as an anesthetic in minor surgery and to induce anesthesia before the administration of a longer-acting anesthetic such as nitrous oxide. Ultra-fast-acting barbiturates are rarely found outside of medical channels and present no abuse problems.

Effects of abuse: The effect of these drugs varies with the strength of the dose, individual tolerance depending on previous use, and when and where taken. A prescribed dose at bedtime will merely induce sleep. Intoxication results when they are taken in larger doses in a social setting such as a party or at a bar, especially when combined with alcohol. With mild intoxication there is a feeling of well-being (euphoria); there is a heightening of self-esteem and a lowering of inhibitions. Increasing intoxication produces reactions exactly like those of alcohol intoxication—staggering due to loss of muscular control, short temper, the "fighting drunk" syndrome of aggressiveness and violence or, in some individuals, depression and withdrawal. Barbiturate abusers suffer the same morning-after hangover miseries as alcoholics including headache, nausea, dizziness, depression and drowsiness that may persist for hours. Impairment of judgment, poor motor control and mood swings may last many more hours, making chronic users unfit to drive or operate machinery. Very high doses increase blood pressure and depress respiration so that less oxygen reaches the heart and brain. Such doses may result in acute poisoning with all the classic signs of shock: shallow breathing, weak pulse, cold and clammy skin, depressed reflexes. Coma and finally death—usually from respiratory failure—may occur unless hospital care is available in time.

Tolerance: With regular use the body gets so accustomed to the presence of the drug that ever larger or more frequent doses are needed to get the desired effects. Unfortunately, tolerance to the lethal level does not develop and as time goes on chronic users may find themselves close to a fatal dose before they get any effect at all. Accidental death may occur when the user is not certain about how much to take because of his increased tolerance, or because he becomes confused and does not remember taking a previous dose or how much of a dose was taken.

Dependence: Two kinds of dependence (addiction) may develop with abuse. Psychological (psychic) dependence, which can develop very quickly, occurs when there is a compulsive desire for the relaxing or hypnotic effects of the drug—a feeling that well-being or sleep is not possible without it. Physical dependence takes longer to develop and is far more dangerous. It occurs when the body has grown so used to the presence of the drug that it reacts violently if the drug is suddenly withdrawn or sharply reduced. Physical dependence on barbiturates and other sedative hypnotic drugs is one of the most dangerous of all drug dependencies.

Barbiturates and pregnancy: A woman who uses barbiturates regularly during pregnancy, especially in high doses, may endanger her baby. Congenital defects and abnormal behavior have been observed in such children. The drug is carried from the mother's bloodstream into the child's through the placenta and after birth the baby suffers the same withdrawal symptoms that are produced by all central nervous system depressants. These may include feeding difficulties, disturbed sleep patterns, breathing problems, irritability and fever.

Withdrawal symptoms: Once physical dependence has developed, suddenly stopping or sharply reducing daily barbiturate doses causes very severe withdrawal symptoms—worse than those that follow morphine or heroin withdrawal. They include anxiety, progressive weakness and restlessness, dizziness, visual distortion, nausea, vomiting, delirium and severe convulsions. With fast-acting barbiturates, reactions come to a peak in about two to three days. Reactions to withdrawal of slow-acting types take seven or eight days to reach their height. When dependence on barbiturates has been very deep, symptoms can last for several months. Treatment consists of slowly reducing the daily intake. While this does not eliminate suffering, it at least decreases the severity of the more serious reactions and lessens the danger of death while the body slowly adjusts. Death occurs in about 5 to 7% percent of those attempting withdrawal without treatment.

Interaction with other drugs: Barbiturate users often take other drugs as well. A common abuse pattern is to take AMPHETAMINES to wake up and to offset the morning-after barbiturate hangover. Then more barbiturates are needed to fall asleep and as the dose increases so does the need for more amphetamines until a vicious cycle develops. Alcohol and barbiturates are another common and dangerous mixture: each one enhances the effect of the other so that a dose of either one—not normally fatal taken alone—can cause death (see SYNERGY). Other drugs which interact with barbiturates are tranquilizers, antihistamines, and opiates which also depress the brain's control over breathing and increase the risk of respiratory failure.

Who uses barbiturates? According to one study, the elderly (especially women) received the most prescriptions for sedative hypnotics. Since age decreases the speed with which drugs are metabolized, people over 65 are particularly vulnerable to their toxic effects and to the development of dependence. In addition, some of the effects of these drugs are often mistaken for senility.

There has been a marked increase in abuse of barbiturates and other sedative hypnotic drugs among young people—even down to the grade school level. One Canadian study revealed that 12.8% of students in grades 7 to 12 had used prescribed barbiturates and 6.8% had used unprescribed pills.

Sources: Barbiturates are legitimately available only by prescription. Their manufacture is strictly controlled by the Drug Enforcement Administration under Schedule II of the Controlled Substances Act. Unlike amphetamines and narcotics, barbiturates are not illicitly manufactured in clandestine laboratories. The supplies that reach the black market are generally stolen or smuggled in from Colombia or Mexico. Government agencies estimate that about 20% of legally produced barbiturates are diverted through illicit channels.

History of Barbiturates

1864	**Two German scientists, von Mering and Fischer, synthesize barbital, a derivative of barbituric acid.**
1903	**Barbital is introduced to medicine under the trade name Veronal.**
1912	**Phenobarbital, a second derivative, is introduced under the trade name Luminal.**
1930s	**Barbiturates are widely prescribed in the U.S.**
1940s	**Studies show that barbiturates are intoxicating and addictive, and that withdrawal symptoms appear when use is stopped.**
1942	**First major campaign against nonmedical use of "thrill pills" is launched.**
	States begin passing laws against nonprescription barbiturates, and black market becomes profitable.
1950s	**Barbiturates become one of the major abused drugs in U.S.**
1960s	**Abuse spreads to youth.**
1970s–1980s	**Barbiturates still widely prescribed and abused. Government estimates that 20% of legally manufactured barbiturates is diverted into illicit channels. A 1988 survey by the National Institute on Drug Abuse indicates that 3.5% of the population had used sedatives without a prescription.**

Traffic and control: As with other dangerous drugs, illegal possession of barbiturates is a criminal offense. The charge is "possession" and the offender is subject to arrest. Without proof of intent to sell, however, sentences are often light.

Synonyms: goof balls, barbs, downers, block busters, and numerous others. Terms tied in with the color of the capsules include: blues or blue devils (Amytal); Mexican reds, red birds or red devils (Seconal); yellow jackets (Nembutal); rainbows or Christmas trees (Tuinal); and purple hearts (Luminal).

behavioral learning theory A psychological theory of alcoholism based on the assumption that alcoholics drink because alcohol consumption is followed by a reduction in anxiety and tension. Since alcohol is a sedative drug, this theory may also apply to the abuse of other sedative drugs. As more is understood about alcoholism, so the theory has become broader in concept. A number of behavior theorists now recognize that factors other than tension reduction may play an important role in the development of alcoholism, including peer pressure, heredity, family drinking styles, specific situational cues such as bars and cocktail parties, and so on. Because behavioral models propose that alcoholism is a conditioned behavioral response, it is suggested that alcoholism or other sedative drug abuse can be helped through modification of stimuli and reinforcement.

behavioral toxicity Behavior that is destructive to the individual or those around him. When aberrant, damaging behavior is due to drug intoxication, withdrawal or overdose, it is more obvious than the impaired perceptions or mood changes caused by chronic use of a drug. If a person has hallucinations and does not act upon them, they would not be detected. If he responds to the hallucinatory event, the behavior becomes evident to others and may culminate in injury or incarceration.

beinsa *Mitragyna speciosa,* a plant native to Burma. There are claims that it can produce sedative effects when chewed or brewed into a tea.

belladonna A plant, *Atropa belladonna,* also called deadly nightshade, that has been known since the Middle Ages as a sedative and a poison. The Romans considered the pupil dilation caused by belladonna a mark of beauty. It can produce hallucinations with severe adverse reactions, and sometimes even extremely small doses can prove toxic. As little as 120 mg of plant material (less than the amount of material in a marijuana cigarette) may result in coma or death. There have been fatalities among children who have eaten deadly nightshade. It contains the alkaloids ATROPINE, HYOSCYAMINE and SCOPOLAMINE and these extracts are used today as ingredients in proprietary drugs. Other plants containing belladonna alkaloids are DATURA, HENBANE, MANDRAKE, PITURI and SCOPOLA.

Benzedrine® (Smith, Klein & French) A brand of AMPHETAMINE sulfate. Generally used for weight control, it has a high potential for abuse and tolerance and extreme psychological dependence often occurs. Overdosage can result in insomnia, irritability and personality changes. It is available in 15 mg transparent capsules containing red and white grains, and in 5 and 10 mg peach-colored tablets.

Synonyms: bennies, benz, peaches, roses, whites.

benzene A toxic volatile hydrocarbon found in paint and varnish removers, gasolines and pesticides. It has an intoxicating effect when inhaled, and has consequently been abused. Prolonged inhalation can result in acute poisoning and liver damage. It is being decreasingly used in industry.

benzine A volatile petroleum distillate used in motor fuels and numerous cleaning fluids. It produces intoxicating effects when inhaled. Acute poisoning can result from prolonged inhalation.

benzodiazepine The chemical source of the class of DEPRESSANT drugs known as minor tranquilizers (or anxiolytics) which includes chlordiazepoxide (Librium), diazepam (Valium), oxazepam (Serax), clorazepate dipotassium (Tranxene) and others. Flurazepam (Dalmane), which is a sedative hypnotic, is also a benzodiazepine derivative. Stronger than meprobamate and tybamate, the benzodiazepine derivatives have gained popularity as safer substitutes for BARBITURATES. Australian authorities credit the replacement of barbiturates with benzodiazepine derivatives for the fall in the Australian suicide rate between 1962 and 1973.

Activity in the body: The benzodiazepine derivatives are readily absorbed in the gastrointestinal tract and quickly though unevenly distributed in the body. Most are metabolized in the liver and slowly excreted in the urine. They are central nervous system (CNS) depressants and act on the brain's limbic system, the center of emotional response. The usual half life is about one day.

Effects: The effects of the benzodiazepine derivatives closely resemble those of the barbiturates, though they produce less euphoria. The drugs relieve tension and anxiety due to emotional stress. They also relax muscular tension caused by anxiety, and have some muscle relaxant activity. They have very little effect on REM sleep in ordinary amounts. They are useful in treatment of seizure disorders.

Adverse reactions are rare but can include drowsiness, loss of coordination, confusion, constipation, rash, jaundice, tremors and—in large doses—fainting. Paradoxical hostility has also been reported.

Use of benzodiazepine derivatives was thought to involve a low risk of tolerance or the development of physical or psychological dependence. This was another factor in doctors' preference for these drugs over barbiturates. When dependence does occur and the drug is stopped, cessation of administration is accompanied by withdrawal symptoms similar to but less severe than those seen in barbiturate and alcohol addiction: convulsions, tremors, muscular and abdominal cramps, vomiting, sweating, insomnia,

Benzodiazepines

Generic name	Trade name
	Short half life (4–20 hours)
Oxazepam	Serax
Lorazepam	Ativan
Temazepam	Restoril
Alprazolam	Xanax
Triazolam	Halcion
	Long half life (24–72 hours)
Chlordiazepoxide	Librium
Diazepam	Valium
Clorazepate	Tranxene, Azene
Flurazepam	Dalmane
Clonazepam	Clonopin
Prazepam	Verstram Centrax
Haalzepam	Paxipam

loss of appetite, and the recurrence and aggravation of the patient's neurosis. These symptoms can last 7–10 days.

The mild tranquilizers are additive with alcohol and other CNS depressants (see SYNERGY), and should be administered very carefully, if at all, in combination with these drugs.

Usage: Medical applications of the benzodiazepine derivatives cover a wide range. Their most common use is as anxiolytics in the relief of symptoms of tension and anxiety resulting from neurosis or stressful circumstances. Other applications include treatment of convulsive disorders, neuromuscular and cardiovascular conditions, and gastrointestinal distress related to anxiety.

Knowledge of the advantages of the minor tranquilizers over barbiturates has spread beyond the medical community to drug abusers, and many of these drugs are available illicitly. Because they produce less euphoria and intoxication than barbiturates, abusers often take them in dangerous combination with other drugs, particularly alcohol; 10% of drivers arrested for DRIVING UNDER THE INFLUENCE have both alcohol and minor tranquilizers in their systems. Similarly, the minor tranquilizers have been used successfully in suicides (and accidental deaths) when ingested with alcohol.

benzoylecgonine A cocaine metabolite which is looked for when testing an individual for drug use. Benzoylecgonine is invariably found in the urine of a cocaine user whether or not cocaine itself is present.

benzphetamine A sympathomimetic amine with pharmacological activity similar to AMPHETAMINES. It is used as an anorectic for weight control and in the treatment of narcolepsy and has a significant potential for abuse. (See DIDREX.)

benzpyrene A carcinogen in MARIJUANA and TOBACCO.

Beta Alcoholism See JELLINEK.

biofeedback A treatment method used in addict withdrawal and rehabilitation. It's aim is to increase motivation to tolerate withdrawal and decrease tension after physical withdrawal is complete. The patient is presented with his ongoing biological information (such as heart rate) by means of biofeedback machines using meters, lights, auditory signals, etc. The treatment then centers on the patient using this information to self-regulate the biological process and control certain autonomic functions. This method of self-regulation is similar to the ancient practice of yoga. The technique is not completely understood and the Biofeedback Society of America, founded in 1969, along with other medical organizations, is continuing to research the subject.

biological models See PHYSIOLOGICAL ETIOLOGICAL MODELS.

Biphetamine® (Pennwalt) A central nervous system stimulant that contains AMPHETAMINE and DEXTROAMPHETAMINE. It is used as an anorectic for weight control. Tolerance can develop within a few weeks and it has a high potential for abuse. Psychological dependence and social disability can occur. Overdosage can result in restlessness, tremors, hallucinations and coma. It is available as Biphetamine 7½ mg in white capsules; Biphetamine 12½ mg in black and white capsules; and Biphetamine 20 mg in black capsules.

Synonyms: black beauties, blackbirds, black mollies.

BHCDA See BUREAU OF HEALTH CARE, DELIVERY AND ASSISTANCE (BHCDA).

black Americans According to the National Institute on Drug Abuse, 61.2% of black males admitted to federally-funded drug abuse treatment programs in 1980 were admitted for heroin abuse, as opposed to 21.3% of white males. As with other available statistics, however, this figure may be the result of several factors unrelated to actual usage. There is a greater likelihood that a black addict will be arrested or otherwise become *known,* for instance. If there is indeed a higher proportion of heroin addicts among blacks it may well be the result of a difference in heroin distribution channels in recent years, and may not mean that there is a predilection for heroin among blacks. Primary heroin distribution centers for urban areas are often located in black sections. Because of this illicit drug traffic pattern, narcotic agents often follow traffickers into black ghettos and this may account for a heavy overrepresention of black addicts.

Treatment programs for black addicts have encountered difficulties in cases where METHADONE maintenance is suggested. Some have suggested that methadone maintenance is a conspiracy against the black community. It is believed, for instance, that methadone renders males impotent and causes both males and females to become sterile. Although these beliefs have been proved false, there is still concern among some people that methadone programs are used for repression.

In the case of alcoholism rates, there are no significant differences in those for black males and white males, though the latest government report shows there has been an increase in the problems and consequences of alcoholism in the last 10 years. As with the white community, alcoholism is a serious problem. Among blacks it is particularly serious, however, because the mortality rate for CIRRHOSIS is nearly twice as high as it is for whites. Studies have suggested that blacks are also more susceptible to CANCER of the upper digestive tract. Blacks suffer as well from a significantly higher rate of hypertension, which is further complicated by drinking. The black community also has a significantly higher rate of alcohol-related homicides.

Economic frustration, unemployment, and racism can exacerbate drug use and drinking, especially in black ghettos.

Among black adolescents there is reported to be a higher abstention rate and a lower rate of heavy drinking than among whites. Due to social, economic and family problems this tendency changes and there is a higher rate of alcoholism among young black adults.

There is a high rate of heavy drinking among black women (11% compared with 4% of white women). This fact is supported by studies that show black women to have lower expectations about life than white women. There is also a higher rate of abstainers among black women—51% compared with 39% of white women. Economic and domestic problems drive some black women to heavy drinking, while the same stresses cause others to abstain from alcohol altogether and focus on a "happier hereafter." Among blacks who drink, twice as many black women as black men report health problems due to drinking. Also, the incidence of fetal alcohol syndrome (FAS) is an estimated 1 to 3 per 1,000 live births.

As is the case with drugs, treatment programs for alcoholism are not recognized or accepted in many black communities, probably because there is often more tolerance for drunkenness than in white communities. Alcoholics Anonymous (AA) groups, for instance, are sometimes perceived by blacks as being strictly white middle-class institutions. Blacks are also less likely to have insurance to pay for alcohol treatment services, and they may lack knowledge about free social services. It should be noted, however, that blacks who are admitted to hospitals and clinics show a stronger motivation to abstain and cooperate more fully in treatment than do white alcoholics.

blackout A chemically induced period of amnesia commonly suffered by chronic alcoholics and not uncommonly by nonalcoholics in conjunction with bouts of extremely heavy drinking over a short period of time. Blackout consists of an individual's inability to recall entire blocks of time during which he was fully conscious, and seems related to the impairment of the brain's information transfer facilities to long-term memory stores. An early sign of progressive alcoholism, the risk of blackout is increased by factors such as fatigue and stress and by the combination of alcohol with such drugs as sedatives, tranquilizers and marijuana. Blackouts are called alcohol amnestic disorder in DSM III (Diagnostic and Statistical Manual, Third Edition).

blood alcohol concentration (BAC) The degree of a person's intoxication can be measured by the concentration of alcohol in his bloodstream. Blood alcohol concentration (BAC), also referred to as blood alcohol level (BAL), measures the weight of the alcohol in a fixed volume of blood.

BAC tests are most often given to motorists suspected of DRIVING WHILE INTOXICATED (DWI), but they are also used in alcohol treatment centers and medical facilities as guides for the treatment of inebriated patients. The percentages of BAC are expressed differently throughout the world: in the United States, for example, BAC for seven parts of alcohol per 10,000 parts of blood is expressed as .07%; in Canada the equivalent would be 70 milligrams per 100 milliliters of blood and would be expressed as 70 mg%; in Sweden it would be recorded as 0.7 promille.

In DWI tests, the percentage necessary for a person to be considered legally intoxicated varies from state to state; from .08% in Idaho and Utah to .10% in the District of Columbia and most other states. A person's BAC can be determined by testing his breath or urine as well as by giving a blood test. Breath analyzers have come into common use, particularly for on-the-spot analysis.

A number of factors contribute to a person's BAC:

(1) Weight: The larger and heavier a person is, the greater his or her blood supply, thus more alcohol can be accommodated. Fatty tissue is a major determinant of a BAC level. Since excess weight is stored in the form of fat, an overweight person's blood supply is not increased in proportion to the additional weight. Therefore a fat person can have a higher BAC than a lean person of the same weight from a given amount of alcohol.

(2) Sex: BAC is generally higher for women. Recent research indicates that women have less of a stomach enzyme called gastric alcohol dehydrogenase that neutralizes alcohol.

(3) Time of consumption: Unless alcohol consumption is limited to less than one full drink an hour, BAC will generally continue to climb. Alcohol is slowly excreted by the body in the following way: oxidization by the liver 95%; breath 2%; urine 2%; perspiration 1%.

(4) Food consumption: Although the effect of food on BAC varies from individual

to individual, in general a full stomach will help to retard the absorption of alcohol.

(5) Quantity: Drink equivalents vary from 1½ ounces of "hard" liquor (gin, scotch, etc.) to 5 ounces of table wine to 12 ounces of normal-strength beer. Two 1¼-ounce shots of hard liquor, and the equivalent in wine or beer, may result in BAC levels of 0.1%.

blood alcohol level (BAL) See BLOOD ALCOHOL CONCENTRATION (BAC).

blood sugar An alcoholic will sometimes suffer from hypoglycemia, a low concentration of sugar in the blood. The condition is apparently due to the interference of alcohol with the normal conversion of carbohydrates into sugar. Alcohol may also indirectly stimulate the hormone insulin, which works to lower blood sugar. Inadequate food intake, common in alcoholics, can also contribute to hypoglycemia. Low blood sugar is also thought to be a possible contributor to the HANGOVER effect.

B'nai B'rith International An international service organization established in 1843 to unite world Jewry for the advancement of the Jewish people and to help create a better world for all. CVS, the Community Volunteer Services of B'nai B'rith, suggests that alcoholism is probably a greater problem than other areas of drug abuse and has begun a concentrated program of prevention. Focusing on a mass media information campaign, the program includes the distribution of literature directed at both the Jewish and general communities.

BNDD The Bureau of Narcotics and Dangerous Drugs, now called the Drug Enforcement Administration (DEA).

B & O Supprettes® (Webcon) A narcotic analgesic containing powdered OPIUM and BELLADONNA extract. It is used rectally for minor to severe pain, and can be habit-forming. Overdosage results in respiratory depression.

boats and drugs Drugs pay for about one of every three recreational boats in Miami and "maybe 50% carry some kind of contraband sometimes," says writer T. D. Allman. In addition, drug TRAFFICKING is behind the piracy of many recreational boats off the Florida coast. Some stolen boats are used to transport drugs while others are illegally seized because they are mistaken for craft belonging to rival drug gangs. Dealers in security equipment, including guns, actually tout their wares at national boat shows in Florida. Sometimes, boating people get involved in drug-trafficking themselves. On August 29, 1987, powerboat-racing champion Benjamin Kramer was arrested for running a drug ring involving the distribution of approximately 550,000 pounds (250,000 kg) of marijuana between early 1980 and mid-1987. The grand jury noted that Kramer was the "organizer, supervisor and manager" of the smuggling operation, which did business in Florida, Illinois and elsewhere in the United States. (See also SMUGGLING.)

T. D. Allman, *Miami: City of the Future* (New York: Atlantic Monthly Press, 1987), 83.
Gilda Berger, *Drug Abuse: The Impact on Society* (New York: Franklin Watts, 1988), 82–83.
James A. Inciardi, *The War On Drugs* (Palo Alto, Calif.: Mayfield, 1986), 184–191.

Boggs Amendment An amendment to the HARRISON NARCOTICS ACT of 1914, the NARCOTIC DRUGS IMPORT AND EXPORT ACT of 1922, and the MARIJUANA TAX ACT of 1937. Enacted in 1951, the amendment increased the penalties for all drug violations. Reflecting the increased concern over drug addiction after World War II, it lumped together—for the first time—marijuana and narcotic drugs and established uniform penalties for offenses: a mandatory minimum sentence of two years for first "narcotic" violators and up to 10 years' imprisonment for repeat offenders. These penalties were raised in 1956 by the Narcotic Drug Control Act.

BOL-148 A congener of LSD-25, d-2-bromolysergic acid tartrate. It is a hallucinogen.

Bolivia Coca cultivation and consumption have been traditional for centuries in Bolivia, but licit demands for coca account for only 12,000 of the estimated 70,000 metric tons that are produced annually. Along with Peru and Colombia, Bolivia is responsible for the majority of cocaine on the world market (see Appendix 3, Tables 39, 43 and 44). Most of the coca cultivated in Bolivia is processed and distributed by Colombia.

Bolivia has averaged more than one government per year since the republic was founded in 1825, and after each change attempts by the U.S. government to resume coca control must begin all over again. Narcotics assistance programs were begun in Bolivia in 1972, for instance, and in 1977 there was an agreement that provided for narcotics control assistance and a study of alternate crops. But a coup by General Garcia Meza in 1980 halted these activities; allegedly Meza had the support of a Mafia group who dominated the cocaine trade. The Bureau of International Narcotics Matters (INM) recently attempted an eradication program designed to reduce Bolivia's coca cultivation to a licit level. The program included both voluntary and mandatory crop eradication and controls. There are an estimated 23,000 farm families growing coca, usually on small holdings of one hectare (2.47 acres) or less. The large number of landowners complicates the eradication problem. Officials now contend that $300 million to $500 million a year is needed to develop legitimate alternatives for coca-farming peasants. This is considerably more than President Bush's so-called Andean initiative, proposing between $100 million to $270 million to finance anti-drug campaigns in Bolivia, Peru and Colombia.

Bontril PDM® (Carnrick) A brand of phendimetrazine tartrate; a stimulant used as an anorectic for weight control. Its activity is similar to that of AMPHETAMINES and tolerance to its effects develops within a few weeks. It has a potential for abuse and can cause personality changes, insomnia, irritability and hyperactivity. Overdosage can result in rapid respiration, hallucinations, restlessness and tremor. It is available in three-layer green, white and yellow tablets.

booting Attempting to prolong the initial effects of a HEROIN injection by injecting a small amount, then withdrawing blood back into the syringe and repeating the process.

booty In their crackdown on drug traffickers, especially major drug lords, federal authorities in the 1980s have taken possession of a wide range of properties and other assets bought with proceeds from illegal drug sales. Law enforcement officials have seized boats, cars, aircraft, businesses, and even real estate purchased with profits of drug kingpins. In fiscal year 1986, total income to the U.S. Department of Justice Assets Forfeiture Fund was about $90 million; under provisions of the 1984 Comprehensive Crime Control Act, some $25 million in cash and property forfeited in federal cases in 1986 was shared with the state and local criminal justice agencies that participated in those cases. Gross seizures by the federal government mushroomed to more than $1 billion in fiscal year 1987, due largely to efforts by U.S. Justice Department agencies and the U.S. Customs Service.

This sharing of proceeds from seized assets with state and local law enforcement officials began in August 1985, following authorization by Congress in the Comprehensive Crime Control Act of 1984. State and local law enforcement agencies share property forfeited to the federal government in proportion to their participation in particular cases—and are thus encouraged to help federal officials make "big busts."

State and local law enforcement agencies have received more than $182 million in cash and property from the federal government since the change in the law. Funds are used to purchase vehicles, firearms and surveillance equipment, as well as to support overtime pay for narcotics officers, funding for informants and new investigative units to go after major drug traffickers.

Defense attorneys object to the aggressive asset seizure policy since the law can be used to keep ill-gotten drug profits from being used to pay attorneys, either by freezing the assets of the accused in pretrial proceedings so that attorneys cannot be paid or by seizing fees allegedly paid from drug proceeds at a later time. Some legal authorities say the practice of seized fees violates the Sixth Amendment right to counsel of choice, interferes with the attorney-client relationship and precludes an effective defense because such cases require specialized expertise.

Nonetheless in a 5-4 ruling in June 1989, the U.S. Supreme Court determined it was permissible for federal prosecutors to seize the assets of those indicted for dealing drugs, including money used to hire a lawyer. Justice Byron White said Congress made no exception for attorney's fees when it allowed seizure of assets. No right exists, the court stated, "to spend another person's money for services rendered by an attorney." The ruling gives prosecutors a powerful tool against drug dealers who hire high-priced lawyers to keep them out of jail.

As the kinks gradually are worked out, the asset-seizure program will likely grow more important. European nations are now considering new asset-seizure laws and in the United States several states have followed the lead of Arizona and Florida, which have both developed sophisticated seizure capabilities. The Police Executive Research Forum and the National Criminal Justice Association have developed and are presently maintaining a training program for local criminal justice investigators using the tools and techniques for financial investigations in asset seizure and forfeiture cases. The training is funded by the Bureau of Justice Assistance. For more information on these training sessions, write or call: Richard Ward, Bureau of Justice Assistance, 633 Indiana Avenue, N.W., Washington, DC 20531. Telephone: (202) 724-5974.

National Institute of Justice, *Research in Action, NiJ Reports/SN 9 202,* March/April 1987, p. 2.

booze As a verb it means to guzzle or drink to excess, usually to get drunk quickly. As a noun, it is an alcoholic beverage, often whiskey, such as that made around 1840 by a Philadelphia distiller named E. G. Booze. Both the verb and the noun predate Mr. Booze by many centuries. It was formerly spelled "boose" from early Germanic sources. From booze comes other terms: "boozing it up," "boozer," and so on.

Bowery A section and street in lower Manhattan, populated largely by derelicts. Although it has been partially rehabilitated, it is still an impoverished area and contains a SKID ROW section. Its inhabitants are the source of the term "Bowery bum." The area was formerly notorious for its cheap theaters, dance halls and drinking gardens.

brain A part of the CENTRAL NERVOUS SYSTEM (CNS), which is made up of the brain and spinal cord. The brain controls almost all the functions of the body through its nerve cell network which reaches all the tissues, and through its regulation of the endocrine hormones.

The brain consists of some 12 billion cells, and has a complex chemistry that is only now being explored. Stimulation of a neuron results in an electrical transmission through the long cell axons that extend from the nerve cell. Transmission from one neuron to another is a chemical process across a microscopic gap (or synaptic cleft) between the cells. We are aware of numerous neurotransmitters (also called biogenic amines) that carry the signal across the gap. They include dopamine, norepinephrine, serotonin and acetylcholine. It is suspected that hundreds of neurochemicals are present in various parts of the brain.

Not all substances in the bloodstream enter the neuron. A blood-brain barrier exists that keeps certain molecules out—proteins, for example. All drugs that have an effect on brain function will, of course, pass the blood-brain barrier. The drugs that are abused usually affect synaptic transmission, others impact on cell membrane permeability.

Alcohol Ethanol affects the neuronal membrane, delaying the exchange of ions and thereby diminishing its electrical excitation. Alcohol interfers with the cell's ability to utilize oxygen and glucose which leads to malfunction and eventually death of the neuron. This explains the brain atrophy seen in chronic alcoholics. A certain amount of function can be regained if the alcoholic becomes abstinent: in this case the remaining neurons take over the lost cell's functions.

Marijuana The precise way in which cannabis affects the brain is not known. Many mental functions are affected by marijuana intoxication, including immediate recall, sensory perception, tracking, attention span, etc. The heavy, consistent ingestion of marijuana produces a chronic cannabis syndrome (amotivational syndrome) in certain people. Since it is LIPID SOLUBLE and the nerve cell membrane is lipid, the drug seems to be retained in the brain for longer periods than alcohol. Studies that show distortions of synaptic structure are suggestive of marijuana's effect, but further work is needed.

Cocaine and amphetamines Both drugs make dopamine available at synapses in the brain in excessive quantities, leading to euphoria, and later paranoid psychosis. When the dopamine is depleted depression occurs.

LSD and Other Hallucinogens Serotonin antagonism may account for the unusual mental effects of these drugs.

Heroin Heroin is locked into specific opiate binding sites and exerts its euphoriant, analgesic and sleep-inducing activity on that basis.

Benzodiazepines A specific benzodiazepine receptor site has been identified. Stimulation results in increased amounts of G.A.B.A., a neurotransmitter. When triggered by a benzodiazepine, reduction of anxiety and sedation occur.

Barbiturates Like alcohol, barbiturates appear to act on the cell membrane. They have effects similar to alcohol on brain cell transmission and the withdrawal syndrome (the DTs) is identical to alcohol withdrawal symptoms which confirms the idea that both drugs have similar mechanisms.

(See also individual drug categories and CENTRAL NERVOUS SYSTEM.)

breathalyzers Machines which detect and measure the blood alcohol concentration (BAC) of a person. They have been used for a number of years by law enforcement agencies in an effort to crack down on drunk drivers. The readings are based on a solid state, semi-conductor reaction to alcohol present in the breath. Recently a portable, handheld breathalyzer has begun to gain popularity in high schools. A number of schools which have purchased them admit that they are reluctant to use them but they hope the presence of a breathalyzer at the school and the students' awareness of the fact will deter alcohol use during school hours. Although there have been no major complaints, it has been hinted that the use of breathalyzers in schools may be the source of potential conflicts over constitutional rights. Breathalyzers are being utilized increasingly by the military, and in areas where the public is at risk.

Breath alcohol has a constant ratio to blood alcohol levels. Breath alcohol levels are multiplied by a factor of 2,300 to obtain blood alcohol levels.

breech births Studies have shown that breech births, in which a fetus emerges with the buttocks, knees or feet appearing first, are significantly higher among mothers addicted to narcotics. (See PREGNANCY for other effects of narcotic use among pregnant women.)

Brevital Sodium© (Lilly) An intravenous anesthetic containing methohexital sodium. A rapid, ultra-short acting BARBITURATE, it is used for short surgical procedures. It may be habit-forming but the rapid onset of effects and brief duration of action makes it less desirable for purposes of abuse.

British System, the In Great Britain the treatment of opiate users is medically oriented and addicts are allowed to obtain and use opiates legally. Widely praised by advocates of heroin maintenance, the system has been recommended as a model for implementation in the United States. The British System has been credited with limiting the use of heroin, preventing the development of a black market, reducing drug-related crimes, and enabling addicts to lead more useful lives.

Before 1967, the system was simply a policy that allowed private physicians to prescribe maintenance doses to opiate users. As heroin abuse increased during the 1960s, however, the approach was altered and in 1967 a government-sponsored program was established. The new program imposed stricter controls on the manufacture, sale and posession of opiate drugs, and required addicts to be registered and treated through clinics or through specially licensed physicians.

It is of interest that the British System of heroin maintenance has become a methodone maintenance system. In 1980, 2,095 of the 2,846 patients in treatment received methadone alone; others received methadone in combination with other drugs; and only 53 patients were given heroin alone.

The British System remains highly controversial, and while some observers view government clinics as a sensible and humane approach to the problem, others maintain that the clinics are not abstinence-oriented and do not handle the problem of addiction. (See also UNITED KINGDOM.)

bromides A group of synthetic sedative hypnotic DEPRESSANTS derived from bromine. Introduced to medicine in 1857 as a treatment for epilepsy, bromides were later widely prescribed as sedatives, though rarely used as hypnotics. Bromides are now considered obsolete and have been replaced by BARBITURATES and BENZODIAZEPINES.

Activity: Bromides are readily absorbed into the bloodstream and have a 12-day half-life. They appear in mother's milk and cross the placental barrier.

Effects: Bromides depress the central nervous system but, like paraldehyde, have little or no effect on the medullary centers and thus do not affect breathing or circulation. In low doses bromides have a typical sedative effect, causing drowsiness and loss of muscular coordination. The substance is cumulatively toxic, however, and larger doses can, paradoxically, cause confusion and agitation.

Dependence can occur, resulting in a disease similar to alcoholism called bromism. Symptoms include tremors, skin rashes, dizziness, delirium and lethargy. Coma and death can result.

Usage: Bromides have been used medically as antiemetics (to suppress vomiting), aphrodisiacs, anticonvulsants and sedatives but they are rarely used nowadays. They are not often used for recreational purposes.

Bromides are not subject to the Controlled Substances Act.

Brompton Cocktail A variable mixture of drugs used in British and American hospices to control terminal pain associated with cancer. Traditionally, it contained heroin, cocaine and an antiemetic like Thorazine. Morphine is equally effective as heroin when given orally after dosage adjustment. Cocaine has been dropped from the formulation in many hospices.

bruxism See TOOTH GRINDING.

Buff-A-Comp© (Mayrand) A buffered analgesic containing aspirin, caffeine, phenacetin and the intermediate-acting BARBITURATE, butalbital. It may be habit-forming and has the potential for abuse. It is also available in capsules and tablets containing 30 mg of codeine in addition to the above ingredients.

bufotenine A HALLUCINOGEN found in the skin glands of certain toads, as well as in several plant species. In Haiti and parts of Central and South America, natives use a snuff, Cohoba, which contains bufotenine as well as DMT and other hallucinogenic substances. Bufotenine produces an LSD-like experience though the illusionary disturbances are less complex. Physical effects are pronounced. The user experiences walking difficulties and paralysis and the face may swell and redden. Typically, the physical effects of the drug appear first. As the effects wane, the user falls into a stupor-like sleep.

Synonym: Yopo (for Cohoba).

buprenorphine A NARCOTIC ANTAGONIST.

Bureau of Health Care, Delivery and Assistance (BHCDA) One of the three organizational components of the Health Resources and Services Administration (HRSA). BHCDA works to improve access to quality health care for populations underserved because of social, economic and cultural factors. BHCDA has a number of alcohol and drug abuse activities underway for close to six million clients through a network of 565 community and migrant health centers (C/MHCs). The C/MHCs' purpose is to focus on alcohol and/or other drug-related clinical symptoms requiring further attention. Through BHCDA, C/MHCs have received funding that enabled them to improve the care of clients who exhibit problems with alcohol and other drugs. The organization has also a heightened public awareness through extensive community education and prevention activities, linkage agreements with local alcohol and drug agencies, and distribution of resource directories and prevention brochures.

BHCDA, as a component of HRSA, is within the Public Health Service (PHS), in the U.S. Department of Health and Human Services.

Vivan Chem, M.A., M.S.W., "BHCDA: A Federal Model for Collaboration," *Alcohol Health & Research World,* 13:1 (1989), 64–67.

Bureau of Narcotics and Dangerous Drugs (BNDD) A law enforcement agency in the U.S. Department of Justice which was created in 1968. It was replaced in 1973 by the Drug Enforcement Administation (DEA).

Bureau of Narcotics, Federal A government agency within the Treasury Department created in 1930. Its goal was to investigate, detect, and prevent violations of laws prohibiting unauthorized possession, sale or transfer of opium, opium derivatives, synthetic opiates, cocaine and marijuana. Transferred in 1968 to the Department of Justice, it was merged with the Bureau of Drug Abuse Control to form the Bureau of Narcotics and Dangerous Drugs. This bureau, in turn, was replaced by the Drug Enforcement Administration (DEA).

business Drug abuse is having an astronomical effect on American business and the American economy. Not only is drug abuse causing lost productivity, its effects are mushrooming throughout other areas of business. A government-sponsored survey by the Research Triangle Group in 1986 showed that the total cost to the economy (adjusted to reflect current dollars due to inflation) was conservatively estimated at $25 billion. A breakdown of the costs showed the following categories:

Lost productivity: Absenteeism, nearly $5 billion; drug-related deaths, $1.3 billion; imprisonment, $2.1 billion; and the loss of employees who left the job to find more lucrative methods (often criminal) to support their habits, $8.3 billion.

Medical expenses: Treatment in hospitals, by private doctors, and in rehabilitation centers, $1.9 billion; Employee Assistance Programs research and training, and the administration of other programs, $367 million.

Crime: Court, police, and prison costs on all levels (federal, state and local), $5.2 billion; crime prevention methods (locks, alarm systems, etc.), $1.6 billion; and the destruction of property during drug-related criminal acts, $113 million.

It was suggested that these incredible costs to business reflect the fact that previous high school age drug abusers are now a part of the U.S. work force. This additional population compounds the loss in productivity created by older drug users on the work force.

Today, the new Bush plan to fight drugs and drug abuse problems carries a price tag of over $8 billion, dwarfing recent drug-fighting budgets, including the $2.1 billion spent in 1985.

The economic cost to the nation from alcohol use and alcohol abuse in 1988 alone was $117 billion.

Alcohol, the most abused drug, accounting for 98,000 deaths annually, was recognized as a problem in industry as long ago as the 1930s and 1940s, and steps were taken to deal with it (see EMPLOYEE ASSISTANCE PROGRAMS). Today the problem of abuse also includes illicit drugs, such as cocaine, marijuana, and prescription drugs (particularly amphetamines). They present an entirely different problem. Because these drugs are illegal, they are usually used secretly and identifying employees involved in such drug abuse is more difficult. There is also the expense factor. While alcohol is relatively inexpensive, an illicit drug habit can easily become more than a person can handle on his or her salary. The cocaine habit, in particular, can cost hundreds of dollars a day to support.

Drug abuse is not centered around a particular level of employment; nor are actual working hours particularly relevant. It should be noted that alcohol and drug abuse know no socio-economic class, ethnic background or gender classification. Secretaries will use drugs (particularly marijuana) on a lunch break; nightshift workers will take amphetamines to stay awake; high-level executives will snort cocaine in the morning to "get going" and will continue to snort the drug during the day to "stay on top." Drug abuse is common practice in *all* occupations. Even the medical profession is not exempt, although doctors see the consequences of abuse more than anyone. Perhaps the pressure, stress and long hours involved in medical practice are responsible, perhaps it is the availability of drugs. Whatever the reason, it has been suggested that nearly 4% of doctors and nurses are drug dependent. The consequences of drug use by members of the medical profession could be staggering when one considers the importance of clear judgment in saving lives. (See HEALTH CARE PROFESSIONALS AND ADDICTION.)

In the area of car production, one of the biggest industries in the U.S., it has been suggested that the poor quality and low sales of American cars are related to the problem of drug abuse among employees and that this problem accounts for the success of imported cars. The problem is not always limited to employees on the assembly line but extends to office personnel; they may cost a company money because of poor bookkeeping. Surveys have shown that drug abusing employees perform at only 67% of their ability. In order for the American car industry to remain in business, it has been suggested that these employees be weeded out or rehabilitated.

Companies are increasingly employing drug detection tests, usually blood and urine tests. IBM, AT&T and 3M are among the private companies that have successfully begun testing job applicants and, when suspicions arise, some of their employees. Fewer than half of the Fortune 500 companies, however, have initiated testing programs, scared off by costs and labor opposition. These tests are generally performed on employees who exhibit the following symptoms: requests for late arrivals and early departures; requests for time off; numerous sick days; and those who are more likely to file a workmen's compensation claim in case of accidents. Companies also are looking for other tell-tale signs among drug abusers: pupil changes, odors, chain smokers who do not use filter tips, and constant licking of the lips. Investigations are also often instigated by other employees who complain about the performance of fellow employees because they are tired of "covering" for them.

The implementation of Employee Assistance Programs (EAPs) can save billions of dollars annually among large corporations. Dr. Robert G. Wiencek, associated with General Motors, states that "for every $1 invested in treatment, General Motors can identify $3 in return for full-time employees who recover completely."

Unless a worker has union backing, or an employment contract that will help defend him, he has little legal protection against drug tests or "the right to search." Workers have occasionally sued for "invasion of privacy" and "defamation of character"; court battles are time-consuming and corporation practices have often been found negligent.

The biggest problems to American industry are loss of productivity and accidents, but there is also the additional problem of theft. Drug habits are expensive and there is a clear relationship between heavy drug use and crime. Employees not only embezzle money, they also take company property and are often involved in "company kickbacks."

Alcohol and drug abuse cost well over $100 billion in lost or impaired productivity each year, according to the latest statistics. And these costs are increasing. Untold millions more dollars are lost as a result of problems linked to substance abuse; increased on-the-job accidents, theft, and in-house security breaches.

Drug abuse, for example, cost the U.S. economy $60 billion in 1983, or nearly 30% more than the $47 billion in 1980. Lost productivity, absenteeism, increased health benefit utilization, accidents, and losses stemming from impaired judgment and creativity are among the drug-related expenses in the estimate. A growing number of companies are now looking to Employee Assistance Programs to help control skyrocketing health care costs.

Employee Assistance Programs address a much broader range of issues, including alcohol, drug abuse and other personal issues. Services of the EAPs are typically free and seem to be one of the best answers to industry's drug-related problems. The General Motors program is well known; the company set up its original alcohol-based programs in 1972 and in 1975 expanded them to include the abuse of other drugs. Unfortunately, despite good success rates, many companies do not want to get involved in treatment programs—possibly because the monetary value of treatment programs is sometimes difficult or impossible to evaluate, or because the company feels it is too small to take on such projects. Small- to medium-sized industries are often the most difficult to reach because of monetary considerations. It is startling to realize that money diverted from legitimate business enterprises to buy illegal drugs could be as much as $100 billion a year (2.5% of the GNP and 8% of discretionary spending), while the costs to individual companies usually exceeds 2.5% of payroll. (See also ABSENTEEISM, ACCIDENTS and WORKPLACE.)

butabarbital An intermediate-acting barbiturate that produces mild sedation and has muscle-relaxing properties. (See BARBITURATES.)

butalbital An intermediate-acting barbiturate used as a sedative hypnotic. (See BARBITURATES and BUFF-A-COMP.)

Buticaps© (McNeil) A central nervous system depressant containing the intermediate-acting BARBITURATE sodium butabarbital. It is used for sedation and hypnotic purposes and psychological dependence can occur. Overdosage can result in severe respiratory depression. It is available in 15 mg lavender and white capsules; 30 mg green and white capsules; 50 mg orange and white capsules; and 100 mg pink and white capsules.

Butisol Sodium© (McNeil) A central nervous system depressant that contains the intermediate-acting BARBITURATE sodium butabarbital. It is used for sedation and hypnotic purposes and may be habit-forming. Psychological dependence can occur. Overdosage can result in severe respiratory depression. It is available in green elixir, 30 mg per 5 ml with 7% alcohol, and in tablets: 15 mg lavender; 30 mg green; 50 mg orange; and 100 mg pink.

butyl alcohol A solvent made by the fermentation of glucose. It should not be confused with ETHANOL, the principal chemical in alcoholic beverages.

butyl nitrite An inhalant drug that first appeared in 1969 and which is similar to AMYL NITRITE. Classified as a volatile inhalant, butyl nitrite inhalation produces a brief but intense lightheaded feeling, the result of lowered blood pressure and relaxation of smooth (involuntary) muscles of the body.

C

caffeine (1, 3, 7-trimethylxanthine) A naturally occurring alkaloid found in many plants throughout the world, caffeine was first isolated from coffee in 1820 and from tea leaves in 1827. Both "coffee" and "caffeine" are derived from the Arabic word *gahweh* (pronounced "kehveh" in Turkish).

Caffeine is a STIMULANT of the CENTRAL NERVOUS SYSTEM. When taken in beverage form, it begins to reach all the body tissues within five minutes; peak blood levels are reached in about 30 minutes. Caffeine has a half-life in the body of about three and a half hours. Normally caffeine is rapidly and completely absorbed from the gastrointestinal tract. Little can be recovered unchanged in urine and there is no day-to-day accumulation of the drug in the body.

Caffeine increases the heart rate and rhythm, affects the circulatory system and acts as a diuretic. It also stimulates gastric acid secretion. There may be an elevation in blood pressure, especially during stress. Caffeine inhibits glucose metabolism and may thereby raise blood sugar levels.

A behavioral stimulant which interferes with sleep and may postpone fatigue, caffeine appears to interact with stress—improving intellectual performance in extroverts and impairing it in introverts. When taken before bedtime caffeine usually delays the onset of sleep, shortens sleep time and reduces the average "depth of sleep." It also increases the amount of dream sleep (REM) early in the night while reducing it overall.

Fatalities resulting from caffeine poisoning are rare: only seven deaths have been recorded to date. The lowest known fatal dose is 3.2 grams administered intravenously. The fatal oral dose appears to be of the order of 10 grams.

While caffeine in moderate doses can increase alertness and talkativeness and decrease fatigue, regular use of 350 mg or more a day results in a form of physical dependence. Interruption of such use can result in withdrawal symptoms, the most prominent of which is sometimes quite severe headache—which can be relieved by taking caffeine. Irritability and fatigue are other symptoms. The regular use of caffeine produces partial tolerance to some or all of its effects.

Regular use of over 600 mg a day (approximately eight cups of percolated coffee) may cause chronic insomnia, breathlessness, persistent anxiety and depression, mild delirium and stomach upset. It may also cause heart disease; researchers at Johns Hopkins University School of Hygiene and Public Health found a modest association between heavy coffee drinking (considered to be five cups or more per day) and a myocardial infarction in young women (a condition in the heart muscle resulting from the formation of a blood clot in the coronary arterial system.) Excessive use of caffeine has been suspected as a factor in cancer of the bladder and renal pelvis, but the evidence is inconclusive. In addition, caffeine consumption has been linked to fibrocystic disease in women, but, again, the evidence so far is inconclusive.

Studies have also indicated that heavy use of caffeine in amounts equivalent to eight or more regular cups of coffee a day is responsible for an increased incidence of spontaneous abortions and stillbirths, breech deliveries, and cyanosis at birth.

Caffeine is probably the most popular drug in the world. It is primarily consumed in tea and coffee but is also present in cola drinks, cocoa, certain headache pills, diet pills, and patent stimulants such as Vivarin and Nodoz. Caffeine belongs to the family of methylxanthines. Theophylline and theobromine are closely related compounds but caffeine is the most potent of the group.

The following chart shows the caffeine content of various products:

Product	Caffeine (mgs)
Coffee (5 oz.)	
Regular Brewed	
percolated	110
dripolator	150
Instant	66
Decaf Brewed	4.5
Instant Decaf	2
Soft Drinks (12 oz.)	
Dr. Pepper	61
Mr. Pibb	57
Mountain Dew	49
Tab	45
Coca-Cola	42
RC Cola	36
Pepsi-Cola	35
Diet Pepsi	34
Pepsi Light	34
Instant/Brewed Tea (5 min. brew)	45
Cocoa	
Cocoa (5 oz.)	13
Milk Chocolate (1 oz.)	6
Drugs	
Vivarin Tablets	200
Nodoz	100
Excedrin	65
Vanquish	33
Empirin Compound	32
Anacin	32
Dristan	16.2

Sara J. Carrillo, "Caffeine Versus the Body," *PharmChem Newsletter,* Vol. 10, No. 3 (April 1981.

"Facts About Caffeine" (Toronto, Canada: Addiction Research Foundation of Ontario, January 1980).

M. B. McGee, "Caffeine Poisoning in a 19-Year-Old Female," *Journal of Forensic Sciences,* Vol. 24, No. 1 (January 1980).

Mark Wenneker, "Breast Lumps: Is Caffeine the Culprit?" *Nutrition Action* (August 1980) (Publication of Center for Science in the Public Interest).

caines A group of synthetic local anesthetics that are sometimes used as adulterants of cocaine. They include Novocaine, Pontocaine and Lidocaine and provide the numbness, and perhaps a little of the euphoria of cocaine. They are to be found in the "legal cocaines" advertised in publications that specialize in drug paraphernalia. They are cocaine look-alikes and sound-alikes with names like "cococaine," "snowcaine," etc.

calabar bean Seeds of the plant *Physostigma venenosum,* which is native to the West Indies. The seeds contain physostigmine, an inhibitor of the enzyme that breaks down acetylcholine, and therefore cause severe adverse reactions.

California, drug cases in Drug abuse makes headlines when Hollywood celebrities are involved. But the problem is also widespread among workers in other industries. Dr. Howard Frankel, medical director of Rockwell's space shuttle division from 1981 to 1983, says from 20% to 25% of Rockwell employees at the Palmdale, California plant (final assembly point for U.S. space shuttles) were high on the job from drugs, alcohol or both. One raid by police on Rockwell's shuttle assembly plant resulted in nine workers being fired. R. Richard Heppe, president of Lockheed California, told a *Time* magazine reporter that "people with these problems are much higher security risks."

Another California problem is CLANDESTINE LABS, now flourishing in the southern part of the state. The labs produce "crystal meth" and other forms of speed, PCP and even synthetic heroin. Nationwide, state and federal authorities raided 647 clandestine drug labs in 1987, an increase from 479 during 1986. Three-quarters of those labs were located in southern California. Clandestine drug labs have been a factor in California's drug underworld since the mid-1960s, when the Hell's Angels motorcycle gang began setting up operations to produce speed. For a total investment of less than $5,000, an underground chemist can make about 10 pounds of crystal meth. Each pound sells for $10,000 to $15,000 wholesale, or up to $150,000 for the 10-pound batch. And the value of the same batch at retail (street) prices may be as much as $15 million.

Gilda Berger, *Drug Abuse: The Impact on Society* (New York: Franklin Watts, 1988), 13, 66, 102, 117.

Michael A. Lerner, "An Explosion of Drug Labs," *Time,* April 25, 1988, 25.

California poppy There are unconfirmed claims that smoking the poppy *Eschscholtzia californica* can produce narcotic-like effects.

calorie A unit of measure used to express the heat- or energy-producing value of food when it is metabolized in the body. Absolute alcohol, on the average, contains about 150 to 200 calories an ounce. Calories contained in alcohol are so-called empty calories because they cannot be stored and do not produce essential vitamins for the body's nutritional needs. The body burns alcohol before it burns food, which is stored and used as fat. Prolonged consumption of heavy amounts of alcohol while cutting down on food can lead to malnutrition and avitamenosis, a condition frequently seen in alcoholics.

Canada The patterns and trends of drug abuse in Canada tend to follow those of the United States, probably because of the geographical proximity, but to a much lesser extent. As in the U.S. smoking and drinking are the two major health problems; but there has been increasing use of marijuana, heroin, codeine, cocaine, and methaqualone. Alcohol-related social costs reached $6.4 billion for Canada and $1.8 for Ontario in 1984. Codeine, a legal drug in Canada, is the most popular psychoactive drug in that country.

It was estimated in 1987 that 1.8 million Canadians (9.5% of the total population of 20 million) have used marijuana at some time. A government survey in 1973 reported

45,000 *known* users and over 10,000 convictions on marijuana-related charges. Regarding heroin, the survey reported 7,719 *known* users. The survey also reported 10,000 known users of other hallucinogens, particularly LSD, PCP and MDA. The use of inhalants was also reported but to a far lesser degree. An earlier survey had shown an increase in the abuse of methaqualone which led to the establishment of a methaqualone treatment program in 1971.

There was a movement in Canada, as there is in the United States, toward the legalization of marijuana. The federal Commission of Inquiry into the Non-Medical Use of Drugs (commonly called the Le Dain Commission) which is conducting a continuing study, suggested that while marijuana should not be legalized, penalties for possession cases should be reduced—no jail sentences for first offenders—and that research on the subject be continued and expanded. As a result of the study, considerable discretion is now used in possession cases. However, convictions for trafficking, importing, exporting and growing marijuana can result in prison terms of up to seven years. If the charges concern narcotics or other dangerous drugs, the penalty can be seven years to life imprisonment.

Treatment programs in Canada generally center around the problem of heroin addication; methadone maintenance is generally used. It should be noted, however, that there has been an increase in methadone abuse recently.

Attitudes toward alcohol consumption, which is one of the country's major health problems, are becoming more liberal as they are in most other developed Western countries. But a 1986 national survey shows that 62% of the population favors a national law that would set the legal drinking age in all provinces at 21 years. Between 1950 and 1987 there was an increase in drinking among youth and women—groups that in the past did not generally drink—and the number of abstainers may have dropped by 50%. Canada's drinking pattern is one of increased consumption on weekends and holidays, though only one-sixth of the consumption takes place in public places. Beer is the most popular drink. Proportions of alcoholic beverages consumed breaks down to 50% beer, 40% distilled spirits, and 10% wine, with the latter two on the increase. Per capita consumption, on a national level, rose 34% between 1966 and 1974. International comparisons for alcohol consumption per person 15 years and over, in 1984, show Canada with 105.9 liters (1 liter equals 1.06 quarts) for beer, 12.5 for wine, and 3.4 for spirits (pure alcohol). The nation's total alcohol consumption per person 15 years and over was 10.2 liters, giving it a ranking of 21st among other countries, tied with the United States. Between 1975 and 1979 sales of alcoholic beverages by value rose 46% from $2.9 billion to $4.37 billion.

A conservative estimate of the entire country put the total number of alcoholics at 503,000 in 1984. In 1986, there were 150,571 alcohol-related traffic offenses. In 1985, there were 880 divorces attributed to alcohol-related problems. There is an acknowledged need for comprehensive training programs to deal with the problem and there are agencies responsible for combating abuse on both the federal and provincial levels. But while most of the provinces maintain research foundations, health facilities and education programs, formal policies aimed at reducing abuse appear to be lacking. In many provinces voluntary and charitable organizations, such as the Salvation Army and Alcoholics Anonymous, have been the most successful in addressing the problem.

Canary Island Broom *Genista canariensis.* There are claims that when smoked or taken orally, this plant can produce narcotic-like effects. It is poisonous even in low doses.

cancer The primary drugs of abuse which seem to be directly related to cancer are alcohol and tobacco—the two most abused drugs in the United States. Recent studies have shown that heavy drinkers who also smoke have a higher incidence of cancer than drinkers who do not smoke or smokers who do not drink. Compared to the rest of the population, alcoholics and heavy drinkers show a high incidence of mortality from cancer of the mouth, pharynx, larynx, esophagus, liver and lungs. Cancer associated with alcohol accounts for 6.1% to 27.9% of the total incidence of all cancer. It has been difficult to separate the effects of drinking from the effects of smoking because most heavy drinkers are also heavy smokers. Alcohol itself has not been shown to be an independent carcinogen, but it is thought to act as a co-carcinogen—a substance that promotes cancer in conjuction with a carcinogen. Studies have indicated that alcohol and cigarettes act synergistically to increase carcinogenic potential, particularly in cancers of the mouth and throat. It has been suggested that the combination of drinking and smoking increases the risk of throat and mouth cancer 15 times above that of the non-smoking non-drinking population.

Studies of marijuana smokers and the incidence of cancer are few and inconclusive; in fact, THC (the active ingredient in marijuana) is sometimes prescribed for cancer patients as a treatment for the nausea and vomiting caused by chemotherapy.

During the 1950s and 1960s extensive studies provided conclusive evidence that cigarette smoking was directly related to lung cancer, heart disease, emphysema and chronic bronchitis. It was further shown that cigarette smoking during pregnancy was hazardous to the unborn child. (See NICOTINE.)

In 1989, U.S. Surgeon General C. Everett Koop released a report on the consequences of smoking that attributed 390,000 deaths to smoking tobacco in 1985. The report stated that major smoking-related diseases were cancer, heart disease, respiratory disease and other conditions, such as stomach ulcers. It indicated that since 1986, lung cancer has exceeded breast cancer as the leading cause of cancer death in women—the relative risk of lung cancer among women smokers has increased more than four times since the early 1960s. Smoking, according to Dr. Koop, now causes more than one of every six deaths in the United States.

Hepatoma (primary liver cancer) is often accompanied by and probably preceded by CIRRHOSIS. Studies have shown that 64% to 90% of victims suffer from both conditions. It has been suggested that liver cancer proceeds in two stages: liver damage due to alcoholism, followed by intervention of a secondary agent which sets off the actual malignancy.

A number of theories seek to explain the increased incidence of cancer in alcoholics and/or smokers. Inadequate nutrition is one of them: lack of nutritious food weakens the body's immune defense system, leaving it vulnerable to cancer-causing agents. Another theory suggests that alcohol itself causes cancer. Known carcinogens have been found in many alcoholic beverages; beer, for example, has been found to contain asbestos fibers from the filters used in its manufacture. Alcohol has also been shown to have an effect on the cell membranes, possibly increasing the ability of carcinogens to affect the cells themselves. Alcohol may also dissolve water-insoluble carcinogens making them more available to various organs.

Richard L. Berke, "U.S. Report Raises Estimate of Smoking Toll," *New York Times,* January 11, 1989, A20.

cannabinoids Derivatives of CANNABIS. Cannabis contains some 60 cannabinoids.

cannabis The Indian hemp plant, *Cannabis sativa.* The resin, flowering tops, leaves and stems contain the psychoactive substance delta-9-TETRAHYDROCANNABINOL (THC).

Cannabis sativa, which probably originated in Central Asia, grows wild practically anywhere but flourishes in temperate and tropical climates. The resin contains the highest concentration of THC; plants grown in very hot, dry climates produce the most resin and are therefore most potent. An herbaceous annual with palm-like leaves, male and female plants occur separately. The female plant is taller, broader and longer-lived than the male and produces more leaves and resin. Although the plant can reach 30 feet, average height is four to eight feet, and it has a hollow, six-sided base that is at least two inches in diameter at maturity.

Cannabis occurs in a variety of grades, depending on climate and method of cultivation, and can be processed to yield several different forms of graduated strength. Plants cultivated for the hemp fiber contain only .05% THC. The name marijuana refers to the leaves and flowering tops which are dried and shredded and usually consumed orally—either smoked in cigarettes or pipes, or prepared in foods or beverages such as tea. It typically contains 0.5–5% THC. Ghanga, which is cultivated and consumed primarily in Jamaica, is made from the flowering tops, leaves and top stems of a specially cultivated female plant and contains about 10% THC. Hash oil is the most potent form of cannabis with a THC content of 20%.

The cannabis family, *Cannabinaceae*, has one other member, *humulus lupulus:* the hops of this plant are used to flavor beer and ale.

Cannabis has been not quite appropriately classified as a HALLUCINOGEN. Although it is true that it *can* produce psychedelic effects in very high doses, it also exhibits some of the characteristics of depressants (sedation), narcotics (analgesia) and even stimulants (enhanced perception). Its defiance of previously established categories seems to merit its being classified a Schedule I drug under the CONTROLLED SUBSTANCES ACT.

The hemp plant has long been cultivated for a variety of commercial, medical, recreational and religious purposes. First documented as early as 2700 B.C. (by the Chinese emperor Shun Nung) as a pharmacologically useful herb, it is probably the oldest cultivated nonfood plant. As a source of fiber for cloth and rope, hemp was a principal crop in 18th century Virginia (one of George Washington's plantations produced it). Its legitimate cultivation in the United States peaked during World War II when Asian sources were cut off by Japanese military conquests. Today hemp fiber has been largely replaced in commercial use by nylon. Other commercial cannabis products include oil for soap and cooking. The seeds are used in bird seed, fish bait and fertilizer.

Cannabis has also been used medicinally for centuries. Its primary use has been as an analgesic, to treat such conditions as open wounds, scorpion bites and skin inflammations. It has also been used as a sedative in cases of mania and hysteria, and as an anticonvulsant. In the U.S., public misconceptions and fears about the "killer weed," and consequent legislation, limited the exploration of its usefulness. But with the first production of synthetic THC by Mechaulam at the Hebrew University in 1966 medical research progressed rapidly. Possible medical applications include relieving pressure on the eyeballs in the treatment of glaucoma. Its most widespread use has been as an antiemetic for the nausea and vomiting of cancer chemotherapy. Cannabidiolic acid, a cannabis alkaloid, is a topical antibiotic. (See also MARIJUANA and HASHISH.)

Capital with Codeine© (Carnrick) A narcotic opiate containing 325 mg of acetaminophen and 30 mg of codeine, that is used as an analgesic for mild to moderate pain. It can produce effects similar to morphine and therefore has a potential for abuse and for the development of dependency. When used with alcohol or other central nervous system depressants it can have an additive effect. Overdosage can result in respiratory depression, cold and clammy skin, muscle flaccidity and extreme somnolence leading to stupor or coma. It is available in pale blue tablets.

carbohydrate Carbohydrate metabolism is affected by the consumption of alcohol, and the blood sugar level may increase or decrease depending on the state of nutrition in the body. When carbohydrate stores are high, alcohol induces hyperglycemia (high blood sugar); when carbohydrate stores are low, hypoglycemia results (low blood sugar). Most distilled liquors have almost no carbohydrates, wine contains some, and beer is very high in carbohydrates. A popular fad diet, the "drinking man's diet," is based on the fact that there are very few carbohydrates in hard liquor. However, liquor does contain a lot of "empty calories," so if someone eats and at the same time drinks large amounts of alcohol, he or she is likely to gain rather than lose weight simply because the calories in liquor will be metabolized before the food calories which are stored as fat.

carbon tetrachloride A toxic hydrocarbon that was a common ingredient in many cleaning fluids. Although it was sometimes inhaled for the intoxicating effect produced, it is extremely dangerous: inhalation can result in headache, confusion, vomiting, and coma or death. Inhaled in large quantities it can cause damage to the nervous system, heart, liver and kidneys. It is especially dangerous when combined with alcohol. Carbon tetrachloride has been barred from consumer products because of its toxic effect.

Carbrital© (Parke-Davis) A sedative hypnotic containing the BARBITURATE pentobarbital sodium along with carbromal, that is used for insomnia. Tolerance can develop along with physical and psychological dependence. It has a significant potential for abuse. Overdosage can result in shallow respiration, coma and possible death. It is supplied as Elixir Carbrital, each fluid ounce containing 2 grains (120 mg) pentobarbital; Carbrital Kapseals with 1½ gr pentobarbital; and Carbrital Kapseals Half Strength with ¾ gr.

cardiac arrhythmia See HEART.

cardiac myopathy See ALCOHOLIC MYOPATHY.

catnip A herb, *Nepeta cataria*. There are claims that when it is smoked it can produce marijuana-like effects, but the likelihood of this is doubtful.

causes See ETIOLOGY.

celebrity drug use A number of famous singers, musicians, dancers and actors have made headlines when heavy drug use and abuse ruined their careers and, in some cases, cost them their lives. Most authorities believe that this notoriety affects the behavior and attitude about drugs of impressionable young people. Such personalities are often role models for the country's youth. When a prominent person—athlete, actor, rock star—does drugs, it seems to send out a message to youngsters that says, "Drugs are okay, they're cool."

Drugs have figured in the tragic deaths of such well-known celebrities as basketball star Len Bias, comic John Belushi, and singer Janis Joplin. Richard Pryor, the actor-comedian, frankly admits that drugs almost killed him. Others who have spoken out about their drug abuse problems include: Elizabeth Taylor, Gelsey Kirkland, Carrie Fisher, Liza Minelli, Drew Barrymore, Suzanne Sommers, New York Giant football star Lawrence Taylor, Los Angeles Dodgers outfielder Darryl Strawberry, and former Pittsburgh Pirates pitching ace Dock Ellis.

Many celebrities have urged fans through talk shows, books, interviews and audience appeals to help in the fight against illicit drug use. Others have contributed their time to public service programs and announcements. However, many in the treatment field question the effectiveness of the celebrities' efforts.

cement, household See GLUE SNIFFING.

central nervous system (CNS) The network of neurons (nerve cells) concentrated in the BRAIN and spinal cord which conduct electrical sensory and motor impulses to and from all parts of the body, via the peripheral nervous system (PNS). The PNS also includes the autonomic nervous system which is divided anatomically and functionally into the sympathetic and parasympathetic branches.

Nerve fibers called axons lead away from neurons and produce and store neurohormones such as norepinephrine, serotonin and acetylcholine. Transmission of an impulse occurs when neurohormones cross the synaptic gap to a neuron or its attached dentrite (a nerve fiber which carries impulses toward a neuron).

The brain is divided into a number of areas which exert control over specific functions: in the brainstem, the medulla oblongata is the center of respiratory, cardiac and vasomotor functions. The reticular activating system, a network of specialized nerve cells within the brainstem, controls alertness. The brainstem also includes the pons and mesencephalon (midbrain), collections of nerve fiber bundles which relay impulses.

Located above the brainstem, the thalamus acts as a central switchboard, directing impulses between the body and brain and within the subcortical area. Projecting from the thalamus, the hypothalamus affects emotional balance, regulates the autonomic nervous system, body temperature and water balance, and controls the dichotomous pleasure/pain and hunger/satiety reactions. Attached to and behind the brainstem, the cerebellum controls coordination, equilibrium and muscle tone. The most highly evolved part of the human brain is the approximately 6 mm outside layer called the cerebral cortex. It controls intellectual functions, (including memory), certain motor functions, language and speech, auditory, visual, and other sensory skills.

Drugs and other toxic substances can alter nervous system function by inhibiting, stimulating or imitating neurohormones, by disturbing their metabolism, or by affecting structures involved in the neurological process. Drugs also specifically affect different parts of the brain and therefore predictably impair certain functions. Drug abuse can cause permanent organic damage.

Depressant drugs, including alcohol and the opiates, interfere with neurohormonal production and absorption by the postsynaptic membrane and exert their principal effect on the medulla. This action explains the danger of respiratory failure that accompanies abuse of these drugs. They also affect the reticular activating system, including sleep, and other areas of the cerebral cortex.

One of the best documented categories of drug abuse pathology is that of brain damage related to alcoholism, though the mechanisms of many of these disorders are not fully understood.

Alcoholics commonly suffer from impairment of judgment, concentration and memory. In their early stages these symptoms can disappear with abstinence, which does not, however, always reverse brain atrophy which occurs as more and more brain cells are destroyed by alcohol.

Factors associated with alcoholism, such as malnutrition, also contribute to the development of both reversible and irreversible brain damage; thiamine deficiency in particular is at least partially responsible for a number of common alcoholic brain disorders. Victims of WERNICKE'S ENCEPHALOPATHY and KORSAKOFF'S PSYCHOSIS, for example, exhibit delirium, tremors, visual impairment, inability to maintain balance and memory failure. Thiamine deficiency also contributes to alcoholic polyneuropathy, another relatively common condition which involves numbness, pain, wasting and impaired function of the limbs, beginning with the legs. Alcoholic amblyopia provides another example. This disorder consists of visual impairment which sometimes involves degeneration of the optic nerves.

Structural damage, such as cerebral edema, congestion and hemorrhage, also occurs with abuse of depressant drugs. Brain injuries also result from accidents attributable to intoxication.

Stimulant substances generally accelerate production and release of neurohormones. Nicotine overloads the nerve cells and blocks synapses by mimicking acetycholine. Stimulants seem to focus on the autonomic nervous system, increasing heartbeat and blood pressure. Hypertension and tachycardia leading to cerebral hemorrhage are risks associated with the abuse of amphetamines and other stimulants. These drugs also keep the user awake by stimulating the reticular activating system, and appear to stimulate the pleasure and satiety centers located in the hypothalamus. Altered patterns of thinking, such as the exaggerated attention to insignificant detail that often occurs on an amphetamine binge, may indicate that there is an effect on the cerebral cortex as well. Cumulative nervous system degeneration has been associated with chronic stimulant abuse.

Cocaine is a very strong CNS stimulant. Specific physical effects include constricted peripheral blood vessels, dilated pupils and increased temperature, heart rate and blood pressure. Cocaine's immediate euphoric effects, which include hyperstimulation, reduced fatigue and mental clarity, last approximately 30 to 60 minutes. Cocaine used at high doses or chronically can have toxic effects. Overdose deaths are a result of seizures followed by respiratory arrest and coma, or sometimes by cardiac arrest or stroke.

Heroin and other opiates act primarily on the thalamus, medulla and cerebral cortex. Large doses stimulate the hypothalamic pleasure center to produce immediate euphoria which is often likened to a "complete body orgasm." Opiates also appear to stimulate or mimic activity of the parasympathetic division of the autonomic nervous system and generally depress the function of affected areas. Opiate overdose sometimes involves coma and cerebral edema.

Hallucinogens, such as LSD, excite a collection of structures known as the limbic system which plays a large role in emotional response and is closely connected to the thalamus and hypothalamus. They also seem to affect those areas of the brain which control auditory and visual reflexes and speech skills. Psychedelics may inhibit nerve impulses by antagonizing the neurohormone serotonin and possibly by mimicking norepinephrine. Reports of permanent brain damage resulting from the use of LSD have been largely unsubstantiated, but long-term psychotic reactions are occasionally reported.

Many studies have been conducted to determine the relationship of chronic marijuana use to the loss of short-term memory, but none has sufficiently explained this phenomenon. It has been postulated that chronic marijuana smoking inhibits production of DNA which chemically stores information. To date there has been no conclusive evidence that structural brain damage, including cerebral atrophy, can result from chronic cannabis consumption.

central pontine myelinolysis A disease characterized by a progressive weakness in the muscles extending from the medulla to the spinal cord. Other symptoms include an inability to swallow and an absence of the gag reflex. A rare disease that is difficult to diagnose, it is most often found in long-time alcoholics suffering from malnutrition. As the disease progresses the patient becomes drowsy and, finally, comatose.

cephalotropic See PSYCHOTROPIC.

charas The Indian term for the resin produced by the flowering top of the female plant of *Cannabis sativa.* It is far more potent than GHANGA in which the leaves, stems and twigs are ground up along with the flowering top.

Chemical Awareness Training Institute A nonprofit national organization specializing in student assistance program training for grades 7 through 12. The institute offers student assistance and group facilitator training for educators and other interested adults, and technical assistance to schools for alcohol and drug use and other related student problems. Training materials and student assistance manuals are available through the institute. Contact: Cheryl Watkins, The Chemical Awareness Training Institute, 21 Muriel Street, Phoenix, AZ 85022. Telephone: (602) 863-9671.

Chemical Diversion and Trafficking Act of 1988 Passed by Congress and signed by President Ronald Reagan on November 18, 1988, the act provides the Drug Enforcement Administration (DEA) with the major authority to mount a "revitalized attack against the clandestine manufacture of controlled substances and to pursue an aggressive program against those who divert certain precursor and essential chemicals for illicit purposes."

The act regulates the distribution of 20 listed chemicals used in the clandestine manufacture of controlled substances, such as methamphetamine, LSD, PCP, cocaine and heroin. Over 2,000 chemical manufacturers, distributors, importers and exporters are required to report all suspicious orders for these chemicals to DEA, maintain sales and distribution records and to make these records available to DEA for inspection.

Importers and exporters are required to adhere to criteria regulating the importation and exportation of listed chemicals. An advance notice and declaration system for all imports and exports of these chemicals enables the DEA to identify consignees and shipments to and from the United States.

The act also provides penalties for certain acts related to the diversion of listed chemicals. These controls, integrated into existing enforcement programs, provide a unified, aggressive stance against chemical diversion and trafficking at both the domestic and international levels.

U.S. Department of Justice, Drug Enforcement Administration, *Drug Enforcement Administration Briefing Book,* from a statement by David L. Weintraub, (April 1989), 44.

Chemical People Institute A nonprofit organization committed to leading communities toward awareness, understanding and action concerning alcohol and other drug problems through the promotion of community task forces. The institute provides community outreach, education and research and has an information center, video library and speakers' bureau. Adults can receive training on the effects of drug and alcohol use through community awareness and development programs. Contact: Sister Michele O'Leary, Chemical People Institute, Duquesne University, Pittsburgh, PA 15282. Telephone: (412) 391-0900.

chat See KHAT.

chia seeds The term is applied to seeds from any plant which belongs to the genus *Salvia*. There have been claims that they produce a marijuana-like effect when smoked.

child abuse See CHILDREN OF DRUG DEPENDENT INDIVIDUALS.

children of drug dependent individuals Most studies in this area deal with children of alcoholics. Unfortunately, the best way to predict the future drinking habits of a child is to study the drinking pattern of his or her parents. One of the most negative effects of having an alcoholic parent is that it predisposes a child to alcohol abuse. Daughters of alcoholics become alcoholic 20–50% of the time and alcoholic mothers seem to exert more influence in this way than alcoholic fathers. Studies have also shown that even if a daughter of an alcoholic parent escapes becoming an alcoholic, she is likely to marry one (see PARA-ALCOHOLIC).

Alcoholic parents often vacillate between being overly affectionate and being abusive and neglectful. This type of treatment is not understood by children and, along with becoming anxious and frightened, they often become confused about their own responsibility for their parents' behavior.

Although some children may seem to cope with the problems of having an alcoholic parent, they run a high risk of developing problems later in life. For instance, some children assume a responsible role and attempt to take care of parents and other siblings; this can lead to the inability to depend on others in later life and the need to always be in control of a situation. The child who always tries to smooth over conflicts and help others in an alcoholic household may deny his or her own feelings of anger and hurt and later in life will be constantly trying to please others. In addition, a child who constantly adjusts to the moods of an alcoholic parent may find himself going through life being manipulated by others. Even if an alcoholic parent stops drinking, the child's problems may not end. He can then no longer use the parent as a scapegoat for misbehavior; he may also feel resentment or hostility because he has become accustomed to handling situations and having responsibilities (these feelings have also been noted in spouses of alcoholics).

Most of the studies concerning other drugs have centered around the effects on an unborn child and the consequent symptoms of withdrawal at birth (see PREGNANCY). However, it would follow that the negative effects of having an alcoholic parent would also be true of having a parent addicted to heroin, cocaine, amphetamines, barbiturates or any mind-altering substance. In a situation where a parent is not rational at all times, the same neglect, instability of home life, and abusive treatment will be present.

There are an estimated one million cases of child abuse and neglect each year in the United States. It has been suggested that one-third of these cases are alcohol-related. How many are attributable to other drug use is not known. Child abuse in the family can be a vicious circle. It is not always the alcoholic parent who abuses a child; often the alcoholic will abuse the spouse who, in turn, will abuse the children as a means of releasing frustration. When a parent is undergoing WITHDRAWAL symptoms from any drug, his or her irritability threshold is very low and this may also lead to child abuse.

The exact connection between child abuse and drug use is not known but studies have shown repetitive cycles from generation to generation. If an adult has been abused as a child, he or she will be more apt to continue the abuse pattern. In regard to alcohol, it was found that nearly one-third of all reported cases of father-daughter incest were attributed to alcohol dependence. Even when drug abuse is not considered the major factor in child abuse, it may aggravate the problem.

As the incidence of child abuse grows, so does public awareness of the problem. Adults who were abused children are now more open about discussing their childhood, both as a way of helping others who have suffered child abuse and as a way of dealing with their own emotional problems. A number of national self-help organizations have been established to help children of alcoholics—both adult COAs and those still in their adolescent years. Neighbors and relatives of battered children are also more forthcoming with reports, and school officials, law enforcement agencies and hospitals are now more conscious of the problem. The number of cases reported, however, is still thought to represent only the tip of the iceberg.

China The cultivation and use of opium has been a tradition in China for centuries. The Chinese and British fought two Opium Wars during the 19th century because Britain was bringing opium into China from India and undercutting the local competition. The

Chinese government, however, contends that the Opium Wars were fought to combat the consumption of opium. In the 1850s and 1860s, when Chinese laborers were brought to the United States to work on the railroads, they were said to have brought the practice of opium smoking with them. Opium smoking rapidly gained popularity in the U.S. and it was the prevalence of "opium dens" that prompted San Francisco to enact the first narcotics ordinance in 1875.

The cultivation of the opium poppy is a laborous undertaking (the labor involved in the short 10-day harvest season can amount to hundreds of hours) and this accounts for the fact that commercial production flourishes mainly in economically deprived countries that have cheap sources of labor available on short-term notice. While opium is cultivated in rural China, the involvement of the Chinese in opium exported from the GOLDEN TRIANGLE has all but ceased to exist. Until the late 1970s the Chinese were regularly involved in smuggling but government regulations, along with internal competition among traffickers, greatly reduced their activities.

In recent years opium intoxication and addiction have been considered political offenses. Although statistics are unavailable, it is thought that drug abuse in China is not a major problem. However, opium is still grown and smoked in remote areas, and control over individual consumption is strong in urban areas.

An alcohol problem in China is acknowledged to exist but to what extent is unknown.

chloral alcoholate A chloral derivative that is converted to CHLORAL HYDRATE in the body.

chloral betaine A synthetic chloral derivative that is similar to CHLORAL HYDRATE but is said to cause less gastric distress. It is used as a sedative.

chloral derivatives CHLORAL HYDRATE, CHLORAL BETAINE, CHLOROBUTANOL, TRICLOFOS SODIUM, and CHLORAL ALCOHOLATE. (See CHLORAL HYDRATE for characteristics.)

chloral hydrate A nonbarbiturate sedative hypnotic which acts as a depressant on the central nervous system. It is produced by passing chlorine gas through ethyl alcohol. The first synthetic sedative hypnotic, it was introduced in 1869 by Oskar Liebreich and was widely used both medically and recreationally. Today it has been largely replaced by newer drugs.

Appearance: Chloral hydrate appears as colorless or white transparent crystals which are soluble in water, olive oil and alcohol. It is available in liquid, capsule or tablet form for oral use, and in suppositories and olive oil enemas for rectal use. The substance decomposes quickly when exposed to light and, in liquid form, quickly develops mold. It has a bitter taste and unpleasant odor.

Activity in the body: Chloral hydrate is absorbed into the bloodstream from the intestinal tract and evenly distributed through the body. It appears in breast milk and crosses the placental barrier; like the barbiturates, it is not advised for use during pregnancy and nursing. The drug's half-life is four to eight hours.

Dosage: The average lethal dose of chloral hydrate is 10 grams. As little as 3 grams have proved fatal, and up to 30 grams have been survived. The recommended sedative dosage is 250 mg three times a day after meals. The usual hypnotic dose is .5 to 1 gm approximately 15–30 minutes before bedtime.

Effects: Like other DEPRESSANTS, chloral hydrate inhibits the transmission of nerve impulses in the ascending reticular formation of the brain, thereby affecting such functions as breathing. As a hypnotic it acts very quickly, producing immediate drowsiness and—within 15–30 minutes—a sound sleep which lasts four to eight hours. Chloral hydrate is considered safer than other hypnotics, particularly BARBITURATES, because it interferes very little with REM sleep, and because it has less effect on the respiratory center in the brain.

In sedative doses, chloral hydrate's effects are similar to those of alcohol and barbiturates: euphoria leading to intoxication and usually resulting in a slight hangover. Common side effects include gastrointestinal irritation and loss of muscular coordination. Overdoses can result in falling temperature, pupil constriction followed by dilation, irregular pulse, delirium, coma, and death within five to 10 hours. Tolerance, along with physical and psychological dependence, can develop; consequently the drug is not recommended for long-term use, especially for patients with histories of drug addiction or abuse. However, the abuse risk for chloral hydrate is only low to moderate. Probably because of its bad taste and gastric effects it is not favored by drug abusers; they generally prefer barbiturates and the newer nonbarbiturates, such as glutethimide and ethclorvynol.

The combination of chloral hydrate and alcohol increases the depressant activity of both drugs (see SYNERGY), intensifying the euphoria and intoxication as well as slowing the breathing and accentuating loss of muscular coordination. Coma can result. This possibly lethal combination has earned chloral hydrate preparations the nicknames "knock-out drops," "Mickeys" and "Mickey Finns."

Chloral hydrate also interferes with anticoagulants and should be used cautiously in combination with other drugs.

Usage: Chloral hydrate is used medically at a post- and pre-operative sedative and hypnotic, particularly in combination with barbiturates. It is used in the first stages of labor, as a nocturnal sedative in the treatment of insomnia, and in the treatment of certain convulsive disorders. Like other sedatives, it is also frequently used in treating withdrawal from other drugs, such as alcohol, barbiturates and narcotics.

Recreationally, it is used to produce the same euphoria and intoxication derived from the use of alcohol and barbiturates, although its use in this regard is infrequent. Morphine and heroin addicts use it as a substitute when their habitual drugs are unavailable.

Chloral hydrate is a Schedule IV drug under the Controlled Substance Act.

chlordiazepoxide Best known under the tradename LIBRIUM, this drug is one of the most commonly prescribed sedatives in the United States. Chlordiazepoxide hydrochloride is a benzodiazepine derivative and is very similar to diazepam and oxazepam. It is sometimes prescribed to relieve symptoms of tension and anxiety. It is used extensively in alcohol detoxification programs for withdrawal.

Appearance and activity: Chlordiazepoxide hydrochloride appears as a colorless crystalline substance which is water soluble. It is absorbed in the gastrointestinal tract, and depresses the limbic system—the center of emotional response. Metabolized chiefly in the liver, it is excreted in the urine and crosses the placental barrier. After oral administration, its effects manifest in about half an hour and peak in two to four hours. Onset after intramuscular injection occurs in 15–30 minutes, and in 3–15 minutes after intravenous administration. The substance has a 24–48 hour half life.

Dosage: In the form of Librium, it is prescribed in two or four daily doses of 5–50 mg. Daily doses can range as high as 100 mg but should not exceed 300 mg. A daily dosage of 300–600 mg can produce physical dependence. No lethal dose has been specified in humans, but 50% of mice fed 620 mg per kilogram of body weight died.

Effects: Like the other sedatives, Librium calms symptoms of anxiety and tension resulting from emotional stress. One of its principal applications is the treatment of alcohol withdrawal symptoms, especially delirium tremens.

Chlordiazepoxide at prescribed doses produces less euphoria than meprobamate, opiates or barbiturates, so psychological dependence may be less of a risk. But as high doses produce the kind of intoxication induced by barbiturates, physical dependence is likely with doses 10 times larger than the recommended therapeutic dose. Withdrawal symptoms for physical dependence are convulsions, insomnia, loss of appetite, tremors and the recurrence of previous symptoms of anxiety. Like other benzodiazepine derivatives, it is additive to other depressant drugs (see SYNERGY), and their combination can result in fatal respiratory depression.

The euphoria produced by large doses makes the drug attractive to drug abusers. It has also been used in enormous amounts in suicide attempts.

It is a Schedule IV drug under the Controlled Substances Act.

chlormezanone A DEPRESSANT drug used as a tranquilizer in the treatment of mild anxiety and tension. It acts without impairing the patient's clarity of consciousness. (See TRANCOPAL.)

chloroform A vaporous ANESTHETIC, more potent than ether, but no longer used therapeutically because it produces serious adverse effects on the liver.

chlorphentermine hydrochloride A sympathomimetic amine with pharmacologic activities similar to AMPHETAMINES. (See PRE-SATE.)

chlorpromazine A neuroleptic which has actions at all levels of the central nervous system and is used as a antipsychotic drug. (See THORAZINE.)

chocolate A very mild stimulant (containing 1.0% CAFFEINE) made from cocoa beans.

chromatography A technique used for urine testing for drugs. Both thin-layer and gas chromatographic methods of urine testing are considered the most useful techniques for detecting drugs with the exception of LSD. (Methods for detecting LSD in both blood and urine are presently restricted to research laboratories.)

chronic A descriptive term for a condition or disease that is characterized by slowly progressing symptoms and which continues for a long time, as opposed to an ACUTE disease or condition which quickly develops into a crisis.

chronic alcohol intoxication Continuous intoxication maintained by repeated consumption of alcohol. The term is also used generally to refer to alcoholism, although many alcoholics are not continually intoxicated.

chronic alcoholic See CHRONIC ALCOHOLISM.

chronic alcoholism As alcoholism is a chronic disorder the term chronic alcoholism is superfluous. It is used, however, to distinguish a long-lasting condition from ACUTE ALCOHOLISM, which is generally used to refer to alcohol intoxication or alcohol poisoning which may be a temporary disturbance.

cigarettes See NICOTINE.

cirrhosis A liver disease that occurs frequently, but not exclusively, in association with alcohol abuse. The word comes from the Greek "kirrhos," meaning orange-colored—the color of a cirrhotic liver. The disease is characterized by scarring and severe dysfunction. (See LIVER.)

citronella An oil with a lemonish odor made from citronella grass. There are unconfirmed claims that it can produce intoxicating effects when inhaled.

clandestine laboratories The past 25 years has seen a rise in the number of illicit, clandestine laboratories. They were first noticed in California in the mid-1960s, when the Hell's Angels motorcycle gang set up operations to produce "speed." They have since been encountered in virtually every part of the United States. Government actions to control the legitimate manufacture and distribution of dangerous drugs contributed to the growth of these labs as demand for psychoactive drugs—stimulants, depressants and hallucinogens—mushroomed.

Clandestine laboratories have also proliferated because of the ease of production and the limited skill needed to operate them. The overall risks are minimal despite sporadic fires and explosions and the threat of discovery and arrest. The potential profits from these enterprises can be enormous. Most clandestine labs are established in rural areas, though occasionally they are located in suburban or urban areas.

Some clandestine laboratories synthesize analogues of controlled substances. These controlled-substances analogues, known popularly as "designer drugs," usually retain the pharmacological properties of controlled substances, but because of slight variations in chemical structure, they are not specifically listed as controlled substances. These analogues carry increased health risks due to their unknown purity, toxicity and potency.

The emergency scheduling provisions of the Comprehensive Crime Control Act of 1984 and the Controlled Substance Analogue Enforcement Act of 1986 are aimed at closing legal loopholes used by individuals who manufacture and distribute these analogues. Nationwide, federal and state authorities raided 647 clandestine labs in 1987, up from 479 during 1986. Three-quarters of the raided laboratories were located in southern California.

U.S. Department of Justice, Drug Enforcement Administration, *Drugs of Abuse,* 1988, 53.

cleaning fluids Although toxic, with the potential to produce brain, liver and kidney damage, cleaning fluids are sometimes inhaled by those seeking an intoxicating effect. (See INHALANTS.)

clonidine A drug widely used to treat narcotic withdrawal that was reported to have success in curbing smokers' tobacco cravings. Recent studies do not confirm this claim. Clonidine was first used in the treatment of hypertension. It is now sold illicitly and may have some abuse potential.

Clonopin© (Roche) An anticonvulsant, containing clonazepam, that is used for the control of seizures. Because it is a BENZODIAZEPINE, tolerance can develop and it has the potential for abuse. When taken with alcohol or other central nervous system depressants it can have an additive effect. Overdosage can result in somnolence, diminished reflexes, confusion and coma. It is supplied in tablet form: 0.5 mg orange; 1 mg blue; and 2 mg white.

clorazepate dipotassium A synthetic BENZODIAZEPINE used in the treatment of anxiety. (See also TRANXENE.)

clortermine A sympathomimetic amine with pharmacologic activity similar to that of AMPHETAMINES. It is used as an anorectic. (See VORANIL.)

co-alcoholic See PARA-ALCOHOLIC.

coca *Erthroxylon coca,* a bush which grows in South America. From 0.65% to 1.25% (by weight) of the alkaloid COCAINE is found in its leaves. South American Indians, particularly the mountain Indians of Peru and Bolivia, mix the leaves with lime to release the cocaine, then chew them for a stimulant effect and for a variety of medicine and religious purposes. Coca was an ingredient of Coca Cola until the U.S. government prohibited its use in 1906. In 1914 its use was controlled by the Harrison Narcotics Act, which incorrectly classified it as a narcotic. Now the coca leaves are decocainized before being used as a flavoring in cola drinks. Maximum estimated 1989 coca production was: Ecuador 319 tons; Colombia 26,620 tons; Bolivia 87,604 tons; and Peru, 138,446 tons, according to figures supplied by the Congressional Research Service, the U.S. State Department and the Drug Enforcement Administration.

coca paste The first extract produced during the manufacture of cocaine from coca leaves. It is made by adding sulfuric acid and kerosene to the leaves. In South America cocaine is not processed into FREEBASE before smoking; it is smoked in the form of coca paste which is dangerous because of the impurities it contains and its high cocaine content.

cocaine An alkaloid found in the leaves of the coca bush, *Erthroxylon coca*. Cocaine affects the central nervous system and induces feelings of euphoria. Used since the time of the Inca Empire, which flourished for hundreds of years in the Andean Mountain region of Peru until the arrival of the white man in the 1500s, Inca priests and nobles chewed coca leaves in order to achieve and enhance their religious experiences. Using coca leaves was originally a mark of the aristocracy, but gradually other members of the male Inca population took up the habit. The Indians discovered that besides helping to resolve religious truths, the magical leaves would prolong physical endurance, retard fatigue and hunger and give a pleasurable feeling of euphoria. Coca was widely used by the men who worked in mines which were located at very high mountain altitudes. Today it is estimated that fully 90% of the adult male Indian population of the region regularly chews coca leaves.

The Indians chew coca leaves along with an alkali, such as bird lime: when mixed with saliva, it acts as an agent to release the cocaine from the leaves. Someone chewing two ounces of coca a day would be taking in 0.7 grams of pure cocaine. Someone taking several doses of "pure" cocaine—actually only 5–35% pure—sold on the street, on the other hand, would be ingesting 6 grams.

The pure cocaine substance benzoylmethylecognine was first identified and extracted from the leaves of the coca bush in the 1850s by the German chemist Albert Niemann.

The use of cocaine in its pure form began in the 1880s. Bavarian soldiers were given it to help them gain endurance and to retard fatigue. Shortly afterward, cocaine was touted in medical circles as a highly effective local anesthetic for certain operations. Experiments were conducted to discover what other disorders and maladies cocaine could cure or sooth, and a small circle of professional people began taking the drug themselves. Sigmund Freud insisted it helped him in his work. He even went so far as to praise cocaine in a series of papers to the public in which he commented favorably on the drug's beneficial properties as a cure for morphine addiction, depression, overeating and alcoholism. But when reports of cases of cocaine addiction and death by overdose began surfacing, Freud immediately ceased taking the drug.

By the early 1900s cocaine had found its way, through patent medicines like Vin Mariani, into the lives of many people. A great deal of cocaine was produced for use in potions and beverages. Coca Cola contained cocaine until 1906 when the company, at the insistence of the U.S. government, removed the ingredient from its recipe.

Both the Canadian government (in 1911) and the U.S. government (in 1914) put legal restrictions on the sale of the drug. Cocaine diminished greatly in popularity and it wasn't until the 1960s that it made a comeback. Its appeal was due in part to the public's acceptance of amphetamines, the effects of which are remarkably similar to cocaine.

Indications are that Europe is on the verge of a cocaine explosion reminiscent of that which began in the United States more than a decade ago. Romolo Urcioli, deputy chief of Italy's Central Antidrug Service, says, "What was only a threat a few years ago is now a reality." Lists of cocaine seizures on the Continent support this view: 1,034 pounds in central France; 770 pounds in Madrid; 230 pounds in Milan, Italy; 460 pounds in Rotterdam, the Netherlands. Charles Gutensohn, head of cocaine investigations, U.S. Drug Enforcement Administration, says: "It's (the coke plague) increasing at a greater rate than any of the enforcement people had anticipated."

In 1986, cocaine seizures topped two tons. The next year, seizures doubled. And, say authorities, they are likely to have doubled again in 1988, when final statistics are totaled. One reason the cocaine glut in the United States was so pronounced in 1989 was that the price of a kilogram had dropped roughly by half, from about $35,000 five years ago to as low as $15,000. In Europe, by contrast, relative scarcity allows dealers to ask up to $65,000 a kilo. Most of the drug originates in Colombia, travels through several other Latin American countries and reaches Western Europe at such major cocaine entry points as Lisbon, Madrid, Barcelona, Milan, Rome, Naples, Rotterdam, Amsterdam, Southhampton, London and Brussels. The *British Journal of Addiction*'s February, 1989 issue warns of a coming epidemic. When the 12-nation European Community eliminates trade barriers and border checks in 1992, the drug will be more readily available. Veteran narcotic agents speak of a "weak line" scenario, in which all of Europe will be as vulnerable as its least patrolled port.

There are several methods of taking cocaine hydrochloride or crystal cocaine. The most common is by "snorting" it into the nostrils through a straw, a rolled paper, or from a tiny "coke spoon." Another method, favored by some heavy users, is to inject the substance directly into the bloodstream—sometimes mixing or following it up with a shot of heroin. Cocaine can also be taken by applying it to the mucous lining of the mouth, rectum or vagina. Oral ingestion of the drug decreases its potency. For a more recent method of using cocaine see FREEBASE and CRACK.

A smokable form of cocaine, crack is smoked in a pipe or mixed with a tobacco or a marijuana cigarette and smoked. Crack became prevalent in New York City in late 1985 and on the American drug scene in early 1986. Crack is inexpensive. However, because of its highly addictive properties the continuous taking of the drug can make it a very expensive habit.

Classification: The effects of cocaine are similar to the effects of the natural substance adrenaline as well to the manufactured stimulants, amphetamines. In its pure form cocaine is a white powder but it is often cut with other drugs or similar looking substances, such as talcum powder or sugar, and very little street-purchased cocaine is in pure form. The Federal Bureau of Narcotics once mistakenly classified cocaine as a narcotic but it is presently classified as a STIMULANT. It is also classified as a legal, though tightly regulated (Schedule II) anesthetic, and used in some surgical operations on the mouth, eyes and throat because of its ability to constrict blood vessels and to be rapidly absorbed by the mucous membranes.

Effects: Cocaine directly affects the central nervous system, causing a definite stimulative sensation. The effects, which only last a very short time, depend on the size of the dose. Small doses will bring about sensations of extreme euphoria; illusions of increased mental and physical strength and sensory awareness; and a decrease in hunger, pain and the need for sleep. Large doses significantly magnify these effects, sometimes causing irrational behavior. For heavy users, the heightened euphoria is often accompanied by intensified heartbeat, sweating, dilation of the pupils and a rise in body temperature. Euphoria can be followed by irritability, depression, insomnia and an extreme condition of paranoia. These effects are similar to those felt by heavy amphetamine users. The belief and feeling that crawling insects are under the skin, may also occur. In some cases, a condition similar to amphetamine poisoning may occur and the user will not only appear extremely restless and nervous, but will experience delirium, hallucinations, muscle spasms and pain in the chest. Male users may be come impotent or incapable of ejaculation. If the drug is injected, abscesses may appear on the skin. Malnutrition and anemia may be experienced because of a decrease in appetite. Many of these symptoms can be reversed simply by halting the drug.

Both heavy and light users will eventually develop some of the same physical side effects: runny nose, eczema around the nostrils, and gradual deterioration of the nasal cartilage. Death from cocaine overdose is rare, although such instances are on the increase. Death usually results from respiratory arrest, heart rhythm disturbances, convulsions or stroke.

Addictive aspects: Physical dependence, though once thought not to occur, may occur. Heavy use when stopped causes hunger, irritability, extreme fatigue, depression and prolonged periods of restless sleep. Psychological dependence is common. Many users become "hooked" on the feeling of euphoria induced by cocaine and their entire being begins to revolve around the next dose. If dependence is severe, a user will experience a deep depression when the effects of a dose wear off.

Tolerance: Tolerance develops to cocaine. The same dose frequently repeated will not produce similar symptoms over a period of time. Many cocaine users find a need to increase the dosage frequently. A lethal dose can be as small as 1.2 grams intravenously, but a heavy user may, through frequent small doses, ingest as much as 10 grams in a day.

Sources: Approximately 70% of the cocaine entering the United States comes from COLOMBIA, and passes through south Florida. Colombia is also responsible for 50% of the world's supply. (See Appendix 3, Tables 39 and 44).

Synonyms: coke, snow, blow, leaf, stardust, flake, C, girl, and many others.

Gordon Wilkin and Stephen J. Hedges, "The Coming Cocaine Plague in Europe," *U.S. News & World Report,* February 20, 1989, 34–36.

cocaine freebase See FREEBASE, COCAINE.

cocktail A drink which is a mixture of a distilled spirit and an aperitif or other flavoring. A cocktail is usually shaken or stirred with ice and then strained into a glass. Although there are various theories, the origin of the term is unknown. It came into popular usage in the United States in the 1920s and although the word is now widely used throughout the world it is considered an American term. Probably the most common cocktail is the martini, a mixture of gin and vermouth. The term has been extended to include COCKTAIL HOUR.

cocktail hour A term referring to the time when COCKTAILS are usually served, either at a social gathering (a 4–6 p.m. cocktail party) or a designated hour at a restaurant, bar or lounge. The term "happy hour" has become popular in recent years.

cocoa *Theobroma cacao,* a bush that grows in Central and South America. The seeds are used to make cocoa powder and chocolate. Cocoa is a mild stimulant containing 1.0% CAFFEINE by weight.

Codalan© (Lannett) A narcotic opiate that contains CODEINE. It is used as an analgesic for degrees of pain that would require less analgesia than morphine. It may be habit-forming. It is available in three varieties: No. 1, orange tablets containing ⅛ gr codeine; No. 2, white tablets with ¼ gr; and No. 3, green tablets with ½ gr. All three varieties contain caffeine, salicylamide and acetaminophen.

History of Cocaine

c.1532	**Pizarro discovers Incas chewing coca leaves in Peru.**
1750	**Coca specimens classified as *Erythroxylon coca.***
1844	**Cocaine, the principal alkaloid in coca leaves, is isolated.**
1863	**A preparation of coca leaves and wine called "Vin Mariani" gains popularity in Europe.**
1878	**Cocaine used for morphine addiction.**
1883	**Bavarian soldiers use cocaine to combat fatigue.**
1884	**Sigmund Freud studies cocaine as a psychoactive drug to treat depression and fatigue.**
	Karl Koller uses cocaine as a topical anesthetic in eye operations.
	William Halstead injects cocaine into nerve trunks as a regional anesthetic.
1885	**Dr. Albrecht Erlenmeyer warns against the use of cocaine to cure morphine addiction.**
1886	**Coca-Cola, containing coca extract, comes on the market.**
1902	**Richard Willstatter synethesizes cocaine.**
1906	**Pure Food and Drug Act prohibits interstate shipment of food and soda water containing cocaine.**
	Coca-Cola Company switches to "decocainized" cola leaves.
1914	**Harrison Narcotics Act lists cocaine as a narcotic.**
1922	**Congress prohibits most importation of cocaine and coca leaves.**
1932	**Uniform Narcotic Drug Act requires licensing for manufacture and imposes criminal penalties for illegal possession.**
1956	**Narcotics Drug Control Act imposes severe penalties for offenses.**
1970	**Controlled Substances Act classifies cocaine as a Schedule II drug.**
1970s-1980s-1990s	**Use of cocaine spreads to all segments of society. An estimated 30–60 tons are smuggled into the U.S. annually. Few American communities are immune to the influx of cocaine.**
1980s-1990s	**Crack cocaine becomes easily available in America's cities. In July 1990 the DEA announced that supplies of cocaine entering major metropolitan areas had declined and that the drug was less pure and more expensive.**

CODAP (Client Oriented Data Acquisition Program) This reporting system provides demographic, diagnostic and outcome data on patients in federally supported drug treatment facilities. The reporting forms can be found in National Institute on Drug Abuse (NIDA) Research Issue Series 12, "Drug Abuse Instrument Handbook."

codeine (morphine 3-methyl ether) A narcotic analgesic, codeine was discovered in 1832 and gets its name from the Greek word *kodeia* meaning, "poppyhead." Like morphine, it is an opiate, a natural opium alkaloid, and appears in the juices of the unripe white poppy pod. The natural yield is rather small (about .5%) so codeine is also synthesized through the methylization of morphine (and is sometimes called "methyl morphine").

Appearance: Codeine appears in two forms. The first, codeine phosphate, is an odorless white crystalline powder soluble in water and slightly soluble in alcohol. The second, codeine sulfate, appears as white crystals which are slightly soluble in water and freely soluble in alcohol. Being more soluble in water, codeine phosphate is used most often in elixirs and in injectable form. Codeine sulfate appears in pill form.

Activity in the body: Taken orally, codeine is absorbed (more rapidly than morphine) from the gastrointestinal tract. It is biodegraded in the liver and appears in the urine. Codeine's effects peak in 30–60 minutes and last three to four hours. Its half life is three to five hours. About 10% of the subtance converts to morphine in the body. Codeine crosses the placental barrier and therefore can affect unborn babies.

Dosage: Codeine can be taken orally, subcutaneously or intramuscularly. As an antitussive, it is prescribed in doses ranging from 5–10 mg; the usual analgesic dose is 15–60 mg. Doses over 60 mg can have stimulatory rather than sedative effects. In hypodermic administration 120 mg of codeine is equivalent to 10 mg of morphine. Death from codeine is very rare and the lethal dose has not be determined.

Effects: Codeine's analgesic effects are very similar to morphine's, although it has only about one-sixth to one-tenth of morphine's potency. It relieves minor pain, producing a mild euphoria and drowsiness. Codeine also dries the respiratory mucosa and affects the autonomic nervous system. Large doses intensify these effects. Tolerance to the drug's sedative effects does develop, but codeine is considered only moderately physically addictive. Psychological dependence is more common: in addition to the desired euphoria, addicts experience loss of appetite, depressed sexual drive, itchiness and, most often, constipation and nausea. Withdrawal symptoms are relatively mild.

Usage: Codeine's most common medical use is as an antitussive in cough syrups, often in combination with non-narcotic pain relievers such as aspirin or Tylenol. Codeine is used for this purpose more than any other drug and is thus widely prescribed. Other medical applications include relief of minor pain of various kinds and relief of constipation, though large doses can cause the latter problem.

Codeine is subject to abuse but the problem is not a big one. Since large doses are required to achieve and maintain the kind of "high" abusers seek, brand name codeine products, which often contain other drugs, are not satisfactory for this purpose. In the 1960s, however, many teenagers drank codeine cough syrups in large quantities for their euphoric effects, and studies have shown that many addicts of harder drugs began their pursuit of artificial euphoria with codeine syrups. The discovery of this abuse led to tighter control over the drug's prescription; consequently recreational use of codeine is no longer such a big problem. Codeine is a Schedule II drug under the Controlled Substances Act. Street terms for codeine tablets are "schoolboys" and "pops." In Canada, the most popular legal psychoactive drug is codeine. Canadians, in 1985, had the fourth highest per capita codeine consumption in the world, after Denmark, Norway and Bulgaria.

Codeine and alcohol: The combination of codeine and alcohol can be dangerous and can result in respiratory arrest and depressed brain activity.

coercive treatment When a drug dependent person is forced into a treatment situation, it is considered coercive treatment. The pressure may arise from a court, "Get into treatment or go to jail"; from one's employer, "If you don't stop drinking, you will be fired"; or from other sources. Since the entry into treatment is not voluntary, the person may have little or no motivation to change and the therapist must induce the desire. It has been found in some cases that if the threat of punishment is maintained, the results of coercion are as good as those for voluntary participation in treatment programs.

coffee See CAFFEINE.

cola An African tree belonging to the Sterculiaceae family. The seeds, kola nuts, contain 2% CAFFEINE and are used to make a mildly stimulative beverage. Kola nuts are an ingredient of the carbonated soft drink Coca Cola.

collapsed veins A common condition among HEROIN addicts caused by frequent injections over a long period of time. When a vein becomes swollen and blocked (collapsed) due to infections known as thrombophlebitis, or by venous thrombosis, an addict will have to start using another vein. Long-term addicts have been known to use veins in the neck, the penis, between the toes and even under the tongue.

Colombia Colombia has the dubious distinction of being the world's principal drug source, a fact which may be attributed to its strategic location on the South American continent and its geographic makeup, as well as to its experience as a well-ordered trafficking community. The major processing and transshipment center for Peruvian and Bolivian coca, Colombia is responsible for 70% of the cocaine entering the United States and for 50% of the world's supply. Colombia is also a major supplier of marijuana to the United States, and opium poppy cultivation has also been found on a limited scale in the country. U.S. drug enforcement officials estimate that 44 tons of cocaine (with a street value of $29 billion) is annually smuggled into the U.S. from Colombia. The country also cultivates coca on some 7,200 acres that yield an estimated 4 tons of cocaine annually. The country's 1989 production of coca leaves in metric tons was 20,000; of marijuana 2,700. Colombia is also the major exporter of marijuana to the U.S., supplying 75% of the market (see Appendix 3, Tables 38, 39, and 44). An estimated 80% of other dangerous drugs entering the U.S., particularly methaqualone, are supplied through Colombia. Most of the illicit drug traffic passes through south Florida, Southern California, the Gulf of Mexico and East Coast port areas.

Trafficking in cocaine and marijuana, the top two money-producers, has a value to the Colombian economy of an estimated $1 to $1.5 billion, perhaps $500 million of which stays in the country and—untaxed and inflationary—undermines the legitimate economy.

While cocaine processing is big business in Colombia, it is interesting to note that three of the chemicals considered essential to the processing of coca into cocaine—ether, hydrochloric acid and acetone—are not produced in the country. Until recently Colombia's principal suppliers for these chemicals were the Netherlands, the Federal Republic of Germany, and the United States. Colombia in turn supplies these three countries with the majority of their cocaine. On January 4, 1983, the Colombian Minister of Economic Development banned the importation of these chemicals in an effort aimed at curbing cocaine smuggling into the U.S.

Although the Colombian government and public do not perceive drug abuse as a major problem, it has been suggested by outside observers that there has been an increase in the use of cocaine, marijuana and methaqualone among Colombian youth. If true, it is certainly not surprising considering the availability of these drugs. In 1981, after two years of inactivity, the National Council on Dangerous Drugs in Colombia initiated a program to reduce the domestic demand for narcotics. With the recent political unrest in the country it is difficult to foresee what government efforts and actions will be effective. There have been reports that guerrilla groups are trafficking drugs as a source of income to pay for arms shipments.

After the August 18, 1989 murder of Senator Luis Carlos Galán, one of Colombia's leading presidential candidates, President Virgilio Barco, vowed to drive the drug dealers out of his country. Eduardo Martinez Romero, a reputed money manager for the Medellín cocaine cartel was the first victim of Barco's executive order, reviving a U.S.-Colombia extradition treaty invalidated by the Colombian Supreme Court in 1987.

The drug lords of Colombia vowed to fight back against both their government's and the U.S. government's crackdown. President George Bush moved promptly to assure U.S. reinforcement of President Barco's imperiled government with an emergency grant of $65 million worth of weapons, material and military training equipment. The U.S. National Drug Control Strategy includes additional funds to assist Colombia, Peru and Bolivia in the fight against drugs.

colorines *Erythrina flabelliformis,* a tropical shrub of the Leguminosae family. There are claims that the seeds are a hallucinogen. In fact, they are toxic.

coma A state of unconsciousness. A person in a coma cannot be aroused even by powerful stimulation.

Committees of Correspondence A nonprofit, government-approved, drug education resource organization that disseminates up-to-date information relating to drug use and abuse issues. Among the items available are a basic information kit containing educational fact sheets, pamphlets and brochures; and a 125-page drug prevention resource manual, including age-appropriate reading and audio/visual recommendations plus special resources for parents, educators, librarians, and health professionals. Contact: Connie Moulton, Committees of Correspondence, 57 Conant Street, Room 113, Danvers, MA 01923. Telephone: (617) 774-2641.

Compazine© (Smith, Kline & French) A brand of prochlorperozine used for severe neuropsychiatric conditions and for nausea. The drug is rarely abused as its effects do not produce euphoria.

compulsion A psychological term used to refer to a force that compels a person to act against his own will. The term is often used interchangeably with the word CRAVING. Compulsion is different from the type of behavior exhibited during withdrawal when the need for a drug is physical.

confidentiality In drug abuse treatment programs, confidentiality—the assured anonymity of participants—is protected by federal and state regulations. Records may only be disclosed with the prior written consent of the person involved.

congener When used in reference to drugs, the term means a chemical relative; a derivative. In reference to alcohol, congeners are the organic alcohols and salts formed in the manufacture of alcoholic beverages. They provide the distinctive flavor and pungency of various beverages; vodkas contain the least congeners and bourbons and brandies the most.

consumption Alcohol consumption is estimated in one of two ways: self-reported consumption which is derived from individual responses to surveys; and apparent consumption which is derived from tax records, official state reports and reports of sales by the alcoholic beverage industry.

Since 1938, apparent consumption of alcoholic beverages in the United States has increased; the largest rate of increase took place between 1960 and 1970 (25%). The rate of growth slowed to 8% in the 1970s. Per capita consumption of alcohol has shown a significant decline since its peak in 1980–81, dropping from 2.76 gallons of pure alcohol per person 14 years old and older in 1978 to 2.65 gallons in 1984. For each person in the U.S. 14 years of age or over, the apparent consumption now averages about 1 ounce of 100% ethanol per day (approximately two drinks). This average is somewhat misleading, however, because one-third of the adult population reports abstaining. Consequently daily average consumption for those who drink is higher: 1.5 ounces of 100% ethanol, or three drinks a day. Even this average is misleading, though, because a small proportion of adults drink far more than the average and the majority drink less. It has been estimated that 11% of the adult population (16 million adults 18 years and older) consume about half of all beverages.

National surveys of drinking practices indicate that the one-third of adults who reported abstaining from drinking was broken down into 40% female and 25% male. In the heavier drinking category (1 or more ounces of 100% ethanol a day), males outnumbered females 14% to 4%. The percentage of drinkers showed a decrease with age except for a rise in the proportion of female drinkers from ages 18 to 20 and ages 21 to 34. Among males, heavier drinking appeared to peak at ages 21 to 34. Among females, heavier drinking peaked during the years between age 35 and 49. Since 1977 surveys have revealed a decrease in the number of abstainers and an increase in the number of drinkers in the lighter category (0.01 to 0.21 ounces of 100% ethanol per day).

Consumption of both beer and spirits declined in 1984, although wine consumption increased slightly. Beer consumption followed a pattern similar to that for total alcohol consumption, reaching the highest level in 1981 and declining each year thereafter. Consumption of spirits continued a long decline that began in 1970, dropping in 1984 to a new low of 0.94 gallons per person. A 1964 international survey ranked the U.S. 22nd out of 32 countries surveyed. The U.S. per capita consumption of spirits (pure alcohol) was 3.6 liters; U.S.S.R. ranked first (7.8). The United Kingdom ranked 24th with a per capita consumption of 2.0 liters. Total alcohol consumption per person 15 years and over in the U.S. was 10.2 liters.

M. M. Horgan, et al. International Survey: *Alcoholic Beverage Taxation and Control Policies.* 6th ed. Brewers Association of Canada, 1986.

contingency A behavior modification procedure frequently used in residential drug abuse treatment settings. Specifically agreed upon behavior and activities are rewarded; failure to act in the way agreed upon is punished. Under this system, the continuation of specified rewards is contingent upon continuation of agreed upon behaviors.

controlled drinking A concept whereby someone deliberately sets a limit on the number of drinks he or she will take, and when he reaches it, stops drinking. In the case of alcoholics, this concept runs directly contrary to the traditional belief that abstinence is the only course to recovery. The authors of the RAND REPORTS are among those who have suggested that alcoholics may resume "controlled" drinking. Their findings show that patients with a relatively short history of problem drinking will have a greater likelihood of success than those with a long history of alcoholism. Generally, patients who are able to control their drinking are younger and have a lower consumption rate than those who are not able to exercise control. The authors point out that with the wider range of treatment possibilities today, therapists can gear treatment to suit the patient rather than impose a uniform abstinence program upon all.

Opponents see the idea of controlled drinking as a tempting illusion presented with scientific authority. They believe that the concept will be most tempting to those alcoholics who are least able to cope with it. They also suggest that the Rand Report studies are faulty; that the time span of the study was too short and that many of the controlled drinkers in the sample were not really gamma alcoholics in the first place (see JELLINEK, E.M.).

In 1970, Mark and Linda Sobell of the University of California began what was to become one of the most controversial studies to date on controlled drinking. Their study compared two different treatment methods: 20 patients were assigned to a behavior-modification program whose goal was to produce moderate drinkers, and another 20 patients received regular hospital treatment aimed at total abstinence. The Sobells published the results of their research, including one- and two-year follow-ups, and claimed that the patients in the controlled-drinking group were able to function better than those who abstained. In 1973, Mary Pendery, a psychologist and alcoholism counselor at the University of California at Los Angeles, began to investigate the Sobells' findings. In an article in the July 9, 1982, issue of *Science,* Pendery and her colleagues attacked the Sobells' results and were highly critical of the Sobells themselves. Pendery stated that the reexamination of the 20 patients who had undergone behavior-modification indicated failure to achieve controlled drinking in all cases except one. No studies currently exist that demonstrate that accurately diagnosed alcoholics (or other addicts) can achieve controlled use. However, the controversy continues between those who see alcoholism as irreversible and those who see controlled drinking as a viable treatment method.

controlled drugs Drugs that are strictly controlled by the CONTROLLED SUBSTANCES ACT. Although alcoholic beverages are sometimes said to be controlled, they are only "regulated" by federal and state laws which govern their sale and purchase. Unlike other controlled drugs, the manufacturers and suppliers of alcoholic beverages are not held accountable for every ounce of the substances involved.

Controlled Substances Act The Comprehensive Drug Abuse Prevention and Control Act of 1970 (Public Law 91-513), Title II, more familiarly known as the Controlled Substances Act (CSA). It is the legal foundation of a federal strategy aimed at reducing the consumption of illicit drugs. The Controlled Substances Act brought up to date and consolidated all federal drug laws since the nation's first law regarding narcotics regulation was passed in 1914 (the HARRISON NARCOTICS ACT). The Drug Enforcement Administration (DEA) of the Department of Justice is responsible for enforcing the provisions of the act. The following material is quoted from *Drugs of Abuse* (Vol. 6, No. 2, July 1979), published by the DEA:

> *Criteria by which Drugs are Scheduled.* The CSA sets forth the findings which must be made to put a substance in any of the five schedules. These are as follows (Section 202b):
>
> *SCHEDULE I*
>
> (A) The drug or other substance has a high potential for abuse.
>
> (B) The drug or other substance has no currently accepted medical use in treatment in the United States.
>
> (C) There is a lack of accepted safety for use of the drug or other substance under medical supervision.
>
> *SCHEDULE II*
>
> (A) The drug or other substance has a high potential for abuse.
>
> (B) The drug or other substance has a currently accepted medical use in treatment in the United States or a currently accepted medical use with severe restrictions.
>
> (C) Abuse of the drug or other substance may lead to severe psychological or physical dependence.
>
> *SCHEDULE III*
>
> (A) The drug or other substance has a potential for abuse less than the drugs or other substances in Schedules I and II.
>
> (B) The drug or other substance has a currently accepted medical use in treatment in the United States.
>
> (C) Abuse of the drug or other substance may lead to moderate or low physical dependence or high psychological dependence.

SCHEDULE IV
(A) The drug or other substance has a low potential for abuse relative to the drugs or other substances in Schedule III.
(B) The drug or other substance has currently accepted medical use in treatment in the United States.
(C) Abuse of the drug or other substance may lead to limited physical dependence or psychological dependence relative to the drugs or other substances in Schedule III.
SCHEDULE V
(A) The drug or other substance has a low potential for abuse relative to the drugs or other substances in Schedule IV.
(B) The drug or other substance has a currently accepted medical use in treatment in the United States.
(C) Abuse of the drug or other substance may lead to limited physical dependence or psychological dependence relative to the drugs or other substances in Schedule IV.

There are eight specific factors which the DEA and the Department of Health and Human Services (HHS) are directed to consider when including a drug or other substance in a particular schedule, or when transferring or removing a substance entirely from the schedules. These criteria, as published by the DEA in *Drugs of Abuse* (Vol. 6, No. 2, July 1979), are:

1. Its actual or relative potential for abuse.
2. Scientific evidence of its pharmacological effect, if known.
3. The state of current scientific knowledge regarding the drug or other substance.
4. Its history and current pattern of abuse.
5. The scope, duration and significance of abuse.
6. What, if any, risk there is to public health.
7. Its psychic or physiological dependence liability.
8. Whether the substance is an immediate precursor of a substance already controlled under this title.

Under the Controlled Substances Act nine major control mechanisms are imposed on manufacturing, purchasing, and distributing controlled substances:

1. *Registration of Handlers.* Any person who handles or intends to handle controlled substances must obtain a registration issued by the DEA. A unique number is assigned to legitimate handlers: importers, exporters, manufacturers, wholesalers, hospitals, pharmacies, physicians and researchers. Prior to the purchase of a controlled substance the number must be made available to the supplier by the customer, thus diminishing the opportunity for unauthorized transactions.

2. *Recordkeeping Requirements.* Full records must be kept of all quantities manufactured, and of all purchases, sales and inventories of all controlled substances regardless of the schedule in which they are placed. Limited exemptions are available to physicians and researchers. Because they are highly abusable substances, records for Schedule I and II drugs must be kept separate from all other records by the handler for expeditious investigations if called for. The system of control makes it possible to trace the flow of any drug from the time it is first manufactured or imported to the actual person who receives it. It also serves as an international check for large corporations who must be concerned about employee pilferage. The mere existence of this requirement can discourage forms of abuse.

3. *Quotas on Manufacturing.* The DEA limits the quantity of controlled substances listed in Schedules I and II which may be produced during any calendar year. Although the statute speaks exclusively in terms of Schedules I and II, certain drugs in Schedules II, IV and V derive from materials listed in Schedule II. Codeine syrups, for example, are made by combining codeine (a Schedule II drug) with other ingredients in a special diluted form. Therefore many narcotic products in Schedules III and V, as well as certain barbiturate combination drugs in Schedule III, are in fact subject to quotas as

well. The DEA uses available data on sales and inventories of Schedule I and II substances, and taking into account Food and Drug Administration (FDA) estimates of drug usage, it establishes aggregate production quotas which set the national limits of production. The overall production limits are subdivided into manufacturing quotas which are granted to the registered manufacturers. To set manufacturing quotas it is necessary to determine how much bulk controlled substance will be purchased by those companies engaged only in the formulation of dosage units. Formulating companies are granted procurement quotas, based on their past usage.

4. *Restrictions on Distribution.* Recordkeeping is required for the distribution of a controlled substance from one manufacturer to another, from manufacturer to wholesaler, from importer to wholesaler, and from wholesaler to dispenser. In the case of Schedule I and II drugs, the supplier must have a special order form from the customer. This form is issued only by the DEA (form 222) to those who are properly registered and is preprinted with the name and address of the customer. The drug must be shipped only to that person. This reinforcement of the registration requirement makes certain that only authorized persons may receive Schedule I and II drugs. For Schedule III, IV, and V drugs, no order form is necessary but the supplier is held fully accountable for any drug shipped to a purchaser who does not have a valid registration.

5. *Restrictions on Dispensing.* There are also restrictions on the dispensing or delivery of a controlled substance to the ultimate user, who may be a patient or research subject. Schedule I drugs may be used only in research situations as currently they have no accepted medical use in the U.S. A prescription order is required for Schedule II, III, and IV medications under the Federal Food, Drug and Cosmetic Act. The determination to place drugs on prescription is within the jurisdiction of the FDA. Schedule II drugs are subject to additional special restrictions: prescription orders must be written and signed by the practitioner and may not be telephoned in except in an emergency. In addition, these prescriptions may not be refilled; the patients must see the doctor again in order to get more drugs. Schedule III and IV drug orders may be either written or oral and with the doctor's authorization may be refilled up to five times within six months of the initial dispensing. Schedule V drugs include many over-the-counter (OTC), narcotic preparations, including many antitussives and antidiarrheals, and here too restrictions are imposed. The patient must be 18 years old, have some form of identification, and have his named entered into a special log maintained by the pharmacist.

6. *Limitations on Imports and Exports.* International transactions involving any drug in Schedule I or II or a narcotic drug in Schedule III must have prior approval of the DEA; international transactions involving a non-narcotic in Schedule III or any drug in Schedule IV or V do not need approval but prior notice must be given to the DEA. Approval to import a Schedule I or II drug is not given unless an importer can show that there is an insufficient domestic supply with no adequate competition. Similarly, exportation of Schedule I and II drugs and narcotic drugs in Schedule III is severely limited: exporters must demonstrate that the drugs are going to a country where they will actually be used and will not be reexported.

7. *Conditions for Storage of Drugs.* The DEA sets requirements for the security of premises where controlled substances are stored. Among the requirements for Schedule I and II drugs are specially constructed vault and alarm systems. For Schedule III, IV and V drugs a vault is optional and the handler may segregate the controlled substance in a secure area under constant supervision. These requirements do not apply to qualified researchers, physicians, export-

ers and wholesalers who handle small quantities of controlled substances. The DEA is presently reviewing requirements for shippers as well as for employees who have access to controlled drugs.

8. *Reports of Transactions to the Government.* The monitoring of all drugs in Schedules I and II and narcotic drugs in Schedule III is carried out by the Automation of Reports and Consolidated Orders System (ARCOS), established in January 1974. Manufacturers, wholesalers, importers and exporters of these drugs must report all manufacturing activities, importations, exportations and all other distributions to the DEA. Inventories must also be filed annually.

9. *Criminal, Civil and Administrative Penalties for Illegal Acts.* Trafficking is defined as the unauthorized manufacture, distribution (that is, delivery whether by sale, gift or otherwise), or possession of with intent to distribute any controlled substance. For narcotics in Schedules I and II, a first offense is punishable by up to life in prison and up to a $4 million fine. For trafficking in a Schedule I and II non-narcotic drug or any Schedule III drug, the penalty is up to five years imprisonment and a $250,000 fine. Trafficking in a Schedule IV drug is punishable by a maximum of three years and up to $250,000. Trafficking in a Schedule V drug is a misdemeanor punishable by up to one year and up to $100,000. Second and subsequent offenses are punishable by twice the penalty imposed for the first offense.

The CSA carefully distinguishes between trafficking offenses (by those who supply illicit drugs to abusers) and use offenses (by those possessing drugs solely for personal use). A use offense is always a misdemeanor on the first offense, punishable by one year and up to $5,000.

Procedures for Controlling Substances The various procedures for controlling a substance under the CSA are set forth in Section 201 of the act. Proceedings may be initiated by HHS, by the DEA, or by petition from any interested person or group: the manufacturer of a drug; a medical society or association; a pharmacy association; a public interest group concerned with drug abuse; or a state or local government agency. When a petition is received by the DEA the agency begins its own investigation of the drug. In most cases this process has led to a report and recommendation to HEW.

International Obligations The CSA further provides that if control of any drug is required by U.S. obligation under international treaty arrangements, the drug shall be placed under the schedule deemed most appropriate to carry out these obligations. As cited in the CSA, the U.S. is a party to the Single Convention on Narcotic Drugs of 1961, designed to establish effective control over international and domestic traffic in narcotics: coca leaf, cocaine and cannabis are included within the legal definitions. A second treaty, the Convention on Psychotropic Substances of 1971, which became enforceable in 1976, is designed to establish comparable control over such drugs as LSD, amphetamines, certain barbiturates and other depressants. Legislation has been passed by Congress authorizing the U.S. to become a signatory to this treaty. Congress ratified this treaty in 1980.

convulsions Involuntary spasmodic contractions of muscles. Convulsions can occur in cases of stimulant OVERDOSE and during CNS depressant WITHDRAWAL. (See also DELIRIUM TREMENS.)

cough medicine Cough medicines are often abused because of their high alcohol content. Some nighttime cough medicines have more than twice the amount of alcohol found in wine and only 15% less than the amount found in some hard liquors. Comtrex Nighttime and Vick's Nyquil Cold Medicine both contain 25% alcohol; Vick's Formula 44D has 10% alcohol; Pertussin Cough Syrup for Children, 8% alcohol; Chlor-Trimeton

Allergy Syrup, 7%; and Robitussin Cough Formula, 3.5%.

Many cough medicines are also abused because of the CODEINE they contain. These can only be obtained with a prescription. An effective antitussive, codeine resembles MORPHINE but its effects are milder. Although it is considered only mildly addictive and instances of addiction are rare, if is often abused for its mild euphoric and sedative properties. Codeine is a Schedule II drug and it is more difficult to obtain a cough medicine containing codeine than it is an over-the-counter (OTC) cough medicine with a high alcohol content, although both can be and are abused. Dextromethorphan, contained in Ramilar and most other OTC cough preparations, has a lower abuse potential than codeine. It has been taken infrequently in large quantities for abuse purposes.

counseling See TREATMENT, REHABILITATION and GROUP THERAPY.

counterculture A culture which rejects key norms and values of the general society at large. The term was coined in the 1960s and was used to describe those who were in favor of the use of such drugs as LSD and marijuana. Many of these individuals were also anti-government, anti-police and anti-war. It was particularly applied to the young adults living in HAIGHT-ASHBURY.

"crack" cocaine First reported in Los Angeles, San Diego and Houston in 1981, crack is cocaine in smokable (freebase) form. It became prevalent on the U.S. drug scene in early 1986; it became a serious problem in New York City in 1985; and in 1988, crack was reported in 28 states and the District of Columbia. Cocaine HCL (hydrochloride) is available on the street today at 55% pure for $100 per gram; crack is available at 75% to 90% pure for $10 per one-tenth of a gram.

The first product made from leaves of the coca plant (grown primarily in Bolivia and Peru) is coca paste. This paste is converted chemically into cocaine base. Dried cocaine base is usually dissolved in ethyl ethes, acetone, or a mixture of both and filtered to remove solid impurities. A mixture of acetone and concentrated hydrochloric acid or ethanol and concentrated hydrochloric acid is added to precipitate cocaine hydrochloride. This precipitate is filtered and dried carefully using bright light to produce the white crystalline powder, cocaine hydrochloride (HCL), otherwise known as cocaine.

Because cocaine HCL will largely decompose if smoked directly, the HCL must be converted back to a relatively pure base state, or freebase, before it is suitable for smoking. Freebase is made either the traditional way by using volatile chemicals, most notably the highly explosive ether, or by a heating and cooling method that produces "crack." In traditional freebase cocaine HCL is mixed with distilled water, a solvent (volatile chemicals) and ether. It is then put over a high flame. Crack is made by mixing cocaine HCL with water and baking soda and cooking the mixture in a pan. Once all the impurities have been cooked out, what remains is a pancake that is cracked into little pieces to be sold.

Crack is smoked in a pipe or mixed in a tobacco or marijuana cigarette and smoked. The term "crack" comes from the crackling sound made when it is smoked before it dries, or from its occasional resemblance to cracked paint chips or plaster. Users pulverize the chips into "pebbles" prior to smoking.

Crack and cocaine can cause seizures, cardiac arrest, arrythmia heart attack, stroke, or respiratory arrest. Effects of an overdose include agitation, increase in body temperature, hallucinations, convulsions, and possible death.

Several street names for crack exist. They include: base, baseball, black rock, cloud nine, conan, crack, crank (also the name for speed or methamphetamine in the Northeast), freebase, gravel, handball, lido, rock, roxanne, serpico, snow, toke, space basing (crack doused with liquid PCP and smoked—also called ghostbusters), super white, white cloud, white tornado.

Data from the 1985 National Household Survey on Drug Abuse show that 21% of the people who have ever used cocaine have used freebase and 8% have used cocaine intravenously. Recent (latter half of the 1980s) cocaine users are more likely to have ever used freebase: 38% of the past month users compared with 20% of the past year users and 10% of those last using cocaine over a year ago. Among high school seniors in the class of 1987, 5.6% reported having tried crack while 4% used it in the past year.

The percent of people admitted to treatment for a primary problem of cocaine abuse, who reported smoking cocaine as their primary route of administration, increased from 1.4% in 1979 to 18.7% in 1984. Between 1984 and 1986, the proportion of cocaine-related hospital emergency room episodes involving smoking of the drug increased from 1 in 15 patients to 1 in 5.

The 1985 National Household Survey on Drug Abuse indicates that among youth (age 12–17), lifetime and past year prevalence of cocaine is highest for Hispanics (7% and 6%), compared to whites (6% and 5%) and blacks (3% and 3%). Among young adults (age 18–25), the rates are highest for whites (28% and 18%), compared to Hispanics (15% and 12%) and blacks (14% and 11%). Among older adults (over age 25), these rates are highest among blacks (7% and 3%), as compared to whites (4% and 1%) and Hispanics (3% and 1%).

Demographic data for cocaine-related emergency room patients from the DAWN system (Drug Abuse Warning Network) in 1987 suggest a predominance of males (66%) and adult patients in their 20s and 30s (85% were 20–39 years of age). Fewer whites than blacks were seen in emergency rooms for cocaine emergencies (28% and 55%, respectively).

Demographic data on cocaine-related death in 1987 were similar to data shown for cocaine emergencies except that the number of whites and blacks were similar (39% and 47%, respectively), while 11% were Hispanics. Eighty percent were male and 79% were 20–39 years of age.

In July 1989, the National Institute of Drug Abuse (NIDA) estimated that the number of Americans using *any* illegal drug on a "current" basis (i.e., at least once in a 30-day period preceding the survey) dropped 37%, from 23 million in 1985 to 14.5 million in 1988. Current use of the two most common illegal substances—marijuana and cocaine—is down 36% and 48% respectively.

The above noted 1989 report stated, however, that crack is responsible for the explosion in recent drug-related medical emergencies—a 28-fold increase in hospital admissions involving smoked cocaine since 1984.

In early 1990 crack was selling on America's streets for $3 to $20 a vial (less than 1 gram). This amount provides a "high" of approximately 20 to 30 minutes duration.

Another devastating result stemming from use of the smokable cocaine derivative, crack, is the drug's serious effect on babies born to mothers using the drug. Studies have indicated thus far that prenatal exposure to crack may result in some permanent impairment.

Experts say that while the babies themselves are free of drugs not long after birth prenatal exposure and postnatal deprivation are likely to take a severe toll.

Each year, according to the National Institute of Drug Abuse (NIDA) researchers, more than 300,000 infants are born with traces of illegal drugs. No one is yet certain how many are being exposed specifically to crack. But few doubt that the needs of these babies will present a challenge to schools, future employers and society. More women than men are now reported using crack in several major American cities, and drug experts say a large number of the new users are young pregnant women.

Crack may produce these negative effects by altering fundamental neurological pathways in the baby's brain, researchers say. The drug crosses the placenta during the first trimester of pregnancy when the brain is forming. The pleasure and reward pathway, based on the brain chemical dopamine, is especially vulnerable to cocaine. Experts believe this might explain the flat (lethargic) moods and emotional poverty seen in some crack babies. Research groups are doing follow-up studies on this phenomenon at the Perinatal Center for Chemical Dependency at Northwest University School of Medicine in Chicago and at the University of California, Los Angeles.

Sandra Blakeslee, "Crack's Toll Among Babies: A Joyless View, Even of Toys." *New York Times,* September 17, 1989.

Maurice L. Hill, *Drug Enforcement Administration Briefing Book: DEA Mission,* U.S. Department of Justice, June 1988.

John C. Lawn, *Drugs of Abuse,* 1988 edition, U.S. Department of Justice, Drug Enforcement Administration (DEA), Washington. DC 1988 (U.S. Government Printing Office).

craving An overwhelming desire or need for a drug that can be either physical or psychological in origin. (See also DEPENDENCY.)

crime A drug user needs a vast amount of money in order to support a habit—usually more than he has access to by legal means. The usual categories of crime indulged in by drug users to support their habits are: theft, drug dealing (buying and selling), confidence games, pimping, prostitution, gambling and forgery.

Studies conducted by the National Institute of Drug Abuse (NIDA) found that many drug users commit more than one type of crime to maintain their habits, although they tend to focus on a particular activity. It was also found that those addicted to drugs at a younger age tend to commit crimes more frequently later on. One NIDA study identifies the types and frequencies of crimes committed by heroin addicts. The survey, which covered 11 years, followed 243 male heroin addicts in Baltimore, Maryland. In total, the men committed more than 473,738 crimes during their years on the street (they were not incarcerated). The study is based on "crime days per year at risk."

A second study by NIDA in Miami, Florida, covered 1,007 drug- and non-drug-using criminals. In the year prior to being interviewed, the individuals committed 355,699 crimes: heroin users were more heavily involved in criminal activities than other drug users or non-users, not a surprising fact considering the expense of a heroin habit. Employed heroin users committed crimes considered less serious than those committed by unemployed users. Of the total crimes committed, 122,484 were drug sales; 8,144 were assaults and robberies; 87,795 involved burglary and other types of theft; 9,514 were forgeries. Only a small portion of the crimes committed resulted in arrest: 248 crimes to one arrest. The ratio of crimes to arrest varied according to the type of illegal activity: 35:1 for assaults and robberies; 102:1 for forgeries; 148:1 for burglaries and other thefts; 761:1 for drug sales.

In 1988, the DEA made a total of 23,972 drug arrests, 14,116 for cocaine alone. Nationally, in 1987, there were 937,400 arrests for drug violations, up 13% from 1986. Drug arrests rose 48% from 1984 through 1988.

The seriousness of the crimes involved grows greater with age. Among youthful addicts there are more muggings and purse snatchings; older addicts commit robberies. Because of black market prices, an addict only realizes one-fourth of the value of stolen merchandise, a fact that accounts for the cost of addiction in relation to the criminality involved. Unfortunately, many members of the public welcome the opportunity to buy black market items at bargain prices and thus provide a ready market for stolen goods.

The business community is also affected by criminality. Not only does business suffer from on-and-off-the-job absenteeism because of drug abuse, it also suffers substantial losses due to theft. Thefts are committed both by low level employees using the cheaper crack and high level employees with $100-a-day habits.

In crimes that involve drug abuse everyone is a victim: the business community, the addict and the non-addict are all hurt. Still, it cannot be generalized that all addicts are criminals. While there is an undeniable connection between crime and addiction, there are a great many people who were engaged in criminal activity before they became addicted, and an equally great number would be involved in criminal activity whether or not they are addicted. There are still others who prefer to give up drugs rather than indulge in criminal activity. Although crimes connected with addiction are usually perpetrated against property, and do not generally involve serious crimes against individuals, such as murder, addicts should not be excused from responsibility. Supportive measures by the courts, treatment and rehabilitation, along with correction, parole and probation would certainly help to reverse the criminal trend.

Although it has been suggested that METHADONE maintenance will reduce criminal activity among heroin abusers, the theory has been challenged by those who offer overwhelming evidence of clinic drugs being bought and sold illegally on the streets. Some addicts have even been known to support their habits by selling their take home supplies or methadone that has been smuggled out of clinics.

As to the involvement of alcohol in criminal activity, it is not clear whether drinking leads to criminal activity or whether involvement in criminal activity leads to drinking. Statistics involving alcohol-related crimes vary widely. In the case of rape offenders, alcohol involvement was from 13% to 50%; in the case of rape victims, alcohol involvement was 6% to 31%. In studies of homicides it was found that from 28% to 86% of the offenders used alcohol and 14% to 87% of the victims used alcohol. There have been a number of theories which have attempted to explain the role of alcohol in criminal and violent behavior. It has been suggested that alcohol releases inhibitions and intensifies certain mental states: the release of anger may enhance the likelihood of violence and aggression. The synergistic combination of alcohol and another drug may result in increased violent behavior.

The relationship of crime to drug abuse is generally confined to the study of those addicted to heroin or alcohol, and much less to those addicted to other drugs. This is probably because of the high cost involved in heroin addiction and the greater incidence of violence related to alcoholism. This is not to say that there is no incidence of crime among those addicted to drugs such as marijuana. Studies of marijuana are generally related to its effects on the body but it has been suggested that it should not be given a clean bill of health in relation to crime. The same holds true for amphetamines and hallucinogens. Use and or habituation can result in mental disorder, confusion, and changes in behavior that can lead to criminal and violent acts. The susceptibility of an individual when he takes a drug, along with the dosage, can also account for criminal involvement. Because there are no conclusive criminal studies of marijuana and other drugs, it is hard to estimate how many crimes would be committed if they were not available.

There is less chance of violent aggressive behavior in heroin addicts while high because heroin tends to diminish aggressiveness. This does not hold true for alcoholics because alcohol tends to evoke aggressiveness; nor is it true of barbiturate users. One would think that because barbiturates are sedative hypnotic drugs, abusers would simply fall asleep. In fact, they become argumentative, overactive and irritable. Studies have found, for example, that members of motorcycle gangs will take "downers" before engaging in street fights and confrontations; this kind of reaction is similar to the aggressive behavior that alcohol often produces. Drug use can produce false feelings and ideas of suspicion and persecution. It can also produce feelings of omnipotence and bravado. These paranoid thought disorders can lead to bursts of violence and hyperactivity which, in turn, can lead to criminal behavior.

The setting in which someone takes a drug, along with his mood and personality, can also alter a drug's action. In other words, no drug is invariably criminogenic.

crime, organized There is a massive involvement of organized crime in drug trafficking largely because it is extremely lucrative. Nationwide, according to the U.S. Department of Justice, drug pushers took in an estimated $130 billion in 1987. At least four organized gangs in Los Angeles alone had traffic in cocaine exceeding $1 million per week.

Organized crime reaped the bulk of these profits, over a 100% increase from 1977, through large-scale highly sophisticated drug operations. "Big time" drug dealers have to obtain the illicit substances (usually overseas), arrange for the processing of the drugs (coca into cocaine, and so on), smuggle them into the country, arrange for the cutting of pure drugs, and then distribute them over a wide geographical area in elaborate trafficking networks. Drug money is often "laundered" or passed through legitimate businesses, some of which are "fronts" in major enterprises, before it is put back into the drug trade.

Two new non-traditional groups have emerged in organized crime in the last two decades—prison gangs which operate inside and outside prison, and outlaw motorcycle gangs. Other drug cartels that have recently appeared are Colombian groups, such as the Medellin cartel, known as "Cocaine Cowboys," and Southeast Asian groups. The common objective is money and the primary tactic is violence. The use of violence is a major problem. In 1981, for example, 25% of all homicides in Dade County, Florida, were the result of drug groups carrying out machine-gun assassinations in public places. Violence among gangs in Los Angeles rose 88% in 1987. These gangs are now spreading from neighborhoods to cities across the United States. One estimate placed Los Angeles street gang members in 49 American cities. Organized crime also engages in weapons trafficking, prostitution, gambling, pornography, and other activities that directly or indirectly involve many innocent people and institutions. There are also reports of public officials at all levels who are being corrupted by drug money, particularly rural police officers who accept large sums to "look the other way" during smuggling operations.

To combat organized crime, the number one crime problem, the Drug Enforcement Administration (DEA) has recently been reorganized; and for the first time the FBI has been brought into the fight to work with the DEA. The Navy, Coast Guard, and U.S. Customs officials are also cooperating in interdicting smuggling operations. In 1988, the DEA made a total of 23,972 drug arrests; 14,116 for cocaine alone. Nationally, in 1987, there were 937,400 arrests for drug violations, up 13% from 1986. Drug arrests rose 48% from 1984 through 1988.

crisis intervention The process of diagnosing and arresting such conditions as overdose, suicide attempts and panic reaction in drug crisis situations. Unconsciousness, low breathing rate, respiratory arrest, fever, extreme high or low pulse rate, muscle rigidity and vomiting in a semi- or unconscious state are signs indicating overdose and the need for immediate drug crisis intervention.

cross-addiction Addiction between drugs within the same group can be mutual or interchangeable. For example, a person addicted to a sedative will in some degree be addicted to all other sedatives, including alcohol. Therefore a person addicted to Librium could prevent WITHDRAWAL SYMPTOMS by taking alcohol and vice versa. The same does not apply to drugs from other groups: if someone is addicted to a sedative, a narcotic would not be effective.

cross-dependence The term is used in much the same way as CROSS-ADDICTION, meaning that dependence between drugs of the same group is mutual or interchangeable.

cross-tolerance If tolerance has developed to one drug it will carry over to another in the same group. For example, alcoholics are more difficult to anesthetize than nonalcoholics. The increased ability to metabolize another drug may be a cause of cross-tolerance, or it may be caused by changes in the tissues of the central nervous system (CNS) which make the system less responsive to the other drug.

cultural stress etiological theories See SOCIOCULTURAL ETIOLOGICAL THEORIES.

cut The act of diluting HEROIN (usually with milk sugar) so that the pusher can make a larger profit. A mixture containing only 5% heroin is the usual product sold to the consumer.

cyclazocine A narcotic antagonist used in the treatment of heroin addiction. An addict who has been withdrawn from heroin and then treated with cyclazocine will not feel the effects of an ordinary dose of heroin. The drug can cause dependence but withdrawal is milder than heroin withdrawal. Cyclazocine has not been used since naltrexone, a more effective and longer lasting antagonist, has become available.

cyclobarbital A short-acting BARBITURATE that is mainly used in hypnosis. Because of the rapid onset of its effects and their short duration it is found undesirable by most drug users.

Cylert® (Abbott) A STIMULANT of the central nervous system that is generally used for children with Minimal Brain Dysfunction (Attention Deficit Disorder). It is a brand of pemoline. Although it is pharmacologically similar to other CNS stimulants (AMPHETAMINES), it does not have a high potential for abuse. Overdosage can result in agitation, restlessness and hallucinations. It is available in 18.75 mg yellow tablets; 37.5 mg orange tablets; and 75 mg tan tablets.

Cystospaz-SR® (Webcon) A depressant containing the intermediate-acting BARBITURATE, butabarbital. It is used as an antispasmodic-sedative and may be habit-forming. It is supplied in blue opaque and clear yellow capsules.

cytisine An extremely poisonous alkaloid found in many plants of the pea family. It was once used as a cathartic and diuretic. Canary Island broom, Spanish broom and Scotch broom, which are sometimes smoked or taken orally, all contain cytisine.

D

Dalmane® (Roche) A sedative, the benzodiazepine flurazepam hydrochloride, used as a hypnotic agent in the treatment of insomnia. It is in widespread use. When used with alcohol or other central nervous system depressants, it can have an additive effect. Overdosage can result in somnolence, confusion and coma. It is available in 15 mg orange and ivory capsules, and in 30 mg red and ivory capsules.

damiana *Turnera diffusa,* a tropical American plant of the Turneraceae family. There are claims that smoking the leaves can produce a marijuana-like effect. It is also purported to be a mild aphrodisiac.

DARE See PROJECT DARE.

Darvocet-N® (Lilly) See DARVON-N.

Darvon® (Lilly) An analgesic that is widely used to moderate pain, Darvon has the pharmacological properties of a NARCOTIC but does not compare with narcotics in analgesic potency. It contains propoxyphene hydrochloride. The use of Darvon with alcohol or other central nervous system depressants can result in additive depressant effects. The drug can produce physical dependence, and is often abused. Overdosage can result in respiratory depression, convulsions, circulatory collapse, pupil constriction, and extreme somnolence leading to stupor and coma. Cardiac arrest and death have occurred. Darvon is supplied in 32 and 65 mg light pink opaque capsules. It is also available mixed with other drugs: Darvon Compound and Darvon Compound-65, each with aspirin, caffeine, and phenacetin; and Darvon with A.S.A., which is aspirin. The combination of propoxyphene with aspirin, or a mixture of aspirin, caffeine and phenacetin, will produce greater analgesia than that of propoxyphene alone. Darvon Compound is supplied in capsules with a light pink opaque body and light gray opaque cap. Darvon Compound-65 is supplied in capsules with a red opaque body and light gray cap. Darvon with A.S.A. is supplied in capsules with a red opaque body and light pink opaque cap.

Darvon-N® (Lilly) A drug that contains propoxyphene napsylate, which is similar to propoxyphene hydrochloride (see DARVON), but differs in that it allows more stable, longer-acting liquid and tablet dosage forms. Like Darvon, it is a mild analgesic and is structurally related to the narcotics but it does not compare in potency. Physical dependence can occur and there is potential for abuse. Overdose symptoms are the same as those for Darvon. Darvon-N has been used to detoxify patients form opiate dependence. Darvon-N is supplied in buff-colored oval tablets; Darvon-N with A.S.A. (aspirin) are oval-shaped orange tablets. Darvocet-N 50, and Darvocet-N 100 (which are propoxyphene napsylate and acetaminophen) are dark orange capsule-shaped tablets.

Data Centers and Clearinghouse for Drugs & Crime Established in 1986, the agency is funded by the Bureau of Justice Assistance, and directed by the Bureau of Justice Statistics of the U.S. Department of Justice. The center responds to requests for drug and crime data; advises about new drugs and crime data reports; conducts special bibliographic searches upon request for specific drugs and crime topics; and publishes special reports on subjects such as assets forfeitual and seizure, economic costs of drug-related crime, drugs and violence, drug laws of the 50 states, drug abuse and corrections, and innovative law enforcement reactions to drugs and crime. The center also prepares a comprehensive, concise report that brings together an array of data to trace and quantify the complete flow of illicit drugs. Contact: Data Center and Clearinghouse for Drugs & Crime, 1600 Research Boulevard, Rockville, MD 20850.

datura A HALLUCINOGEN found in the poisonous Jimson weed plant, *Datura stramonium,* which is a member of the potato family (Solanaceae). The active ingredients in the substance are the BELLADONNA alkaloids, atropine, scopolamine and hyoscyamine. Leaves and seeds of this extremely dangerous plant have been used as poisons and hallucinogens for centuries. Users smoke the dried leaves. The leaves have also been used in asthma powders and in the anti-asthma cigarette, Asthmador.

Synonyms: angel's trumpet, devil's apple, devil's weed, Jamestown weed, Jimson-weed, stinkweed, stramonium, thorn apple.

dawamesk A green cake popular in North Africa, made from sugar, spices, orange juice and the tops of the CANNABIS plant. It is eaten for its hallucinogenic effects and it was in the form of dawamesk that cannabis was first introduced to Europe in the mid-1800s.

DAWN See DRUG ABUSE WARNING NETWORK.

DAYTOP Oldest and largest drug-free therapeutic program in the United States. The program features a residential center for persons 13 years old and older who have a severe drug abuse problem, outreach centers that treat adolescents who have a moderate drug problem, and specialized services, such as: an adolescent program, a young women's group, a siblings group and an adult outpatient service. Contact: DAYTOP, 54 West 40th Street, New York, NY 10018. Telephone: (212) 354-6000.

DEA See DRUG ENFORCEMENT ADMINISTRATION.

deadly nightshade See BELLADONNA.

decriminalization See LEGAL ASPECTS.

delirium Many drugs, including some which do not have a mental effect, can cause a delirium in large doses or in average amounts in people who are sensitive to them. A delirium, also called a toxic psychosis, is marked by confusion, disorientation, clouding of consciousness, hallucinations and delusions. Distractibility, inability to concentrate and agitation are often observed.

delirium tremens A serious condition of WITHDRAWAL from barbiturate-type drugs and alcohol, commonly referred to as the D.T.'s. This condition is considered a medical emergency and the patient should be hospitalized immediately. Symptoms may include vivid and terrifying auditory, visual and tactile hallucinations; profound confusion; disorientation; severe agitation and restlessness; insomnia; fever; and abnormally rapid heartbeat. Sedation may be required, but extreme caution should be used in order to avoid oversedation, for a drug dosage that would suppress all symptoms would also seriously depress the patient's respiration. The D.T.'s can last for three to four days, or can persist intermittently for several weeks.

delta alcoholism See JELLINEK.

delusions A belief or firm fixed idea that is not amenable to reason, rationality or evidence to the contrary. Delusions are common among those who are under the influence of a hallucinogen or large doses of stimulants, and can be dangerous. During the "LSD era" several deaths were reported because some users were under the delusion that they could walk on water or fly. Delusions may be persecutory or grandiose in quality.

dementia A condition described by the *Diagnostic and Statistical Manual* (see DSM III) as "a loss of intellectual abilities of sufficient severity to interfere with social or intellectual functioning." The deficit is multifaceted and involves memory, judgment, abstract thought and other cortical functions. Changes in personality and behavior also occur. Alcoholism, or nutritional deficiencies associated with alcoholism, are two of its many possible causes. Early symptoms, which can vary, include a slow deterioration of personality and intellect. Judgment, insight, speech and motor activity are affected. Personal habits deteriorate and eventually, if the dementia is progressive, the patient may require total nursing care.

Demerol® (Winthrop) A narcotic (a brand of MEPERIDINE hydrochloride) used as an analgesic for moderate to severe pain and as a sedative. Its activity is similar to that of morphine: it can produce the same type of dependence, and it has a high potential for abuse. Respiratory depression and coma may result from overdosage, and if Demerol is combined with alcohol or other central nervous system depressants an additive effect can occur. High dose abuse and withdrawal can result in seizures (seen with no other narcotics). It is available in white scored tablets of 50 and 100 mg, and as a banana-flavored syrup (nonalcoholic) of 50 mg per ml. For parenteral use it is available in vials, ampules and disposable syringes.

denial An addicted person's inability to perceive the existence of a drinking or drug problem. It differs from lying in that it is a true distortion in thinking. It is one of the main defense mechanisms addicts employ to deal with life and this posture distinguishes them from nonaddicts. Relatives and friends will also often "deny" an alcoholic's problem to protect him. Denial should be dealt with quickly in alcohol treatment: by recognizing his denial for what it is, an alcoholic becomes more aware of his problem and his role in its creation.

Denmark Drug abuse began to be noted as a problem in Denmark early on in World War II, around 1940. As the problem increased, particularly morphine abuse, the government took action and passed the Euphoric Drugs Act of 1955. It empowered the Minister of the Interior to limit the use of certain drugs to medical purposes. In the 1960s, as abuse grew more widespread and included the use of cannabis and amphetamines along with morphine, the government switched its attention to peddlers and stiff penal rules for drug offenses were introduced in 1965. A 1968 study revealed that out of 350,000 school-age youths, 42,000 had used drugs (90% of the cases involved the use of marijuana). A follow-up study in 1970 showed that while the use of marijuana and other drugs showed a steady increase it was on a smaller scale than before. Despite a new wave of legislation and increased penalties, the Danish attitude toward drug abuse (similar to that of Great Britian) is that addiction is first and foremost a medical problem and is a manifestation of disease.

Since the mid-1970s the number of addicts seems to have stabilized at around 6,000 to 10,000, out of a total population of almost six million. Abuse is dominated by heroin—most of which is brought in from Southwest Asia—but also includes the use of barbiturates, amphetamines and cannabis. Although the abuse of LSD was once pronounced it is now negligible. Today the average age of drug abusers is 26–27 (70% of the addicts being over 25). As most addicts make their debut around the age of 18, this means an abuse career of from six to 10 years. The incidence of new addicts each year is not known but is estimated to be around 500 to 800 per year. The rising age of addicts reflects the fact that few are able to stop their abuse—only 5% a year.

Although the number of addicts has stabilized somewhat, the consequences of abuse have increased considerably. Along with the strain on penal institutions because of growing offenses against property, there is also an increase in organized crime—a relatively new development in Denmark. The number of deaths from drug abuse in the 26–27 age group is second only to vehicle fatalities, although it is possible that some of the deaths—particularly those attributed to heroin—are actually the result of other complications (see SYNDROME X).

Drug addicts in Denmark can receive treatment in two ways, from general practitioners or from publicly financed treatment centers (youth centers). Treatment in youth centers is generally on an outpatient basis and includes the use of therapeutic communities. There is, however, relatively little use of prescribed drugs in the treatment of heroin abuse, and methadone treatment of long duration is limited. The program includes counseling, social and psychological support, and vocational rehabilitation. There is now a plan to rapidly expand facilities for youth centers.

A relatively large number of addicts seek treatment from general practitioners. This is partly a result of lack of places in treatment centers, and partly because many addicts prefer the more medical type of treatment.

A majority of drug addicts are not in contact with either general practitioners or treatment centers. A total of 2,000 addicts were in touch with a treatment institution in 1981, but only a small portion received prolonged treatment. Because of this fact, there is a growing trend toward strengthening established social institutions and training more social workers. There are also plans to set up more youth centers to house drug abusers within the penal system.

In Denmark there has always been a liberal attitude toward alcohol consumption; the national drinking pattern has been one of frequent but temperate consumption. The majority of consumption takes place in the home and mostly beer is involved. Although there has been some increase in preference for distilled spirits during recent years the basic pattern remains unchanged.

Because the Danish government believes that the regulation of alcohol consumption is suitable only if agreed to by the majority, it limits control to the taxation of alcoholic beverages. There is a National Commission on Alcohol, but its purpose is advisory; public responsibility for prevention and control of alcohol-related problems is left in the hands of county-level government. Because the consumption of both wine and distilled spirits rose twice as fast as beer between 1967 and 1977, there is a growing number of problem drinkers in the country. It is responsible for an increase in alcohol-impaired driving offenses and in admissions to psychiatric hospitals for alcohol-related problems. Mortality rates for alcoholism and the incidence of liver cirrhosis have also increased in the last 10 years. An international comparison survey of alcohol consumption per person 15 years and over in 1984 shows Denmark ranked 13th out of 32 nations in total alcohol consumed. Danes drink 12.9 liters per person per year (note: 1 litre equals 1.06 quarts).

dentistry Alcoholism and the abuse of other sedative drugs can complicate dental surgery. Dentists should, therefore, be informed or be on the lookout for warning signs of drug abuse. Care should be taken in the use of anesthetics since both cross-tolerance and synergistic effects can result from alcohol-sedative drug-anesthetic combinations. If a patient has a sedative drug in his system while undergoing dental surgery, the initial phase of anesthesia will be followed by a synergistic reaction that can produce a potentially dangerous situation.

Routine dental examinations can frequently disclose symptoms of alcoholism, such as long-term neglect; enlarged parotid glands (the largest salivary glands); and general deficiencies in oral hygiene. Alcoholics have a rate of permanent tooth loss that is three times that of the general population and they are more likely to consult dentists for emergency treatment than for routine care. The abuse of any drug is likely to lead to the neglect of oral care. Poor nutrition, which is common among drug users, can also lead to tooth decay and loss.

Department of Defense, drug testing Because officials believe that the nation's national security calls for drug-free personnel, the military now gives over 3 million drug tests a year to its approximately 2.5 million soldiers, sailors and marines. These tests are designed currently to detect six types of drugs: cocaine, marijuana, amphetamines, barbiturates, opiates and PCP. The armed forces now conduct about one out of every two drug tests in the nation. According to Defense Department figures, the military drug program costs over $47 million a year. It is the first and most thorough drug-testing program in the country.

Since "blanket testing" began in 1981, drug taking has reportedly declined significantly in all military services. Advocates contend that these results prove that testing leads people to stop using drugs. Opponents say that the results are misleading. Many experts argue for extending the military's drug-testing program to the space and defense industries. Massive drug testing in privately owned businesses and in nonmilitary agencies of the government raises a special set of legal and ethical questions.

Gilda Berger, *Drug Testing* (New York: Franklin Watts, 1987).

Department of Housing and Urban Development (HUD) drug-free program HUD and the National Association of Housing and Redevelopment (NAHRD) provide extensive information to Public Housing Authority management personnel and residents on what they can do to help make public housing drug free. The program is ongoing and is nationwide. Contact: Department of Housing and Urban Development, National Association of Housing and Redevelopment Officials, National and Regional Conferences on Drug-Free Public Housing, 451 Seventh Street, S.W., Washington, DC 20202 (Room 10214). Telephone: (202) 755-8247.

dependence There are two aspects to dependency: physical and psychological. A person can be dependent in either one of these ways or in both. Dependency can occur after periodic or prolonged use of a drug and its characteristics vary according to the drug involved. In 1964 the World Health Organization recommended that the term "drug dependence" be substituted for the term "drug addiction" because the latter term was too general. (See also ADDICTION, PHYSICAL DEPENDENCE and PSYCHOLOGICAL DEPENDENCE.)

depressants Drugs which act on and slow down the action of the CENTRAL NERVOUS SYSTEM (CNS), diminishing or stopping vital body functions. OPIATES, BARBITURATES, ALCOHOL and INHALANTS are depressants. Alcohol and sedatives are the most commonly used and abused depressant drugs. Their action is irregular because they do not depress all parts of the CNS at once. They work primarily on the brain, depressing psychomotor activity and relieving tension and anxiety. When the sedative level in the blood begins to fall, psychomotor activity increases, producing agitation. The term "depressant" may be misleading because such drugs actually elevate a person's mood initially. The word "depressant" has no direct relationship to "depression" except that consistent use of CNS depressants can result in psychological depression.

depressed communities Unlike boom towns, depressed communities show a decline in economic growth and/or population. They are generally long-established stable areas that have declined over a period of time. Because employment opportunities are limited, young people generally leave such communities and the population therefore tends to be older than average. Although increases in drug abuse are usually low, alcohol abuse tends to be higher—probably a reflection of individual rather than mass reaction, and of differences in the ethnic and religious make-up of communities. Although there is less money to be spent on alcohol it is still a ready sedative for problems and is often cheaper than other forms of recreation. It can also be indulged in at any time of day. (See also ELDERLY.)

depression Depression is a mood or state of despondency which, in normal individuals, is characterized by feelings of inadequacy, pessimism (particularly about the future) and lowered activity. In pathological cases, depression is an extreme state of unresponsiveness to stimuli, along with feelings of hopelessness, delusions of inadequacy and self-deprecation.

Medications are often prescribed as a treatment for depression. But drug abuse frequently results in depression. Long-term use or large doses are generally followed by depression, however. Consequently, amphetamines are worthless and possibly harmful in many cases. Abusers of illicit amphetamines are usually depressed individuals who seek the feeling of self-worth and added energy that the drug will produce.

Cocaine is sometimes used to overcome depression because it produces feelings of euphoria, increased alertness and great power. When cocaine is used regularly and for a long period of time and then discontinued, depression will return and generally in a more severe form. More cocaine is then needed to combat the depression, which leads to a perpetuation of the habit. This vicious circle is also true of amphetamine use.

Depression tends to be a major withdrawal symptom of most drug use. In the case of heroin addiction, depression, along with craving and anxiety, is not just a short-term symptom but may continue for years and often leads to a relapse. Depression is also a frequent symptom of withdrawal from alcohol, caffeine, and nicotine.

Depression is a disorder often associated with alcoholism. While it may be a reason for drinking, it is usually a result of drinking. Alcohol is often consumed for its euphoric effects and the feeling of self-confidence that it induces. These pleasant feelings, however, are quickly followed by depression and prolonged drinking almost always leads to a deterioration of mood.

Suicide attempts are common among addicted and abusing individuals. Doctors sometimes prescribe sedatives in an attempt to calm the patient, but they usually worsen the depression. Attempts are most common during active use but may occur post-withdrawal.

Depressive states are commonly found among the elderly, perhaps because they often feel of little use to society and wonder what they have to live for. ANTIDEPRESSANTS, a major classification of recently developed drugs, are often prescribed to improve mood in severely depressed patients. Antidepressants are generally divided into various categories (see DRUG CLASSIFICATION chart on p. xxiv). Antidepressants are occasionally abused for their sedative side effects when mixed with alcohol.

deprivation A psychological theory that suggests addiction is caused by disturbance and deprivation in early infancy. If deprived of a significant emotional relationship during his or her early years, so the theory goes, an individual will later develop primitive, excessive and insatiable demands which will result in the failure of interpersonal relationships. Long suppressed feelings of loss and rejection will reawaken, and rather than destroy another, the person will turn his anger inward or obliterate it by drug use. Deprivation as a cause of addiction is very theoretical and of late has little support. Deprivation, however, can clearly be a result of growing up in an addicted family.

desensitization A technique employed to decrease tension in situations that can lead to the use of drugs. Patients are repeatedly subjected to situations that would ordinarily make them tense and reduce their self-control, such as being offered a "fix" by an old friend. They are then taught and practice methods to achieve relaxation of the tension.

Desoxyn® (Abbott) A central nervous system stimulant containing methamphetamine hydrochloride, that is used primarily as an anorectic for weight control. A member of the AMPHETAMINE group of sympathomimetic amines, it has a high potential for abuse. Tolerance and severe psychological dependence, along with social disability, can occur. Overdosage can result in restlessness, tremors, rapid respiration and hallucinations. It is supplied in 2.5 and 5 mg white tablets, and in gradumet (long-acting) tablets (inert, porous, plastic matrix which is impregnated with Desoxyn) of 5 mg white, 10 mg orange and 15 mg yellow.

DET (diethyltryptamine) A completely synthetic HALLUCINOGEN similar to DMT. Like DMT, the drug is easily produced in home laboratories. DET produces an experience similar to a DMT trip except that it is milder and of even shorter duration.

detoxification The process by which drugs that have produced physical dependence are withdrawn from the addicted individual. This is usually accomplished by gradually reducing the dose of the drug, or, more commonly, a similar (cross-tolerant) medically prescribed drug. It is accomplished in a gradual and stepwise fashion to reduce dangerous or uncomfortable physical symptoms.

Detoxification from narcotics most frequently is accomplished by replacing the drug of addiction (often heroin) with methadone and then tapering the daily dose of methadone. An alternative method of suppressing the withdrawal symptoms of heroin is the use of a non-opiate, non-addictive drug called Catapres (clonidine) is also used. Detoxification usually takes about one week and is rarely medically complicated because opiate withdrawal symptoms are not life threatening even if untreated.

Detoxifications from sedatives, including alcohol, barbiturates, and benzodiazepines, is more medically crucial since withdrawal from these substances may produce serious complication such as seizures, delirium tremens and uncontrolled fever leading to death. The preferred and medically approved method for detoxification from sedatives involves the use of cross-tolerant medications, such as Librium, Serax or phenobarbital, which are administered in an initial dose sufficient to prevent withdrawal but not cause sedation. The dosage is then gradually reduced. While sedative withdrawal can be life threatening, it is worth noting that most addicted people, regardless of the drug they use (e.g., alcohol, heroin, barbiturates), who stop using do so without medical supervision. For alcohol or narcotic dependent people with a history of uncomplicated withdrawal, "non-medical" or "social setting detox" may be reasonable. Barbiturate addiction, however, is variable and extremely dangerous and should always be treated in a hospital setting. Addicted (habituated) individuals abstaining from stimulants (e.g., cocaine and amphetamines) and marijuana can experience symptoms of psychic misery, including anxiety and depression; however dangerous or chemically treatable their condition, physical symptoms are not present. Withdrawal from these substances may require tremendous psychological and social support (especially with stimulant abstinence) and patients may become suicidal, but detoxification (gradual withdrawal of the substance or its replacement) is not of value.

Detoxification is not a definitive treatment of addiction but a purely medical, first step in treating physical dependence. (See DEPENDENCE and WITHDRAWAL.)

Dexedrine® (Smith, Kline & French) An AMPHETAMINE (a brand of dextroamphetamine sulfate) usually used as an anorectic for weight control. It has been extensively abused and extreme psychological dependence and social disability can occur. It is a Schedule II drug. It is supplied in elixir; in 5 mg orange tablets; and in orange and brown Spansule capsules of 5 and 10 mg.

Synonyms: copilots, dexies.

dextroamphetamine A synthetic AMPHETAMINE. A central nervous system stimulant, it is used in the treatment of narcolepsy, Minimal Brain Dysfunction in children and as an anorectic. (See DEXEDRINE.)

dextromoramide An analgesic with a potency greater than morphine. It is a synthetic OPIATE and classified as a Schedule II drug.

diabetes The principal manifestation of diabetes is hyperglycemia (high blood sugar) and there has been some controversy about whether diabetics should be allowed to consume alcoholic beverages. Although small amounts of alcohol taken close to or with a meal generally produce little change in blood sugar levels, excessive consumption during a time of fasting can cause problems, and so can the consumption of sweet dessert wines, ports or liqueurs. When taken during a fasting state, alcohol can enhance the blood sugar-lowering action of insulin and interfere with the body's ability to produce its own glucose. Alcohol should not contribute more than 6% of the total calories consumed each day by a diabetic, because it can, on the simplest level, disrupt diet control, stimulate the appetite and provide extra calories. It is best for diabetics to consult their physicians about including alcohol in their diets. Alcoholics can develop diabetes because of destruction of insulin-producing cells in the pancreas.

diacetylmorphine The semisynthetic opiate derivative HEROIN, first produced in 1898.

diazepam A minor tranquilizer, diazepam is best known under the brand name VALIUM, which was at one time recently the number one prescribed drug in the United States. In 1974 Americans spent $500 million on 50 million prescriptions. Valium's liberal dispensation for anxiety and as a sleeping aid made it a socially acceptable drug of abuse: it has been known to play as large a role in middle-class American life as cocktail parties and little-league baseball.

Diazepam appears as a colorless crystalline powder which is insoluble in water and slightly soluble in alcohol. After oral administration it is quickly and completely absorbed by the gastrointestinal tract, with effects manifesting in 15–30 minutes. The onset of effects from intramuscular injection is erratic. There is immediate onset of effects by intravenous injection. Diazepam is detoxified in the liver and metabolites are excreted in the urine and feces. The drug acts on the brain's limbic system, but does not interfere with the peripheral autonomic system. It has a half life of 20–50 hours and crosses the placental barrier.

Diazepam is prescribed to alleviate neurotic tension and anxiety which prevent a person from coping with daily life. It is also prescribed as a sleeping pill. Its anticonvulsive properties warrant its use, alone and in conjunction with other drugs, to control muscle spasms in such conditions as cerebral palsy, paraplegia, petit mal and myoclonic seizures. It is also used to treat the symptoms of alcohol withdrawal. Both physicians and "street drug users" use diazepam to calm anxiety and panic induced by hallucinogenic drugs.

For mild to moderate anxiety it is prescribed in two or three daily doses of 2–5 mg, and in severe anxiety three or four daily doses of 5–10 mg are prescribed. A lethal dose of diazepam in humans has not yet been specified, but 50% of mice fed 758 mg per kilogram of body weight died. Therefore, it can hardly be used for suicidal purposes except in combination with other central nervous system (CNS) depressants which makes it highly lethal.

A benzodiazepine derivative, diazepam's common side effects include initial drowsiness, unsteadiness and weakness. High doses cause intoxication similar to that produced by alcohol and barbiturates. When taken with alcohol or other central nervous system depressants it can have an additive effect. Tolerance along with physical and psychological dependence also occurs. Withdrawal symptoms include convulsions, tremors, cramps and sweating.

Valium, a brand name of diazepam, is a favorite drug of minor abusers. It is available illicitly but probably a bigger problem is the fact that it is overprescribed for minimal anxiety. Doctors have been known to prescribe it freely to patients who insist they require a tranquilizer. Matters are complicated when a prescription is not limited to a certain number of refills, and Valium users have been known to take them freely when they know they will be well supplied. Supervision of the patient on diazepam or other benzodiazepines is essential despite their safety insofar as overdose is concerned. Situational anxiety does not seem to warrant constant tranquilization. Another question in the Valium controversy is whether, in the absence of Valium, a patient would resort to barbiturates or alcohol—which are much more dangerous—or not use any drug at all.

Illicit Valium (sometimes known as "Vs") is used by abusers who take large quantities to achieve intoxification. It is also frequently used to ease the crash experienced after amphetamine or cocaine abuse.

Although over two hundred times the normal dose of Valium has been survived, the drug is still often used in suicide attempts. Some of these attempts have been successful, particularly in cases where alcohol was taken with the Valium.

Diazepam is a Schedule IV drug under the Controlled Substances Act.

Didrex® (Upjohn) A central nervous system stimulant that contains benzphetamine hydrochloride, and which has a pharmacological and chemical activity similar to that of the AMPHETAMINES. It is used as an anorectic for weight control. Psychological dependence and social disability can occur and the drug has a potential for abuse. It is supplied in 25 mg yellow and 50 mg peach press-coated tablets.

diethylpropion A synthetic drug similar to the AMPHETAMINES in its activity but with less central nervous system stimulation. It is usually used as an anorectic. (See TENUATE.)

diethyltryptamine See DET.

digestion Alcohol, when taken in very small quantities, may aid digestion if gastric motility is impaired. It allows freer salivation in "dry mouth" associated with stress, which in turn triggers increased gastric motility, the gentle motion which is beneficial to digestion and empties the stomach. Heavier doses, however—more than a glass or two of wine—can result in increased acid secretion causing gastritis and peptic ulceration.

dihydrocodeine A semisynthetic narcotic analgesic that is related to codeine and has a similar activity. (See SYNALGOS.)

dihydrocodeinone A synthetic codeine derivative, also oxycodone. (See PERCODAN.)

dihydromorphinone An opium derivative that is used as an analgesic; also called hydromorphone. (See DILAUDID.)

Dilaudid® (Knoll) A narcotic analgesic that contains hydromorphone, a MORPHINE derivative. It is used for moderate to severe pain and is habit-forming. Physical dependence can occur. Although it has the same activity as morphine, Dilaudid is much more potent and does not produce such adverse reactions as nausea and vomiting and it is therefore highly sought after by narcotics users. It is available in ampules for injection and in rectal suppositories. In tablet form it is supplied in 1 mg green tablets; 2 mg orange tablets; 3 mg pink tablets; and 4 mg yellow tablets.

dill There are claims that when they are dried and smoked dill seeds can produce a mild high. This is extremely doubtful.

dimethyltryptamine A psychedelic drug that is manufactured synthetically in England. (See DMT.)

diphenoxylate A Schedule V drug that is chemically related to the narcotic MEPERIDINE and may be habit-forming. Used in the management of diarrhea, it slows intestinal motility. (See LOMOTIL.)

dipipanone A synthetic OPIATE that is used as an analgesic. Its potency is less than morphine but dependency can develop. It is a Schedule II drug.

dipsomania A term that refers to an uncontrollable craving for alcohol, it is sometimes improperly used as a synonym for alcoholism. The term is obsolete in the United States.

disease concept of alcoholism Despite the misconception that the disease concept of alcoholism is of recent origin, studies point out that as early as the first century the Roman philosopher Seneca distinguished between a man "who is drunk" and a man "who has no control over himself." Benjamin Rush, an 18th century American physician, expounded further on the theory. By the 19th century the disease concept was widely accepted by the medical community, and in 1952 JELLINEK elaborated further on the developments of alcohol addiction. Although Jellinek's theories on the progression of the major symptoms are seriously questioned, the disease concept of all chemical dependency is backed today by the World Health Organization and the American Medical Association.

Because addiction is designated as a disease, the guilt stigma—often in itself a stimulus for further drinking—is lifted from the patient, and social support rather than punishment is emphasized. Opponents of the concept argue that addiction may be a symptom of a number of separate problems and that to be classified as a disease there should be some abnormality of the anatomic or biologic structure. Under this definition, however, all behavioral and psychiatric disorders would be eliminated from the classification of disease. Opponents further suggest that calling addiction a disease fosters irresponsibility and passivity in the patient. Proponents of the concept, on the other hand, argue that along with lifting the "guilt stigma," making addiction a medical disease problem means that some of the personal economic costs are handled by insurance, disability payments and workmen's compensation. Although some clinicians feel the disease concept may not be completely adequate, they generally believe it to be the most sound basis for a 20th century approach to the problem.

diseases There are numerous diseases which are caused by extended, heavy use of drugs, and others in which drug abuse may play a significant role. The use of alcohol and tobacco are major contributors to various diseases of the HEART, LIVER, LUNGS, PANCREAS and STOMACH. Heavy drug use can also damage the BRAIN and CENTRAL NERVOUS SYSTEM, and TETANUS and HEPATITIS are common among heroin addicts. Diseases attributable to poor NUTRITION are common among drugs users in general. Not only can drug use be harmful to the individual, it can also be harmful to the fetus. (See also PREGNANCY and CANCER.)

disorientation A state of mental confusion in which the person has no concept of time, place, situation or identity. A variety of drugs—stimulants, depressants, hallucinogens—can produce this effect. Accidental deaths may result from cases of disorientation where the individual has no idea when, or even if, he took a previous dose of a drug.

distillation The process of heating fermented mash, collecting the alcohol content that vaporizes, and then collecting the recondensed alcohol as a distillate. Using the distillate as a base, any number of potable spirits can be produced by aging and flavoring techniques. Thought to have been a discovery of the Arab cultures, distillation became common practice in Europe around 1000 A.D.

diviner's sage *Salvia divinorum,* a plant belonging to the mint family. The Mazatec Indians of Mexico chew the leaves or brew them as a beverage for their hallucinogenic effects.

d-lysergic acid diethylamide tartrate 25 LSD 25. (See LSD.)

DMT (N-dimethyltryptamine) A fast-acting HALLUCINOGEN similar in structure to PSILOCIN, the hallucinogenic substance to which PSILOCYBIN is converted in the body. Organic DMT is found in the seeds of the shrubs *Piptadenia,* in the flesh of the climbing vine *Banisteriopsis caapi,* and in the roots of *Mimosa hostilis.* It can also be easily synthesized. DET and DPT are close chemical variants.

Effects: Within five to 10 minutes after ingestion, DMT produces an LSD-like experience which lasts from 30 to 60 minutes. Because the effects do not last long, DMT is sometimes referred to as the "businessman's LSD" or the "businessman's lunchtime high." Unlike LSD, it affects only visual perceptions, not auditory and tactile ones. It can cause lack of coordination and spasticity, physical effects which are not associated with LSD. Physical and psychic effects appear simultaneously. The DMT experience can be quite intense and, for many who try it, frightening and nightmarish.

Addictive aspects: As is the case with all of the hallucinogens, DMT does not produce physical DEPENDENCE.

Tolerance: As with all hallucinogens, short-term reversible tolerance to the drug rapidly develops.

Sources: Easily synthesized, DMT is produced in "basement" laboratories and sold illicitly. It's use has declined in recent years as has that of other hallucinogens. It is an important component of COHABA, a snuff used in Haiti and parts of Central and South America, which also contains BUFOTENINE.

Synonyms: businessman's LSD, businessman's lunchtime high.

DNA Deoxyribonucleic acid, an organic substance found in the chromosomes of living cells. It is vital in the storage and replication of hereditary information, and also plays an important role in protein synthesis. RNA is the other main type of nucleic acid.

Do It Now Foundation (DIN) A non-profit publisher of low-cost drug, alcohol, and health education materials which are distributed nationally and internationally. Founded in 1968 and supported entirely by its sales, DIN distributes approximately seven million pieces of literature a year. The foundation believes that ignorance about drugs can be as dangerous to an individual as drugs themselves, and consequently publishes materials in both primary and secondary prevention as well as general information.

Dolene® (Lederle) A mild analgesic, containing propoxyphene hydrochloride, that is a NARCOTIC in pharmacological properties but is less potent. It can produce psychic and physical dependence and has potential for abuse. Taken with alcohol or other central nervous system depressants, it can have an additive effect. It is supplied in 65 mg pink capsules. Dolene Compound-6, which also contains aspirin, caffeine and phenacetin, is supplied in pink and brown capsules. Dolene AP-65, which contains propoxyphene and acetaminophen, comes in pink oval-shaped tablets.

Dolonil® (Parke-Davis) A depressant that contains phenazopyridine hydrochloride, hyoscyamine hydrobromide, and the short-to-intermediate acting BARBITURATE, butabarbital. It is used for inflammation of the lower urinary tract, and may be habit-forming. Dolonil is supplied in dark maroon coated square tablets.

Dolophine Hydrochloride® (Lilly) A synthetic narcotic analgesic that contains METHADONE hydrochloride, and has multiple action similar to MORPHINE. It is used for severe pain and for detoxification and maintenance in the treatment of narcotic addiction. Drug dependence, similar to morphine dependence, can occur and Dolophine has the potential for abuse. It is supplied in ampules for injection and in 5 and 10 mg tablets.

DOM (STP) (2, 5-dimethoxy-4-methyl amphetamine) A synthetic HALLUCINOGEN with a structural resemblance to both AMPHETAMINES and MESCALINE, DOM is sometimes classified as an adrenergic hallucinogen because it produces physiological changes typical of such adrenergic agents as epinephrine.

The synthesis of DOM was reported in chemical literature in 1964 and first came to public attention in 1967 when FDA chemists identified it as one of the active constituents of STP. Today STP is a common synonym for DOM, although the original STP was a variety of drug mixtures and not all of them contained DOM.

DOM is considerably more potent than either amphetamines or mescaline, which it resembles in its chemical structure. On a weight for weight basis it is less potent than LSD but the effects last somewhat longer: effects are perceptible about one hour after ingestion and reach their highest intensity three to five hours after ingestion. They subside in 12 to 18 hours. Psychological effects the next day are only rarely reported.

It is difficult to know how much DOM is available today. Users may buy DOM and receive some other drug, or they may receive DOM when they think they are buying something else.

Effects: Physiological changes include an increase in heart rate and systolic blood pressure, dilation of the pupils, and a slight rise in body temperature. Other changes that may occur include nausea, tremors, and perspiration. The intensity of these changes appears to be a result of the dose. Psychological effects also vary with the dose. Doses of approximately 3 mg produce euphoria and "enhanced self-awareness," while doses above 5 mg produce hallucinations. Some users may experience vivid visual imagery on closing their eyes along with a change in their perception of time. Eventually images may be seen with the eyes open. The predominant emotional state of the user is usually one of happiness. The experience is clear to the user after it is over and insight is retained throughout.

Addictive aspects: Physical dependence does not develop to DOM.

Tolerance: It is similar to other hallucinogens in that tolerance to its effects develops with regular use. This tolerance is rapidly developed but also rapidly reversed when use stops.

Sources: DOM is produced by "basement" chemists who supply the illegal drug market.

Frederick G. Hofman, *A Handbook on Drug and Alcohol Abuse* (New York: Oxford University Press, 1975), pp. 171–173.

Richard R. Lingeman, *Drugs from A to Z* (New York: McGraw-Hill Book Company, 1974), pp. 236–238.

Dona Ana A cactus, *Coryphantha macromeris,* native to Texas and Mexico, which contains the psychedelic alkaloid macromerine. It is eaten or brewed into a tea and has about one-fifth the potency of mescaline.

dopamine The immediate precursor of norepinephrine in the body, dopamine is found especially in the adrenal glands and exhibits adrenergic effects. It is a neurotransmitter and is important in the action of amphetamines and cocaine. Dopamine deficiency is thought to be a primary defect in Parkinson's disease. Dopamine hydrochloride is a synthetic drug which affects the autonomic nervous system and is used in the treatment of shock syndrome and congestive heart failure. Cocaine and amphetamines are thought to have their major effects resulting from disturbing dopamine transmission.

Doriden® (USV Pharmaceutical) A nonbarbiturate HYPNOTIC that contains glutethimide and is used for insomnia. Because it does not cause respiratory depression it is also used as a preanesthetic. Physical and psychological dependence can occur. Overdosage, which is difficult to treat, can result in central nervous system depression, coma, pupil dilation and loss of tendon reflexes. Taken with alcohol or other CNS depressants, Doriden can have an additive effect. It is supplied in white scored tablets of 0.5 gm and 0.25 gm; and in 0.5 gm blue and white capsules. Doriden is called CIBAs on the street. Glutethimide is frequently abused in combination with codeine or other narcotics in a mixture called PACs.

Dover's powder An obsolete remedy which contained 10% opium and ipecac. It was given to induce sweating during a febrile illness.

doxepin A tricyclic ANTIDEPRESSANT that is manufactured as Apapini and Sinequani.

DPT (dipropyltryptamine) A little-known synthetic HALLUCINOGEN related to DMT and DET.

dram In fluid measurement, 1 dram is equal to 1/8 of an ounce. There are 1 1/3 drams in a teaspoon. In terms of alcohol, the word dram is often used interchangeably with the word "shot." "Dram-drinking" and "dramming" were used in the 17th century to refer to habitual drinking. A dramshop was a barroom.

dram shop law A law which imposes legal liability upon a person, usually a tavern keeper, who supplies alcoholic beverages to a person who becomes intoxicated and causes injuries or damages to himself or another as a result.

Drinamyl® A drug manufactured in England, which combines amphetamine sulfate and amobarbital. See DEXAMYL. It is supplied as purple tablets which are often referred to by abusers as "purple hearts" or "French blues."

driving and drugs Although there have been numerous studies on the effects of alcohol on driving skills, there is less information available concerning the effects of other drugs.

One 1981 study, by Dr. Kenneth W. Terhune and James C. Fell for the National Highway Traffic and Safety Administration, covered 497 drivers injured in motor vehicle accidents and treated at a hospital. The sample was considered conservative because only drivers who consented to blood analysis were included. The results of the study showed 38% of the drivers had alcohol or some other drug in their system: alcohol was found in 25% of the drivers; tetrahydrocannabinol (THC—the active principle in marijuana) in 9.5%; and tranquilizers in 7.5%. Two or more drugs had been ingested by 10% of the drivers. A negligence rate of 74% was found in drivers who were legally intoxicated (BAC of .10%). Drivers with lower alcohol levels had a negligence rate of 54%, and those with THC in their system had a rate of 53%. In comparison, drug-free drivers had a negligence rate of 34%. Drivers with tranquilizers in their system were considered negligent in 22% of their accidents. This evidence, along with the results of similar studies, strongly suggests that marijuana interferes with driving skills, perception, coordination, attention, visual awareness, reaction time, and so on. Another danger is that performance decrements may persist for some time, possibly several hours beyond the time that someone actually feels "high" and he may drive without realizing that his ability is still impaired.

When drugs are combined there can be an additive effect on driving skills; even when drugs are used in therapeutic doses and not in the amounts used by abusers. Even over-the-counter sleeping aids can have more of a depressant effect on the central nervous system when combined with alcohol. In highway accidents where the driver has taken more than one drug, alcohol is almost always found to be one of the drugs.

Each year nearly 50,000 people die on U.S. highways and over half of these fatalities are alcohol related. Accidents involving alcohol also result in injuries to more than a half million people, more than $1 billion in property damage, insurance costs and medical services and several hundred thousand arrests.

The majority of alcohol-related accidents occur at night and a larger proportion of men than women are involved (perhaps partly because of drinking patterns as women tend to drink at home). One of the biggest menaces on the highway is the problem drinker who has previous arrests for offenses involving alcohol. Studies indicate that people with severe drinking problems are disproportionately involved in all kinds of crashes. Single vehicle accidents are alcohol or drug related in 75% of the cases.

About 50% of all fatally injured drinking drivers are less than 30 years old. From 40–60% of all fatal crashes involving young people are alcohol related. Not only are they inexperienced in both drinking and driving, they are more likely to combine alcohol with another drug. (See also BLOOD ALCOHOL CONCENTRATION and MOTHERS AGAINST DRUNK DRIVING.)

dropper A medicine dropper which is used for injecting heroin when a needle is attached to its tip. The bulb acts as a plunger and the glass portion acts as the barrel. A dropper is sometimes favored over a regular hypodermic because it gives an addict more control over injecting the heroin. They are also commonly used when no hypodermic is available.

Drug Abuse Warning Network (DAWN) A network started in 1972 by the Bureau of Narcotics and Dangerous Drugs to provide information on medical and psychological problems associated with the effects of drug use. The network's aim is to identify patterns and trends in drug use and to pinpoint those drugs that are bringing users into emergency facilities. Data is received from such sources as general hospital emergency rooms, medical examiners and coroners, and crisis intervention centers and fed into DAWN; there are approximately 15,000 new case descriptions a month. The network issues quarterly reports describing current drug emergencies and whether or not the people concerned are in treatment. Presently funded and administered by NIDA, it derives information from 26 metropolitan areas and detects trends in which drugs are being used for their psychic effects, suicide, dependence, and so on.

drug addiction See ADDICTION and DEPENDENCE.

drug automatism Taking drugs without being aware of the amounts; a state that often occurs with heavy barbiturate use when tolerance has developed. In order to produce sleep, the user takes more of the drug because of an amnesia about the amount previously taken.

drug culture See SUBCULTURE, DRUG.

Drug Enforcement Administration (DEA) The lead agency in narcotic and dangerous drug suppression programs at the national and international levels and in federal drug law enforcement. Established in 1973 to replace the Bureau of Narcotics and Dangerous Drugs, the DEA was created to enforce the Controlled Substances laws and regulations. To this end, it investigates and prosecutes organizations and individuals involved in the growing, manufacture, or distribution of controlled substances destined for illicit traffic in the United States. In order to expand its facilities and become more efficient, the DEA began working with the

Federal Bureau of Investigation (FBI) in January 1982. (See FEDERAL BUREAU OF INVESTIGATION.)

drug interaction See SYNERGY.

drug testing Taking a urine sample from an individual suspected of illegal drug use, or screening large groups of people, is quite common today. Many U.S. companies (the U.S. Bureau of Labor Statistics reports 43% of the nation's largest firms) have implemented drug-screening programs for job applicants, employees or both. A 1986 executive order signed by former President Ronald Reagan authorized drug testing throughout the federal government. More than 50 government agencies, including the Agriculture and Interior departments, have moved to start up testing programs. In addition, the federal government now requires a urine test of railroad employees involved in serious accidents.

This proliferation of drug testing of both public and private sector workers has, however, initiated a growing number of legal challenges from civil libertarians and labor leaders who view the antidrug campaign as an ominous invasion of privacy. They argue that such testing is an "unreasonable search" barred by the Fourth Amendment to the U.S. Constitution. In February 1989, the U.S. Supreme Court, in its first rulings on the drug-testing issue, upheld, by a 7-to-2 vote, the constitutionality of the government regulations that require railroad crews involved in accidents to submit to prompt urinalysis and blood tests. The Court also upheld, 5 to 4, urine tests for U.S. Customs Service employees seeking drug enforcement positions.

The U.S. armed services conduct about one of every two drug tests in the nation. According to the Defense Department, the military drug program costs over $47 million a year. Blanket testing for military personnel began in 1981 and today the military gives about 2.3 million drug tests a year to its 2.14 million soldiers, sailors, marines and airmen. Urine testing first became a part of military life during the Vietnam War. Thus far, random drug testing has survived all challenges in the military courts, including *Murray* v. *Haldeman* in 1983 and *Committee for GI Rights* v. *Callaway* in 1975. A recent survey indicates that drug abuse in the armed forces dropped from 27% in 1980 to 9% in the fall of 1985. See also GAS CHROMATOGRAPHY/MASS SPECTROMETRY; HAIR ANALYSIS; RADIOIMMUNOASSAY; SUPREME COURT DRUG DECISIONS, U.S.; THIN LAYER CHROMATOGRAPHY.

Robert Augoroia, "Protect Safety, Not Drug Abuse," *American Bar Association Journal,* August 1, 1986, 35.

Gilda Berger, *Drug Testing* (Franklin Watts: New York, 1987), 76–87, 100–114.

Alain Sanders, "A Boost for Drug Testing," *Time,* April 3, 1989, 62.

drug trafficking See TRAFFICKING, SMUGGLING, GOLDEN TRIANGLE, GOLDEN CRESCENT and FRENCH CONNECTION.

Drug Use Forecasting System Program developed by the National Institute of Justice in the U.S. Department of Justice, collects vital information and drug use data based on urine tests of persons arrested in 11 cities. The program's purpose is to track drug use trends among urban defendants suspected of dangerous crimes. The Drug Use Forecasting System (DUF) conducted the urine tests on a sample of more than 2,000 arrestees between June 1987 and November 1987.

James K. Stewart, National Institute of Justice, *NIJ Reports*/SNI208, March/April 1988.

drunk The term for a person under the influence of alcohol or in a state of intoxication. The term is also used to describe a drinking spree.

dry drunk A person who has stopped drinking but continues to crave alcohol. As used by Alcoholics Anonymous, it refers to someone who has not attained true SOBRIETY but exists in a state of "white-knuckled sobriety," and is usually irritable and depressed because of his or her effort not to drink.

DSM III R (revised) The third edition of *Diagnostic and Statistical Manual* of mental disorders, including substance use disorders. It is currently in use and contains the criteria for diagnosing a variety of substance abuse conditions. It is currently being revised for a fourth edition.

DUI Driving under the influence. (See DRIVING AND DRUGS.)

Duradyne DHC® (O'Neal, Jones & Feldman) A NARCOTIC analgesic, containing dihydrocodeinone bitartrate along with aspirin, caffeine and acetaminophen, that is used for moderate to severe pain. It may be habit-forming and repeated administration can produce drug dependence. If used with alcohol or other central nervous system depressants, an additive effect can occur. A Schedule III drug, it is supplied in green scored tablets.

DWI Driving while intoxicated. (See DRIVING AND DRUGS.)

dynorphin A potent ENDORPHIN found in the cow's pituitary gland. It is about two hundred times more powerful than morphine and one of the most potent endorphins yet discovered.

dysphoria A generalized feeling of discomfort, malaise or unhappiness that accompanies WITHDRAWAL. All abused drugs can occasionally produce a dysphoric state. Antonym: euphoria.

E

ebriate To intoxicate or inebriate.

ebriety See INEBRIETY.

economic impact See BUSINESS, EMPLOYEE ASSISTANCE PROGRAMS and ABSENTEEISM.

ecstasy (MDMA) Street name given to 3_14 methylenedioxymethamphetamine (MDMA), a combination stimulant and hallucinogen related to methamphetamine and MDA; currently illegal. MDMA was originally synthesized in the early 1900's and is considered the licit parent (and now the illicit offspring) of MDA (the "love drug") and methamphetamine ("speed").

In March 1989, the West German chemical company Imhausen-Chemie was found by German prosecutors to have been involved in the illegal production and sale of MDMA. Authorities said the firm had supplied U.S. drug traffickers with 374 pounds of MDMA, worth up to $27 million on the street. Company officials claimed they were unaware the substance was illegal. Called "Adam," "ecstacy," or "X-TC", on the street, this is a synthetic psychoactive (mind-altering) drug with hallucinogenic and amphetamine-like properties. Its chemical structure is very similar to two other synthetic drugs: MDA and methamphetamines, which are believed to cause brain damage. MDMA is a so-called designer drug, which, according to the Drug Enforcement Agency (DEA) became a nationwide problem as well as a serious health threat in the 1980s. It was implicated in several deaths. Promoted by a few individuals as an aid to psychotherapy, it became the focus of a short-lived controversy. In no way accepted or approved by any responsible group of psychotherapists, the use of this drug has either rapidly declined or is going unnoticed. (See MDA, METHAMPHETAMINE.)

Ectasul (SR, JR, & III)® (Fleming) A drug used for sinusitus and hay fever that contains ephedrine and AMOBARBITAL. It may be habit-forming. Ectasul SR contains 60 mg ephedrine and 60 mg amobarbital; Ectasul JR contains 30 mg ephedrine and 30 mg amobarbital; and Ectasul III contains 15 mg ephedrine and 9 mg amobarbital.

ED50 See EFFECTIVE DOSE OF A DRUG.

effective dose of a drug (ED50) This term refers to the dosage of a drug which produces a certain effect in 50% of the people tested, whereas 25% of those tested require a higher dosage and 25% require a lesser dosage to produce the same effect.

Eighteenth Amendment The amendment under which the manufacture, transportation and sale of intoxicating beverages were banned, beginning Prohibition on January 17, 1920. It was repealed by the Twenty-first Amendment in 1932.

Elavil® (Merck, Sharp & Dohme) An ANTIDEPRESSANT with sedative effects that contains amitriptyline. While the mechanism of its action is not known, Elavil is used to alleviate endogenous depression. When used with central nervous system depressants it can have an additive effect. Although abrupt cessation can result in mild nausea, headache and malaise, these withdrawal symptoms are not indicative of addiction. Patients who are potentially suicidal should not have access to large quantities of the drug as severe overdosage can result in convulsions, congestive heart failure, coma and death. It is supplied in 10 mg round blue tablets; 25 mg yellow tablets; 50 mg beige tablets; 75 mg orange tablets; 100 mg mauve tablets; and 150 mg capsule-shaped blue tablets. It is also available in 10 mg vials for injection.

elderly Current statistics reveal that "senior citizens," individuals over 65 years of age, comprise 10% of American society. By the year 2000 the number will have doubled to 20% of the population. In view of this increase and the fact that most of us will one day belong to this age group, it is important to recognize the special substance abuse problems facing the elderly.

Misuse and abuse of medications and other drugs is pronounced among people over 65 for several reasons. Many older people suffer from a variety of physical ailments for which they receive prescription medications and for which they also buy non-prescription, over-the-counter drugs. Old age is also often fraught with emotional problems which may prompt further medication. In addition to experiencing frustration as a result of physical deterioration, older people frequently have a new life-style forced on them by retirement and react, not unnaturally, with feelings of loneliness, boredom and uselessness. Lowered incomes and the acute awareness of mortality that comes when more and more of one's friends and relatives die add to their distress. As a result, many older people request and receive tranquilizers and other sedative medicines as well as resort to alcohol to alleviate their feelings. People over 65 consume more than 25 percent of all prescription drugs, at a cost between $2.5 billion and $3 billion a year, and even more non-prescription, over-the-counter preparations.

Many older people, then, regularly ingest significant quantities of several drugs. Unconscious, habitual drug taking can have seriously debilitating effects, especially in old age when the system is more sensitive. People over 60 experience adverse drug reactions twice as frequently as the rest of the population. Because the body of an elderly person has a higher fat content than that of a younger person, fat soluble drugs remain in the system longer. Less effective metabolism in old age also contributes to the accumulation of such substances, making the elderly particularly vulnerable to drug interactions. Lack of communication between older patients and their doctors (and, often, they have several doctors) can result in the prescription of contradictory medication—sometimes with serious results. Doctors often fail to explain adequately the purpose and effects of the drugs they prescribe, and it has been suggested that older patients may also self-prescribe over-the-counter medications and experiment with friends' and neighbors' medications which do not complement their prescribed drugs. Forgetfulness may also lead them to take larger than safe quantities of drugs or fail to take doses of an essential drug.

One of the most dangerous effects of drug interaction arises with the use of alcohol, the foremost form of substance abuse among older people. To numb the feelings of loneliness and uselessness, many elderly people increase their alcohol intake, while some others have longstanding problems with alcohol. About 10–15% of people over 65 have drinking problems, and 1–5% of the elderly population is estimated to be alcoholic.

As with other drugs, alcohol's effects intensify in old age. The combination of alcohol's solubility in fat and the increased fat content of the body may produce higher concentrations of acetaldehyde in the blood and brain, and therefore more prolonged and toxic effects than in younger individuals. Slower metabolism may induce WITHDRAWAL symptoms and prompt the older drinker to increase his drinking to alleviate them.

This lowered tolerance magnifies the addictive effects of alcohol and of the CNS depressants which are so commonly used by older people, and so greatly increases the risks of taking the drugs together. Another common and dangerous practice is combining alcohol with medication for heart conditions, since alcohol acts as a cardiac muscle toxin in large amounts.

The diagnosis and treatment of alcoholism also presents special problems. Some of the symptoms of alcoholism, such as forgetfulness and incoherence, may be interpreted as signs of senility; thus the real problem may go undetected. Alcohol can also mask pain and other symptoms of physical illness.

Older chronic drinkers, who are predominantly male, are more likely to deny their problem than younger alcoholics, possibly because of culturally derived prejudices common to the generation. Some professionals in alcohol rehabilitation methods have suggested that social activity programs which break the pattern of lonely solitary drinking is a relatively easy way to treat alcohol problems in older people, especially if the problems have developed only since the onset of old age. The comparative ease of this kind of treatment should not be assumed, however.

Chemical abuse in nursing homes is a particularly sensitive issue for the elderly. Less than 5% of the elderly are currently confined to such institutions; two-thirds are women, and their average age is 82. Recent years have produced reports of overmedication of nursing home patients with high-power tranquilizers and antidepressants, even when their use is not necessary. Constant tranquilization can seriously incapacitate a patient as well as simulate symptoms of senility or physical ailments from which he has not previously suffered. The tranquilizer Thorazine, for example, induces symptoms of Parkinson's disease. Such deceptive symptoms may prompt attending physicians, insufficiently aware of the medication's effect or of the patient's condition, to prescribe more medication. Routine administration of sedatives makes life easier for nursing home *staff*. Advertisements for some drugs promote this misuse of medication by stressing the product's value in "patient management," rather than patient care. In *The Tran-*

quilizing of America, Richard Hughes and Robert Brewin labeled this practice "the chemical pacification of the elderly." They blamed doctors for their negligence, irresponsibility and general lack of knowledge about geriatric medical problems. Geriatric specialists are few in the United States, and doctors who treat all age groups sometimes exhibit impatience with their older patients, who generally have numerous complaints and demand a great deal of time and attention. The elderly frequently have little chance of recovery and little money. Sometimes doctors terminate the visits and silence the complaints of what they consider a cantankerous group by simply writing prescriptions which are not really necessary. Hopefully, with increasing postgraduate education in geriatrics, this practice may be on the decline.

A recent phenomenon to come out of the pervasive drug scene in the United States is older people selling drugs. The elderly, law enforcement officials say, are being lured into the drug trade by the big money involved. And, say authorities, their relative age is "the best cover around." In Baltimore recently, three men, ages 65 to 69, were arrested at their social club on drug conspiracy charges after police found 308 bags of cocaine worth $7,700.

Other police reports around the country have revealed instances of drug dealing by seniors in Washington, D.C.; Putnam, Connecticut; Trenton, New Jersey; Jacksonville, Florida. In New York, a 70-year-old man was linked to an intercity drug ring after authorities seized 850 pounds of Asian heroin. And in Puerto Rico, a 90-year-old man and his 70-year-old wife were arrested after police found $45,000 worth of cocaine and heroin in their home.

George Sunderland of The American Association of Retired Persons (AARP) acknowledges that senior citizens are being drawn into the drug scene. Among the reasons are money, excitement, less severe punishment if caught and "feeling back in the mainstream—a big-time operator." Northeastern University criminologist James Fox notes that "as the population is getting older, so is the criminal population."

Sam Meddis, "Seniors' New Deal: Drugs," *USA Today,* June 29, 1989.

electric shock In the treatment of alcoholism, conditioning with electric shock was once used in AVERSION THERAPY. It is currently used to treat patients suffering from depression, especially those who are unresponsive to antidepressant medication.

elemicin An alkaloid found in NUTMEG and believed to produce mild hallucinogenic effects.

emetine An emetic drug which induces nausea. It is used in AVERSION THERAPY.

Empirin Compound with Codeine® (Burroughs Wellcome) An analgesic used for moderate pain. It is habit-forming. A Schedule III drug, it contains aspirin, caffeine and phenacetin, along with codeine. No. 1 has ⅛ grain codeine; No. 2 had ¼ grain; No. 3 has ½ grain; and No. 4 has 1 grain (65 mg.)

Employee Assistance Programs (EAPs) First begun in the 1930s and 1940s by such companies as Kodak and DuPont, EAPs are now an established part of today's alcohol and drug abuse programs. Between 1950 and 1973 the number of EAPs grew from 50 to 500; in the last 15 years the programs have grown to more than 5,000 (covering over 400 major U.S. companies). Most of the original programs dealt only with alcoholism but the increase in drug abuse has forced them to expand.

The National Institute on Alcohol Abuse and Alcoholism estimates that 50% of people with job performance problems suffer from alcoholism; this results in a loss of production to companies estimated at $30 billion a year. Medical care costs alone are estimated to be $50 billion. Because alcoholism is a progressive disease, often taking 10 to 15 years to reach its middle stages, the worker suffering from alcoholism has often reached a position of responsibility in his or her company. The Stanford Research group has estimated that by treating workers with a drinking problem industry saves about $6,000 annually for each alcoholic employee. A rehabilitated high-level executive could alone save a company millions of dollars on a project no one else is equipped to handle. Although employers once sought to weed out "troublesome" employees, they now realize the need to provide help. The National Institute on Drug Abuse (NIDA) reported in late 1988 that in 1984 estimated annual costs to society of drug abuse was around $60 billion, and of this amount over $33 billion was believed to result from lost employee productivity due to drug use.

Voluntary associations, labor unions and organizations for employees in both public and private sectors are among the sources that provide EAPs. Labor unions are the most recent supporters of these programs, probably because initially they were suspicious that companies were trying to "spy" on drinkers in their ranks. The success of the programs in restoring their members to good health has obviously changed their minds, and most successful programs often depend upon labor union support.

The U.S. Department of Health and Human Services has found that the highest rate of recovery from alcoholism occurs in the office or factory rather than the clinic or hospital program. Perhaps EAPs have greater leverage because while problem drinkers are generally not intimidated by threats of losing family, possessions, reputation or pride, they are usually deeply concerned about losing their jobs.

A person's place of work provides helpful structures for early intervention and confrontation. Deterioration of job performance is usually apparent before physical signs of alcoholism appear. Managers and supervisors are trained to look for unsatisfactory performance and at this time an employee is generally sent off to an EAP where a variety of counseling services are available. The basic orientation of most programs is alcoholism identification and intervention, but actual treatment methods differ from company to company. While some care for their employees in-house, others refer them to community-based agencies that are more professionally equipped to handle the problem. Other companies refer employees to Alcoholics Anonymous or other self-help groups.

Public opinion about EAPs differs widely. In the case of airlines, some people say they will not fly with a company that has admitted an alcoholism problem among its employees. On the other hand, there are people who say they won't fly with a company that *doesn't* have an EAP. Regardless of how public opinion sways, companies have found that they have at least a 50% recovery rate among employees who had to choose between getting treatment and losing their jobs. In some cases between 70% and 80% of employees return to their jobs "recovered."

Despite the success rate of many programs there are numerous companies that evaluate on a cost-benefit analysis basis, and because the monetary value of benefits is sometimes difficult or impossible to evaluate, EAPs are not implemented. This prevents many small and medium-sized businesses from participating in such programs. There is also a strong need to reach women, minorities and those in high-income levels. High-level employees, in particular, often work in isolated conditions with minimal supervision and if approached may feel that EAPs are only for low-level employees.

An effective EAP program will consist of: top management support, company policy statement of needs, supervisory training, client services, external linkages (for employee referral to treatment programs), employee education and evaluation.

Alcoholism is still the cause of most cases of poor job performance related to drugs. This is probably because, unlike heroin and cocaine, alcohol is not only legally available, it is socially acceptable.

enabling A term that refers to attempts (usually made by relatives and friends) to protect an alcoholic from the consequences of drinking. Although aimed at helping the alcoholic, such attempts "enable" the person's drinking pattern to continue unchecked. (See also PARA-ALCOHOLIC.)

encounter groups See GROUP THERAPY.

endocrine etiological theories A theory which suggests that dysfunction of the endocrine system may lead to the development of alcoholism. Hypoglycemia, a result of a pituitary-adrenocortical deficiency, is thought to cause symptoms that can stimulate drinking. Alcohol can temporarily elevate blood sugar and relieve the hypoglycemia, but it eventually intensifies the condition and can cause a dependence on increasingly larger amounts. Because alcohol is a sedative drug it is likely that this theory can also be applied to the use of other sedative drugs. Up to now there has been no strong evidence to support this physiological approach to the cause of alcoholism.

endorphins OPIOID biochemical compounds that are produced by the body and resemble the opiates in their ability to promote a general sense of well-being and induce analgesia. The term is used generically to refer to all endogenous opioid compounds and it implies a pharmacological activity as opposed to a specific chemical formulation. Endorphins have thus far been found only in vertebrate animals. They are not abusable or addictive.

enkephalins Short chain amino acids that have opioid actions. Endorphin is becoming a collective name for the long chain and short chain endogenous opioids.

enzyme multiplied immunoassay technique (EMIT) A method used for rapid urine screening for drugs of abuse produced by Syna Corporation.

epena The Waika Indians of Brazil grind up the bark of the epena tree to make a snuff that produces hallucinogenic effects.

ephedrine A synthetic cardiac and central nervous system stimulant that is used for asthma and other allergies, hypotension and narcolepsy. It is used mainly as a bronchial dilator and vasoconstrictor of the nasal membranes.

epidemiology The medical study of the occurrence and prevalence of disease. The term is often applied to the study of a disease that affects large numbers of people in a community, such as alcoholism.

Epsilon Alcoholism See JELLINEK.

Equanil® (Wyeth) A minor tranquilizer that contains MEPROBAMATE. It has a potential for abuse and may produce physical and psychological dependence. Excessive doses can cause the rapid onset of sleep, with pulse, blood pressure and respiratory rates being reduced to basal levels. Equanil is supplied in white scored 200 and 400 mg tablets; 400 mg red and white capsules; and 400 mg yellow coated tablets called Equanil Wyseals.

Erthroxylon coca The coca bush containing the alkaloid COCAINE.

erogenics Synonymous with STIMULANTS; drugs that increase the capacity of physical and mental functioning.

Esgic® (Gilbert) An analgesic with a mild sedative effect that contains caffeine, acetaminophen, and the BARBITURATE butalbital. It is generally used for headache pain and may be habit-forming. Esgic is supplied in yellow compressed tablets containing 50 mg of butalbital.

esophagus In comparison with the general population, smokers, heavy drinkers and alcoholics show a high incidence of esophageal CANCER. Patients with cirrhosis of the liver have blockages of the veins returning blood from the abdominal cavity to the heart. In an effort to overcome the obstruction, esophageal varicosities develop. These are enlarged veins that can easily rupture causing bleeding that can be profuse. The esophagus itself may tear as a result of irritation and vomiting associated with alcoholism

ethanol Ethyl alcohol, the principal chemical in distilled spirits, wine and beer. An inflammable liquid, it is produced by the reaction of fermenting sugar with yeast spores. Distillation can produce 96–100% ethanol, also called ABSOLUTE ALCOHOL. (See also ALCOHOL.)

ethchlorvynol (brand name Playcidyl) A nonbarbiturate sedative hypnotic. Its overdose symptoms are similar to BARBITURATES and dependency can occur. It is frequently abused and can sometimes be detected by causing an apple-like odor on the breath.

ether A volative anesthetic obtained by the distillation of alcohol with sulfuric acid. Its medical usage began in the early 1800s and because of its intoxicating effects (similar to alcohol), ether sniffing became quite popular. It was also taken orally for a quicker onset of effects and less expensive intoxication than alcohol. Ether is seldom used today as an anesthetic or a euphoriant.

ethical issues, drugs and In *Drug Abuse: The Impact on Society,* Gilda Berger discusses at length the fundamental question: ''Is violating people's rights justifiable when protecting the community against drugs? Or is it better to stick to the letter of the law and risk letting drug criminals get away?''

Various national polls as recent as the summer of 1989 show that the American public considers drug abuse the nation's number one problem. Government officials at all levels—national, state and local—have increased efforts and taken stronger measures to combat drugs. Despite notable victories, most authorities (including William J. Bennett, director of the Office of National Drug Control Policy) seem to agree by and large that the war against drugs and drug abuse is being lost. This had led to even tougher strategies, some of which have been sharply criticized. Chief among them are drug testing and greater penalties (including seizures of personal assets of drug dealers and, in some instances, users) for drug violators. Certain state governors, big-city mayors and other lawmakers have urged the U.S. Congress to create a death penalty for drug dealers. The purpose of the various stronger measures being discussed and considered is, of course, to send a powerful message to both drug sellers and users that the country is serious in its determination to control the drug epidemic. Critics say measures that violate individual rights when attempting to protect communities from the drug scourge are wrong. These opponents to more severe punishment, while admitting the nation has serious problems of drug abuse, maintain that more effective ways must be found to prevent drug abuse and misuse—and help users live productive, noncriminal lives. Historically enforcement has been of negligible value in controlling or eliminating drug use.

Gilda Berger, *Drug Abuse: The Impact on Society* (Franklin Watts: New York, 1988), 119–127.

ethinamate A nonbarbiturate mild sedative hypnotic that is effective when deep hypnosis is not needed. (See VALMID.)

ethnopharmacology The study of human beings in relation to drug use, with special emphasis on the social, cultural and historic aspects of the subject.

ethyl alcohol See ETHANOL.

ethylmorphone hydrochloride An OPIUM derivative.

etiology The science of causes, particularly the investigation of the causes and origins of disease and abnormal conditions.

ETOH, Alcohol & Alcohol Problems Science Database In September 1988, the NIAAA announced public availability of its in-house science data base—ETOH. The data base is available to all subscribers to BRS Information Technologies (via BRS Colleague/BRS Search or BRS After Dark), a commercial data base vendor in Latham, New York. (For further information, call BRS at 1-800-468-0908 or 1-800-345-4277.)

The formal name of the National Institute on Alcohol Abuse and Alcoholism (NIAAA) data base is Alcohol and Alcohol Problems Science Database. ETOH, derived from chemical shorthand for "ethanol," is the BRS label for the NIAAA data base. ETOH's 60,000 bibliographic citations include abstracts dating back to the 1960s. In addition to journal articles (62% of the collection), the citations include conference papers and proceedings (14%), books and monographs (10%), reports, dissertations, and some unpublished research studies. The data base's collection of fugitive literature in alcohol is said to be unique.

NIAAA reports that by the year 2000, the data base is expected to hold more than 100,000 records. For a normal fee, the *ETOH User Guide* can be purchased directly from BRS Information Technologies, Latham, New York.

Ellen T. McGinn, "ETOH: The NIAAA Data Base—What It Is and What to Expect from It," *Alcohol Health & Research World,* 13:1, 1989, 24–27.

euphoria A feeling of elation and extreme well-being that can be achieved with a variety of psychoactive drugs.

ex-addict The term is generally applied to someone who is no longer addicted to a drug. It usually implies abstinence for some minimum length of time (six months, one year, two years, etc.), rather than detoxification alone. It also implies a change in lifestyle, characterized by such measures as employment, lack of arrests, school enrollment, improved relationships and continuing or completing treatment. The term is felt by many clinicians to be inaccurate, since addiction is considered to be a chronic condition. The term recovering addict is suggested by many as more accurate.

experimental drug use A short-term nonpatterned trial period of drug use, usually motivated by curiosity or by the desire to assess anticipated drug effects. Experimental use of drugs most often occurs in the company of one or more friends or social acquaintances. It can lead to a heavier involvement in drug use.

eyes Traditionally considered the "windows to the soul," the eyes can also reveal a good deal about a person in relation to drug abuse. Bloodshot eyes, for example, may betray the use of marijuana or of heavy alcohol consumption, while dilated pupils are the classic telltale sign of LSD and stimulant ingestion. Although most types of drugs exert some effect on the eyes, no ocular diseases or other damage to the eyes seems to be precipitated by short or long-term use of any recreational drug, with the exception of alcoholic amblyopia. This rare disease occurs most commonly in male alcoholics who also smoke. It involves painless, progressive blurring of the vision which is thought to be the result of a toxic reaction in the orbital portion of the optic nerve. If unchecked, the disease may progress to include degeneration of the optic nerve, but it is otherwise reversible with abstinence and a vitamin and mineral treatment program.

By affecting areas of the brain which control sensory perceptions, large doses of alcohol disturb the vision and other senses. Alcohol congests blood vessels in the eyes, causing "red eye." It also relaxes certain eye muscles, thereby interfering with the eyes' ability to focus, and slows adjustment reactions. These two effects result in double vision—common in those who are intoxicated. Nystagmus, involuntary oscillation of the eyeball, may also be present in cases of sedative intoxication. Horizontal nystagmus is most common in barbiturate and other sedative intoxications, but PCP can also cause vertical nystagmus.

Constricted pupils accompany opiate use, but extreme tearing, dilated pupils and double vision occur during withdrawal. Dilated pupils are also a part of the experience of using hallucinogens, certain solvents and stimulants, and can cause photophobia.

Psychedelic drugs produce intense visual hallucinations, often consisting of brightly colored geometric designs which are seen especially when the eyes are closed. These hallucinations, prolonged afterimages, and sensory interaction such as hearing colors and seeing sounds (synesthesis), all seem to be manifestations of the drug's effect on the central nervous system.

Cocaine gained international recognition in the nineteenth century after Freud and his colleague Koller endorsed it as a local anesthetic for eye surgery. The drug acts directly to anesthetize the corneal sensory nerve, but it is rarely used medically any more. THC (the active ingredient in marijuana), however, is beginning to enjoy professional approval in the treatment of open angle glaucoma, which it relieves by lowering pressure within the eyeball.

F

fake coke In 1982 the Food and Drug Administration (FDA) issued a warning against fake coke—or cocaine substitutes—white powders that look like cocaine and are sold openly to members of the drug culture through the U.S. mail and in HEADSHOPS. Many of these substitutes contain local anesthetics such as lidocaine, procaine and tetracaine, and can be as hazardous as cocaine itself. Although they are not controlled substances, these substitutes are subject to FDA regulation and the FDA has asked all manufacturers and distributors to help stop their dissemination. Adverse reactions can include collapsed blood vessels, lowered blood pressure and depressed heart muscle strength. Some of the trade names for these cocaine substitutes are: Toot, Florida Snow, Supercaine and Ultracaine.

false negative, false positive Terms used to indicate erroneous results in tests which measure the presence (positive) or absence (negative) of something. In a screening for drugs, for example, *a false positive* means that the test indicated the presence of a drug when in fact none was there, and a *false negative* means just the reverse. Whether a result of personal or computer error, or of errors associated with the collection or transportation of specimens, or improperly performed tests, nearly all drug-testing techniques are susceptible to false or erroneous test results, especially when improper techniques, identification or storage occurs.

familial etiological theories Sociocultural theories on the cause of alcoholism that emphasize the important role the family plays in the development of drinking patterns. Some studies have shown that among siblings of alcoholics there is two to 14 times more alcoholism than among siblings of nonalcoholics. It has been suggested that children will tend to follow parental modes of coping with stress, tension and anxiety. It is also possible to apply familial etiological theories to the abuse patterns of other drugs. (See also CHILDREN OF DRUG DEPENDENT INDIVIDUALS.)

Families in Action (FIA) The nation's first community-based parents' group formed to prevent drug abuse among children and teenagers. Founded in De Kalb County, Georgia, in 1977, it now has over 3,000 members. The group collects and distributes relevant information about young people and drugs and conducts research on the effects of drugs. FIA has established the Drug Information Data Base of over 70,000 documents and the U.S.Library of Congress lists the group as a national referral center.

family problems See FAMILIAL ETIOLOGICAL THEORIES, YOUTHS, CHILDREN OF DRUG DEPENDENT INDIVIDUALS, ORAL FIXATION and SPOUSE ABUSE.

family therapy See TREATMENT and REHABILITATION.

Fastin® (Beecham Laboratories) An anorectic used for weight control that contains phentermine hydrochloride and has a pharmacological activity similar to that of AMPHETAMINES. Because of this similarity Fastin has a significant potential for abuse and tolerance develops quickly. Overdosage can result in restlessness, rapid respiration, confusion and hallucinations. It is supplied in blue and white capsules.

fatty liver A reversible condition of the liver that results from heavy drinking. It is characterized by an excessive accumulation of fat in the liver and liver dysfunction. (See also LIVER.)

FBI See FEDERAL BUREAU OF INVESTIGATION.

Federal Bureau of Investigation (FBI) On January 21, 1982 the U.S. Attorney General announced that the FBI and the Drug Enforcement Administration (DEA) would have concurrent jurisdiction over violations of the federal drug laws. The announcement was a result of the serious drug trafficking problem in the United States and the need for a more concentrated effort at all levels. Under the new alliance, the DEA will report to the Director of the FBI and the FBI will then be given concurrent jurisdiction with the DEA for investigations of violations of the Controlled Substances Act. The DEA will continue to be the lead organization in the federal government's efforts to direct the assault on traffickers and to assist state and local enforcement, but the alliance will serve to open new fronts in the war on drugs and insure that the skills and resources of both agencies will be used to the best advantage. Drug enforcement investigators now have the backing of more than 1,500 trained FBI agents. They also have access to ISIS, the Investigative Support Information System of the FBI, and the OCIS, the Organized Crime Information System which retrieves, organizes and analyzes information developed in organized crime investigations.

In the first few months of the alliance, FBI narcotics investigations increased from 100 to over 800, and joint FBI/DEA investigations increased from a handful to about 200. In 1989, the DEA reported that arrests of drug traffickers and dealers have increased 200% in the past seven years and the rate of prosecutions has increased 300%.

fenfluramine hydrochloride A synthetic drug chemically related to the AMPHETAMINES. It is used as an anoretic. (See PONDIMIN.)

fentanyl A narcotic analgesic and opium derivative. Fentanyl is about one hundred times more potent than morphine. It is generally used intravenously as a pre-operative anesthetic, for brief anesthesia or for post-operative pain. In terms of drug abuse, anesthesiologists and nurse anesthetists have been known to self-administer the drug to provide sedation and sleep. Compulsive use becomes a possibility. Fentanyl is also the basis for the manufacture of CHINA WHITE (methylfantanyl) which is even more potent, and is a street drug. Because it is so potent overdose is a possibility. (See SUBLIMAZE.)

fetal alcohol syndrome (FAS) Identified in 1973 by Kenneth L. Jones and David W. Smith of the University of Washington in Seattle, fetal alcohol syndrome is the name applied to alcohol-related birth defects. Jones and Smith replicated studies done a few years earlier by Christie Ulleland, also of the University of Washington.

Born to mothers who have used alcohol excessively during pregnancy, children with fetal alcohol syndrome exhibit a number of characteristics, including growth deficiencies, mental retardation and physical malformations. FAS is the third leading cause of congenital mental disorders, ranking behind Down's syndrome and spina bifida, and is the only one which is preventable.

Certain features are commonly found in cases of FAS. The victims usually fail to reach normal length both before and after birth; they are below normal weight and have a tendency to remain thin and small as they grow older; and they tend to have elongated folds in their eyelids, causing eye slits. A short nose, low nasal bridge, narrow upper lip, small chin and flat midface, and indistinct philtrum (the vertical groove between nose and mouth) are among the other physical abnormalities that occur. Approximately 30% of children with FAS have heart defects. Central nervous system effects of FAS include retarded mental and motor development, hyperactivity, tremulousness and a poor attention span. Mental deficiency is the most common sign of fetal damage and even when placed in supportive atmospheres, such children show no improvement with time.

Alcohol consumed by a pregnant woman passes freely across the placental barrier into the baby's bloodstream. The concentrations are at least as high as those in the mother and the fetus is not equipped to handle such amounts. (See PREGNANCY.)

Mineral and vitamin deficiencies resulting from maternal drinking may also be harmful to the fetus. Although research in this area is still in its early stages, it is known that insufficient amounts of calcium, magnesium and zinc all play an important role in fetal development. Fetal malformations may also be caused by a deficiency of vitamins, particularly folic acid, which is common in alcoholics.

It is not yet known exactly how much alcohol is harmful to a fetus, and it should be noted that most documented cases of FAS have been children of women whose drinking meets the criteria of alcoholism. Many organizations, such as the National Institute on Alcohol Abuse and Alcoholism, and the American Medical Association Panel on Alcoholism, recommend complete abstinence from alcohol during pregnancy. They consider this the wisest course because the effects of even a small amount of alcohol are still unknown. The March of Dimes, along with some other organizations, does not emphasize complete abstinence since they feel the suggestion may unnecessarily frighten a woman whose custom is to have a drink or two in the evening even during pregnancy. Organizations who take this view point out that millions of social drinkers have healthy babies and they feel it is better to raise the consciousness of drinkers by alerting them to the dangers instead of counseling complete abstinence.

Until more is known, caution or abstinence is the recommendation of most agencies and organizations.

Finland The use of cannabis, LSD and amphetamines was first detected in Finland during the late 1960s. At this time, too, the use of barbiturates and minor tranquilizers increased. In 1968 the National Board of Health withdrew amphetamines from the market and doctors were required to obtain a special license in order to prescribe their use in individual cases. These legal restrictions, however led to illicit smuggling and illegal manufacture. Cannabis became popular, particularly among youths, and was often combined with the use of alcohol. These increases in drug abuse led to an extensive study by the National Board of Health in 1971. As a result, rules for prescribing drugs were re-evaluated and a permanent system to monitor drug use was established.

A follow-up study was done in 1977 which showed a decrease in the use of barbiturates and minor tranquilizers but a compensatory use of antidepressants and neuroleptics (major tranquilizers). From 1979 to 1980 the use of neuroleptics once again showed an increase.

There is a high incidence of respiratory ailments in Finland due to the cold moist climate and treatment has centered on codeine—the traditional ingredient in most analgesics and cough medicines. Codeine accounted for 80–90% of narcotic use in Finland until 1972 when the Board of Health revised the control of codeine and consumption decreased significantly. As the use of methaqualone increased, it too was placed under the same sort of control, and doctors had to follow certain rules in prescribing the drug and keep detailed records of the patients concerned. In 1977 methaqualone use was restricted to hospitals only. The government's concern and actions have led to a decrease or leveling off in the abuse of most drugs and it continues to monitor the situation closely.

Alcohol problems are a concern in Finland, although the per capita consumption is far less than in other European nations. Finland ranked 25th of 32 nations included in an international alcohol consumption comparison in 1984. Total alcohol consumption was 8.2 liters per person age 15 and older. (Note: 1 liter is equal to 1.06 quarts). The pattern of abuse which prevails today is one of occasional but heavy consumption, and more than half of the alcoholic beverages consumed are strong liquors rather than wine or beer. The State Alcohol Monopoly controls distribution, and restricted centers where alcohol is available are mainly in cities. Because of this, illegal distilling is popular in rural areas and it has been suggested that 10% of alcohol consumed in Finland is illegally distilled. At present, the government's emphasis in trying to control alcohol consumption is placed on increased supervision of public drinking places—places where cultural trends and habits are likely to form.

Fiorinal® (Sandoz) An analgesic used for tension (or muscle contraction) headache. It contains aspirin, phenacetin, caffeine and Sandoptal (the BARBITURATE, butalbital). It may be habit-forming and psychological dependence can occur. Overdosage can result in respiratory depression, confusion, hypotension and coma. It is supplied in two-tone green capsules, and white compressed tablets. Fiorinal with Codeine® is used for more severe pain. It is supplied in capsule form: No. 1, ⅛ grain codeine, red and yellow; No. 2, ¼ grain codeine, gray and yellow; No. 3, ½ grain codeine, blue and yellow.

flashback A little understood phenomenon of the MEMORY that is reported by a small percentage of users of hallucinogenic drugs, whereby the individual reexperiences the drug state days, weeks or months after the original experience. Stressful or other dissociative states, such as falling asleep or waking up, may precipitate flashback. They may represent a form of state dependent learning: when the nervous system is aroused and ego functioning is diminished, the physical and psychological state induced by LSD or other hallucinogens is reproduced and intensified visual and other perceptions experienced and stored during the drug "trip" surface. Since the body eliminates LSD within 24 hours after ingestion, prolonged retention of the substance cannot explain flashback. Nor does the drug affect the brain's structure in any way.

Flashback has been known to occur with large doses of amphetamines and may be provoked by marijuana and such substances as antihistamines, nitrous oxide and even caffeine.

Florida, drug cases in A 1986 article in *U.S. News & World Report* entitled "America on Drugs," by John Lang and Ronald Taylor, stated that in Florida, TRAFFICKING has grown so phenomenally in recent years that it has become the biggest source of income in the state. In 1986, cocaine arrests rose 80%, the burglary rate went up 30%. Other crimes that generate enough cash for a quick fix have also risen in areas of the state where crack is sold. Miami is known currently as the "capital of the money-laundering" industry. (See "LAUNDERY.") One indication that huge amounts of drug money pass through Miami banks, says Gilda Berger in *Drug Abuse: The Impact on Society* is the big annual cash surplus of the Florida banking system. Florida banks routinely report cash surpluses of $6 to $8 billion a year, more than double that of other state banking systems around the country. Says Berger, "Experts guess that over half of the surplus is drug money."

Agents of the U.S. Treasury Department believe that more than one-third of all Miami banks share in the huge profits made in laundering illegal drug money. Most of the laundered money, of course, ends up in the pockets of the international drug lords. In 1982, the Drug Enforcement Administration (DEA) found the Great American Bank guilty of money laundering—an estimated $94 million in illegal drug profits covering a 14-month period.

fluorocarbons A group of hydrocarbons, chlorinated or fluorinated, that are now used chiefly as refrigerants. They were widely used as aerosol propellants prior to 1978 and were subject to abuse because of their intoxicating effects when inhaled. In 1978 the U.S. Environmental Protection Agency under the Toxic Substance Control Act banned fluorocarbons and chlorofluorocarbons from use in household consumer products.

flurazepan A BENZODIAZEPINE derivative. (See DALMANE.)

fly agaric A HALLUCINOGEN which is obtained from the *Amanita muscaria* mushroom. The mushroom is also used as a fly poison, which explains the origin of the drug's name.

Effects: Fly agaric produces various PSYCHOTOMIMETIC reactions which are similar to but less intense than those produced by LSD and PSILOCYBIN. As mentioned in the entry on HALLUCINOGENS, it is suspected that the Norse tribesmen used this drug to stimulate warlike rage before going into battle.

The mushroom is consumed whole or mixed with milk or water. As the hallucinogen passes through the system, it remains chemically unchanged. Thus, it is a practice among some users to "recycle" the urine of a person who is intoxicated.

forfeiture sanctions See BOOTY.

formaldehyde A pungent gas formed in the body in small amounts by the oxidation of methyl alcohol. It is toxic but is usually broken down into nontoxic units by the liver. When a large amount of alcohol has been consumed the liver works first to break down and metabolize the ethyl alcohol. Methyl alcohol builds up and when it is finally metabolized, a modest amount of formaldehyde is produced. Formaldehyde is thought to be partially responsible for the hangover effect and may also be responsible for certain withdrawal symptoms.

Fourth Amendment and drug abuse The chief argument against the practice of "blanket" drug testing is that it violates the Fourth Amendment, which protects against "unreasonable searches." The fourth Amendment to the U.S. Constitution states:

> The right of the people to be secure in their persons, houses, papers and effects, against unreasonable searches and seizures, shall not be violated, and no warrants shall issue, but upon probable cause, supported by oath or affirmation, and particularly describing the place to be searched, and the persons or things to be seized.

The Fourth Amendment applies *only* to government searches. It does not legally limit the power of private employers or school officials, except if the principle of fairness—the idea that general searches of innocent people are unfair and unreasonable—is violated.

An exception to the Fourth Amendment is the "administrative search." For example, airport, border, courthouse and certain regulated industry searches have all been determined permissible under the Constitution. Administrative searches (to justify blanket searches) in drug cases have been repeatedly rejected by federal and state courts. Prisons are the only institutions that have the Supreme Court's permission to conduct blanket searches.

Gilda Berger, *Drug Testing* (Franklin Watts: New York, 1987), 50–54.

Fox, Ruth, M.D. (1897–1989) Prominent psychoanalyst who, in 1959, became the first medical director of the National Council on Alcoholism. A native New Yorker, Dr. Fox performed pioneering research on the use of Antabuse, a chemical used widely in alcoholism treatment today. She was founder and first president of the American Medical Society on Alcoholism and Other Drug Dependencies in 1954. Writer, researcher and lecturer, Dr. Fox also maintained a private practice and was one of the first psychoanalysts willing to accept alcoholics as patients. She was a fellow of several groups: the American Psychiatric Association, the New York Academy of Medicine, the American Academy of Psychoanalysis, the American Health Association and the American Society of Clinical Hypnosis. A graduate of Rush Medical College, Chicago, she also studied in Paris, Vienna, and Frankfurt and interned at the Rockefeller Foundation in Beijing. Dr. Ruth Fox won many national and international honors. She died at a nursing home in Washington at age 93 on March 24, 1989.

France Until recently, recreational drug use in France consisted primarily of the use of alcohol, particularly wine, and tobacco. Changing cultural habits, however, are altering the pattern to include a broad range of narcotics, marijuana, amphetamines and barbiturates. This is not to say that drugs were not previously used (hashish was introduced in the 19th century), only that they have recently gained in popularity.

In a country where approximately one-tenth of the population derives its income directly or indirectly from the production and sale of alcoholic beverages, particularly wine, alcohol has understandably been the object of strong economic, as well as cultural, emphasis. In 1976 a World Health Organization survey of 26 countries ranked France first in per capita annual consumption of 100% ethanol (16.5 liters), twice the consumption rate in the United States. Wine, which is generally less expensive than such non-alcoholic beverages as soft drinks or fruit juices, is regularly consumed with meals and is viewed as a natural part of the daily diet. According to 1983 statistics, 46% of the French population drinks wine on a daily basis; 31% imbibes occasionally; and 23% abstains. Although there has been a recent increase in the consumption of beer and distilled spirits, wine is still the most popular beverage.

Recent statistics indicate, however, that per capita wine consumption is on the decline: in 1960 the average French citizen drank 120 quarts of wine annually; in 1982 the annual consumption had dropped to 80 quarts. While the study claims that the majority of French people have replaced wine with non-alcoholic beverages, the statistical decline may, in fact, simply reflect the rising popularity of beer and hard liquor, the consumption of which has increased threefold since 1960. In 1984, a survey of 32 countries concerning alcohol consumption per person 15 years and over ranked France second in total alcohol consumption (18.2 liters per person), third in wine consumption (105.1 liters) and 26th in per person beer consumption (52.8 liters).

Statistics on alcohol-related physical and mental illnesses reflect the important role wine and other alcoholic beverages traditionally assume in French culture. In a country of some 53 million, roughly two million individuals (2.6% of the population) suffer from alcoholism. The consumption of red wine accounts for 70% of these cases. Another three to five million people are considered problem drinkers. Alcohol consumption is the third leading cause of death in France after cardiovascular diseases and cancer. In 1978 there were approximately 30.2 deaths per 100,000 people from cirrhosis and 6.6 deaths per 100,000 people from alcoholism and alcohol psychosis. It has been estimated that alcohol abuse also accounts for half the country's murders and a quarter of its suicides. The overall cost of alcoholism to the French government in 1977 was estimated at over $4 billion; of this amount taxes on alcoholic beverages compensated for only a third.

Nearly all drugs of abuse are found in France, particularly in the metropolitan areas and around the southern ports. Marseilles, in particular, achieved worldwide notoriety during the days of the FRENCH CONNECTION, and there is reason to believe that heavy trafficking and clandestine laboratories still exist in the area. France's long Mediterranean coastline and its proximity to Southwest Asia facilitates smuggling and provides almost ideal conditions for the illicit drug trade. During the 1960s and 1970s most of the heroin for the U.S. market came through France—an estimated 10 tons annually. Morphine base and opium from Turkey and other Middle Eastern countries was converted to heroin in French laboratories and then shipped on. At the time, most of the heroin was exported and little was consumed in France itself. This pattern has now changed and heroin use is appearing with increasing frequency in France. Over the last decade heroin has played an increasingly important role as a drug of choice among abusers.

The pattern of drug use in France generally closely resembles the pattern in other Western countries. In addition to heroin, cannabis use (especially hashish) has spread to all ages and social groups. The use of cocaine is also increasing; not only is France one of the primary points of entry to Europe for cocaine traffickers (generally arriving by way of commercial airliner or boats or ships, from South America), much of the cocaine passing through French airports actually stays within the country. From 1980 to 1981, cocaine seizures increased 150%. In 1988, however, cocaine seizures dropped to 458 pounds, down from 1,728 pounds seized in 1987.

Hallucinogens and psychedelic drugs are not used frequently in France. PCP, which has been a problem in the United States, has barely made an appearance on the illicit market. The pattern of amphetamine and barbiturate abuse follows the steady increase found in other European countries but has not reached the magnitude seen in the U.S.

In 1970 and 1971 the French government initiated new treatment programs for drug abusers and severe penalties for use and possession. The legislation of the early 1970s also increased official awareness of drug abuse and addiction as a medical rather than behavioral problem. It provided more possibilities for effective treatment and made treatment compulsory for addicted criminal offenders. The legislation did, however, provide clemency for individuals who sought treatment voluntarily.

The French government has not been trying to handle its problem alone. In 1971 the United States and France signed a protocol agreement which sought to stop the flow of heroin from France into the U.S. French authorities were stationed in the U.S. and the U.S. Bureau of Narcotics and Dangerous Drugs maintained an office in France. This agreement was renewed in 1976, and in 1981 it was extended for an additional five years. France has also become active in worldwide organizations aimed at stemming drug abuse, particularly the United Nations Commission on Narcotics.

Although drug use in France has continued to increase in recent years, particularly in the over-25 age group, there has been a decrease in the likelihood of teenagers to indulge in heavy drug use—an encouraging sign for the future.

When the 12-nation European Community eliminates trade barriers and border checks in 1992, authorities fear that cocaine will be more readily available than ever. Veteran narcotics agents say all of Europe will be as vulnerable as its least patrolled port.

freebase, cocaine In its normal street form cocaine hydrochloride is not effective when smoked; an alkali and solvent is required to convert it to cocaine alkaloid, called "freebase." The process involves heating ether, lighter fluid, or a similar flammable solvent with cocaine—a potentially dangerous process that could lead to burns. It can also be produced by adding bicarbonate of soda (baking soda) and ether to street cocaine and smoking the mixture. The result is a purified cocaine base which is smoked in a special pipe with wire screens, or sprinkled on a tobacco or marijuana cigarette. When smoked it produces a sudden and intense high that lasts for less than two minutes.

Crack cocaine is the preprocessd smokable form of cocaine and after conversion to a purified form known as "free base" can be highly potent and addictive.

Freebase has a lower vaporizing temperature than cocaine hydrochloride, therefore smoking does not destroy it. It is rapidly absorbed by the lungs and carried to the brain in a few seconds. The brief euphoria that results is quickly replaced by a feeling of restless irritability. The posthigh after freebase can be so uncomfortable, in fact, that in order to maintain the high, users often continue smoking until they either run out of cocaine or until they are completely exhausted.

The custom of smoking cocaine originated in the 1970s in Peru, and quickly spread through the South American countries and into the United States. In South America cocaine is not processed into freebase before smoking; it is smoked in the form of coca paste, the extract produced during the manufacture of cocaine from coca leaves. Smoking coca paste is extremely dangerous because of the impurities it contains.

Synonyms: white tornado, freebase, baseball, snowflake.

French Connection Led by Jean Jehan, the French Connection was a group of French underworld figures who were the major suppliers of heroin to the U.S. from the 1930s until 1973 when a concentrated international law enforcement effort smashed the ring. Jehan was later arrested in France but was held only briefly, then released.

While it was flourishing, the French Connection dominated heroin trafficking; it had control of smuggling and a monopoly on heroin laboratories. It also had a working relationship with Italian criminals that guaranteed the American market to the French: apparently the agreement was to the effect that if the French sold only to the Italians in America, the Italians in Europe would stay out of the traffic. Of necessity, this agreement required the closest understanding between the highest level of the criminal underworld in Italy and its counterpart in the U.S.

Although the French Connection was wrecked, it has been suggested that it is not really dead. Heroin laboratories were found in France in February of 1978 and September of 1979; two months later a French chemist was arrested at a clandestine heroin laboratory in Italy. In March 1980, another small lab was seized outside Marseilles, France. Among those who were in contact with the people managing the laboratory was Jean Jehan. In June 1980, three laboratories were seized in and near Milan, Italy; following the raids the French police arrested Jehan at Marseilles. Jehan was released in September of 1980, at the age of 82, for reasons of ill health.

The U.S. government considers these events warning signals that the French Connection may be showing signs of life. If this is true, they suggest it will resurface as the Franco-Italian Connection.

Freon A FLUOROCARBON. It was frequently used as a propellant for aerosols prior to 1978 when fluorocarbons were banned from use in household consumer products.

fructose It is thought that fructose, a natural sugar in fruits and honey, may speed up the rate at which ethanol is metabolized. The degree of acceleration involved is not known but is thought to be small. The addition of fructose to one's diet is not a practical sobering agent but may slightly reduce hangover effects.

fumo d'Angola Brazilian for CANNABIS. This Brazilian reference to Angola, a Portugese colony in Africa, supports the theory that African slaves may have been the first to bring cannabis to South America.

G

Gamma alcoholism See JELLINEK.

gas chromatography/mass spectrometry (GC/MS) A drug-screening test that claims to be 99.9% accurate. GC/MS is considered as effective in recognizing chemicals as fingerprints are in identifying people. It is the only test accepted in most courts of law as proof of drug use beyond a reasonable doubt.

The GC/MS machine, which costs around $15,000, must be operated by highly skilled, specially trained technicians. To run the test, a tiny amount of urine sample is injected into a port in the gas chromatograph. The moving gas then carries the sample through a long narrow tube packed with a special chemical. As it passes through the tube, the various molecules in the sample are attracted, whether strongly or weakly, to the chemical in the tube. The various molecules arrive at the end of the tube at different times.

The molecules then pass into a mass spectrometer, which ionizes the molecules and sends them through an electromagnetic field that pulls on the individual molecules with varying force (depending on the mass, weight and electric charge of each ion.) Thus, they're further separated. At the end, the machine automatically produces a chart indicating precisely which molecules are in the urine sample and the specific amount of each kind of molecule.

The GC/MS test can cost as much as $80 per sample. It is strictly a laboratory tool and cannot conveniently be used on location in a factory, a plant or an army base, for example. Simple, fast and relatively accurate new tests for drug abuse are presently being developed for on-site use in doctors' offices, clinics, offices, factories, or even in the home.

Gilda Berger, *Drug Testing* (Franklin Watts: New York, 1987), 38–41.

gaseous anesthetics See NITROUS OXIDE.

gasoline Inhaling gasoline fumes can produce an intoxicating effect similar to alcohol. Extensive inhaling can produce hallucinations, confusion, delirium and coma. Lead poisoning is a possible outcome. (See also INHALANTS.)

gastrointestinal tract The gastrointestinal tract is the term applied to the part of the digestive system which includes the stomach and the small and large intestines. (The digestive tract includes the complete food canal from the mouth to the anus.)

Food is converted into soluble or emulsified material that can be absorbed by the blood and circulated for distribution and utilization by the various tissues of the body. This conversion is achieved by the secretions and enzymes of the gastrointestinal tract. Digestion begins in the mouth, where chewing reduces the food to a fine texture and where the action of the saliva begins the alteration of starch. The juices and enzymes of the stomach then continue the process as hydrochloric acid; pepsin and rennin act upon the protein components of the food. When the partially altered mass enters the small intestine there is further enzymatic action by the bile and the pancreatic secretions, and the conversion of starch, sugar, fat and protein is completed. The residue that cannot be utilized by the body passes into the large intestine and is excreted as waste from the rectum.

Drugs taken by mouth begin to enter the blood through the walls of the stomach or through the upper portion of the small intestine.

Alcohol passes through the mouth to the stomach where about 20% of it absorbed. The rest is absorbed in the upper small intestine. The ingestion of alcohol has been widely associated with inflammation of the stomach, particularly inflammation of the stomach's mucous membranes. Although small amounts of alcohol (a glass or two of wine) can stimulate the appetite, high concentrations of alcohol depress the appetite and produce hypersecretion and gastric irritation, which cause nausea and vomiting. In addition, alcohol delays the emptying time of the stomach. Consistent drinking impairs pancreatic enzyme function, producing diarrhea. Prolonged and excessive use of alcohol may result in more serious erosion of the stomach membrane, ranging from inflammation to ulceration and hemorrhage. In addition, many alcoholics suffer from malnutrition because their main caloric intake consists of alcohol.

Barbiturates and other sedative and hypnotic drugs are rapidly absorbed into the body through the upper portion of the small intestine. The presence of food in the stomach slows down the absorption of these drugs, as it does with alcohol. The moderate, medically prescribed use of barbiturates seems to have little or no direct adverse effect on the gastrointestinal tract. The abuse of these drugs, however, can produce symptoms like those of alcohol intoxication—nausea and vomiting. Unlike alcoholics, barbiturate addicts are not likely to suffer serious malnutrition or gastric irritation.

The popular stereotype of a heroin addict is someone who is emaciated, sallow-complexioned and obviously unhealthy. The most authoritative studies have shown that addiction to opiate derivative drugs "is not characterized by physical deterioration or impairment of physical fitness aside from the addiction per se. There is no evidence of change in the circulatory, hepatic, renal or endocrine functions." (Arthur B. Light and

Edward G. Torrance, in *A.M.A. Archives of Internal Medicine,* 44, [1929]:876.)

In terms of the effects on the digestive system, and on the gastrointestinal tract in particular, the opiates are sometimes constipating (in fact, codeine and opium itself have been used as treatments for diarrhea). Some addicts must use laxatives to aid elimination.

Cocaine is easily absorbed by the mucous membranes and is usually sniffed: it is not taken orally because it is hydrolyzed by the gastrointestinal secretions. Perhaps because cocaine is absorbed and eliminated by the body so quickly it does not seem to have any adverse effects on the gastrointestinal tract. Freud is said to have successfully prescribed cocaine for a patient with gastric distress probably because of its local anesthetic action.

In the case of cigarette smoking, Dr. Vincent P. Dole of Rockefeller University made an interesting comparison: "Cigarette smoking is unquestionably more damaging to the human body than heroin." He made this statement after examining and testing many heroin addicts who had been addicted for a long time. Most of the nicotine in cigarettes is absorbed through the buccal membranes of the mouth and the lungs, but nicotine is also readily absorbed through the stomach and is quickly distributed to the brain, body organs and all the body fluids. It is a stimulant to both the central and peripheral nervous systems and, as is the case with amphetamines, caffeine and other stimulants, even moderate doses can result in prolonged gastric secretions which can lead to the formation of peptic ulcers. Recent information from the office of the U.S. Surgeon General seems to confirm Dr. Dole's assessment.

Very heavy use of cannabis has been associated with temporary intestinal disorders such as diarrhea, abdominal cramps and inflammation, but it does not seem to have any long-term effect on the gastrointestinal tract. The synthetic psychedelic drugs, such as LSD, seem to have no effect on the gastrointestinal tract but organic psychedelics, such as peyote or "sacred mushrooms," sometimes cause nausea and vomiting at the beginning of a "trip." Again, these drugs do not seem to have any long-lasting effects on the digestive system.

gay drug users See HOMOSEXUALS.

Gaysal® (Geriatric) An analgesic (generally used for arthritis) and a sedative. It contains sodium salicylate, acetaminophen, aluminum hydroxide and the BARBITURATES, phenobarbital and secobarbital. It may be habit-forming and dependence can occur. Gaysal-S has the same formula minus the barbiturates.

Gemonil® (Abbott) An anticonvulsant that contains metharbital (a synthetic derivative of barbital) and is used for the control of seizures. It is a BARBITURATE of long duration and slow action and may be habit-forming. Physical and psychological dependence can occur and, when taken with alcohol or other central nervous system depressants, it can have an addictive effect. Overdosage can result in drowsiness, irritability, dizziness and coma. It is supplied in 100 mg tablets.

generics When applied to drugs, the term means the chemical description of the drug's class as opposed to a commercial brand or trade name for the same compound. For example, Valium is a trade name for diazepam, the generic name.

genetics See HEREDITY.

genetotropic etiological theory A theory that the satisfaction of all nutritional needs will end the desire for alcohol. The theory was first advanced by R. J. Williams, who suggested that alcoholism is related to a genetically determined biochemical defect. Although Williams' theory has been discredited it is known that nutrition may well play a role in the cause of alcoholism. (See also NUTRITION.)

Germany The pattern of drug abuse in Germany has changed drastically in the past two decades. Initially, the country was troubled by the abuse of LSD, other psychedelic drugs, and hashish. Today the main problem is heroin, followed closely by cocaine.

In 1980 the number of heroin addicts was estimated between 80,000 and 100,000 and it has been suggested that one out of every 20 Germans has experimented with various dangerous drugs. Of particular concern is the fact that government surveys show an increase in the number of heroin abusers under the age of 21. The increase in abuse tends to go along with an increase in illicit drug trafficking and smuggling (a 7% increase between 1977 and 1980 in recorded cases). Government surveys show there is an excessive supply of heroin and cocaine at extremely low prices despite increased police seizures. In 1980, 95% of heroin seizures came from Southwest Asia; preliminary figures for the first few months of 1981 indicate that Southeast Asia heroin accounted for 30% of the seizures. It is thought that much of the increase in heroin abuse is due to Germany's geographical position as a supply route for illegal drug smuggling across Western Europe.

Recently officials have expressed concern about a renewed wave of cocaine abuse. In 1988, 1,302 pounds of cocaine were seized up from 638 pounds in 1987. One DEA official said that Germany, in fact all of Western Europe, was only about five years behind the United States in cocaine use and availability. One reason is that among professional people, cocaine is seen as the "in" drug, harmless, according to myth.

Early in 1970 the government initiated a crash program to deal with drug abuse. In-depth surveys were begun and funding was made available for research into the reasons behind the increase. Law enforcement was strengthened to try to halt illegal trafficking; a system of public education on the dangers of narcotics was set up; and improvements were made in the medical assistance available to addicts. In the late 1970s the program was further expanded; international contacts were beefed up and cooperation with neighboring countries on border control was greatly increased.

Since the initial crash program of the early 1970s, 50 institutions are now available to abusers for long-term therapy. Former addicts have access to vocational rehabilitation institutions, and under federal law employers can now be reimbursed for 60–80% of salary for up to two years if they employ a former addict.

Educational programs aimed at combating drug abuse take the form of government booklets and pamphlets, and public media education through television. These informative and educational efforts are carried out by the Federal Center for Health Education, an agency subordinate to the Federal Ministry for Youth, Family Affairs, and Health. Future government programs call for an intensification of these existing programs, particularly with regard to epidemiological research. A recent government study revealed that the increase in drug abuse coincides with the German people's search for solidarity, autonomy, hedonism and spirituality. It was suggested that those particularly liable to addiction are those who feel they do not belong to any society and believe they are getting "too little from life." This theory would demonstrate why it is so difficult to identify these people at an early age and why it is so important to educate them at an early age. Consequently, the government has concentrated its public health education measures on the following target groups: children prior to at-risk age (8–12 years); young people in high-risk groups (13–17 years); parents with children in these two age groups; "mediators" who work with these age groups and parents; and representatives and decision-makers of institutions responsible for structuring and implementing preventive measures.

The problem of alcohol abuse is also serious in Germany and the country reports one of the highest levels of consumption of absolute alcohol in the world. The annual level of consumption, according to a 1974 report, was approximately 14.8 liters per person aged 15 and over. In 1984, that figure had dropped slightly to 14.3 liters per person 15 years and over (1 liter equals 1.6 quarts). Although a very high level, it was below those of Portugal (23.4) and France (22.4) during the same period. The high consumption in West Germany is not surprising in view of the fact that almost all meals and social occasions are accompanied by beer, wine and other alcoholic beverages. A slight decline in consumption was reported from 1975–78 (a drop of 0.3 liters); this drop was significant because until 1975 the level had been steadily rising.

Based on reports from Frankfurt and Hamburg, the following types of programs for alcoholics are available: self-help groups, treatment centers and advice bureaus. The best known of the self-help groups is Anonymen Alkoholiker, modeled after AA in the United States, which has approximately 800 groups throughout West Germany. Self-help groups with religious affiliations are sponsored by Protestants, Catholics and Jews. Advice Bureaus are numerous throughout the country and are usually located in clubs, health services, churches and various other organizations. The first centralized center for the intoxicated opened in Hamburg in the mid-1970s and was primarily designed to provide a place where individuals suspected by the police of being drunk could sober up overnight. The center was considered necessary because there were reports of people dying in police ''coolers'' because they were in need of medical attention. At the center a doctor examines each person and those in need of medical care are sent on to a hospital; those who are merely drunk are kept in the center overnight at their own expense. Other cities throughout the country are considering opening such centers.

glue sniffing See INHALANTS.

glutethimide A nonbarbiturate hypnotic usually prescribed for insomnia. It has a rapid onset. (See DORIDEN.)

Golden Crescent In the late 1970s, following a drop in illicit opium from the GOLDEN TRIANGLE, three Southwest Asian countries emerged as the leading opium producers in the world: Pakistan, Afganistan and Iran. Most of the trafficking of Southwest Asian heroin is carried on by Turkish nationals who smuggle heroin which has been converted from opium grown in Southwest Asia and processed in illicit laboratories in eastern Turkey and western Iran. Current trends indicate that increasing numbers of other Southwest Asian nationals (Lebanese and Syrians) are moving into the European heroin market. Southwest Asian heroin has enjoyed great success in Europe because it is less expensive and of higher quality than Southeast Asian heroin.

The Federal Republic of Germany has become the major market for Turkish traffickers (partly because of the large number of Turkish guest workers there), although the Netherlands has also experienced a recent influx of smuggled heroin. Italy is also beginning to play an increasingly important role in international heroin trafficking. Being a key transit point for Southwest Asian heroin reaching other Western European nations, Italy is also a location for heroin conversion laboratories and a major source area for the increasing quantities of heroin reaching the U.S. Italy has become an important consumer country for heroin, too. Italian authorities estimate that between 40,000 to 50,000 Italians may use heroin on a daily basis.

For years the governments of Southwest Asian countries have viewed the abuse of heroin as an American problem. Although narcotics have been used in Asia throughout history, there are now more addicts in Asia than there are in the U.S. and heroin addiction is quickly becoming epidemic. The trend is troubling local governments and making them take a closer look at the international war on narcotics.

Three consecutive bumper opium harvests, beginning in 1980, have produced a stockpile, and officials believe there is little hope of controlling the supply soon. Because of the excess supplies, dealers are cutting prices—the price of street heroin has halved since 1980—and are looking for new markets. It is estimated that Asia already accounts for 60% of world heroin use, and addiction among people under 21 is growing at an alarming rate.

There are several reasons for the increase in heroin abuse in the area. In addition to excess supplies and cheap prices, Asians have become more open to drug use in recent years: there has been a shift in population from rural to urban areas; people have started to earn more money and have become alienated from traditional ways; and in many households both parents now work, leaving children unsupervised. In Burma, Thailand, Pakistan and Afganistan traffickers are often government insurgents or independent tribal leaders who are almost impossible to control. Furthermore, the process of refining heroin is increasingly taking place in Asian laboratories.

Golden Triangle An area that includes regions in eastern Burma, northern Laos and Thailand. It emerged in the 1960s and 1970s as the largest producer of illicit opium in the world and, until recently, dominated the heroin market in Western Europe. The growing of opium poppies is thought to have been introduced to the region by Chinese political refugees and further encouraged by Europeans as a source of revenue. Chinese traffickers, using the Netherlands as the main importation and distribution area, virtually controlled the heroin market; arranging for the purchase of raw opium, overseeing its conversion (usually in laboratories in and around Bangkok and Hong Kong), and managing an international smuggling network. In the late 1970s there was a reduction in trafficking due to several factors: rivalry among the various Chinese groups of crime syndicates, law enforcement efforts against major Oriental traffickers, and a drop in opium production due to poor crops.

With the decrease in heroin from Southeast Asia, the European market was successfully challenged by other traffickers,

Major Areas of Heroin Addiction in Asia

Country	Addicts (in thousands)	Population (in millions)	Percentage
Burma	60	35	0.17
Hong Kong	50	5.5	0.9
Iran	300–500	40	1.0
Malaysia	250	14	1.8
Pakistan	120	87	0.14
Singapore	7	2.5	0.28
Thailand	400–600	48	1.0

These figures are based on Asian and U.S. government estimates.

SOURCE: *The Wall Street Journal*, Thursday, January 12, 1984. Reprinted by permission.

mostly Turkish nationals smuggling heroin converted from opium grown in Southwest Asia (see GOLDEN CRESCENT) and processed in western Iran and eastern Turkey. Since the late 1970s Southwest Asian heroin has enjoyed great success because it is less expensive and generally more potent than heroin from the Golden Triangle. In 1989 the major suppliers production of opium in metric tons were Burma 1,300, Afghanistan 750, Iran 300 and Laos 250 tons.

government corruption, drugs and In certain drug TRAFFICKING areas, government corruption is widespread. In south Florida, for instance, drug-related corruption among law enforcement personnel has been commonplace; so much so, in fact, that new scandals are no longer considered that newsworthy.

Drug traffickers in some countries have even tried to take over governments. In 1980, for example, Bolivia's General Luis Garcia Menza, a major cocaine trafficker, staged a military coup and established close ties between the government and the nation's drug enterprises. Both major political parties reportedly have ties to the principal drug dealers; police and armed forces personnel do not act, either from fear or because they, too, have taken bribes.

Bolivian Attorney General Carlos Mavro Hoyos summed up the role of traffickers in politics: "Narcotics traffickers are becoming a superstate because of their enormous wealth. But if we allow ourselves to be intimidated by fear or by the power of these people, our future will be more and more uncertain."

Sometimes traffickers have links with international terrorist groups, such as the Palestine Liberation Organization, M-19 leftist rebels in Colombia and Peru's Maoist Shining Path guerrillas. Governments in several countries—Bolivia, Colombia, Thailand, Pakistan—have reportedly used weapons provided for antidrug activities to kill those who happen to disagree with their politics.

U.S. government officials long suspected that Panamanian leader General Manuel Antonio Noriega accepted payoffs in the millions of dollars to allow drug shipments to pass through his country enroute to the United States. Yet Noriega was put on the payroll of the U.S. Central Intelligence Agency in the mid-1970s as the then head of his country's intelligence service. In 1988, however, federal prosecutors in Miami won indictments accusing Noriega of helping Colombian drug lords smuggle tons of cocaine into the U.S. In January 1990, the deposed dictator surrendered in Panama to U.S. officials of the Justice Department and was flown to Miami, where he is incarcerated in the city's federal courthouse awaiting trial on counts that could put him away for 210 years and cost him $1 million in fines.

In July 1989, Cuba announced that four high-ranking army officers had been executed after conviction by court-martial of conspiracy to ship tons of cocaine and marijuana to the United States. The four included General Arnaldo T. Ochoa Sanchez, a highly decorated war hero. The death sentence imposed by special military tribunal represented the biggest scandal since Fidel Castro took power in Cuba 30 years ago. Evidence presented at the trial suggested that President Castro's brother, Raul, Cuba's defense minister, may have been aware of the drug trafficking. Fidel Castro complained that the United States withheld information that could have helped his government uncover the drug ring sooner.

grand mal convulsions Convulsive seizures that can occur during WITHDRAWAL from barbiturates or alcohol or less frequently from Demerol (there have been extremely rare instances of such convulsions occurring during other narcotic withdrawal). They generally occur 24 to 48 hours after cessation of drinking and a third of those who experience convulsions also go on to have DELIRIUM TREMENS. Grand mal convulsions are less common in barbiturate withdrawal and do not occur as quickly as they do in the case of alcohol withdrawal. Convulsions can also occur in drug OVERDOSE.

grog A mixture of rum and water, sometimes served hot. It was named for Edward Vernon (1684–1757), a British admiral, who ordered his men's daily ration of rum to be diluted with water because he feared they were becoming habitually intoxicated. The name given to the mixture came from the admiral's sobriquet, "Old Grog." This term referred to Vernon's habit of wearing a coat made of grogham (a wool-silk-mohair combination) in inclement weather. The term is also extended to refer to any liquor.

group therapy A drug treatment and rehabilitation technique which involves group rather than individual treatment as a way of emphasizing that a patient's problems are not unique. Usually fewer than a dozen patients are involved in a group, which allows for maximum participation, and the group is generally led by a psychiatrist, a psychologist or a social worker. Members open up their problems to the scrutiny of others and discuss them as a group. This communal type of therapy also allows members to benefit vicariously from the resolution of other members' problems. The technique is sometimes preferred over large group meetings, such as Alcoholics Anonymous or Narcotics Anonymous, where extensive and intimate exploration of a problem is limited.

gum opium Raw OPIUM.

H

habit Dependency on drugs. (See ADDICTION.)

habit-forming Manufacturers of drugs use the term "Warning: May be habit-forming" if there is a possibility that tolerance can develop and physical or psychological dependency can occur.

habituation The process of forming a habit; also a synonym for DEPENDENCE. Dependence or ADDICTION are preferable terms because they are more specific.

Haight-Ashbury, the A district in San Francisco, California, which during the mid-1960s was a gathering spot for counterculture youths whose lives centered around hallucinogenic drugs, particularly LSD.

hair analysis Hair analysis, while still in the developmental stage, promises a complementary type of drug detection for various criminal justice and forensic applications. Techniques of hair analysis are essentially the same as those of radio immunoassay of urine and offer the same general detection sensitivity. The National Institute of Justice (NIJ), presently engaged in a pilot study, says that it appears present laboratory-based hair analysis methods will be refined and made more amenable to larger scale applications. When this occurs, say NIJ officials, hair analysis will become a technique complementary to urinalysis, expanding the criminal justice system's ability to detect and monitor illicit drug abuse. Analysis of a few strands of hair offers the potential to detect drugs absorbed by the growing human hair over a longer time period; urinalysis, on the other hand, is limited to detecting drugs consumed within the previous three days.

U.S. Department of Justice, National Institute of Justice, *NIJ Reports/SNI 202*, March-April 1987, 4.

Haldol® (McNeil) A major TRANQUILIZER that contains haloperidol and which is used in the treatment of acute or chronic psychosis. When taken with alcohol or other central nervous system depressants it can have an additive effect. Overdosage can result in respiratory depression and hypotension. It is supplied in 0.5 mg white tablets; 1 mg yellow; 2 mg pink; 5 mg green; 10 mg aqua; as a concentrate of 2 mg per ml; and in ampules for injection.

Hale House A rehabilitation home for drug-affected babies in the Harlem district of New York City, it was founded in 1969 by octogenarian Mother Clara Hale, who has devoted her life to helping children born to drug abusers. Her success in caring for so-called crack babies has been outstanding.

half-life of drugs The amount of time it takes for the body to remove half of a drug dose from the system. For drugs with a half-life of 24 hours or more, such as Valium, half of the first dose may still be in the body when the next dose is taken 24 hours later. After several days the cumulation in the body can be fairly large, and if alcohol or another central nervous system depressant is taken the result can be additive. Cumulation levels off within a week. (See also SYNERGY.)

halfway house A home for formerly institutionalized individuals, such as alcoholics, drug addicts, mental patients or ex-prisoners. It is a transition point as they move from inpatient care to outside life. The halfway house movement developed in the 1970s, and mushroomed in the 1980s. It is based on the belief that to be effective such houses should have only a small number of residents and maintain an informal "homelike" atmosphere. Primarily for the homeless who need support and protection, rather than medical care, until they can again take their place in the community, halfway houses are generally staffed by non-professionals and provide residents with food, shelter and a therapeutic environment. Professionals are available for any needed medical care. Halfway houses are sometimes referred to as transitional housing for recovering drug addicts and alcoholics. These people need or want ongoing therapy as they begin their transition back into society.

hallucinogens (From *hallucination*—a sensory experience that does not relate to external reality.) Hallucinogens are drugs that act on the central nervous system and produce mood changes and perceptual changes varying from sensory illusion to hallucinations. Because some of these drugs have the ability to "mimic" psychotic reactions—loss of contact with reality, hallucinations, mania, and schizophrenia—they are sometimes called psychotomimetic drugs. The term psychotogenic, which refers to the production of a psychotic-like state, is also applied. In addition, because of their perceptual effects qualities, the hallucinogens are sometimes called psychedelics.

Hallucinogens are classified as Schedule I drugs under the CONTROLLED SUBSTANCES ACT, and include LSD, MESCALINE, PEYOTE, DMT, PSILOCYBIN (PSILOCIN), MARIJUANA, and TETRAHYDROCANNABINOLS, among others. Apart from marijuana (which has not quite appropriately been placed in this classification although it can produce some psychedelic effects) the most widely used of the hallucinogens are LSD, mescaline, DOM (STP), and psilocybin (psilocin). LSD and DOM (STP) are synthetic compounds, as are other hallucinogens such as MDA, MDMA, and TMA. Mescaline and psilocybin are naturally-occurring substances which can also be synthesized. Some of the less widely used hallucinogens occur only in natural materials such as MORNING GLORY SEEDS, NUTMEG, and certain varieties of mushrooms.

Numerous pharmaceuticals and other drugs can produce hallucinogenic reactions. Such drugs are not classified as hallucinogens, however, since the primary reaction sought from them is not a hallucinogenic one.

Hallucinogenic drugs have been in use at least 5000 years. In many parts of the world they have traditionally been used in religious and ceremonial occasions and continue to be so used today. The peyote cactus (containing mescaline) was first used by the Aztec Indians of Mexico and is still used by the American Indians of the Native American Church as a sacrament in religious ceremonies.

The Indians of Central America and Mexico have long used *Psilocyba mexicana,* a mushroom which contains the hallucinogens ocybin and psilocybin. They call it "food of the gods." It is believed that Norse tribesmen used *Amanita muscaria* mushrooms to bring on a feeling of rage before going into battle. This mushroom, also known as FLY AGARIC, contains hallucinogenic agents which produce effects similar to those induced by LSD. The word berserk comes from the bearskin shirt which these warriors wore in battle.

More recently, because many of these drugs mimic psychoses, it has been hoped that they could be beneficial in the research and treatment of various mental illnesses. But while many therapeutic claims have been made for these drugs, as yet none have proven safe or effective in the treatment of mental disorders.

Effects: Most drugs affect individuals differently depending on the amount taken, the past experience of the user, the method of administration, and whether or not the drug is used concurrently with another substance. Reactions to the hallucinogens are particularly variable and often depend on the context in which the drugs are taken and the mental condition of the user. Variations in composition and purity also contribute to the idiosyncratic effects of these drugs.

In low doses the drugs commonly alter moods and perceptions, though they do not necessarily produce hallucinations or other psychotic-like reactions. Mood changes may range from euphoria to depression. Perceptual changes may be pleasant and quasi-mystical or frightening and unpleasant. Typically, sensory perceptions are heightened. In high doses the drugs may also produce hallucinations.

The onset of the hallucinogenic experience may be fast or slow depending on the drug itself and the manner in which it is used. Duration is also variable. Occasionally the user will experience a prolonged reaction or a recurring reaction to a hallucinogen. In such cases, the effects may continue for an extended period after the drug is taken or there may be a spontaneous recurrence of the original experience weeks or even months later. The latter experience is sometimes called a FLASHBACK.

Interestingly, a user is generally aware that his experiences are distortions of reality. With some of the more powerful hallucinogens, however, he may lose all sense of reality. Though this state usually passes quickly, a few cases exist where the individuals have become permanently psychotic, perhaps from the stress of the experience or from the precipitation of an underlying schizophrenic disorder.

Physical effects of the hallucinogens are also wide ranging. Adverse effects such as headache, nausea, blurred vision, sleeplessness and dilation of the pupils are all common. Other effects include loss of appetite, increased body temperature, vomiting, lowered or raised blood pressure, decreased or increased heart or respiratory activity, trembling, dizziness, profuse perspiration and numbness of extremities. Some of the hallucinogens are also known to produce convulsions on occasion.

Though hallucinogens are relatively nontoxic—there are no known cases of death caused by heavy doses—individual psychological reactions to them can be lifethreatening. BAD TRIPS and prolonged or recurring reactions have brought on delusions which have caused serious accidents, even suicides and homicides. And though not confirmed conclusively, research suggests the LSD increases the risk of spontaneous abortion among pregnant women.

Among drug users, it is a common belief that the perceptual effects of LSD and other hallucinogens stimulate creativity. This has not been confirmed by objective studies. Studies done with marijuana have actually demonstrated that musicians when comparing recordings they made under and not under the influence of the drug rated their "straight" session better consistently.

Addictive aspects: Chronic users of hallucinogens can become psychologically dependent on these drugs, but it is generally agreed that no physical DEPENDENCE develops. Even after long use no WITHDRAWAL symptoms are known to develop when the drugs are given up. Psychological dependence is manifested by a compelling need to use the drug involved. The mental state induced by the drug becomes so much a part of the user's life that to be without it seems abnormal. Thus the user craves the mental state induced by the drug.

Tolerance: Regular use of certain hallucinogens, such as LSD, will rapidly produce tolerance but it disappears after a few days abstinence. Tolerance is not generally an issue as few people would use a drug such as LSD or mescaline on a daily basis. However, users tolerant to the effects of LSD exhibit CROSS-TOLERANCE to mescaline and to psilocybin. Tolerance to hashish and marijuana do not develop. Due to the very long half life of cannabinoids regular use leads to a state where even a *smaller* than initial dose can raise an existing steady blood level and produce the high. Regular users need less, not more to feel the effects.

Sources: Only limited amounts of certain hallucinogens are produced commercially in government-authorized laboratories for research or treatment. Most of the synthetic hallucinogens can be readily manufactured and these along with the naturally occurring hallucinogens are sold illicitly.

Traffic and control: Because they have a potential for abuse and no accepted medical benefits, most of the hallucinogens are federally regulated under Schedule I of the CONTROLLED SUBSTANCES ACT (CSA). The drugs under Schedule I are basically research substances for which there is no known or accepted medical use in the United States. They can be manufactured only in federally-regulated laboratories for research purposes. They cannot be sold by prescription. Researchers using the drugs must administer the substances directly to their subjects, although small amounts of THC have been given to cancer patients to take home for the treatment of nausea from chemotherapy.

Morning glory seeds, nutmeg, jimson weed and the like are not subject to any specific legal regulations. In some states PEYOTE is used legally by the Native American Church.

Synonyms: illusionogenics, psychedelics, psychotomimetics, psychotogenics, mind-expanding or mind-manifesting drugs, acid (refers mainly to LSD).

Samuel M. Levine, *Narcotics and Drug Abuse* (Cincinnati: the W. H. Anderson Company, 1973).

Robert J. Wicks and Jerome J. Platt, *Drug Abuse: A Criminal Justice Primer* (Beverly Hills, Cal.: Enziger Bruce & Glencoe, Inc., 1977).

hangover A condition that follows alcohol intoxication by eight to 12 hours. It is characterized by general malaise; nausea and vomiting; dizziness; dry mouth and thirst; sensitivity to movement, bright lights and loud sounds; a splitting headache; anxiety or depression. A person who is "hung over" may experience one, several, or all of the above symptoms. There are probably a number of factors involved in the cause of a hangover, but they are not completely understood. Because many of the symptoms are similar to those of hypoglycemia it is believed that lowered blood sugar may be a factor (blood glucose levels are at their lowest during a hangover). Another element may be stress reaction: the stress of intoxication is often heightened by guilt resulting from uninhibited behavior, lack of sleep, and heavy smoking. Dehydration and acidosis are also contributors to the post-intoxicated hangover state.

There is speculation that the hangover syndrome is a symptom of early withdrawal—that overdrinking has established a dependency and the body is reacting because of a need for more alcohol. Consuming alcohol ("hair of the dog that bit you") will sometimes alleviate or reverse hangover symptoms, supporting the theory that a hangover may indeed be early withdrawal. However, hangover is a general term and it is likely that small amounts of alcohol reverse the symptoms only in regular heavy drinkers and that the discomfort of occasional or light users may have a different cause. But while drinking a small amount of alcohol may correct metabolic rebound, there is a danger that it will lead to another bout of excessive drinking or simply delay the symptoms of hangover.

hard drugs, hard narcotics Opium, morphine, and cocaine, along with their derivatives, are considered by addicts to be hard narcotics. Marijuana and non-opiates, on the other hand, are called soft drugs. This dichotomy is not realistic or scientific. Soft drugs like alcohol and tobacco are likely to be more harmful over a period of time than hard drugs.

harmal *Peganum harmal,* an herb containing the psychedelic alkaloids HARMINE and HARMALINE. The plant is native to India and countries of the eastern Mediterranean.

harmaline A psychedelic alkaloid found in the herb HARMAL. It is also the active alkaloid in *Banisteriopsis caapi,* native to Peru. (See also AYAHUASCA.)

harmine A psychedelic alkaloid found in *Banisteriopsis caapi,* a plant native to the Amazon River basin. The substance is extracted by boiling pieces of the vine in water. Harmine produces reactions similar to those induced by LSD and mescaline. South American Indians use the substance in religious ceremonies and as a healing agent. (See AYAHUASCA.) Harmine is also found in the herb HARMAL, native to India and countries of the eastern Mediterranean.

Harris-Dodd Act A drug abuse control act passed in 1965 that has since been superseded. (See CONTROLLED SUBSTANCES ACT.)

Harrison Narcotic Act The first law in the United States to regulate narcotics. Passed in December 1914, it became effective in 1915 and was designed primarily to channel the flow of opium and coca leaves and their derivatives and to make their transfer a matter of record. Forms issued by the Collector of Internal Revenue were required for all transfers of the drugs between manufacturer, wholesaler, retailer and doctor. A tax was also levied on the narcotic. The act also required the registration of all those who dealt in the production or transfer of narcotics, with the exception of warehousemen and common carriers, nurses who were under a doctor's supervision, and government officials who had drugs in their possession for official duties. The Federal Bureau of Narcotics was not in existence in 1915 and enforcement of the act was carried out by the Collector of Internal Revenue and the Narcotic Unit of the Bureau of Prohibition, both agencies of the Treasury Department. Under the law the only way an unregistered person could legally possess one of these drugs was when he had obtained it through a doctor's prescription.

haschischins, Le club des A French club attended by literary men with the purpose of experimenting with hashish. It was founded in 1844 by the French novelist Theophile Gautier.

hashish From the Arabic *hashish,* "dry grass," the word "hashish" is also associated with a semi-legendary religious cult in

11th century Persia. The cult was headed by Al-Hasan ibn-al Sabbah, the so-called "Old Man of the Mountain," who lead a branch of the Isma'ili sect of Shi'ite Muslims in a number of terrorist murders committed for political and religious reasons. Known as the Hashishi, the sect has been linked to the use of hashish, though there is no concrete evidence of this. Our word "assassin" comes from the name of this sect.

Hashish is the resinous extract of the hemp plant, CANNABIS SATIVA. It is obtained by boiling the parts of the plant that are covered with resin in a solvent, or by scraping the resin from the plant. The resin, which contains the active principal TETRAHYDROCANNABINOL (THC), is then formed into cakes or lumps that range from brown to black. Hashish is a very potent form of cannabis; its THC content may range from 5–12% by weight compared with 5–10% for the most potent forms of MARIJUANA, and 1% for Mexican marijuana. An even more potent form of cannabis with a THC content of about 20–80% is known as LIQUID HASHISH (Hash Oil).

In America hashish is usually smoked, sometimes in a waterpipe which regulates the intake and cools the smoke. In North Africa hashish is smoked or eaten in a confection known as *majoon* or DAWAMESK, a sort of cake made of sugar, vanilla, almonds, pistachios, and spices, along with the hashish. In India hashish is known as *charas*.

The effects of hashish, like those of marijuana, depend a great deal on the user, on the dosage, and—in particular—on the potency of the drug. In the 19th century a group of French literary figures, including Gautier, Baudelaire, Hugo, Balzac, and de Nerval, formed a group known as LE CLUB DES HASCHISCHINS. They ingested hashish in the dawamesk form, a more unpredictable way of consuming it than smoking because it is difficult to control the dose. The effects which these men describe in their writings vary a great deal and were almost certainly linked to their individual imaginations and personalities and the atmosphere in which they took the drug. Gautier had hallucinations of "hybrid creatures, formless mixtures of men, beasts, and utensils; monks with wheels for feet and cauldrons for bellies," while Baudelaire saw "an exquisite harmony of proportion . . . through space." The effects experienced by most users are quite similar to those produced by smoking potent marijuana. Large amounts of ingested hashish, on the other hand, can lead to such a degree of intoxication that extreme perceptual distortion and anxiety may result. Psychotic episodes rarely last for more than 48 hours after the hashish has been ingested. While it is true that hashish may bring on psychotic episodes, it may also be the case that it does so only in those who already have shown signs of potentially psychotic behavior (antecedent psychopathology) before taking any drugs or those who are idiosyncratically sensitive to the drug.

A typical American hashish user is white, male, aged 18–25, with some college education. Use is limited almost exclusively to those who also use marijuana. In spite of its relative scarcity, use of hashish is increasing in the U.S. because of a growing preference for higher potency cannabis.

Classification: Hashish is a very potent form of CANNABIS SATIVA. Marijuana and all other cannabis drugs come from this one species, but different varieties and different growing climates affect the potency. Hashish, which is the resin of the upper leaves and flowering tops of the female plant, is usually produced from plants grown in areas of fairly high altitude and high temperature because they tend to produce a greater amount of resin. The principal psychoactive ingredient in all forms of cannabis is Delta-9 Tetrahydrocannabinol, or THC, found in the resin on the undersurface of the flowers and leaves. Hashish is classified as a hallucinogen (a Schedule I classification under the CONTROLLED SUBSTANCE ACT).

Effects: The effects may include distorted perception, depersonalization or "double consciousness," spatial and time distortions, intensification of scents, tastes, colors, and sounds, and visual hallucinations. The effects are similar to those produced by marijuana, but usually they are more intense because of the higher potency of hashish.

Addictive aspects: Hashish is not physically addictive, and withdrawal symptoms are non-specific. Psychological dependence is a danger; this has been seen primarily in North Africa and India where use is quite heavy but infrequently in the U.S.

Tolerance: Tolerance to hashish does not develop. Due to high blood levels of THC someone who has smoked hashish regularly will need a smaller dose to achieve the same "high."

Sources: Most of the hashish in the U.S. is smuggled in from Morocco, Nepal, Pakistan, Afghanistan and Lebanon. The principal suppliers of marijuana to the U.S. market, Colombia, Mexico and Jamaica, do not produce significant quantities of hashish. This is probably due to differences in the amounts of resin produced by the plants in different climates (more resin is produced in dry areas at high altitudes) and to cultural and traditional practices.

Traffic and control: The use of hashish in the U.S. is apparently on the rise but it is difficult to estimate how much is being used because seizures by the authorities fluctuate widely from year to year: from 700 pounds in 1970 to over 50,000 pounds in 1973–74, for example. Although most seizures are relatively small, one large seizure will completely change the figures for a given year. In 1978, for instance, 2,999 pounds were seized; but in 1979 a total of 43,233 pounds were taken which included one huge seizure of 41,676 pounds of suspected Lebanese hashish from a ship off Sandy Hook, New Jersey. In May 1988, the Drug Enforcement Administration seized a record amount of 75,000 pounds in San Francisco.

Synonyms: hash, Goma de Mota, soles, charas.

Hawaiian wood rose, baby A plant, native to Hawaii and Asia, whose seeds contain lysergic acid amide. When eaten they produce psychedelic effects similar to but milder than LSD.

Hawaiian wood rose, large Similar to HAWAIIAN WOOD ROSE, BABY but only half as potent.

head shop Head shops, which have sprung up across the country in recent years (there are an estimated 15,000 to 30,000), sell assorted drug paraphernalia. Their stock includes everything from roach clips and water pipes to hypodermic syringes and cocaine spoons. They also carry publications which give advice on drugs to buy and how much to pay, and others that provide gardening tips on how to grow your own marijuana and mushrooms. They sell kits to convert street cocaine to FREEBASE that can be smoked and that will produce a more intense high than when it is snorted. Not only are head shops a place to make contacts for the purchase of an illicit drug, they also sell certain uncontrolled drugs. Butyl nitrite, which is technically not a drug and is usually sold as a room deodorizer, is sold as an inhalant. It is a vasodilator which expands blood vessels and produces a three to five minute "high." The Food and Drug Administration has no control over this substance and it is sold in head shops under such tradenames as "Bullet" and "Rush." (See FAKE COKE.)

The increase in drug abuse among adolescents may be due in part to the prevalence of head shops. They are, in fact, "learning centers" for inexperienced users and handy shopping centers for experienced ones. The existence of head shops is a continuation of the casual public attitude toward drug use. Children who start out using marijuana, as most do, can go to a head shop to purchase a roach clip and come away with a knowledge of much harder drugs.

Head shops not only sell paraphernalia, they glamorize, condone and advocate the use of drugs. The head shop business is turning into a multi-million dollar industry. Some states have attempted to control the sale of drug paraphernalia, but their laws are usually ineffective. In response to the need for legislation, the Drug Enforcement Administration has drafted a Model Drug Paraphernalia Act. It will cover the control of all equipment, products and materials of any kind which are used, intended for use, or designated for use in planting, propagating, cultivating, growing, harvesting, manufacturing, compounding, converting, producing, processing, preparing, testing, analyzing, packaging, repackaging, storing, containing, concealing, injecting, ingesting, inhaling, or otherwise introducing into the body a controlled substance in violation of the Controlled Substances Act. The act will further amend the offenses and penalties section of the Controlled Substances Act to cover the possession of such drug paraphernalia. It has been successfully adopted by a number of municipalities and states and is being considered by others.

health care professionals and addiction By some estimates, as many as one in eight physicians is or will be chemically addicted. The percentages among other health care professionals are believed to be equally high. Some theorize that this phenomenon is due to medical workers' constant exposure and easy access to addictive substances.

In 1972, the American Medical Association (AMA) launched the "impaired physician movement" in a special study that called on doctors to report debilitated colleagues and recommended state and local medical societies oversee treatment. Today, all 50 state medical societies have impaired-physicians committees. Nurses, dentists and other professional groups have followed suit.

The AMA currently lists 124 programs to which doctors are referred by state committees, including many that specialize in medical addicts. The AMA estimates that roughly 85% to 90% of impaired physicians stay "clean" for at least two years after treatment. A recent Mayo Clinic study put the recovery rate at 83%.

Some critics say there is still too much denial on the subject among professionals and urge more candor about the problem, beginning with frank discussion in medical schools. As a result, the rehabilitation of addicted health care professionals has become a significant sub-specialty of the drug-treatment field.

David Gelman, Andrew Murr and Regina Elam, "Docs in Need of Detox," *Newsweek,* May 29, 1989, 61–62.

heart A muscular organ which rhythmically contracts and relaxes to pump the blood throughout the body. The heart is one of the body's most complex organs and it is susceptible to temporary and permanent damage from a variety of causes.

Heart disease does not necessarily result from drug abuse, although most toxic substances do affect heart action in some way. LSD and other hallucinogens can cause temporary tachycardia (increase heart rate) as well as occasional bradycardia (lowered heart rate). One of the most consistent physical effects of smoking marijuana is increased heartbeat, possibly caused by increased secretion of epinephrine, a hormone which stimulates the heart. Marijuana-induced tachycardia usually peaks about 15 minutes after the drug is smoked and subsides almost completely while psychological effects are still noted. The rate increase correlates directly to dosage and, with large doses of THC, the heartbeat can almost double. Pulse rate was once considered an effective gauge of how much marijuana a subject had smoked, but the theory has been discarded since the heartbeat is affected by so many other factors. Tolerance to the tachycardia will occur in chronic users. Very high doses of THC in sequence will change the tachycardia to a bradycardia due to tolerance development.

Inhalation of aerosols and volatile solvents may cause death from cardiac arrest. Trichlorethane and the fluorohydrocarbons, especially, exhibit strong toxic effects on the myocardium (heart muscle) and can produce cardiac arrhythmia and edema (fluid accumulation) in the heart and other organs. Necrosis, fatty degeneration of the heart, liver and adrenal glands, and myocarditis, inflammation of the heart muscle, have resulted from abuse of these drugs.

In the past AMYL NITRITE, a depressant inhalant was often prescribed to relieve chest pain associated with heart problems such as angina pectoris. It increases the heart rate considerably by dilating the blood vessels and relaxing the smooth heart muscle. The inhalant enjoys widespread but decreasing recreational use, primarily to enhance and prolong sexual pleasure.

Heroin and other narcotics generally reduce heart rate, although vast fluctuations can occur during heroin withdrawal. Moreover, heroin addiction exposes the heart, as well as the liver, to diseases which are attributable to the method of administration rather than to the drug itself. Endocarditis, an infectious inflammation of the heart's inner lining and valves, usually occurs in addicts with some history of heart problems and is caused by staphylococcus and other antibiotic-resistant bacteria and fungi. (Endocarditis that occurs in non-users is usually caused by a variety of streptococcus.) Antibiotics are used in the treatment of this disease, which is characterized by nodules on the edges of the heart valves. Scarring impairs valve function, blood clots can develop, and fatal congestive heart failure can result. The disease has a high mortality rate when its development follows drug injection.

Using unclean needles also makes heroin addicts susceptible to tetanus, which creates an imbalance in the autonomous nervous system and consequent cardiac instability. Disruption of heart rhythm regulation can lead to cardiac arrest.

Stimulants such as cocaine and amphetamines obviously increase heart rate and can expose users to the risk of heart disease. Amphetamines have the added effect of strengthening myocardial contraction. Cardiac arrhythmia occurs with these drugs in direct proportion to their overall toxicity, and cardiac arrest is a frequent result of their abuse.

Of the stimulants, nicotine is certainly the most widely publicized and effective substance in inducing heart disease and other circulatory damage. Including such conditions as coronary artery disease, arteriosclerosis, and hypertension, heart disease accounts for more than 50% of deaths related to smoking cigarettes.

Nicotine mimics acetylcholine, blocking the impulses that acetylcholine normally transmits, and affecting nerve synapses to produce greater excitability. These effects combine with nicotine's release of ephinephrine to overwork the heart—stimulating it without providing for the return of additional blood to the organ.

Epinephrine stimulated by nicotine also releases fatty acids into the blood, and one of the major risks of heavy smoking is the early development of coronary heart disease (CHD), a progression of arteriosclerosis consisting of an accumulation of fats in the lining of the large to medium-sized arteries to the heart. Coronary heart disease claims almost a million Americans each year, and smokers are twice as likely as non-smokers to die from it.

Studies have indicated that the risk of coronary heart disease in the non-smoking population can sometimes be lowered by very light consumption of alcohol (up to one ounce a day). Alcohol increases levels of high density lipoproteins (HDL) which break up cholesterol deposits in the arteries. Heavy alcohol consumption, however, does not have this beneficial effect and instead increases the likelihood of sudden death from CHD and alcoholic myocarditis.

Alcoholics commonly suffer from hypertension (high blood pressure) but this condition cannot be attributed solely to alcohol use; like alcoholism itself, it frequently results from stress. Long-term chronic consumption of alcohol can cause alcoholic cardiomyopathy, a disease of the heart muscle associated with coronary artery disease, in which the organ becomes large and flabby and inefficient in its action. Ethanol, or more precisely its metabolite, acetaldehyde, directly depresses myocardial function and damages mitochondria (as in the liver). Symptoms of cardiomyopathy include difficulty in breathing, swelling of the feet and ankles, fatigue, palpitations and chest pain. Heart failure can follow. Alcoholism and malnutrition combine to produce heart disease which involves thiamine deficiency.

Chronic alcoholism can also combine with previous heart trouble to produce irregular heartbeat. Because cardiac arrhythmias can also involve previously unaffected nonalcoholic individuals during binges of heavy drinking (with an especially high incidence during the Christmas season), it is frequently referred to as the "holiday heart syndrome." Abstinence eliminates the problem.

The combination of the heavy use of alcohol and other drugs—marijuana, for example—is especially dangerous because the cumulative effect can tax the organ past its capacity.

Daniel & Dorothy Girdano, *Drugs—A Factual Account* (Reading, Ma.: Addison-Wesley Publishing Co., 1973).

Frederick G. Hofmann, *A Handbook on Drug and Alcohol Abuse, The Biomedical Aspects* (New York: Oxford University Press, 1975).

Ralph W. Richter, editor, *Medical Aspects of Drug Abuse* (Hagerstown, Md.: Harper & Row, 1975).

heavy drinker One who drinks in excess of the normal limits of moderation as defined by his or her society.

hedonistic A term meaning "pleasure-seeking" that is often used to describe the motivations of chronic drug users. There is little justification for this as addicts generally use drugs to alleviate discomfort.

heliotrope A plant of the genus *Heliotropium*. There are claims that when the flowers are brewed as a tea they can produce a tranquilizing effect.

hemochromatosis A condition that involves excess deposits of iron in the body tissues which can cause extensive damage. The cause of this relatively uncommon disorder is not known, though alcoholism is associated with many cases. It can be a cause of CIRRHOSIS, and has been found to be prevalent among heavy and chronic users of wine that contains a large amount of iron.

henbane *Hyoscyamus niger*, a fetid Old World herb. Its leaves yield an extract containing hyoscyamine that has properties similar to belladona.

hepatitis An inflammation of the liver that occurs frequently in alcoholics and in addicts who administer drugs with dirty syringes. In the case of alcoholics the inflammation is due to the alcohol and usually subsides quickly (see LIVER). Intravenous drug users get hepatitis from viruses. This type is contagious and can be much more serious causing permanent liver damage or death.

hepatoma A cellular cancer that affects the liver and is often associated with CIRRHOSIS. It is also known as hepatocarcinoma.

herbals Certain plants were dried and used as medicinal agents before modern medicine emerged. The herbals are now enjoying renewed interest along with the movement toward natural foods. Some herbals have psychoactive effects while some are inert and can be used as teas. Potentially toxic herbals include poke root and ginseng preparations. Instances of lead and pyrolizidine poisoning have been reported.

heredity The sum of qualities and potentialities that are genetically handed down through families.

Studies using natural and adopted children have been made to try to determine whether environment or genetics causes a predisposition to alcoholism. The results strongly suggest that a vulnerability to alcoholism is inherited. It is a recognized fact that alcoholism is common in certain families and studies point to both genetic and environmental factors. In addition, it has been shown that inherited traits may ward off alcoholism; possibly because of excessive production of acetaldehyde in the metabolic process (Orientals show a low incidence of alcoholism and a high level of acetaldehyde). Although heredity may play a primary role, it is generally agreed that other factors are also involved for the development of alcoholism.

Several studies have been conducted to determine the genetic or heredity susceptibility to drugs other than alcohol, but they are as yet inconclusive.

There are numerous drugs that pass through the placenta during pregnancy and reach the unborn child, including alcohol, THC, nicotine, heroin, methadone and morphine. Some of these drugs also enter the mother's milk. Babies are likely to go through WITHDRAWAL SYMPTOMS at birth if the mother is a chronic user of narcotic drugs. Long-term effects on babies born with withdrawal symptoms are inconclusive, and there is an obvious need for further research in the field. Studies indicate babies born to methadone maintained mothers are small and slow at birth but "catch up" in approximately 3 years. Whether babies addicted at birth are more apt to develop addiction is unknown. (See also PREGNANCY.)

heroin A narcotic, diacetylmorphine, derived from morphine, which it greatly resembles. Heroin is a central nervous system depressant that also relieves pain. It was developed in 1898 by the Bayer Company in Germany. Found to be more potent than morphine, its name comes from the German word *heroisch* (powerful, heroic). Originally the drug was considered a better analgesic than morphine, a more efficient cough suppressant and a non-addictive cure for morphine and opium withdrawal symptoms. It took some 12 years for the medical profession to realize that heroin was at least as addictive as morphine.

The Harrison Narcotic Act of 1914 was the first attempt to control the use of heroin medically. By 1924 its manufacture in the United States was prohibited and law enforcement agencies were made responsible for its control. Nevertheless, more than 20 years went by before all existing stocks on hand were surrendered. The dangers involved in heroin use became recognized worldwide, and by 1963 it was used medically in only five countries and manufactured in only three.

Meanwhile, heroin was steadily replacing opium and morphine on the street. An international black market with underground laboratories and well-organized smuggling operations grew rapidly. Two things made such operations fairly easy—the comparatively simple chemical equipment needed to convert morphine to heroin, and the reduced bulk of heroin compared to morphine.

Appearance: Pure heroin is a white, crystalline powder with a bitter taste. It is soluble in water. Until recent years, most of the heroin smuggled into the United States was supplied from Southeast Asian opium sources and was converted to heroin in clandestine laboratories in the area of Marseilles, France. After this supply was curtailed (see GOLDEN TRIANGLE), production of the drug increased in Mexico, which remained the major source for several years. Simpler, faster methods than those used in Marseilles resulted in impurities, which gave the Mexican heroin a brown color.

Effects: Heroin depresses the central nervous system in a way similar to alcohol and barbiturates but, unlike those drugs, it also relieves pain. While abuse of alcohol and barbiturates can increase belligerent behavior by removing inhibitions, heroin acts to depress aggression as well as appetite and sexual drive. Other effects include constipation and suppression of the coughing reflex. Depending on the method of administration, heroin induces varying degrees of euphoria; orgasmic reactions have been reported to follow intravenous injection. After a ''fix'' a sense of well-being replaces feelings of depression or low self-esteem and this is followed by a semiconscious dreamy state—''going on the nod.''

Administration: Addicts usually inject (''shoot up'' or ''mainline'') heroin into a vein. Although it can also be mixed with a liquid and swallowed, sniffed like cocaine, placed under the tongue, and even smoked—as it was occasionally in Vietnam where it was cheap, potent and plentiful—these methods of administration are rarely used by addicts in the U.S. This is because of the high cost of the drug; addicts need a number of fixes a day and want the maximum effect from their supply. Also, heroin has a disagreeable taste and the ''rush'' that addicts crave (an intense feeling similar to orgasm) only follows intravenous injection.

Many people ''sniff'' in an attempt to avoid becoming addicted. The cautious first-time user who tries swallowing or sniffing heroin often graduates to ''skin popping'' or ''joy popping'' (subcutaneous injection of heroin) but the effects are comparatively mild and there is no ''rush.'' Some users continue at this level, sniffing or skin popping, trying to avoid addiction. However many ''sniffers'' and ''skinpoppers,'' become addicted. Most people who become addicted have gone on to mainlining already.

Before preparing the powder for injection the user measures out what he thinks is his usual dose. This can be difficult to estimate because the heroin sold on the street has been adulterated (diluted or ''cut'') many times as it passes down the line from the large distributor to the street pusher. Since an epidemic of malaria among addicts in the 1940s, QUININE has often been used to cut heroin. Quinine also enhances the ''rush'' effect and gives heroin diluted with milk sugar a bitter taste. Other adulterants include mannitol (a mild laxative) and milk sugar. Talcum powder is sometimes used as an adulterant and can be extremely dangerous because it does not dissolve in the bloodstream.

To prepare an injection the addict dilutes the heroin powder in a little water, puts it into a spoon or other device known as a ''cooker'' and holds it over a match, candle, cigarette lighter or other single flame until the mixture has boiled for a few seconds. After the liquid is filtered through a piece of cotton to remove any solid impurities and drawn up into a syringe or medicine dropper attached to a hollow needle, it is ready for injection.

If the user is skin popping, the needle is pushed under the skin in any convenient place; if mainlining, the usual area that is chosen is the large vein inside the elbow. A tourniquet is applied between the vein and the heart, the needle is inserted and the syringe is pulled up to draw blood (a step called ''verifying'' or ''registering'') to make sure the needle is in a vein and not in muscle tissue or flesh. The bulb or syringe is then pushed down to inject the heroin and the rush follows immediately. Some users employ the process of BOOTING to prolong the initial effects. When heroin is booted, a small amount is injected and then blood is withdrawn back into the syringe and the process is repeated.

Dangers of heroin use: Abcesses at the site of the injection are common and the preferred vein may inflame after repeated use. Veins in the thigh, wrist or foot may then be used. Addicts who have run out of usable veins may resort to skin popping and end up covered with sores. One of the great dangers in mainlining is the chance of hitting an artery instead of a vein. The result is extreme pain at best, and permanent necrosis and scarring of the arm or leg at worst. Infection from unsterile needles is an ever-present danger. Along with abcesses, serum hepatitis, tetanus, and endocarditis (infection of the heart lining) can also occur as well as HIV virus caused by sharing dirty needles. While numerous studies have indicated that heroin is not physiologically harmful, and does not cause brain deterioration, it is characteristic of addicts to neglect their health. Because the drug suppresses hunger, malnutrition is common and chronic bronchitis often develops as a result of suppression of the cough reflex. Addicts are also prone to accidents and violent death, living as they often do in contact with the underworld that controls the distribution of heroin. Many must become small-time pushers themselves to earn their own supply.

The greatest danger of heroin use is death from what the media calls an overdose. Actually, the heroin sold on the street has been adulterated so much the addict is unlikely to get a large enough amount to suppress respiration. Most deaths are due to what medical examiners now call acute reactions. These include hypersensitivity with pulmonary edema, infections, complications associated with the adulterants used and the combination of heroin with alcohol or barbiturates (see SYNDROME X). In New York City on February 4th, 1991 it was reported that at least a dozen heroin addicts had been killed by a batch of heroin that contained the tranquilizer methyl fentanyl that made it 27 times more powerful than heroin alone.

Heroin and pregnancy: Women addicts run a high risk of complications during pregnancy and childbirth. The most common medical problems are anemia, heart disease, hepatitis and pneumonia. Children born to addicted mothers have a significantly higher mortality rate, are smaller than average and often show signs of acute infection. Some are also born physically addicted because they develop varying degrees of withdrawal symptoms within a short time after birth and require detoxification.

Tolerance: Tolerance to heroin builds rapidly and stronger doses and more frequent shots are needed to produce the effects craved. Some addicts inject ''speedballs'' (heroin and amphetamines or cocaine), increasing the danger of acute reactions and death. Unlike barbiturates, virtually unlimited tolerance to heroin can build up; but there is still always a lethal dosage. Tolerance to heroin carries over to other opiates (all drugs derived from opium) as well as to opioids (synthetic drugs that resemble opium alkaloids and their derivatives).

Dependence: Both psychological and physical dependence develop rapidly with regular use of heroin. In psychological dependence there is an uncontrollable craving for the drug's effects. In physical dependence the body comes to rely on the drug to avoid withdrawal sickness.

Withdrawal symptoms: Although withdrawal symptoms from heroin are neither as severe nor as dangerous as those associated with depressants, especially barbiturates, they are bad enough. Their severity depends on several factors—how long an addiction has lasted, how frequently a fix is needed, the general state of health, and whether withdrawal is forced or voluntary. The first symptoms are usually noticed just before the time for the next regular shot. They include restless sleep, gooseflesh (from quitting ''cold turkey''), tremors, yawning, irritability, joint and muscle pains, abdominal cramps, chills alternating with profuse sweating, runny nose, nausea, vomiting, diarrhea, urinary incontinence, shortness of breath, and muscle spasms (''kicking the habit''). Reactions usually peak in a few days and linger for about one week. Although physical withdrawal symptoms subside in a week or so, psychological craving can continue for months and even years, making treatment difficult and causing many addicts to resume their habits. A protracted abstinence syndrome has been observed in which for many months addicts experience sleep disturbance, anxiety and physical discomfort.

Treatment: Treatment for heroin addiction other than simple detoxification has changed greatly in recent years. Long-term residential centers (Daytop, Synanon, Phoenix House), now modified to address the problems of multiple drug use, including alcohol, still exist and are the most restrictive and longest duration treatments. Shorter term residential programs of one to three months are becoming more common and are structured similarly to alcohol rehabilitation centers providing detoxification, education and the development of habits, skills, and strategies useful in recovery. An approach based on a chemical dependency, not a single substance dependency, is becoming more accepted as most ex-heroin users have been found to develop problems with alcohol. Methadone maintenance provides opiate addicts with a long acting, orally administered, affordable and, when administered properly, non-intoxicating dose of a prescribed narcotic. For a portion of patients treated it is effective. By breaking the drug procuring cycle it has been useful in allowing people to lead stable, productive lives. Another portion of patients use methadone for a short period of time and then detoxify. For many patients the results are less positive and they remain drug involved, with chaotic lives and all the attendant risks. The factors in selecting good candidates for methadone and how best to use it (i.e.: how much and what types of counseling and other services to provide) remain obscure and are often debated.

Who uses heroin?: There are now an estimated 1.5 million heroin users in America. Heroin-related deaths increased 18% between 1981 and 1988, when 1,100 people in the U.S. died from the drug. Although once concentrated in metropolitan areas, heroin use has spread to all levels of society from the inner city ghettos to the prosperous suburbs. Narcotics have become a problem on college campuses and in rural as well as city high schools. No class, race, educational level or community is free from the problems of heroin abuse. The major, most visible social evils and criminal activities, however, are found in large cities. A heroin habit is expensive: in one city it was estimated to average $10,000 a year. For the addict who must support his habit through theft this means stealing some $50,000 worth of goods because they can be fenced for only one-fifth their value. Heroin addicts are not apt to commit violent crimes (bartiburate users have the highest rate) but many have been found to have criminal records before they become dependent on drugs.

In 1989, however, users started to snort cocaine, a stimulant, and then quickly snort heroin—the "smoke speedball." Authorities say the speedball has the potential for catching on with white-collar drug addicts.

Traffic and control: Heroin is listed in Schedule I of the Controlled Substances Act of 1970 as a drug most susceptible to abuse. It is completely illicit in the U.S. and it is not considered to have any medical value. Its manufacture, importation and use are illegal but in spite of strenuous control efforts a black market flourishes. When the manufacture and smuggling of heroin from Southeast Asia through Marseilles, the well-known FRENCH CONNECTION, was curtailed many operations shifted to Mexico. Between 1986 and 1988 the amount of Mexican heroin entering the U.S. doubled, according to the National Narcotics Intelligence Consumers Committee. Most of the heroin supplying the U.S. market today comes from Southwest Asia (see GOLDEN CRESCENT). It has enjoyed great success because it is more potent and less expensive than heroin from Southeast Asia.

Smuggling by land and by sea is very difficult to control. When enforcement efforts are increased in one border area or seaport, drug smugglers quickly switch to another. The profits of the illicit drug trade

History of Heroin

1874	**Heroin is isolated from morphine.**
1898	**Bayer Company of Germany produces heroin commercially and it is found to be more potent than morphine.**
1900	**Heroin is recognized as being addictive, though it was originally thought to be a cure for opium and morphine addiction. U.S. authorities estimate 250,000 to 1 million users.**
1914	**Harrison Narcotics Act taxes manufacture, importation and distribution of heroin.**
1924	**Manufacture is prohibited in the U.S. and heroin becomes available on the black market.**
1930s	**Abuse becomes widespread and the French Connection becomes main supplier of U.S. market until broken up in 1973.**
1965	**Drs. Dole and Nyswander present methadone maintenance program to treat heroin addiction.**
1970	**Controlled Substances Act classifies heroin as a Schedule I drug.**
1980s	**Government authorities estimate 400–750,000 users in U.S. Southwest Asia becomes the major supplier.**
1990s	**Government authorities estimate 1.5 million users in U.S. Heroin-related hospital emergencies rose 9.5% from 1987 to 1988.**

are so great that the risk of being caught is disregarded and others are always waiting to take the place of those arrested. To make things more difficult, world-wide organized crime is deeply involved in heroin manufacture, smuggling and distribution as well as in prostitution and in the sort of crimes which many users must commit to support their habits.

Synonyms: H, big H, horse, Harry, hairy, junk, joy powder, Mexican brown or mud, smack, white stuff, thing.

Edward M. Brecher, ed., *Licit and Illicit Drugs* (Boston: Little, Brown and Company, 1972).

Sidney Cohen, *The Substance Abuse Problems* (New York: The Haworth Press, 1981).

"Facts About Opiates" (Toronto, Canada: Addiction Research Foundation, 1980).

Richard R. Lingeman, *Drugs from A to Z* (New York: McGraw-Hill Book Company, 1974), 101–112.

Jack Margolis, *Complete Book of Recreational Drugs* (Los Angeles: Price/Stern/Sloan Publishers, Inc., 1978), 227–231.

Mike McQueen, "Heroin Cracks Cocaine Market," *USA Today*, July 7, 1989, 3A.

hexane A major volatile solvent that is found in plastic cement. (See INHALANTS.)

hexobarbitol A short-acting BARBITURATE. Its rapid onset and short duration of action makes it undesirable for purposes of abuse. It is sold under the trade name Sombulex.

high Being under the influence of a drug. The term usually refers to a state of pleasurable intoxication and drug euphoria. A "high" associated with alcohol is often expressed by uninhibited behavior which borders on or lapses into the irresponsible. It is an ironic effect of the sedative nature of the drug that the "high" phase actually involves sedation of those areas of the bran that would normally guard against abnormal behavior by producing inhibitions. The high induced by such stimulants as amphetamines or cocaine is actually the opposite of a high produced by alcohol.

high blood pressure Also referred to as HYPERTENSION. A number of studies have linked high blood pressure to heavy alcohol consumption.

hippie A member of the nonconformist social movement of the mid to late 1960s, often referred to as the "counterculture." The hippie subculture developed in the Haight-Ashbury section of San Francisco and in New York City on the Lower East Side.

Hippies rejected many of the predominant values of mainstream American culture, which they characterized as "The Establishment." Emphasis was laid on pacifism, communal living and rejection of material ambitions. Non-conformist modes of dress were encouraged, including long hair and beads. The use of drugs, particularly hallucinogens, was advocated by hippies as a means of increased awareness.

histamine A compound found in human tissue and highly concentrated in the skin, lungs and stomach. It is responsible for the dilation and increased permeability of blood vessels and plays a major role in allergic reactions. It is also a potent stimulator of gastric acid secretion. Release of histamine occurs very quickly after an intravenous injection of heroin, morphine or codeine and can cause intense itching, sometimes over the entire body. Histamine can also cause a reddening of the eyes and a fall in blood pressure. The latter can result in dizziness and sometimes shock.

holiday heart syndrome An irregularity or disturbance in the heart (arrhythmia) which can occur after a period of heavy alcohol consumption. (See also HEART.)

holistic medicine A medical approach that deals with a patient's whole complex of needs rather than just treating a diseased or malfunctioning part of the body. Along with traditional bio-medical techniques and nutrition, holistic medicine employs exercise plans, diet regimes, methods of self-healing, and suggests different, less stressful ways of living. Frequently several teams of health care workers are involved in a patient's treatment.

homicide See CRIME.

homosexuals The needs of homosexual chemically dependent individuals are being specifically addressed in certain specialized treatment centers. Historically much was written about elevated rates of chemical dependency among gay and lesbian individuals, but these previous "statistics" were established by self-report surveys and by observing treatment populations. There are no valid statistics on what percentage of the population is homosexual. Currently most authorities agree that homosexuals may have more difficulty accessing treatment and may have socially complicated recoveries. Whether homosexuals have higher rates of chemical dependency than other groups is not known. The *Pride Institute* in Minnesota is a valuable resource for information and referral sources for gay and lesbian individuals.

hormone A body chemical secreted into the bloodstream by the endocrine glands, and which brings about specific effects in tissues throughout the body.

hormones, male sex See SEX.

hot lines Telephone numbers that can be called for information and help. They are often toll-free and generally operate on a 24-hour basis. Hotlines cover a wide range of problems—from battered women, runaways and child abuse to mental health and drug problems. Some are very specific, such as the cocaine hotline and the number for Alcholics Anonymous.

Hughes Act The act that established the National Institute on Alcohol Abuse and Alcoholism in 1970. This federal legislation was named after its sponsor, Senator Harold Hughes.

Hycodan® (Endo) A narcotic antitussive for cough relief that contains hydrocodone bitartrate (a CODEINE derivative) and homatropine methylbromide. It has a potential for abuse and can produce drug dependence. When used with alcohol or other central nervous system depressants it can have an additive effect. Overdosage can result in depressed respiration, somnolence and muscle flaccidity; with extreme overdosage cardiac arrest and death may occur. It is supplied in white scored tablets and as a cherry-flavored syrup.

Hycomine© (Endo) A narcotic antitussive for cough relief. It contains hydrocodone bitartrate (a CODEINE derivative) and phenylpropanolamine for nasal congestion. It has the potential for abuse and can produce dependence. Hycomine is supplied as an orange fruit-flavored syrup. Hycomine-Pediatric is a green fruit-flavored syrup.

hydrocodone A synthetic CODEINE derivative that is used as an antitussive. It is a Schedule II drug. (See HYCODAN.)

hydromorphone A semisynthetic MORPHINE derivative. Used as an analgesic, its potency exceeds that of morphine. (See DILAUDID.)

hyoscine, hyoscyamine See SCOPOLAMINE.

hyperactive A condition of excessive or pathological activity, most often seen in young children. It is also called attention deficit disorder (ADD). Stimulant drugs are sometimes used in the treatment of children and adults with ADD. Their hyperactivity is characterized by constantly moving, handling, touching, and otherwise drawing attention (usually critical) to themselves. It seems paradoxical that stimulants can be helpful in a condition where hyperactivity is present, but studies have shown that the use of stimulants can decrease aggressive behavior and hyperactivity and improve concentration and attention. Since a deficit in concentration may be the cause of the hyperactivity this improvement in concentration may be the key action of the stimulant. This use of stimulants is controversial, however, and some authorities suggest that hyperactivity may be due to situational or personality factors, and that stimulants may aggravate the condition they were prescribed to alleviate. It has also been suggested that use of stimulants may condition children to psychotropic drug use in later years, but this has not been proven. Adequate treatment of ADD may actually reduce probability of later chemical dependancy.

hyperglycemia Unusually high blood sugar level.

hypertension High blood pressure. This condition has been associated with excessive consumption of alcohol. PCP, cocaine and amphetamines produce temporary hypertension.

hypnosis In recent years hypnosis has gained popularity as a way of controlling habits, particularly among smokers. Originally identified with the work of Anton Mesmer in the 1770s, hypnosis gained a certain respectability in 1843 when James Braid published a book entitled *Neurypnology* which served to remove the taint of "occultism" from the procedure. Hypnosis has been questioned right up to the present, however. Today it is recognized as a process, not a therapy, but one that can be successfully utilized in combination with therapy.

The recent popularity of hypnosis has led to an increase in untrained and incompetent practitioners entering the field, which has caused the American Society of Clinical Hypnosis and the International Society of Hypnosis to take a strong stand against unskilled hypnotists. Lacking training, they are unaware of the importance of trance states and there can be untoward and possibly dangerous consequences.

(Hypnosis also refers to sleep, and drugs that produce sleep are called HYPNOTICS.)

hypnotic A drug used to induce sleep. Hypnotics slow down the action of the central nervous system. This group of drugs includes BARBITURATES and nonbarbiturates.

hypodermic administration See ADMINISTRATION.

hypoglycemia Low blood sugar level. This condition is occasionally seen in alcoholics.

hypotension Abnormally low blood pressure. Hypotension may be caused by drugs, especially narcotics, sedatives or diuretics.

I

iatrogenic addiction Addiction to a drug that has resulted from the drug being prescribed by a physician for medical purposes.

ibogaine A psychedelic alkaloid found in the roots, stems and leaves of *Tabernanthe Iboga,* and also in the plants *Peschiera lundii, Stemmademia donnellsmithi, S. galleottiama* and *Conopharyngia durissma* which are native to Africa, Asia and South America. It has hallucinogenic effects similar to those of LSD and it is also a STIMULANT. The alkaloid was isolated in 1901 and synthesized in 1966. Iboga extracts, or ibogaine, are still sold in Europe in tonics and stimulants. Used in Africa by hunters stalking game, iboga has the effect of allowing the user to remain motionless for long periods of time while remaining conscious and mentally alert. Indian tribes in South America use iboga in a rite of passage into adulthood and it is known as the Ordeal Bean.

ice Like crack, ice is not a new drug but a smokable version of an old one—crystallized methamphetamine, better known as "crystal meth" and "speed" during the 1960s and 1970s, when it was usually taken as pills or injected. Injected methamphetamine abuse is still reported to be high in California. The first appearance of ice in the U.S. was in Hawaii (1989), where it sells for around $50 in cellophane packets ("paper") that contain about a tenth of a gram, good for one or two "hits." But smoking ice provides users a high that usually lasts eight hours or more. This compared with the brief (less than 30 minutes) high for crack cocaine. Ice is as addictive as crack and produces similar bouts of severe depression and paranoia, as well as convulsions. It is possible that prolonged stimulant use can result in long-lasting psychological damage. Other side effects: aggressive behavior, hallucinations, and fatal kidney failure.

Ice has become Hawaii's No. 1 drug problem. It is smuggled in from illegal labs in South Korea and the Philippines. Methamphetamine is produced in clandestine labs across the U.S., especially in California, Oregon, and Texas. Ice was reported to be making serious inroads in the U.S. and some officials predicted it would soon outstrip crack cocaine in overall use. This possible epidemic is as of yet difficult to document and may not occur. The fact that methamphetamine already exists in the U.S. in a relatively cheap and available form (pills and "crystal") may make ice less of a marketing phenomenon than crack.

Hawaii's ice trail can be traced back to South Korea (where it's called *hiroppon*), which, along with Taiwan, leads the world in the manufacture and export of the drug. Koreans learned about methamphetamine from the Japanese, who invented the stimulant in 1893. Japan banned use of the drug they call *shabu* in the 1950s, and though use in recent years has leveled off in that country, it remains the drug's largest market.

The little that is known about ice's effects on newborns is alarming. As with cocaine babies, ice babies tend to be irritable and have difficulty with early bonding. Some have severe tremors and cry for 24 hours without stopping; they have to be swaddled to be held.

Most clinics are treating ice addiction as they would cocaine and other stimulant addiction but report that ice addiction is proving more difficult to "kick."

illusions Distorted or mistaken perceptions that differ from hallucinations and delusions because they always involve the distortion of external stimulus patterns. Illusions may be of various sorts and include distortions of space, perspective and movement. For a person suffering from illusions, a crack in a wall may, for example, be seen as a crawling snake.

impairment A term used to describe both short and long-term damage to an individual caused by the use of drugs. A drug may interfere with an individual's ability to function in society, for instance. Signs of such social dysfuncton or impairment may be skipping meals; not attending school or work; difficulty in sleeping, walking or talking; and general confusion.

inability to abstain A characteristic of JELLINEK's fourth category of alcoholism, the term is used to describe someone who although unable to abstain from drinking for even a day, can sometimes control the amount consumed on any given occasion.

India Although no comprehensive survey has been taken to assess the magnitude of drug abuse in India, research studies sponsored by the Ministry of Social Welfare in selected cities showed alcohol and tobacco to be the most commonly abused drugs. Although the prevalence rate of drugs such as cannibis, LSD, heroin and opium was very small, it should be noted that cannabis, in various potent forms, is often used in religious ceremonies. While there has been an increase in the use of GANGA (a form of cannabis that is midway in potency between charas and bhang) among college students in recent years, the drug has been mostly used for experimental purposes. Previously drug use was associated with the more impoverished sections of the population.

Charas, a potent form of cannabis, has been forbidden since the mid-1940s. There is heavy smuggling of the drug from Tibet, though, and most of the supplies pass through India before being channeled into other countries. An increase in trade has prompted the Indian government to consider stronger penalties for smuggling.

Although there have been partially successful attempts to abolish the caste system in India, alcoholism and drug abuse are still conditioned by the system which is based on religion and affluence. There are a number of individual patterns even within the various religions. The Islamic religion forbids drinking but some Moslems drink; Sikhism forbids smoking but some Sikhs smoke; Christianity permits the use of alcohol but some Christians abstain. The Brahmins, the highest caste among Hindus, are not allowed alcohol but are permitted to use ghanga. Thus there is no single pattern of substance use and abuse.

India claims that alcohol is the most commonly abused drug, but the term "abuse" has a much wider connotation in India than in other countries and includes not only addiction but also occasional and experimental use of alcohol. By most Western standards "experimental" and "occasional" is more *use* than abuse. Compared with other nations, India, actually has a low rate of alcohol abuse—somewhere in the range of 0.2–1.9% of the total population. But when you consider the lack of money and facilities available for treatment, these figures represent an enormous burden.

Thus far the Indian government is focusing a substantial portion of its study of drug and alcohol problems on the student population. This group is more readily available to the centers conducting the research, and is easier to communicate with than the rest of the population. There is also a higher incidence of drug use among college students than among other groups.

As of the late 1980s there were few centers in the country devoted exclusively to the treatment of drug and alcohol abuse. Although there are limited inpatient facilities in mental and psychiatric departments of general hospitals, the government tends to feel that "it is not desirable to promote specific and separate treatment facilities for drug addicts." In outpatient programs the principal method of treatment emphasizes the use of antagonistic drugs such as Antabuse.

Indian Alcoholism Counseling and Recovery House Program A private nonprofit drug and alcoholism residential treatment program with primary and secondary alcohol and drug use prevention components for American Indians of all ages. The program works with youths and parents to provide education and guidance about Indian traditions through a combination of classes, alternative activities, culturally specific programs, support groups and community functions. Parenting and life skills training classes are also provided for all ages. Contact: 375 South 300 West, Salt Lake City, Utah 84101. Telephone: (801) 328-8515.

Indian Health Service (IHS) alcoholism and substance abuse programs The IHS is an agency of the U.S. Department of Health and Human Services (DHHS) and now provides primary health care for approximately 800,000 American Indians and Alaskan Natives through a system of some 200 hospitals, clinics and health stations. The IHS also assists in funding several urban Indian health clinics. More than 300 alcohol and drug abuse programs providing prevention, education, outpatient, inpatient, aftercare, half-way house and drop-in center services are funded by the IHS and contracted by tribes and native organizations. Through this specialized health care delivery system, approximately 800 physicians and 2,000 hospital, clinic and public health nurses respond daily to the many consequences of alcohol and other drug use, abuse and dependence. The IHS also has developed and now conducts a training program for its professional staff members. This effort was accelerated with enactment of Public Law 99-570, the Anti-Drug Abuse Act of 1986. Further information about the IHS training programs can be obtained from the Indian Health Service, Alcoholism and Substance Program Branch, Room 6A-63, 5600 Fishers Lane, Rockville, MD 20857. Telephone: (301) 443-4297.

Eva Marie Smith, M.D. "Service for Native Americans," *Alcohol Health & Research World*, 13:1 (1989), 94–96.

inebriate An alcoholic.

inebriety ALCOHOLISM or excess drinking.

infancy See PREGNANCY and ORAL FIXATION.

infection Infection from unsterile needles is a serious danger to addicts who inject drugs. Two of the most common diseases associated with unclean needles are AIDS and HEPATITIS. Thrombophlebitis and bloodstream infections from contaminated injections are also a hazard. (See also ADMINISTRATION, AIDS, and LIVER.)

inhalants Inhaling substances for their euphoric and intoxicating effects has had a long history of use and abuse. Thousands of years ago people inhaled the vapors from burning spices and herbs, particularly in religious ceremonies. Today people use commercial inhalants which are usually broken down into two categories: anesthetic gases and volatile hydrocarbons. Inhalants are absorbed through the lungs and their effects have a rapid onset but are usually of short duration.

Anesthetics: The anesthetics NITROUS OXIDE, ETHER and CHLOROFORM were used recreationally long before they were used medically. Discovered in the 1700s, they were most often abused by students and physicians and "inhalant parties" were popular during the 19th century. Although some abuse of gaseous and vaporous anesthetics, which produce effects similar to alcohol intoxication, still exist today, the trend now is toward the use of volatile hydrocarbons and organic solvents.

Volatile hydrocarbons and organic solvents: Volatile hydrocarbons, used commercially as aerosols and solvents, are compounds of distilled petroleum and natural gas and include gasoline, kerosene, benzene and other related chemicals. Varnish, varnish removers, paint thinners and lacquers, lighter fluid, nail polish remover, cleaning solutions, spot removers, glues and cements and various aerosols are common household products containing organic solvents. Toluence, acetone, naphtha, cyclohexane, carbon tetrachloride and various alcohols are some of the active chemicals found in these products.

Absorbed by the lungs, vapors rapidly enter the bloodstream and are then distributed to the brain and liver. Because most solvents are fat soluble they are quickly absorbed into the central nervous system and consequently depress such body functions as heartbeat and respiration. In fatty tissue, accumulation occurs less rapidly. The kidneys metabolize and excrete some solvents; others are eliminated unaltered, primarily through the lungs. When the lungs are the route of elimination the solvent odor will linger on the breath for several hours.

After the quick onset of effects, the duration can usually be measured in minutes; maximum duration is probably an hour depending on the substance and the dosage. Among the effects generally felt are excitement, the lowering of inhibitions, restlessness, uncoordination, confusion and disorientation, and—after prolonged inhalation—delirium and coma. The effects are similar to alcohol intoxication and intoxication from other sedatives, though some inhalants are reported to produce psychedelic-like effects. In industrial settings, where chemicals are inhaled for prolonged periods in unventilated areas, they are toxic. Prolonged exposure can result in nausea, vomiting, muscular weakness, fatigue and weight loss. There can also be extensive damage to the kidneys, liver, bone marrow and brain. Most people who inhale substances for their giddy and intoxicating effects stop long before these more serious symptoms appear.

In moderate doses inhalants can produce sedation, changes in perception, impaired judgment, fright and panic—symptoms which in some cases have resulted in accidental deaths. Some inhalants seem to be capable of sensitizing the heart to adrenaline, a substance which is present in the body and is manufactured in greater quantities in times of stress. This has been thought to be a cause of cardiac arrhythmia fatalities in some cases. In larger doses inhalants produce sleep, unconsciousness and even seizures. Long-term effects of inhaling are usually reversible after drug use is stopped. Permanent brain, liver or kidney impairment can occur. Chromosome damage among inhalant abusers is still under study by researchers and the effects of blood abnormalities are still not proven.

Inhalants are often referred to as "deliriants," drugs capable of producing illusions, hallucinations and mental disturbances. While these effects are possible, they usually only occur in cases of overdose.

Dependence: Physical and psychological dependence have occurred in cases of long-term abuse but solvents are not considered as dangerous as other DEPRESSANTS, such as alcohol and barbiturates. Tolerance can develop and a user will need a larger dose in order to get the same effect. There have also been reports of withdrawal symptoms among solvent abusers, such as hallucinations, chills, abdominal cramps and delirium tremens. Studies have shown that a cross-tolerance can develop between solvents and other central nervous system depressants, such as alcohol. In addition there is a SYNERGISTIC or additive effect when alcohol or barbiturates are taken with certain solvents.

Patterns of abuse: Recreational use of inhalants is usually seen in young teenagers (particular boys) between the ages of 13 and 15, probably because they have access to many common household products that contain organic solvents and do not have access to the more conventional drugs. Consistent inhalant users tend to be disturbed individuals. The use of inhalants by prisoners in institutions, retarded and mentally ill people, and people in economically deprived communities has also been reported, probably because common household products are the only substances readily available. Alcoholics who are trying to forestall withdrawal symptoms are also known to inhale solvents when alcohol is not available. In some countries (e.g., Ireland) inhalant use among teenagers is more widespread than in the U.S.

TOBACCO and MARIJUANA, as well as various other substances which are inhaled through smoke and absorbed through the lungs are classified as inhalants. Cocaine is also often referred to as an inhalant although it is sniffed and actually absorbed through the membranes of the nostrils.

AMYL NITRITE, a rapidly acting stimulant inhalant that dilates the blood vessels and is used particularly to intensify and prolong sexual orgasm, is also often classified as an inhalant although it, too, is absorbed through the membranes of the nostrils.

In the 1960s glue-sniffing became a nationwide concern as numerous deaths were reported. A campaign was mounted against it and received mass media coverage. Studies reported that most deaths (approximately six out of nine) were actually the result of asphyxiation because the person (usually a child) placed a plastic bag over his head to intensify the effects of the fumes. It has been suggested that the nationwide attention given to the campaign may have actually alerted potential users to the substance and contributed to the extensive abuse.

Inhalants are absorbed through the lungs, one of the most rapid routes to obtaining a "high." Various methods are employed, including putting the substance on a piece of cloth and then inhaling the fumes; spraying or placing the substance in a paper bag and then inhaling (known as "huffing"); and, in the case of pressurized gases, filling a balloon then waiting for the vapor to warm before inhaling.

Local and state governments now prohibit minors from purchasing certain substances, particularly plastic model glues. The abuse of organic solvents will most likely continue, however, because of the large variety of household products on the market which contain them.

input-output model for treatment A method of matching alcoholic clients with the most suitable treatment center for successful results. It was proposed by the authors of the RAND REPORT. "Input" is divided into client and treatment inputs. The first lists client characteristics, such as symptoms, drinking history, social background and physical characteristics, that might be relevant in determining the best type of treatment. The second lists the type and amount of treatment available at a particular center, such as the techniques used, and the characteristics of the therapists and the facility. The success of the treatment (the "output") depends on the appropriateness of the treatment chosen.

insomnia A disturbance of the biologic rhythm of waking and sleeping, insomnia is characterized by insufficient or poor sleep, and fatigue during waking hours. Common complaints of insomniacs include difficulty falling asleep and frequent awakenings during the night. A detailed study of a person's insomnia is generally not made because sleeping pills can usually provide a simple, apparently effective but very short-term cure. Although true insomnia does exist, there can be numerous other causes such as depression, misinformation about sleep requirements, and a preoccupation about getting enough sleep. Certain drugs, such as amphetamines, can also cause insomnia. Alcohol can cause sleeplessness in some individuals and relaxation and sleep in others. The majority of chemically dependent people complain of insomnia. It almost always resolves in recovery.

instability and crisis etiological theory A sociocultural theory that suggests that social factors which produce heavy stress may cause the onset of alcoholism. In other words, turning to alcohol to alleviate stress may begin a cycle in which a stressful event leads to heavy drinking which, in turn, causes more stress and more drinking. This theory may also apply to the use of other drugs.

Institute for Social Research Located at the University of Michigan in Ann Arbor, the institute reports annually on the drug use and related attitudes of America's high school seniors and young adults. The findings come from an on-going national research and reporting program entitled Monitoring the Future: A Continuing Study of the Lifestyles and Values of Youth. The program is funded by the National Institute on Drug Abuse (NIDA). Lloyd D. Johnston, Ph.D., is program director for the Michigan institute and is co-author, with Patrick M. O'Malley, Ph.D., and Jerald G. Bachman, Ph.D., of the 1975–87 report. For additional information, contact the authors at: Institute for Social Research, The University of Michigan, Ann Arbor, MI 48106-1248.

Institute on Black Chemical Abuse A nonprofit national and international organization that addresses the alcohol and other drug abuse problems of all age groups in the black community. It offers prevention, intervention and assessment, treatment and public education programs. Training and internship seminars are available on an ongoing basis throughout the year. Materials are provided through its resource center and a free quarterly newsletter is sent on a request basis. Contact: Peter Bell, Institute on Black Chemical Abuse, 2614 Nicollet Avenue South, Minneapolis, MN 55408. Telephone: (612) 871-7878.

insurance Although insurance companies paid out large sums during the first half of the 20th century to cover complications and secondary manifestations of alcoholism, the disorder of alcoholism itself went undiagnosed and untreated. The Kemper Insurance Companies and Wausau became the first, in 1964, to provide coverage for the treatment of alcoholism, and other companies began to follow suit. Early coverage was generally restricted to inpatient care and it wasn't until the mid-1970s that it began to be extended to some outpatients facilities. Kemper was again the leader in providing group health coverage for outpatient treatment in qualifying nonhospital alcoholism centers. By 1979, 24 states had enacted legislation concerning the coverage of alcoholism; some mandated coverage, others required coverage to be available as an option. Insurance coverage for the treatment of other substance abuse was still ignored, however, and it wasn't until very recently that it was recognized as an area where coverage was needed. Treatment for those addicted to heroin, cocaine, etc., is still often limited to

EMPLOYEE ASSISTANCE PROGRAMS set up by an individual company, and these programs, in turn, are often limited to large corporations that can afford to finance them.

On October 1, 1983, Medicare, which covers approximately 29.4 million eligible Americans, implemented a new hospital reimbursement system that affects a large number of alcohol and drug abuse treatment centers. Under the new system, referred to as *prospective payment,* hospitals are reimbursed with fixed payments, determined in advance, rather than the previous cost-based payment method. The Health Care Financing Administration (HCFA) has announced that alcohol or drug abuse treatment services provided at psychiatric facilities will be temporarily exempt from the new system *if* they meet HCFA criteria (a key criterion is that the unit be under the direction of a psychiatrist). The preset rates of the new system are based on an extensive list of Diagnosis Related Groups (DRGs) which cover most illnesses. The HCFA established 470 DRGs which are based on specific diagnosis, patient age and sex, treatment procedure and clinical and statistical analysis of all cases treated. The system was designed to curb the rapid growth of Medicare costs in recent years but according to authorities in the field of substance abuse treatment, it will most likely negate any advances in treatment achieved in the past. For example, the National Association of Alcoholism Treatment Programs estimates that the average length of stay in a hospital, including detoxification, is 28.5 days. According to the new system, Medicare payments are based on an average 11.3 day stay. They also reflect the cost of living and differences in hospital wages in different parts of the country.

The DRG-based payment plan will be watched very closely by private insurance carriers and also by self-insuring employers to see if it works, particularly in the area of costs. It is possible that the new system could set a trend that will become the norm in the future. If this does occur, most drug treatment authorities concur that it will be a major setback in recent research breakthroughs. The new system does not allow for continuing care and neglects the fact that different modes of approach and treatment are required by different patients. Authorities contend that the treatment of alcoholism cannot be restricted to an 11-day regimen, and suggest that the patient's family will be the ultimate victim as it will be left to pay additional treatment bills.

The limit on detoxification coverage, either through the new Medicare system or through private insurance carriers, does not reflect the recent upsurge in DUAL ADDICTION which requires longer detoxification. In addition, few companies cover treatment for family members of a drug-dependent person even though they are often involved in the problem.

Perhaps one of the reasons why there has been little motivation to develop an insurance plan with broad coverage that extends into the area of substance abuse, is that affluent people often pay for drug abuse treatment without health insurance coverage and often receive their treatment in expensive settings. Treatment coverage is generally not available to disadvantaged members of minority groups because many of them do not belong to a group insurance plan and cannot afford an individual policy.

The National Institute on Alcohol Abuse and Alcoholism estimates that the cost of treatment per year, per client, is $13,730 for hospital alcoholism treatment (the new Medicare system will reimburse approximately $2,300); $20,780 for hospital detoxification; $4,730 for an intermediate long-term alcoholism treatment service; and $740 for an outpatient treatment program. Although alternative programs (halfway houses, residential programs, etc.) are less expensive, they have not generally been included in insurance coverage and most are not covered by the new Medicare system. Because recent research data seems to indicate that treatment of a drug user will decrease subsequent health care costs, it would seem there is a need for a movement by insurance carriers to encourage their clients to cover treatment programs and prevent the progression of drug use and its costly effects.

intemperance Excessive or habitual drinking.

International Commission for the Prevention of Alcoholism and Drug Dependence (ICPA) Founded in 1952, ICPA is a nonsectarian, nonpolitical organization of the United Nations operated exclusively for scientific and educational purposes. It seeks to reveal the impact of alcohol and other drug dependencies upon the economic, political, social and religious life of nations, and to point up effective preventive actions. The commission is made up of 250 prominent men and women from around the world. The number of invited representatives is based on the population of a country.

international drug control High-level meetings on international drug policy were held during the White House Conference meeting, February 28–March 2, 1988, in Washington, D.C. Attending were experts from the international community, the U.S. government, and the private sector plus conferees and White House Conference participants. They discussed ways to improve the effectiveness of the U.S. international drug policy.

Participants concluded that international enforcement and diplomatic activities initiated by the United States will never be sufficient to eradicate the illicit drug trade. These are only part of the solution. The U.S. is currently the world's largest consumer of illicit drugs: 60% of all such drugs now produced in the world are being used in this nation. So long as this country provides such a lucrative market for illicit drugs, it was decided, no amount of federal resources will be enough to stop the flow of illicit drugs from foreign lands. The conclusion was that the long-term, permanent solution is reduction in the demand for illegal drugs by Americans.

It was stressed, too, that many policy questions relate to issues of individual responsibility and the protection of the individual, which are fundamental to a democratic society. Any antidrug policy that is to have widespread public support must carefully balance the wide latitude given to individuals in U.S. society against the need for society to protect itself from that which seeks to destroy it.

These six general recommendations were made by conference attendees:

1. International narcotics issues must be given a much higher priority in the formulation of U.S. foreign policy.
2. U.S. drug eradication programs overseas must be refocused and strengthened.
3. Congress should review the legislation creating the narcotics certification process.
4. The activities of U.S. law enforcement officials engaged in narcotics enforcement overseas should be strengthened.
5. The U.S. Department of Treasury should convene a meeting, or series of meetings, on international drug money laundering to develop specific suggestions for improving international cooperation in the investigation and confiscation of illicit, drug-related assets and profits.
6. The U.S. should intensify its efforts to exchange expertise and information with other countries on effective prevention and treatment programs to combat illegal drug use.

The above recommendations were included in the final report, issued in June 1988, by Chairman Lois Haight Herrington, The White House Conference for a Drug-Free America.

Since that time, it appears U.S. efforts to slow cocaine traffic from Peru, Bolivia and Colombia, which have cost taxpayers $72 million since 1972, have been ineffective. The U.S. Department of State's inspector general, Sherman Funk, told a Senate subcommittee in late July 1989 that coca production in Peru and Bolivia has increased every year—with less than 1% of the illegal drugs seized. Eradication has not succeeded either, the subcommittee concluded.

In addition, the inspector general's audit, updated through July 1989, found: inadequate security to protect U.S. drug agents; no contingency plans to evacuate the agents; and, intelligence data that was useless.

At the same time, Assistant Secretary of Defense Stephen Duncan stated that the military is ready for a greater role in the drug war abroad. Congress has called for using U.S. military to join the effort in Peru, Bolivia and Colombia.

All this came in the wake of then drug czar William Bennett's declaration that crack cocaine was the number one target of his drug policy recommendations to President George Bush—issued in a special report in early September 1989. On September 5, 1989, the president, consistent with Section 1005 of the Anti-Drug Abuse Act of 1988 (21 U.S.C. 1504) transmitted his administration's 1989 National Drug Control Strategy for congressional consideration and action.

International Drug Enforcement Conference (IDEC) Held in Guatemala in March 1988, this was the sixty such conference dealing with the international drug trafficking situation, as well as the cooperative narcotics enforcement efforts of the attending 30 nations throughout the Americas, Europe, Asia and Africa. David L. Westrate, assistant administrator, Drug Enforcement Administration, reported on IDEC VI before the U.S. Senate's subcommittee on Terrorism, Narcotics and International Operations, Foreign Relations Committee, on April 5, 1989. The hallmark of the enforcement effort emerging from the IDEC was, according to Westrate, the "IDEC Initiative," simultaneous operations fully coordinated among member nations. Westrate said: "The greatest import of the 'IDEC Initiative' lies in its makeup and its methods—the identification and recognition of a common concern, and the mounting of mutual action." The assistant administrator, DEA's report is available from the U.S. Department of Justice's *Briefing Book,* DEA Mission, Public Affairs (April 1988). John C. Lawn is administrator of the Drug Enforcement Administration.

intervention In the treatment of drug abuse, intervention strategy is the therapist's direction of or influence on a client's actions. Many interventions are formulated by families, friends and co-workers of alcohol and drug abusers with the help of a therapist. The goal of an intervention is to get the abuser into treatment.

interview, structured An interview with a client or subject that follows a set form, usually for purposes of systematic data collection. No deviation from the series of questions is permitted.

interview, unstructured An interview format that uses the responses of the client or subject as a stimulus for subsequent inquiries. This method of questioning exploits unusual answers and attempts to obtain in depth data on pertinent issues.

Ionamin© (Pennwalt) A central nervous system stimulant that contains phentermine resin and is used as an anorectic for weight control. It is chemically and pharmacologically related to AMPHETAMINES and consequently has a significant potential for abuse. Overdosage can result in rapid respiration, tremors, confusion and hallucinations. It is supplied in 15 mg yellow and gray capsules, and 30 mg yellow capsules.

Ipecac© (Lilly) A syrup used as an emetic to induce vomiting in cases of poisoning. It contains 7 gr of ipecac per 100 ml. If it is absorbed instead of vomited it can exert a cardiotoxic effect.

Iran Opium Abuse has long been widespread in Iran, but until very recently it was used in a different form from the one known in the United States. In Iran opium is eaten or smoked. The goals of the abusers also differ. Iranians do not seek opium's euphoric, mind-altering effects; they use it mainly to deaden the realities of life among the poor. Use is particularly widespread in rural areas among poor farmers. Opium is also used extensively among the sick and aged to numb pain.

In 1972 it was estimated that there were 110,000 registered and 200,000 unregistered opium addicts. Since 1980 the use of heroin has become widespread in Iran, as it has in other Asian countries (see GOLDEN CRESCENT), and there are now an estimated 300–500,000 heroin addicts in a population of 40 million.

Large amounts of cannabis which is either cultivated in Iran or imported from neighboring countries, are also used, usually in the form of hashish and ghanga. The hashish is more potent than most types of marijuana used in the U.S.

In the past, Iran responded favorably to requests from other countries to cut back on the amount of opium it produced and exported. While Iran was ruled by the Shah, constructive steps were taken; in 1955 he imposed a ban on domestic opium production, although he later permitted some legal production to meet the requirements of registered addicts. In 1969 the cultivation of the opium poppy was made a government monopoly under very stringent laws that imposed harsh fines and prison sentences for possession, trafficking, importing and exporting of opium and hashish.

As the Shah's hold on Iran weakened, law and order began to break down; the ban on cultivation began to be ignored and there was a major increase in illicit export. In 1979 when the Shah and his government were overthrown by the Ayatollah Khomeini regime, the government structure that had held production and trafficking in check over the years collapsed. Police and military forces who had enforced the narcotics laws were diverted from their primary tasks and became involved in internal security. In addition, many of those who had staffed law enforcement units became political outcasts and were considered enemies of the people. Since 1979 Iran has become a major country in the GOLDEN CRESCENT, the primary source of heroin smuggled into Europe and on to the United States. The political chaos in Iran has diverted government attention to other priorities and trafficking has become much easier. In addition to Iran's role as a major source and transit country, it has also become a significant producer of heroin and morphine base in clandestine laboratories.

In 1989, Iran was third among the major suppliers of opium, producing over 300 metric tons. It ranks behind Burma (now Myanmar) and Afghanistan, and just ahead of Laos, as a major world supplier of opium.

If the current turmoil in Southwest Asian countries continues it can be expected that traffickers will continue to exploit the situation and the flow of heroin will probably increase.

Ireland Ireland lies just outside the mainstream of drug trafficking in Europe, but there has been an upward trend in drug abuse during the last few years. It has been suggested that the increase is due to the relatively recent industrialization of Ireland; others theorize that it is due to recent restrictive government measures concerning drug abuse and a rebellion among the people who feel their rights are now being impinged. Still others attribute the increase to the country's political unrest.

Government recognition of the problem led to the Misuse of Drugs Act of 1977, which strictly defined controlled substances but which is more flexible than previous legislation. Under the law, heavier penalties were to be enforced for serious offenses, while penalties on minor offenses were to be less severe. In cases where drug dealing or possession is suspected, the 1977 law supersedes normal provisions that protect individuals from warrantless search and seizure.

Although the Irish are striving for more effective methods to control drug abuse, they have not yet found any satisfactory solutions. Treatment programs and facilities are available only around Dublin; in other areas drug addiction is usually treated by local psychiatric services. In Dublin itself there is just one treatment facility. While it provides 24-hour service seven days a week, its detoxification unit contains only nine beds and is run mainly for suicide cases. Patients are usually discharged within 24 hours and are sent on to an outpatient facility on Usher's Island. This latter facility provides daily counseling, occupational therapy and group therapy and deals mainly with adolescents who have behavioral disorders related to drug abuse.

For those patients who have made a determined effort to overcome addiction, there is a therapeutic community in the town of Coolemine, near Dublin. Therapy involves social rehabilitation through self-help.

The abuse of alcohol in Ireland far exceeds the abuse of other drugs. The Irish spend 12% of their income on alcoholic beverages, a higher percentage than any other country. This is probably due to the high excise tax on alcohol, which the government treasury is heavily dependent on as a source of revenue. To any individuals, the thought of Ireland is likely to conjure up images of heavy drinking, boisterous pubs and alcohol-related problems. However, by international standards, alcohol consumption in Ireland is quite low; when adjusted by population figures it is beneath that of the U.S. It should be noted that there is a high percentage of nondrinkers among the Irish: in 1974 it was 43% of the population over the age of 15, although its percentage has been declining annually at a rate of 2.9%. Consequently, the average consumption of alcohol (in 1984, total alcohol consumption was 9.7 liters [1 liter equals 1.06 quarts] per person 15 years and over, as compared to 10.2 liters in the U.S. and 18.2 liters in France) is maintained by heavier consumption on the part of the drinking population.

The high percentage of abstainers in Ireland is probably due to the number of temperance movements and reaction to the high rate of alcoholism among alcohol users. These movements were very common in the 19th century, and one in particular had disastrous results. In the 1840s, a vigorous crusade led by a Catholic priest resulted in thousands pledging never to drink. There was a physician in Draperstown, Northern Ireland, however, who had been experimenting with the use of ether and the news quickly spread that it was a pleasant substitute for alcohol. Not only was it cheap, because unlike alcohol it was not subject to tax, the effects were quick and even when used several times a day there were no hangover effects. In fact, the effects wore off so quickly that a person exhibiting signs of drunkenness was usually sober even before he reached a police station. The sniffing of ether in Draperstown and in other parts of Ireland became epidemic for some time and it wasn't until the 1920s that ether abuse finally died out.

Although beer has long been the traditional drink in Ireland, the consumption of wine and distilled spirits has increased in recent years. The relatively high cost of alcoholic beverages does not seem to deter those who drink and evidence suggests that the expenditure for alcohol rises at least in proportion to income.

Admissions to mental hospitals for the treatment of alcoholism increased by over 300% from 1965 to 1977, and the upper socioeconomic group has one of the highest hospital admission rates. The average hospital stay, however, is much shorter for this group than for the average unskilled worker.

isocarboxazid See MONOAMINE OXIDASE (MAO) INHIBITORS.

isopropyl alcohol A major component of rubbing alcohol that has solvent properties similar to ethanol and is poisonous if taken internally. It has replaced ethanol for many uses because it is less expensive.

Italy Aside from alcohol, abuse of drugs in Italy is a relatively new occurrence. Probably because it is less expensive than other drugs, hashish is the most commonly abused drug, but in urban areas there has also been a recent trend toward the abuse of heroin, cocaine and other "hard drugs." The increase in cocaine use recently prompted the deputy chief of Italy's Central Anti-drug Service to say, "What was a threat a few years ago is now a reality." A major clandestine laboratory near Genoa was busted up in 1988 and 230 pounds of cocaine were seized by agents in Milan. In fact, the number of pounds of cocaine seized in Italy in 1988—2,832—was a significant increase from the 708 pounds seized in 1987. Among six major Western European countries only Spain had a higher record than Italy for seizure of cocaine. The use of heroin is thought to have risen 600% since 1976 and may well become the country's most abused drug. Because of its geographic location, Italy has been an important transit country. Heavy trafficking and processing of heroin in the late 1950s led to the establishment of a Rome branch office of the U.S. Bureau of Narcotics and Dangerous Drugs. The office was moved to Paris, France, in 1969 when it was believed that activity had shifted to that area. The FRENCH CONNECTION, active from the 1930s to the 1970s involved Italian underground criminals: raids of clandestine heroin laboratories in Italy during 1980 suggest that either the French Connection is not really dead or it has been replaced by a Franco-Italian Connection. The source of opium found in Italy is Southwest Asia (see GOLDEN CRESCENT), and trafficking continues to increase in the early 1980s.

The pattern of entry for cocaine was usually from Peru and Colombia through Lisbon, Madrid or Frankfurt. Most seizures were made at non-airport locations and the cocaine was generally smuggled in by Italians in Milan, Rome, and Naples.

Until new legislation was passed in 1973 to alter the definition, drug addiction was not considered a disease in Italy but was instead considered a criminal act. The new laws provide for harsher penalties for traffickers and pushers and allow addicts to be treated as "sick individuals."

Treatment programs in Italy during the early 1970s generally centered on those addicted to hashish and marijuana, although doctors are obligated to report persons using narcotics. In 1979 general health care was nationalized in Italy; medical care is virtually free but because of the scarcity of bed space people are generally detoxified, or dried out, then released. The exception to this occurs with heroin addicts. Because of the recent increase in heroin use and because the addicts are now considered "sick," there are numerous specialized services available, especially therapeutic communities.

There have been no national surveys concerning alcohol abuse in the last 30 years. Alcohol is not considered a problem in Italy and the consumption of wine in particular is viewed as a social event that centers around meals. Although Italy is one of the top wine producing countries in the world, there has been a shift in per capita wine consumption over the past 15 years. In 1968 per capita consumption was 116 litres; in 1979 per capita consumption had decreased to 90.1 litres. In 1984, however, there was an upward shift and consumption increased to 118.6 liters (1 liter equals 1.06 quart), placing Italy second of 32 countries in an international comparison survey. There has been an increase in the consumption of both beer and distilled spirits, as well. In fact, Italy's total alcohol consumption in 1984 stood at 15.1 liters per person 15 years and over, sixth highest of the 32 nations included in the survey. Exportation of wine is increasing and wine that was previously shipped to

France to be mixed with French wine is now simply exported directly to other countries. This situation has triggered a French-Italian wine war which continues to escalate.

Because drinking in Italy is traditionally associated with wine, and wine consumption is generally associated with meals and is an integral part of family life, public drunkenness is not a common occurrence. Moreover, alcohol control laws do not regulate wine or beer because they are not considered alcoholic beverages, a reflection of the traditional wine culture of the country. The government of Italy does not recognize alcohol abuse as a major health care concern and since 1979, when health care was nationalized, alcohol abuse has become a relatively "forgotten problem" with the only treatment usually found in private facilities.

While no recent surveys have been conducted on alcohol abuse, and research into social attitudes is lacking, there is a bill pending in the Italian Parliament to restrict advertising for distilled spirits. There is also an attempt to form a permanent national commission on alcohol problems which would collect data and suggest reforms. Because alcohol consumption is so closely tied to the family and home, the history and background of this aspect of Italian culture will have to be extensively explored before contemporary problems of alcohol abuse can be dealt with.

M. M. Horgan, et al. *International Survey: Alcoholic Beverage Taxation and Control Policies*. 6th ed. Brewers Association of Canada, 1986.

IV Intravenous. (See ADMINISTRATION.)

J

J.M. Foundation Created in 1924 by philanthropist Jeremiah Milbank (1887–1972) to enhance the nation's health, rehabilitation and educational programs, the J.M. Foundation began funding projects related to alcohol and other drug abuses in 1983. Since then, the organization has funded 88 projects, totaling $2.75 million, in the areas of medical education, national voluntary organizations, public policy and children of alcoholics. The foundation also has initiated several conferences for grantmakers on alcohol and other drug issues. The foundation's most prominent alcohol-related project is the J.M. Foundation Medical Student Scholarship Program in Alcohol and Other Drug Dependencies, begun in 1985. Contact: Joseph S. Dolan Program Officer, The J.M. Foundation, 60 East 42nd Street, New York, NY 10165.

Jamaica The cultivation and use of *ganga*, as marijuana is called in Jamaica, has been going on for over 100 years and is thought to have been introduced by indentured laborers from India. In the past it was generally smoked only by isolated social groups but in recent years use has spread to all ages and segments of society; an estimated 60–70% of the island's population now ingests ganga in one form or another. Although the Jamaican government has made attempts to control usage (ganga has been illegal since 1913), the drug is such big business that most law enforcers turn their backs on incidents of cultivation, use and possession. It has been suggested that marijuana is the basis of the Jamaican economy and the United States government claims that 10% of the U.S. marijuana market comes from Jamaica. The usual route is through South Florida, by both plane and boat.

In 1989, Jamaica was one of the top three suppliers of marijuana with production of 400 metric tons. Only Mexico and Columbia produced more marijuana.

Ganja is particularly important to the RASTAFARIANS and their way of life. Reggae music, which popularizes Rastafarians, is known worldwide and many of the lyrics condone and encourage the use of ganja. Popular Rastafarian musicians, including the late Bob Marley, are idols of young people in the U.S. and throughout Europe who are influenced by the songs praising the "mystical herb."

Members of Jamaica's medical profession are more than aware of the health hazards involved in the widespread use of ganja, although they are often criticized as having a "middle-class bias." Dr. John Hall, consultant physician with the Jamaica Ministry of Health, has been conducting research on the effects of marijuana for a number of years. Among the clinical observations that he has made is the fact that the seasonal upsurges in stomach hemorrhages tend to occur during the twice-yearly marijuana harvests, and the fact that the whites of the eyes often turn brown among heavy users of marijuana. Neither of these two phenomena have appeared in published research and Dr. Hall is continuing studies in both areas.

The use of ganja is more widespread among men than women, although both women and children are known to consume marijuana in a beverage called "green tea." Common conditions among heavy ganja users are impotence, low blood sugar and a bronchitis-type of cough. Apathy and a tendency to retreat from reality are also noted among heavy users. The extensive poverty in Jamaica may contribute to the use of marijuana as an escape from problems, but as with all chemical dependency it causes a vicious circle when users become dependent and lose all power to overcome economic conditions.

As in other countries throughout the world, Jamaica also has an alcoholism problem. Jamaican rum, known the world over, is inexpensive and readily available. The consumption of rum by all socioeconomic classes is a major problem. In the last decade cocaine use has become a growing problem as well. Jamaica (and the West Indies in general) is a distribution point for U.S. bound cocaine.

Japan Prior to 1945 there were no substantial drug abuse problems in Japan although some cocaine and opium addicts did exist. After World War II, however, serious problems arose; they can be divided into three separate periods. Immediately following the war, during Japan's reconstruction period, stimulants were in great demand particularly among students, night laborers and entertainers. Though the abuse of stimulants began in the major cities it soon spread and was prevalent throughout the country. The government enacted the Stimulants Control Law (1951) and amended its Mental Health Law to provide for compulsory hospitalization of those addicted to stimulants. The increased law enforcement, treatment of addicts, and intensive public campaigns seemed to have conquered the problem by the late 1950s.

No sooner was the stimulant problem seemingly brought under control than widespread heroin abuse appeared on the scene. While there had been heroin abuse since World War II, it suddenly increased to the point where in 1961 it was estimated that there were some 40,000 addicts. Government countermeasures included strengthening penalties for offenders, and the compulsory hospitalization of additcs. After 1964 there was a sharp decrease in the amount of heroin abuse and for several years the country entered a period of declining drug problems.

In the 1970s stimulant abuse again surfaced and rapidly spread throughout the country. The government amended the Stimulants Control Law and increased the penalties for violation to the same level as those for heroin offenses. It also strengthened control over stimulant precursors. As a result, there was a 30% reduction in 1974 but it was only temporary. At the present time stimulant abuse is considered the most serious drug problem in Japan. Approximately 20,000 users were arrested in 1980 and increases seem to run at 20–30% annually. The actual number of abusers is estimated to be 10 times the number known to authorities. The 30–39 age group is the most affected (38%); 31% are in the 20–29 age group; and 10% are under 19 years old. The latter group has shown a large increase in abuse over the past few years. Methamphetamine is the stimulant most abused, and is usually administered by injection. There is negligible illicit domestic manufacture and little is diverted from licit channels. The drug is usually smuggled from Korea and Taiwan. Street prices run from $600 to $800 U.S. dollars per gram of pure substance. Public health and social problems have resulted from the widespread stimulant abuse. An individual's economic and social life is seriously hampered by his psychological dependence on the drug. In addition, "amphetamine psychosis"—or the occurrence of hallucinations and illusions—has been responsible for a marked increase in traffic accidents, arson and murder. The large profits from illicit sales have also brought about an increase in organized crime.

Marijuana is second to amphetamines in substance abuse today. The 20–29 age group in particular has shown a slow but constant increase in abuse. Heroin offenses in 1980 reached a very low level. As for opium, it has never constituted a problem in Japan; most offenses involve ignorance of the law when poppies are grown for ornamental purposes. Under the Opium Law of 1954 the cultivation of the opium poppy is only permitted under license, and the government monopolizes its import, export, and domestic purchase.

Japanese government's measures to reduce drug abuse include a nationwide eradication campaign, the establishment of a council to check the dependence-producing properties of new drugs, and harsher penalties for abusers. On an international level, Japan cooperates with the United Nations in the field of drug abuse.

Social consumption of alcoholic beverages is widely accepted and deeply ingrained in Japan. This attitude has led to a pattern of infrequent but heavy consumption on special occasions. In a recent survey 52% of the Japanese polled considered alcohol a part of their lives, while 35% considered abstinence harmful to social life.

A 1984 international comparison survey of alcohol consumption per person 15 years and over placed Japan 27th among the 32 nations surveyed. Total alcohol consumption was 7.8 liters (1 liter equals 1.06 quarts) per person; beer consumption was 53.6 liters; wine (including sake) was 17.0 liters; and spirits (pure alcohol) was 2.7 liters per person.

Sake, a fermented rice wine, is the preferred beverage among middle-aged and older Japanese, though young people are drinking beer more and more. There is some actual encouragement of drunkenness during festive celebrations and a favored gift to hosts at social functions is distilled spirits. A general trend toward westernization since World War II and wider advertisement of alcoholic beverages seems to have resulted in increased levels of drinking, particularly among women and youths. Although habitual heavy drinking is limited to 4% of the male population and 1.6% of the female population, a survey in 1976 reported that 85% of the male population drinks and 52% of the female population. The rate of drinking was heaviest among males between 40 and 49 years old. According to definitions established by the Japanese government, 2.5% of the total population of the country may be considered alcoholics. In 1977 the national rate of hospitalization for a primary diagnosis related to alcohol abuse was 12.8 per 100,000 population. The rate of mortality from liver cirrhosis was 13.8 (male deaths were three times that of female deaths); and 3.6% of the hospital beds in the country were occupied because of alcoholism or alcohol related diseases. Alcohol was also involved in 12% of all traffic fatalities in 1977. The economic cost of alcohol abuse, including premature death, absenteeism and medical care is calculated to be 260 billion yen (about $1.3 billion) annually.

Drug Control Law Violations in Japan, 1954–1981

Law	Narcotic Control Law		Opium Law		Cannabis Control Law		Stimulants Control Law	
Year	Number of Cases	Number of Persons	Number of Cases	Number of Persons	Number of Cases	Number of Persons	Number of Cases	Number of Persons
1954	1,527	2,092	25	30	16	17	53,221	55,664
1955	1,280	1,753	157	181	42	52	30,670	32,140
1956	1,060	1,575	128	140	27	33	4,876	5,047
1957	1,013	1,365	144	173	25	29	787	781
1958	1,616	2,073	63	76	7	13	268	271
1959	1,394	1,714	137	147	28	30	332	372
1960	1,667	1,987	310	315	9	10	426.	476
1961	2,023	2,442	190	199	22	24	459	477
1962	1,773	2,176	203	208	34	34	530	546
1963	2,135	2,571	402	417	144	147	1,061	971
1964	707	792	419	425	158	164	969	908
1965	1,035	1,090	890	902	255	259	885	736
1966	899	974	917	920	157	158	838	722
1967	592	638	702	705	301	298	867	710
1968	298	361	1,136	1,148	392	410	1,088	791
1969	210	239	377	377	426	413	915	735
1970	212	245	230	230	707	733	2,453	1,682
1971	256	229	207	202	831	717	4,431	2,634
1972	354	341	253	251	853	726	7,702	4,777
1973	455	429	310	287	799	761	14,260	8,510
1974	436	393	176	171	781	720	9,771	6,119
1975	268	232	158	140	971	909	13,590	8,422
1976	195	165	184	185	1,064	960	17,929	10,919
1977	201	125	191	191	1,225	1,096	24,022	14,741
1978	136	102	140	142	1,771	1,253	30,287	18,027
1979	147	103	217	217	1,571	1,314	31,991	18,552
1980	241	158	269	264	1,745	1,433	34,808	20,200
1981	144	98	261	262	1,596	1,346	36,855	22,331

SOURCE: *A Brief Account of Drug Abuse and Counter-Measures in Japan, 1981*. Japan Ministry of Health and Welfare.

Government controls on alcohol abuse include a stiff penalty for public drunkenness and a permissible blood alcohol level for drivers of 0.25 grams of ethanol per 1,000 grams of blood (about one drink). There are as yet, no school programs for the prevention of alcoholism, and no limitation on the advertising of alcoholic beverages. There is, however, a government funded organization called the Liaison Conference for Alcoholic Problems which coordinates its prevention and treatment programs with private organizations such as the All Nippon Sobriety Society (Japan's version of Alcoholics Anonymous).

Jellinek, E. M. (1890–1963) The founder of the Center of Alcohol Studies and Summer School of Alcohol Studies, formerly at Yale University and now centered at Rutgers University. Jellinek was also a cofounder of the National Council on Alcoholism and was consultant on alcoholism for the World Health Organization. He was also the author of *The Disease Concept of Alcoholism.* In this influential study Jellinek distinguished between five categories of alcoholism which he referred to as Alpha, Beta, Delta, Epsilon and Gamma.

1. *Alpha Alcoholism:* Sometimes known as problem drinking, it represents a continual purely psychological dependence or reliance upon alcohol's effects to relieve emotional or bodily pain. It can develop into Gamma alcoholism but often continues in the same state for years with no signs of progression. The damage it causes is usually limited to disturbances in the person's family or social relationships and does not lead to loss of control. There are no withdrawal effects.

2. *Beta Alcoholism:* Possibly as a result of poor nutritional habits or of the customs of certain social groups, the person who suffers from this kind of alcoholism eventually develops medical complications such as cirrhosis or alcoholic polyneuropathy. Beta alcoholism is not associated with physical or psychological dependence and withdrawal symptoms do not appear but the condition can develop into Gamma alcoholism.

3. *Gamma Alcoholism:* This type of alcoholism causes the most damage to an individual's health and to his interpersonal relationships. Recognized by Alcoholics Anonymous, it is apparently the dominant form of alcoholism in the United States. It is characterized by acquired increased tissue tolerance; adaptive cell metabolism; physical dependence (craving and withdrawal symptoms); and loss of control. In Gamma alcoholism psychological dependence progresses to physical dependence.

4. *Delta Alcoholism:* The predominant form of alcoholism in France and other countries where there is significant wine consumption, Delta alcoholism is characterized by an acquired tolerance to alcohol. Unlike Gamma alcoholism which is characterized by loss of control, Delta alcoholism involves the inability to abstain. The person can control his or her intake but cannot stop drinking for even a few days; his consumption, although heavy, is steady, not "explosive."

5. *Epsilon Alcoholism:* The term refers to periodic alcoholism. Less is known about this category than the other four.

Though clinicians tend to no longer refer to Jellinek's categories as different types of alcoholism, the patterns he described and the research he performed are still useful and valid today. The current definitions of alcoholism differentiate less the issues of physiological versus psychological dependance. (See ALCOHOLISM.)

Jones Miller Act (1922) Federal legislation that established fines of up to $5,000 and imprisonment of up to 10 years for anyone involved in the trafficking of narcotics. At the time, drug use, especially heroin, was considered a national epidemic. As finally adopted, Jones Miller, or the Narcotics Drug Import and Export Act, approved May 26, 1922, led to the establishment of the Federal Narcotics Control Board, composed of the secretaries of state, treasury and commerce. A key measure of the act was the prohibition of in-transit shipments of narcotics.

Just Say No Foundation A nonprofit national and international research-based drug prevention program for children and teenagers. The program offers youth the opportunity to join Just Say No clubs, where members gain information skills and support to resist peer pressure and other influences to use drugs. It provides educational, recreational and service activities designed to foster and reinforce the attitude of intolerance toward drugs and drug use. The foundation supports and offers clubs, materials, handbooks, a club book, a quarterly newsletter, on-site training and coordination of events, such as the annual Walk Against Drugs. Contact: Tom Adams, Just Say No Foundation, 1777 N. California Blvd., Walnut Creek, CA 94596. Telephone: (800) 258-2766; in California (415) 939-6666.

K

kava A beverage made from the roots of the shrub, *Piper methysticum,* which produces a mild marijuana-like high. It also has a sedative action and if enough is consumed will produce sleep. The roots are also sometimes chewed.

kerosene See INHALANTS.

Ketaject® (Bristol) A nonbarbiturate rapid-acting general anesthetic that is normally used for short surgical procedures; with additional doses, however, it can be used for longer operations. It contains ketamine hydrochloride, which is related to phencyclidine, and has the potential for abuse. Ketaject is supplied in vials for injection. (See KETAMINE HYDROCHLORIDE.)

Ketalar® (Parke-Davis) Contains ketamine hydrochloride and is the same as KETAJECT. See KETAMINE HYDROCHLORIDE for abuse potential.

ketamine hydrochloride A nonbarbiturate rapid-acting general anesthetic that is normally used for short surgical procedures. Discovered in 1961, it was frequently used during the Vietnam War. Manufactured as KETAJECT and KETALAR it is supplied in vials for injection. It is an abused drug but not in its liquid form since injection only produces a rapid onset of sleep. Drug abusers evaporate the liquid by heating it and reducing it to a fine white powder. It is then sprinkled on marijuana or tobacco and smoked, or it is snorted. The crystalline powder is called "green" and has both depressant and psychedelic effects similar to those of phencyclidine but is much shorter in duration. It relieves tension and anxiety, is purported to be a sexual stimulant, and intensifies sounds and colors. Large doses produce delusions and hallucinations. When taken with alcohol or other central nervous system depressants the drug can have an additive effect. It is frequently a drug of abuse of medical personnel.

khat An East African plant, *Catha edulis,* whose leaves and buds are chewed or brewed as a beverage. It is said to produce stimulant effects similar to but milder than those induced by amphetamines, and psychological dependence can develop. It is also spelled chat, q'at and kat.

Korsakoff's psychosis A disease (syndrome) that usually only affects people who have been drinking heavily and steadily for many years, although it has also been found in nonalcoholics who suffer from extreme nutritional deficiencies. Identified in 1897 by the Russian psychiatrist Sergei Korsakoff (1854–1900), who founded the Moscow school of psychiatry, the disease is characterized by short term memory failure resulting in confusion, disorientation, and emotional apathy. The person is often unaware of his or her condition and usually remains quite cheerful. The disease, usually preceded by WERNICKE'S ENCEPHALOPATHY, is irreversible.

L

LAAM (levo-alpha-acetylmethadol) A narcotic analgesic agonist. LAAM is an opioid that has been tried as an alternative to METHADONE. Unlike methadone which must be taken daily, LAAM is taken only three times a week, and appears to provide a sustained level effect. It was discontinued in the early 1980s due to possible link to liver tumors.

laboratories See CLANDESTINE LABS.

lacquer thinner Sometimes inhaled for its intoxicating effects, lacquer thinner usually contains the liquid hydrocarbon TOLUENE.

lactose See MILK SUGAR.

La Guardia Report In 1938 New York City Mayor Fiorella La Guardia commissioned a study on marijuana use. The report suggested that marijuana might have valuable therapeutic applications and found no evidence that its use might lead to the use of opiates. The report has since been succeeded by more contemporary studies, but when it was published in 1944 as *The Marijuana Problem in the City of New York, by the Mayor's Committee on Marijuana* it was a landmark study and is still cited today, especially by those who favor the legalization of marijuana.

laudanum Originally any of various opium preparations, it is now a tincture (alcoholic extract) of opium. Laudanum was first compounded by Paracelsus in the 16th century. Before it was discovered to be addictive, it was used extensively in the 19th century to treat various illnesses.

"laundering" Drug dealers have the problem of hiding the massive amounts of money they collect; this activity is called "laundering." It involves converting "dirty" money from drug dealing and making it appear "clean" (i.e., from legitimate sources). Because of the volume often involved, banks cooperating in this laundering feed huge amounts of small bills into high-speed money counters. And when the volume is really heavy, they sometimes just weigh the piles of money. For example, 300 pounds (136 kg) of $20 bills is worth $3.6 million.

Money-laundering schemes are complex and thus difficult to uncover; it is equally as difficult to gather evidence required to prosecute those involved. Criminal violations can result in a maximum penalty of five years in prison and a $500,000 fine.

Miami, Florida is known as the capital of the nation's money-laundering business. According to one estimate, posh Brickwell Avenue houses offices of more than 100 banks from some 25 to 30 different countries. In addition, there are over 40 branches of overseas and out-of-state banks, plus some 50 agencies representing foreign banks. One authority said there are more banks than supermarkets in Miami. Agents of the U.S. Treasury Department believe that over one-third of all Miami banks share in the huge profits made in various illegal drug money laundering schemes.

In recent years, money-laundering centers have sprung up around the world—Hong Kong, Panama, Cayman Islands, Montevideo (Uruguay), Nassau (Bahamas), the Netherlands Antilles—offering services ranging from secret accounts to dummy corporations with hidden ownership. According to police and launderers, the basic fill for recycling money of dubious origin is 4%, while the rate for drug cash and other "hot" money is 7% to 10%.

Gilda Berger comments in *Drug Abuse: The Impact on Society:* "Not only is the drug trade extracting a great deal of money from drug users and robbing the government of millions of dollars in tax revenues, it is also buying its way into the very heart of American's trade and industry."

Gilda Berger, *Drug Abuse: The Impact on Society* (Franklin Watts: New York, 1988), 71–74.

L-Dopa (Levodopa) A drug mimicking the neurotransmitting dopamine that is currently used in the treatment of Parkinson's disease. It has been used experimentally, without particular success, as a possible counteragent to the acute effects of alcohol intoxication and alcoholism. It has been used experimentally to block cocaine craving, also with little success.

Timothy Leary Prominent 1960s pro-drug social psychologist who coined the expression "Turn on, tune in, and drop out" to describe the change of consciousness brought on by drug use. When he first uttered the expression, he was indeed describing a common phenomenon of that era. (See HIPPIES.) Dr. Leary, then a Harvard professor, was dedicated to establishing the unhindered use of psychedelics for "seekers of self-knowledge." He proposed that useful self-knowledge was obtained by the use of psychedelics. While he profited economically from publishing royalties and paid speaking engagements, his ideas are not considered psychologically or philosophically sophisticated.

legal aspects of drug use The legal foundation for the government's strategy for combatting abuse of drugs and other substances is the CONTROLLED SUBSTANCES ACT of 1970. The basic provisions of the law were strengthened by the Congress in 1984 and again with the Anti-Drug Abuse Act of 1986. A major segment of the latter, the Narcotics Penalties and Enforcement Act, provides for mandatory minimum sentences. The most common and well-known control mechanism is the criminal penalty for trafficking. Trafficking is defined as the unauthorized manufacture, distribution or possession of a drug with intent to distribute. Criminal penalties are based on the drug "Schedules" listed in the act.

Federal trafficking penalties for such Schedule I and II controlled substances as heroin, cocaine base, PCP, LSD, Fentanyl and Fentanyl Analogue, dependent on such factors as first or second offense and quantity/mixture, vary greatly. For example, the penalty for trafficking in cocaine, first offense, 500–4,999 gm mixture, is not less than five years and not more than 40 years. If death or serious injury results, it is not less than 20 years and not more than life. Fine of not more than $2 million individual; $5 million other than individual.

Federal trafficking penalties for marijuana, hashish and hashish oil, dependent on prior offense record and quantity/mixture, also vary considerably. For instance, the penalty for a first offense when the quantity involved is 50 to 100 kg is not more than 20 years; if death or serious injury occurs, it is not less than 20 years, not more than life. Fine up to $1 million individual, $5 million other than individual. Marijuana is a Schedule I controlled substance. Schedule IV drug is punishable by a maximum of three years in jail and up to a $250,000 fine individual, $1 million not individual. Trafficking in a Schedule V drug is punishable by up to one year in prison and up to a $100,000 fine individual, $250,000 not individual. Second and subsequent offenses are punishable by twice the penalty imposed for the first offense. The Controlled Substances Act carefully distinguishes between trafficking offenses (those who supply illicit drugs to abusers) and use offenses (those possessing drugs solely for personal use). Possession for one's own use of any controlled substance in any Schedule is always a misdemeanor on the first offense, and is punishable by one year in jail and up to a $5,000 fine. A first offender under the age of 21 may receive up to one year probation and thereafter motion court for expungement of all records. When compared to some countries, particularly Turkey where not only the penalties but the jails themselves have a reputation for harshness, the U.S. is considered lenient. (See Appendix III, Tables 2 and 3.)

The National Organization for the Reform of Marijuana Laws (NORML) is the most active group attempting to decriminalize the use of marijuana and remove the country's estimated 30 million marijuana users from the criminal justice system. In recent years some states have changed their laws and no longer treat possession of a small quantity of marijuana for personal use by adults as a felony: Alaska, California, Colorado, Maine, Massachusetts, Minnesota, Mississippi, Nebraska, New York, North Carolina, Ohio and Oregon now provide written citations for offenses and charge small fines or extend probation. This procedure replaces the system of arrest, prosecution and jail sentences. In Alaska there are no state laws prohibiting the private possession and cultivation of marijuana for personal use in the home by adults. As a result of follow-up surveys in these states NORML cites substantial monetary savings to the criminal justice system, public approval of the new laws, only a slight increase in the number of first-time marijuana users, and a decline in frequency of use. The move toward decriminalization appears to have halted recently as research uncovers a number of adverse consequences of marijuana use.

As of November 1982, 33 states had enacted legislation authorizing programs of legal access to THC for victims of cancer and glaucoma. In addition, three state supreme courts, Washington, Illinois and Michigan, have held marijuana penalties unconstitutional on the grounds that they deny equal protection because marijuana was classified with far more dangerous drugs, including narcotics.

In June 1982, a committee appointed by the National Academy of Sciences released a detailed report that endorsed marijuana decriminalization. The report concluded, however, that marijuana is not a single drug but a complex preparation containing many biologically active chemicals, and recommended that comprehensive studies of the affects on the health of the American public be undertaken. Both the president of the academy and the director of the National Institute of Drug Abuse rejected the committee's recommendation to eliminate criminal penalties.

The only legally grown marijuana in the United States is found on a federal government farm in Faulkner County, Mississippi. It is operated by scientists from the Research Institute of Pharmaceutical Sciences of the University of Mississippi. A 5.6 acre farm with more than 100 varieties of cannabis plants, it has been under contract to the National Institute on Drug Abuse (NIDA) since 1968. The drug is grown under carefully controlled conditions strictly for research and therapeutic purposes, and is sent through NIDA to approved researchers. The farm has a sophisticated analysis laboratory located nearby. Here the crude plant material is extracted and filtered off to yield a resin extract that is then dissolved in ethanol. Various levels of the cannabinoids in each specimen are pinpointed; some are then isolated and synthesized. All crude plant material is carefully labeled as to seed origin, plant sex, and dates of planting and harvest, so that uniform study results can be obtained.

The increased cost of importing marijuana due to interdiction has stimulated domestic production, which rose 10% from 1982 to 1986. As a result, the total amount consumed by Americans rose 22% from 1982 to 1986. The three largest marijuana-producing states are Oregon, California and Kentucky. One official has said that the marijuana growers are the bootleggers of the 1980s and 1990s.

legal high A term for substances that can alter the mind and produce a HIGH and are readily available without a prescription. For example, NUTMEG, DILL MOUTHWASHES with a high alcohol content, CLEANING FLUIDS, airplane GLUE, etc.

legalization In the late 1980s the concept of legalizing or decriminalizing (regulating like alcohol) the use of currently illicit drugs became hotly debated. Due to drug related crime many so-called conservatives began to consider decriminalization as a possible step to reducing crime. While it is more publicly debated than in the past it probably still remains a minority opinion among enforcement and treatment groups. Many general opinion surveys indicate a significant increase in the number of people who believe the measure would reduce crime and violence.

Lemmon The manufacturer of QUAALUDE. The company produced this drug with their name stamped on the tablet. A Lemmon

714 was the 300 mg size. On the street these came to be known as "Lemmons" or "714s." Quaaludes were widely adulterated with substances other than methaqualone. This drug has been withdrawn from the pharmaceutical market by the manufacturer because of its widespread misuse.

lesbian drug users See HOMOSEXUALS.

lethal dose The dosage of a drug that results in death. There are so many factors involved, however, including the amount taken, the purity of the drug, what it was taken in combination with, the physical state of the person taking it, and so on, that it is impossible to say what actually constitutes a "lethal" dose. Depending on the conditions, it could be an extremely small amount.

lettuce There are claims that both wild lettuce and head lettuce sold in supermarkets can produce marijuana-like effects when dried and smoked. This is extremely doubtful, however, and any effects that are felt are probably a result of the person hyperventilating while smoking.

levallorphan A narcotic antagonist used to lessen respiratory depression caused by the use of narcotics. (See LORFAN.)

Levo-Dromoran® (Roche) A synthetic NARCOTIC that contains levorphanol tartrate and acts as a highly potent analgesic for moderate to severe pain. It can be habit-forming and has an addictive potential similar to morphine. It is supplied in ampules, vials, and 2 mg white, scored tablets.

levorphanol An OPIOID NARCOTIC ANALGESIC similar to but more potent than morphine. Levorphanol tartrate is applied in many of the same ways as other opioids, including relief of moderate to severe pain in cases of renal or biliary colic, myocardial infarction and pain associated with cancer. It also supplements nitrous oxide in pre- and post-operative anesthesia. The effects of levorphanol peak in 60–90 minutes and last four to eight hours. It is prescribed in quantities of 2–3 mg to be taken orally or subcutaneously; a dose that is equivalent to 10 mg of morphine.

Levorphanol achieves the same analgesic effects as morphine, but side effects typical of morphine, such as nausea, constipation, and vomiting, occur less frequently. The drug can cause respiratory depression, and use of narcotic antagonists may be called for to counteract it.

Although tolerance and dependence do occur, levorphanol is not subject to great abuse.

Available from Roche in 2 mg tablets, as well as in ampules and vials for injection, it is marketed as LEVO-DROMORAN and is a Schedule II drug under the Controlled Substances Act.

Librax® (Roche) A minor TRANQUILIZER that combines Librium (chlordiazepoxide hydrochloride) and Quarzan (clidnium bromide, an anticholinergic drug), both developments of Roche research. Dependence can occur if the recommended dosage is exceeded. When taken with alcohol or other central nervous system depressants it can have an additive effect. Overdosage can result in diminished reflexes, somnolence, confusion and coma. Librax is supplied in green capsules containing 5 mg Librium and 2.5 mg Quarzan.

Libritabs® (Roche) A sedative-tranquilizer that contains chlordiazepoxide, a BENZODIAZEPINE derivative. Both psychological and physical dependence can occur if the recommended dosage is exceeded. When taken with alcohol or other central nervous system depressants it can have an additive effect. Overdosage can result in diminished reflexes, somnolence, confusion and coma. It is supplied in 5, 10 and 25 mg green tablets.

Librium® (Roche) One of the most widely prescribed sedative-tranquilizers. It contains chlordiazepoxide hydrochloride (a BENZODIAZEPINE derivative) and is used to reduce both simple and severe forms of tension, anxiety and fear. It is also used to detoxify alcoholics and other sedative-dependent people. Chemically and pharmacologically it is similar to diazepam and oxazepam. Physical and psychological dependence can occur if the recommended dosage is exceeded and it has a significant potential for abuse. As is the case with other central nervous system drugs, use with alcohol or other CNS depressants can produce an additive effect. Overdosage can result in diminished reflexes, somnolence, confusion and coma. Librium is supplied in ampules for injection, and in capsule form; 5 mg green and yellow; 10 mg green and black; 25 mg green and white.

lidocaine A synthetic local anesthetic that has a relatively weak effect on the central nervous system and consequently has little potential for abuse.

lighter fluids See INHALANTS.

lipid soluble A substance, such as THC, that is soluble in fats and fatty tissues. Lipid solubility is usually associated with insolubility in water.

liquid hashish Hashish is made only from the resin of the plant *Cannabis sativa;* liquid hashish is made from plant material which is ground or chopped up. It is turned into liquid form by distillation. Considerably more potent in liquid form, as little as one drop can produce a HIGH. It is smoked (a very small amount is put on a cigarette) and it can be ingested orally, but because of its potency it has to be used in cooking or put into wine. When it is smoked, the smoker can regulate the degree of his high by spacing out the intake. (See also HASHISH.)

liquor A term generally used to refer to spirits, rather than beer or wine, but it may cover any alcoholic beverage. During its early English usage the word referred to any mixed liquid, or to any measured solution of a solid in liquid. During the 17th century the term became specifically associated with alcoholic beverages.

liver The liver is located in the upper right hand side of the abdomen and is partially protected by the lower rib cage. Weighing about three pounds in adults, it is the largest and most metabolically complex organ in the human body. Its functions include circulation, metabolism, excretion, immunology and detoxification. Seventy-five per cent of the blood carried to the liver comes from the intestinal tract; the liver is, therefore, the first to receive digested material.

Alcohol abuse has directly harmful effects on the liver. Ninety percent of the alcohol a person consumes must be oxidized, or detoxified, in the liver and both alcohol and acetaldehyde (a metabolic product of alcohol) can scar the liver and break down its tissues. This damage affects all parts of the body since the liver cannot then convert vitamins and foods into forms usable by the other organs and tissues, or perform its many other functions.

There are several distinct types of *alcoholic liver disease* that can result from heavy drinking. In its mild form, it is characterized by an accumulation of fat in the liver and is the most common liver disease found in hospitalized alcoholics. Alcoholic hepatitis is a more acute and serious form of the disease. It involves inflammation of the liver and cell death and can be accompanied by fever, jaundice and an abnormal accumulation of fluid in the abdominal cavity. *Alcoholic hepatitis* has a mortality rate of 10% or more. The most serious form of alcoholic liver disease is cirrhosis which is characterized by scarring of the liver with fibrous tissue and breakdown of the liver structure. This disease is irreversible although it is not always fatal.

One does not have to be an alcoholic to fall victim to an alcoholic liver disease—heavy social drinking can also result in damage to the liver. Nor will an adequate diet protect a heavy drinker from liver injury, as many people believe, though malnutrition may certainly contribute to liver damage. The liver can repair itself to a remarkable degree, however, and with the exception of cirrhosis, most liver diseases can be corrected to some extent through proper diet (high protein, high vitamin content) and rest—provided the individual stops drinking.

Acute hepatitis is the most common medical complication that results from injecting drugs such as heroin or methedrine. Narcotics themselves seem to have little direct affect on the liver; hepatitis is transmitted through the use of contaminated needles. In one study, 76% of addicts with a history of hepatitis had their first episode within 24 months of starting to use a needle; 50% within the first year. Some 30% of addicts who get hepatitis have recurring bouts of the disease. The first symptoms of hepatitis are nausea, vomiting, jaundice and pain in the upper right side of the body.

Liver dysfunction has been reported in adolescents who have abused inhalants, particularly cleaning fluid preparations. Abuse of glue, the most popular inhalant among young abusers, does not seem to affect the liver.

In studies of the effects of cannabis on the liver, no laboratory evidence was found of liver dysfunction in heavy smokers, with the exception of individuals who used cannabis in conjunction with alcohol.

The use of LSD and other psychedelic drugs does not seem to result in liver damage. In the case of cocaine, studies have shown that from 10% to 20% of the cocaine administered was excreted unchanged in the urine and that "the liver can detoxify one minimal lethal dose of cocaine in an hour" (Richter).

Ralph W. Richter, ed., *Medical Aspects of Drug Abuse* (Harper & Row, 1975), 61.

lobelia There have been claims that smoking the dried leaves of the plant, *Lobelia inflata,* can produce a marijuana-like effect. It does not have a significant potential for abuse because of extremely unpleasant side effects, such as nausea and vomiting.

Lomotil® (Searle & Co.) An antidiarrheic. A snythetic drug containing diphenoxylate hydrochloride and atropine sulfate, it is chemically related to the narcotic MEPERIDINE. Because of its similarity to meperidine it has addiction potential and the prescribed dosage should be strictly adhered to. Overdosage can result in severe or even fatal respiratory depression. It is supplied in white tablets and in liquid form.

lophophorine An alkaloid contained in PEYOTE.

Lorfan® (Roche) A NARCOTIC ANTAGONIST that contains levallorphan tartrate. It is used in cases of deliberate and accidental opioid overdose for the treatment of respiratory depression. If used in the absence of a narcotic it can *cause* respiratory depression, or if the respiratory depression has been caused by a barbiturate or other nonnarcotic agent, it can increase the depression.

Lotusate® (Winthrop) A short-acting BARBITURATE that contains talbutal and is used as a hypnotic sedative. It can produce dependence and has a high potential for abuse.

LSD (d-lysergic acid diethylamide, lysergide, LSD-25) A semisynthetic drug derived from the alkaloid lysergic acid which is found in ergot, a parasitic fungus or "rust" that grows on rye and other grains.

LSD was originally synthesized in 1938 by two Swiss chemists. Five years later in the spring of 1943 one of its co-discoverers, Dr. Albert Hofmann, inadvertently ingested some of the drug. He experienced restlessness and dizziness followed by a mild delirium in which he experienced "fantastic visions of extraordinary vividness accompanied by a kaleidoscopic play of intense colouration." To make certain that LSD was the source of these visions Hofmann took another dose, 25 mg, which today is considered to be two and a half times the normal dose for a major trip. He again experienced intense visual changes and also synesthesia, or the merging of senses: "sounds were transposed into visual sensations so that from each tone or noise a comparable coloured picture was evoked changing in form and colour kaleidoscopically."

After 1943, LSD was "a drug in search of a use" (Edward M. Brecher in *Licit & Illicit Drugs,* p. 349). The United States Army tested it for use as a brainwashing agent and as a way of making prisoners talk more readily, and it was stockpiled by the armed forces for possible use in disabling an enemy. Psychiatrists, believing that its effects mimicked a psychotic state, used LSD on themselves and on staff members of mental hospitals in order to better understand mental illness. LSD came into widespread use as an adjunct to psychotherapy in the late 1940s and early 1950s in the U.S., England and Europe. It was used on chronically withdrawn, seriously ill mental patients and had initially promising results. Longer term and more careful follow-up studies were not as favorable, but the ultimate scientific proof of its effectiveness in psychotherapy has not been established.

Until the 1960s self-administration of LSD was mostly restricted to a small number of intellectuals. In *The Doors of Perception* (1954), Aldous Huxley's favorable reports of his experiences with MESCALINE, another hallucinogen whose effects are similar to those of LSD, encouraged others to explore the possibilities of mystical visions and the potential for increased creativity. The illicit use of LSD on a broad national scale began in the U.S. around 1962. Prior to this time, almost all the LSD available in the U.S. and Canada was produced by Sandoz Laboratories. New Food and Drug Administration (FDA) laws and restrictions on LSD and other investigational drugs was followed by an *increase* in the availability and use of LSD. This was helped by Dr. Timothy Leary, an instructor at Harvard University, who left Harvard in 1963 under a cloud of scandal because of his activities involving LSD. He became a media figure overnight and used his newfound fame to propagandize ("turn on, tune in and drop out") for LSD on a national and international scale.

LSD is commonly prepared as a tartrate salt which is soluble in water. When pure it is a white odorless crystalline material, but street preparations are generally mixed with colored substances. LSD may be manufactured in capsule, tablet, or liquid form. It is always taken orally but it has been injected in clinical situations. LSD is one of the most potent drugs know to man: dosages are measured in micrograms—millionths of a gram—and 25–150 micrograms constitute a dose. Because such small amounts are required, LSD is often impregnated on sugar cubes, blotter paper or small gelatin squares. In relation to other psychedelic drugs, LSD is considered to be 200 times as potent as psilocybin and 5,000 times as potent as mescaline (according to Richard R. Lingeman in *Drugs from A to Z,* p. 132).

When taken orally the effects of LSD are usually felt within an hour. They can last from six to 12 hours and usually peak after three to five hours. LSD can be considered "the king of psychedelics" because it produces the most intense effects of "mind-expansion" with little or no adverse physical side effects. The subjective experiences that LSD induces can be spectacular. Sensory perceptions are altered and intensified so that colors appear brighter and sounds become magnified or are perceived as patterns; there is a merging of senses (synesthesia) so that sounds become swirling patterns of vivid color; perceptions of time and space are distorted so that seconds may seem like an eternity and objects become fluid and shifting. The user may experience himself as being both within and without himself, or as merged with an object or another person. Hallucinations, visions, religious revelations and personality insights have all been reported. The majority of users have both pleasant and unpleasant reactions to the drug, but for those whose overall reaction has been positive, the unpleasant side effects are seen as transitory and valuable in terms of self-knowledge.

As the use of LSD became more widespread in the 1960s, the incidence of "bad trips" also increased. One of the main reasons was because LSD was now available to everyone—including schizophrenics and schizoid personalities who are the most likely to experience adverse effects. On a totally "bad trip," the user may feel that he no longer has control of the psychological effects experienced and may want to end the drug state immediately. The most common reaction to a bad trip is one of acute anxiety or panic, often accompanied by a fear of insanity. Confusion, depression and paranoia may also result.

One widely publicized adverse effect of LSD is the FLASHBACK—a reexperiencing of the effects of the drug weeks or even months after taking it. There are a few theories that seek to explain flashbacks, but none of them are conclusive: one is that flashbacks are induced by stress, fatigue or the use of other drugs. Flashbacks seem to occur most frequently in people who have used LSD repeatedly.

The size of a lethal dose of LSD is not known and so far there are no well-documented reports of human deaths attributable to the action of LSD. In 1967 it was reported that the drug caused damage to white-blood-cell chromosomes in test tubes; however, subsequent studies produced mixed results and to date there has not been any conclusive evidence of its deleterious effects on the chromosomes. Also, it has not been proven that brain damage or other permanent psychological or physical change is caused by LSD.

Use of LSD appears to be related to an increased risk of spontaneous abortion among pregnant women. It may also be linked to a higher than normal incidence of congenital abnormalities in newborns. However, as chronic users of LSD are also likely to be users of other drugs, it is difficult to establish what effects are due to each particular drug.

Use of LSD peaked in the late 1960s and, after a steady decline, seemed to have stabilized in the 1970s. In the early 1980s there appeared to be increasing interest in LSD, but little hard evidence that there was much increase in the actual use of the drug. In a nationwide comparison of drug trends among high school students in 1975–1980, the Institute for Social Research found that 9.3% of high school seniors used hallucinogenic drugs at some time in 1980 compared to a rate of 11.2% in 1975.

Prevalence rates for LSD did not change significantly for any age group between 1985 and 1988. Lifetime prevalence is highest among 26–34 year olds (18%).

Early typical users of LSD were generally creative-type personalities, college students and hippies. Regular users in the late 1970s and the 1980s are not confined to these groups, though; in one comparative study of regular users of LSD, occupations included plumbers, longshoremen, janitors and tractor mechanics.

Classification: LSD is classified as a HALLUCINOGEN, a Schedule I drug under the CONTROLLED SUBSTANCES ACT.

Effects: The effects of LSD depend on the quality of the drug and, largely, on the psychological and emotional state of the user and the setting in which the drug is taken. Effects can also vary in an individual, so that one experience may be pleasant and the next unpleasant.

Physiological effects: LSD is quickly distributed to the brain and throughout the body. It acts on the central and autonomic nervous systems. All traces of LSD are gone from the brain after 20 minutes although its effects last for many more hours. It is metabolized in the liver and kidneys and excreted in the feces.

There is no evidence that even long-term, high dosage use of LSD results in any permanent damage to the body or brain. However, like all other drugs, it should not be taken by people who are unstable or those with psychotic tendencies.

Physiological effects are associated almost entirely with the central and autonomic nervous systems. They include increased blood pressure, a rise in body temperature, dilated pupils, and a rapid heartbeat. Occasionally trembling, nausea, loss of interest in food, chills and flushing occur. Body motor skills may be impaired.

Psychological effects: Organic hallucinogenic drugs producing LSD-like effects have been used by people throughout the world, especially in North and South America, for thousands of years in religious ceremonies because of the mystical experience they offer, purportedly bringing the user closer to God and nature. They are called "mind-expanding" drugs because that is what they do—break down the barriers which keep an individual locked into his "normal" perception of the world, and free his mind to other ways of perceiving the universe. Users have reported experiences ranging from hallucinations, visions, synesthesia, great euphoria and feelings of well-being and "oneness" with the world, to anxiety, panic, fear, depression and despair. Prolonged anxiety and psychotic reactions following the use of LSD have occurred. Reactions to the drug are very much related to the expectations of the user, which may account for many of the "bad trips" which happened after nationwide warnings against LSD in 1962.

History of LSD

1938 **Drs. Albert Hofmann and W. A. Stoll, chemists at Sandoz Laboratories (Basel, Switzerland) discover d-lysergic acid diethylamide while experimenting with ergot fungus.**

1943 **Dr. Hoffmann accidentally absorbs a synthesized compound in the lysergic acid series and experiences "fantastic visions." He later deliberately self-administers LSD and again experiences visions.**

1949-1954 **LSD widely studied for use in the treatment of mental disorders, epilepsy and alcoholism.**

1956-1960 **Early recreational use of LSD by the medical and psychiatric community and their friends.**

1962 **Drs. Timothy Leary and Richard Alpert of the Harvard Center for Research in Human Personality treat inmates at the Massachusetts Correctional Institute.**

Thalidomide scare focuses attention on LSD. As fears arise, laws banning LSD appear.

1963 **Government investigates Leary and Alpert who then leave Harvard under a cloud of scandal with much national publicity.**

Black market in high quality LSD begins. Adulterated, contaminated or improperly manufactured LSD appears.

1965 **New York is the first state to pass legislation against possession, use and sale.**

1967 **LSD is reported to damage white-blood-cell chromosomes in test tubes.**

1968 **Incidents of "bad trips" and flashbacks increase across the nation. Use of LSD peaks in the late 1960s.**

1970s-1980s **Use steadily declines and stabilizes in the 1970s. Early 1980s show an increasing interest in LSD but little evidence of actual increase in use. Prevalence rates didn't change significantly in the late 1980s. Lifetime prevalence is highest among 26 to 34 year olds (18%).**

Addictive aspects: Physical DEPENDENCE does not develop with LSD.

Tolerance: If used daily, tolerance to the effects of LSD can develop rapidly but it will disappear after a few days abstinence. Because the very nature of the drug limits its use (few individuals, if any, would take LSD on a daily basis), tolerance is not generally an issue.

Sources: "Basement chemists" have been readily able to obtain the materials for synthesis of LSD and it is fairly easily made. Supply has equalled demand.

Traffic and control: In 1978 the U.S. Drug Enforcement Administration seized 386,543 doses of LSD; in the first quarter of 1979, the DEA seized over 800,000 doses. While this enormous increase may be due to an increase in use, figures on one-year use by seniors in high school compiled nationally by the Institute for Social Research do not show such a pattern.

Synonyms: acid, the beast, blotter acid, blue cheer, Blue Star, California sunshine, chocolate chips, the cube, dots, the ghost, the hawk, microdots, pellets, sacrament, windowpane.

LSM Lysergic acid morpholide, a chemical substance related to LSD.

Luminal® (Winthorp) A hypnotic sedative and long-acting BARBITURATE that contains phenobarbital. It is often used to control seizures. Physical dependence can occur as the drug can be habit-forming and tolerance will develop. A Schedule III drug, it is supplied in sugar-coated 16 and 32 mg oval tablets and in ampules for injection.

lungs The two conical, saclike organs where respiration, or the exchange of gases between blood and the external atmosphere, takes place. Cartilaged passageways of smooth muscle, called bronchi, conduct air to smaller bronchioles which terminate in alveoli. It is in the alveoli, tiny membranous air sacs filled with vast networks of blood vessels and capillaries, that the absorption of oxygen and the emission of carbon dioxide occur. The sympathetic and parasympathetic nerve fibers regulate respiration through their respective effects on the blood vessels and bronchi of the lungs.

Although sedatives do not seem to inflict direct damage to the lungs, their effect on the medulla, the brain's respiratory center, explains the danger of death by respiratory failure that may result from the abuse of these drugs. High doses of barbituates, volatile solvents, tranquilizers and alcohol can cause oxygen deficiency and difficulty in breathing that can result in apnea—temporary suspension of breathing—and death by suffocation. Many alcoholics are also smokers and a correlation between alcohol abuse and respiratory disorders, such as bronchitis and emphysema has been established through association with heavy smoking.

STIMULANTS such as amphetamines, cocaine, caffeine and nicotine, increase respiratory rate and depth, causing labored breathing. In the case of an overdose, however, their effects during the depressive phase can cause death from respiratory failure. The long-term effects on the lungs from smoking cocaine freebase are unknown.

Abuse of the addictive stimulant nicotine, through smoking, definitely leads to serious lung damage, though this is attributable to the particulate and gaseous contents of tobacco smoke rather than to the action of nicotine. Tars and other particles in the smoke damage the lungs in several ways. By trapping air they cause alveolar ruptures, scarring and inflammation. The decreased surface area of the lungs severely inhibits exchange of gases and causes emphysema victims to suffer from very labored breathing, which can make them barrel-chested. Twenty thousand American smokers die from emphysema each year.

Furthermore, the hydrocarbons in cigarette tar contain carcinogens and co-carcinogens which promote the development of cancerous cells in the lungs and other parts of the body. Cancerous cells eventually replace functioning respiratory cells. Lung cancer, which is the second major cause of deaths from smoking (after coronary heart disease), claims approximately 84,000 Americans annually.

Cigarette smokers risk even further damage to the lungs from such gases as ammonia, formaldehyde, acetaldehyde and hydrogen cyanide, which are contained in cigarette smoke and irritate and eventually kill the mucus-producing and ciliary cells lining the respiratory tract. This destruction of the respiratory system's protective mechanisms sharply increases the smoker's susceptibility to bronchial inflammation (bronchitis) and other infectious diseases.

Heroin abuse increases the likelihood of pulmonary infections such as abcesses and pneumonia, not because of the drug itself but because of the unsanitary conditions under which heroin is often administered—through unsterilized or shared needles. Usually attributable to staphylococcus, such diseases are common among addicts. In addition, "street" heroin is often contaminated or adulterated with binding agents, such as talc or cellulose, which can lodge in the small vessels of the lungs and cause fibrosis and thrombosis.

Heroin itself can depress respiration and decrease the volume and diffusing capacity of the lungs. Pulmonary hypertension and even cardiopulmonary collapse can follow the reduction of lung function. Narcotic overdose can involve abnormally fast or slow breathing, congestion and edema. This last condition manifests as froth which fills the bronchial tree, comes out through the nose and mouth, and can cause death by suffocation. Autopsies of overdose victims have revealed fluid-filled lungs weighing five and six times the normal weight.

In general, psychedelic drugs produce no characteristic adverse effects on the lungs or on respiration. There have been reported cases of LSD precipitating asthma but it is not known if the individuals involved suffered from asthma before taking the drug, in which case the asthma may have been the result of a panic reaction of the LSD.

The effects of marijuana smoking on the lungs have not yet been satisfactorily established. No causal relationship has been established between marijuana use and emphysema or lung cancer. In fact, until early in this century marijuana was used in the United States to treat a variety of illnesses, including asthma. Like tobacco, marijuana contains tars that may conceivably produce deleterious effects. On the other hand, cancer-causing chemicals in marijuana smoke are present in amounts 50–70% higher than in old-fashioned, high tar cigarettes. Furthermore, the marijuana smoker deliberately inhales and holds the smoke in his lungs as long as possible, placing the irritants and carcinogens in long and direct contact with lung tissue. As people continue to use marijuana over the years that it takes to develop a symptomatic lung cancer, we may see primary malignancies on the lungs due to cannabis. Chronic heavy daily use can significantly impair lung function. Excessive smoking of hashish and other forms of potent marijuana have produced bronchial irritation, asthma and chronic catarrhal laryngitis.

M

mace The dried arillode of the nutmeg seed. It is mixed with hot water to form a beverage which has psychedelic properties.

macromerine An alkaloid found in the cactus DONA ANA. It has psychedelic properties similar to, but far less potent than, mescaline which is found in the peyote cactus.

macronodular cirrhosis A contemporary classification of a type of cirrhosis that is similar to POSTNECROTIC CIRRHOSIS which follows liver inflammation or hepatitis. (See also LIVER.)

Madagascar periwinkle *Catharanthus roseus*. The leaves of the plant produce stimulant and hallucinogenic effects when smoked but can cause extremely severe adverse reactions.

magic mushrooms PSILOCYBIN. (See also MUSHROOMS, SACRED.)

mainline, mainlining Injecting heroin into a vein, particularly the main arterial vein of the arm. (See ADMINISTRATION.)

maintenance therapy See METHADONE.

malaria The disease was once suffered by a significant number of narcotic addicts, but is now almost eradicated in the United States. An epidemic of malaria, spread by contaminated needles, occurred in New York City in 1939. QUININE them became a popular dilutant of heroin on the East Coast. Although it supresses malarial symptoms, it is not the reason why very few cases of heroin-related malaria are seen. Instead, the malarial plasmodium has been eradicated in North America, and the causative agent would have to be introduced into the country from abroad.

Mallory-Weiss syndrome Lacerations of the esophagus due to frequent vomiting and morning retching. It is a condition found commonly in most alcoholics but is not limited to them. The syndrome can lead to massive hemorrhage and surgery is usually necessary to stop the bleeding.

mandrake *Mandragora officinarum*. An herb that grows in southern Europe and northern Africa. It contains anticholinergic belladonna alkaloids and can cause severe adverse reaction.

Mandrax® A British brand of methaqualone, a non-barbiturate sedative hypnotic. It has a significant potential for abuse. Tolerance can develop and physical and psychological dependence can occur.

MAO inhibitors See MONOAMINE OXIDASE (MAO) INHIBITORS.

marijuana The dried flowering tops, leaves, and stems of the Indian hemp plant *Cannabis sativa,* which contain the psychoactive substance TETRAHYDROCANNABINOL (THC) and are usually smoked in cigarettes ("joints") or pipes. Marijuana is a tall, leafy weed which grows best in hot dry climates like Central Asia, where it probably originated, but also grows wild in most parts of the world. An herbaceous annual with palm-like leaves, it has a hollow six-sided base, which is about two inches in diameter at maturity. The plant grows four to eight feet high.

Probably the oldest cultivated nonfood plant, the hemp plant has been a valuable source of products for man's commercial, medical, religious and recreational use for thousands of years. Its cultivation in the eastern hemisphere, both for its fibers and its psychoactive substance, has been widely chronicled. The earliest known written reference occurs in a Chinese pharmacological treatise dating from 2737 B.C. and attributed to the Emperor Shen Nung who, according to tradition, was the first to teach his people the medicinal value of cannabis. In India the first known reference to marijuana is found in the *Atharva Veda* which probably dates back to the second millenium B.C. There are references to marijuana on cuneiform tablets from Asia Minor dating back to 650 B.C., and some believe there are references to the drug in the Bible, in Homer, Herodotus, Pliny, Dioscorides, *The Arabian Nights,* and Marco Polo's writings. It is not known exactly when cannabis was introduced to Western Europe but it must have been very early; an urn found near Berlin, Germany, containing marijuana leaves and seeds is believed to date back to 500 B.C. Marijuana was also in early use in all parts of Africa.

The first record of marijuana in the New World dates from 1545 when the Spaniards introduced it to Chile, although it has been suggested that African slaves who used marijuana as an intoxicant and as a medicine brought it to Brazil earlier in the 16th century. It is not known if the Pilgrims brought marijuana to Plymouth but the plant was introduced to Virginia in 1611 and cultivated for its fiber. It was brought to New England in 1629 and until the end of the Civil War it was a major crop in North America and played an important role in colonial economic policy. In 1765 George Washington was growing hemp at Mount Vernon, presumably for its fiber, though some say Washington was interested in the medicinal and intoxicating qualities of his plants.

Raised for thousands of years as a source of fiber, the hemp plant has also been used in medicine for centuries. The *United States Pharmacopeia* listed it as a recognized medicine in 1850 under the name *Extractum Cannabis* (extract of hemp) and it appeared in the list until 1942. During the latter half of the 19th century, American doctors used cannabis in the treatment of pain, convulsive disorders, hysteria, asthma, rheumatism and labor pains. Cannabis preparations were on the shelves of every pharmacy and were widely prescribed until medical use of the plant was prohibited in 1937.

Marijuana was also used recreationally during the last half of the 19th century and became quite popular in the early part of the 20th century. In 1856, *Putman's Magazine* published an account of hashish-eating by a 16-year-old Poughkeepsie, N.Y., resident named Fitz Hugh Ludlow who had read and been influenced by De Quincey's *Confessions of an English Opium Eater*. Ludlow continued to experiment with hashish and marijuana extracts over the next few years and published an expanded account of his experiences in *The Hasheesh Eater*. Marijuana "tea pads," resembling opium dens, were established in New York about 1920. They were tolerated in much the same way that speakeasies were tolerated and by the 1930s there were an estimated 500 of them in New York City alone. During the 1920s New Orleans was a center of marijuana use as black musicians made it part of the jazz scene. Prohibition and the unrestrained lifestyles of the Roaring Twenties contributed to the spread of marijuana use, and until it began to be linked to the crime wave which swept the country during the 1930s (a link that was magnified by the sensational reports of yellow journalism) it was largely considered innocuous.

The belief that the nationwide upsurge of depraved criminal behavior was closely linked to the growing use of marijuana was particularly encouraged by Harry Anslinger, commissioner of the Federal Bureau of Narcotics. He conducted a personal campaign (felt by some individuals to be primarily an effort to gain political power) against the "killer weed" which resulted in state legislation banning marijuana. It also resulted in the passage of the 1937 Marijuana Tax Act which, while it did not actually ban marijuana on a federal level, outlawed the nonmedical, untaxed possession or sale of the drug. Anslinger's campaign was based on the contention that marijuana was "criminogenic," that is, it directly caused criminal behavior. In 1939 New York Mayor Fiorello La Guardia appointed a committee to study the use of marijuana, particularly in New York City. The committee cleared the drug of the criminogenic charge and further testified to its relative harmlessness. The committee's report was not published until 1944, however, when stereotypes fostered by Anslinger, and such propaganda films as *Reefer Madness,* were already strongly imbedded in the consciousness of the American people who were too preoccupied with World War II to pay it much attention anyway. During the 1955 Senate committee hearing Anslinger testified that marijuana use inevitably led to heroin addiction—an apparently false allegation that stuck in the public mind.

Despite the lurid stories of sexually depraved and criminal behavior which resulted from smoking marijuana, cannabis use continued to spread. Encouraged by the "Beat Generation," represented by such authors as Jack Kerouac, during the 1950s marijuana found a broad new audience: the American middle class and intelligentsia. In the 1960s it gained even more widespread popularity on college and high school campuses, becoming almost a symbol of American youth and the generation gap that separated young people from their parents.

During the 1970s and 1980s marijuana use had spread to all strata of American society and to all age groups. The increase in its popularity has brought with it a growing lobby for its legalization, which recent legislation does not reflect. The Controlled Substances Act of 1970 deems marijuana a Schedule I drug ("no known medical use"), and makes possession of it a misdemeanor. The sale, transfer, and intent to sell marijuana are felonies. A 1972 presidential commission suggested that the government focus on controlling traffic of the drug rather than on prosecuting recreational users of it. President Nixon rejected the recommendation.

In 1989, the three biggest suppliers of marijuana were Mexico (4,750 metric tons), Colombia (2,700 metric tons) and Jamaica (406 metric tons). The street value of a pound of marijuana grown in the U.S. is $1,660. Hawaiian marijuana is more expensive and costs $2,800 per pound in that state and $5,800 per pound on the East Coast.

After caffeine, nicotine and alcohol, marijuana is the fourth most popular abused substance in the world. Despite its illegal status in the United States, there are an estimated 16 million regular users (according to *Marijuana Under the Microscope,* a reprint from the Drug Enforcement Administration magazine, Vol. 7, No. 1, March 1980, p. 9), and the number of users increased each year until 1978. Since that time the two most reliable surveys, the high school senior survey and the household survey (performed by the Alcohol, Drug Abuse and Mental Health Administration of the U.S. Department of Health and Human Services), have shown significant drops in marijuana use. For example, in 1977 nearly 17% of all 12 to 17 year olds reported past-month use of marijuana; this figure dropped to 11.5% during the month prior to the 1982 survey. Similarly, in the 1979 survey, 35.4% of all young adults (aged 18–25) reported past-month use (an all time high), but by 1982 this figure had dropped to 27.4% A 1988 report by the National Institute on Drug Abuse placed current use of marijuana at 18 million for the 12 and older population. Among 24 to 40 year olds, 16% reported using marijuana at least once in the past month. This decrease in use is attributed to a change in attitude among young people. In 1978, 35% felt that regular marijuana use was associated with great risk; by 1982, this figure had risen to 60%. In his book *Marijuana: Costs of Abuse, Costs of Control* (Westport, Conn., 1989), economist Mark A. R. Kleiman of Harvard's Kennedy School of Government says the total amount of THC (TETRAHYDROCANNABINOL, the active ingredient in the plant) consumed by Americans actually rose 22% from 1982 to 1986. John P. Sutton of the Drug Enforcement Administration says Americans now grow "the most potent marijuana in the world." In many states, the law remains unchanged while actual enforcement policies testify to a diminishing concern among police officers with recreational users of marijuana.

Classification: Marijuana is classified as a HALLUCINOGEN, a Schedule I drug under the Controlled Substances Act of 1970.

Activity: The active principal in *Cannabis sativa* is delta-9-tetrahydrocannabinol (THC) which was first synthesized in 1966 at Hebrew University, Israel. It is most concentrated in the resin but is distributed throughout the plant, except in the root and seeds. Absorbed slowly and incompletely by the stomach, THC is much more effective when smoked and absorbed by the lungs. It is distributed to all the organs and almost completely metabolized in the liver. It is LIPID SOLUBLE, and deposits form in fatty tissues. It crosses the placental barrier and is excreted in the urine and feces. THC is insoluble in water and destroyed by heat. Its half life, the time required to eliminate half of the dose from the body, is 28–56 hours.

Dosage: It is impossible to say how much marijuana constitutes an effective dose since different varieties contain different concentrations of THC. The THC content can vary from 1% to 5% and more. Jamaican and South American marijuana contains the most THC while domestically cultivated marijuana contains about 1%. When smoked, THC's effects manifest in a few minutes, peak in 10–30 minutes and last two to three hours (depending on the potency). About 50% of the THC content of a marijuana cigarette is lost in burning and in the side-stream smoke; the rest is available for absorption if the ROACH is consumed. If a joint contains 1000 mg of 1% THC, it would have 10 mg of the active ingredient and about 5 mg would be available for absorption. Since the brain only receives its share by weight, approximately 0.05 mg of THC would arrive in the brain during the first few minutes.

After eating THC, effects materialize in 30–60 minutes, peak in two to three hours, and last three to five hours. THC is only one-half to one-third as effective when eaten as it is when smoked.

A lethal dose has never been established since no deaths directly related to the action of marijuana have been reported. Research with mice indicates that for a human weighing approximately 154 pounds a lethal dose of marijuana containing 1% THC would be 15 pounds smoked or 30 pounds eaten—all at once.

Effects: The effects of marijuana are highly subjective and are affected by a number of variables such as the quality of the drug, the dosage, the experience and expectations of the user and his environment. In very high doses, THC can produce hypnotic and psychedelic effects, including time and space distortions, enhanced sensory perceptions, euphoria and free-flowing thoughts. Adverse psychological reactions such as anxiety and paranoia can occur, usually in novice users. Some writers have described an "amotivational syndrome," which occurs with regular marijuana use, especially among the younger age groups. They claim that some chronic smokers became lethargic and lose their ambition and interest in everything except smoking marijuana. It has been counterproposed, however, that a person who is predisposed to this kind of life-style might simply find reinforcement of his views and desires in the sedative effect of marijuana.

The most common physiological effects reported with moderate use are dryness of the mouth and throat, an increase in pulse rate and heart action (tachycardia), increase in appetite (especially for sweets), red eyes, slight impairment of reflexes and psychomotor coordinated tasks such as driving, and sometimes nausea due to dizziness or anxiety. These symptoms are transitory and disappear after a few hours except for impaired driving skills which can last up to 10 hours.

During 1982 three major reports reviewed research findings to date. They are the reports of the Institute of Medicine (IOM), World Health Organization (WHO) and the National Institute on Drug Abuse (NIDA). Their general conclusions were similar and are briefly reported here. The NIDA study makes the following points: adolescents are beginning to smoke marijuana at an earlier age; marijuana is being used intensively by adolescents of both sexes; and the marijuana now available is five to 10 times more potent than it was a half dozen years ago. These facts are all unprecedented in history, especially in a demanding, highly industrialized society. Adolescence is a vulnerable period when coping mechanisims are learned and psychological maturation should be taking place. Instead, the report states, many youngsters are intoxicated on marijuana during a good part of their waking hours. The IOM conclusion is worth quoting: "What little we know now about the effects of marijuana on human health—and all we have reason to suspect—justifies serious national concern." The WHO summary states that "intermittent use of low potency cannabis is not generally associated with obvious symptoms of toxicity. Daily or more frequent use, especially of the highly potent preparations, may produce a chronic intoxication that may take several weeks to clear after drug use is discontinued." More recent research has demonstrated marked disturbances in depth perception, time judgment, and coordination during cannabis use. Coupled with surveys that indicate that many traffic accidents occur to people using cannabis derivatives, these facts raise a significant public health concern about driving vehicles or operating machinery after use.

A recent Canadian study on the effects of marijuana on the fetus has found a link between marijuana smoking and temporary exaggerated tremors, vision problems, and startle reflexes among the babies of mothers smoking five or more marijuana cigarettes per week during pregnancy. There are sparse reports of evidence of a fetal cannabis syndrome that resembles the fetal alcohol syndrome. (See PREGNANCY.)

Marijuana and alcohol: People who smoke marijuana are also apt to drink alcohol. According to findings of the National Commission on Marijuana and Drug Abuse, alcohol and tobacco are the two substances most commonly used by regular marijuana smokers. When alcohol is taken with marijuana there is greater impairment of motor and mental skills than with either drug alone (see SYNERGY). Among the young (under 21) there seems to be a growing trend toward the combined use of alcohol and marijuana.

Addictive aspects: The use of marijuana does not produce physical dependence but psychological dependence and the euphoric and sedative effects can result after long-term chronic use. Abstinence may result in feelings of irritability, nervousness or insomnia but these pass quickly.

Tolerance: Studies have shown that moderate and infrequent use of marijuana does not produce tolerance. Most experts agree, however, that heavy daily use produces tolerance to the tachycardia. "Reverse tolerance" has been suggested, a syndrome characterized by the user needing progressively smaller doses to achieve a HIGH. This phenomenon has been attributed (1) to the theory that smoking marijuana is a learned behavior, in the sense that with use the smoker learns how to smoke more efficiently and to recognize the effects of the drug more quickly and (2) to the fact that because of the very long excretion period of the drug and its lipid solubility, blood levels may remain at a subintoxification level but be rapidly raised by small additional quantities used.

Sources: In 1980, 75% of the U.S. marijuana market was supplied by Colombia; Mexico supplied 8% (a decrease in recent years); Jamaica supplied 10%; and 7% was grown domestically. Domestic cultivation is centered in seven primary states: California (where it is estimated that marijuana is the state's largest cash crop worth over $1 billion annually), Hawaii, Oregon, Arkansas, Missouri, Kentucky and Florida.

mazindol A stimulant drug whose activity is similar to that of the amphetamines. Some patients notice mild sedation from it. It is found in the anorectic SANOREX.

MDA (3, 4-methylenedioxyamphetamine) A semisynthetic drug produced by modifying the major psychoactive components of nutmeg and mace. It can also be produced from safrole, the oil of sassafras. The drug was first synthesized in 1910.

The effects of MDA combine some of the properties of MESCALINE and AMPHETA-

History of Marijuana

c.2737 B.C.	Reference to marijuana in Chinese pharmacology treatise.
c.2000 B.C.	Reference to marijuana found in India.
c.500 B.C.–1500 A.D.	500 B.C. urn containing marijuana found near Berlin, Germany.
	Cloth made from hemp in Europe.
1545	Hemp plant introduced to Chile.
1611	Hemp is cultivated by early colonists in Virginia.
1850	U.S. Pharmacopeia lists marijuana as a recognized medicine.
1856	Putnam's Magazine publishes an account of Fitz Hugh Ludlow's marijuana-eating experiences.
c.1875	"Hasheesh houses" modeled after opium dens begin to appear.
1920s–1930s	Commerce in marijuana for recreational use begins to increase during Prohibition.
	"Tea pads" spring up in major cities.
	Marijuana linked to crimewave of the 1930s.
1937	Marijuana Tax Act outlaws nonmedical, untaxed possession or sale.
1944	La Guardia Report in NYC clears the drug of being criminogenic and attests to its relative harmlessness.
1950s–1960s	Recreational use grows in the 1950s and becomes widespread in the 1960s on college and high school campuses.
1970	Controlled Substances Act lists marijuana as a Schedule I drug, and makes possession a misdemeanor; sale, transfer and intent to sell are felonies.
1970s–1980s	Use spreads to all segments of society and increases each year until 1978–79. In 1979 35.4% of young adults (aged 18–25) report use in past month; in 1982 27.4% report past month use. In 1988, 28 million Americans (14%) had used marijuana, cocaine or other illicit drugs at least once in the past year. The lifetime rate of marijuana use for youths (12 to 17) was 17%; the rate for young adults (18 to 25) was 56%.
1990s	Marijuana producers appear set to be the "bootleggers" and "moonshiners" of the decade.

MINES. Physical effects with low doses include pupil dilation, increased blood pressure and pulse rate; with high doses, there may be an increase in body temperature, profuse sweating and muscular rigidity. A sense of physical well-being with heightened tactile sensations may occur with low doses, while high doses may produce illusions and hallucinations. Subjective reports emphasize warm loving feelings (it has been called "the love drug" and "speed for lovers") and the desire for close communication and increased reflectiveness. This drug was believed by some to induce age regression and was used experimentally in psychotherapy as a way of helping a patient to relive specific childhood experiences. It was not found to be useful. While this phenomena happens with other hallucinogenic drugs, it occurs so regularly with MDA that it seems to be inherent in the pharmacology of the drug itself. MDA can be highly toxic—even fatal—in various dosages depending on the individual's sensitivity to it.

The average dose of MDA is from 50 to 150 mg. The effects begin to be felt about 30 to 60 minutes after ingestion and they last about eight hours. Mental and physical exhaustion may follow the use of MDA.

Tolerance to MDA does not develop. No physical or psychological dependence has been conclusively demonstrated. (See ECSTASY.)

MDMA See ECSTASY.

Mebaral® (Breon) A long-acting BARBITURATE that contains mephobarbital. It is used as a sedative hypnotic particularly in the treatment of epilepsy, its anticonvulsive action being much stronger than its hypnotic effect. Physical and psychological dependence can occur and when used with alcohol or other central nervous system depressants it can have an additive effect. Overdosage can result in respiratory depression; severe overdosage can result in coma and death. It is supplied in white scored tablets of 32, 50, 100 and 200 mg.

Media-Advertising Partnership for a Drug-Free America, Inc. Organization responsible for development and distribution of some of the most sophisticated drug awareness messages. It has generated millions of dollars worth of media time to disseminate well-designed, effective public service announcements. The partnership also conducts research to help target these messages. Contact: Tom Hendrick, % The American Association of Advertising Agencies, 666 Third Avenue, New York, NY 10017. Telephone: (212) 661-5447.

media and entertainment, drug use in The White House Conference for a Drug Free America's final report, in June 1988, stated: ''For too long some media have glamorized illicit drugs and portrayed their use as socially acceptable.'' Members of the film and television industries, musicians and gatekeepers of national news, the report said, ''were often viewed as unresponsive to attempts to fight illicit drug use.'' The report went on to explain that although the media have certainly been part of the problem, they must now become an ''ever-growing'' part of the solution. To accomplish this end, the conference set forth eight recommendations:

1. Every segment of the media and entertainment industries must ensure or continue to ensure that its programming avoids any positive portrayal of illicit drug use, and that responsible industry executives reject as unacceptable any programming that does not meet this standard.
2. Every segment of the media must establish a comprehensive public campaign against illicit drug use.
3. Media employers must adopt for all media workplaces a strong antidrug work policy that covers every employee.
4. Local media must work closely with community leaders and citizens groups to combat the use of illicit drugs.
5. Media messages must also increasingly target people who do not now use illicit drugs and minority populations.
6. The movie rating system, conducted by the Motion Picture Association of America, must take a stronger stance against illicit drugs.
7. The media must adhere to existing guidelines restricting alcohol and tobacco advertising that targets youth.
8. Student-run media, including high school newspapers and college print and broadcast outlets, must actively disseminate accurate information about illicit drug use.

Melfiat® (Reed-Provident) An anorectic drug containing phendimetrazine tartrate that is used for weight control. Its activity is similar to that of the AMPHETAMINES. Tolerance can develop within a few weeks and psychological dependence and social disability can occur. As with other anorectics it has a high potential for abuse. Overdosage can result in restlessness, tremors, rapid respiration, confusion and hallucinations. The drug is supplied in round orange 35 mg tablets, and in 70 mg tablets that are white with speckles of red.

Mellaril® (Sandoz) An anti-psychotic that contains thioridazine and is used for acute or chronic psychoses. When taken with alcohol or other central nervous system depressants it can have an additive effect. It is supplied in 10, 15, 25, 50, 100, 150 and 200 mg tablets, and as an concentrate containing 30 mg per ml and 100 mg per ml.

memory Memory is defined as the power or process of reproducing or recalling what has been learned in the past and retained. In this literal sense, what is remembered can be given a more or less sharply defined position in time and space.

Neither the mechanisms of memory itself, nor those of memory loss induced by drugs or other factors, are well understood at present, but both continue to be the subject of much scientific study. The memory process includes immediate short-term and long-term storage and retrieval facilities which appear to be centered in the brain's limbic system. Electrical stimulation of this area has enabled some patients to recall long-forgotten events and other information.

Information storage seems related to such chemical structures as proteins and nucleic acids. Pituitary hormones may also contribute to the memory process. Information appears to be filed chronologically and by sense; that is, there is a separate memory "file" for vision, hearing, taste, and so on.

Symptoms of memory loss, regardless of the cause, include inability to concentrate, absent-mindedness, poor sequence retention and general temporal confusion. A number of recreational drugs interfere, probably chemically, with the transfer of information from short-term to long-term memory, preventing users from storing and remembering information received while intoxicated. Scientists have been studying a theory known as "state dependency": it postulates that information received under intoxication can be recalled only when that state is reproduced, but so far findings have been inconsistent. Storage blockage is known to occur with the use of alcohol, marijuana, heroin and other depressants. Furthermore, information that is stored during drug intoxication may be distorted and therefore disturb the reasoning process.

Heavy drinkers commonly suffer "alcoholic haze," a reversible memory disturbance which correlates to the amount of alcohol ingested. After years of chronic alcoholism this condition can progress to more severe memory failure which abstinence may correct to some degree. Irreversible memory disturbance is an aspect of organic brain damage. In KORSAKOFF'S PSYCHOSIS, patients experience extreme difficulty in retrieving information from short-term memory. They are unable to "store" new memories.

Many chronic alcoholics frequently suffer lapses of memory called "blackouts" in which they lose all recollection of entire blocks of time during which they were conscious. This too is attributed to severe impairment of information storage facilities and can happen to anyone—not just alcoholics—when very large quantities of alcohol are ingested quickly. Risk of blackout is increased by fatigue and by the combination of alcohol and other sedative drugs.

Myriad studies on the effect of marijuana on memory processes have yielded a variety of results. Some have shown that only immediate recall is affected during intoxication and that this is due to the user's inability to concentrate. Other reports state that the transfer of information from short-term to long-term memory is impaired while the user is high but that there are no long-term effects. Marijuana's suppression of nucleic acid synthesis may be responsible for this effect, which is significant in light of the large numbers of students of both high school and college age who smoke marijuana during school hours. If memory storage is impaired, information received while the person is high will not be remembered and clearly learning cannot take place at the student's full capacity. However, marijuana smoking is a learned behavior in a number of ways and many users have reported being able to overcome the drug's effects on memory storage by concentrating harder on the material at hand.

Use of hallucinogens like LSD has caused a rare but well-known phenomenon of memory disturbance known as FLASHBACK, in which the user's drug experience is so vivid and impressive that it becomes firmly implanted in the memory and can be re-experienced long afterward. No satisfactory explanation for flashbacks has been developed. The perceptual distortion which results from taking psychedelic drugs has also included temporal confusion in which the user projects a memory into his present situation.

Hardin & Helen Jones, *Sensual Drugs* (New York: Cambridge University Press, 1977).

Elizabeth Loftus, *Memory* (Reading, MA: Addison-Wesley Publishing Company, 1980).

Robert O'Brien and Morris Chafetz *The Encyclopedia of Alcoholism* (New York: Facts on File Publications, 1982).

Menrium® (Roche) A preparation that contains chlordiazepoxide and esterified estrogens and is usually used for the treatment of menopausal syndrome. It can produce dependency and it can have an additive effect when taken with alcohol or other central nervous system depressants. Overdosage can result in diminished reflexes, somnolence, confusion and coma. Menrium 5–2 is supplied in green tablets: Menrium 5–4 in dark green tablets; and Menrium 10–4 in purple tablets.

meperidine A NARCOTIC ANALGESIC meperidine hydrochloride is best known by the brand name DEMEROL. It is an OPIOID, a synthetic opiate, similar pharmacologically but not structurally to morphine, and is one-tenth as potent. Eislab & Schaumann introduced the drug, also known as penthidine, to the medical profession in 1939, proclaiming its usefulness in reducing spasms of the smooth muscles of the stomach and small intestine. The discovery of its analgesic properties some time afterward produced a wave of excitement among doctors, who believed the drug had morphine's effect without being addictive. This supposition was subsequently proven false.

Appearance: Meperidine hydrochloride appears as a fine white crystalline powder. It is odorless, soluble in water and alcohol, and slightly soluble in ether. Its melting point is between 186–189 degrees fahrenheit.

Activity: Rapidly absorbed and metabolized in the liver, meperidine brings relief in 15 minutes when taken orally and in 10 minutes when administered hypodermically. Its effects peak in one hour and last two to four hours, which is briefer than morphine's effects. The drug's half-life is three to four hours. Meperidine crosses the placental barrier and appears in mother's milk.

Dosage: For pain relief, meperidine is administered orally, intramuscularly or subcutaneously every three to four hours in doses of 50–200 mg. The lethal dose has not yet been determined; 1200 mg have been fatal and 2000 mg have been survived. Cases of extreme tolerance have been recorded in which the addict's daily habit reached 3000–4000 mg. Intravenous administration should be slow and in diluted solution to accommodate the higher potency of the drug through that route.

Effects: Meperidine relives moderate to severe pain and produces a euphoric effect less intense than that of morphine. It is a respiratory depressant and has proved fatal when administered to patients suffering asthmatic attacks. In therapeutic doses meperidine causes the side effects usually associated with narcotic drugs, such as dizziness, nausea and sweating. Larger doses can cause tremors, twitches and seizures.

Tolerance: Tolerance to meperidine's sedative effects develops more quickly than tolerance to its analgesic action. The drug's short duration necessitates repeated administration to maintain euphoria and this accounts in part for the uncommon development of meperidine dependence. Special care should be exercised with patients receiving other narcotic-analgesic and sedative hypnotic drugs. Symptoms of addiction include extreme drowsiness, respiratory depression and cold clammy skin. Abusive doses can result in circulatory collapse, cardiac arrest and death. Withdrawal symptoms are dose related, as with all opiates. Unlike other opiates, meperidine withdrawal may produce seizures.

Usage: Used medically for the short-term relief of moderate to severe pain, meperidine often serves, in combination with other drugs, as a pre-operative analgesic, particularly in obstetrics. After morphine, meperidine is the second most widely used analgesic for severe pain.

Recreational use of and addiction to meperidine occurs most frequently, though not exclusively, among members of the medical profession to whom the drug is most readily available.

Availability: Winthrop manufacturers meperidine hydrochloride in white tablet form under the brand name Demerol. The drug is also available in syrups and injectable form.

mephobarbital A long-acting BARBITURATE that exerts a strong sedative and anticonvulsive action but has a relatively mild hypnotic effect. Onset of action is from 30 to 60 minutes; duration is from 10 to 16 hours. It is manufactured as MEBARAL and appears in tablet form. It is converted in the liver to PHENOBARBITAL but is less effective as a sedative than phenobarbital. Mephobarbital is used in the treatment of epilepsy, anxiety, tension and apprehension.

meprobamate A sedative hypnotic, first marketed under the name MILTOWN in tribute to the New Jersey town where it was developed in the early 1950s. Meprobamate was heralded as a unique drug which relieved anxiety without producing undue sedation. It enjoyed instant popularity and liberal prescriptions were given to patients suffering from anxiety and tension. As early as 1956 reports of addiction appeared, encouraging caution in its prescription but curbing its use only slightly. In the late 1960s over a million pounds of meprobamate were manufactured and distributed.

Meprobamate is a bitter white powder, slightly soluble in water and freely soluble in alcohol. Readily absorbed in the gastrointestinal tract and rapidly distributed throughout the body, meprobamate is metabolized by the liver and excreted by the kidneys. It crosses the placental barrier and appears in mother's milk. Cases of congenital malformation associated with meprobamate use by pregnant women have been reported.

The drug depresses the central nervous system, with effects peaking in two hours. It has a half-life of four to ten hours. Usual oral doses range from 1200–1600 mg daily, divided into three or four doses. A dose of 800 mg taken at one time may cause sleep and daily doses above 2400 mg are not recommended. Overdose can cause respiratory depression, coma and death. No lethal dose has been established, however, although 20,000–40,000 mg have been survived.

Less potent than the minor tranquilizers derived from benzodiazepines (Librium, Valium), meprobamate is used for muscle relaxation and sedation. It is prescribed for the short-term relief of symptoms of anxiety. Large doses can result in euphoria and intoxication similar to that induced by BARBITURATES, including such symptoms as slurred speech and loss of coordination and muscular control.

Adverse reactions include drowsiness, dizziness, headache, visual impairment, nausea, vomiting, rash, prickly or burning sensations and diarrhea.

Tolerance, along with physical and psychological dependence can develop with meprobamate use. Withdrawal symptoms include tremors, insomnia, gastrointestinal distress, convulsions and hallucinations, as well as the recurrence, in magnified degree, of the symptoms of anxiety which lead to the use of the drug.

Meprobamate exhibits cross-tolerance to barbiturates and is potentiated by other central nervous system depressants. Accidental deaths have occurred from combinations of meprobamate and other depressants and it has been used in suicide attempts—usually unsuccessfully.

Meprospan® (Wallace) A nonbarbiturate minor TRANQUILIZER that contains MEPROBAMATE. It is used for the relief of tension and anxiety and as a muscle relaxant. Tolerance can develop and physical and psychological dependence can occur. When taken with alcohol or other central nervous system depressants it can have an additive effect. Overdosage can result in drowsiness, stupor, coma and respiratory collapse. It is supplied as Meprospan 200, yellow-topped capsules; and as Meprospan 400, blue-topped capsules.

mescal A beverage made from plants of the genus *Agave* (maguey, pulque) which grow in the southwestern United States. It has an intoxicating effect. Also a slang term for PEYOTE.

mescaline The principal alkaloid in the peyote cactus, *Lophorphora williamsii,* found in northern Mexico and Texas.

Mescaline was one of the first hallucinogens to be chemically isolated. Arthur Heffter (1860–1925), a German chemist and professor of pharmacology, was studying peyote and individually tested four alkaloids that were isolated from the cactus. On November 23, 1896, Heffter took 150 mg of mescaline hydrochloride and reported: "2:00 p.m. Violet and green spots appear on the paper during readings. When the eyes are kept shut the following visual images occur . . . carpet patterns, ribbed vaulting, etc. . . . Later on landscapes, halls, architectural scenes (e.g., pillars decorated with flowers) also appear. The images can be observed until about 5:30 p.m. Nausea and dizziness are at times very distressing. . . . In the evening well-being and appetite are undisturbed and there is no sign of sleeplessness."

The chemical structure of mescaline was determined in 1918. Mescaline attracted widespread intellectual interest in the early part of the century by such people as Havelock Ellis, Weir Mitchell and Aldous Huxley, but today it is rarely available licitly.

Mescaline is usually taken orally but it can be inhaled by smoking ground peyote buttons, or, more rarely, it can be injected. It is considerably less potent than LSD. Average doses range from 300 to 500 mg. Of the alleged mescaline samples analyzed at the Addiction Research Foundation in Toronto, Canada, nearly 90% were not mescaline; usually they contained either PCP or PCP combined with LSD.

Mescaline offers the user the opportunity to achieve a hallucinogenic state without undergoing all of the preliminary emetic effects of peyote, and to achieve it more rapidly. The hallucinatory effects of peyote and mescaline are reported to be fairly similar to the effects of LSD.

Classification: Mescaline is classified as a HALLUCINOGEN, a Schedule I drug under the CONTROLLED SUBSTANCES ACT. It is in the same chemical group of drugs as TMA and MDA and is chemically related to adrenaline.

Effects: Common mental effects include euphoria, heightened sensory perception, a dream-like state, sometimes with hallucinations or synesthesia, and difficulty in thinking. At low doses the effects appear within one to three hours and lasts for four to 12 hours or more. Physical effects include dilation of the pupils, an increase in body temperature, some muscular relaxation and sometimes vomiting. At higher doses mescaline may also induce fever, headache, low blood pressure and depressed heart and respiratory activity.

Addictive aspects: No physical dependence on the effects of mescaline develops regardless of the frequency of usage.

Tolerance: Tolerance to mescaline, like to all hallucinogens, develops rapidly and is very short lived. Mescaline is rarely taken on the kind of regular basis that would allow tolerance to develop. When tolerance is observed, CROSS-TOLERANCE to other hallucinogens occurs.

Sources: Mescaline can be made synthetically or from peyote cactus. The heads or "buttons" of the cactus are dried and then sliced, chopped, or ground and sometimes put in capsules.

Jan G. Bruhn, "Three Men and a Drug: Peyote Research in the 1890s," *The Cactus and Succulent Journal of Great Britain,* vol. 30, no. 2, 1977, pp. 27–30.

"Facts About Hallucinogens," pamphlet, Toronto, Canada: Addiction Research Foundation, 1980.

Frederick G. Hofmann, *A Handbook on Drug and Alcohol Abuse* (New York: Oxford University Press, 1975), pp. 169–171.

Jerome Jaffe, Rovert Petersen, and Ray Hodgson, *Addictions: Issues and Answers* (New York: Harper and Row Publishers, 1980), pp. 61–61.

metabolism The process by which the body uses food, water and oxygen to sustain itself. The process begins with absorption of a substance, such as food or a drug, into the body system and continues until the substance is excreted. There are two metabolic processes: anabolism and catabolism. Anabolism is the chemical change that turns the introduced substance into the complex substances of which the body is built. Catabolism involves the breaking down process of energy production. See individual drug categories for specific metabolic patterns.

methadone An OPIOID. A synthetic NARCOTIC ANALGESIC, methadone was first introduced during World War II when it was developed by German chemists (the brand name DOLOPHINE is a tribute to Adolph Hitler). Though structurally dissimilar to morphine, it shares its effects. Methadone is best known for its application in the controversial Methadone Maintenance program, which some experts believe has been our most useful tool in the treatment and rehabilitation of heroin addicts.

Appearance and activity: Methadone is an odorless white crystalline powder which is soluble in water, alcohol and chloroform and insoluble in ether. The body absorbs and responds to the substance in much the same way as it does to morphine (see MORPHINE for details).

Dosage: As an antiussive, methadone is prescribed in 1–2 mg doses to be taken every four to six hours. For pain relief, 2.5–20 mg are prescribed intramuscularly or orally ever 3–4 hours. Doses in the Methadone Maintenance program range from 20–120 mg orally and effects last from 24–48 hours, whereas the average addict's dose of heroin lasts only four to six hours.

Effects: The effects of methadone resemble those of morphine and heroin in most respects. The drug produces the same euphoria and drowsiness but does not slow the respiration as much as heroin. Most importantly, it produces cross-tolerance to that drug, thereby blocking its effects. It is this quality that makes the drug useful in heroin addiction therapy. It also reduces the craving for opiates. Methadone is as likely as heroin to produce dependence and withdrawal symptoms are more prolonged. Symptoms include pain in the bones, sweating and diarrhea.

Usage: Methadone is used to relieve chronic pain of moderate to severe intensity. Methadone is also useful as an antitussive and as a detoxicant for patients withdrawing from heroin and morphine. The drug's primary use today is in Methadone Maintenance programs aimed at helping heroin addicts overcome their addiction and accompanying destructive life-style. The program includes weaning the addict away from heroin and providing him with the counseling and training needed to rejoin society in a constructive capacity. The program has been applied at numerous rehabilitation centers all over the United States and abroad and its philosophy and results have been the subject of longstanding debate and disagreement.

There are two types of programs: the original high-dose model developed in the early 1960s by Drs. Vincent Dole and Marie Nyswander, and the low-dose model. Both models use the oral administration method; the dose is generally in liquid form and dissolved in fruit drinks. In the high-dose model, the treatment begins by increasing the patients' tolerance until he can accommodate a daily dosage of between 50 and 120 milligrams. The low-dose model stabilizes the patient on 30 milligrams or less a day.

The patient leaves urine samples which are tested for signs of morphine (heroin is excreted as morphine) and other drugs. Although methadone blocks heroin's effects, some patients continue to use heroin, and other opiates. Abuse of cocaine, alcohol and barbiturates has been well documented among methadone patients. Once he has demonstrated responsibility and commitment to rehabilitation, the patient is allowed to take home a one- and later a three-day, or six-day supply of methadone.

Detoxification is effected by gradually reducing the methadone content of the mixture. Some patients, however, find their psychological dependence more difficult to overcome than their physical addiction. Many either revert to their heroin habit or require indefinite methadone treatment. Opponents of the programs focus their arguments on the fact that it replaces one addiction with another and that it is doubtful that the patient will ever withdraw from methadone.

The positive aspects of methadone treatment are the following: cross-tolerance may reduce craving and block opiate effects. The oral administration of methadone is especially important because it breaks the ritual of injecting and eliminates infection. Finally, and maybe most significantly, methadone can be obtained legally. The heroin addict can satisfy his dependence without reverting to criminal activities and, at the same time, work under a controlled program to free himself of his addiction.

Statistics on the success of the Methadone Maintenance programs differ and it remains a controversial issue. New problems have arisen as a result of the program: large quantities of legal methadone are diverted to the illicit drug market each year, for example, and in 1973 there were more methadone-related deaths than heroin-related ones in New York City. On the other hand, the treatment developed by Drs. Dole and Nyswander has certainly enabled large numbers of heroin addicts to reshape their lives and to rejoin society, free of their crippling addictions. Methadone maintenance seems to be the most effective way yet of accomplishing that goal.

Some critics argue that methadone maintenance is little more than "chemical slavery" and say it does not give addicts the hope of being drug free. (There are an estimated 500,000 heroin addicts in the U.S. today.) Researchers counter that if it is a choice between lifelong therapy or addiction to a dangerous drug, such as cocaine or heroin, the choice is clear. Dr. Marvin Snyder, director of the task force on medication development at the National Institute on Drug Abuse (NIDA), says, "Drug addiction is a chronic, ongoing disease. If you have to take a therapeutic drug for the rest of your life, so be it."

Commercial availability: Methadone is manufactured in tablets, syrups and injectable forms. Brand names include DOLOPHINE (also known as dollies), METHADONE HYDROCHLORIDE DISKETTES. and Methanex.

Methadone and alcohol: Investigations have shown a considerable amount of crossover between the use of alcohol and heroin. Alcoholism among heroin addicts is frequent. Studies have suggested that alcohol is the drug most frequently abused before the initial use of heroin, and that addiction has already occurred. When heroin is not available, heroin addicts will often use alcohol as a substitute to relieve their withdrawal symptoms. The figures on the prevalence of alcoholism among methadone-maintained addicts vary from 20% to 50%.

Alcoholism among methadone-maintained addicts not only interferes with the rehabilitation process, it also causes dangerous side effects. Because a majority of heroin addicts have had an episode of viral hepatitis,the consumption of large amounts of alcohol may aggravate a pre-existing liver condition and progress rapidly to CIRRHOSIS. In addition there is the increased danger of a synergistic effect between the depressant properties of alcohol and methadone. Mortality rates for methadone patients who are also alcoholics are much higher than for those who are not alcoholics.

Alcoholism plays a disruptive role in the rehabilitation process of heroin addicts. A patient suffering from alcoholism is likely to become aggressive and refuse to follow rules often leading to the termination of his methadone therapy. Premature discharge from a program can also occur because the alcohol interferes with proper detoxification from heroin. After detoxification from heroin and withdrawal from methadone, alcoholism is not necessarily alleviated, and because of the complexities of CROSS-ADDICTION alcoholism can be the single most important obstacle that prevents a heroin-addicted individual from functioning in society. Because many alcoholism programs will not accept methadone-maintained patients, methadone treatment programs should be oriented toward dealing with alcoholism.

methadone "clone" A therapeutic agent designed to break a cocaine user's physical and psychological dependence on the drug. An idea championed by Senator Daniel Patrick Moynihan (D-NY) and given the catch phrase "methadone clone," it has yielded few encouraging results.

Research into the biology of cocaine addiction is also beginning to show that a methadone-like substance for cocaine addicts will be neither simple to develop nor necessarily effective. Cocaine does not produce the kind of easily duplicated physical tolerance and dependence of heroin.

The idea behind providing methadone, with its narcotic activity, is that it reduces the craving for heroin. Both heroin and methadone are opiates, and tolerance develops to opiates. However, when the body is subjected to cocaine-like stimulants, stable narcotic-like tolerance does *not* develop, so a chemical as similar to cocaine as methadone is to heroin could overstimulante nerve cells the way cocaine itself does, significantly affecting the way a person acts or thinks.

Researchers seem to agree, though, that pharmacological agents combined with various non-chemical therapies could be useful. Current treatment methods, which rely heavily on self-help group sessions and one-on-one counseling, have produced mixed results.

The new therapeutic drugs under development are not intended as a replacement for cocaine but to help addicts past the initial anxiety, depression and craving of going "cold turkey"—and to give support structures and therapy a chance to work. Agents that have shown success thus far include: antidepressants, believed to restore a brain chemical depleted by cocaine that carries signals from one nerve to another; and anti-epileptic drugs that block the erratic nerve cell firing that results from cocaine use.

Joanne Silberner, "A Technical Fix for Cocaine Addiction," *U.S. News & World Report,* April 17, 1989, 61.

Methadone Hydrochloride Diskettes® (Lilly) A synthetic narcotic analgesic whose activity is similar to that of morphine. It is used for detoxification and maintenance treatment in cases of narcotic addiction. It is long-acting and, when doses are given daily, its effects last 24–48 hours. Tolerance can develop and physical and psychological dependency can occur. The drug has a high potential for abuse. Overdosage can result in respiratory depression; circulatory collapse, cardiac arrest and death can occur. It is supplied in 40 mg pillow-shaped, peach-colored tablets. It is a Schedule II drug under the CONTROLLED SUBSTANCES ACT.

methamphetamine A synthetic amphetamine used as an anorectic. (See DESOXYN and AMPHETAMINES.)

methanol Methanol (also known as methyl alcohol or wood alcohol) is a colorless flammable liquid that can be mixed with water in all proportions. It is a poison and, because it oxidizes slower than ethyl alcohol, the formaldehyde produced may cause blindness even in small doses. When used as a denaturant for ethanol it makes the latter unfit for drinking. Methanol is also called wood alcohol because at one time it was primarily produced as a by-product of wood distillation. Today methanol is produced synthetically and is generally used as a solvent or antifreeze. People have died from unknowingly drinking wood alcohol in bootleg whiskey or moonshine. Others have died after knowingly consuming it in the absence of their usual alcoholic beverages. Initially it has intoxicating effects.

methaqualone (2-Methyl-3-[2-methylphenyl]=4[3H]quinazolinone) First synthesized in 1951 in India as an antimalarial drug, methaqualone was introduced to the American medical market in the mid-1960s for the treatment of insomnia and anxiety and was believed to have none of the abuse potential of short-acting barbiturates. Because it was alleged to be safe and non-addictive it became quite popular with individuals looking for a new safe high. Since that time, however, many instances of addiction and overdose have been reported and its high abuse potential has been documented in scientific research.

Intoxication from methaqualone is similar to intoxication from barbiturates and alcohol. The risks are the same: death by overdose, accidents due to confusion and impaired motor coordination. Coma has been known to occur following 2.4 grams of methaqualone; 8 to 20 grams have produced severe toxicity and death. Like barbiturates, methaqualone has a SYNERGISTIC effect when used with alcohol and other central nervous system depressants. Overdose can result in delirium, restlessness, excessive tension and muscle spasms leading to convulsions. An addict should not discontinue the drug abruptly and to avoid the risk of convulsions during withdrawal, a patient should be detoxified in a hospital.

As more doctors have become aware of the abuse and addictive potential of methaqualone, their willingness to prescribe it has declined. This has resulted in a large traffic in illicitly produced tablets. The most commonly produced imitations are of the brands Quaalude and Mequin, both of which, before they were withdrawn from the market, contained 300 mg of methaqualone. The imitations may contain between 10 and 150 mg of methaqualone, between 20 and 300 mg of diazepam (Valium), or combinations of other substances. The level of diazepam found in just one tablet may at times be enough to render the user unconscious. Other imitations may be so weak that a small handful of pills are needed in order to get high—a danger if someone accustomed to a weak form unknowingly obtains an identical-looking but much more potent form.

The heaviest concentration of users of illicit methaqualone was between high school age and the mid-30s.

Appearance: Methaqualone is a white crystalline powder with little or no odor and a bitter taste. It is stable in light and air, and soluble in alcohol and ether. It is slightly soluble in water.

Classification: Methaqualone is a nonbarbiturate sedative hypnotic. LEMMON, the last manufacturer of methaqualone under the brand names Quaalude and Mequin, removed the drug from the market in the early 1980s because of its widespread abuse. Methaqualone was placed in Schedule II in 1973, then rescheduled to Schedule I in 1984.

Effects: Methaqualone is readily absorbed from the gastrointestinal tract. It is transported in the plasma and is distributed in the body fat, the liver and the brain tissue. Relatively low doses (75 mg four times a day) lead to sleep. With hypnotic (sleep-inducing) doses there may be transient "pins and needles" sensations prior to sleep. Excessive dreaming and sleepwalking sometimes occur. Hangover is frequent. Side effects can include nausea, vomiting, stomach discomfort, sweating, hives, rapid heart beat and lack of appetite.

Users who take the drug for pleasure typically resist its sedative effects in order to achieve a dissociative high similar to that induced by barbiturates. They generally take larger doses, 600–900 mg, or more if TOLERANCE has developed. Users experience a pleasant sense of well-being, an increased pain threshold, loss of muscle coordination and a prickling of the fingers, lips and tongue. The "high" is reputed to enhance sexual performance; there is little evidence of this, however, and it is more likely that, like alcohol, the drug acts on the central cortex of the brain to release normal inhibitions.

Addictive aspects: Psychological dependence occurs with methaqualone. Physical dependence also develops producing distinctive WITHDRAWAL symptoms similar to those occurring with barbiturate dependence: headaches, severe cramps, convulsions and tremors. Symptoms of withdrawal also include irritability and sleeplessness followed by mania and delirium tremens. Many authorities believe that the potential for methaqualone addiction and abuse are as serious as those of barbiturates and heroin.

Tolerance: Tolerance to the drug's euphoric effects develops at a more rapid rate than tolerance to its respiratory depressant effects, increasing the danger of overdose.

Sources: Legitimate supplies are now unavailable in the United States. There is a strong black market of lookalike capsules or tablets that may or may not contain actual methaqualone. A large amount of illicit methaqualone arrives in the U.S. from Columbia. Mandrax is a European name for methaqualone in combination with an antihistamine.

metharbital A long-acting BARBITURATE with anti-convulsant properties similar to those of MEPHOBARBITAL and PHENOBARBITAL. Metharbital is a derivative of BARBITAL, to which it is converted in the liver. Milder and less toxic than phenobarbital, it is manufactured as GEMONIL. It is used in the treatment of grand mal, petit mal, myoclonic and mixed types of seizures.

methyl alcohol See METHANOL.

methyldihydromorphinone An analgesic. A semisynthetic MORPHINE derivative, used mainly in the treatment of cancer, it is a Schedule II drug and is more potent than morphine. It is also known as Metopon.

methylmorphine See CODEINE.

methylphenidate A central nervous system stimulant with action somewhat like that of the AMPHETAMINES. It is used in the treatment of narcolepsy and also in the treatment of hyperkinetic children. (See RITALIN.)

methyphenobarbital A long-acting barbiturate with an onset time of up to one hour and duration of action up to 16 hours. It is also known as MEPHOBARBITAL. (See BARBITURATES and MEBARAL.)

methyprylon A central nervous system depressant and hypnotic used in the treatment of insomnia. Its action is similar to that of the BARBITURATES but it is chemically unrelated. (See NOLUDAR.)

metopon See METHYLDIHYDROMORPHINONE.

Mexico Since 1970 there have been several investigations aimed at estimating the prevalence of drug use in Mexico. The surveys reported that inhalants were the most commonly abused substances, followed by amphetamines, cannabis and tranquilizers. Use of heroin, LSD and cocaine was reported by only a small percentage of the population in Mexico City and the northern region of the country. The surveys were conducted in hospitals and treatment centers, in the general population through household surveys, among students and the imprisoned population, and among other high risk groups. Although the surveys indicate certain problem areas, the government acknowledges that they are far from comprehensive and that the actual number of abusers is unknown.

In a 1980 survey carried out in a representative sample of the school population (14–18 year olds) of Mexico City and its metropolitan area, 12.3% of the students reported some pattern of abuse. This figure was further broken down to: 10.7% light users; 1.1% moderate users; and .5% heavy users. The percentage of heavy users increased to 5.6% when alcohol and tobacco were included. When compared to a 1976 survey, the frequency of regular use did not show a significant increase. There was an increase, however, in the percentage who had "ever used" a drug. A recent study carried out in Mexico City among younger children (11–14 years old) reported that 27% had used inhalants. In a 1984 international comparison of alcohol consumption per person 15 years and over, Mexico was 31st among 32 nations included in the survey. Mexico's total alcohol consumption was 4.2 liters (1 liter equals 1.06 quarts) per person.

The kinds of drugs that are abused vary greatly among different groups and according to geographical areas. It should be noted that most surveys were carried out in metropolitan areas and not in the numerous rural communities. Use of non-medical drugs was most common among the male population under 25 years of age; the abuse of medically used drugs was more common among the female population of the same age.

Nearly all health institutions in the country provide some sort of service for drug abusers. There are also small pilot programs in which new approaches to the treatment of high risk groups are tried and evaluated—particular attention has been given to those who use inhalants. Centros de Integración Juvenil, a civil association and one of the biggest organizations specializing in treatment facilities, has received government funding. Since 1970 the association has established 32 centers in 28 cities. Before 1981 every young person who asked for treatment was accepted; after 1981 the admission policy had to be modified because of the number of applicants and now only the most severe cases are accepted.

For thousands of years Mexicans used "native" hallucinogens in religious rites; peyote and sacred mushrooms were the most common. In recent years the use of these substances has dwindled but a kind of occultism centered around these hallucinogens has sprung up in other countries—largely influenced by the writings of Carlos Casteneda—and generated a movement of those who want to experience Mexico's wondrous drugs. Consequently the Mexican government has to contend with trafficking in "occult" drugs, as well as the current exoteric drugs of abuse.

Because of its border situation, Mexico has also long been a center for other kinds of drug trafficking. Until the late 1970s Mexico was the primary source for the marijuana market in the United States. This dubious distinction has since been bestowed on Colombia. From 1977 to 1978 Mexico's share of the U.S. marijuana market dropped from 40% to 18%; from 1978 to 1980 it declined to 8%. But in 1989, Mexico again led big suppliers in marijuana production. Metric tons produced there were 4,750, leading Colombia's 2,700 metric tons. Significant traffic in diverted amphetamine powder and other illicit drugs from Europe and the U.S. via Mexico has been well documented, along with trafficking in illicit methaqualone. The majority of these drugs now pass through Colombia because of concerted efforts by both the U.S. and Mexican governments.

In past years Mexico was also involved in heroin trafficking. When the FRENCH CONNECTION fell apart, Mexico became a main supplier of heroin to the U.S. During the mid-1970s it was estimated that 60% of the heroin consumed in the U.S. was of Mexican origin. Mexican "brown" heroin was at that time assayed at about 17% heroin—a high percentage when compared with the other heroin available, which assayed at about 2–3%. Mexico had a corner on the market for only a short time, though, and has since been replaced by the GOLDEN CRESCENT.

Mexican poppy cultivation dates back to World War II. Shipments from Europe were all but cut off due to the war and the New York Mafia began to finance Mexican production. Poppy cultivation in Mexico declined until its brief comeback in the mid-1970s. Opium fields are still cultivated today in rural areas but only an insignificant amount of the drug is exported.

In 1969 the United States and Mexico signed an agreement calling for joint action against drug trafficking. Called "Operation Cooperation," it resulted in the confiscation of many tons of drugs, particularly marijuana, and the arrest of many smugglers. In addition the Mexican government has made numerous changes in its National Health Code and many chemicals are now subject to strict control. In 1989, Mexico, under President Carlos Salinas de Gortari, is prosecuting some formerly untouchable drug lords and officials, notably José Antonio Zovvilla Pérez, former chief of the Federal Security Directorate.

Penalties for drug use and possession have also undergone changes. There is no bail or bond now for individuals charged with a narcotics crime: they must stand trial and, if convicted, there is no parole or suspended sentence. Long pre-trial imprisonment can be expected in Mexico because the courts are backed up with pending cases.

micronodular cirrhosis A contemporary classification for a kind of cirrhosis that is similar to PORTAL CIRRHOSIS, the most common cirrhosis found among alcoholics. (See CIRRHOSIS.)

milieu therapy A socioenvironmental therapy that is an essential part of inpatient treatment. In this therapy the behavior and attitudes of the staff and the activities perscribed for a patient are determined by the patient's interpersonal and emotional needs. This interaction between patient and staff includes learning how to interact with others without letting anger turn to violence; learning to talk to people about things other than drugs; and learning to ask for help when it is needed.

military See AMERICAN MILITARY.

milk sugar Lactose crystals that are used to dilute heroin. It resembles heroin in appearance.

Miltown® (Wallace) A widely used minor tranquilizer that contains MEPROBAMATE and is used for the relief of tension and anxiety. It has a significant potential for abuse, and both physical and psychological dependence can occur. When taken with alcohol or other central nervous system depressants it can have an additive effect. Overdosage can result in drowsiness, stupor, respiratory collapse, coma, shock and death. It is supplied as Miltown in 400 mg white scored tablets, and 200 mg white sugar-coated tablets; and as Miltown 600, white capsule-shaped tablets containing 600 mg of meprobamate.

Miltrate® (Wallace) A minor tranquilizer that contains MEPROBAMATE (for tension and anxiety) and pentaerythritol tetranitrate (to relax smooth muscle). It is used for the relief of pain associated with coronary artery disease. Miltrate has the potential for abuse and both physical and psychological dependence can occur. When taken with alcohol or other central nervous system depressants it can have an additive effect. It is supplied as Miltrate-10, white tablets containing 10 mg of pentaerythritol tetranitrate; and Miltrate-20, orange tablets containing 20 mg of pentaerythritol tetranitrate. Each variety contains 200 mg of meprobamate.

minerals See NUTRITION.

mixed addiction See POLYDRUG USE.

mixed cirrhosis A combination of macronodular and micronodular cirrhosis. (See CIRRHOSIS.)

mixing drinks Changing alcoholic beverages in the course of a drinking session. Though commonly thought to cause or intensify a hangover, the fact is the alcohol content and concentration of the drinks are actually to blame. Mixing drinks can, however, be a factor in how rapidly a person becomes intoxicated. If, for example, beer is taken first and then followed by whiskey, the beer slows the absorption of the whiskey and its effects are somewhat delayed. If whiskey is taken first and then beer, the result is more rapid intoxication because the beer reinforces the concentrated rush of the whiskey to the bloodstream.

MMDA A derivative of the alkaloid myristicin found in nutmeg. It has psychedelic properties and purportedly intensifies present experiences, as opposed to MDA which intensifies experiences in the user's past. It is the same as MDA except that its chemical formula includes a 3-methoxy group.

Model Drug Testing Policy The International Association of Chiefs of Police has information and a model policy for use by state and local law enforcement agencies that they use to implement antidrug programs. Contact: Model Drug Testing Policy, International Association of Chiefs of Police, 1110 N. Glebe Road, Suite 200, Arlington, VA 22201. Telephone: (703) 243-6500.

moderate drinking Occasional drinking or a regular habit of drinking small amounts of alcohol; a level and frequency of drinking consistent with the pattern in the community and resulting in no pathological behavior or consequences.

monoamine oxidase (MAO) inhibitors Central nervous system stimulants that are used in the treatment of moderate to severe depressive states. The main types are isocarboxazid (Marplan), phenelzine (Nardil) and tranylcypromine (Parnate). They are effective. Adverse reactions can be severe. When used in combination with many other types of drugs—depressants, stimulants, narcotics—such an intense additive effect can be produced that death may result. The same is true when MAO inhibitors are taken with common foods that contain tyramine, such as cheese, herring, salami and chocolate. MAO inhibitors are considered extremely dangerous drugs and are usually only administered under close medical supervision.

moonshine Potstill corn whiskey that is not aged to any extent and is usually made secretly. Like pure alcohol it has a clear color and raw taste. It is also called "white lightning," a name which is well merited. When the government first started imposing taxes on whiskey in the late 1700s, distillers began setting up stills in concealed places, usually working at night (hence the name moonshine). In parts of Tennessee, Kentucky, North Carolina and other areas of the rural South, moonshining is still carried on and in some areas moonshine is now legally available.

morning drinking Sometimes engaged in to relieve the symptoms of a HANGOVER, morning drinking is a significant warning sign that indicates probable alcoholism.

morning glory seeds The seeds of certain members of the bindweed family *Convolvulaceae,* which contain HALLUCINOGENIC substances similar to those found in LSD—principally lysergic acid amides, d-isolysergic acid amide, chanoclavine, and clymoclavine. All of these substances are also found in the fungus ergot, *Clavicips purpurea,* from which LSD was first synthesized. The active ingredients in morning glory seeds have about one-tenth the potency of LSD-25.

As with so many of the organic hallucinogens, morning glory seeds have long been used by native peoples of America in religious ceremonies and as healing agents. The Aztecs were the first to discover their hallucinogenic possibilities and the Aztec word *ololiuqui* is now used to refer to all varieties of the seeds. It is believed that the Aztecs used the word only when referring to the seeds of one species, *Rivea corymbosa. Tlitliltzen,* it is thought, was the Aztec name for morning glories of the genus *Ipomoea.*

Effects: As might be expected, the effects of morning glory seeds are somewhat like those of LSD. The user may experience perceptual disturbances, mood changes and even psychomimetic reactions. Physical effects are wide-ranging: nausea, vomiting, intense headache, drowsiness, diarrhea, chills, impaired vision, decreased blood pressure and even shock can result from their use. The onset of the experience is 20–45 minutes after ingestion and duration can be upwards of six hours. Cases of prolonged reactions or FLASHBACKS following ingestion of morning glory seeds have been reported.

Sources: Several seed varieties commonly planted in gardens are used, including Heavenly Blue, Pearly Gates, Blue Star, Flying Saucers and Wedding Bells, but those sold commercially are often covered with methyl mercury to prevent spoilage. Some may also be covered with vomit-inducers which have been applied to discourage psychotropic use. As a result, many users grow their own seeds.

The appearance of morning glory seeds on the illicit drug market is rare as LSD is readily available and preferred. When the seeds are used, they are first pulverized or ground and then soaked in water. The liquid is strained and drunk.

Traffic and control: No laws regulate the sale of morning glory seeds.

Synonyms: ololiuqui, bador, loquetico, tlitliltzen, bindweed, Heavenly Blue, Pearly Gates, Blue Star, Flying Saucers, Wedding Bells.

morning shot For an alcoholic, the first drink of the day (see MORNING DRINKING). For an addict, it is the first narcotic shot of the day.

morphine A NARCOTIC ANALGESIC, the principal alkaloid of OPIUM. The isolation of morphine around 1802 is usually attributed to Serturner, who named the drug for Morpheus, the god of sleep and dreams. The most potent naturally occurring medication known for pain relief, it remains the standard by which all other analgesics are judged.

Complete synthesis of morphine was achieved in 1952.

Appearance: Morphine constitutes by weight about 10% of opium, the coagulated exudate of the poppy plant, *Papaver somniferum,* which also contains codeine and about twenty other alkaloids. Because pure morphine is only slightly soluble in water, morphine sulfate is the form most commonly used both medically and recreationally. It appears as odorless white crystals, or white crystalline powder, which loses water on exposure to air and darkens on exposure to light. Morphine sulfate is soluble in water, slightly soluble in alcohol and insoluble in chloroform and ether. Morphine hydrochloride is also occasionally used in injections.

Activity in the body: Readily but slowly absorbed from the gastrointestinal tract, morphine acts directly on the central nervous system, specifically affecting pain receptor neurons. After initial stimulation, the drug depresses the cerebral cortex and medullary centers.

Within 24 hours, 90% of the total excretion process is complete. Like other narcotics and depressant drugs, morphine crosses the placental barrier. Babies of addicted mothers usually exhibit withdrawal symptoms soon after birth.

Dosage: Recommended dosage for relief of moderate to severe pain is 10 mg/70 kg (approximately 154 pounds) bodyweight. When taken orally, morphine produces longer-lasting effects but it is only about one-tenth as potent as when it is injected intramuscularly. With subcutaneous injection, pain relief manifests in 20–60 minutes and lasts four or five hours. Intravenous administration brings almost immediate pain relief and effects peak within 20 minutes. Analgesia lasts a much shorter time when morphine is injected intravenously.

Toxic and lethal doses vary with individual tolerance; 120 mg taken orally and 30 mg injected intravenously have caused no toxic reactions in a non-addicted person, though less than 30 mg have caused death by respiratory depression on some occasions. Addicts have been known to take daily doses of up to 5000 mg because of tolerance.

Effects: Morphine is prized for its ability to relieve almost any kind of pain—particularly dull, continuous pain—along with the fear and anxiety associated with such suffering. In addition to analgesia, the drug produces drowsiness (and, in sufficient doses, sleep), euphoria, and impairs mental and physical performance. When given to people who are not experiencing pain, initial doses can produce dysphoria—heightened fear and anxiety—rather than euphoria. Vomiting after the first dose is common. Morphine decreases the motility of the genitourinary and gastrointestinal tracts (causing constipation), depresses respiration, and decreases hunger and sometimes the sex drive (although in some people, especially women, it can enhance sexuality by disinhibition). It may also have the effect of delaying ejaculation in men. (It has been suggested that opium's popularity in 19th century India was largely due to that effect.) In women, morphine use can cause menstruation to become irregular; with daily use some women stop menstruating altogether. Studies indicate that narcotic use also decreases the likelihood of pregnancy.

Typical adverse effects include nausea, vomiting (which is not always experienced as unpleasant) and sweating. Yawning, lowered body temperature, flushing of the skin, a heavy feeling in the limbs and itchiness around the face and nose are also usually present, along with pupillary constriction and consequent dimming of vision.

In overdose, the effects described above are magnified. Respiratory depression can be severe enough to cause coma and death—respiratory failure (apnea) is in fact the principal danger of morphine abuse. The skin of overdose victims is cold, clammy and bluish, and the pupils are so constricted they become pinpoint. Skeletal muscles become flaccid.

Overdose also frequently involves pulmonary congestion and edema. Until the patient can be admitted to emergency hospital care, he should be kept awake by walking, administering smelling salts and by stimulating the skin. NALOXONE (Narcan) is a specific antidote for opiate overdose. Given intravenously it will restore a comatose, barely breathing patient to consciousness within seconds.

Tolerance: Tolerance and severe psychological and physical dependence develop quickly with regular use of morphine. Psychological dependence develops before actual physical craving. Tolerance, however, develops only to morphine's depressant effects and not to other physical effects such as constriction of the pupils. Morphine exhibits CROSS-TOLERANCE and dependence to other narcotics, and its depressant effects are prolonged and intensified when used with other depressant drugs.

Up to a threshold of 500 mg a day, the severity and duration of WITHDRAWAL symptoms from morphine depends on the quantity of the drug regularly ingested. Usual symptoms include nausea, lacrimation, yawning and sweating alternating with chills. Withdrawal from morphine generally lasts 36–73 hours.

Usage: When morphine was introduced to the medical profession, it was hailed as a powerful analgesic effective in the relief of all kinds of pain and, falsely, as it turned out, as a cure for opium addiction. Opium, either in the form of laudanum (a hydroalcoholic tincture) or in a form suitable for smoking, was already a popular "remedy" for every imaginable ailment—and some imaginary ones. Morphine quickly replaced opium in many applications, though it did not cure opium addiction. In the 1850s, with the advent of the hypodermic syringe which made possible almost immediate relief from pain and anxiety, morphine proved especially valuable and doctors prescribed it liberally. Unfortunately, the new drug proved equally popular among recreational users, particularly in conjunction with the hypodermic needle. Morphine could be purchased at the local drugstore or through the mail in powder, tablet or liquid form. Hypodermic kits were also readily available. Compared to alcohol it was a "respectable" intoxicant and was heartily recommended by many of those who tried it. During the Civil War it served as a priceless surgical anesthetic and analgesic. Doctors distributed supplies of the drug, along with hypodermic syringes, to

History of Morphine

c.1803	**Serturner, German pharmacist, isolates morphine from opium.**
1825	**Morphine is first used in medicine as an analgesic and is thought to be a cure for opium addiction.**
1853	**Hypodermic needle is introduced and used to inject morphine.**
1866	**Morphine use during Civil War in U.S. creates an estimated 400,000 addicts.**
1870s	**Franco-Prussian War in Europe creates morphine addicts.**
1874	**Heroin is isolated from morphine.**
1906–1920	**Legislation regulates cultivation and distribution of opium, outlaws prescriptions of narcotics to addicts and imposes criminal penalties.**
1920s	**Heroin, because of its higher potency and illicit availability, becomes favored over morphine.**
1952	**Complete synthesis of morphine is achieved.**
1970	**Prescriptions containing morphine are classified as Schedules II and III drugs under the Controlled Substances Act.**
1980s	**Morphine rarely appears on the illicit market and addicts are generally members of the medical profession or hospital personnel.**

soldiers for use at home to ease the continuing pain of battle wounds. It was not until several decades after the war that doctors realized their mistake in assuming that injections of morphine carried no risk of addiction because when administered this way the drug bypassed the digestive tract. Approximately 2% of the population (400,000 people) was estimated to be suffering from the "army disease"—opiate or morphine addiction. Many of the addicts were doctors.

Today opiate addicts prefer the more potent and shorter-acting heroin. Morphine rarely appears on the illicit market and most addicts nowadays are probably members of the medical profession or hospital personnel who have access to the drug. Morphine is generally used as a sulfate rather than in its pure form. Recreational users inject the drug, take it orally in capsules or liquid solution, heat and inhale it, or absorb it from rectal suppositories. It is also often taken in combination with stimulant drugs such as amphetamines or cocaine, in order to counteract the depression, weakness and dizziness it produces, as well as to increase the analgesic effect.

Current medical applications of morphine include severe pain, cough suppression, relief of diarrhea, and as a preanesthetic to relieve the fear and anxiety associated with surgery and to reduce the amount of anesthetic needed. It is not recommended for patients suffering from bronchial asthma or other respiratory depression.

Morphine is a Schedule II drug under the CONTROLLED SUBSTANCES ACT.

Synonyms: M., morph, dreamer, Miss Emma, M.S.

morpholinylethylmorphine Another name for PHOLOCODINE, a semisynthetic morphine derivative.

Mothers Against Drunk Driving (MADD) A community action group that seeks to change the legal system's casual response to drunk driving and the whole climate of acceptance and tolerance of the drunk driver. The group was organized in 1979 by a mother whose daughter was killed by a drunk driver. Headquartered in Hurst, Texas, the organization has recently gained nationwide attention: petitions instigated by MADD have been instrumental in the recent rise in the drinking age to 21 in all states. The organization is also aimed at helping those who have been victimized by drunk drivers. National Office, Box 541688, Dallas, Texas 75354-1688.

mouth The mouth is the entry into the digestive tract and any impairment to its functions, which include mastication, salivation, swallowing, tasting and speaking, will subsequently affect the functioning of the digestive system.

Of all the recreational drugs, alcohol and tobacco have the most directly harmful effects on the mouth. Alcohol alone has not been proved to be carcinogenic but it is believed to act as a "co-carcinogen" in conjunction with a substance that is carcinogenic, such as tobacco. Studies have shown that alcohol and cigarettes act synergistically (see SYNERGY) to increase the potential for cancer, especially in the mouth and throat. Most heavy drinkers are also heavy smokers and it is estimated that people who drink and smoke heavily run a risk of developing cancer which is 15 times greater than that of nondrinkers and nonsmokers. One theory states that the carcinogens in tobacco have easier access to the mucous membranes of the mouth if the cells are bathed in alcohol, with its solvent effects. Another theory suggests that alcohol and tobacco independently affect the mucous membranes. Tobacco may contribute to cancers of the roof of the mouth, of the nasopharynx (which connects with the nostrils), of the larynx and of the lungs. Pipe and cigar smoking increase the incidence of cancer of the lip and jaw. Alcohol plays more of a role in cancers of the floor of the mouth, the lower pharynx and the esophagus—areas where contact is most direct.

Few other drugs of abuse produce directly harmful effects on the mouth. Marijuana smoking often produces dryness in the mouth and throat, and many users of amphetamines and other stimulants have experienced teeth grinding, but these symptoms disappear quickly.

Many opiate users neglect oral and personal hygiene and this results in rampant tooth decay. However, a large segment of the population—particularly the poor—receives unsatisfactory dental care, so it is difficult to establish if dental neglect is due to poverty or drug abuse.

mouthwash Numerous mouthwashes contain high percentages of alcohol. Listerine, for example, has 26.9%, while most hard liquor (gin, vodka, whiskey) contains about 40% alcohol. While they do have a potential for abuse, the main concern posed by mouthwashes containing alcohol is that an alcoholic who legitimately uses one may develop a craving for more. In addition, an alcoholic who is abstinent may be started on a relapse by drinking mouthwash. Mouthwashes may also produce adverse reactions in people taking ANTABUSE. Other mouthwashes with a high alcohol content are: Cepacol, 14%; Scope, 18.5%; and Signal, 15.5%.

MPTP A synthetic heroin-like designer drug that produces permanent symptoms closely resembling the stiffness and tremors of Parkinson's disease. Ironically, an outbreak of MPTP-induced Parkinson's in California has led to a breakthrough in medical knowledge and treatment of the disease, which afflicts many Americans.

multihabituation See POLYDRUG USE.

multimodality programs A drug treatment program that uses a variety of treatment approaches.

muscarine See FLY AGARIC.

muscimol See FLY AGARIC.

muscles The effects of drug abuse on the muscles range from a slight muscular weakness that allegedly follows marijuana use to the severe, permanent muscular damage that can result from alcohol and heroin abuse. The mechanisms of most of these disorders remain unclear although the symptoms are well known and frequently encountered.

Tranquilizers such as VALIUM (diazepam) act as muscle relaxants and are commonly used in the treatment of spastic disorders. Cumulative effects of abuse of such depressants (including barbiturates, alcohol, sedatives and narcotics) can cause muscular necrosis, or cell death. Alcohol abuse in particular has been recognized as a causative agent in the development of muscle disease. In their early stages, muscle diseases caused by alcohol can be reversed through abstinence.

Alcoholic myopathy is probably a direct effect of ethanol or acetaldehyde on the muscle cells. The subclinical form of alcoholic myopathy develops in as much as one-third of the alcoholic population and is indicated by abnormally high levels of the enzyme creatine phosphokinase, which is produced by muscle cells. Lactic acid levels also rise and victims may suffer muscle cramps and tenderness. If the patient does not stop drinking, his condition may worsen.

Sudden severe muscle cramps, pain or swelling of the arms and legs after heavy alcohol consumption are usually signs of acute alcohol myopathy, a localized, benign condition which also improves with abstinence. Myoglobinuria, a condition characterized by muscle fiber necrosis, fluid leakage and high enzyme levels may appear later. If undetected, it can progress and cause renal insufficiency and death.

Chronic alcoholic myopathy progresses slowly, often painlessly and without myoglobinuria, and involves weakness and atrophy of the limbs (usually the legs).

Alcoholic cardiac myopathy is a progressive weakening of the heart muscle fibers that often leads to severe disability and death.

Wasting of the muscles also occurs with the abuse of AMPHETAMINES, accompanying and partially resulting from weight loss. Amphetamines and other stimulants increase skeletal muscle tension while relaxing smooth muscles of the bronchi and intestine. After several days of a speed run, the user experiences pain in the muscles and joints and distinct tremors. These involuntary movements, which have also been noted in connection with alcohol and sedative abuse, sometimes temporarily continue to trouble the individual after he or she has stopped using the drug.

Heroin's usual effect on the muscles is to reduce muscular activity of the hollow organs. Muscle spasms are a well known recognizable symptom of withdrawal from narcotic drugs and can involve the facial muscles as well as entire limbs (hence the expression "kicking the habit"). Muscular rigidity is a usual condition in babies born of addicted mothers.

It is still unclear whether disorders related to heroin abuse constitute toxic or allergic reactions. Several disorders seem to be associated with adulterant agents used to dilute street heroin. Acute rhabdomyolysis, for example, manifests within a few hours after injection as skeletal muscular pain, tenderness, swelling and weakness in the extremities. In this condition, muscular fibers can undergo structural change with or without necrosis. Random or total necrosis can also occur, sometimes accompanied by edema and hemorrhage.

Years of subcutaneous or intramuscular heroin injection can also cause muscular fibrosis or abcesses as well as chronic infections. Permanent muscular contractions—"frozen" limbs or extremities—can result from muscular scarring.

Bacterial infection is a common complication of heroin use in unsanitary conditions. It strikes the muscles in the form of pyomyositis, which involves fever and swelling and tenderness of the limbs. Extensive areas of dead muscle have been found in some cases. Muscular rigidty and convulsions are frequently present during tetanus infections and can interfere with respiration.

Another muscular disorder associated with heroin addition is the "crush syndrome," which afflicts overdose victims. It sometimes appears as massive swelling of the extremity which received the injection. Localized limb compression has been seen in individuals who lost consciousness.

Marijuana and hallucinogenic drugs have only a slight affect on the muscles. The muscular weakness previously mentioned in connection with marijuana smoking is not universally accepted as an effect of cannabis use, although the drug has been used medically as a muscle relaxant since the mid-19th century. Extremely high doses of cannabis may, however, cause involuntary jerking of the muscles and the lower extremities and sometimes other parts of the body.

LSD and other psychedelics generally constrict smooth muscles of the uterus, blood vessels and bronchioles. Skeletal muscles may show tremor and weakness but, again, these effects do not commonly result from the use of these drugs.

mushrooms, sacred Several varieties of mushrooms with hallucinogenic properties have been used for centuries by Mexican Indians in religious rites and ceremonies. When eaten, the mushrooms affect mood and perception in a way similar to LSD and MESCALINE. They contain the active alkaloids PSILOCYBIN and PSILOCIN (psilocin changes to psilocybin in the body). In 1958 Dr. Albert Hofmann, who synthesized LSD, isolated psilocybin and later synthesized it. The psilocybin which is sold on the illicit market today is more often than not another chemical compound, such as LSD or PCP.

Another name for sacred mushrooms is teonanactl which means "flesh of the gods" or "god's flesh." The most common types of mushrooms are *Psilocybe mexicana, Conocybe siliginoides, Psilocybe aztecorum, Psilocybe zapotecorum, Philocybe caerulescens* and *Stropharia cubensis.* Effects begin 20–30 minutes after ingestion and the duration can be from six to 12 hours. Peak effects are usually felt in one hour and include visual hallucinations. The mushrooms can be lethal in large doses. Psilocybin, which is expensive to synthesize, is a Schedule I drug under the CONTROLLED SUBSTANCES ACT.

music and drugs It has been suggested that currently popular music and currently popular drugs go hand-in-hand. This suggestion of a link between the two dates back to the 1880–1920 era, a time of widespread poverty when the great majority could only obtain inexpensive drugs, such as alcohol and tobacco, and an inexpensive form of entertainment—in this case "the blues" because it was basically guitar or piano music requiring only one performer.

Dixieland jazz which was popular during the blues era but came into its own after World War I, is associated with the use of alcohol and the limited use of cocaine (a habit brought home by World War I servicemen). The National Prohibition Act of 1919 which aimed at curtailing the use of alcohol, actually enhanced the desire for it and people would drink anything that even resembled it, such as wood alcohol.

From 1930 to 1942, the "swing era" was prominent and coincided with the repeal of Prohibition. The availability of alcohol and an atmosphere of permissiveness lead to a boom in legitimate dance halls and nightclubs. This was also a time when many Americans, musicians included, were called into service for World War II and newly developed "music and dance rooms" in many popular hotels were forced to close. Those who could afford it and who were not involved in the war effort attended private "jam sessions" and the small groups that evolved developed "bop" music. With the development of bop music, which was somewhat restless and angular compared to previous forms, came an increase in heroin abuse.

The interaction of music and drugs was further demonstrated in the decade from the late 1940s to the late 1950s when the soft, intimate sounds of the newly evolved "cool" music was enjoyed by a host of marijuana users who preferred quiet intoxication.

In the 1960s "electric" sounds became popular and there was an increase in the use of hallucinogens, and acid rock parties centered around the use of LSD. As the drug's popularity waned in the 1970s, the use of amphetamines, barbituates and other dangerous drugs took over. People continued to use alcohol, which became known as the gateway drug.

Musicians and singers have long inhabited an environment that is conducive to drug abuse: along with the irregular pay, frequent traveling, contact with the criminal underworld in order to get bookings, and irregular working hours, there is the pressure and tension inherent in performing itself. Musicians are also apt to abuse drugs because of their desire to perceive "life" more deeply and come up with unusual visions which they can express through their music. The lyrics of songs often contain references to LSD, marijuana, alcohol and cocaine and the "good" feelings they can produce. Adolescents in particular are greatly influenced by popular singers and by song lyrics, sometimes even unconsciously. They often model their own life-styles on those of their idols'. Recently many of the same entertainment people who once used illicit drugs have undergone treatment and are now encouraging their fans to achieve a natural high. (See also RASTAFARIANS.)

mydriasis Dilation of the pupils of the eyes that occurs with intoxication from hallucinogens, scopolamine, atropine, cocaine and amphetamines. Mydriasis does not occur from the use of marijuana, barbituates or alcohol. (See also EYES). It is seen in withdrawal from opiates.

myoglobinuria A syndrome characterized by severe muscle pain, along with weakness, tenderness and swelling. It can be accompanied by cardiac arrhythmias, respiratory failure and renal insufficiency (the latter possibly leading to death). Depressant drugs (barbiturates, alcohol, narcotics) have been known to be responsible for muscle necrosis resulting in myoglobinuria. There is also a syndrome of myoglobinuria referred to as "heroin user's myoglobinuria" which is thought to be related to heroin adulterant mixtures.

myristicin An alkaloid found in NUTMEG and thought to produce hallucinogenic effects.

N

N_2O See NITROUS OXIDE.

nail polish remover A volatile hydrocarbon that is inhaled for its intoxicating effects. (See INHALANTS.)

nalbuphine A synthetic narcotic agonist/antagonist analgesic chemically related to oxymorphone and naloxone. (See NUBAIN.)

Nalline® (Merck, Sharpe, & Dohme) A narcotic antagonist which is no longer available. It contained nalorphine hydrochloride and was used in the treatment of opiate drug overdose to counter respiratory and central nervous system depression. (It did not counter respiratory depression caused by barbiturates or other drugs.) A small dose of Nalline could also be used to avoid full-blown withdrawal symptoms. The drug was used in the NALLINE TEST to ascertain whether or not an addict who had stopped using narcotics had resumed his habit.

Nalline test A test which used the narcotic antagonist NALLINE, to determine if an addict had returned to the use of drugs. If a narcotic was present in the person's system Nalline would reverse its effects and the pupils would dilate. The Nalline test has been replaced by the NARCAN TEST.

nalorphine A semisynthetic morphine antagonist. (See NALLINE.)

naloxone A nearly pure narcotic antagonist that is used to reverse the effects of overdose, particularly respiratory depression. It is effective only with opiate overdose and does not act on barbiturates. (See NARCAN.) Its actions last a few minutes.

Naloxone Challenge Test See NARCAN TEST.

naltrexone A nearly pure opiate antagonist that was developed in 1963. It does not produce opiate withdrawal symptoms with sudden discontinuation, and it is long-acting, effective orally, and relatively free of side effects. It has been used to discourage opiate use by being administered on a regular basis, thus blocking opiate effects.

nanogram A billionth of a gram. Laboratory testing of abused drugs, such as THC, is often reported in nonograms per milliliter (a thousandth of a liter).

Narcan® (Endo) A narcotic antagonist that contains naloxone hydrochloride. It is used to reverse depression effects caused by narcotics (natural and synthetic) and also to diagnose recent opiate use. Unlike many other narcotic antagonists it does not produce respiratory depression; in the absence of narcotics it exhibits relatively little pharmacological activity. It will not reverse the effects of respiratory depression caused by non-opiate drugs.

Narcan test Similar in procedure to the NALLINE TEST, this test is used to determine opiate dependence. Both tests rely upon the narcotic antagonistic properties of the drugs to induce visible symptoms of the presence of opiates, such as pupillary dilation.

narcotic Narcotics are medically defined as central nervous system depressants with analgesic and sedative properties. Under United States laws, narcotics are considered to be addictive drugs that produce physical and psychological dependence and include opium and its derivatives, heroin, morphine and codeine. Also included are synthetic substances that can produce morphine-type addiction (Demerol, methadone, etc.). Under the Harrison Narcotics Act of 1914, the first U.S. law regulating narcotics, cocaine (which produces psychological but not well-defined physical dependence) was included in the classification but it has been removed under contemporary legislation. Cocaine is still classified as a narcotic in some states, as is marijuana, but many states have taken corrective action on these improper classifications. Both narcotics and non-narcotics are included under the CONTROLLED SUBSTANCES ACT.

Narcotic Addict Rehabilitation Act (NARA) Enacted in 1966, this federal law established civil commitment of drug abusers to an in-hospital phase of treatment and an aftercare phase in their home communities. In addition, the act provided assistance and support to states and municipalities in developing facilities and treatment programs. Title I of the program covered narcotic addicts charged with certain federal offenses who desired to be committed for treatment in lieu of prosecution. Persons eligible under Title II of the act were addicts convicted of federal crimes who were committed by the court. Title III covered addicts who voluntarily wished to apply for commitment. The National Institute of Drug Abuse (NIDA) was responsible for patients under Title I and the Department of Justice was responsible for those covered under Titles II and III. NARA has been repealed and the federal hospitals at Lexington and Fort Worth have been closed.

narcotic antagonist A drug that counteracts or blocks the effects of opiate narcotics. In sufficient doses, these drugs can block such physiological effects as the development of tolerance and physical dependency, and can reverse or prevent toxic effects. Some narcotic antagonists have been developed by chemically altering natural or synthetic opiate narcotics. In dependent persons who have not been detoxified, a low dose of an antagonist can also produce dilation of the pupils and this property has been employed for identifying persons who are physically dependent (see NALLINE TEST and NARCAN TEST). Among the best known antagonists are naloxone (NARCAN) and naltrexone (TREXAN).

Narcotics Anonymous (NA) A self-help organization, founded in 1953, composed of individuals who meet regularly to stabilize and facilitate their recovery from drug addiction. Their rehabilitation involves a 12-step program identical to the one adopted by Alcoholics Anonymous. The organization also publishes informational pamphlets and a quarterly publication, *Voices of Narcotics Anonymous*. Organization now has 12,000 chapters in the U.S., and chapters in 40 other countries. The group is open to any drug user and assesses no dues or fees. Members rely on the therapeutic value of one addict helping another.

Narcotics Education, Inc. A private non-profit organization, founded in 1954, that conducts nationwide educational programs for the prevention of drug addiction and alcoholism. The group publishes two subscription publications, *Winner,* a magazine for children in grades three to six, and *Smoke Signals,* a monthly issue on topics related to tobacco. Pamphlets, books and filmstrips are also available for purchase or rental.

nasal septum The dividing wall inside the nose between the nostrils. Individuals who snort cocaine heavily on a regular basis are inclined to suffer severe nasal problems, including erosions and perforation of the septum. (See COCAINE.)

National Asian Pacific American Families Against Substance Abuse A nonprofit organization committed to eliminating alcohol and other drug use and/or abuse among Asian Pacific American families. Contact: Patrick Okura, National Asian Pacific American Families Against Substance Abuse, 6303 Friendship Court, Bethesda, MD 20857. Telephone: (301) 530–0945.

National Association of Broadcasters (NAB) abuse programs Professional organization with 17 antidrug and antialcohol abuse campaigns underway. Campaigns include Team Up Against Drugs, Project Workplace, and America Responds to AIDS. These programs are co-sponsored by grassroots organizations, the federal government, corporations, as well as small businesses, schools and parent groups. Contact: The National Association of Broadcasters, 1771 N Street, N.W., Washington DC 20036. Telephone: (202) 429–5447.

National Association of State Alcohol and Drug Abuse Directors (NASADAD) An organization, founded in 1978, that is composed solely of directors of state alcoholism agencies (SAAs) and single state agencies (SSAs) for drug abuse prevention. NASADAD's purpose is to represent and promote the interests of state agencies before Congress and federal agencies, with the aim of encouraging and developing comprehensive programs in each state. The organization is based on two predecessor organizations: the National Association of State Drug Program Coordinators, established in 1971, and the Council of State and Territorial Alcoholism Authorities, established in 1974.

National Basketball Association (NBA) drug policy and abuse program The Commissioner's Office of the NBA and the National Basketball Players Association have worked together to develop a comprehensive policy and program to rid professional basketball of illicit drug use. The policy, forged as part of contract negotiations, has the support of players, coaches and management. For the NBA, contact: Carolyn Blitz, National Basketball Association, 645 Fifth Avenue, New York, NY, 10022. Telephone: (212) 826–7000. For the National Basketball Players Association, contact: Charles Grantham, NBPA, 15 Columbus Circle, New York, NY 10023. Telephone: (212) 541–6608.

National Center for Health Statistics (NCHS) The federal government's principal vital and health statistics agency. For more than a quarter of a century, NCHS data systems have covered the full spectrum of concerns in the health field from birth to death, including overall health status, lifestyle and exposure to unhealthy influences, the onset and diagnosis of illness and disability, and the use of health care. NCHS is part of the Centers for Disease Control within the Public Health Service (PHS), U.S. Department of Health and Human Services.

The NCHS mission involves such functions as data collection and analysis, data dissemination, research in statistical and survey methodology, technical assistance in the United States and foreign countries, and cooperation in ongoing programs involving state, national and international organizations. To meet the priority data needs for public health, NCHS works closely with other federal agencies as well as research and academic institutions. The center has more than a dozen data systems for collecting information and also responds to requests for special analysis of data that have already been collected. Contact: Scientific and Technical Information Branch, National Center for Health Statistics, 3700 East-West Highway, Room 1057, Hyattsville, MD 20782. Telephone: (301) 436–8500.

National Clearinghouse for Alcohol and Drug Abuse Information (NCADAI) A successor organization to the National Clearinghouse for Drug Abuse Information. NCADAI was established in 1988 to serve as the federal government's focal point for the collection and dissemination of drug abuse information. In this capacity, NCDAI collects, classifies, stores and disseminates scientific and general information on drug abuse and drug misuse; develops information resource materials; and maintains an inventory of over 300 publications that are distributed to the public without charge in response to phone or mail inquiries. The inventory includes publications targeted to various audiences (parents, educators, students, community program workers, for example). NCADAI also supports the nationwide Regional Alcohol and Drug Abuse Resources (RADAR) program, consisting of satellite information centers affiliated with federal, state and local government agencies, universities and training centers.

National Coalition of Hispanic Health and Human Services Organization (formerly COSSMHO) National, nonprofit organization that promotes the health and well-being of the Hispanic community. It conducts substance abuse demonstration and training programs among other activities. A materials development program provides books, brochures and curricula and training materials. The *Reporter* newsletter is available quarterly and reports on activities and health-related information. Contact: National Coalition of Hispanic Health and Human Services Organization, 1030 15th Street, N.W., Suite 1053, Washington, DC 20005 Telephone: (202) 371–2100.

National Collegiate Athletic Association (NCAA) drug program In its member institutions, the NCAA provides resources for drug education for student-athletes, provides funding to assist allied conferences in their drug education programs and places special emphasis on drug prevention in its various youth programs, such as YES (Youth Education through Sports) Clinics and National Youth Sports Programs. Drug education material is distributed each year to more than 100,000 freshmen in member institutions. The NCAA also conducts a comprehensive drug-testing program for student athletes participating in its National Collegiate Championships and in post season football bowl games. Contact: NCAA, Frank D. Uryasz, Hall Avenue and 63rd Street, P.O. Box 1906, Mission, KS 66201. Telephone: (913) 384–3220.

National Commission on Marijuana and Drug Abuse Appointed by President Nixon in 1971, the commission was comprised of nationally prominent citizens who undertook a two-year examination of drug use, misuse and abuse. They concluded that old ways of looking at things, and old definitions required a new set of terms and perspectives. The commission issued two reports (1972, 1973) that defined issues, provided data on drug-using behavior, assessed its social impact, and formulated a rationale toward a coherent social policy regarding illicit drugs. It also recommended the decriminalization of marijuana. President Nixon rejected the recommendation.

National Crime Prevention Council (NCPC) The council offers a number of drug abuse prevention materials. The McGruff Puppet Program "Drug Prevention and Child Protection Program" features a puppet version of messages and songs for children, from kindergarten through grade 6. The 32-lesson curriculum is designed to cover a full year and includes 12 drug or alcohol abuse prevention lessons for each grade level. The council also offers a drug abuse prevention kit, which is a multimedia package for elementary school age children. It contains cassettes, puzzles, games and activity sheets. This is available free from the center, as is a monthly newsletter for interested adults. Contact: National Crime Prevention Council, 733 15th Street N.W., Suite 540, Washington, DC 20005. Telephone: (202) 393–7141.

National Federation of Parents for Drug Free Youth (NFP) A nonprofit membership organization of local parent groups and other concerned citizens committed to deal with and prevent alcohol and other drug use by young people. The federation has a parent networking component, a materials clearinghouse, and a youth training seminar called REACH AMERICA. Contact: National Federation of Parents for a Drug Free Youth, Karl Bernstein, 8730 Georgia Avenue, Suite 200, Silver Spring, MD 20910. Telephone: (301) 585–5437.

National Hispanic Family Against Drug Abuse A nonprofit alliance of individuals, organizations, and communities actively working together as partners for a drug-free future for all Hispanics. Contact: National Hispanic Family Against Drug Abuse, 1511 K. Street, N. W., Washington DC 20005, c/o Rodolfo B. Sanchez. Telephone: (202) 393–5136.

National Hospital Discharge Survey (NHDS) Conducted since 1964 on an ongoing basis by the National Center for Health Statistics (NCHS), the NHDS collects data from a sample of nonfederal hospitals with six or more beds and an average length of stay under 30 days. The sample is stratified by geographic region and hospital size. Discharges are randomly sampled at each participating hospital.

Each record in the NHDS describes a hospital episode for a single patient. These items are provided for each episode (or discharge): age, sex, race, marital status and length of stay for the patient; size and regional location of the hospital; and up to seven diagnostic codes describing the patient's condition and treatment. (The NHDS also codes up to four surgical procedures.) Starting with 1979, the diagnostic codes used in the NHDS come from the ninth revision of the International Classification of Diseases, Clinical Modification (ICD-9-CM).

Estimates of alcohol-related morbidity based on the NHDS sample are probably underestimates, not only because the hospital sample is limited, but also because morbidity among individuals who are not hospitalized (those who seek outpatient treatment or no treatment) is not reflected in NHDS data. In addition, the stigma associated with alcohol abuse may lead to a reluctance on the part of some health professionals to report an alcohol-related diagnosis. In short, numbers and rates reported usually reflect the prevalence of alcohol-related discharges (hospital episodes) and not the prevalence of alcohol-related diagnoses among individuals discharged from hospitals.

Frederick S. Stinson, Mary DuFour, M.D., and Darryl Bertolucci, "Alcohol-Related Morbidity in the Aging Population," *Alcohol Health & Research World,* NIAAA, 13: 1, (1989), 80–87 (Epidemiologic Bulletin No. 20).

National Institute on Alcohol Abuse and Alcoholism (NIAAA) A component institute of the Alcohol, Drug Abuse and Mental Health Administration (which it predates), NIAAA was established in 1971. Its mandate is similar to the NATIONAL INSTITUTE ON DRUG ABUSE (NIDA) and it is charged with providing "leadership, policies, and goals for the federal effort in the prevention, control, and treatment of alcohol abuse and alcoholism and the rehabilitation of affected individuals."

NIAAA has published four special reports to the U.S. Congress as part of its information program; the first in 1971, followed by others in 1974, 1978 and 1981. The reports focus on advances in knowledge in the field of alcoholism, effects on health, causes, and treatment methods. The findings are described in extensive detail.

Various research projects in the field are also funded by NIAAA; the most well-known is probably the controversial RAND REPORTS.

National Institute on Drug Abuse (NIDA) Established in 1972, NIDA is a component institute of the Alcohol, Drug Abuse and Mental Health Administration. its mandate is similar to that of the NATIONAL INSTITUTE ON ALCOHOL ABUSE AND ALCOHOLISM. NIDA is charged with providing "leadership, policies, and goals for the federal effort in the prevention, control, and treatment of narcotic addiction and drug abuse, and the rehabilitation of affected individuals." Although drug abuse services are now administered primarily at the state level under the new Alcohol, Drug Abuse and Mental Health block grant, NIDA continues to be responsible for providing national leadership in the critical areas of research, research training, data collection and analysis, information dissemination, and technical assistance and it is the lead agency responsible for federal efforts to reduce the demand for drugs.

National Nurses Society on Addictions (NNSA) Started in 1975 as the National Nurses Society on Alcoholism, NNSA has recently completed, with the American Nurses Association (ANA), *Standards of Addictions Nursing Practice with Selected Diagnoses and Criteria*. The document establishes 12 standards for the specialty of addiction nursing. The NNSA also employs a process of setting forth the following objectives of certification in nursing:

- assure quality of care
- provide credentials for employers and third-party payers
- expand opportunities for advancement
- motivate nurses to participate in continuing education in order to expand knowledge and alternatives in approaches to nursing practice
- inject a greater measure of prestige and peer recognition into clinical practice.

The NNSA has recently announced that it will facilitate the selection of five candidates for professional-in-residence scholarships to the Betty Ford Treatment Center in Rancho Mirage, California. The scholarships, funded by the center, are designed to impact on the nursing profession's awareness of alcoholism and drug addiction. For more information on the professional-in-residence program, contact: Fred Sipe, training coordinator, Betty Ford Center, 3900 Bob Hope Drive, Rancho Mirage, CA 92270. Telephone (619) 340–0033. For additional information concerning NNSA and its certification program, contact: Nellie Nelson, chair, NNSA Certification Committee, National Nurses Society on Addictions, 2506 Gross Point Road, Evanston, IL 60201. Telephone (312) 475–7300.

National Organization for the Reform of Marijuana Laws (NORML) A volunteer citizen action group founded in 1970 to seek changes in U.S. laws regarding marijuana. NORML lobbies for legislative reform of laws, collects and disburses educational material, and provides speakers for interested groups in an effort to end criminal penalties for the possession, use and cultivation of marijuana. An organization of 25,000 members, NORML brought legal action against the Federal Drug Enforcement Administration to make marijuana legally available for medical uses, and was instrumental in the passage of legislation which now allows marijuana to be used as medicine in 33 states. In 1989 NORML failed in its petition to the Drug Enforcement Agency (DEA) to reclassify marijuana as a Schedule II drug (it is currently a Schedule I drug) to make it easier to obtain for medical purposes.

National Parents' Resource Institute for Drug Education, Inc. (PRIDE) Based at Georgia State University, PRIDE is a non-profit organization which provides parents, educators, physicians, counselors and other concerned citizens with the most current research information on drug abuse. It also helps in the organization of parent groups, parent-school teams and community action groups.

National Prohibition Act See VOLSTEAD ACT.

Native American Church See PEYOTE.

Navy Drug and Alcohol Abuse Treatment Program This program provides both outpatient and residential treatment for U.S. Navy and Marine Corps personnel with diagnoses of drug or alcohol abuse and/or dependency. It accepts patients from across the United States. Contact: Navy Drug and Alcohol Drug Abuse Treatment Program, Navy Drug and Alcohol Drug Abuse Prevention and Control Division, Naval Military Personnel Command (MNPC-63), Washington, DC 20370, Captain Leo A. Cangianelli. Telephone (202) 694–8008.

Nembutal® (Abbott) A BARBITURATE sedative that contains pentobarbital sodium. It is used as a sedative, a hypnotic and as preanesthetic medication. Nembutal may be habit-forming and has a high potential for abuse. Physical and psychological dependence can occur. Overdosage can result in circulatory collapse, respiratory depression, diminished reflexes and coma. It is supplied in several forms: Nembutal Granulet 100 mg tablets; Nembutal Sodium Capsules: 30 mg, yellow; 50 mg, orange and white; 100 mg yellow; Nembutal Elixir, 18.2 mg per ml teaspoon; and Nembutal Sodium Solution in ampules and vials for injection.

Synonyms: nebbies, nemmies, nemish, nimby, nimbies, yellow bullets, yellow dolls, yellow jackets and yellows.

Netherlands, The Heroin abuse is on the increase in the Netherlands, just as it is throughout Western Europe. In 1980 the estimated number of heroin addicts was between 10,000 and 12,000. In 1983 the number was estimated to be 15,000: with a population of 14 million this means about 0.1% of the population is affected. Roughly one-third of the heroin addicts belong to ethnic minority groups: Surinamese and Mollucans. Annual consumption of heroin in 1980 (based an an assumed average daily intake equivalent to 50 milligrams of pure heroin) was 182–219 kilograms. Because European addicts generally smoke heroin rather than inject it, consumption rates are somewhat higher than in the United States. As in the rest of the European market, nearly all the heroin originates in Southwest Asia.

The Netherlands has some of the most relaxed hashish legislation in Western Europe. At one time youth centers in Amsterdam permitted the open sale of the drug. There are no estimates of the number of cannabis users in the general Dutch population. However, the percentage of high school students using cannabis is estimated to be 4%.

There are 20 Consultation Bureaus dealing with drug abuse problems in the Netherlands. They are centered in large and medium-size cities and towns. There are also numerous branches and consulting facilities in smaller areas. The bureaus are funded by grants from the government: 60% is paid by the Ministry of Welfare, Public Health and Culture and 40% by the Ministry of Justice since the bureaus also act as probation offices. In 1983 the consultation bureaus had an estimated 7,200 drug clients. Beside the bureaus, there are counseling centers and day treatment centers financed by local authorities. (The government contributes 90% of all local expenditures as long as the authorities meet certain conditions which conform to its grant scheme for Social Assistance and Services for Youth and Young Adults.) Several religious organizations, private psychiatrists and general practitioners also offer outpatient treatment for drug addicts.

Detoxification centers, addiction clinics and therapeutic communities (offering treatment to those addicted to various drugs including alcohol) help addicts on an inpatient basis. The Health Insurance Funds Act and the Exceptional Medical Expenses Compensation Act finance most of the inpatient treatment centers. Psychiatric and general hospitals also treat drug addicts and together they account for some 650 admissions per year.

Alcohol consumption is widely accepted by the Dutch: 93% of the male population drinks and 82% of the female population. Only 3% of the population recommends abstinence from alcoholic beverages. Two-thirds of the nation's annual consumption takes place in the home and an overwhelming majority approve of drinking by adolescents when they reach the legal age of 16. Although consumption is widespread, less than a quarter of the population drinks daily. Beer is the preferred alcoholic beverage by a vast majority of the country's drinkers. Beer consumption per person 15 years and over in 1984 was 106.3 liters (1 liter equals 1.06 quarts), wine 19.4 liters and spirits (pure alcohol) 3.0 liters. In total alcohol consumption, the Netherlands ranked 18th among 32 nations—11.0 liters per person 15 years and over.

In 1975 the number of hospital admissions for alcohol-related problems numbered 2,357, up from 1,724 in 1973. This increase prompted a governmental inquiry that was intended to lay the groundwork for the country's first official policy on alcohol. A problem of equal or greater concern is abuse of other drugs aggravated by alcohol. Until an official body is created to oversee the government's as yet undetermined policy, prevention and treatment efforts for alcohol-related problems remain in the hands of private agencies, particularly the National Commission on Alcoholism, a national temperance organization. Indications are that a number of programs are forthcoming from nationalized industries, law enforcement groups and medical associations. Rotterdam and Amsterdam are now major entry ports for cocaine for Western Europe, most of which originates in Colombia.

New York City, drug cases in One of the nation's most severe drug abuse sites, New York City has an estimated 200,000 heroin addicts, some 50% to 60% of them believed to be infected with the HIV virus. In recent years—especially during the 1980s—the city's proportion of intravenous drug abusers who have developed AIDS has increased dramatically. Eight of 10 children with AIDS have drug-abusing parents and nine of 10 are black or Hispanic. Fifty-three percent of all the city's AIDS-related deaths involve intravenous drug users.

A recent survey showed that murders in New York City rose 20% from 1985 to 1986; the Citizens Crime Commission says most of the rise could be blamed on the growing use of crack cocaine and other drugs. Deputy Chief Francis Hall, head of the New York Police Department's narcotics division says, "The escalated use of cocaine has truly changed the drug problem." Eric Brettschneider, of the New York City Human Resources Administration, points out that the numbers of cases of neglected or abused children rose 50% from June 1985 to June 1986—an increase attributed to the use of crack by parents. An estimated one-third to one-half of all the babies born to crack-using mothers have serious neurological problems. In 1986, the New York City police began seizing automobiles of suspected cocaine buyers and sending police teams into "head shops'' to confiscate large numbers of the glass pipes commonly used for smoking crack. New York's former mayor Edward Koch wrote in the *New York Law Journal* that the actions were ''legitimate applications of the law against an extremely serious threat.'' Koch also suggested that a top federal priority should be to convert military bases scheduled to be fully or partially closed into drug treatment centers or prisons for drug offenders.

A 1988 study conducted by the National Institute of Justice (NIJ) showed that in New York City, the percentage of men arrested on any charge who tested positive for any drug, excluding marijuana, was over 80%. The percentage of men arrested who tested positive for cocaine was about 78%.

In 1988, the Police Department instituted a police saturation technique featuring the Tactical Narcotics Team, or T.N.T. Still, drug dealers ply their trade brazenly, with seemingly little fear of arrest. Police Commissioner Benjamin Ward (since retired) often noted that the city's drug problem is a complicated one, rooted in poverty and joblessness. He added that New York has committed ''more resources to the war on drugs than any other municipality in the country.'' The city committed (in 1989) more than $116 million over two years just to ''special antidrug offensives.'' In 1990 the T.N.T. is being reduced in size due to need for personnel in street crime prevention.

In Brooklyn alone, felony drug arrests quadrupled between 1983 and 1987, swelling to more than 4,000 cases and constituting over 40% of the district attorney's caseload. In 1988, the police made more than 90,000 narcotics arrests in New York City—almost one-third of all arrests made by police in the city. In 1987, 27.1% of arrests made were for drug offenses. Police estimate that in the near future, the number of such arrests will be higher.

Overall, illicit drugs seem a part of city life as never before. Indeed, in some areas, crack has so glutted the market that the price of a vial has dropped to $3 from $5. Bronx District Attorney Robert T. Johnson noted recently, ''It's incredible; they are selling the stuff right around the courthouse.'' Spotting a drug transaction in midtown Manhattan is not uncommon.

A former New York city commissioner of health, Stephen C. Joseph, supported the concept of pharmacological treatment for cocaine. He says, ''Without such a commitment to cocaine treatment research, any hope we have of stemming the national epidemic of substance abuse and its concomitant medical and social problems will be as insubstantial as the smoke from a crack pipe. Mr. Bush must not lose this chance to make a long-term contribution to the war on drugs.'' Meanwhile, former Mayor Koch announced during his reelection campaign plans to sharply expand the city's jail system and add 775 new officers to the NYPD's 1,400-member narcotics division—at a cost of between $70 million and $100 million in the next two years. Newly elected Mayor David N. Dinkins announced in early 1990 that the above plans have been put on hold temporarily due to a city budget crisis.

Gilda Berger, *Drug Abuse: The Impact on Society* (Franklin Watts: New York, 1988).

Peter Kerr, ''Koch Seeking 775 More Police Officers for an Anti-Drug Blitz,'' *The New York Times*, August 10, 1988.

Michael Marriott, ''New York's Worst Drug Sites: Markets of Death and Despair,'' *The New York Times*, June 1, 1989.

New Zealand Aside from alcohol and tobacco, which are the major health hazards in New Zealand, cannibis is the most abused drug and most of it is produced locally. LSD and the synthetic drug, bromo-DMA (which has effects similar to LSD), were popular during the 1970s but their use has been rapidly declining. Heroin abuse is also down; principally because the drug is in short supply and consequently costs $500-$700 a gram. The GOLDEN TRIANGLE is the traditional source of heroin for New Zealand and indications point to a bumper crop in 1983 which may mean heroin will be more readily available in the future. Amphetamine and barbiturate use remain fairly widespread and have proved difficult to monitor. Deaths classified by the police as "drug-related" usually involved the use of these two drugs.

In 1977 the New Zealand government established a Caucus Committee to recommend legislative and administrative action to control the misuse of licit and illicit drugs. A 1978 act substantially increased the penalties for possession and dealing. The maximum penalty for dealing is now life imprisonment.

One of the government's most important though circumscribed powers is the use of listening devices. This power was introduced in 1979 and there is no doubt of its value in monitoring the activities of those thought to be dealing in drugs. In the year ending March 1982, for example, prosecutions resulted from nearly all warrants in force. If it had not been for the use of listening devices several of the biggest drug importers in New Zealand would not have been apprehended.

All members of the police force are now trained in drug identification and are expected to handle drug offenses in the course of their normal duties. Police units are also upgrading their intelligence network and new units are concentrating their efforts on stemming such national trends as the buildup of drug organizations, chemist shop burglaries, and criminal gangs. The government attributes the declining use of hard drugs to these concentrated efforts. The effort is not just concentrated on hard drugs in particular: from January through November 1982, 604.5 kilos of cannabis leaf material were seized.

Along with stepping up police action, the government is continuing its work in the education field and in the treatment and rehabilitation of addicts.

As in most other countries, alcohol remains the major drug of abuse. Among a population of just over three million, surveys estimate that there are some 50,000 "chronic alcoholics," and another 200,000 "excessive drinkers." Adolescents have easy access to alcohol and the pattern of consumption relates to this fact. Annual per capita consumption of absolute alcohol rose from 5.8 liters in 1965 to 8.4 liters in 1975. In 1987, estimated consumption of absolute alcohol per person of mean population aged 15 years and over was: beer 6.4 liters (1 liter equals 1.06 quarts), wine 1.8 (table) and 0.6 (fortified), and spirits 2.1, for a total of 10.9 liters, up 0.2% from 1986. Figures are from the Alcoholic Liquor Advisory Council in Wellington. In 1977, 45% of fatal traffic accidents were attributed to alcohol; hospital admission rates because of alcoholism are also up. The social cost of alcoholism to the country is overwhelming and there is an acknowledged need for new clinics to deal with the problem. Existing efforts to control alcoholism are indirect and tend to target the potential problem rather than the existing one. Recent revisions of regulations concerning the sale and public consumption of alcohol, and stricter enforcement of legislation concerning drunk driving will not handle the problem without concerted educational measures.

NIAAA See NATIONAL INSTITUTE OF ALCOHOL ABUSE AND ALCOHOLISM.

nicotine ($C_{11}H_{14}N_2$) Used for centuries by natives of the Americas, nicotine was first encountered by Europeans during the 16th century explorations of the New World. It was named in honor of Jean Nicot who claimed that it had great medicinal potential. Columbus noted that Indians "drank the smoke" from dried leaf roots, not for medicinal purposes, but rather for the paradoxical stimulant-sedative effects it had on the mind and body. To date no therapeutic or healthful applications of nicotine have been found.

Nicotine is a potent oily alkaloid found in concentrations of 2–5% in the tobacco plant,

Nicotiana tabacum. Native to South America, the plant is now cultivated in areas throughout the world. Pure nicotine is colorless and has a strong odor and acrid taste. It is highly poisonous and, when dissolved in water, has been used as a potent insecticide. Volatized somewhat by heat, nicotine is inhaled as smoke from cigarettes, cigars and pipes. It is also ingested through chewing and snuffing tobacco. It is estimated that nearly 45 million Americans smoke tobacco, making it the most addictive drug in the United States.

Since colonial times nicotine has supported a large and prosperous tobacco industry. Despite its ill effects on people's health, it was consumed as fast as it could be supplied. One Bohemian observer in 1662 indicated that "the common people are so given up to the abuse that they imagine they cannot live without several pipes of tobacco a day—thus squandering in these necessitous times the pennies they need for their daily bread." The use of tobacco was prohibited by the Roman Catholic Church as early as the 17th century, and Russian czars were known to torture smokers. The Sultan of Constantinople imposed the death penalty for smoking in 1633, but "even the fear of death was of no avail with the passionate devotees of the habit."

Before the 20th century most nicotine was taken by chewing tobacco, smoking pipes and cigars, and inhaling snuff. In the early 1900s cigarettes became the most popular method of taking nicotine. This popularity came about for several reasons. First, public health warnings stated that chewing tobacco had been shown to cause tuberculosis. Unaware of the high risks of cigarette smoking—irreparable damage to the lungs, heart, blood and nervous system—people switched to smoking instead. Second, the cigarette industry began using automatic machinery for mass production which lowered the price of cigarettes. The industry also embarked on extensive advertising campaigns. Third, and probably the foremost reason for the public switch, was the fact that a new "milder" type of Virginia tobacco was used in cigarettes and it allowed for deeper inhalation.

As cigarette smoking increased in popularity so did the number of anti-smoking leagues and campaigns. Several states enacted cigarette prohibition and other states passed laws prohibiting the sale of cigarettes to young people. Despite the campaigns and regulations, however, the production of cigarettes increased from 4.2 billion (1900–1909) to 80 billion (1920–1929); by 1970 the figure had jumped to 583 billion.

In 1964 the first Surgeon General's report was issued. Entitled *Report of the Surgeon General's Advisory Committee on Smoking and Health,* it received extensive media coverage and convinced many smokers of the risks they were taking. For a while cigarette sales dropped. President Johnson signed legislation, effective on January 1, 1966, requiring all cigarette packs and cartons to carry the statement: "Caution: Cigarette smoking may be hazardous to your health." In 1971 cigarette advertising was banned from radio and television. The ban resulted in increased print advertising and in 1977 the U.S. Department of Agriculture reported that cigarette companies had spent $779 million that year alone on promotion and advertising. The tobacco industry is one of the world's wealthiest enterprises.

In early 1989, U.S. Surgeon General C. Everett Koop issued a federal report which concluded that the number of deaths attributed to smoking in 1985 was at 390,000. Smoking, the report said, was a major cause of stroke and the third-leading cause of death in the U.S. An estimated 50 million Americans continue to smoke. By mid-1988, more than 320 local communities had adopted laws or regulations restricting smoking. New state laws enacted in 1987 restricting smoking in public places exceeded the number passed in any preceding year. Two major differences between the 1964 report and Dr. Koop's 1989 report were that the first did not mention the hazards of inhaling smoke from others' cigarettes and did not find that smoking was conclusively a cause of heart disease.

There has been an increase in recent years in the manufacture of filter and low-tar low-nicotine cigarettes. Brands of cigarettes now on the market have tar and nicotine yields ranging from 1 mg to 20 mg. Although low-tar and nicotine cigarettes may be safer, there is no such thing as a "safe" cigarette. Because of the smaller amount of nicotine, however, people may become less dependent and eventually stop smoking altogether. Opponents of "safer" cigarettes argue that users will find them less satisfying and simply smoke more of them, which will make the health risk even greater.

Studies have shown that smokers are more likely to use other drugs, particularly alcohol and marijuana. This is especially disturbing in the light of teenage smoking statistics. A 1979 government survey showed there were 1.7 million teenage girls and 1.6 million teenage boys who smoked. It is thought that peer pressure, the "kick" of risk-taking, and parental use of cigarettes are the main reasons why teenagers begin smoking. School and government-funded anti-smoking programs are becoming increasingly popular and they have obviously had some success: during the period 1974–1979 the number of teenage smokers dropped from 15.6% to 11.7%.

Classification: Nicotine is both a transient STIMULANT and a SEDATIVE to the central nervous system and to both voluntary and involuntary muscle systems. It is physically and psychologically addictive and some studies indicate that it is even more addictive than heroin. The ingestion of nicotine results in a transient stimulation or "kick" because it causes a discharge of epinephrine from the adrenal cortex. This stimulates the central nervous system, as well as other endocrine glands which cause a sudden release of glucose ("blood" sugar). Stimulation is then followed by depression and fatigue, leading the abuser to seek more nicotine to restimulate the adrenals. Meanwhile, stress causes a rise in the acidity level of urine, thus enhancing the elimination rate of nicotine and the further need for more nicotine. Many people who try to break this vicious cycle and are not able to, become further depressed. Perhaps the most devastating social effect of nicotine is that it leaves its countless addicts feeling guilty and/or powerless.

Effects: Pure nicotine is highly poisonous, and only a drop or two (about 50 mg) on the tongue can kill a person within minutes. Ingesting a cigarette or cigar may well prove lethal or, at the least, produce serious physical and mental reactions. There are approximately 15–20 mg of nicotine in a typical cigarette (although some of the newer low-nicotine brands contain as little as 0.5) but usually less than 1 mg reaches the bloodstream. The amount can vary according to how frequently the smoker inhales, whether or not the cigarette is filtered, the type of filter, and so on. Nicotine taken in smoke takes only 60 seconds to reach the brain, but has a direct effect on the body for up to 30 minutes. For this reason, smokers who are dependent on nicotine—and virtually all regular smokers are—generally find that they need at least one cigarette every half hour. This can add up to about a pack and a half per day. It is difficult to discern the exact effects of nicotine since it is taken in combination with many other substances found in tobacco. Cigarette smoke is mainly comprised of a dozen gases (particularly carbon monoxide) and the particulate matter, nicotine and tar. The tar in a cigarette (approximately 15 mg, though as little as half this amount is found in low-tar brands) disposes the user to a high expectancy rate of lung cancer, emphysema and bronchial disorders. The carbon monoxide in the smoke increases the chances of being vulnerable to cardiovascular diseases. But in any case, nicotine plays a significant role in many serious diseases, most of which have high fatality rates. Bronchial and cardiovascular disorders are increased by the effects that nicotine has on bronchial and heart muscles, and the arteries. Chronic bronchitis and emphysema are particularly common diseases among smokers. Nine-tenths of those who suffer Buerger's disease are smokers: this affliction involves the progressive constriction of the vascular system, particularly in the legs. By impeding blood circulation, it eventually leads to arterial occlusions. These cause gangrenous conditions that often lead to amputation. For much the same reason, users of nicotine have at least a 70% greater chance of suffering from coronary and cerebral occlusions which manifest as heart attacks and strokes.

The risk of congestive heart failure is also increased by the effects of nicotine. Coronary and cerebral thromboses (blood clots in the blood vessels of the heart or brain) and emboli (dislodged particles which break off from a main clot and travel through the vascular system) are also precipitated indirectly by nicotine since the vasoconstriction increases the possibility of blood flow interference.

Bronchial and pulmonary dysfunction are caused partly by the displacement of oxygen by the carbon monoxide in cigarette smoke (especially in the case of emphysema), and by the irritant effect of the tars.

The most specific and serious of all long-term effects of smoking is lung cancer, which proves to be fatal in well over 90% of cases. Relatively rare in the early 1900s, today lung cancer is a leading cause of death from cancer. An average male smoker runs a 10-times greater risk of death from lung cancer than a nonsmoker: women smokers run a 5-times greater risk. The tar in a cigarette contains many constituents known to cause cancer in experimental animals. The hair-like cilia on the membranes of the lungs (which work to keep the lungs clean) can become damaged or paralyzed by the tar and when the cilia are not working properly the lungs become vulnerable to pneumonia and chronic obstructive pulmonary disease. Cancer of the esophagus, mouth, lips, and larynx are also associated with cigarette smoking.

Cigar and pipe smoking do not have as great an effect on health as cigarette smoking, probably because the smoke is not usually inhaled. Pipe and cigar smokers do run a greater risk of cancer of the oral cavity, however, and lip cancer is increased by pipe smoking.

Nicotine has many deleterious effects on pregnant women and lactating mothers. Women who smoke run two times the risk of having a stillborn infant. Most babies born of women smokers are smaller than normal and they are also frequently premature. Babies sometimes suffer overt signs of nicotine addiction and withdrawal, and are often afflicted with related mental and physical impairments. Miscarriages are much more likely among smokers, and congenital heart defects (those occurring at birth) are more likely if the father smokes. In addition, women who smoke generally have earlier menopause and, if they also take oral contraceptives, are even more prone to cardiovascular and cerebrovascular diseases than other smokers, this is especially true for women over 30. Lactating mothers excrete nicotine directly through breast milk, and pregnant women transport it through their blood supply to the fetus.

Smoking among women increased dramatically during World War II when women began "doing men's work." It is now estimated that slightly under 30% of the adult women in the United States are smokers. While the number of male smokers has dropped sharply over the last 20 years there has been no similar decline for women. The number of teenage girls who smoke is larger than the number of teenage boys.

Besides the many serious long-term effects of nicotine, there are also less severe short-term ones. Sweating, vomiting, and throat irritation number among them, along with others that typically lead to more serious conditions over longer periods: increased heart rate and blood pressure, leading to myocardial dysfunctions and arteriosclerosis; a drop in skin temperature accompanied by increased respiration which may cause chronic hyperventilation; and dimness or blurring of vision culminating in blindness, a condition known as Tobacco Amblyopia.

Effects on nonsmokers: Research studies indicate that the health of nonsmokers can be affected by the toxic substances, particularly carbon monoxide, that are released in the air around them by smokers. Nonsmokers are also subject to eye and nasal irritation, headache and cough from cigarette smoke. In many parts of the United States recent legislation and regulations now restrict smoking to certain areas or prohibit it altogether.

Addictive aspects: Casual use of even small amounts of nicotine (three or four cigarettes, for example) can develop into a definite physical and psychological dependence on the drug in just a matter of days. The dependence increases until it reaches a fairly stable level at which the user stays for many years; often for the rest of his life. At least 75% of smokers attempt to overcome their addiction. Interruption of nicotine use leads to a WITHDRAWAL syndrome, featuring irritability, depression, and preoccupation with the lack of smoking. It generally takes a full year to break the habit. Fatigue, dizziness, headache and shortness of breath are physical characteristics of withdrawal, which usually subside rapidly. Because smoking is sometimes used as a tranquilizer during periods of stress, or as a pleasure enhancer after meals, during coffee breaks and in such social situations as parties, the psychological difficulties involved in withdrawal (quitting) can be far worse than the physical difficulties.

To help people break their dependency on the drug, a number of nicotine "cogeners" (chemically similar substances) have been developed to displace it. Lobeline is the most common of these. It is used in Nikoban, and marketed as an aid to breaking the habit but is thought by many to be little more than a placebo. Nicotine chewing gums and pills have also been employed in this way, but they usually give the user as much nicotine as he gets from smoking and hence have little effect on breaking the nicotine habit unless used in a programmed tapering dose regimen.

Smoking-withdrawal clinics and support groups have become particularly popular in the last 15 or 20 years, although the majority of people who stop smoking still tend to do it on their own without outside help. The National Clearinghouse for Smoking and Health reports that from 1966 to 1970 the number of ex-cigarette smokers in the adult population rose by 10 million; from 19 million in 1966 to 29 million in 1970. Nearly half of all living adults who ever smoked have quit, according to Dr. Koop's 1989 report. Smoking has been reduced from 40% of adults in 1965 to 29% in 1987.

Tolerance: The body rapidly develops tolerance to the short-term effects of nicotine, thus making it more likely that the habit will take hold. Increased and more frequent dosages taken in order to satisfy the craving for nicotine are also quickly adapted to.

NIDA See NATIONAL INSTITUTE ON DRUG ABUSE.

niopo Pods from the plant *Acacia niopo* which grows in Venezuela. They are ground up and used as a snuff which produces psychedelic effects.

nitrous oxide (N_2O) A general anesthesia normally used in dentistry. It is also called nitrogen oxide and has the common name "laughing gas." When supplemented with other agents it is used for surgical anesthesia. It was previously used as a propellant for canned whipped toppings but has been discontinued due to abuse. It has been abused for its eurphoric effects and mild hallucinations. Sustained inhalation of nitrous oxide without adequate oxygen can result in anoxia (arrested respiration) and death. It is available in small cannisters, which are used to fill balloons and then inhaled.

Noctec® (Squibb) A sedative hypnotic that contains CHLORAL HYDRATE, and is used for nocturnal sedation and as a pre- and post-operative medication. It may be habit-forming and when taken with alcohol or other central nervous system depressants it can have an additive effect. It is supplied as Noctec Syrup, a flavored syrup containing 500 mg per ml teaspoon; and as Noctec Capsules in 250 mg and 500 mg red capsules.

Noludar® (Roche) A sedative hypnotic that contains METHYPRYLON and is used for insomnia. Physical and psychological dependence can occur and it has the potential for abuse. When taken with alcohol or other central nervous system depressants it can have an additive effect. Overdosage can result in somnolence, respiratory depression, confusion and coma. It is supplied in 300 mg amethyst and white capsules, and in 50 mg and 200 mg white tablets.

nonaddictive abuser A person who on occasion misuses or over uses alcohol or other drugs but who on most occasions does not demonstrate loss of control, compulsion or dangerous use.

North Conway Institute (NCI) Founded in 1951 by a group of concerned clergy and lay persons, the institute is an outgrowth of the Yale University School of Alcohol Studies. It is an interfaith, ecumenical, non-profit organization, governed by a board of church people, which works as a catalyst with religious and secular organizations in all areas of alcohol and drug problems. In addition to holding an annual seminar, NCI also serves as a resource center.

Norway Although Norway has one of the most stringent approaches to alcohol consumption (and drunk driving) in the world, the government's attitude toward the abuse of other drugs has not changed in recent years even though there has been an increase in use. According to the government, existing programs will be continued and general preventive measures will be taken but no new treatment programs will be implemented. This is because the government looks upon the drug abuse problem as a symptom of personal, family and social problems.

Up to 1940, drug dependence was not considered a problem in Norway. During the 1940s there was an increase in the use of tranquilizers, particularly in the middle and older age groups. By 1965 use of drugs had spread to younger people and the favorite substance was usually marijuana or hashish. Abuse of tranquilizers continued and amphetamines began to make their appearance.

Illicit trade in drugs has, until recently, not been an issue in Norway. In addition, possession of narcotic drugs (with the exception of heroin) is legal. Distribution, possession and use of marijuana, hashish and LSD are unlawful. As of 1976, the government reported that there was no heroin problem in Norway, although methadone and some morphine-based drugs had gained popularity. Doctors were specifically warned not to prescribe methadone.

Addicts with complex and serious addiction problems receive treatment in mental health institutions. But because the government believes that drug dependency is not an illness but a symptom of personal or social problems, a generally accepted treatment model for drug dependency does not exist. Instead, the problem is approached from the standpoint of prevention. Along with educational programs, the government believes in implementing programs that help the youth of the country channel its energies and demands for acceptance in new directions.

Developments since 1975 have included the establishment of therapeutic communities modeled after Daytop and Phoenix House in the United States. As of 1983, regional contact groups have been set up in various counties to establish contact between country doctors, schools, social services, and the police and prison systems in an effort to coordinate information and help on drug abuse questions. Tighter pharmaceutical control has also been implemented and these recent controls may be an indication that dependency on drugs other than alcohol is being acknowledged as a specific problem in need of special attention.

Although there is very little information available concerning the specific nature of treatment for alcoholics, in 1980 the Norwegian government proposed over 30 measures to reduce alcohol consumption. While the level of consumption is substantially below that of other European countries, it has nonetheless been increasing each year. According to a 1979 report in *News of Norway,* the consumption level rose by approximately 156% between 1955 and 1979. This notable increase no doubt accounts for the stringent approach to alcoholism in the country. A driver with a blood alcohol concentration of 0.05% or more must serve a minimum of three weeks in prison, and if a person causes a motor vehicle accident while drunk there is no insurance compensation. In addition, there is a ban on advertising alcoholic beverages in the print media and a ban on winemaking in the home. In an international comparison of alcohol consumption per person 15 years and over for 1984, Norway ranked 30th among the 32 nations included in the survey. Total alcohol consumption was 5.2 liters (1 liter equals 1.06 quarts) per person 15 years of age and older.

noscapine An opium alkaloid that is used as a cough suppressant in cough medicines. It is a Schedule IV drug under the Controlled Substances Act.

Nubain® (Endo) A synthetic NARCOTIC agonist-antagonist analgesic which is chemically related to both OXYMORPHONE and NALOXONE. A potent analgesic, it is used for the relief of moderate to severe pain, as a pre-operative anaylgesia and as a supplement to surgical anesthesia. Nubain contains nalbuphine hydrochloride and caution should be used in prescribing it to a person with a history of narcotic abuse because psychological and physical dependence, along with tolerance, can develop. Nubain is supplied in ampules for injection. If it is administered intravenously onset of action occurs in two to three minutes; onset time is less than 15 minutes if administered intramuscularly or subcutaneously. Analgesic activity can range from three to six hours.

Numorphan® (Endo) A potent analgesic that contains the opium derivative OXYMORPHONE and is similar to morphine in its effect. It may be habit-forming and physical dependence can occur. A Schedule II drug, it is supplied in suppositories, solution (for injection), and in 10 mg tablets.

nutmeg The dried seed of *Myristica fragrans,* an evergreen tree indigenous to East India. MACE, its seed coat, has similar properties. Both are common cooking spices as well as HALLUCINOGENS. The two hallucinogenic substances in both nutmeg and mace are elemicin and myristicin, which are closely related to MESCALINE and TMA.

Because of their unpleasant side effects, nutmeg and mace have limited popularity. They are used chiefly by prison inmates who have little access to other drugs and by teenagers as substitutes for illegal drugs.

In their powdered forms the substances may be brewed into a tea and then drunk or added to a hot beverage such as hot chocolate. Some users add them to orange juice or to mashed potatoes.

A normal dose is one to two tablespoons, or about 10 grams. Occasionally these substances are snorted but they are poorly absorbed when used this way and can be irritating and mildly painful. They can also be obtained in an oil form which is nearly unpalatable.

Effects: Commonly, nutmeg and mace produce a euphoric or intoxicating effect not unlike a mescaline high, in conjunction with unpleasant physical effects such as nausea and dizziness. In high doses—over 20 grams—the substances can produce more intense effects, ranging from strong visual hallucinations to feelings of fear, anxiety and sometimes acute panic. Physical reactions intensify with higher doses: vomiting, rapid heartbeat, excessive thirst, bloodshot eyes, temporary constipation and difficulty in urinating are all typical. Physical reactions may begin within 45 minutes after ingestion; psychological effects usually occur after one to two hours. The effects generally last two to four hours an then begin to subside, though the user may experience residual effects for up to 24 hours.

Sources: Nutmeg and mace are common grocery store items and are found on the spice shelves of most households and eating establishments.

Traffic and control: No laws regulate the sale of these substances.

nutrition Nutritional deficiencies often accompany prolonged use of drugs. Drugs may decrease the appetite, change the sense of smell and taste, and alter metabolic processes that can result in hindered absorption and hastened excretion, and impair the use and storage of nutrients. However, lifestyle and social class are the major determining factors in the nutritional state of users.

When an addict is in a drug-induced state he is often disinterested in food, and in the case of an alcoholic the individual will often prefer to devote his time and energy to drinking instead of eating. If funds are limited, an addict will generally use his money for drugs rather than food. The neglect of good eating habits is also a consequence of the disorganized life addicts lead and street addicts often experience large weight losses. Drugs do not contain vitamins, proteins or minerals so replacing food intake with drugs will obviously cause problems. Alcohol does contain calories but they are not the kind of calories that can be stored for later use, nor do they aid in building body tissue as carbohydrates, proteins and fats do.

The use of marijuana often brings on periods of increased appetite; the same is true of morphine early in the addictive process. The foods craved, however, are usually high in carbohydrates and low in nutrition (''junk'' foods such as soda, candy and other sweets). These foods are often picked for their convenience and low cost.

Some drugs are actually taken to depress the appetite. When taken in large doses, anorectics, particularly cocaine and amphetamines, can lead to ketosis—the process in which a low carbohydrate diet causes the body's fat stores to be broken down for energy faster than they can be used by the body. Body protein can eventually waste away during prolonged and heavy amphetamine or cocaine use.

Barbiturate users experience a decrease in the absorption of thiamine and an increase in urinary ascorbic acid. Barbiturate and heroin users also have low serum B vitamin levels. A bad diet, especially insufficient consumption of leafy green vegetables, can cause low folate (folic acid) levels, further complicating their B-complex deficiencies. Heroin users frequently suffer from acute and chronic infections which can alter their nutritional needs. Hepatitis, a common occurrence among heroin users, can cause decreased appetite and nausea.

Some drugs, however, will increase appetite and result in weight gain. This is particularly true of phenothiazines, such as Thorazine®.

Drug use, particularly alcohol, can also impair the digestion of food and the absorption of nutrients into the blood, thus causing malnutrition. Alcohol can also interfere with the activation of vitamins by the liver cells, which often results in deficiency diseases. Some theorists suggest that vitamin deficiencies play a role in the initial development of alcoholism but this theory has not been proven and most nutritional deficiencies appear as a result of alcoholism, not the cause. Alcohol is absorbed rapidly from an empty stomach and more slowly from a full stomach. Consequently, nutrition plays an important role in the rate that alcohol is absorbed. In spite of the extreme toxicity of alcohol and some other drugs, good diet can prevent or retard much of the damage to the liver and central nervous systems, so maintaining good nutrition in the active abuser is important. Chronic drinkers may suffer from malsorption of folate thiamin and B12. The diarrhea which alcoholics often suffer from causes a loss of fat and fat soluble vitamins, water, electrolytes and minerals. A damaged liver has difficulty in converting vitamins into their usable forms, and it cannot store vitamins well. The body needs increased amounts of vitamins and proteins to restore the damage that alcohol does to tissues and from bleeding. So the nutrient deficiencies of the alcoholic are multiple and severe with malnutrition compounding the effects of alcohol on almost every body system.

Nutrition also plays an important role in the treatment of alcoholism. High protein diets and massive amounts of B vitamins are prescribed, along with regularly scheduled meals, because the lowering of blood sugar at any time of day increases craving for alcohol and other drugs. Although good nutrition is not a cure for alcoholism, an alcoholic who is properly nourished may find it easier to abstain. The correction of nutritional problems is also an important part of rehabilitation in the case of other drugs.

nystagmus Involuntary rapid eyeball movement. It is a common symptom of toxic reaction resulting from PCP or sedative use. (See also EYES.)

O

Obetrol® (Obetrol) A single entity AMPHETAMINE that is used as an anorectic for weight control and in the treatment of narcolepsy and Minimal Brain Dysfunction. Tolerance can develop and as with other amphetamines, psychological dependence and social disability can occur. It has a significant potential for abuse, and when taken with alcohol or other central nervous system depressants it can have an additive effect. Overdosage can result in restlessness, tremors, rapid respiration, hallucinations and confusion. It is supplied in 10 mg blue and 20 mg pink tablets.

ODPHP See OFFICE OF DISEASE PREVENTION AND HEALTH INFORMATION CENTER.

Odyssey Resources, Inc. Founded in 1966 as a treatment center for adult drug addicts in New York City, Odyssey Houses are now located in other parts of the United States as well as in Australia and New Zealand. They are drug-free, therapeutic communities which are psychiatrically oriented and believe that personal growth can replace the need for drugs. Odyssey Houses now treat a wide range of patients: adolescents, alcoholics, female addicts with children, and child abuse victims.

Office for Substance Abuse Prevention (OSAP) Created by the Anti-Drug Abuse Act of 1986 as a new agency to develop a multidimensional prevention program with a fresh perspective and new resources. The agency's mission is to review government policy related to alcohol and other drug abuse; operate a clearinghouse; operate a grant program; support development of model programs; conduct prevention workshops; coordinate research findings; and develop prevention materials. Contact: Elaine Johnson, Ph.D., Director, Office for Substance Abuse Prevention, 5515 Security Lane, Rockville, Maryland 20852. Telephone: (301) 443-0365.

Office of Disease Prevention and Health Information Center (ODPHP) Agency helps the public locate health information through identification of resources and an inquiry and referral service. Formerly the National Health Information Clearinghouse, the center also prepares and distributes publications and directories on health promotion and disease prevention topics. Contact: P.O. Box 1133, Washington, DC 20013-1133. Telephone: (800) 336-4797; (202) 429-9091 (DC metro area).

Office of Workplace Initiatives (OWI) Established in February 1987 by the National Institute on Drug Abuse (NIDA), OWI develops policies and provides leadership for the implementation and administration of a national program to eliminate the use of illegal drugs in the workplace. The program includes research, treatment, training and prevention activities, as well as projects related to development of a comprehensive Drug-Free Workplace program, which covers policy development, supervisory training, employee education, employee assistance and drug-testing components. Contact: NIDA, Office of Workplace Initiatives, 5600 Fishers Lane, Rockville, Maryland 20857. Telephone: (301) 443-6245.

ololiuqui See MORNING GLORY SEEDS.

onset In drug research, the term is used to mean the first time a person uses a particular drug. It is also used to refer to the initiation of the "withdrawal syndrome." Age of onset is a major variable, often studied by epidemiologists alone and in relation to other variables.

Operation Primavera A 10-day campaign by Colombian authorities in early 1984 that became the most successful bust of cocaine laboratories in Colombian history. The successful operation netted a total of 26 plants capable of producing 6.6 tons of cocaine per week. Authorities confiscated 1.3 tons of cocaine in base and finished form, plus unprecedented quantities of chemicals used in the manufacture of cocaine. Enough chemicals were seized to make 104 tons of cocaine, a third of the estimated annual cocaine output of Colombia, Bolivia and Peru combined. The seizures underscored a little noted but crucial fact of life in the $130 billion cocaine business: the drug trade is a two-way street. That is, the cocaine flows from mostly Third World producers to the United States and other industrialized nations, but the chemicals and other materials needed—ether acetone, methyl ethyl ketone, potassium per manganate—to turn coca leaves into cocaine flow from the industrialized nations to the Third World.

William R. Doesner, "The Chemical Connection," *Time*, February 20, 1989, 44–45.

Operation Snowcap An important mutual action initiative in which the U.S. Drug Enforcement Administration has been involved since 1987. Operation Snowcap is a three-year multifaceted campaign created to significantly reduce the supply of illicit cocaine reaching the United States from Latin America. It was developed by DEA and the U.S. State Department's Bureau of International Narcotics Matters (INM) and has been closely coordinated with appropriate U.S. agencies. The overall strategy is to extend to other Latin American countries a various interrelated aerial, waterway and ground enforcement/reduction programs that were previously proven successful in coca reduction efforts (particularly in late 1986) under Operation Stop Prop/Blast Furnace in Bolivia. At present, Snowcap operations are coordinated with law enforcement officials in 12 Latin American countries.

U.S. Department of Justice, Drug Enforcement Administration, Statement of David L. Westrate before U.S. Senate Subcommittee on Terrorism, Narcotics and International Operations, *Drug Enforcement Administration Briefing Book,* April 1989, Washington, D.C., 3.

opiates Specifically, refers to the two opium alkaloids, MORPHINE and CODEINE, and the semisynthetic drugs derived from them, such as HEROIN (diacetylmorphine) and hydromorphine hydrochloride (Dilaudid). Morphine and codeine, along with opium, are sometimes referred to as natural opiates, and their derivatives as semisynthetic opiates. *Classification:* narcotic analgesic agonists [RIS 27:220–161 entries; opium, RIS 27:222–14 entries]. RIS stands for the U.S. Department of Health and Human Services Research Issue Series, of which there are 29 at this writing.

opioids Synthetic drugs with characteristics similar to OPIATES.

opium A narcotic which acts as a depressant on the central nervous system (CNS). Unlike other CNS depressants, however, such as barbiturates and alcohol, narcotics also relieve pain.

Opium is made by air drying the juice which has been extracted from the unripe seed pods of the oriental poppy *(Papaver somniferum).* The resulting brownish gum is then formed into bricks or cakes which eventually harden.

There is evidence that opium has been used since prehistoric times. The opium poppy is thought to have originated in Asia Minor and was first used medicinally in Egypt. From there, its use spread to Greece. Arab traders carried it to India and China, where it was used to control dysentery and for its euphoric and sedative effects. Opium use became so widespread in China and was considered so harmful that the Chinese government tried to control its importation, sale and use. This was opposed by the British because it interfered with their profitable trade in opium grown in India, and led to the Opium War (1839–42). The British won the war and as a result, opium cultivation and importation were legalized in China and Chinese emigrants carried the habit of opium smoking to the United States and elsewhere.

In the early 1500s, the physician Paracelsus made a tincture of opium (powdered opium dissolved in alcohol) he called laudanum; it was the first medicinal form of opium. In Europe laudanum was used to relieve pain and control dysentery, and as a cough suppressant and sedative. It became a standard drug until the end of the 19th century when its use began to decline. Several other opium mixtures were developed in the 1700s and 1800s but the most important was paregoric, a tincture of opium combined with camphor. Although considered an old-fashioned remedy today, it is still used to control diarrhea and is listed in Schedule III of the Controlled Substances Act. However, it is obtainable in some places without a prescription and heroin addicts often resort to it when they cannot get their usual "fix."

The danger of developing dependence on these staple opium remedies was not well understood, and by the end of the 19th century many people including famous poets and writers had become addicted. After doctors became aware of the problem, laws were passed making opium and its derivatives available only on prescription. The first of these was the 1914 Harrison Narcotics Act which placed opium under strict federal control. Other legislation followed, culminating in the Controlled Substances Act of 1970 which regulated all drugs likely to be abused. The drugs are listed under five schedules according to their abuse potential. Heroin is a Schedule I drug, and drugs containing narcotics such as opium are listed in Schedule II.

The chemical substance (alkaloid) in opium which causes its effects is morphine. Morphine was first extracted from opium in 1803 and because it was found to be a more effective drug, the medical use of opium began to decline. Except for a few prescription drugs, it is rarely used medically today. Only two of the alkaloids extracted from opium—morphine and the milder codeine—are still in clinical use.

When heroin, a derivative of morphine, was developed in 1898 it was heralded as a better pain killer than morphine and a highly effective cough suppressant. Considered to be nonaddictive, physicians used heroin to treat opium and morphine addicts until the drug's own—even worse—addictive effects were recognized. By that time addicts whose opium and morphine supplies had been cut off by stringent laws, and the underworld, had discovered the far greater potency of heroin. By the early 1900s heroin had replaced both opium and morphine on the street and the era of the "junkie" was born. Today the manufacture and use of heroin is completely illegal in the United States and it is considered to have no medical use.

Opium smoking, the most common form of abuse, is practiced mostly in China, Hong Kong and Southeast Asia. It was introduced into the United States by Chinese immigrants in the 19th century. More recently some American soldiers acquired the habit during the war in Vietnam. Illicit use of opium in the United States, however, is mostly confined to such opium-containing remedies as paregoric which is used intravenously—with disastrous results on the veins—by heroin addicts when they are cut off from their regular supplies. The use of opium per se is not a major drug problem in America—the main problems lie primarily with morphine and its derivative heroin. In 1989, the four major producers of opium in the world, in terms of metric tons, were Burma 1,300; Afghanistan 750; Iron 300; and Laos 250.

Appearance: Raw opium comes in a solid mass of varying shape weighing from one-half to five pounds. It is processed in several ways.

Though now rarely used, granulated opium is a medically approved drug for treating diarrhea.

Powdered opium is more finely ground than the granulated variety. It is used in the manufacture of a few prescription drugs, notably PANTOPON and B & O SUPPRETTES.

Dissolved in water, filtered, then boiled down into a sticky paste the substance becomes the preparation used by opium smokers.

Dissolved in alcohol, the substance becomes the tincture of opium used in making laudanum and paregoric.

Broken down chemically into its alkaloids (chemical substances found in all plants), the substance yields morphine and codeine.

Effects: Used medically, opium dulls sensations of pain, controls diarrhea because it has a constipating action, suppresses coughing, induces drowsiness, alleviates anxiety, and gives a feeling of euphoria or well-being. It is the drug's euphoric effect which the opium abuser is seeking, as well as its ability to make him indifferent to hunger, sexual urges, tension and anxiety. Unlike barbiturates, alcohol and other drugs, narcotics do not trigger aggresive behavior. On the contrary, they usually make the user docile and dreamy.

There can also be unpleasant side effects with opium use such as nausea and vomiting, but the user is normally indifferent to these reactions because they are quickly followed by sedation and euphoria.

Tolerance: Opium tolerance develops as inexorably as tolerance to barbiturates and other CNS drugs. With regular use, dosage must be steadily increased to achieve the desired effects. As dosage increases dependence can develop.

Dependence: Long-term use of opium can cause both psychological and physical dependence. With psychological dependence, the user has a craving for the drug and feels life is not worth living without it. With physical dependence, the body grows to rely on the drug to take over some of its normal functions. When the drug is stopped or sharply reduced, physical reactions of varying degrees of severity follow.

History of Opium

5000 B.C.	**Opium is known in Mesopotamia and mentioned in Assyrian medical texts.**
1500 B.C.	**Used as an anesthetic by Egyptian physicians.**
c.7th century	**Opium poppy is brought to China via Middle East and India.**
1200	**Used in the Middle East as a medicine and an intoxicant.**
1541	**Paracelsus, Swiss alchemist, introduces laudanum and it becomes popular throughout Europe.**
1650	**Opium smoking becomes rampant in China.**
c.1803	**Morphine is isolated from opium and used medically in 1825.**
1839-1842	**Opium War between China and England.**
1866	**Use of opium and morphine during Civil War in U.S. creates estimated 400,000 addicts.**
1870s	**Sales of patent medicines containing opium proliferate in Europe and America.**
1875	**San Francisco passes first ordinance against opium dens.**
1909	**Legislation is passed making opium smoking a criminal offense.**
1914	**Harrison Narcotics Act taxes manufacture, importation and distribution of opium and products containing opium.**
1920s	**Opium dens operate in most U.S. cities.**
1930s	**Opium abuse almost completely replaced by heroin.**
1931	**Agreement for Control of Opium Smoking in the Far East is signed at Bangkok.**
1942	**Opium Poppy Control Act prohibits cultivation except under license in U.S.**
1946	**Iran prohibits opium cultivation.**
1948	**World Health Organization becomes responsible for narcotics control. Only a few nations are allowed to cultivate opium for export.**
1970	**Controlled Substances Act classifies medicines containing opium as Schedules II, III and V drugs.**
1971	**Turkey agrees to stop cultivation of opium poppies in 1972.**
1980s	**Opium itself not a major abuse problem in the U.S. In the Middle and Far East it is still smoked or eaten.**

Withdrawal: When physical dependence has developed, opium users experience a number of withdrawal symptoms if the drug is suddenly stopped. These develop rapidly and reach their height in two or three days; they continue for a week or more before subsiding, although it may take as long as six months for some effects to wear off. There are occasional fatalities among deeply dependent users who are in poor health but opium withdrawal is much less dangerous to life than barbiturate withdrawal.

The symptoms of opium withdrawal are the same as those for other narcotics: anxiety, restlessness, yawning, tears, runny nose, nausea, diarrhea, cramps, general body aches, gooseflesh and dehydration.

Source: The opium poppy is grown in China, Southeast Asia, Mexico, Turkey and Lebanon. The amount of raw opium required by legitimate drug houses to manufacture morphine and other prescription drugs is only a fraction of the supply available. The rest makes its way into black market laboratories in Europe and elsewhere to produce illicit heroin and morphine.

Traffic and control: Raw opium is too bulky for profitable long-distance smuggling and does not present a major traffic and control problem in the U.S. Even morphine is in the form of a solid block before it is processed into a soluble salt. In North America the real problem is heroin. It has only half the bulk of morphine and control of smuggling is extremely difficult and requires international cooperation.

Synonyms: O, op, black pills, black stuff, gum, hop, tar.

oral administration See ADMINISTRATION.

oral fixation A psychoanalytic theory that was suggested by some to be the cause of alcoholism. The earliest stage of psychosexual development occurs during the time when an infant's only means of achieving security and release from tension is through stimulation of the oral cavity. According to the oral fixation theory, if an infant is deprived of a warm and loving relationship during this time, he will be traumatized and will continue to seek gratification of his primary emotional hunger. In other words he becomes fixated at the oral stage of development and his unconscious desire for warmth and nurturance cannot be satisfied in normal interpersonal relationships. An alcoholic seeks liquid nourishment as a way of generating sensations of warmth and satisfaction, much as an infant seeks to fill his emptiness through oral ingestion. Along with this need for gratification, there is the alcoholic's feelings of anger and rage at parents who failed him—a rage which he redirects through alcohol consumption. Current research tends to disprove this theory as a cause of addiction.

organic disorder A disorder which is the result of known or hypothesized pathological changes in the tissues, as opposed to a functional disorder which is a condition in which one or more of the normal activities of the organism cannot be properly performed, though there is no known pathological change in organic structure.

organic solvents See VOLATILE HYDROCARBONS and INHALANTS.

organized crime See CRIME, ORGANIZED.

OSAP See OFFICE FOR SUBSTANCE ABUSE PREVENTION (OSAP).

outreach The effort to reach out to a drug dependent person who does not voluntarily enter a treatment situation is called outreach. It may be made by street workers who are recovered addicts or health care workers visiting places where addicts are found. It is also done by public media, such as TV, radio and magazines.

overdose The ingestion of a drug in an amount larger than the body's system can deal with. Whether accidental or deliberate, overdose is a great danger in the use and abuse of drugs.

A deliberate overdose of a drug, particularly a short-acting barbiturate such as amobarbital, secobarbital or pentobarbital, is a widely used method of suicide. Studies have shown that a high percentage of those who use this method are also alcoholics. Although the amount of a barbiturate required to produce a lethal dose can vary from person to person, it is usually in the range of 10–15 times a normal dose. Cardiovascular collapse precedes respiratory depression in a lethal dose and is followed by coma and death.

Accidental overdose can result from a variety of factors. In recent years the increase in polydrug use has been a leading factor in overdose cases, particularly the use of alcohol with other drugs. Because of the synergistic effect, even a small, normal dose of a drug can prove fatal when taken with alcohol. The combination of barbiturates and amphetamines, often taken by amphetamine dependent people to bring themselves down from a "wired up" state or to ward off withdrawal symptoms, can also prove fatal. In polydrug use a person can never be completely certain what his or her reaction will be to a combination of drugs, and overdoses are common.

An overdose of an amphetamine, which is a central nervous system stimulant, is characterized by hyperactivity, restlessness, tremulousness and mental confusion. In severe overdose the symptoms are delirium, stroke, cardiac arrhythmia and convulsions, followed by circulatory collapse and coma. The lethal dose of an amphetamine is not known but it is estimated to be 5–10 mg per kilogram of body weight for a nontolerant person. Among some individuals, however, a much smaller dose can prove fatal, while a habitual user who has developed tolerance can consume a much larger dose. Tolerance to amphetamines builds quickly and the need for larger amounts is the primary factor in overdose.

Overdose of cocaine, also a central nervous system stimulant, has symptoms similar to amphetamine overdose. In cases of acute toxicity, death can occur in as little as two to three minutes or in as long as 30 minutes. Lethal doses vary according to the method of administration. Ingested cocaine is less toxic than cocaine that is injected; 120 mg taken intravenously is said to be a lethal dose but as little as 20 mg applied to mucous membranes can also be lethal in sensitive individuals.

Overdoses of barbiturates, which in normal doses act as central nervous system depressants, relieve tension and anxiety and produce drowsiness and sleep, are common. When the desired effect is not achieved by a normal dose, a user will often increase the dosage. Another cause of overdose is when a user takes repeated doses because he is in a state of mental confusion and cannot remember how many doses he has already taken. Symptoms of overdose include cold sweaty skin, a weak rapid pulse, breathing that is either slow or rapid and shallow, and coma. Treatment for barbiturate overdose by support of breathing and heart action is usually effective if the person is discovered in time.

Heroin overdose is characterized initially by lethargy and stupor, followed by a prolonged coma. Death from an overdose can sometimes be prevented by an injection of a narcotic antagonist. Deaths that are reported as heroin overdoses are generally inaccurate. Because death from heroin is a slow process, the sudden death of an addict is more likely to be caused by such complications as a combination of heroin and alcohol or a sensitivity to an adulterant. (See SYNDROME X.) Overdose patients admitted to hospitals often show signs of pulmonary edema, pneumonia, shallow breathing and coma. A lethal dose of heroin is related to a person's tolerance level and increases as tolerance increases. A lethal dose for a nonaddict has been variously estimated at between 120 and 500 milligrams. Addicts have been known to survive injections of 1800 milligrams. Overdoses have occurred when an addict's tolerance is low and also in cases when he has taken heroin that is unusually potent. Addicts can never be sure what percentage of the mixture they have purchased is pure heroin. Sometimes a dealer will give a buyer a "hot shot"—a deliberate overdose—if the latter is suspected of being an informer.

There is no known lethal dose of marijuana, although it can produce highly toxic reactions whether it is taken orally or injected. Prolonged heavy use can result in chronic bronchitis, asthma and pulmonary disorders.

An overdose of hallucinogens (LSD, mescaline, psilocybin, and so on) is not likely to be fatal. Large doses can produce unconsciousness, however. One of the great dangers associated with the use of hallucinogens is that they impair the user's judgment, and deaths have been reported to have occurred while a person was under the influence of such a drug. Temporary panic states can occur, and sometimes chronic psychoses occur that last for months.

Deaths have resulted from the use of inhalants but, as in the case of glue sniffing, the cause of death is most likely to be from suffocation because a plastic bag has been placed over the head to enhance the effects. In the case of solvents, a high dose can produce general sedative-anesthetic effects—drowsiness, stupor, respiratory depression and unconsciousness. In extremely heavy use death has been reported from inhibited breathing. The fluorocarbons in aerosols have been associated with deaths due to cardiac arrhythmia.

over-the-counter medications (OTC) OTC drugs are those that may be purchased without a prescription. Some of the estimated 350,000 OTC products (with annual sales of between $5 billion and $7 billion) are subject to abuse, particularly those that contain analgesic, sedative or stimulant ingredients. Among the most abused are cough syrups, sleeping aids and appetite depressants (diet pills).

OWI See OFFICE OF WORKPLACE INITIATIVES (OWI).

oxazepam A BENZODIAZEPINE derivative that has a relatively slow onset of action but long-lasting effects. It is used to relieve tension, anxiety and muscle spasm; to produce sedation; and to prevent convulsions. (See SERAX.)

Oxford Group A nondenominational, theologically conservative, evangelical group that attempted to recapture what its members referred to as "primitive Christianity." It was started in 1908 by Frank N. D. Buchman, an ordained Lutheran minister from Allentown, Penn. Bill Wilson, the founder of ALCOHOLICS ANONYMOUS, included a number of the Group's principles in the AA philosophy (self-survey, restitution, confession). Originally called the First Century Christian Fellowship, it became popularly known as the Oxford Group during the 1920s and 1930s because of Buchman's preaching among Oxford students. In its final years the group was known as the Moral Re-Armament or MRA.

oxycodone A semisynthetic MORPHINE derivative, it is a narcotic used as an analgesic. Its potency is similar to that of morphine. It produces sedation as a side effect. (See PERCOCET and PERCODAN.)

oxymorphone A semisynthetic MORPHINE derivative whose analgesic potency is much higher than morphine. It is sold under the trade name Numorphan® (Endo).

P

Pacific Institute for Research and Evaluation Health Professionals as Preventors Organization concerned with prevention of alcohol abuse and other drug abuse. Since 1985, a team of researchers and program development specialists has sought to extend prevention and early intervention to settings that offered access to youth, demonstrated a keen interest in the welfare of young people, and did not consistently address youth alcohol and other drug prevention and early intervention issues.

The group works with officials at the Alcohol, Drug Abuse, and Mental Health Administration (ADAMHA) to locate potential funding sources. Grants supporting the project have come from such sources as The Pew Charitable Trusts, The J. M. Foundation and IBM. A major current project involves nationwide promotion of *Substance Abuse: A Guide for Health Professionals*, jointly developed by the Pacific Institute and the American Academy of Pediatrics in 1988.

The basic philosophy of this organization is that all health professionals can and should aid youth in avoiding alcohol and drug abuse and related problems as a crucial component of the national effort to combat these problems. Contact: Michael D. Klitzner, Ph.D., Project Director, Health Professionals as Preventors, Pacific Institute for Research and Evaluation, 8521 Leesburg Pike, Vienna, VA 22180.

Pakistan Pakistan is faced with a twin problem in the area of drug abuse. Not only has the poppy, the source of opium, been cultivated since time immemorial, the cannabis plant grows wild in the northern areas of the country. In the face of small landholdings, the absence of employment opportunities, depleted soil and inadequate irrigation, it is not hard to understand the temptation to sell and gain an easy profit from these products. During the 1960s only a fraction of the total production of opium and cannabis was consumed within the country; the majority found its way into illicit foreign trade. It has been estimated that 50% of the heroin smuggled into the United States, and 85% of the heroin smuggled into Great Britain, was from Pakistan.

The government of Pakistan, aware of the complexity, magnitude and repercussions of drug abuse within the country as well as the serious implications of illicit exportation, set up a Pakistan Narcotics Control Board in 1973. In 1979 the Prohibition (Enforcement of Hadd) Ordinance was set into effect by the government: it imposed a complete ban on the production, processing, manufacture, sale and use of all intoxicating drugs. The ordinance introduced Islamic disciplines into the domain of drug abuse and the deeply religious bent of the people has helped to assure their determination to combat the drug problems.

Poppy cultivation in Pakistan was formerly divided into three diverse areas: (1) settled districts; (2) merged areas; and (3) tribal areas. In settled areas, poppy cultivation was under license of the government (licensed production is now forbidden by law); it was understood that the entire harvest would be turned over to the government and after processing would be issued by the government opium factory for scientific, medical and quasi-medical uses. In merged and tribal areas, cultivation was not governed by licensing and was largely administered according to tribal customs. Following the enactment of the Prohibition Ordinance, the government of Pakistan appealed to tribal elders to respect the drug and alcohol law according to Islamic injunctions against the use of intoxicants. Most of the tribal leaders responded and the 800 tons of opium produced in 1978–79 was reduced to 100 tons in 1979–80, and further reduced in 1980–81 to 85 tons.

The withdrawal of poppy cultivation has imposed an enormous socio-economic hardship, particularly in neglected areas of the country. One of the major problems facing the Pakistan government today is to find a viable alternative crop that will produce a sufficient economic return. Approximately $45 million of the U.S. Aid Program package has been designated to help in the development of rural areas. The Buner Project, a development already implemented in Thailand, is currently underway. These projects include road-building, providing water supplies for villages and crops, supplying farm credit, land leveling and terracing, and improving livestock health and production.

In a country where it is reported that between 450,000 and 800,000 people abuse various types of drugs, it is not enough to ban the cultivation of poppies. The Pakistan Narcotics Control Board, in cooperation with the United Nations, is also involved in a detoxification and after-care program for drug abusers and addicts. It is a slow and costly process, however: in 1979 only seven detox-

Total of Major Narcotic Drugs Seized in Pakistan by Drug Law Enforcement Agencies

Drug	Quantity Seized	Quantity Seized	
	(1973–79)	(1980–81)	
Heroin	28 Kgs.	93,575	Kgs.
Morphine	146 Kgs.	1,168	Kgs.
		233	Ampules
		672	Injections
		4,501	Tablets
Mandrax (Methaqualone)		1,530,362	Tablets
Other Opiates		45,075	Tablets
Opium	48,611 Kgs.	11,647	Kgs.
Cannabis	171,507 Kgs.	72,951	Kgs.

SOURCE: Pakistan Narcotics Control Board.

ification and rehabilitation centers were in operation. The government's program for the future calls for another 12 centers and 20 specialized hospitals. Between March 1979 and June 1981, the centers claim to have detoxified 6,000 addicts. A lack of properly trained and organized narcotic law enforcement agents has led the government to establish a forensic laboratory for chemical analysis and testing. In 1980 the Pakistan government negotiated a contract with the Federal Republic of Germany to conduct a survey on the exact extent of drug abuse in the country, covering patterns of abuse, age, sex, availability, income group, and so on.

Although the amount of narcotic drugs seized during the years 1980–81 (see chart) is extremely impressive, the crux of Pakistan's problem is still one of substituting a profitable crop in place of the poppy.

Opium production in Pakistan in 1987 remained at between 135 and 160 metric tons, according to the U.S. Drug Enforcement Administration (DEA). In mid-1989, prospects brightened in Pakistan when Haje Minza Izqbal Baig, described as a heroin kingpin, surrendered to Pakistani police.

panaddiction See POLYDRUG USE.

pancreas A small glandular organ located below and behind the stomach and connected to the small intestine at the duodenum. The pancreas secretes insulin and glucagon—hormones which regulate the blood's glucose level—and enzymes necessary for the digestion of proteins, carbohydrates and fats. A failure to produce sufficient insulin results in diabetes mellitus.

Most drugs have little direct effect on the pancreas whether taken in therapeutic or abusive doses. Alcohol, however, appears to stimulate pancreatic secretion while prompting spasms which obstruct pancreatic duct outflow. The pressure on the pancreatic ducts causes tissues in the organ to swell, and the resulting condition is pancreatitis.

Malnutrition may also be partly responsible for pancreatitis which can occur after bouts of heavy drinking but more frequently develops after years of excessive alcohol consumption. Chronic alcoholics show a particularly high incidence of both acute and chronic pancreatitis. It does not develop in all alcoholics, however; cirrhotic patients are more than twice as likely to develop pancreatitis than those without cirrhosis.

Symptoms of pancreatitis include severe abdominal pain, nausea, vomiting, abdominal bleeding, digestive distress and diabetes mellitus, in varying degrees of severity. Abstinence from alcohol and a low-fat diet can relieve the acute state of the disease, which is evidenced by abnormally high concentrations of serum amylase. Pancreatitis can sometimes produce striking mental changes due to electrolyte disruptions in the suffering individual. More severe cases can involve pancreatic necrosis, hemorrhage and scarring.

Chronic relapsing pancreatitis is relatively common among alcoholics, who are also more likely than the rest of the population to develop carcinoma of the pancreas. Pancreatitis is rare in non-alcoholics.

Pantopon® (Roche) A narcotic analgesic that contains hydrochlorides of OPIUM alkaloids. It is used in place of morphine for the relief of severe pain. In addition to the action of morphine, it exhibits the action of codeine and the other alkaloids present in opium. It can be habit-forming and dependency can occur. Pantopon has a high potential for abuse. It is supplied in 1 ml ampules for injections; each ml contains 20 mg hydrochlorides of opium alkaloids.

papaverine An alkaloid of opium in the benzylisoquinoline class that has no central nervous system or analgesic effect. It is usually used as a cough suppressant and in the treatment of cardiovascular disease. Dependency does not develop, and because it does not produce euphoric effects it is not an abused drug.

Papaver somniferum The oriental opium poppy plant from which opium and its derivatives are produced.

para-addict (usually co-addict) A person who has a close relationship with an addict (a parent, spouse, or employer, for example), and because of the relationship is also an indirect victim of the disease and its effects. A co-addict (or para-addict) also needs counseling in many cases and will often find that his or her needs have been vicariously served by the relationship in some way. There is often an attempt by co-addicts to assign blame, particularly in the case of wives who feel at fault because of their husbands' addiction. Denial of a person's addiction problem may also be a fault of co-addicts. Denial only delays the treatment which should begin immediately. Problems for a co-addict can also continue after a person stops using. During the time an addict is using, his or her spouse will often take control of the household; when the addiction stops the addict is no longer dependent, and the co-addict may feel unnecessary, unneeded, and unappreciated. NAR-ANON and AL-ANON are organizations that help the friends and relatives of addicts and alcoholics in these types of situations.

parahexyl A synthetic cannabinoid resembling THC. (See PYRAHEXYL.)

paraldehyde A synthetic non-barbiturate sedative hypnotic. Discovered in 1829, it was first used medically in 1881 and was long considered one of the safest hypnotics. It enjoyed widespread use. Paraldehyde is now thought to be inconvenient and slightly dangerous, however, and has been largely replaced by barbiturates and benzodiazepines.

Appearance and activity in the body: Paraldehyde appears as a colorless inflammable liquid with a strong bitter taste and odor. Taken orally or by injection, it is rapidly absorbed by the body and metabolized in the liver. Up to 28% of the substance is exhaled which gives the breath a characteristic pungent odor. Paraldehyde crosses the placental barrier, and large doses can depress neonatal respiration.

A problem encountered with paraldehyde relates to the substance's quick absorption of oxygen. When exposed to air, it oxidizes to strong acetic acid and loses a great deal of its effectiveness. Since the products of decomposition can be very dangerous, sometimes causing death, strict guidelines for the storage of paraldehyde must be observed. It is stored in amounts no greater than 30 mg and at temperatures no higher than 25 degrees centigrade. It must be discarded if not used within 24 hours after opening.

Dosage: Paraldehyde is administered in doses ranging between 5–30 mg. As little as 12 mg has proved fatal to patients with liver disease, and over 100 mg have been survived.

Effects: Although paraldehyde acts much more quickly than chloral hydrate, barbiturates, alcohol and other depressants, its effects are very similar, including intoxication and diminished reflexes. Hypnotic doses induce sleep in as little as 10 minutes and the drug's effects last from four to eight hours. Respiration is not significantly depressed nor is circulation affected. Oral administration causes burning of the mucous membranes, and intramuscular injection causes severe permanent injury if the injection is close to the sciatic nerve. Intravenous administration is both difficult and dangerous: difficult because paraldehyde reacts with plastic syringes, and dangerous because the minimal injectable anesthetic dosage and the lethal dosage are extremely close.

Tolerance to depressants develops with the use of paraldehyde. Dependence can also occur, especially in the case of alcoholics who receive the drug in withdrawal treatment. Abusive doses can cause stomach bleeding, blood dysfunctions and, in some cases, a deep coma similar to ether anesthesia. Symptoms of WITHDRAWAL from paraldehyde parallel those that occur with alcohol withdrawal.

Usage: Paraldehyde is used most commonly in connection with withdrawal treatments for alcoholics, particularly those suffering from delirium tremens. It is also used to treat insomnia, convulsions and tetanus, and as an obstetric anesthetic and analgesic.

Despite its addictive qualities, paraldehyde is not commonly abused, probably because of its bitter taste, unpleasant and identifiable odor, and its burning effect on the mucous membranes.

Availability: Paraldehyde is available as a liquid to be administered orally with juice, as rectal suppositories, in olive oil or cottonseed oil enemas and in injectable form. It is a Schedule IV drug under the CONTROLLED SUBSTANCES ACT.

paranoia In this case, a drug user's constant fear of arrest which leads him to take obsessive and extensive steps to avoid being caught buying or possessing drugs. Unlike the imaginary paranoia of a psychotic, a drug user's paranoia may have a basis in fact.

Paranoid states do occur in withdrawal states and with the use of amphetamines, cocaine, phencyclidine and hallucinogens. The user has delusional thoughts that he is being persecuted, or that he is all-powerful (megalomaniacal).

paraquat A herbicide which has recently been used by the Drug Enforcement Administration (DEA) to eradicate marijuana crops on federal land areas in the United States. The U.S. government has also been encouraging the spraying of paraquat in South American countries.

In July 1979, the United Nations Narcotics Laboratory issued the following statement about paraquat: ". . . the toxic properties of paraquat are such that the handling of the concentrate requires care. Although fibrosis of the lung can result from the ingestion of paraquat, there is no known instance of this occurring in humans following the ingestion of paraquat. Furthermore, residues of sprayed formulations on cannabis would not be sufficient to cause toxic effects to the marijuana user."

Opponents of paraquat use include the National Organization for Reform of Marijuana Laws, the Sierra Club, Friends of the Earth, the National Coalition Against the Misuse of Pesticides and several citizen action groups, who argue that the spraying poses a serious health threat to the estimated twenty-nine million marijuana smokers in the U.S. The government claims that it is not paraquat that is the issue, but rather marijuana. They further claim that farmers use an estimated four million pounds of paraquat annually over an estimated 10.7 million acres for the control of weeds among crops. A suit brought against the DEA by the above mentioned groups resulted in a court order on September 13, 1983, temporarily restraining paraquat spraying because the DEA had not assessed the environmental impact before beginning the operation. The day after the court ruling, the Reagan Administration announced that spraying would be suspended for the rest of the 1983 growing season. It has not been reinstituted. Recent studies sponsored by the Centers for Disease Control (CDC), in Atlanta, indicate that the original fear of the health consequences of paraquat spraying was an overreaction.

paregoric A narcotic that acts as a central nervous system (CNS) depressant. Paregoric is an opium tincture (powdered opium dissolved in alcohol) combined with camphor and has an alcohol content equivalent to 90 proof whiskey. It has been used medically since its first appearance in the early 1700s. Although considered an old-fashioned remedy today, it is still medically accepted and used principally to treat diarrhea.

In the 19th century the danger of addiction to opium-containing medicines was not well understood and abuse of paregoric and laudanum (an earlier tincture of opium) was common. Countless people, including a number of famous poets and writers, developed at least psychological dependence on them.

Well into the 20th century mothers gave paregoric to their babies not only to control infant diarrhea but also to quiet their crying and put them to sleep. There is no way of estimating the harm this practice caused before the Narcotics Act of 1914 placed opium and its products under federal control, making them available only on prescription. Paregoric is a Schedule III drug under the CONTROLLED SUBSTANCES ACT of 1970.

Today paregoric is in demand by heroin addicts when heroin is not available. Paregoric is a liquid and most addicts drink it, requiring about a quart a day to get the effects they need. Others inject it intravenously after processing it to remove the camphor and alcohol. At one time, addicts sometimes added the antihistamine tripelennamine to paregoric and the mixture was referred to as "Blue Velvet." Because the intravenous injection of Blue Velvet resulted in plugged veins and sometimes death its popularity quickly waned.

Tolerance and physical dependence can develop with heavy use over a long period of time. If it does, stopping suddenly or sharply reducing the accustomed dosage can bring on the same symptoms as those that follow opium withdrawal.

It is used medically to detoxify newborns addicted to narcotics.

Richard R. Lingeman, *Drugs from A to Z* (New York: McGraw-Hill Book Company, 1974), p. 203.

Jack Margolis, *Recreational Drugs* (Price/Stern/Sloan Publishers, Inc., 1978), pp. 311–312.

parenteral The injection of a substance, either intravenously, intramuscularly or subcutaneously, as opposed to oral ingestion.

Parest® (Parke-Davis) A rapid-acting sedative hypnotic that contained METHAQUALONE hydrochloride and was used for sedation and sleep. It was taken off the market because of widespread abuse.

parica A psychedelic snuff used by the Yekwana Indians in Venezuela. It is made from the bark of the virola tree.

passion flower *Passiflora incarnata.* The leaves and stems of this plant contain a small amount of the alkaloid harmine. There are claims that they produce mild psychedelic effects when they are smoked or brewed in a tea.

passive inhalation Small amounts of smoke enter the lungs of non-smokers when they are in the presence of marijuana or tobacco smokers. This amount is minute even in closed unventilated places. It is practically impossible to become "high" from passive inhalation of marijuana. Any "contact high" is the result of psychological identification with the smoker rather than THC intoxication.

There has been growing concern over the possible adverse health effects of "secondary" or passive inhalation resulting from tobacco smokers since the U.S. Surgeon General's report on smoking and tobacco issued in early 1989. The increased concern has resulted in activity in several policy-making areas: smoking restrictions in public places by some states, cities and federal agencies, smoking restrictions in the workplace and on all commercial domestic flights under six hours duration, lawsuits against tobacco manufacturers, warning labels and even proposed bans on print advertising tobacco products.

In a preliminary report issued in May 1990 the Environmental Protection Agency (EPA) asserted that secondhand smoke caused more than 3,000 cases of lung cancer in nonsmokers each year in the United States. If the report is adopted it could designate cigarette smoke as an environmental hazard along with carcinogens such as benzene and radon. An Australian Federal Court ruled in February 1991 that an advertisement by the Tobacco Institute claiming there was "Little evidence and nothing which proved scientifically that cigarette smoking causes disease in nonsmokers" was false and that scientific evidence demonstrated that secondhand smoke could cause respiratory diseases in children, asthma attacks, and lung cancer.

Pathibamate® (Lederle) A sedative that contains tridihexethyl chloride and MEPROBAMATE. It is used in the treatment of peptic ulcers and colon disorders, particularly when they are accompanied by tension and anxiety. It has the potential for abuse and physical and psychological dependence can occur. When taken with alcohol or other central nervous system depressants it can have an additive effect. Overdosage can result in stupor, coma and respiratory collapse. It is supplied as Pathibamate-400, yellow scored tablets containing 400 mg of meprobamate; and Pathibamate-200, yellow coated tablets containing 200 mg of meprobamate.

pathological drinker A problem drinker or alcoholic. A person who handles unconscious problems or discomforts by excessive drinking.

pathological intoxication A radical change in a person's behavior which usually takes the form of aggressive explosive rage, and follows the ingestion of a small amount of alcohol that is insufficient to produce intoxication. Deep sleep ends the episode and there is no memory of the outburst. This condition, which is fairly rare, is thought to be due to hypersensitivity to alcohol. Pathological intoxication also occurs after head injuries or in cases of severe liver disease. It seems unrelated to classical alcoholism and appears to be an idiosyncratic biological reaction similar to an allergy.

PCP Phencyclidine hydrochloride. (Chemical name: 1-[1-phenylcyclohexyl] piperdine.)

PCP was first developed in 1959 as one of a new class of anesthetic agents, known as dissociative anesthetics because they detach or dissociate patients from all bodily sensations so that no pain is felt during surgery. It was found that patients often became agitated, delusional and irrational while recovering from the anesthetic effects of PCP, however, so use was discontinued. It was used in veterinary medicine until the late 1970s when it was replaced by an equally effective anesthetic with fewer side effects.

PCP is a white crystalline powder which is readily soluble in water or alcohol. It has a distinctive bitter "chemical" taste. PCP can be mixed easily with dyes and turns up on the illicit drug market in a variety of tablets, capsules and colored powders. It is normally used in one of three ways: it is snorted, smoked, or eaten. It can also be injected but it is not often used this way. When smoked it is most often mixed with another substance such as mint leaves, parsley, tobacco or marijuana.

PCP is easily manufactured and is in plentiful supply wherever there is a demand. It is also commonly found as an adulterant—or complete misrepresentation—in mescaline, psilocybin and LSD. Most "THC" (tetrahydrocannabinol) sold is actually PCP. Marijuana is frequently "dusted" with PCP to increase its market appeal. Crack cocaine mixed with PCP is known as Bazooka or Space Base. Less frequently it is found as a substitute for cocaine and heroin or as an adulterant in these drugs. It is often difficult to know if PCP is a component of a drug, and it is sold by at least 100 different street names.

PCP was first introduced in the latter part of the 1960s as a street drug and quickly gained a reputation as a chemical that could cause bad reactions and wasn't worth the risk. It was then used to dilute or replace other drugs that were more expensive or more difficult to synthesize.

In the 1960s, PCP was commonly sold as THC, a synthetic marijuana that is costly to manufacture and is never available. As ersatz THC, the drug spread nationwide and increasingly users began wanting PCP itself. The use of PCP among young adults in the United States jumped from 9.5% in 1976 to 14% in 1977. PCP usage has been in steady decline since 1979. A 1988 report by the National Institute on Drug Abuse indicates that PCP was used by 2.9% of high school seniors that year as compared to 7.0% in 1979. (NIDA Drug use, Drinking, and Smoking: National Survey Results From High School, College, and Young Adult Populations 1975–1988).

PCP is unusual in that it appears to have a higher percentage of undesirable reactions than any other commonly used psychoactive drug. In spite of its many bizarre and unpleasant effects it has enough desirable qualities to make it in demand. Dr. Ronald Siegel, a Los Angeles psychologist, tested and interviewed 310 adult users and all agreed that on every occasion there were unpleasant negative aspects to the PCP experience. The positive effects described by Dr. Siegel's users included heightened sensitivity to outside stimuli, dissociation, elevation in mood, inebriation and relaxation. Only one in 12 reported experiencing euphoria.

Voluntary patients at Metropolitan State hospital with a history of PCP abuse without current major behavioral, mental or physical disorders reported experiencing the following effects sometime during PCP abuse:

> 80% reported organicity: forgetfulness, difficulty in concentrating, thinking clearly and understanding, etc.;
> 75% reported behavior dyscontrol: physical violence, aggression and agitation;
> 74% reported estrangement: feelings of derealization and depersonalization;
> 60% reported paranoia: transient suspiciousness;
> 55% reported altered mood states: elation to depression;
> 41% reported hallucinations: tactile, visual or auditory;
> 20% reported suicidal impulses.

PCP has sedative effects, and interactions with other CENTRAL NERVOUS SYSTEM depressants such as ALCOHOL and BENZODIAZEPINES can lead to coma or accidental overdose. Use of PCP among adolescents may interfere with hormones related to normal growth and development as well as with the learning process. According to the University of Michigan's Institute for Social Research, as of 1980 9.6% of high school seniors had used PCP at some time, 4.4% in the previous year. The incidence of male users is about two-thirds larger than female users. Typically, PCP users are young single males of all ethnic backgrounds.

Classification: PCP is a dissociative anesthetic with mixed neurologic and autonomic activity, originally developed as an anesthetic. It is difficult to classify accurately as different doses produce different effects: they may resemble the actions of a sedative, stimulant, analgesic, anesthetic or HALLUCINOGEN. PCP is really in a class by itself—the Student Organization for the Study of Hallucinogens has called it a "delusionogen."

Effects: At low to moderate doses physiological effects include a slight increase in breathing rate and a more pronounced rise in blood pressure and pulse rate. Respiration becomes shallow, and flushing and profuse sweating frequently occur. Generalized numbness of the extremities and muscular incoordination may also develop. At high doses there is a drop in blood pressure, pulse rate and respiration. This may be accompanied by nausea, vomiting, blurred vision, vertical nystagmus (flicking up and down of the eyes), drooling, loss of balance and dizziness. Large amounts of the drug can cause convulsions and coma; several deaths have been associated with PCP use.

Psychological effects with small doses include distinct changes in body awareness, similar to those associated with alcohol intoxication. Effects of higher doses mimic certain primary symptoms of schizophrenia such as delusions, mental turmoil and a sensation of distance from one's environment. Illusions and hallucinations, usually of hearing, occasionally of vision, have also been reported following administration of large amounts of the drug. Bizarre behavior of many types sometimes occurs in response to them. Speech is often blocked and to the outsider it may also appear meaningless. Paranoid thinking is common. Users may react with frightening violence in response to imagined threats. Because PCP has anesthetic action, touch and pain sensations are dulled and the user may severely injure himself without knowing it. He may be difficult to control in a hospital situation.

Addictive aspects: The popularity of PCP indicates some degree of psychological dependence. Physical dependence and WITHDRAWAL in humans has not been observed.

Tolerance: In two studies published in 1978 tolerance was reported, making increased doses of PCP necessary to produce the same effects. The degree of tolerance developed is still unknown.

Sources: PCP is difficult to control by law because it is easily and inexpensively synthesized. The starting chemicals are in widespread industrial use; very simple equipment is needed; and no special skill is required. The drug is manufactured only in illicit laboratories within the U.S. and efforts to control the precursors have been only partly successful.

Synonyms: angel dust, horse tranquilizer, animal tranquilizer, tic, dust, crystal, superweed, rocket fuel, street drug, peace pill, Shermans.

PDR The PHYSICIANS' DESK REFERENCE.

peer pressure Perhaps the most vulnerable individual to confront the growing social acceptance of drug use in the United States is the adolescent. Peer pressure, the *desire* and *need* to belong to a certain group and to *show* that one belongs, has long been cited as a reason for adolescent drug use and abuse.

In 1989 there were 6,500 emergency room visits related to the use of marijuana and they primarily involved adolescents. PCP accounted for 3,668 emergency room visits and 176 deaths. In 1990 a nationwide survey conducted for the National Institute on Abuse reported 91% of senior high school students had tried alcohol at least once and 33% had five or more drinks in a row within the last two week period.

Peers may pressure adolescents to try a drug at a stage when their sense of individual identity is still undeveloped and the need to be accepted is very strong. Adolescents may also use drugs with peers in order to relax and be comfortable as much as from the pressure to conform to the dictates of the group. Because of peer pressure, children are also likely to adopt the group's attitude toward drugs.

pemoline A central nervous system stimulant that is most commonly used in the treatment of Minimal Brain Dysfunction. Because it has an activity similar to that of AMPHETAMINES dependency can occur. (See CYLERT.)

pentazocine A potent ANALGESIC and mild NARCOTIC ANTAGONIST that was first synthesized in 1961 by Sterling-Winthrop. Pentazocine resembles codeine and morphine in most of its properties. It is used for the relief of moderate to severe pain and as a supplement to anesthetics. When given to a patient who has previously received a narcotic, it may act as a narcotic antagonist and withdrawal symptoms are experienced. The drug is best known by the brand name TALWIN and Talwin NX (Winthrop) and is one of the 100 most prescribed drugs.

Appearance and activity: Pentazocine is a white crystalline substance soluble in acidic aqueous solution. It is extensively metabolized in the body, with only 13% appearing in the urine.

Dosage and effects: Talwin is prescribed orally in doses of 30–50 mg every three or four hours. In intravenous administration, 30 mg is equivalent to 10 mg of morphine but the duration of effects may be less than morphine. Pentazocine's analgesic effects materialize more quickly than morphine's, in as little as 15–30 minutes with oral administration and in two to three minutes with intravenous administration. They include euphoria and the usual range of narcotic effects. Like DARVON, the drug can cause hallucinations, disorientation and confusion.

Usage: Talwin's abuse is related to its medical use and is partially a result of overprescription. It is abused on the street in a combination of Talwin and pyribenzamine ("T's and blues"), often intravenously. It is a Schedule IV drug under the Controlled Substances Act. The tablets have recently been reformulated to contain NALOXONE and they are now sold as Talwin NX to make intravenous use undesirable because if injected the Naloxone will negate the effects of the Talwin but if taken orally the Talwin will be effective. Talwin itself will produce withdrawal in individuals dependent on opiates due to its partial antagonist properties. It should never be given to methadone maintained or actively narcotic addicted individuals. Death due to Talwin overdose is known. (These deaths may have been due to the talcum powder contained in commercially available tablets.)

pentobarbital A short-acting barbiturate that is used as a sedative hypnotic. In the depressant category, it is one of the most sought after drugs by abusers. It is sold under the trade name NEMBUTAL. (See also BARBITURATES.)

Pentothal® (Abbott) A short-acting central nervous system depressant that contains thiopental sodium. It is used intravenously to induce hypnosis and as an anesthesia for brief procedures. It is also used in the control of convulsive states and for narcoanalysis in psychiatric disorders. Overdosage can result in respiratory depression and paralysis. This Schedule III drug should only be administered by a trained anesthetist.

peptides, endogenous See ENDORPHINS.

Percocet-5® (Endo) A semisynthetic narcotic analgesic that is used for mild to moderate pain and for sedation. It contains 5 mg of oxycodone hydrochloride and 325 mg acetaminophen. It can produce morphine-type drug dependency and has a potential for abuse. When taken with alcohol or other central nervous system depressants it can have an additive effect. It is supplied in white scored tablets.

Percodan® (Endo) A semisynthetic narcotic analgesic that contains oxycodone hydrochloride. Its activity is similar to morphine and it is usually used for analgesia and sedation. It may be habit-forming and has a significant potential for abuse. Tolerance, along with physical and psychological dependence can develop. When used with alcohol or other central nervous system depressants it can have an additive effect. Overdosage can result in respiratory depression, muscle flaccidity, somnolence and coma; severe overdosage can result in circulatory collapse, cardiac arrest and death. It is supplied as Percodan: yellow scored tablets containing 4.50 mg of oxycodone hydrochloride and 0.38 mg of oxycodone terephthalate; and Percodan-Demi, pink scored tablets containing half the above amounts. It is sold and sought after on the street. Most street varieties come from pharmacies that are involved in selling and rebuying drugs (pill mills).

periodic alcoholism Also known as Epsilon alcoholism as defined by JELLINEK, it is characterized by sporadic bouts of excessive drinking which are followed by intervals of controlled drinking or abstinence.

peripheral neuritis See ALCOHOLIC POLYNEUROPATHY.

personality trait theories In this case, personality trait theories seek to explain the reasons for the addictive personality. These theories concentrate on determining a specific set of characteristics that would be associated with the development of drug abuse. Although studies have not identified a particular set of personality traits that distinguish drug users from other groups, the following traits were most often observed: low thresholds for frustration, ambiguity and dissonance; high levels of hopelessness, anxiety and helplessness; negative self-image; and feelings of isolation and depression. It should be noted that it is often difficult to determine if these traits preceded drug use or were a consequence of it. Studies have clearly supported the emergence of traits after onset of addiction.

Peru For more than 2,000 years Peruvians have grown and chewed coca. Today the government permits and licenses substantial cultivation of coca for traditional domestic use as well as for pharmaceutical purposes. Despite government controls, however, coca cultivation expanded in 1989 to an estimated 110,000 metric tons; only 12–14,000 tons are used licitly. About half of the cocaine consumed in the United States is provided by Peru; most of it is processed and distributed by Colombia. Peru has a weak economy (their gross domestic product has been shrinking in recent years and in mid-year 1989 inflation was running at 25% a month) and cocaine trafficking provides several hundred million dollars. It is the principal and often only income for thousands of farmers—an income that is many times the daily wage for growing other crops. Coca is an attractive crop for farmers because it is a deep-rooted plant with a life span of about 30 years. In addition, it can be harvested three to six times a year and grown in poor soil unsuitable for other crops. Officials admit to having difficulty developing legitimate alternatives for coca-farming unless economic growth opens markets for alternative products.

The smoking of coca paste is of particular concern to the Peruvian government. In this semi-refined state, coca contains harmful impurities such as cement, large amounts of coca alkaloids and kerosene, and inhaling it into the lungs can be extremely dangerous. Recent reports show an increase in smoking coca paste among high school youths.

In 1980 the government doubled its resource commitment to curbing production in excess of that used for licit purposes. In a cooperative effort with the U.S., 1,500 acres of coca were eradicated in 1980 and 57 laboratories were destroyed. In 1981 a five-year eradication and enforcement project was initiated by the Bureau of International Narcotics Matters (INM) concurrently with a five-year plan by the Agency for International Development (AID) to diversify agricultural development. By mid-1982 about 5% of coca cultivation had been abandoned and other cultivations were not being fully harvested.

Peru is part of President George Bush's September 1989 National Drug Control Strategy which proposes $100 million to $270 million going into a superfund to finance the so-called Andean-Peru, Colombia and Bolivia Initiative. Already the plan has its critics in the Congress and, indeed, in some parts of the administration. The major criticism is cost.

pethidine A generic name for MEPERIDINE.

Pew Charitable Trusts, The A Philadelphia-based national foundation with a longtime interest in the health field. In 1971, the trusts awarded their first grants to train health professionals in the area of alcohol and drug abuse. More recently, they have established health professional training as one of three primary components of their drug abuse and alcohol abuse programs, which also include prevention and early intervention programs for children and youth and research on prevention. Other projects in this area have included support for Johns Hopkins University's establishment of a center for teaching and clinical practice in alcoholism. In addition, the trusts are supporting the Society of General Internal Medicine through the American College of Physicians to develop a curriculum in alcohol and other drug abuse education for general internal medicine faculty. The George Washington University School of Medicine and Health Sciences is also receiving support from the trusts in the field of educating health professionals to meet the challenge of alcohol and other drug abuse. Contact: Nadya K. Shmavonian, Program Officer, The Pew Charitable Trusts, 3 Parkway, Philadelphia, PA 19102-1305.

peyote A spineless cactus, *Lophophora williamsii,* native to central and northern Mexico whose top crown, or button, is a hallucinogenic drug. The button is dried, then ingested by holding it in the mouth until it is soft and then swallowing it whole. Generally it takes three to four buttons to achieve a "trip." The buttons may be cut up and eaten in pieces or cooked into a slush and then mixed with juices or drunk alone.

Peyote was first used by the Aztecs and then by other Mexican Indians to enhance awareness in religious ceremonies. It is a very nauseating drug and vomiting is considered a part of the purgation by Indian peyotists. Peyote purportedly produces a deep insight into reality, along with highly complex sensory experiences. The richly colored "kaleidoscope" type of hallucination is one of its most sought-after affects by abusers.

In the 1800s the use of peyote spread northward to the American Indians and "peyote cults" began to spring up. As total abstinence from alcohol was required in peyote cults, and this was a time when alcohol use was becoming epidemic among the Indians, many tribes encouraged the use of peyote. Indian leaders who were striving to maintain peace with the white men also encouraged the use of peyote among their tribes because those using it were less hostile to the white men.

An attempt, particularly by missionaries, to have peyote outlawed by the various western states, gained some success but many state legislatures which enacted such laws eventually repealed them to permit ritual use in religious services.

During the 1950s and early 1960s it was a simple matter to purchase peyote buttons; mail order companies advertised them in numerous publications. The drug's availability led to widespread abuse, particularly among college students. LSD also became popular during the 1960s and the government's attitude and the public hostility toward its use influenced the attitude toward peyote. Investigations were conducted into the possible dangerous effects of peyote.

In 1969, the federal government granted the Native American Church of North America the legal right to consume peyote in their religious services. The church claims some 250,000 members in the U.S. and Canada. The principal supporters of this move were anthropologists and psychiatrists. They suggested that there is something to be learned from the long use of peyote among Indians. Their ability to take a potentially dangerous drug and to use it without suffering harmful side effects, warranted continued study. When peyote is taken, the Indians use safeguards far greater than those employed by some LSD users. Peyote services are held at strictly defined times; no one is allowed to leave a meeting so consequently a hallucinating person is not allowed to wander off by himself; and customarily there are meetings the following morning until well after the time it has taken for the drug's effects to wear off.

Peyote is currently the only hallucinogen whose use is sanctioned by the United States government, but only for those who are members of the Native Church of North America. In 1990 however, the Supreme Court in upholding an Oregon law, held that the states had the right to ban peyote use even when used for religious purposes.

pharmaceuticals Pills, capsules, liquids, medicinal suppositories, lotions and other preparations that have a medical use.

pharmacogenic orgasm The pleasurable sensation (see RUSH) felt by a HEROIN addict after intravenous injection. (See also ADMINISTRATION.)

pharmacokinetics A study, made over a period of time, of a drug's action and movement through the body. The processes studied include the dynamics of absorption, distribution and excretion.

pharmacological etiology (iatrogenic addiction) Drug addiction as a result of the medical administration of drugs can, and has, been a cause of drug abuse. Although this was probably one of the main causes of addiction during the 19th century, it is not as prevalent in the modern world. The majority of physicians are now quite aware of the addictive qualities of drugs, although some are still inclined to prescribe them freely simply because it is easier to cover symptoms than take the time to treat, if possible, the causes of an illness. On the other hand, some patients have been known to complain that physicians are overcautious in the prescription of drugs; a complaint that is most common in patients who are recovering from surgery and are in extreme pain. No extensive studies have been made to determine the effects of medical narcotic use for short periods of time (several days to a couple of weeks), to discover the extent of withdrawal symptoms (if any) when a drug is stopped, or to find out if patients develop a craving or substitute another drug for the one that has been withdrawn. It is known, however, that after a week of full doses of a narcotic, tolerance and some degree of withdrawal may be seen. With barbiturates the process may take a few weeks and with the benzodiazepines it can take months.

phenacetin A central nervous system depressant and synthetic analgesic used for the relief of minor pain (headache and neuralgia) and also to reduce fever. In prescription drugs it is generally combined with other drugs such as butalbital and codeine. Phenacetin in large amounts can cause kidney damage.

Phenaphen with Codeine® (Robbins) A narcotic analgesic that contains codeine phosphate and acetaminophen. No. 2 and No. 3 are used for mild to moderate pain; No. 4 is used for moderate to severe pain. Tolerance, along with psychological and physical dependence can develop. It has a significant potential for abuse, and when taken with alcohol or other central nervous system depressants it can have an additive effect. Overdosage can result in respiratory depression, somnolence, muscle flaccidity and coma. It is supplied as Phenaphen with Codeine No. 2, containing 15 mg codeine in black and yellow capsules; No. 3 containing 30 mg in black and green capsules; and No. 4 containing 60 mg in green and white capsules. It is also available as Phenaphen without codeine, containing 325 mg acetaminophen (Tylenol).

phenazocine A synthetic narcotic analgesic, derived from OPIUM, that is used for acute and chronic pain. Classified as a Schedule II drug, it has a potency that exceeds morphine.

phencyclidine (PCP) An anesthetic which was once used for childbirth but is no longer available licitly. (See PCP.)

phendimetrazine tartrate A central nervous system stimulant whose activity is similar to that of the AMPHETAMINES. It is used as an anorectic for weight control and has a significant potential for abuse. Tolerance can develop within a few weeks. Phendimetrazine tartrate is found in many marketed anorectics.

phenelzine See MONOAMINE OXIDASE (MAO) INHIBITORS.

phenmetrazine A central nervous system stimulant that is used as an anorectic for weight control. Its activity is similar to that of the AMPHETAMINES and it has a significant potential for abuse. (See also PRELUDIN.)

phenobarbital A long-acting BARBITURATE with an onset time of up to one hour and a duration of action up to 16 hours. It is used as a sedative hypnotic and anticonvulsant. (See also LUMINAL.)

phentermine A central nervous system stimulant whose activity is similar to that of the AMPHETAMINES. It is used as an anorectic for weight control and has a significant potential for abuse. (See also IONAMIN.)

phenylpropanolamine A synthetic drug that effects the autonomic nervous system. Used as a mucous membrane decongestant and as a treatment for allergic conditions, it is found in over-the-counter preparations for colds and weight control. It has significant stimulant effects and is a frequent drug of abuse among adolescents, who purchase it on a mail-order basis.

phenytoin A central nervous system depressant that is used mainly as an anticonvulsant in the treatment of epilepsy. Its highly selective action effects only motor centers and it has little or no hypnotic or sedative action. The use and dosage of phenytoin should be carefully monitored because of numerous severe side effects. It is marketed as Dilantin and appears to have no abuse potential.

pholcodine An OPIATE derivative that is used as a cough suppresant in England and France.

Phrenilin® (Carnrick) An analgesic that is used for head pain associated with tension and upper respiratory infection. It contains 15 mg of the BARBITURATE sodium butabarbital, 325 mg of acetaminophen and 40 mg of caffeine. Because it contains a barbiturate, it may be habit-forming. It is supplied in pale violet tablets.

Physicians' Desk Reference (PDR) An annual volume listing commercial drug preparations. Drug users refer to it for pill identification and drug descriptions. A PDR for non-prescription drugs is also available.

physiological models of etiology One of the three major categories of theories about the cause of alcoholism. As alcohol is a sedative drug it is possible that their theory can be expanded to include the use of all sedative drugs.

Theories belonging to this group postulate that individuals are predisposed to develop alcohol problems because of an organic defect and underlying biological malfunction. To date, however, there is only limited genetic evidence about the role that physiology plays in alcoholism.

Physiological theories include those dealing with the endocrine system and nutritional needs of the body. Because one cause alone may not account for alcoholism or the abuse of other sedative drugs, physiological etiological theories are generally considered in conjunction with psychological and sociocultural theories. (See also GENETOTROPIC ETIOLOGICAL THEORIES and ENDOCRINE ETIOLOGICAL THEORIES.)

physostigmine An acid derivative of an alkaloid extracted from the seeds of the calabar bean. It is used to reverse toxic effects on the central nervous system (hallucinations, delirium, disorientation, etc.) caused by drugs which have produced anticholinergic poisoning. (See also ANTILIRIUM.)

Pil-Anon Family Program A self-help support organization founded in 1978 and sponsored by PILLS ANONYMOUS, for the families of chemically dependent people. It is based on the 12-step program of Alcoholics Anonymous.

Pills Anonymous World Service (PA) A self-help, self-supporting group with a 12-step program based on that of Alcoholics Anonymous. The only requirement for membership is a desire to stop taking pills and/or other mood altering chemicals. Founded in 1975, the group also sponsors PIL-ANON FAMILY PROGRAM for the families of those who are chemically dependent.

piloerection The involuntary bristling or erection of hair (gooseflesh), which is an objective diagnostic sign of opioid withdrawal and therefore opioid dependency.

pinpoint pupils See EYES.

piptadenia A hallucinogenic snuff used by Indians in Venezuela and Colombia. It is made from the seeds of shrubs in the mimosa family *(Leguminosae)*.

pituri *Duboisia hopwoodii*, a plant that grows in Australia and whose leaves are chewed by Aborigines for a stimulating effect. After the initial stimulation, it can cause severe adverse effects.

Placidyl® (Abbott) A sedative hypnotic that contains ethchlorvynol and is used for insomnia. It has the potential for abuse and when taken with alcohol or other central nervous system depressants can have an additive effect. Overdosage can result in severe respiratory depression and deep coma. It is supplied in capsule form: 100 mg round red; 200 mg round red; 500 mg oblong red; and 750 mg oblong green.

Plegine® (Ayerst) A brand of phendimetrazine tartrate that is used as an anorectic for weight control. Chemically and pharmacologically it is similar to the AMPHETAMINES; thus it has a high potential for abuse and can cause psychological dependence and social dysfunction. Overdosage can result in restlessness, confusion, hallucinations and coma. It is supplied in yellow scored tablets of 35 mg.

Plexonal® (Sandoz) A BARBITURATE sedative that is used for anxiety, tension and insomnia. It contains barbital sodium, butalbital sodium, phenobarbital sodium, scopolamine and dihydroergotamine. Tolerance can develop along with physical and psychological dependence and it has a significant potential for abuse. Overdosage can result in shallow respiration, coma and possibly death. It is supplied in white sugar-coated triangular tablets.

PMB 200 & PMB 400® (Ayerst) A sedative preparation that contains Premarini (conjugated estrogens) and MEPROBAMATE. It is usually used for menopausal syndrome when accompanied by tension and anxiety. It has a potential for abuse and can produce physical and psychological dependence. When overdosage occurs, sleep ensues rapidly and blood pressure, pulse and respiratory rates are reduced to basal levels. PMB-200, supplied in green tablets, contains 200 mg of meprobamate; PMB-400, supplied in pink tablets, contains 400 mg of meprobamate.

polydrug use The use of two or more drugs simultaneously. This may be done for a variety of reasons: to enhance or POTENTIATE one drug's effects; to neutralize or counteract undesirable effects of one of the drugs; or to achieve a less expensive HIGH by combining an inexpensive drug with a small amount of an expensive one. The practice of polydrug use is becoming more and more popular and single drug users now tend to be in the minority. There are an infinite number of combinations; probably the most popular is marijuana and alcohol. Other favorites are barbiturates and alcohol, barbiturates and amphetamines, analgesics with tranquilizers or sedatives, and more recently, sleeping pills and codeine. Heroin users will supplement their habit with barbiturates if the only heroin they can obtain is highly diluted. The practice of polydrug use is also known as multihabituation.

polystyrene cement Model airplane glue, sniffed for its intoxicating effects.

Pondimin® (Robins) An anorectic that is used for weight control. It is a brand of fenfluramine hydrochloride. Unlike other anorectics that have an amphetamine activity, Pondimin produces more central nervous system depression than stimulation. When taken with alcohol or other CNS depressants it can have an additive effect. It has a significant potential for abuse and psychological dependence can occur. Overdosage can result in agitation, confusion, hyperventilation and pupil dilation. It is supplied in orange scored tablets of 20 mg.

portal cirrhosis Named for the portal vein which transports blood from the stomach, intestines and spleen to the liver, it is the most prominent type of cirrhosis and the one most frequently found among alcoholics. It is also known as Laennec's, nutritional or alcoholic cirrhosis.

postintoxicated state A general term used to refer to the agitated state immediately following a drinking bout. It has no specific meaning and is sometimes used to refer to a HANGOVER or to the symptoms attributed to WITHDRAWAL.

postnecrotic cirrhosis A form of CIRRHOSIS that follows hepatitis or other liver inflammations and is sometimes found in alcoholics.

potentiation The ability of one drug to increase the activity of another drug taken simultaneously. The overall effect is greater than the added total effects of each drug taken alone. Also called supradditive. (See also ADDITIVE EFFECT and SYNERGY.)

Pre-Sate® (Warner/Chilcott) An anorectic that contains 65 mg chlorphentermine hydrochloride and is used for weight control. Its activity is similar to that of the amphetamines and consequently it has the potential for abuse. Dependency can occur. Overdosage can result in restlessness, aggressiveness, hallucinations and panic, and can progress to convulsions and coma. It is supplied in blue tablets.

pregnancy When a woman is pregnant, her health and nutrition are crucial not only to her own well-being but also to the developing baby's. Almost everything that a pregnant woman ingests passes directly from her bloodstream through the placenta to the fetus. Since there is no chemical known to science which has proved to be entirely harmless during all phases of pregnancy, most doctors today advise women not to take *any* drug during pregnancy unless there is a specific need for it, and then only under the strictest medical supervision, in the amounts and at the times specified by the physician. This restriction on drug intake applies not only to medically prescribed drugs but also to recreational drugs and even to over-the-counter, self-prescribed remedies such as aspirin.

Women who are heroin addicts suffer a high incidence of complications during pregnancy, including toxemia, abruptio placentae, retained placenta, postpartum hemorrhage, premature births by weight, breech deliveries and high neonatal morbidity and mortality (George Blinick, Robert C. Wallach, and Eulogio Jerez, "Pregnancy and Menstrual Function in Narcotics Addicts Treated with Methadone," *American Journal of Obstetrics and Gynecology,* Dec. 15, 1969). These complications, however, are also associated with poverty, malnutrition and a lack of prenatal care—conditions which affect many women addicts in the United States. Babies born to opiate-addicted women often display withdrawal symptoms soon after birth including tremors, irritability, a shrill cry, restlessness and watery stools. These characteristics lead to the term of babies born with "monkeys on their backs." These symptoms may be accompanied by vomiting, fever, twitching, yawning and sneezing. The severity of the symptoms seem to be in direct proportion to the amount of heroin consumed on a daily basis by the mother. Babies born to mothers who are addicted to methadone, barbiturates and tranquilizers can also experience withdrawal. Cocaine and amphetamine: involved babies can demonstrate severe symptoms of CNS damage at birth due to drug effects in the womb. Some of this damage may be of long duration or permanent.

A recent survey (1988) found that 11% of women in 36 hospitals studied around the country had used illegal drugs in pregnancy. Experts said new data suggested that 370,000 newborns a year nationwide faced the possibility of health damage from their mothers' drug abuse. The survey was compiled by the National Association for Perinatal Addiction Research and Education. The study indicated that health consequences of prenatal cocaine exposure, for instance, could cause lasting brain damage, seizures after birth, premature birth, retarded fetal growth, breathing lapses and absence of part of the gut plus structural abnormalities in genital and urinary organs. During 1990 the first of the "crack babies" attended school, and (at the writing of this book) it is still too early to tell the long-term developmental effects crack will have on children. Dr. Elaine M. Johnson, director of the Federal Office of Substance Abuse Prevention (OSAP), said drug use in pregnancy cuts across racial and socioeconomic lines and maternal age groups, especially since cocaine has become so widespread.

Heroin addiction in pregnant women can also present other hazards to infants. One hospital study of 22 addicted women showed a low birth weight in 56.5% of their infants (compared to 13.7% for the hospital as a whole), and a mortality rate at the time of birth of 17.4% compared with 2.2% for infants of nonaddicted mothers. The deaths were not attributed directly to the infants' withdrawal symptoms, but were associated with problems due to their low birth weight, poor nutrition and lack of prenatal care.

Studies have shown that cigarette smoking during pregnancy is hazardous to the unborn baby. Babies born to women who smoke have a two to three times greater chance of being born premature than babies of non-smoking mothers and they are on the average 150–240 grams lighter (C. M. Fletcher and Daniel Horn, *Smoking and Health,* World Health Organization publication, 1970). In addition, babies of mothers who smoke during pregnancy are twice as likely to be aborted, to be stillborn, or to die soon after birth.

During the 1960s and 1970s there was much publicity linking the use of LSD to birth defects and chromosome damage. While studies have not ruled out the possibility, there has been no conclusive evidence that the use of LSD by either the mother or father increases such risks. However, a study reported evidence that the incidence of spontaneous abortion (miscarriage) *is* higher among women who use LSD.

Dr. Peter A. Fried, professor of psychology at Carleton University in Ottawa, Canada, conducted the first extensive research on the effects of marijuana on the human fetus. In a study (1978–1983) of more than 700 expectant mothers, Dr. Fried found evidence of a link between marijuana smoking and exaggerated tremors, vision problems and startle reflexes among their babies. Although there was no increase in stillbirths or the risk of miscarriage, babies of mothers who smoked marijuana were born a few weeks sooner. THC in marijuana does cross the placental barrier and enters the fetus's system where it has an effect on the central nervous system. Babies of mothers who smoked five or more marijuana cigarettes per week "consistently display many more tremors in their arms, legs, and lower jaw than do infants of non-users," according to Dr. Fried. He also reported a tendency of the babies to display more startle reflexes in the absence of obvious external causes. In addition, in a test given three days after birth, Dr. Fried found that the babies showed abnormal responses in reacting or habituating to a light which was shone on them, which suggests "subtle alterations in the nervous system." All of these symptoms disappeared within a month.

There is incontrovertable evidence that alcohol consumption during pregnancy is dangerous to the fetus. When a pregnant woman drinks, the alcohol passes through the placenta and reaches the bloodstream of the fetus in about the same concentrations as in the mother. Since the fetus lacks the mature metabolism and elimination capabilities of an adult, alcohol is more toxic to its system. The most severe damage to a developing fetus caused by heavy drinking is known as FETAL ALCOHOL SYNDROME which is characterized by growth deficiences, physical malformations and mental retardation. The problem is especially severe among American Indians. Studies show that on some reservations in the Plains, the Southwest and Canada 5% to 25% of children are affected. Worldwide, the rate at which children are born with disabilities caused by alcohol is 1% or less, experts say. A safe limit of alcohol consumption during pregnancy has not been established. Some experts and organizations such as the NATIONAL INSTITUTE ON ALCOHOL ABUSE AND ALCOHOLISM recommend complete abstinence during pregnancy, arguing that since the effects of even small amounts of alcohol are unknown, the wisest course is to abstain completely. Others point out that millions of moderate social drinkers (whose alcohol intake is three ounces or less a day of ABSOLUTE ALCOHOL) have perfectly healthy babies. These experts and organizations prefer not to frighten patients whose custom may be to have a drink or two in the evening, but rather to counsel them on the potential dangers of drinking during pregnancy. Rather than strictly prohibiting their patients from drinking, they suggest instead that moderation is the wisest choice.

Another aspect to be considered in relation to the use of drugs during pregnancy concerns the administration of analgesics and anesthetics to women in labor and during childbirth itself. These drugs, which are intended to make birth easier for the mother and to help in emergency situations, all directly affect the fetus. These medical drugs in combination with whatever recreational or self-prescribed drugs a woman may be using can have a synergistic effect which can stupefy the infant throughout the first days of his life. Furthermore, many drugs which were once common obstetrical medications have recently been discovered to be unsafe.

In order to ensure the healthy and natural development of a child, safeguard the health of the mother during and after pregnancy and enhance the birth experience, the consensus of opinion is that pregnant women should abstain from all unnecessary chemicals and medication and should indulge only minimally in alcohol consumption.

Jane E. Brody, "Widespread Abuse of Drugs by Pregnant Women Is Found," *The N.Y. Times,* August 30, 1988.

Gina Kolata, "Alcohol Abuse by Pregnant Indians Is Crippling a Generation of Children," *The N.Y. Times,* July 19, 1989.

Preludin® (Bohringer Ingelheim) An anorectic that is used for weight control. A brand of phenmetrazine hydrochloride, its activity is similar to that of AMPHETAMINES and tolerance can develop within a few weeks. It has a high potential for abuse and psychological dependence and social dysfunction can occur. Overdosage can result in rapid respiration, confusion and hallucinations. It is supplied in 25 mg square white tablets; 50 mg round white tablets; and 75 mg round pink tablets.

prisoners and drug use According to a 1986 survey of inmates in 275 state correctional facilities, 35% of 13,711 prisoners surveyed reported that they were under the influence of drugs at the time they committed their current offense, compared to 32% in the 1979 survey. In the month before their current offense, 43% of state prison inmates were using illegal drugs on a daily or near daily basis; 19% were using a major drug—heroin, methadone, cocaine, PCP or LSD—on a daily or near daily basis.

Many inmates said that they began to use drugs, particularly major drugs, only after their criminal careers had already started. Half the inmates who had ever used a major drug and three-fifths of those who had ever used a major drug regularly did not do so until after their first arrest.

Other findings of the survey:

- Inmates were more likely to report that they were under the influence of cocaine but less likely to report using heroin at the time of the offense than in earlier surveys. Alcohol, marijuana and hashish were the drugs most frequently used at the time of the offense.
- Almost 80% of inmates reported that they had used drugs at some time in their lives; 52% said that they had used a major drug. Interestingly, white inmates and female inmates were more likely than others to have been regular major drug users at some time in the past. Among those who had used drugs, about half said that they began their use by age 15.
- The majority of inmates (81%) were not daily major drug users in the month before they committed the offense for which they were sentenced to prison. About one-seventh (13%) of inmates appear to fit the pattern of drug addicts who committed crimes for gain.
- Of state prisoners sentenced for robbery, burglary, larceny, or a drug offense, 50%

State Prison Inmates under the Influence of Drugs, by Type of Drug at the Time of the Current Offense, 1974, 1979, and 1986

Type of Drug	Percent of All Inmates Who Were under the Influence of a Drug at the Time of the Offense		
	1974	1979	1986
Any drug	25.3%	32.3%	35.4%
Major drug			
Cocaine	1.0%	4.6%	10.7%
Heroin	16.2	8.7	7.0
PCP	—	2.3	2.2
LSD	—	2.0	1.6
Methadone	1.7	.7	.8
Other drug			
Marijuana or hashish	10.3%	17.6%	18.6%
Amphetamines	5.3	5.2	4.2
Barbiturates	5.5	5.7	3.3
Methaqualone	—	—	1.6
Other drugs	3.0	1.6	3.9

NOTE: Individual drugs may not add to total under "any drug" because an inmate may have been under the influence of more than one drug.

—Indicates that the drug was not asked about in that year.

Drug Use History of State Prison Inmates, by Race and Sex, 1986

	Percent of All Inmates Who:				
		Used Drugs			
				In the Month before the Offense	
	Never Used Drugs	Anytime in the Past	Regularly in the Past	At All	Daily
Any drug[a]	20.4%	79.6%	63.4%	52.3%	42.6%
Race					
White	20.0%	80.1%	65.0%	53.9%	44.8%
Black	20.8	79.2	62.0	50.9	40.7
Other	19.8	80.1	62.8	49.8	38.8
Sex					
Male	20.0%	80.0%	63.8%	52.6%	42.8%
Female	28.0	72.0	57.6	47.0	39.3
Major drug[b]	47.6%	52.4%	35.8%	24.7%	18.6%
Race					
White	43.2%	56.8%	38.9%	26.5%	19.3%
Black	52.5	47.6	32.7	23.0	17.9
Other	44.1	55.9	35.1	24.0	17.5
Sex					
Male	47.7%	52.3%	35.6%	24.5%	18.3%
Female	46.1	53.9	40.0	29.6	24.3

[a]Includes major drugs (see note b) and marijuana or hashish, amphetamines, barbiturates, methaqualone, and all other drugs.
[b]Includes cocaine, heroin, PCP, LSD, and methadone.

Drug Use by State Prison Inmates, by Conviction Offense, 1986

Conviction Offense*	Percent of Inmates Convicted of Each Offense Who:	
	Were under the Influence of a Drug at the Time of the Offense	Had Used a Drug Daily in the Month before the Offense
All offenses	35.3%	42.7%
Violent offenses	33.4%	39.2%
Murder	28.3	34.1
Manslaughter	20.0	23.4
Rape	32.0	34.3
Sexual assault	24.9	24.5
Robbery	41.9	50.3
Assault	28.6	34.4
Kidnapping	37.2	44.3
Other violent offenses	31.8	31.0
Property offenses	38.7%	48.4%
Burglary	42.8	52.3
Arson	30.6	39.1
Auto theft	33.6	46.0
Fraud	29.2	37.8
Larceny	39.1	49.2
Stolen property	29.7	42.9
Other property offenses	33.4	32.1
Drug offenses	42.7%	51.4%
Possession	42.8	49.6
Trafficking	42.3	52.4
Other drug offenses	49.6	51.0
Public-order offenses	25.1%	33.3%
Weapons	19.4	26.8
Other public-order offenses	27.2	35.8
Other offenses	26.7%	25.3%

*Most serious offense for which the inmate was sentenced to prison.

Likelihood of Major Drug Use for State Prison Inmates, by Offense, 1986

Conviction Offense*	Percent of Inmates Who Had Used a Major Drug Daily in the Month before the Current Offense
All offenses	18.6%
Drug offenses	30.1%
Property offenses	21.8
Violent offenses	15.6
Public-order offenses	13.0
Other offenses	7.8
Drug possession	30.8%
Drug trafficking	30.0
Other drug offenses	25.9
Larceny	24.9
Burglary	23.3
Robbery	22.9
Kidnapping	20.5
Fraud	18.9
Auto theft	16.9
Stolen property	16.2
Other violent offenses	16.0
Other public-order offenses	13.9
Arson	13.5
Murder	12.3
Assault	11.2
Weapons	10.5
Manslaughter	9.2
Rape	9.2
Other property offenses	8.6
Sexual assault	6.2

NOTE: Major drugs include cocaine, heroin, PCP, LSD, and methadone.

*Most serious offense for which the inmate was sentenced to prison.

Major Drug Use History of State Prison Inmates, by Current Offense, 1986

Conviction Offense*	Percent of All Inmates Who:				
		Used a Major Drug			
				In the Month before the Offense	
	Never Used a Major Drug	Anytime in the Past	Regularly in the Past	At all	Daily
All offenses	100.0%	100.0%	100.0%	100.0%	100.0%
Violent offenses	60.1%	52.6%	50.0%	52.0%	45.7%
Murder	13.5	10.0	9.9	10.7	7.4
Manslaughter	4.2	3.0	2.8	2.2	1.6
Rape	5.6	4.0	3.0	3.2	2.1
Sexual assault	6.6	3.7	3.5	1.5	1.5
Robbery	18.6	22.0	19.7	22.8	25.7
Assault	9.1	7.6	8.6	9.9	4.9
Kidnapping	1.6	1.8	1.9	1.5	1.9
Other violent offenses	1.0	.7	.7	.3	.7
Property offenses	28.6%	30.6%	34.5%	28.1%	36.5%
Burglary	14.3	17.5	17.8	16.3	20.7
Arson	.8	1.3	.5	.3	.5
Auto theft	1.5	1.2	1.7	1.0	1.3
Fraud	4.2	2.7	4.4	2.8	3.9
Larceny	5.4	5.0	7.2	5.3	8.1
Stolen property	1.9	2.1	2.3	2.2	1.7
Other property offenses	.6	.7	.6	.2	.2
Drug offenses	4.7%	11.2%	8.7%	15.1%	13.9%
Possession	1.3	4.3	3.1	5.3	4.8
Trafficking	3.2	6.4	5.1	9.3	8.7
Other drug offenses	.1	.5	.4	.5	.4
Public-order offenses	5.8%	4.9%	6.3%	4.1%	3.6%
Weapons	1.7	1.2	2.0	1.3	.8
Other public-order offenses	4.1	3.7	4.3	2.8	2.8
Other offenses	.9%	.7%	.5%	.7%	.3%

NOTE: Major drugs include cocaine, heroin, PCP, LSD, and methadone. Percents may not add to totals because of rounding.

*Most serious offense for which the inmate was sentenced to prison.

Seriousness of Drug Use and Age of Onset for State Prison Inmates, by Type of Drug, 1986

Type of Drug	Percent of All Inmates Who: Had Ever Used Drugs	Had Used Drugs Regularly	Median Age of First: Use	Regular Use
Any drug	79.6%	62.4%	15 yrs	15 yrs
Major drug	52.4%	35.1%	17 yrs	18 yrs
Cocaine	43.9	22.2	19	20
Heroin	25.2	16.9	18	18
PCP	16.2	5.6	17	17
LSD	22.2	8.3	16	16
Methadone	7.8	2.6	19	19
Other drug	78.0%	57.8%	15 yrs	15 yrs
Marijuana or hashish	76.0	54.5	15	15
Amphetamines	30.4	16.2	16	17
Barbiturates	37.1	11.9	16	16
Methaqualone	23.0	7.9	17	17
Other drugs	15.4	7.9	17	17

Median Age at First Criminal Justice Contact and at First Drug Use for State Prison Inmates, 1986

	Median Age					
		Race			Sex	
	All Inmates	White	Black	Other	Male	Female
Criminal justice contacts						
First arrest	17 years	17 years	17 years	17 years	17 years	20 years
First probation	16	16	16	16	16	20
First incarceration	19	19	19	19	19	23
First drug use						
Any drug						
First use	15 years	14 years	15 years	14 years	15 years	16 years
First regular use	15	15	16	15	15	16
Major drug*						
First use	17 years	16 years	18 years	16 years	17 years	18 years
First regular use	18	17	19	18	18	19

*Major drugs include cocaine, heroin, PCP, LSD, and methadone.

Drug Use Prior to First Incarceration, by Race and Sex, for State Prison Inmates, 1986

Type of Drug Use	Percent of All Inmates Who Reported Using Drugs in the Month prior to the Offense that Resulted in Their First Incarceration					
	All Inmates	Race			Sex	
		White	Black	Other	Male	Female
Any drug						
Any use	50.7%	52.4%	49.3%	47.0%	50.8%	47.8%
Regular use	36.9	39.5	34.5	32.6	36.9	36.8
Major drug*						
Any use	22.7%	24.9%	20.6%	18.4%	22.3%	29.9%
Regular use	13.8	14.6	13.3	10.0	13.5	21.6

*Major drugs include cocaine, heroin, PCP, LSD, and methadone.

Onset of Drug Use in Relation to First Arrest for State Prison Inmates, 1986

Type of Drug Use	Percent of Inmates Who Began Using Drugs:						
	All	Before First Arrest		In Same Year as First Arrest	After First Arrest		No Such Use Reported
		More than 1 Year	One Year		One Year	More than 1 Year	
Any drug							
First use	100%	38.7%	8.1%	10.6%	5.1%	16.7%	20.7%
First regular use	100	26.1	6.4	8.3	4.8	16.6	37.8
Major drug[a]							
First use	100%	14.8%	4.5%	6.0%	4.5%	22.2%	48.0%
First regular use	100	8.0	2.7	3.5	3.0	17.7	65.1

NOTE: Percents may not add to 100 because of rounding.

[a]Major drugs include cocaine, heroin, PCP, LSD, and methadone.

Onset of Regular Drug Use, by Race and Sex, for State Prison Inmates, 1986

Type of Regular Drug Use	All	Before First Arrest: More than 1 Year	Before First Arrest: One Year	In Same Year as First Arrest	After First Arrest: One Year	After First Arrest: More than 1 Year	No Such Use Reported
Any drug							
Race							
White	100%	29.1%	6.2%	8.8%	4.8%	15.1%	35.9%
Black	100	22.9	6.5	7.8	4.8	18.3	39.7
Other	100	26.4	6.8	8.5	4.9	14.3	39.0
Sex							
Male	100%	26.0%	6.4%	8.3%	4.9%	16.8%	37.5%
Female	100	28.4	5.9	8.1	3.1	10.8	43.6
Major drug[a]							
Race							
White	100%	9.9%	2.9%	4.3%	3.6%	17.4%	61.9%
Black	100	6.1	2.5	2.7	2.3	18.0	68.4
Other	100	6.8	1.5	4.2	2.8	18.7	66.0
Sex							
Male	100%	7.9%	2.6%	3.4%	2.9%	17.9%	65.3%
Female	100	10.9	3.9	6.0	3.2	15.2	60.8

Percent of Inmates Who Began Using Drugs Regularly (all columns except Type of Regular Drug Use).

NOTE: Percents may not add to 100 because of rounding.

[a]Major drugs include cocaine, heroin, PCP, LSD, and methadone.

Onset of Drug Use in Relation to First Arrest for Drug-Using State Prison Inmates, 1986

When Drug Use Began	Any Drug: Ever	Any Drug: Regularly	A Major Drug*: Ever	A Major Drug*: Regularly
Total	100.0%	100.0%	100.0%	100.0%
Before first arrest				
More than 1 year	48.8%	42.0%	28.5%	22.9%
One year before	10.3	10.3	8.6	7.6
In same year as first arrest	13.4%	13.4%	11.5%	10.2%
After first arrest				
One year after	6.5%	7.8%	8.7%	8.5%
More than 1 year	21.0	26.6	42.7	50.8
Number of cases	355,285	278,864	233,038	156,386

Percent of Drug-Using Inmates Who Used (all columns except When Drug Use Began).

NOTE: Percents may not add to 100 because of rounding.

*Major drugs include cocaine, heroin, PCP, SD, and methadone.

Daily Use of Major Drugs for State Prison Inmates, by Conviction Offense, 1986

Type of Drug Use and Conviction Offense	Percent of All Inmates
Daily use of a major drug in the month before the offense	
No	81.4%
Yes	18.6%
Conviction offense for daily users:	
Crimes for gain	13.0%
Robbery	4.8
Burglary	3.8
Drug trafficking	1.6
Larceny	1.5
Other property offenses	1.3
Violent offenses*	3.7%
Other	1.8%

NOTE: Percents may not add to totals because of rounding.

*Excluding robbery.

Major Drug Use History and Convictions for State Prison Inmates, 1986

Convictions	Percent of All Inmates Who:				
		Used a Major Drug			
				In the Month before the Offense	
	Never Used a Major Drug	Anytime in the Past	Regularly in the Past	At All	Daily
Prior convictions					
As a juvenile only	10.7%	13.3%	8.3%	11.0%	9.5%
As an adult only	37.0	33.2	38.7	30.7	35.9
Both as a juvenile and as an adult	26.6	37.2	44.2	44.3	45.4
Number of prior convictions					
None	25.7%	16.4%	8.8%	14.0%	9.2%
1	22.8	19.9	16.8	17.2	14.8
2	16.6	17.4	16.7	13.8	16.1
3–5	22.3	26.8	31.4	28.9	30.4
6–10	8.8	13.5	16.5	15.2	18.2
11 or more	3.7	6.0	9.8	10.9	11.3

NOTE: Major drugs include cocaine, heroin, PCP, LSD, and methadone.

Employment by Major Drug Use History for State Prison Inmates, 1986

Employment Status in Year before Incarceration	Percent of All Inmates Who:				
		Used a Major Drug			
				In the Month before the Offense	
	Never Used a Major Drug	Anytime in the Past	Regularly in the Past	At All	Daily
Total	100.0%	100.0%	100.0%	100.0%	100.0%
Employed	73.4%	67.9%	67.5%	67.0%	60.0%
Full-time	61.6	54.5	56.7	59.0	49.5
Part-time	11.8	13.3	10.8	10.0	10.6
Unemployed	26.6%	32.1%	32.5%	31.0%	40.0%
Looking for work	16.5	19.8	18.9	16.9	19.8
Not looking for work	10.1	12.4	13.7	14.1	20.2

NOTE: Major drugs include cocaine, heroin, PCP, LSD, and methadone. Percents may not add to totals because of rounding.

Participation in Drug Treatment Programs for State Prison Inmates, 1986

Extent of Program Participation	Percent of All Inmates
Ever participated in a treatment program	29.6%
Number of times in treatment	
Once	17.7%
Twice	6.5
3–5 times	4.3
6 or more times	.9
In a program in the month before current offense	3.7%
Most recent treatment was while incarcerated	15.7%
Currently in treatment	6.2%

Bureau of Justice Statistics Special Reports are prepared principally by BJS staff. This report was written by Christopher A. Innes. Susan Kline provided statistical review. Frank D. Balog edited the report. Marianne Zawitz provided assistance on data presentation. Marilyn Marbrook, publications unit chief, administered report production, assisted by Yvonne Shields, Christina Roberts, and Jeanne Harris.

The design and collection of the data was directed by Phyllis Jo Baunach, formerly of BJS. Data collection was carried out at the Bureau of the Census by Marilyn Monahan, Susan Schacter-Ryan, Gregory Wells, and Rita Williamson under the supervision of Larry McGinn, Gertrude Odom, and Robert Tinari.

July 1988, NCJ-111940

Income Source by Major Drug Use History for State Prison Inmates, 1986

Source of Income	Percent of All Inmates Who: Never Used a Major Drug	Used a Major Drug: Anytime in the Past	Used a Major Drug: Regularly in the Past	In the Month before the Offense: At All	In the Month before the Offense: Daily
Wages or salaries	85.3%	85.2%	83.3%	84.5%	77.3%
Benefits	22.3	21.4	25.9	22.1	22.8
Family or friends	23.3	30.5	25.1	29.6	30.5
Illegal income	9.6	23.4	27.9	35.5	47.6
Other income source	4.0	4.0	4.1	3.0	3.8

NOTE: Income source refers to any source of income during the year before the current incarceration. Percents add to more than 100 because more than one source of income could be mentioned by each inmate.

Past Drug Dependency by Race and Sex for State Prison Inmates, 1986

Drug Use Dependency	Percent of All Inmates: All Inmates	Race: White	Race: Black	Race: Other	Sex: Male	Sex: Female
Ever dependent on drugs in past	27.8%	31.6%	23.7%	28.3%	27.4%	35.8%
Major drug*	20.4%	22.2%	18.6%	18.4%	20.0%	28.3%
Cocaine	10.0	10.4	9.6	9.2	9.8	13.7
Heroin	13.6	14.1	13.1	11.4	13.2	22.0
PCP	1.7	2.2	1.1	2.0	1.7	1.5
LSD	1.5	2.7	.3	1.9	1.6	.6
Methadone	1.2	1.7	.6	1.2	1.1	2.9
Other drug	14.5%	18.6%	9.9%	17.8%	14.4%	16.1%
Marijuana or hashish	8.8	10.3	7.1	11.9	9.0	5.9
Amphetamines	4.8	7.7	1.7	6.2	4.8	6.4
Barbiturates	3.4	5.3	1.4	5.1	3.4	5.2
Methaqualone	1.3	2.1	.5	1.9	1.3	1.7
Others	1.4	2.2	.5	1.9	1.3	2.3

NOTE: Dependency data, like drug use data, are based on self-reports by inmates. Percents may add to more than totals because more than one drug could be mentioned by each inmate.

*Major drugs include cocaine, heroin, PCP, LSD, and methadone.

were daily drug users, and about 40% were under the influence of an illegal drug at the time they committed the crime. These proportions were higher than those reported by inmates convicted of other crimes.

- In addition, the greater an offender's use of major drugs, the more prior convictions the inmate reported—less than 13% of those who had never used a major drug had six or more prior convictions, compared to about 30% of daily users of major drugs.
- Major drug users among prisoners surveyed were more likely than nonusers to report they had received income from illegal activities during the time they were last free (48% vs. 10%).
- Twenty-eight percent of inmates reported a past drug dependency. The drugs most frequently mentioned were heroin (14%), cocaine (10%), and marijuana or hashish (9%).
- Thirty percent of inmates said that they had participated in a drug treatment program at some time—12% more than once. About 50% of the inmates who had taken part in a program had received their most recent treatment while they were incarcerated.

The survey of state prison inmates was designed and sponsored by the U.S. Department of Justice, Bureau of Justice Statistics (BJS), with data collection done by the Bureau of the Census. A special report entitled *Drug Use and Crime,* based on the State Prison Inmate Survey, 1986, was prepared by Christopher A. Innes, Ph.D., Bureau of Justice Statistics with assistance from members of the BJS staff.

See tables that follow.

Christopher A. Innes, *Drug Use and Crime,* State Prison Inmate Survey, 1986, Bureau of Justice Statistics Special Report, July 1988, NCJ-111940.

problem drinker A vague and outdated term for one who experiences personal, social, vocational and/or health problems whenever he or she drinks. Problem drinkers are almost always HEAVY DRINKERS but there are exceptions. Often the distinction between problem drinking and alcoholism is a matter of degree or depends on whether tolerance is present and withdrawal symptoms appear when the drinking is stopped. Newer definitions of alcoholism do not require tolerance and withdrawal to be present and therefore "include" problem drinkers.

procaine A local anesthetic (Novocain®) whose action prevents the initiation and transmission of nerve impulses. It has a rapid onset of action (two to five minutes) and its duration is one to one and a half hours depending on the type of block, the concentration and the individual patient. Procaine is used as a dilutant in cocaine. Procaine, sometimes in combination with cortisone, has also been used in sports events to allow a participant who is in pain to continue in a contest.

progression The risk of moving from experimental or occasional drug use to regular social/recreational use and on to dysfunctional use. It has been suggested that the use of "soft" drugs, such as marijuana, may lead to the use of "hard" drugs, such as heroin. The progression risk is also found in the manner of administration of a drug; when applied to heroin it can be the escalation from intramuscular or subcutaneous injection to mainlining (intravenous use).

Project Cork Institute The institute's origins lie in Project Cork, a program created in 1977–78 by Operation Cork, a program of the Kroc Foundation. It started as a limited effort within Dartmouth Medical School to develop a model curriculum on alcohol-related issues for undergraduate medical education. In 1978, a resource center was created with a collection of more than 9,000 items, plus a computer-based cataloguing system. Access to the collection was enhanced through a bimonthly newsletter, *Alcohol Clinical Update,* now in its seventh year of publication.

Starting in 1981, Dartmouth Medical School provided the support necessary to maintain the project's identity. In 1984, a gift from the Joan B. Kroc Foundation provided funds for the establishment of The Project Cork Institute. The institute is now an autonomous entity on the Dartmouth Medical School campus, has an independent board, and operates nationally to promote education and training of physicians and other health service professionals in the diagnosis and treatment of individuals and families affected by alcoholism and other forms of chemical dependency.

In early 1988, the institute's data base was made available nationally when it was loaded onto BRS Information Technologies, a commercial data base reference service.

Project Cork Institute's historical involvement with the Dartmouth health service has expanded to collaboration with the American College Health Association (ACHA) for the creation of alcohol and other drug abuse standards for member institutions. The institute also has contractual arrangements to assist other organizations, such as the Indian Health Service, in devising curriculum and support materials for training primary care clinicians. Contact: Jean Kinney, M.S.W., Executive Director, Project Cork Institute, Dartmouth Medical School, Hanover, NH 03756.

Project DARE A cooperative law enforcement and education effort through which police officers help provide classroom lessons and presentations on drug abuse in the elementary schools throughout the Los Angeles metropolitan area. Contact: Lieutenant Roger Combs, Project DARE, Los Angeles Police Department, 1550 N. Los Angeles Street, Los Angeles, CA 90012. Telephone: (213) 485-4865. Program has been cited as an example of effective criminal justice programs and resources in the U.S.

Prolixin® (Squibb) An antipsychotic that contains fluphenazine hydrochloride and is generally used for psychotic disorders. Prolixin is not an abused drug. It is supplied in 1 mg pink tablets; 2.5 mg yellow tablets; 5 mg green tablets; and 10 mg coral tablets. It is also available in an orange-colored and flavored elixir.

proof An official measurement, usually made with an alcoholometer or hydrometer, of the amount of absolute alcohol in a distilled spirit. The American system of proof measurement is based upon the percentage of absolute alcohol in the liquor at 60 degrees F. The proof measurement is double the percentage of alcohol: 100 proof = 50% alcohol. The British system is based upon a comparison of equal volumes of liquor and water at 51 degrees F. In some states the term "proof" means to show identification for one's age, as in admission to a bar to purchase alcohol.

propoxyphene A SYNTHETIC ANALGESIC. Propoxyphene hydrochloride was first synthesized in 1953 by Pohland and Sullivan. It was first marketed in 1957 as DARVON by Lilly & Co., who claimed that the new drug was as effective as codeine but did not share its side effects or addictive nature. Propoxyphene is in fact very similar to codeine and methadone, except that it lacks an antitussive effect. Nearly 20 million prescriptions for Darvon are written annually, making it one of America's most widely used narcotics. It is clearly addictive and has high abuse potential.

Appearance and activity: Propoxyphene hydrochloride is an odorless bitter-tasting white crystalline solid, soluble in water and slightly soluble in alcohol. It also occurs as propoxyphene napsylate which is not water soluble. The effects of the drug peak in two to two and a half hours. This drug has not been determined safe for use during pregnancy.

Dosage: Propoxyphene is prescribed in 32–65 mg doses to be taken three or four times daily: 90–120 mg is equivalent to 60 mg of codeine, and 100 mg of the napsylate form is equivalent to 65 mg of the hydrochloride form. The drug is not prescribed for children. Intravenous administration is not recommended either—it is very irritating and results in damage to the veins and soft tissue.

Effect: Darvon and other forms of propoxyphene produce the drowsiness and euphoria typically associated with morphine and codeine, as well as pain relief. The drug acts as a CNS depressant and has side effects such as dizziness, headache and nausea. It brings on withdrawal symptoms when given to addicts of heroin and other opiates. Overdoses can cause gastrointestinal distress, convulsions, respiratory depression, circulatory collapse and even coma and psychosis. In cases of overdose, a narcotic antagonist such as NALOXONE should be administered. Tolerance and physical and psychological dependence can develop.

Usage: Propoxyphene is used medically to relieve mild to moderate pain and occasionally for withdrawal treatment for morphine and heroin addiction. Recreational use does occur but very large doses (over 500 mg) are required to achieve and maintain a "high" and hallucinations may also occur. Such high levels of ingestion are dangerous and can result in side effects. Overdosage can result in convulsions, depressed respiration, coma and death. The medical profession agrees that Darvon is abused.

Availability: Propoxyphene hydrochloride is commercially available as Darvon, football-shaped capsules colored light pink, red and gray, or red and pink (Darvon is known on the street as "pinks" or "red and grays"). The drug is also available in combination with aspirin and other drugs, in capsule or tablet form. DOLENE is another brand name, while Darvon-N and such variations refer to the napsylate form.

Propoxyphene is a Schedule IV drug under the Controlled Substances Act.

propoxyphene napsylate See PROPOXYPHENE. The substance differs from propoxyphene hydrochloride in that it allows more stable liquid dosage forms and tablet formations. It is also longer acting than the hydrochloride.

prostitution Many women and men, particularly street addicts, obtain money for drugs through prostitution; some work on their own, and others are involved in ORGANIZED CRIME. There is a high incidence of AIDS and other sexually transmitted diseases among addicts involved in prostitution. An addict who supports a habit in this way is also apt to become more deeply addicted: it provides an escape from a dismal life.

Although the likelihood of pregnancy may be reduced for addicts, when it occurs the effects of addiction are passed on to the child in many instances. (See also PREGNANCY.)

protopine A crystalline alkaloid found in small quantities in opium and some papaveraceous plants.

psilocybin The active hallucinogenic ingredient of the mushroom *Psilocybe mexicana* and some of the other psilocybe and conocybe species. Ritual use of psilocybin among Mexican and Central American cultures is known to date back to at least 1500 B.C.

Some tribes of Indians in Mexico have used certain mushrooms with hallucinogenic properties in their religious ceremonies for centuries. These mushrooms, specimens of the genera *Conocybe Stropharia,* and *Psilocybe* were considered to be sacred and were named *teonanacatl,* or flesh of the gods.

In 1958 Albert Hofmann, a Swiss chemist, isolated psilocybin and its congener, psilocin, from *Psilocybe mexicana.* Psilocybin is the only naturally occurring hallucinogen identified thus far that contains phosphorus.

In pure form psilocybin is a white crystalline material, but it may also be distributed in crude mushroom preparations, in intact dried mushrooms, or as a capsule containing a powdered material of any color. It is usually taken orally but may also be injected. Doses generally vary from 4 mg to 5 mg, although 20–60 mg is not unusual. The potency of psilocybin lies somewhere between that of mescaline and LSD and the effects are reported to be much like those of LSD.

Classification: Psilocybin is a hallucinogen. It shows cross-tolerance to LSD and mescaline.

Effects: When taken orally psilocybin is one of the most rapid-acting hallucinogens: initial effects may be felt 10 to 15 minutes after ingestion. Reactions often reach maximum intensity after about 90 minutes and do not begin to subside until two to three hours later. The effects of psilocybin usually last five to six hours in all but doses larger than 8 mg probably prolong their duration. Physiological effects include increased pulse rate, respiratory rate and body temperature, dilated pupils and elevation of systolic blood pressure. Larger doses, 13 mg or more, can produce dizziness, lightheadedness, abdominal discomfort, numbness of tongue, lips or mouth, nausea, anxiety and shivering. Psychological effects with small doses may include mental and physical relaxation, detachment from surroundings and sometimes coexisting feelings of anxiety or elation. With larger doses individuals may experience difficulty in thinking and concentrating, visual distortions and other changes in perception.

Addictive aspects: Physical DEPENDENCE on psilocybin has not been reported.

Tolerance: Tolerance to psilocybin does develop, and there is a CROSS-TOLERANCE to the effects of LSD and MESCALINE. As with all hallucinogens tolerance rapidly develops and rapidly passes.

Sources: It is difficult to estimate how much psilocybin is available to users. Some may be extracted from mushrooms for street sale, and some may be synthesized. Some users grow their own mushrooms. Psilocybin can be bought as a liquid or powder or as whole mushrooms. Much of what is sold as psilocybin is actually PCP and, sometimes, LSD.

Synonym: sacred mushroom.

psychedelic See HALLUCINOGEN.

psychoactive Drugs that alter thinking, perception, emotions or consciousness are termed psychoactive. They are sought after by drug abusers.

psychodrama Acting out a problem. A form of group psychotherapy used at times in drug rehabilitation to heighten a person's awareness of his problem, it is thought to provide more immediacy than simple discussion. Under the direction of a therapist, a member of the group portrays himself while another member takes on the role of the person associated with the problem—spouse, parent, employer or whoever. Sometimes role-reversal is also used; the member takes on the role of the person he believes is associated with his problem.

psychological dependence A broad general term which refers to a craving or compulsion to continue the use of a drug because it gives a feeling of well-being and satisfaction. The term HABITUATION is frequently used interchangeably with the term psychological dependence; the syndrome is also known as behavioral, psychic or emotional dependence.

In chronic drug use psychological dependence is considered more serious and more difficult to deal with than physical dependence. Psychological dependence can vary in intensity from a mild preference for a drug to a strong craving for it. The World Health Organization defines psychic dependence as "a feeling of satisfaction and a psychic drive that requires periodic or continuous administration of a drug to produce a desired effect or to avoid discomfort." An individual can be psychologically dependent on a drug and not physically dependent and the reverse is also true (but very rarely occurs). Newer definitions of dependence or addiction use criteria that include psychological dependence as sufficient criteria for a diagnosis.

psychological models of etiology Along with sociocultural and physiological theories, this is one of the three major categories of theories on the cause of chemical dependency.

The theories are based on the assumption that some element in the personality structure leads to the development of addiction. Although studies have failed to come up with specific personality traits that differentiate addicts from other people, there is evidence that once a pattern is established addicts have certain traits in common; a low tolerance to stress; insecurity; depression; negative self-image; and dependency. It is not clear whether these traits are a result of addiction or precede addiction because most studies have been conducted on people already addicted. (See also ORAL FIXATION and BEHAVIORAL LEARNING THEORIES.)

psychosis A mental state characterized by defective or lost contact with reality. In toxic psychosis, acute or chronic psychotic-like behavior results from impairment of brain cell function; symptoms can include extreme confusion, hallucinations, disorientation, depression and aggressive behavior. Schizophrenic and manic depressive psychosis are examples of what has been called functional psychoses (not caused by drugs or a separate physical dysfunction such as fever).

psychostimulant See STIMULANT.

psychotogenic Drugs that frequently produce hallucinations and delusions when taken in large doses. In smaller doses they produce euphoric effects.

psychotomimetic Drugs that produce hallucinations and alter perception; many of the effects resemble forms of psychosis. Psychotomimetic drugs are usually stimulants and psychedelics.

psychotropic The term is used interchangeably with psychiatric and is applied to drugs used to treat mental disorders (e.g., antipsychotics and antidepressants).

Public Affairs Committee A nonprofit educational organization founded in 1935. Its purpose is to "develop a new technique to educate the American public on vital economic and social problems and to issue concise and interesting pamphlets dealing with such problems." The committee offers an extensive variety of pamphlets dealing with substance abuse and its consequences.

public drunkenness The most visible kind of alcoholic, a public inebriate has symbolic significance for all alcoholics. The English Parliament in 1606 considered public intoxication a legal matter and this approach was brought to America. In 1980 the number of arrests for public drunkenness numbered more than 1.1 million. In 1971 the Uniform Alcoholism and Intoxification Treatment Act was established to decriminalize alcoholism and intoxication and to approach them from a health standpoint. The act states that "alcoholics and intoxicated persons may not be subjected to criminal prosecution because of their consumption of alcoholic beverages but rather should be afforded a continuum of treatment in order that they may lead normal lives as productive members of society." The act has helped to destigmatize alcoholism and to reduce the number of alcoholics who are incarcerated, but it has not brought chronic public inebriates into treatment voluntarily or kept them in treatment. While some treatment programs often write off public inebriates as unlikely to recover, a number of specialized programs have demonstrated good recovery rates in this population over many years.

Puerto Rico From 1966 to 1972 heroin was the major drug of abuse in Puerto Rico, excluding alcohol. From 1972 to the present, there has been a significant increase in polydrug use and a preference for marijuana; heroin use has shown a noticeable reduction, cocaine a noticeable increase.

Heroin use in Puerto Rico closely follows the pattern set by Puerto Ricans living in the United States. In 1976 there were an estimated 125,000 opiate addicts in New York City and one-third were Puerto Rican (Puerto Ricans at that time comprised 12% of the metropolitan area population). The increased addiction statistics for Puerto Ricans living in New York are thought in part to be due to the unfavorable conditions in which they live, often in poor slum areas, with poor access to treatment along with the cultural differences and the physical separation from parents and other relatives. Although there have been mass migrations to the U.S. in the past, a recent trend seems to be a return to Puerto Rico, perhaps as a result of dissatisfaction with poor economic opportunities and with being an ethnic minority in a country where they are citizens.

In the past 20 years drug addiction has become a social problem of epidemic proportions in Puerto Rico, a result of both economic and sociocultural factors. The unemployment rate has been steadily increasing since 1970, particularly among young males. Education is closely tied to the unemployment rate, and although 50% of the work force has completed 12 years of schooling, the highest rate of unemployment persists among those who dropped out of school between grades 6 and 12. In 1978 the per capita income was $2,678; while this was high compared to most Latin American countries, it still left 60% of the island's families living below the federal poverty level. The life-style of the island's inhabitants has also changed drastically, particularly since Puerto Rico became a U.S. territory (1898) and its inhabitants became citizens (1917). There have been rapid changes in industrial development, occupation patterns (women are joining the work force), and social structures.

The Department of Drug Addiction Services (DAS), created in 1973, has the responsibility for reducing alcohol and drug dependence and addiction. According to the DAS, heroin use among its clients declined from 63% in 1975–76 to a current 45%. Marijuana use rose from 19% to 46% in the same time period. Arrests and interventions for drug-related incidents, reported by the Criminal Investigation Bureau of the Police of Puerto Rico, reflect the same pattern. Polydrug use has also increased. Among young clients, 88% admitted use of marijuana and inhalants. The popularity of cocaine has increased in the past few years and, in polydrug use, cocaine is becoming the secondary drug of abuse. Only in a small number of cases is it the primary drug of abuse.

While drug abuse trends in Puerto Rico generally follow the trends on the mainland, there is one exception: the use of inhalants. The popularity of inhalants as an intoxicating drug waned in the U.S. quite a number of years ago, but in Puerto Rico they are still extensively used particularly by young people.

Authorities in Puerto Rico acknowledge a shortage of treatment centers, particularly centers to deal with young people using drugs such as marijuana. They tend to agree that a major problem on the island is the fact that marijuana is classified with heroin under the Controlled Substances Act and most treatment centers are now designed for heroin addicts. There are plans for future treatment centers to help young people, women and the elderly, particularly detoxification centers, hotlines, and therapeutic communities. Puerto Rico is well aware of its drug problem and its lack of treatment facilities, and plans to emphasize a community approach to treatment and prevention education. This approach has also been directed toward the alcohol problem on the island.

The consumption of alcoholic beverages is a deeply ingrained tradition in Puerto Rico and is increasingly becoming more of a problem. Undoubtedly, the same economic and sociocultural factors that are thought to account for the abuse of other drugs are the root cause. In 1978, 18.6% of the per capita income was spent on alcohol, the most popular beverage being the locally produced rum which is known and highly prized throughout the world.

Statistics show that "heavy drinkers" (three out of every 10 drinkers fall into this category) tend to be males between the ages of 20 and 49, and the age at which this group begins drinking grows younger all the time. From 1979–80, 92% of all arrests for drunkenness were for drunk driving and the rate of deaths per 100,000 miles traveled by car was twice that of the U.S.

pyrahexyl A semisynthetic derivative of cannabis which has similar effects.

pyribenzamine An antihistamine (also called PBZ and manufactured by Geigy). Its generic name is tripelenamine. There was a short-lived fad of injecting "Blue Velvet," a mixture of pulverized pyribenzamine tablets and boiled paregoric. There were numerous deaths from plugged veins, thought to have been a result of the talc used as a filler in the tablets. Pyribenzamine has been combined with Talwin as "Ts and blues," the "blues" referring to the color of the scored 50 mg tablets. The combination is injected intravenously.

Q

Quaalude® (Lemmon) A non-barbiturate sedative hypnotic that contained methaqualone. The Lemmon Company removed the drug from the market in the early 1980s because of its widespread abuse. It was prescribed for daytime sedation and to produce sleep, and was once thought to be nonaddictive. It was supplied as Quaalude-150, white scored tablets containing 150 mg methaqualone; and Quaalude-300, 300 mg white scored tablets. The most common illicit methaqualone produced today resembles the original Quaaludes. It is a Schedule II drug under the Controlled Substances Act. (See also METHAQUALONE.)

Quibron Plus® (Mead Johnson) A bronchodilator that contains theophylline, guaifenesin, ephedrine and butabarbital, and is usually used in the treatment of bronchial asthma, bronchitis and emphysema. It may be habit-forming. It is supplied in yellow capsules and as an elixir.

quinine A bitter crystalline alkaloid derived from the bark of the cinchona tree that is used as an antipyretic, antimalarial medicine. After an outbreak of malaria among heroin addicts in New York City in the 1930s, quinine became a popular dilutant of heroin. In the amounts found in street heroin, quinine cannot cure malaria but when the solution is dissolved for injection the quinine may kill the malaria parasite. Quinine is also added because it is thought to enhance the "rush" felt after injection, and because it has a bitter taste. Heroin is often diluted with milk sugar (lactose) which masks its bitter taste, so quinine is added to provide the bitterness in case an addict wishes to taste-test the heroin before buying it to ensure its potency. Some addict deaths labeled "heroin overdose" are thought to be due to sensitivity to intravenous quinine.

R

RADAR Network Support RADAR is the acronym for Regional Alcohol and Drug Awareness Resource. The National Clearinghouse for Alcohol and Drug Information (NCADI) is the hub of the RADAR Network, which consists of the state clearinghouses, information centers of national voluntary organizations and the Department of Education's regional training centers. Network members use NCADI products and services to respond to local needs for information and technical assistance. Individuals can obtain information from NCADI on how to contact the RADAR center in their state. Contact: NCADI, P.O. Box 2345, Rockville, MD 20852. Telephone: (301) 468-2600.

radioimmunoassay (RIA) Similar to the EIA (enzyme immunoassay) drug-testing method, the radioimmunoassay (RIA) machine adds antibodies to the urine that are specific to the target drug. These added antibodies attach to any drug molecules that are present. The antibodies are "tagged" with radioactive molecules, which send out tiny particles and rays in a process known as radioactivity. The antibodies with their attached radioactive molecules can be located because of their radioactivity. The emission of radiation during the test indicates the presence of the drug. A widely used RIA test is marketed under the trade name Abuscreen (its biggest customer is the U.S. military). The RIA machine is a more complex piece of equipment than the EIA, thus requiring more training for its technicians. It can, however, do more drug tests faster than most other approaches.

Gilda Berger, *Drug Testing* (New York: Franklin Watts, 1987).

Rand Report In 1971 the National Institute on Alcohol Abuse and Alcoholism (NIAAA) sponsored and subsidized the Rand Corporation, an independent nonprofit research organization, to prepare an analysis of NIAAA's comprehensive alcoholism treatment program. In June 1976, the Rand Corporation published its findings in a report entitled *Alcoholism and Treatment*.

The highly controversial report contained the following conclusions and considerations:

Treatment: A slightly higher rate of remission was reported for clients who underwent treatment than for those who had a single contact with a treatment center (the terms "single contact" and "untreated" were used synonymously in the report). As the amount of treatment increased, there were slight additional advantages.

Remission rates: Treated clients, 70% (results varied little from one treatment program to another); untreated clients with Alcoholics Anonymous attention, nearly 70%; untreated clients (natural remission), 50%. Throughout the report the term "remission" was used to include both abstention and "normal drinking." Normal drinking was used to cover consumption in moderate quantities where no serious signs of impairment were present.

Relapse rates: The report stated that "relapse rates for normal drinkers are no higher than those for long-term abstainers." The study further suggested "the possibility that for some alcoholics moderate drinking is not necessarily a prelude to full relapse."

Other conclusions of the report: No pattern was found to suggest that one program was better for a client than another. The study did conclude, however, that "recovery from alcohol dependency may depend on mechanisms quite unrelated to the factors that led to excessive drinking in the first place."

Future considerations of the report: If future research were to confirm the initial conclusions of the survey, total abstinence would not be the only goal of treatment. Research would be needed to determine which alcoholics could return to normal drinking. And if the study's theory that the results of most programs are uniform was corroborated, in regard to a client's drinking and other behavior patterns, then less expensive methods of treatment could be used.

Throughout the report, the authors pointed out the limitations of their sample: that conclusions about behavior were not based on controlled experimental data, just observation; that the time frame of the study was limited and the size of the sample was small; and that future behavior would not necessarily conform to the survey data. These limitations noted by the authors were seized upon by critics. They claimed that the report was actually harmful and deluded alcoholics into believing they could actually resume drinking without disastrous results. Critics suggested that the samples were not randomly selected and that a large portion of interviewing was done over the phone by people with only limited training. They also questioned whether all the clients in the survey were actually alcoholics. They noted, too, the time period involved (18 months after a client entered treatment) and said that previous studies over substantially longer periods had rejected the conclusions given in the report.

Rand Report II. A second report, published in January 1980, under the title *The Course of Alcoholism: Four Years After Treatment,* was a continuation of the previous study. Although not a "retraction," the second report modified many of the conclusions in the original. The authors suggested that the issues were more complex than originally suggested and characterized the second report as another phase of continued study.

Also sponsored by NIAAA, the second study was a follow-up on the sample clients involved in the first study. The report confirmed the earlier finding that some alcoholics are able to return to social drinking. For most alcoholics, however, they found that total abstinence seemed to be the surest method of maintaining remission.

The Rand Report II concluded that for younger unmarried alcoholics (under 40 years old), who were often under social pressure to drink, attempts at abstinence might be more stressful than non-problem social drinking. For older married alcoholics who remained abstinent there was less likelihood of relapse.

The report found that 46% of the 900 men studied were in remission, with 28% abstaining and 18% drinking socially. The study showed that alcoholics who entered treatment programs were highly unstable in their ability to refrain indefinitely from problem drinking, with many relapsing several times during the four years and entering various treatment programs from time to time. The highest rate of long-term abstinence was found among men who regularly attended AA; although it was shown that they were just as likely to have relapses as those who did not attend. The worst prognosis was for short-term abstainers (less than six months); they had a much higher rate of relapse and many more alcohol-related deaths.

The authors of this four-year study, the most comprehensive and extensive to date (at a cost of half a million dollars), do not recommend a particular treatment approach nor do they recommend that an alcoholic resume drinking. What the report does is to raise questions about the nature and treatment of alcoholism. Less controversial in its findings, the second report received less criticism and press coverage than the first. Both reports rely heavily on self-report and evaluation, which due to the nature of denial in addiction places the findings in question. The return of 18% to "social drinking" has never been supported by any observer rated study and is believed false by many treatment professionals.

Rastafarians In 1930, when Ras Tafari was crowned Emperor of Ethiopia and took the name Haile Selassie, the first Rastafarians appeared in Jamaica and looked to Selassie as their messiah. Their objective was—and still is—to revitalize and promote their African heritage.

The Rasta God is called Jah and some orthodox followers grow dreadlocks (long unaltered locks formed by washing the hair and allowing it to dry without combing) as a symbol of their devotion. The Rastafarians believe the smoking of GANJA (the Jamaican word for marijuana, taken from the Hindu) is one of their strongest shared experiences and look on ganja as a divine herb important to their spiritual, mental and physical health. Most probably marijuana was introduced to Jamaica by indentured laborers from India in the mid-1800s and there are estimates that between 60% and 70% of the island's population now ingests ganja in one form or another. The "herb" (as it is often referred to) has been illegal to use, possess and sell since 1913 but the police are usually nonchalant about enforcing the law and the ganja trade has been unofficially tolerated. Recently, however, the Jamaican government has felt the trade was slipping out of control and called in the U.S. Drug Enforcement Administration for assistance.

The Rastafari smoke ganja in "spliffs," five-inch cone-shaped rolls made from paper or cornhusks. It is also brewed in a green tea and this is the form usually used by women and children. Ganja tea is a major folk remedy often used for rheumatism, sleeping difficulties and especially male impotence. It is also used as an external tonic for wounds, infections and allergies. Kali (the Hindu black goddess of strength) is the most potent grade of ganja.

Reggae music brought the Rastafari to worldwide attention in the late 1960s and was especially popularized by the late Bob Marley. The lyrics of many reggae songs reflect the near-worship of the "mystical herb," as the Rastas refer to it. (See also JAMAICA.)

Rauwolfia serpentina A DEPRESSANT obtained from the dried root of a small climbing shrub of the *apocynaceae* family, which is native to India and known in English as SNAKEROOT. Indians have used it for 2,500 years in powdered form as a tranquilizer for such conditions as snakebite, hypertension, insomnia and insanity. It is the source of the drug RESERPINE.

Activity: Rauwolfia serpentina is rapidly absorbed from the gastrointestinal tract, widely distributed throughout the body, and excreted slowly in the urine and feces. It depresses the central nervous system at the hypothalamic level, suppressing the sympathetic branch of the autonomic system. Rauwolfia serpentina crosses the placental barrier and also appears in breast milk.

Dosage: The recommended dose for hypertension is 0.5–3.0 mg, and the dosage suggested for emotional disorders is 0.1–2.0 mg.

Effects: Rauwolfia serpentina is an antihypertensive drug which calms symptoms of anxiety such as headache and palpitations without analgesia. It lowers the blood pressure, slows the pulse, causes pupil constriction, and increases gastrointestinal secretion (and should therefore be used cautiously in patients with peptic ulcers and ulcerative colitis). Unlike the minor tranquilizers, Rauwolfia serpentina does not potentiate other CNS depressants, nor does its use lead to tolerance or physical or psychological dependence.

Side effects reported in conjunction with the use of Rauwolfia serpentina include infrequent paradoxical excitation, increased respiratory secretions, gastrointestinal hypersecretion, nasal congestion, nausea, vomiting, diarrhea, drowsiness, depression, rash, impotence, and anorexia in babies of women treated with the drug.

Usage: The Indians who first ground up the Rauwolfia serpentina root and used it to treat hypertension and insanity applied the substance wisely. It is still used in the treatment of mild hypertension and, with additional drugs, for more severe hypertension. It should not be used in patients who are suffering from or prone to depression; it induces a depression which has been known to be severe enough to result in suicide, particularly after withdrawal from the drug.

Availability: Rauwolfia serpentina is manufactured as tablets under the name of the root and Raudixin and Harmonyl. It is also available in tablets mixed with thiazides and potassium chloride.

reassurance A simple therapeutic method of decreasing a client's anxieties or fears by assuring him that his reactions are excessive or his fears groundless. Reassurance is given with sincerity and certainty along with positive, realistic evidence of the needlessness for the anxiety that is being experienced.

receptor sites Sites within the body where chemical substances interact to produce pharmacological actions. Receptors recognize a substance by its chemical configuration and electrical charge, distinguish it from others, and transmit the signal indicating the presence of the substance which brings about pharmacological action in the target tissue. Opiate receptor sites have been identified in the brain, intestines and spinal cord. Endogenous opioid peptides, or ENDORPHINS, were discovered in 1975 and the discovery of others has followed. Very little is known, however, about where and how the endorphins are produced, and what their exact role is in modulating pain and mood. Receptors have been identified for benzodiazepines but not for alcohol.

recovery A term often used in the treatment of alcoholism which has no clear definition. It may be applied to a stable remission of symptoms over a period of time. In the case of Alcoholics Anonymous, however, it means complete *abstinence* for a significant period. Such periods of abstinence may be punctuated by relapse, however. The state of recovery during abstinence is characterized by improving psychological, interpersonal, and spiritual well-being. Recovery can be described as repairing and reversing the effects of addiction in a holistic sense.

recreational drug use The U.S. Commission on Marijuana and Drug Abuse defined recreational/social drug use as that which occurs in social settings among friends or acquaintances who wish to share a pleasurable experience. Unlike EXPERIMENTAL DRUG USE recreational and social use tends to have more of a pattern but is considerably more varied in terms of frequency, duration and intensity. Regardless of the duration of use, it tends not to escalate in either intensity or frequency.

However, in his September 1989 National Drug Control Strategy Report to the President, William J. Bennett, who was director of the Office of National Drug Control Policy, stated that non-addicted casual and regular users of drugs remains "a grave issue of national concern." Bennett said the so-called nonaddicted recreational users of illicit drugs number in the millions, "and each represents a potential agent of infection for the non-users in his personal ambit."

rectal administration See ADMINISTRATION.

red eye See EYES.

Reggae music and drugs Reggae music makes positive and frequent reference to marijuana use and the Rastafarian lifestyle. It also describes poverty and oppression in the West Indies. It was reggae music that called attention to the Rastafari in the late 1960s—the first Rastafarians appeared in Jamaica and looked to the late Emperor of Ethiopia, Haile Selassie, as their messiah. The lyrics of many reggae tunes reflect the near worship of the "mystical herb," as the

Rastas refer to Ganja, the Hindi word for marijuana. (See also RASTAFARIANS.)

rehabilitation The techniques used to help drug users give up the drug (or drugs) to which they are addicted, and make them feel that they can be useful and respected among their families, friends and community. After detoxification, some sort of rehabilitation is generally needed as follow-up treatment because even though a person is now *physically* free of dependence, their thinking and behavior patterns have not changed. Detoxification usually occurs in a hospital but only a small number of hospitals have rehabilitation centers. Rehabilitation centers are more apt to be private and are often situated in suburban or rural areas with pleasant surroundings. Whether or not a rehabilitation center is part of the plan, nearly all modes of treatment emphasize membership in Narcotics Anonymous or Alcoholics Anonymous. In general rehabilitation refers to teaching and supporting the skills needed to change life patterns and psychological responses learned while on drugs. (See also HALFWAY HOUSES, GROUP THERAPY, and EMPLOYEE ASSISTANCE PROGRAMS.)

reinforcement, positive and negative Positive reinforcement is a process by which a response to a stimulus is strengthened usually by rewarding the response. Negative reinforcement is the reverse process; a response to a specific stimulus is punished. When a response has been frequently rewarded or punished so that it becomes regularly elicited or avoided, the organism has been conditioned. During classical conditioning the stimulus may be paired with a second stimulus, and it will evoke a similar response.

relapse The return to the use of a drug and to old behaviors following a seemingly satisfactory adjustment. Relapse may be related to, the availability of the drug, mixing with friends who are still addicted to the drug, returning to an old environment, or for reasons of physiology or personality. Although relapse may be related to depression or frustration, it also occurs with overconfidence. When a patient has made progress in treatment he often feels ready to handle difficult situations which he may not be ready for. Alcoholics Anonymous and Narcotics Anonymous use the term "slip" for a short relapse that is followed by return to treatment (or AA/NA).

relaxation training Any number of techniques that are used to achieve relaxation, usually concentrated in part on muscle tightness. Anxiety states may be contributed to by muscles that are in a state of chronic tension. A feedback loop exists between tensed muscles and psychological tensions. If muscle tension can be relaxed by biofeedback, self-hypnosis or progressive muscle relaxation exercises, it can reduce anxiety. Even when drugs are required for anxiety reduction, relaxation training improves the effect of the anti-anxiety drugs. Psychological techniques to effect thought content and images are also utilized.

Release Based in England, with headquarters in London, Release is a national 24-hour welfare and advice agency which specializes in urgent problems, particularly in the area of drugs and criminal law. Staffed by both professionals and volunteers, Release provides counseling, advice, education and information on drug use and abuse.

REM (rapid eye movement) One of the various stages of sleep, and the stage in which a person dreams. All the orders of the sleep cycle are biologically essential, and when deprived of REM a person may become hostile, irritable and anxious. Barbiturates and other sedatives suppress REM, and alcohol, at some consumption levels, also reduce REM sleep.

remission According to *Webster's Second International Dictionary,* remission is defined as "a temporary and incomplete subsidence of the force or violence of a disease or of pain." Since it is extremely difficult to say when someone is completely recovered from a drug abuse problem, the term "remission" is often used instead of the word "cured."

Repan® (Everett) A sedative and analgesic that contains 50 mg of butalbital (an intermediate-acting BARBITURATE), caffeine, phenacetin and acetaminophen. It is used for the relief of pain associated with nervous tension. Because it contains a barbiturate it can be habit-forming and dependence can occur. It is supplied in yellow tablets.

reserpine A DEPRESSANT and TRANQUILIZER. Reserpine is an alkaloid of RAUWOLFIA SERPENTINA and can also be synthesized. In the last 20 years, it and other Rauwolfia derivatives have been significant in the treatment of patients suffering from psychotic disorders.

Appearance and activity in the body: Reserpine is an odorless white, off-white or yellowish crystalline powder. It is insoluble in water, slightly soluble in alcohol and freely soluble in acetic acid.

Rapidly absorbed in the gastrointestinal tract and widely distributed throughout the body, reserpine crosses the placental barrier, appears in breast milk and is excreted in the urine and feces.

Dosage: Recommended dosages of reserpine range from 0.1–1.0 mg, with 0.5 mg daily suggested for hypertension. Administered intravenously, effects begin to manifest in one hour and last six to eight hours. The onset of effects with intramuscular injection is slower, but they can last 10–12 hours.

Effects: Reserpine's effects resemble those of Rauwolfia serpentina. The drug alleviates anxiety and tension without causing disequilibrium or loss of motor control. It lowers blood pressure. Reserpine does not have anticonvulsant or antihistaminic properties. Tolerance and dependence do not develop. The drug can induce depression, and its cardiovascular and central nervous system depressant effects continue after use of the drug has stopped.

Usage: Like Rauwolfia serpentina, reserpine is used to relieve hypertension. It is no longer used psychiatrically due to the very significant depression it can induce. It has a low abuse potential and is not available on the black market.

Availability: Reserpine is manufactured as tablets under the names Diutensen®, Diupres®, Hydropres®, Regroton® and Reserpine®, and in injectable form under the name Serpasil®.

reverse tolerance A condition in which the response to a certain dose of a drug increases with repeated use. In marijuana use, consistent users sometimes claim to require lesser amounts to achieve the desired effect. Some experts attribute this to more efficient smoking and earlier identification of the symptoms of marijuana intoxication than to reverse tolerance. However, the long period of persistence of TCH in the blood may result in circulation blood levels that are raised to noticeable levels by small additional ingested quantities, resulting in the appearance of reverse tolerance.

rhinophyma A skin condition of the nose characterized by swelling, redness and, often, broken capillaries. It is also called whiskey nose and is sometimes caused by excessive drinking over a prolonged period. (See also ACNE ROSACEA.)

Ritalin® (CIBA) A central nervous system stimulant that contains methylphenidate hydrochloride. It is used in the treatment of narcolepsy, Minimal Brain Dysfunction, and to treat patients showing withdrawn senile behavior. Tolerance can develop and it has a potential for abuse. Physical and psychological dependence can occur. Overdosage can result in agitation, tremors, convulsions and hallucinations. It is supplied in 5 mg pale yellow tablets; 10 mg pale green tablets; and 20 mg peach-colored tablets.

RNA Ribonucleic acid. RNA is a protein found in the chromosomes of all living cells and is one of the two main types of nucleic acid (the other is DNA). RNA plays an important part in the storage and replication of hereditary information and in protein synthesis.

Robitussin A-C® (Robins) An expectorant and cough suppressant that contains 100 mg of guaifenesin and 10 mg codeine phosphate. It can be habit-forming. It is supplied as an amber-colored elixir with 3.5% alcohol.

rock groups See MUSIC AND DRUGS.

role models, drug use by When prominent people, be they athletes, actors, musicians or singers, make headlines because of drug use, young people who are working hard to develop their own professional skills may become disillusioned. Some youngsters may then start to distrust their own ambitions and question their goals.

In recent years, prominent athletes, rock stars, actors and, on occasion, political and government leaders or their spouses have been found to be heavily dependent on drugs. Their notoriety may affect the public's behavior and attitude about alcohol and other drugs. Some of these celebrities go on to use their experiences to try to prevent others from experiencing the problems they have had. Perhaps the most noted—and notable—example of the latter is Betty Ford, wife of former President Gerald Ford. In 1982, the former First Lady established a treatment center in her name in Mirage, California. Mrs. Ford had courageously admitted to the American people that she was in recovery from alcohol and drug dependency. In 1989, Kitty Dukakis, wife of Democratic presidential candidate Michael Dukakis, governor of Massachusetts, revealed that she had entered a treatment program for alcoholism following her husband's national election defeat. Former Senator John Tower (R, Tex), on the other hand, with a reputation for hard drinking, never once admitted to serious drinking problems or alcoholism despite his rejection by the Senate Armed Services Committee as U.S. secretary of defense. Most committee members agreed that the major issue in their deliberations was Tower's drinking.

While considerable good may come from celebrities announcing that they have had alcohol or other drug problems and have dealt with them, the opposite effect may result from prominent personalities not able to deal with such problems.

rubbing alcohol A poisonous nondrinkable solution made with isopropyl alcohol rather than ethyl alcohol or ethanol. It is used externally for medicinal purposes.

rum fits (withdrawal seizures) Convulsive seizures of the grand mal type in which the patient loses consciousness. They are associated with withdrawal from alcohol and appear to develop in a minority of alcoholics. Rum fits often appear in clusters, and can start as early as 12 hours after reduced intake or abstinence. They may be associated with DELIRIUM TREMENS, the most serious form of withdrawal. Named for withdrawal seizures seen in sailors when ships ran out of rum. They are also seen with withdrawal from other sedatives, especially barbiturates.

S

sacred mushrooms See MUSHROOMS, SACRED.

Salvia divinorum A plant belonging to the mint family. Its leaves are chewed or brewed into a tea for their hallucinogenic effects.

Sanorex® (Sandoz) An anorectic that contains mazindol and is used for weight control. Its activity is similar to that of the AMPHETAMINES and tolerance can develop within a few weeks. It has a significant potential for abuse and psychological dependence can occur. Overdosage can result in restlessness, tremors and rapid respiration. It is supplied in 1 mg elliptical white tablets, and in 2 mg round white scored tablets.

San Pedro cactus *Trichocereus pachanoi.* A native of Peru and Ecuador, the stem of the plant is peeled and eaten or brewed into a beverage for its psychedelic effects.

Sansert® (Sandoz) A sympatholytic antagonist to epinephrine and similar drugs. Used for the prevention or reduction of intense, frequent vascular headaches, it causes vasodilation and increases the tone of alimentary tract muscles and other smooth muscle tissue. It contains 2 mg of methysergide maleate. Chemically related to LSD, in large amounts it can produce similar effects and therefore may have the potential for abuse. It is supplied in bright yellow tablets.

sassafras *Sassafras officinal albidum.* Though there are claims that it has psychedelic properties, none are known. The plant contains the toxic ether safrole.

S.B.P. Plus® (Lemmon) A sedative hypnotic that contains three BARBITURATES—50 mg sodium secobarbital, 30 mg sodium butabarbital, and 15 mg phenobarbital—along with 2.5 mg homatropine methylbromide. It is used to induce sleep. Tolerance can develop and both physical and psychological dependence can occur. The drug has a potential for abuse. It is supplied in orange scored tablets.

scheduled drugs See CONTROLLED SUBSTANCES ACT.

schizophrenia A mental disorder characterized by withdrawal from reality. It involves emotions, drive, behavior and thinking. Several drugs subject to abuse, such as alcohol, PCP, amphetamines, cocaine, and hallucinogens, can produce schizophrenic-like symptoms in an individual that can last for some time.

School Program to Educate and Control Drug Abuse See SPECDA.

scopolamine A belladonna alkaloid. It is a nonbarbiturate sedative hypnotic that has been used as a "truth serum." Large doses can produce hallucinations and are accompanied by adverse toxic reactions. It appears as scopolamine hydrobromide in several nonprescription sedatives such as Sominex.

Scotch broom *Cytisus scoparius,* a toxic plant containing CYTISINE.

Seconal® (Lilly) A sedative hypnotic that contains secobarbital sodium, a short-acting BARBITURATE. It is used for insomnia and for pre-operative sedation. It can be habit-forming and when taken with alcohol or other central nervous system depressants can have an additive effect. Both physical and psychological dependence can occur and it has a high potential for abuse. Overdosage can result in respiratory depression, depression of reflexes, lowered body temperature and coma. It is supplied as Seconal Sodium in 30 mg, 50 mg and 100 mg orange-red capsules. It is also supplied as an elixir, in suppositories, and in ampules and hyporets for injection.

Sedapap® (Mayrand) A sedative hypnotic that contains 648 mg of acetaminophen and 16 mg butabarbital (a short-acting BARBITURATE). It is generally used as an analgesic for arthritic and rheumatic conditions and for tension headache. It can be habit-forming and can produce dependence.

sedative A drug that causes somnolence and reduces the acuity of mental activity and alertness.

sedative hypnotic A type of sedative that has rapid action on the brain causing sleep or trance-like states. All sedatives depress the central nervous system.

sedativism Addiction to a sedative drug. The word is also used to describe excessive use of sedatives, or dual or multiple dependence on sedatives.

Sed-Tens Ty-Med® (Lemmon) A sedative hypnotic that contains 50 mg of amobarbital (an intermediate-acting BARBITURATE) and 7.5 mg homatropine methylbromide. It is used for spasm-tension, nausea and vomiting during pregnancy and for motion sickness. It can be habit-forming and has a significant potential for abuse. Physical and psychological dependence can occur. It is supplied in oblong tablets that are white with pink specks.

seizures See CONVULSIONS and GRAND MAL CONVULSIONS.

self-help groups See TREATMENT, REHABILITATION, ALCOHOLICS ANONYMOUS, NARCOTICS ANONYMOUS and HALFWAY HOUSES.

self-help book publishing Self-help books on themes such as alcoholism, drug addiction, child abuse, gambling, etc., are so prevalent now that, according to Edwin McDowell of the *New York Times,* "they have become known in publishing circles as 'bibliotherapy,' or the continuation of the recovery process through books." In fact, many bookstores have sections labeled "Recovery" or "Abuse" or "Addiction." Linda Grey, president of Bantam Books, thinks, "It speaks to something desperate in our society that there is such a demand."

It does indicate, among other things, that open and frank discussion of once-taboo subjects is now socially acceptable. McDowell says that publishing companies are hesitant to estimate sales figures or revenues generated by the explosion of recovery books, but that they are in the "tens of millions of dollars, out of a $5 billion trade book industry."

Dara Tyson, spokesperson for the huge Waldenbooks chain, says that recovery and addiction books are among the company's fastest-growing categories. She says the sale of audio cassettes based on these books has also greatly increased.

A number of the biggest-selling books about substance abuse and recovery have been and are still being published by recognized recovery groups and rehabilitation centers, including Alcoholics Anonymous; Comprehensive Care of Newport Beach, California; Fair Oaks Hospital of Summit, New Jersey, some of whose books are published by Villard Books, a division of Random House; and Health Communications of Pompano Beach Florida. Another big recovery book program is that of the Hazelden Foundation in Center City, Minnesota, which has been in existence for more than 40 years.

One of the most popular self-help books is *Adult Children of Alcoholics* by Janet Woititz (Health Communications, 1983). It has sold approximately 1.1 million copies in trade paperback. The book is an account of how to cope with alcoholic parents.

Edwin McDowell, "In Land of Addictions, Shelves Full of Solace," *New York Times,* June 21, 1989.

sensitivity A general term which may refer to an allergy or to a hypersensitivity to alcohol or a drug. It is sometimes used as an explanation of why an individual may be prone to addiction.

Serax® (Wyeth) A central nervous system depressant that contains the BENZODI-

AZEPINE oxazepam and is used to treat anxiety and tension. Tolerance can develop and it can produce physical and psychological dependence. When taken with alcohol or other CNS depressants it can have an additive effect. It is supplied in 10 mg pink and white capsules; 15 mg red and white capsules; 30 mg maroon and white capsules; and 15 mg yellow tablets.

serotonin A neurotransmitter, like adrenalin and acetylcholine, that transmits messages in the brain. There are numerous theories about the relationship of serotonin and LSD; LSD seems to either inhibit the action of serotonin or compete with it. One theory suggests that when serotonin is blocked, subconscious material takes over a person's consciousness and alters perception. Another theory suggests that when LSD inhibits serotonin's orderly manner of transmitting messages, the brain is overcome with so many messages that it cannot handle them. A third theory postulates that LSD monopolizes the monoamine oxidase enzymes which would otherwise be acting on serotonin to produce metabolites. Without normal metabolism there is a possibility that BUFOTENINE might develop as a byproduct, and bufotenine itself might produce the hallucinations. All of these theories, especially the latter, are still experimental and have yet to be proved, and the function of serotonin itself is still not completely understood. Serotonin activity is reduced in some types of depression.

Sernyl® An anesthetic and analgesic containing PHENCYCLIDINE that was used in veterinary medicine.

Services for Alcohol Abuse and Alcoholism Highlights report from the 1987 National Drug and Alcohol Treatment Unit Survey (NDATUS) conducted by the National Institute on Alcohol Abuse and Alcoholism (NIAAA) and the National Institute on Drug Abuse (NIDA). NDATUS is a voluntary survey designed to be a census of all known drug abuse and alcoholism treatment facilities in the United States. Data include types of services provided, client capacity and census on the point-prevalence data (October 30, 1987), client demographic characteristics, and funding amounts and sources. The report is available from National Clearinghouse for Alcohol and Drug Information.

sex Aphrodisiacs have traditionally been defined as substances which increase sexual drive and pleasure, and the search for effective aphrodisiacs has been going on since time immemorial. Folklore is full of references to foods, herbs, drinks, love potions and medications which are reputed to stimulate the sexual appetite. A modern redefinition of aphrodisiacs, however, takes into account the subjective pleasure experienced, not just changes in sex drive. Within this context, a number of drugs are believed to be aphrodisiacs. With a few exceptions, they do not directly affect the genitourinary tract but act on the brain in such a way as to relieve the user of social and sexual inhibitions, making him more apt to express sexual feelings. Research on the effects of such drugs has been limited by small numbers of sample subjects, lack of control groups, reliance on drug-dependent subjects who are in treatment, and an under-representation of women. It is also difficult to give an accurate account of the specific effects that drugs have on sexual behavior and response because they vary from person to person and from time to time in the same individual, depending on the dose, the expectations and desires of the user and the setting in which the drugs are used.

While small doses of alcohol depress the cerebral cortex and provoke uninhibited behavior, larger doses and chronic use adversely affect neural control and coordination and inhibit sexual performance. Hormonal changes due to large amounts of alcohol include increased breakdown and reduced synthesis of testosterone, the male sex hormone which influences the development of masculine secondary sex characteristics, and the lack of which makes sustained penile erection difficult. Alcohol may also stimulate the production of leutinizing hormones which increase sexual drive, leaving the male user in the frustrating position of being sexually stimulated though unable to perform. Male alcoholics sometimes suffer from testicular atrophy and impotence while female alcoholics may experience menstrual irregularity and even amenorrhea (absence of menses).

Low doses of barbiturates and other sedative hypnotics affect the higher cortical functioning of the brain: this reduces anxiety about sexual matters, allowing some individuals to express themselves more freely. Many people are extremely sensitive to even low doses of these drugs, however, and experience a decrease in sexual drive, excitement and orgasm. As with most other substances, high doses and chronic use interfere with sexual pleasure.

The use of STIMULANT drugs, especially amphetamines and cocaine, seems to increase sexual drive at low doses. In addition to enhancing sensory perception and heightening emotional response, this type of drug impedes the venous drainage of erectile tissue and thus prolongs sexual stimulation. (Cocaine is often applied directly to the genitals and prolongs intercourse, partly through anesthetization.) However, at higher doses they decrease sensation, causing delay or failure to ejaculate in men and failure to achieve orgasm in women. Some consistent abusers of stimulant drugs report disinterest and distaste for sexual activity, especially those who administer amphetamines or cocaine intravenously.

According to a 1982 research project conducted at the Haight-Ashbury Free Medical Clinic, a significant number of men and women who had suffered some sexual dysfunction prior to using heroin reported an improvement in sexual functioning when they first began to use the drug. The women reported an increase in relaxation and a lessening of inhibitions, and the men reported delayed ejaculation. Long-term use of heroin has a negative effect on sexual functioning, though, decreasing sexual drive and generally impairing performance. Menstrual irregularity, frigidity and reduced fertility are relatively common among female heroin addicts, while males commonly experience impotence due to decreased testosterone production. These problems occur not only with the use of heroin but also with other opiate drugs, but they usually rectify themselves after withdrawal from the drug.

The effect of hallucinogens on sexuality is inconsistent. Some users are completely disinterested in sex, consumed instead by more profound perceptions, while for others the pleasure of the sexual act is enhanced and heightened in intensity. Erotic feelings may remain on a mental level, with strong spiritual/mystical overtones, rather than on a physical level.

Marijuana and other cannabis drugs relax the part of the brain which records and stores social inhibitions. It can also enhance sensory awareness, stimulating sexual pleasure. The psychological effects of marijuana are not uniform, however, and the drug produces no direct physical reaction which stimulates sexual desire or performance. Like alcohol, large doses of cannabis affect the pituitary gland which may lower the testosterone level. In women it can reduce the production of follicle-stimulating and leutinizing hormones, temporarily reducing sexual drive.

One substance that has been used as an aphrodisiac for centuries is YOHIMBE, a crystalline alkaloid derivative isolated from the bark of the yohimbe tree, found in central Africa. While some researchers recognize this substance as an aphrodisiac, others believe that any increase in sexual powers is probably due to suggestion. Stimulant effects occur with high doses—which can also be highly toxic.

Two other substances which reputedly act as aphrodisiacs are methaqualone (Quaalude), and amyl nitrite, or "poppers." Although frequently used as sex drugs, neither directly affects sexual functioning. Methaqualone dilates the capillaries just below the surface of the skin, producing a tingling sensation which could, depending on the setting and the individual, enhance sexual enjoyment. Amyl nitrite is sold as an "incense" in HEAD SHOPS under a variety of brand names, such as Rush and Locker Room. A vasodilator, it produces a brief high and is alleged to subjectively prolong orgasm. Its relaxation of the anal sphincter also helps to explain its popularity among the gay population.

The research that has been done seems to substantiate the idea that when drugs are used infrequently and at low doses, they can increase the sex drive and enhance sexual pleasure. But pleasure and performance diminish when individuals move from low to high doses and from infrequent to chronic use.

sinsemilla Spanish word meaning "without seed" (*sin* meaning "without," and *semilla* meaning "seed"). Sinsemilla is the seedless flowering top of the female cannabis plant when it is unpollinated by the male plant. In 1988, sinsemilla accounted for 54% of the cannabis eradicated in the United States, up from the 26% eradicated in 1983, according to the Drug Enforcement Administration. The THC (tetrahydrocannabinol, the principal psychoactive chemical) content of sinsemilla can be four to six times that of ordinary marijuana. Samples analyzed by drug agents in 1987 averaged 7.67%, with some samples as high as 20%.

Maurice L. Hill, "Marijuana," *DEA Briefing Book,* Washington, D.C., April 17, 1989, 14.

Shiva See SIVA.

Siva A Hindu god who is credited with bringing cannabis to the world.

SK-Bamate® (Smith, Kline, & French) A central nervous system depressant that contains MEPROBAMATE and is used as a tranquilizer for states of anxiety and tension and to produce sleep. Physical and psychological dependence can occur and it has a significant potential for abuse. Overdosage can result in stupor, coma and respiratory collapse. It is supplied in 200 and 400 mg white tablets.

SK-65® (Smith, Kline & French) An analgesic containing 65 mg of PROPOXYPHENE hydrochloride, along with aspirin, phenacetin and caffeine, that is used for mild to moderate pain. Pharmacologically, it is similar to narcotics but does not compare in potency. Psychological and physical dependence can occur, and it has a potential for abuse. When taken with alcohol or other central nervous system depressants it can have an additive effect. Overdosage can result in respiratory depression, extreme somnolence progressing to coma and circulatory collapse. It is supplied in gray and white capsules.

skid row A hangout for alcoholics and vagrants. Also a term for a convalescent ward in a narcotics hospital. The term originated in Seattle, Washington, when the city's first sawmill was constructed in 1852. The set of tracks over which logs were hauled were called skids and the road was soon called Skid Row. As the area became dilapidated the term took on the meaning it has today.

skinning, skin popping Subcutaneous injection of a narcotic. This type of injection provides a slower onset of the effects of the drug. Intravenous injection (MAINLINING) results in immediate onset of effects. Addicts usually begin by sniffing a drug, move on to skin popping, and then to mainlining. Abcess formation and, rarely, tetanus are complications of subcutaneous use. (See also ADMINISTRATION.)

smoking See NICOTINE.

smuggling It has been estimated that over 90% of the illicit drugs consumed in the United States are produced in foreign countries. Supplies originate in diverse areas but basically they come from Latin America, Southeast Asia and Southwest Asia.

Shipment into the U.S. is accomplished in a variety of ways. Large-scale professional smugglers use commercial planes and ships for trafficking, but they also tend to use small private aircraft. A private plane is often used on a one-time only basis, to avoid detection, and landings are made at makeshift airfields in rural areas. Small boats are also used extensively for trafficking; often they are disguised as charter fishing craft. Drug trafficking networks are not always this sophisticated, however. Often they employ amateur couriers who are relatively safe from arrest. The couriers are well paid and use every conceivable way of concealing drugs, either on their person or among their possessions. Drugs have been found in suitcases with hollow bottoms; in toy dolls and animals; pressed thin and placed in books. Other innovative smugglers have been known to hide drugs in body cavities; soak their clothes in a drug solution; or swallow balloons or condoms filled with a drug and later excrete them.

Most illicit drugs are smuggled into the U.S. by way of New York City, Florida, California, and Texas. The Drug Enforcement Administration is responsible for developing interdiction intelligence and participation in cooperative efforts with the U.S. Customs Service, the U.S. Coast Guard, and the U.S. Border Patrol (part of the Immigration and Naturalization Service), which provide the principal anti-smuggling operations at ports of entry and along land and water borders. These cooperative efforts are having an effect. The South Florida Task Force, for example, which was established in 1982, seems to have reduced the flow into this key trans-shipment point. Although smugglers appear to have diversified their traffic lanes into Texas, the Carolinas and the Northeast, the Task Force has at least kept them off balance and similar task forces are now being established in these new areas as well.

In 1980 an estimated four metric tons of heroin were smuggled into the U.S.; about 60% was refined from opium cultivated in Southwest Asia, 25% from Mexico and the balance from Southeast Asia. Approximately 44 metric tons of cocaine, the top illicit income producer, were smuggled into America in 1980, nearly all of it from South America, particularly Colombia. The traffic in marijuana, which also generates tremendous profits (an estimated $24 billion), was also principally a Colombian operation (75%). The rest came from Jamaica (10%) and from Mexico (8%); the balance was home-grown domestic. There has also been an extensive increase in the amount of other dangerous drugs brought into the U.S. illegally—such as amphetamines, barbiturates and methaqualone—which have been diverted from legitimate sources or manufactured in highly sophisticated clandestine laboratories many of which are in Europe. A large quantity of these drugs are channeled through Colombia. In 1980 the Drug Enforcement Administration began to take note of large seizures of methaqualone tablets (loads of 1,000 or more pounds) which were arriving surreptitiously in the Southeast U.S. The seizures were often the result of citizen complaints about mysterious aircraft landing on rural roads. The nature of these seizures suggest that authorities are probably only seeing the tip of the iceberg in drug smuggling.

Today, two drugs—cocaine and heroin—constitute the most serious threat to the United States. Virtually all cocaine in the United States is derived from coca grown in Peru (60%), Bolivia (30%) and Colombia (10%). Eighty percent of the cocaine in this country is processed in Colombia and shipped by Colombian drug traffickers.

Opium and its most dangerous derivative, heroin, are smuggled into the United States from major producer countries such as Burma, Afghanistan, Iran, Laos, Pakistan and Thailand.

Colombia is the major source of marijuana sold in the United States, providing roughly 40% of the total United States supply. Mexico provides 25% of the marijuana smuggled into the U.S. and 10% comes from other countries. The remainder of the U.S. marijuana market is supplied by domestic cultivation, primarily in Oregon, California, Kentucky and Hawaii.

A subcommittee of the U.S. Senate recently estimated the global trade in illicit drugs at $500 billion a year. Of that, about $300 billion was earned by smugglers, dealers, wholesalers, pushers and money launderers—and roughly one-third of those drug sales are of cocaine.

snakeroot See RAUWOLFIA SERPENTINA.

sniff, sniffing To inhale a drug through the nostrils. Also referred to as SNORTING. (See also ADMINISTRATION.)

snort, snorting To inhale a drug through the nostrils. Also a term for COCAINE and HEROIN. (See also ADMINISTRATION.)

sober A term used for a person who is not under the influence of alcohol or other psychoactive drugs. It is also used to describe an alcoholic who is no longer drinking. To be considered "legally sober" a person must have a blood alcohol concentration (BAC) of 0.05% or less in some states. Such a person is not, however, as sober as one who has had nothing to drink.

sober up, sobering up To become detoxified after drinking. Other than kidney dialysis there is no known way of speeding up the detoxification process. A 150-pound person will usually take an hour to metabolize ¾ of an ounce of absolute alcohol.

social class There are different attitudes toward drug abuse among the various social classes in the United States. For example, it has been found that as education and income rise, there is also a rise in the frequency of drinking and in the number of drinkers. Upper-class groups generally have a more permissive attitude toward drinking and do not regard it as a moral problem. This attitude is taken less often by lower socioeconomic groups which generally contain a greater number of abstainers. Drinking patterns also differ among social classes: upper-class groups do more drinking in cocktail party settings and lower-class groups are more apt to drink in pub atmospheres. There is less of a difference in drinking patterns between men and women in upper social classes and they also appear less often in alcoholism statistics than men and women of lower-class groups. Often this is because their style of drinking is less visible and they are usually protected by people close to them who help to hide their alcoholism. In lower social classes individuals who drink in public places are more visible and therefore more likely to encounter trouble with the police. In the treatment of alcoholism, it has been shown that those in lower social classes drop out of therapy more often than those in the middle and upper classes. Despite a reputation as an elite or "high class" drug, cocaine has been a drug of abuse used by heroin addicts and others since the early 1900s.

In the 1960s due to ignorance and poor scientific method cocaine was considered non-addictive and innocuous by uninformed clinicians. Its use in visible celebrity circles increased and provided clear evidence of its addictive potential. Just as cocaine use was leveling off in college student and middle-class populations in the mid 1980s, the advent of smokable crack cocaine resulted in an epidemic increase in cocaine use and addiction, especially among young and poor minorities.

There are generally more heroin addicts among lower-class groups centered in the slums of metropolitan areas. This high incidence of abuse is attributed to the easy availability of narcotics "on the street," to feelings of defeat and helplessness in individuals living in these areas. Social class factors are also responsible for the relapse of rehabilitated addicts who return to their old neighborhoods. The goal of therapeutic communities such as SYNANON is to move ex-addicts into drug-free settings.

Amphetamine use does not seem to be centralized in any particular socioeconomic group. Amphetamines have been used by housewives (often as anorectics); by students studying for exams; by truck drivers who need to stay awake on long trips; and by athletes who wish to excel.

Inhalants are sometimes called the "scrubwoman's high" because of reports of cleaning women becoming high from the use of cleaning solvents. Although there may be some truth to this, the use of inhalants has spread to all social classes. Certainly glue sniffing among children has not been confined to those of a particular social class, although chronic inhalant abuse is found most often among Mexican American and American Indian youngsters.

Barbiturate use is generally found in middle- and upper-class individuals, particularly women. Anxiety, depression and insomnia were problems that were often simply accepted in past years. Today they may cause some people to rush to the doctor for treatment. Instead of trying to help a patient face and handle the problems that cause anxiety, many physicians will simply prescribe a barbiturate or a benzodiazepine as a sedative hypnotic.

LSD and other hallucinogens first became popular among college students and can thus be linked to middle and upper social classes. As they became readily available on the illicit market, their use spread to all social classes. This phenomenon is not limited to hallucinogens but is seen in the increased use of many other drugs.

Marijuana, one of the most (if not the most) abused drug in the United States, is certainly not restricted to a particular social class; whether because of its availability or its relatively inexpensive cost, its use is widespread. Marijuana use seems to be as prevalent among the teenage children of blue-collar workers as it is among college-educated adults in their 30s—it has been said that marijuana is "the opiate of the masses."

The reported high incidence of drug use among minority populations is sometimes the result of socioeconomics and sometimes not. Because black Americans and Hispanics often fall into the lower socioeconomic groups, social class certainly has a bearing on their drug use. According to the most recent statistics of the National Institute on Drug Abuse (NIDA), blacks, who now comprise 12% of the nation's population, account for 50% of hospital patients given emergency treatment for heroin abuse, including cases involving overdoses, 55% of those treated for cocaine and 60% of those treated for PCP. Drug use among the elderly may not necessarily be based on economics but may be rooted in feelings of loneliness and uselessness to society. The relationship of social class to addiction is very unclear. It is believed that social class may have its biggest effect on access to treatment and relapse factors and may therefore affect the course of addiction more strongly than the etiology.

social drinking The term usually refers to moderate drinking on social occasions. It is also used to refer to drinking in a way that is acceptable to a certain cultural group.

sociocultural etiological theories One of the three major groups of theories on the cause of addiction, the other two being theories based on physiological and psychological causes.

Sociocultural etiological theories focus on relationships between various factors in society. For example, different cultures set different standards for what is considered the appropriate use of alcohol; cultural support for the consumption of alcohol is high in France but among Jews, Moslems and Mormons there is a cultural proscription against the use or abuse of alcohol. This same pattern is true of countries that have a long tradition of opiate use (Iran, Pakistan) and countries with a long history of coca use (Peru, Bolivia), whereas the abuse of both cocaine (derived from coca) and opium are frowned upon in the United States.

Cultural stress factors may also contribute to the abuse of drugs, such as crises generated by external events; social instability; family patterns of drug use, and so on. Traumatic events seem to lead to heavy consumption, particularly among women.

Although sociocultural theories are receiving wide support as the cause of addiction, they are generally considered in conjunction with the two other etiological theories—physiological and psychological—since no one theory alone seems to completely explain the causes.

sodium butabarbital An intermediate-acting BARBITURATE usually used to produce sedation and sleep.

Solfoton® (Poythress) A sedative hypnotic that contains 16 mg of the long-acting BARBITURATE phenobarbital. It is used for sedation and to produce sleep. Both physical and psychological dependence can occur and it has the potential for abuse. Overdosage can result in respiratory depression and coma. It is supplied in pale green uncoated tablets; light pink sugar-coated tablets; and yellow and brown capsules.

solvents See VOLATILE HYDROCARBONS and INHALANTS.

Sominex® An over-the-counter (OTC) sleep aid that can be potentially harmful because it contains SCOPOLAMINE. Some of the significant side effects of scopolamine are blurred vision, confusion, delirium and heart effects. Scopolamine is generally used to dry up secretions and there is no evidence that the amount in Sominex can be an aid to sleep. In 1975 the Food and Drug Administration recommended that scopolamine be removed from sleep aids but thus far no action has been taken.

South Africa Dagga (cannabis) has long been used in South Africa, particularly among the Bantu people. The South African mine workers often use dagga as an energizer during their work day. With the exception of alcohol, the abuse of other drugs was practically unknown until the late 1960s when it appeared that the age of narcotics—and stimulants and depressants—had arrived.

In 1969 the government appointed a committee of inquiry to investigate the extent of drug use. It was found that there was increasing experimentation among young people, and in 1971 the Substances and Rehabilitation Centres Act was passed. It provided penalties for drug dealing, and use of or possession of dangerous drugs. It also established a National Advisory Board on Rehabilitation Matters which was instructed to plan and coordinate measures to combat drug use and provide treatment for those persons dependent on drugs. The act also provided for the establishment of both government and private rehabilitation centers and their inspection. Any drug-dependent person who voluntarily desires treatment may apply for admission to a center but the 1971 act also provided for compulsory treatment in cases where a magistrate decided it was necessary. The provisions of the act apply not only to the abuse of dangerous drugs but also to alcohol abuse which has long been recognized as a problem in South Africa.

Along with the establishment of treatment centers, the government is also establishing national drug education programs. Voluntary welfare organizations are also working on the drug problem. The most active organization is the South African National Council on Alcoholism and Drug Dependence (SANCAD).

Spanish broom *Spartium junceum,* a toxic plant containing CYTISINE.

SPECDA Acronym for New York City's School Program to Educate and Control Drug Abuse. SPECDA is a cooperative program of the New York City Board of Education and the Police Department. Police help provide classes and presentations on drug abuse while simultaneously concentrating on enforcement efforts within a two-block radius of schools to create a drug-free corridor. For further information contact: Captain Eugene Burke, New York City Police Department, One Police Plaza, Room 200, New York, NY 10038. Telephone: (212) 374-5112.

Special Action Office for Drug Abuse Prevention (SAODAP) An agency established by the Office of the Presidency in 1972 to review and evaluate the functions and policies of all government agencies involved in the area of drug abuse, and to establish policies and provide direction necessary to properly coordinate government efforts. It is no longer in existence.

spirits A term commonly used to refer to the alcoholic essence of a fermented substance. It is also a synonym for alcoholic beverages, as distinguished from the many varieties of chemical alcohols and denatured ethanols which are nondrinkable. It refers to distilled beverages rather than beer or wine.

Sports Drug Awareness Program Started by then Attorney General William French Smith in June 1984, this program was developed in conjunction with the National High School Athletic Coaches Association, the International Association of Chiefs of Police, the National Football League and the NFL Players Association to provide 5.5 million high school athletes with drug abuse prevention information. Additional organizations that have since joined in the program include: the Federal Bureau of Investigation, the Office of Juvenile Justice and Delinquency Prevention, the National Basketball Association, National Hockey League, Major League Baseball, the National Federation of Parents for Drug Free Youth, the National Association of Broadcasters, the National Federation of State High School Associations and the Sporting Goods Manufacturers Association. The goal of the program is to prevent drug abuse among school-age youth, with special emphasis on the role of the coach and the student-athlete (there are some 48,000 men and women coaches in 20,000 high schools across the country who can, the idea goes, help reach the 5.5 million student-athletes). Each participating entity involved uses its unique constituency by directing prevention information and messages toward the 57 million young people now in kindergarten through college. Contact: Ronald J. Taethric, Demand Reduction Section, Office of Congressional and Public Affairs, Drug Enforcement Administration, 1405 I Street, N.W., Washington, DC 20537. Telephone: (202) 786-4096.

U.S. Department of Justice, Drug Enforcement Administration, *Demand Reduction Bulletin* "Sports Drug Awareness Program," August 1986.

sports and drugs The use of drugs by competing athletes dates back a hundred years or more; then the popular drugs to use for increased performance were alcohol and caffeine. Today the use of drugs by athletes is far more widespread and while any number of drugs are used, the most popular are amphetamines, steroids, cocaine and alcohol. Drug use is not limited to professional athletes: it has also been found on both the college and high school levels.

The reasons for drug use vary. Amphetamines are taken to diminish pain or fatigue, to increase strength and endurance, to provide greater concentration, intensify aggressiveness and the desire to achieve. Steroids are taken during training in order to gain weight and increase body mass. Most other drugs are used during actual competition.

There has been a recent campaign among athletic organizations, particularly the National Football League and the International

Olympic Committee, to eliminate the use of drugs. Olympic contestants are aware that they will be tested for evidence of drugs during the Games; in professional football the testing is usually sporadic and players are never sure when they will be tested. The use of drugs by football players was prohibited in 1972. Up to that time it had been common practice for team doctors and trainers to hand out amphetamines and a 1970 survey had shown that 60% of National Football League players took the drugs on a regular basis. Although heavy drug use was violently denied by football officials, a survey taken a year after use was prohibited suggested that many players were continuing to take amphetamines and turning to illicit sources when they were unable to obtain them legally. The testing controversy continues today with many players protesting the practice as an "invasion of privacy."

Amphetamine use by athletes was first reported in the 1940s. They were used by top athletes primarily in endurance sports such as cycling, track, swimming and football. Amphetamines increase respiratory flow, the metabolic rate and cardiac output. They also increase alertness and intensify aggressiveness. In moderate to large doses, they also have an analgesic effect. This ability to relieve pain and increase drive and strength makes amphetamines extremely sought after by athletes involved in contact sports. There are adverse reactions to the use of amphetamines, however: irritability, restlessness, insomnia and impotence, not to mention the possibility of dependence. Amphetamine deaths have also occurred in sports, usually as a result of the drug's cardiovascular effect in combination with heat and overexertion.

The International Olympic Committee defines "doping" as using substances alien to the body in abnormal amounts or by abnormal methods with the aim of taking unfair advantage during competition. If such a substance is used to treat an illness, the fact must be reported. Testing for drugs in Olympic competitions has become mandatory and during the IX Pan American Games held in Caracas, Venezuela, in August 1983, tests proved positive in a number of cases. The presence of steroids was found in eight weightlifters, one an American, and they were stripped of their medals. When this was revealed, 12 U.S. track athletes left the games to return home. The reason for their departure and withdrawal from the Games was not given and it is unsure at this time if it was a protest move or fear of involvement. All competitors were aware they would be tested but the equipment used was so sophisticated and advanced that for the first time it was possible to detect the use of steroids up to a year previously.

Ben Johnson, the Canadian sprinter who set a record at the 1988 Summer Olympics in South Korea, was ultimately disqualified for using anabolic steroids. In June 1989 he admitted for the first time that he had used performance-enhancing drugs, starting as early as 1981.

The aim of an athlete who takes steroids is muscle hypertrophy. Steroids increase body mass because they improve nitrogen utilization and increase the appetite, though some authorities suggest that fluid retention rather than weight gain actually occurs. Steroids can have adverse reactions on liver function, can diminish libido and cause testicular atrophy along with hypertension. Steroids are generally taken during training periods and not just before a competition.

Testing at the Pan American Games was conducted by a highly advanced laboratory in East Germany (which also has the approval of the Olympics Committee) and involved a two-step procedure. First a urine sample was taken immediately after a competitor had taken part in an event. If the test was positive, the athlete's national Olympic Committee was notified and a second sample was taken in the presence of a committee member. If this test also proved positive, the Pan American committee was notified and then had to decide on a course of action. The U.S. Olympic Committee has endorsed the testing and has announced that it will cooperate with the testing procedure in the future.

Narcotics are sometimes used by athletes when there is a need to perform in spite of pain. But the problem appears to be growing and is a matter of considerable concern by league officials and club owners in pro baseball, basketball and football. Alcohol, tranquilizers and other sedatives are sometimes abused because they have a calming effect on tension, anxiety and tremors. When they are employed it is usually with a certain amount of caution so that oversedation is avoided.

In a June 1982 *Sports Illustrated* article, former Miami Dolphin, New Orleans Saint and San Diego Charger, Don Reese, described in graphic detail the course of his growing dependence on cocaine during his career with the National Football League. Stating that cocaine "controls and corrupts" professional football, Reese told the painful story of how he acquired an expensive habit and how it involved daily freebasing with other players and memory blackouts during games. Cocaine was readily available to NFL players, he said, not only from dealers who sometimes attend practices but also from respected veteran players.

Typical reactions to Reese's confession included accusations that he must be mentally unbalanced to have fallen prey to such a habit and that, accordingly, his allegations must be dismissed. Nevertheless, insiders' reports reveal that as many as 60% of pro football players may regularly snort and freebase cocaine. Coaches and players consistently deny the existence of any drug problem yet continue to oppose urine tests to detect the presence of drugs. The result, as Reese points out, is that "what you see on the tube Sunday afternoon is a lie. When players are messed up, the game is messed up. The outcome of games is dishonest when playing ability is impaired."

In June 1986, Len Bias, star basketball forward at the University of Maryland died of a cocaine reaction the day after he signed a lucrative professional contract with the Boston Celtics. Don Rogers of the Cleveland Browns professional football team died the same month of a similar drug overdose. In his 1987 autobiography, *L.T.: Living on the Edge* (written with David Falker), Lawrence Taylor, the legendary New York Giants linebacker, told of using drugs, particularly cocaine, and crack, during the 1988 football season.

Drug abuse in baseball drew national attention in 1984 and 1985 with a sensational criminal trial of players with the Pittsburgh Pirates of the National League. The then commissioner of baseball, Peter Ueberroth, proposed mandatory periodic random drug testing for major league players.

During the 1987 season, the New York Mets' star pitcher, Dwight Gooden, one of the most successful pitchers in the majors, returned to the game after a program of drug therapy at the Smithers Drug Rehabilitation Center. During spring training that year, Gooden had failed a routine urine test. He has since waged a successful battle against drug dependence and is back pitching for the Mets.

Under Commissioner Ueberroth's testing program, seven athletes were suspended in the 1986 season. They were then allowed to return to play only if they donated 10% of their 1986 salaries to a substance abuse prevention program, agreed to random drug testing and did 200 hours of drug-related community service. Since that time, several baseball teams have moved toward comprehensive drug-prevention and drug-testing programs. Some critics have attacked Ueberroth's drug-testing plan on grounds that its effectiveness is weakened or destroyed if results are made known to a third party. They believe for testing to help the user, findings must be kept confidential. Otherwise, the theory goes, the individual (player) loses trust in the process. Other skeptics say baseball's drug-testing plan places all the emphasis on testing and eliminating drug users; it shows little or no concern for helping players who are "doing drugs." Still other critics say that any attempt to rehabilitate drug users is destined to fail if the drug-testing program is handled like a criminal procedure.

Enormous profits are generated by sports events in the United States. While sports fans encourage and demand victory and condone aggressiveness from athletes, it is not difficult to understand why competitors use drugs to achieve what the public wants. Nor is it hard to see why owners, trainers and officials in the various sports want to please the public. Until competitors and management are educated to the dangers of drug use, it will probably continue and grow worse.

Gilda Berger, *Drug Testing* (New York: Franklin Watts, 1987), 109–113.

Edward F. Dolan Jr., *Drugs in Sports* (New York: Franklin Watts, 1986), 74–75, 102–107.

spouse abuse Drug abuse and family violence are clearly connected, particularly violence involving drinking. Although it is a significant problem in the United States, family violence is often ignored, perhaps because of an unwillingness on the part of society to interfere in private lives.

While women are more often seriously injured because of their physical disadvantage, men or women may be the aggressor in cases of spouse abuse. It is estimated that there are some 1.7 million such assaults a year. The FBI's *Uniform Crime Report* indicates that 25% of all murders are committed within families and of these half are spouse killings. Women are just as likely to kill their spouses as men, and they often cite abuse as the motivation.

In what often becomes a vicious circle, spouse abuse is related to child abuse (see CHILDREN OF DRUG DEPENDENT INDIVIDUALS). A man may beat his wife, for example, and she may, in turn, take out her anger and resentment on the children. In addition, a husband or wife who abuses his or her spouse may also abuse the children.

Violent behavior toward spouses and children often emerges and is intensified when chemical dependency is present in a family. Chemical abuse and family violence are highly correlated statistically and are major co-risk factors. Referral for one problem should always result in careful evaluation for the other. They appear to be mutually casual and to complicate and to intensify each other as problems. Drug use and family violence can also be part of a cycle that repeats itself from generation to generation: children from abusive families learn coping patterns (the use of drugs and then violence to resolve problems and reassert control) from the same individuals who teach them to love. In this way, loving and hitting become linked in their minds.

American society in general tolerates a high level of violence and perhaps because of this acceptance victims often hide the fact that they have been abused. A fear of reprisal or lack of understanding by the community is particularly common among women. Feelings of helplessness and despair, along with guilt that she may have failed in a marriage, may lead a wife to feel that she has gotten what she deserves. Women are also likely to remain in an abusive situation because of the fear of divorce and its social and economic impact.

It had been suggested that abused wives have a masochistic streak that keeps them with abusive husbands. There is no evidence for this idea and in fact when reporting abuse is encouraged and safe shelter provided, more women leave abusive relationships and seek help from health care and law enforcement personnel.

Initial violence between spouses can lead to more violence. If the abused spouse does not seek help it is taken as a sign of acquiescence and generally leads to more violence.

It has only been recently that women have tended to report spouse abuse to the police. In the last few years alternative help has also been made available to abused women through various women's centers and "hotlines" for battered wives. Men are much less likely than women to report abuse for reasons of pride. It has been estimated that 280,000 men are beaten by their wives each year. Although the number is small compared to the estimated six million abused wives, it is nevertheless significant.

Violence can also occur in more subtle forms; a drug user can emotionally neglect or psychologically abuse his or her family to such an extent that it causes severe damage. The results of emotional or mental abuse can be as destructive as physical abuse.

Alcohol is acknowledged to be the major drug leading to spouse abuse in the U.S. According to one estimate, 80% of all cases of family violence include drinking—either before, during or after the incident (Jerry Flanzer, *The Vicious Circle of Alcoholism and Family Violence,* Alcoholism 1, No. 3, Jan./Feb. 1981, pp. 30–32). Both moderate and problem drinkers are more frequently involved in incidences of violence than light drinkers. Treatment programs designed to help victims of battering are frequently not capable of addressing alcohol problems. In addition, alcohol counselors themselves do not always know about the mechanics of family violence. Since the two problems are closely linked addiction treatment programs are becoming increasingly sensitive to issues of physical abuse and family violence programs are becoming more sensitive to addiction issues.

spree A period of use, particularly one of prolonged excessive use and usually associated with addiction.

Stadol® (Bristol) A narcotic agonist-antagonist that contains butorphanol tartrate. It is a potent analgesic, equivalent to morphine, and is used for moderate to severe pain. It has a potential for abuse and dependency can develop. Because of its antagonist properties it should not be given to patients with a physical dependence on narcotics and it is not recommended for those who have a history of drug abuse. Adverse reactions to Stadol include sedation, nausea and sweating. Overdosage can result in respiratory depression. It is supplied in vials for intravenous and intramuscular injection. Onset of effects when administered intravenously is within 10 minutes and duration of effects is three to four hours.

Statobex® (Lemmon) An anorectic that contains phendimetrazine tartrate and is used for weight control. Tolerance can develop within a few weeks and because it is chemically and pharmacologically related to the AMPHETAMINES it has the potential for abuse. Psychological dependence and social dysfunction can occur. Overdosage can result in restlessness, tremors, rapid respiration and a confused hallucinogenic state. It is supplied as Statobex, oblong green tablets of 35 mg; and Statobex-D, 70 mg tablets that are white with green specks, and 70 mg capsules that are green and white.

status epilepticus Repetitive convulsive seizures which follow each other with no intervening periods of consciousness. It can result from rapid withdrawal from anticonvulsant or sedative drugs, or it may be spontaneous. Status epilepticus is also possible during use of amphetamines and cocaine. In the case of grand mal status epilepticus the seizures may persist for hours or even days and can be fatal.

stereotypy Persistent and often mechanical repetition of senseless words or acts. It is characteristic of schizophrenics and is often seen in amphetamine, phencyclidine and cocaine abusers and alcoholics.

steroids See SPORTS AND DRUGS.

stimulants Drugs that stimulate the central nervous system and increase the activity of the brain or spinal cord. They produce greater energy, increase alertness and produce a feeling of euphoria. Amphetamines, antiobesity agents and cocaine are highly abused stimulants. Caffeine and nicotine are also classified as stimulants but have a lesser effect on the body.

stomach The stomach is the hollow muscular organ located between the esophagus and the upper small intestine (duodenum). Its function include storing and diluting ingested food, secreting gastric juices containing enzymes and other substances important to digestion and nutrition, and contracting to further hasten the breakdown of food through agitation.

Sedatives depress the entire metabolic and digestive process. The abuse of alcohol compounds this general disruption by directly damaging the stomach because it increases hydrochloric acid secretion. Factors such as stress and malnutrition often accompany alcoholism and can also contribute to its deleterious effects.

Some 20–25% of ingested alcohol is absorbed in the stomach, and the rest in the duodenum. The rate at which the stomach empties its contents (motility) is extremely important in alcohol absorption and effect. A patient who has had part of his stomach removed becomes intoxicated very quickly on small amounts of alcohol because of quick absorption by the duodenum. Conversely, the presence of food can slow alcohol absorption in the stomach and thus diminish the drug's effect.

Small doses (dilutions of up to 10% alcohol) stimulate salivation and gastric secretion and increase motility. Large doses anesthetize the stomach, irritate the organ's lining and affect the brain to reduce appetite. High concentrations of alcohol can also cause spasms of the pylorus, the opening between the stomach and the duodenum, which may manifest as retching. Alcohol also reduces motility, which causes acid to accumulate and results in hyperacidity.

Acute and chronic gastritis, inflammation of the stomach and its mucous membrane, frequently develops as a result of heavy drinking and is commonly evidenced by nausea, vomiting, diarrhea and belching. Acute gastritis can subside after a few week's abstinence but more severe cases are persistent. Membrane erosion, possibly culminating in ulceration, can occur with long-term alcohol abuse. The alcoholic also risks stomach hemorrhage, particularly when alcohol and a drug such as aspirin are combined. Hemorrhage is especially dangerous in the presence of alcoholic gastritis and peptic ulcer since malnutrition may impair coagulation.

Stimulants resemble alcohol in their effect on the stomach. Abuse of this kind of drug increases gastric acid secretion which, in turn, increases the risk of ulcers. Some individuals are so sensitive to caffeine that even relatively small amounts of coffee can make them nauseous and induce vomiting.

Narcotic drugs generally slow digestion by reducing gastric secretion and decreasing motility. Heroin can induce spasms in the stomach's smooth muscle; in fact, addicts often exhibit increased muscular tone in the smooth muscle of the stomach, duodenum and intestines. Opiates produce constipation and are used to treat diarrhea. Heroin addicts are also susceptible to viral infections such as tetanus, which often involves gastrointestinal bleeding. Hypermotility, gastrointestinal cramps, nausea, vomiting and anorexia are symptoms of opiate withdrawal.

Synthetic derivatives of belladonna, stramonium (Jimson weed), and henbane—anticholinergics employed for centuries as poisons and as major components of witches' brews—have been used to reduce gastric secretion and peristalsis in the treatment of gastritis and peptic ulcer. Psychedelic drugs do not seem to share this effect; instead they sometimes cause nausea and vomiting.

Cannabis derivatives are being used medically to control the nausea, vomiting and anorexia associated with chemotherapy. A few reports of inflammation of the stomach after long-term heavy use of strong cannabis preparations have emerged from Eastern countries, but it is not known if this is due to the cannabis use or to diet or other factors. There is little evidence that marijuana or other cannabis products have any direct effects on the stomach.

Sidney Cohen, *The Substance Abuse Problems* (New York: Haworth Press, 1981).

Frederick G. Hofmann, *A Handbook on Drug and Alcohol Abuse* (New York: Oxford University Press, 1977).

Esteban Mezey, "Effects of Alcohol on the Gastrointestinal System," *Practice of Medicine*, Vol. VII, Ch. 36 (Hagerstown, Md.: Harper & Row, 1970).

Ralph W. Richter, ed., *Medical Aspects of Drug Abuse* (New York: Harper & Row, Publishers, Inc. 1975).

stramonium An alkaloid found in the DATURA plant. It has deliriant effects similar to BELLADONNA, which belongs to the same plant family.

stroke Research by Lois Caplan, M.D., Tufts University, Boston, reveals that using common "street drugs," can increase the risk of stroke dramatically, sometimes after just one dose. Most often linked to strokes are cocaine in any form or dose, heroin and stimulants that come in pill form but that are crushed up and injected.

Stroke occurs when sudden increases in blood pressure rupture blood vessels; particles from crushed pills lodge in capillaries; talc used to dilute drugs overstimulate the immune system and injures blood vessels; blood vessels spasm and shut off the brain's blood flow.

Tim Friend, "Street Drugs Can Raise Stroke Risk," Health and Behavior, *USA Today*, January 19, 1989, 5D.

strychnine An extremely dangerous and toxic central nervous system stimulant that affects the spinal cord first and the cerebrum last. Though rarely used today, it can increase muscle tone in gastrointestinal stasis, debility and paralysis. Its value has been questioned because of the narrow margin between its therapeutic and toxic action.

subculture, drug An alternative life-style that centers around knowledge of drugs, use of drugs and obtainability of drugs. Members of a drug subculture share norms of behavior that are disapproved by the general culture, which gives them a certain respect and admiration in the eyes of adherents.

Sublimaze® (Janssen) A narcotic analgesic that contains 0.05 mg fentanyl and whose activity is similar to that of MORPHINE and meperidine, but it is much faster acting and its effect does not last as long. It is used as a pre- and post-operative sedation supplement. A potent analgesic, it has a high potential for abuse and dependency can occur. It is supplied in 2 ml and 5 ml ampules for injection.

substance abuse A general term used to describe the abuse of drugs.

Substance Abuse Narcotics Education Program (SANE) A law enforcement and education effort similar to PROJECT DARE, in which police officers help provide classes and presentations on drug abuse. Contact: Lieutenant Mark Klugman, Los Angeles County Sheriff's Department, SANE Unit, 11515 S. Colima Road, Bldg. D111, Whittier, CA 90604. Telephone: (213) 946-7263.

Substance Abuse Treatment Programs and National Cocaine Hotline Set up by Dr. Mark Gold, noted drug abuse authority, to provide 24-hour information and referral services for drug users and parents. Counselors provide guidance and referral to local public and private treatment centers and family learning centers. Contact: Mark Gold, M.D., Cocaine Hotline, 1-800-COCAINE, Fair Oaks Hospital, One Prospect Street, Summit, NJ 07901. Business telephone: (201) 522-7000.

succinylcholine A central nervous system depressant that acts as a skeletal muscle relaxant during surgery.

suicide The intentional taking of one's own life, suicide is generally a result of a depressive state. But there are "accidental" as well as intentional suicides, and these may result from a synergistic effect when depressant drugs are taken together. Because the combination of drugs results in confusion, an individual may take additional doses of a drug without concern for or memory of previous doses.

Taking a barbiturate overdose is a common manner of attempting suicide, particularly among women. Barbiturates are most often prescribed for insomnia, and depression and insomnia often go hand-in-hand. In a non-tolerant person a small amount can constitute a lethal dose, consequently even when doctors are careful not to prescribe more than two week's supply at one time, it is no guarantee against suicide attempts. Accidental deaths from barbiturates combined with alcohol (both sedative drugs) are even more common than planned suicides using just barbiturates.

The benzodiazepine derivatives, which are prescribed as tranquilizers, are very often used in suicide attempts. Valium, a minor tranquilizer, is one of the most widely prescribed drugs. The lethal dose of Valium alone is not known, and individuals ingesting 200 times the average dose have survived. Successful suicides involving Valium are usually a result of its being combined with another depressant.

Attempted or achieved suicides from amphetamines and hallucinogens are generally not the result of an overdosage of a particular drug, but are due to a psychotic state induced by taking the drug in the first place. When an individual's controls are reduced and a paranoid reaction sets in, he or she may impulsively attempt suicide. Accidental suicides have occurred when a person under the effects of a hallucinogen, particularly LSD, imagined that he could stop traffic or fly through the air.

Women are known to have a higher *attempted* suicide rate than men (they are also acknowledged, as a group, to experience depression more often) but men have a higher *completed* suicide rate. Among alcoholic women the number of attempted suicides far exceeds the number among the general female population, and completed suicides among female alcoholics is 23 times that of the general population.

Studies have shown that addicts are at a particularly high risk of attempting suicide, and those who commit suicide have attempted to kill themselves more often than nonaddicts who commit suicide. Studies have also shown that between 15% and 64% of those who attempt suicide and up to 80% of successful suicides were drinking at the time of the event. Combining alcohol with other drugs is probably responsible for a large number of suicides and accidental deaths.

Because depression is usually the cause of suicide, individuals undergoing post-withdrawal depression symptoms from phencyclidine, amphetamines, cocaine, or alcohol, are watched very closely.

Glen Evans and Norman L. Farberow, Ph.D., *The Encyclopedia of Suicide* (New York: Facts On File, 1988).

Robert O'Brien and Morris Chafetz, M.D., *The Encyclopedia of Alcoholism* (New York: Facts On File, 1983).

supra-additive An interaction of drugs (synergistic or potentiating) in which the effect of two drugs in combination is greater than it would be if the effects were ADDITIVE.

Supreme Court drug decisions, U.S. In 1966, the Supreme Court ruled that compulsory blood tests are bodily searches. It said that the Fourth Amendment applied to such searches and that a compulsory blood test could be conducted only if there is "a clear indication that in fact . . . evidence will be found.''

Prisons are the only institutions that have the Supreme Court's permission to conduct blanket searches. The decision stemmed from a 1984 federal case in New York's Southern District Court—*Storms* v *Coughlin.* The court determined that the constitutional right concerning privacy of prisoners gives way when it conflicts with prison security needs.

The only Supreme Court decision concerning the right to search students in public school involved a Piscataway, N.J. student. In *New Jersey* v. *T.L.O.,* January 1985, a teacher reported a female student found smoking cigarettes in the girls' room. The student was in violation of a school rule permitting smoking in designated areas only. The girl denied the charge and the assistant vice-principal thereupon opened the student's purse and discovered a package of rolling papers. Suspecting possession of marijuana cigarettes, or ''joints,'' the assistant vice-principal then searched the student's purse and uncovered evidence of drug dealing. The Supreme Court stated that the Fourth Amendment prohibits unreasonable searches and seizures in public schools. But what constitutes ''reasonable'' depends upon the context in which a search is conducted. The assistant vice-principal was deemed within his rights in searching the purse, because he had reasonable grounds to believe the student had ''violated or [was] violating either the law or the rules of the school.''

In another matter involving drugs, on December 1, 1986, the Supreme Court refused to hear a challenge brought by jockeys concerning the requirement that they submit to random testing. Some experts maintain this ruling doesn't uphold mandatory drug testing and believe that the question one day must be heard and settled by the Supreme Court.

In March 1989, the Supreme Court upheld, by a 7-to-2 vote, the constitutionality of government regulations that require railroad crews involved in accidents to submit to prompt urinalysis and blood tests. The justices also upheld, 5 to 4, the legality of urine tests for U.S. Customs Service employees seeking drug enforcement posts. The decisions could help the Bush Administration in its effort to increase urine testing in the workplace.

A 1986 executive order by former President Reagan authorized drug testing throughout the federal government. To date, approximately 50 agencies have moved to start such programs. Thus far, some 14 challenges have been brought and are currently making their way through the appellate courts. Opponents of government screening tests argue that it is an ''unreasonable search,'' prohibited by the Fourth Amendment.

Some legal scholars are concerned with the court direction in future cases. ''Will it be limited to safety-sensitive positions or broadened to include any public employee who is a role model?'' asks Michigan Law Professor Yale Komisar. Other experts doubt that the Supreme Court will uphold random drug tests for a broad spectrum of government employees.

Gilda Berger, *Drug Testing* (Franklin Watts: New York, 1987).

Alain Sanders, ''A Boost for Drug Testing'' *Time,* April 3, 1989, 62.

Surital® (Parke-Davis) A rapid, ultra-short-acting barbiturate containing thiamylal sodium that is used as an intravenous anesthetic. It may be habit-forming but the rapid onset and brief duration of action make it undesirable for purposes of abuse.

susceptibility General term indicating higher than average risk for a condition. With respect to alcoholism, a genetic factor has been demonstrated to contribute to susceptibility. Previously held ideas about character defects causing addiction have not been supported by research.

Sweden As in most European countries, alcohol is the most widely abused substance in Sweden. There are some 300,000 to 400,000 alcoholics in a population of more than eight million. According to Thomas Nordegren of the nation's Committee on Health Education, an average of 16 people die each day as a direct result of their addiction. In comparison, Sweden has 50,000 regular users of cannabis, and 15,000 "mainliners" who inject narcotic drugs (especially heroin) directly into the bloodstream. Opium, morphine, cocaine, amphetamines, tranquilizers and solvents are also abuse problems in Sweden.

The Brewers' Association of Canada published statistics in 1986 showing that out of 32 selected countries Sweden is 20th in terms of consumption of "pure alcohol." The average consumption per capita (for those aged 15 and above) was 2.6 liters, slightly greater than the amount consumed in neighboring Norway (1.7 liters), and slightly greater than the amounts consumed in Denmark (1.9 liters), but less than the United States (3.6 liters). Sweden's total alcohol consumption per person 15 years and over in 1984 was 6.4 liters. (Note: 1 liter equals 1.06 quarts.) Since alcoholism is by far the greatest drug abuse problem in Sweden, one can see why the country has taken some effective measures to cope with it.

Since the 19th century Sweden's strong voluntary temperance movement has received a good deal of government assistance and approval. Some 400 temperance societies were in existence before the beginning of the 20th century. Between 1922 and 1955 the government operated a passbook rationing system to hold down the alcohol consumption rate. During that time men over 25 years of age were entitled to purchase up to three liters of spirits per month, while women of the same age could obtain the same amount over a three-month period. Rationing was enforced by the adoption in 1922 of the Bratt system under which a state-owned company, Vin-Spritcentralen, was given control of all alcohol sales. This plan was adopted immediately after an all-out prohibition scheme was vetoed.

Parliament abandoned the rationing system in 1955 and transferred the burden of restricting alcohol use to the National Tax Board. Taxes were imposed according to the alcohol content of a beverage. (Today taxes on alcoholic beverages account for about 7% of the state income tax.) The state-controlled company, Systembolaget, was given a monopoly on the retailing of alcoholic beverages, while Vin-Spritcentralen became responsible for the importation and wholesale trade.

By the 1960s other drug abuse problems had arisen. The intravenous injection of central nervous system stimulants and opiates, the smoking of marijuana and hashish, the sniffing of solvents (mostly by young teenagers) and the abuse of amphetamines and tranquilizers (which had hit the market in the 1930s) were all prevalent. Parliament formed a tough plan of action in 1968 to cope with both alcohol and drug abuse. Police and customs units were beefed up to keep drugs not only off the streets but out of the country. Stricter penal laws were instituted and since Swedes are generally not producers of drugs, but rather buyers, dealers and couriers, much of the new control efforts were aimed at limiting imports from drug-producing countries in Asia, Europe and North Africa. Toward this end, the government vowed to take an increasingly active role in international efforts to stem drug smuggling. For example, it participated in the activities of the agency known as the Single Convention of Narcotic Drugs, established in 1961.

In 1978 the Swedish Parliament adopted a new strategy in the fight against alcohol and drug abuse. Legislation was enacted that relates alcohol and drug problems to their social context rather than treats them simply as crimes. Since then the primary task of the government has been to educate the public about the dangers of drug abuse and to help addicts to get treatment to overcome their dependency disorders.

In order to gain an overview of the problem and educate the public, the government has several agencies that provide its central Crime Prevention Council with statistics on alcohol and drug abuse. The National Board of Education, for instance, reports on drug abuse among sixth to ninth graders and high school sophomores; the National Defense Research Institute obtains similar information for 18 year olds; and the Stockholm police even check for needle marks on people taken into custody. These statistics are helpful because they help target certain segments of the population for special attention. For example, it has been shown that nearly three-fifths of all incarcerated criminals are drug and alcohol abusers.

Treatment has become a major element in Sweden's crackdown. Before 1978 public drunkenness was treated as a crime and offenders were arrested. Since that time, however, it has been seen as a small part of a larger social and sometimes medical problem. Now if offenders are taken into custody, they are dealt with leniently and usually turned over to proper counselors rather than jailors. The government has taken the view that drug addicts and alcoholics "often are people whose narcotics abuse is a consequence and an expression, among other things, of their psychological and social difficulties and perhaps it is an unconscious attempt to alleviate these or modify them." (Drug Addicts Care Committee, quoted from *Facts on Narcotics and Narcotics Abuse*).

The addicts's "escape into abuse" is thought to result from Sweden's increasing industrialization and its accompanying ills: unemployment and the extreme pressure to increase productivity and efficiency. Because government statistics show that drug abusers are likely to attend school irregularly and eventually turn to criminal activities, Parliament has vowed to help alleviate the problem at its source. Offenders thought by police to pose a threat to themselves or others may be taken into immediate custody and given compulsory treatment and counseling on an intensive and/or long-term basis. Although forced into such programs, the long-range goal is for addicts to take voluntary control over their own recovery and well-being. As noted in the introduction to Sweden's Care of Alcoholics and Drug Abusers Act of 1982: "The possibility to inflict treatment on a person without his consent must never lead to the consequences that society takes over the individual's responsibility for his own life."

Sweden has also tightened up its laws against "pushers" or dealers. Criminal acts are classified as misdemeanors, offenses and felonies, in ascending order of seriousness. Narcotics felons are considered among the most serious offenders in Sweden's justice system and may be sentenced to a minimum of 10 years in prison. Drunk driving is taken very seriously: convicted offenders whose blood tests show an alcohol concentration of 1.5 promille or more may be incarcerated for 12 months. Wiretapping is now legal when it is necessary to track down drug dealers, and there are stringent controls over the importation and sale of the hypodermic syringes and needles used by "mainliners."

The Fact Sheets on Sweden on "Alcohol and Drug Abuse" (1982) notes that the great majority of the 10,000 to 15,000 heavy drug abusers in the nation live in the large urban areas; but while the problem has leveled off in the cities it appears to be rising in outlying districts. Sweden offers considerable help to people who want to kick their abuse problems. The nation's mental hospitals contain 20 outpatient wards and an additional 200 beds in drug addiction wards, and they have specially trained addiction-care teams, as do many prison wards. There are some 30 boarding institutes with over 300 beds for addicts, and many private homes also provide beds and care. Once abusers are almost ready to re-enter society, they may go to "halfway homes." Here they associate almost exclusively with addicts and ex-addicts and have peer support in learning how to get back in touch with the "straight" world.

"Alcohol Policy in Sweden" (Stockholm 1982, 2nd rev. ed.) Swedish Council for Information on Alcohol and Other Drugs.

"Care of Alcoholics and Drug Abusers (Certain Cases) Act" (Departementens Reprocentral, Stockholm: 1982). Prepared by the Ministry of Social Affairs, International Secretariat.

"Fact Sheets on Sweden" (The Swedish Institute, Stockholm: September, 1982)

"Facts on Narcotics and Narcotics Abuse" (Liberforlag, Stockholm: 1979). Arranged by the Narcotics Group of the Crime Prevention Council of the National Swedish Board of Health and Welfare, Committee on Health Education.

Thomas Nordegren, "Alcohol and Alcoholism in Sweden," part of *Social Change in Sweden* series, no. 23 (Swedish Consulate General, New York: 1981). Prepared for the Swedish Information Service.

Thomas Nordegren, "Narcotics Abuse and Care of Drug Addicts in Sweden: Problems and Development Tendencies," part of *Social Change in Sweden* series, no. 21, 1980.

Report 81: *On the Alcohol and Drug Situation in Sweden* (Swedish Council for Information on Alcohol and Other Drugs, Stockholm: 1981).

sympathomimetic amines Drugs that act on the autonomic nervous system which controls involuntary muscles. Sympathomimetic drugs are used in the treatment of a number of conditions, including bronchial asthma, glaucoma, respiratory failure, mucous membrane congestion and shock. Some of these drugs also act systemically as stimulants of the central nervous system and they are the ones most sought after by drug abusers.

Synalgos® (Ives) An analgesic that contains drocode, promethazine hydrochloride, aspirin, caffeine and phenacetin. It is used for the relief of moderate to moderately severe pain in situations when a mild sedative is also needed. It may be habit-forming and has the potential for abuse. Tolerance, along with physical and psychological dependence, can occur. When taken with alcohol or other central nervous system depressants it can have an additive effect. It is supplied as Synalgos (without drocode) in maroon and white capsules; and as Synalgos-DC (with 16 mg drocode) in blue and white capsules.

Synanon Founded in 1958 by Charles E. Dederich, the Synanon Church operates communities in which drug addicts, alcoholics and other character-disordered people can learn a better way to live. The first of its kind, Synanon once served as a model for numerous other therapeutic communities in the United States and abroad. Synanon communities are still located on two rural properties, one in central California and the other in Houston, Texas. Anyone with a problem of drug or alcohol addiction, delinquency or criminal behavior, or other character disorder is eligible for admission. There is no set entrance fee but individuals who can afford to contribute to their care are expected to do so. The Synanon Church also acquires and distributes food to charitable organizations, and has established the Synanon College, a California-approved vocational college offering a wide variety of classes.

Syndrome X In *Licit & Illicit Drugs* (Little, Brown and Company, 1972) Edward M. Brecher and the editors of Consumer Reports used the term Syndrome X to describe the high incidence of deaths reportedly due to *heroin overdose*. Before 1943, few—if any—deaths among addicts were attributed to heroin overdose. During the 1950s, however, nearly 50% of such deaths were attributed to this cause, and by 1970, when some 800 addicts in New York City died, the figure had risen to 80%. According to Mr. Brecher, it is unlikely that these deaths were due to heroin overdose for several reasons. First, it is known that even large doses of heroin are not likely to kill. Second, most deaths attributed to heroin overdose occurred very suddenly; in true cases of heroin overdose the initial symptoms are stupor and lethargy, generally followed by coma—a process that can take up to twelve hours. Death can be forstalled effectively by administering a narcotic antagonist, such as NALOXONE. And, third, says Brecher, most addicts whose deaths are reportedly due to overdose are individuals who have developed a tolerance to the drug so that only an extremely large dose of heroin would not cause their deaths.

If a person is known to be addicted to a particular drug and is suddenly found dead, the natural suspicion and assumption is that the drug caused the death. If a heroin addict dies with the syringe still in his arm, or witnesses report that just minutes before he died he was injecting heroin, the obvious conclusion is death by overdose. Such evidence would be circumstantial, though. According to Brecher "a conscientious search of the United States medical literature throughout recent decades has failed to turn up a single scientific paper reporting that heroin overdose . . . is in fact a cause of death among American addicts."

A 1966 study by Dr. Milton Helpern, Chief Medical Examiner for New York City, found that massive pulmonary edema (flooding of the lungs with fluid) was a conspicuous condition in alleged overdose deaths, and that these deaths occurred very suddenly. It is these two characteristics that have been labeled Syndrome X. Dr. Michael M. Baden, an associate of Dr. Helpern, suggested that the majority of deaths are due to "an acute reaction to the intravenous injection of the heroin-quinine-sugar mixture" and to classify them as heroin overdose is a misnomer. There were also other factors suggesting that the deaths were not due to heroin overdose: most of the victims were long-term addicts, a fact which rules out the possibility that they had not developed tolerance; in some cases a number of addicts used the same heroin and only one died; there was an absence of high heroin concentration in tissue surrounding the point of injection and no evidence of heroin overdose in the urine of victims; and there was no evidence that the heroin was any "purer" than the addicts were accustomed to.

Author Edward Brecher suggests several possible causes for Syndrome X deaths. Clearly, heroin itself could not be the cause since the high incidence of deaths among addicts is a recent phenomenon and heroin has been used for a long time. The first Syndrome X deaths occurred in the early 1940s when quinine was first added to heroin after an outbreak of malaria hit New York City addicts. More deaths occurred in the 1950s when addicts began taking central nervous system depressants, especially barbiturates and alcohol. Previously, addicts had generally refrained from alcohol use but after World War II when heroin was in short supply many turned to alcohol as a substitute. A 1967 New York study involving the deaths of 588 addicts, found alcohol present in 43% of the cases. At the Haight-Ashbury Medical Clinic, 37% of the addicts attending used barbiturates when withdrawal symptoms began; 24% used alcohol for the same reason.

In 1970 two noted entertainers died of what was reported as "heroin overdose." The musician Jimi Hendrix was known to use both barbiturates and alcohol, and the singer Janis Joplin was known to be a heavy drinker. She had, in fact, been drinking heavily with friends the night she injected herself with heroin and died.

Great Britain has also studied the question of heroin overdose. The presence of quinine was all but ruled out since quinine is not used to "cut" heroin in Great Britain. However, although inconclusive, the British studies appear to confirm the alcohol-barbiturate-heroin theory.

Despite the accumulated evidence that there must be a cause other than heroin overdose for these deaths, research in the area is minimal and the classification remains.

synergistic effect See SYNERGY.

synergy When two or more drugs are taken together, the combined action increases the normal effect of each drug. The condition is also referred to as POTENTIATION. Potentiation and synergy is when you add one plus one and get three. ADDITIVE EFFECT would give you two. Because of this phenomenon, an amount of a drug that might normally be safe can have a devastating effect if taken with a drug that acts synergistically with it.

For example, a small amount of alcohol combined with a very small dose of a barbiturate can have a much greater effect than alcohol or a barbiturate taken alone. In this instance the mechanism is due to competition for enzymes in the liver. When the two drugs are taken together the enzyme system that processes them is overwhelmed because it does not have the capacity to metabolize both at the same time. In the case of alcohol and a barbiturate drug, which compete for the same enzymes, alcohol is always processed first. The barbiturate meanwhile accumulates in the blood where it has an exaggerated effect on the body and the mind. This delayed metabolization of the barbiturate can result in tripling or quadrupling of its potency when it enters the central nervous system.

The Third Special Report to the U.S. Congress on Alcohol and Health defined an interaction between alcohol or other central nervous system depressants, and a drug as "any alteration in the pharmacologic properties of either due to the presence of the other." The report classified three different types by interactions:

(1) Antagonistic, in which the effects of one or both drugs are blocked or reduced;
(2) Additive, in which the effect is the sum of the effects of each;
(3) Supra-additive (synergistic or potentiating), in which the effect of the two drugs in combination is greater than it would be if the effects were additive.

The supra-additive effect is the most dangerous because it can at times prove fatal. Although not quite as dangerous, the antagonistic effect can be hazardous when the therapeutic effects of one drug are reduced by the presence of the other.

Drugs also have a half-life: this is the amount of time it takes for the body to remove half of the drug from the system. For drugs with a half-life of 24 hours or more, such as Valium, half of the first dose may still be in the body when the next is taken. After several days the buildup can be fairly large, and when alcohol or another central nervous system depressant is taken the result can be devastating.

synhexyl See PYRAHEXYL.

synesthesia The crossover of sensory effects. This phenomenon is most common during hallucinogenic use; colors may be smelled, sounds may be seen. Seeing stars after a blow on the head is a form of non-drug synesthesia.

synthetic marijuana THC. In the 1960s the term was falsely used for PCP.

synthetic narcotics Narcotics that are produced entirely within a laboratory, as opposed to pharmaceutical products which are derived directly or indirectly from narcotics of natural origin. The two most widely used synthetic narcotics are meperidine and methadone. Synthetic narcotics resemble morphine in their action and sometimes have greater analgesic potency. Consequently tolerance and dependence develop with their use and they are all susceptible to abuse.

T

talbutal An intermediate-acting BARBITURATE usually used to produce sedation and sleep.

tachycardia An increase in heart rate. (See HEART.)

Talwin® (Winthrop) A potent analgesic that contains pentazocine and is equivalent in effect to CODEINE. It is an agonist-antagonist and is used for the relief of moderate to severe pain and as a preanesthetic. It has a high potential for abuse and both physical and psychological dependence can occur. Its antagonist qualities are significant and the drug will precipitate withdrawal in opiate dependent people. In large doses Talwin can cause acute central nervous system manifestations of hallucinations and disorientation. Its formulation has been changed by the addition of NALOXONE (Narcan) so that when abusers attempt to inject it intravenously its euphoric effects are blocked. It is supplied as Talwin Compound in white capsules: Talwin Hydrochloride in peach-colored scored tablets; and Talwin Lactate in vials and ampules for injection.

Taractan® (Roche) An antipsychotic that contains chlorprothixene and is used for the management of manifestations of psychotic disorders. It has little potential for abuse or dependency. Overdosage can result in respiratory depression, hypotension, and convulsions. It is supplied as a fruit-flavored elixir; in ampules for injection; and in 10 mg, 25 mg, 50 mg and 100 mg tablets.

TARGET A nonprofit service organization dedicated to helping students cope with alcohol and other drugs. Associated with the National Federation of State High School Associations, TARGET's audience includes student-athletes, debaters, coaches, administrators, parents and others involved in extracurricular activities. Contact: Richard Stickle, TARGET, National Federation of State High School Associations, 11724 Plaza Circle, Kansas City, MO 64194. Telephone: (816) 464-5400.

TCA Tricyclic ANTIDEPRESSANT, the major category of antidepressants.

Tedral® (Parke-Davis) A bronchodilator containing theophylline, ephedrine hydrochloride and the sedative PHENOBARBITAL. It is used for bronchial asthma and other bronchospastic disorders. Because of the presence of the barbiturate phenobarbital, which is added to counteract the stimulant ephedrine, it may be habit-forming. It is supplied as Tedral Elixir: red cherry-flavored elixir with 15% alcohol; Tedral: uncoated white scored tablets; Tedral SA: double-layered uncoated coral and white tablets which contain butabarbital instead of phenobarbital; Tedral Expectorant: white tablets; and Tedral Suspension: yellow licorice-flavored suspension.

telepathine HARMINE.

temperance In the early 1800s the word temperance, usually synonymous with moderation, took on the meaning of *abstinence* in reference to alcohol. A group of Litchfield, Connecticut, residents formed the first temperance organization in 1789 when they pledged total abstinence. In 1826 a national organization, the American Temperance Society, was formed. Churches supported the movement, particularly Methodist and Presbyterian churches, and by the 1830s temperance societies across the country numbered over 1,000, gaining most of their strength in rural areas. Leaders of the movement used moral attacks as a method to persuade people to join their cause. After the Civil War the movement became even more popular and in 1872 the Catholic Church formed the Total Abstention Union. In 1874 the Woman's Christian Temperance Union, which is still active, was formed. In the early 1900s the movement concentrated on legislative measures, which led to PROHIBITION in 1920.

temposil A compound calcium carbamide which produces an ANTABUSE effect. It is used in the treatment of alcoholics participating in recovery programs. Effects last only 12 to 24 hours whereas the effects of Antabuse can extend four to five days before the danger of a reaction passes. It has not been approved for use in the United States but is administered in treatment programs in Canada and Japan.

Tenuate® (Merrell-Dow) An anorectic that contains diethylpropion hydrochloride and is used for weight control. Tolerance can develop and because it is chemically and pharmacologically similar to the AMPHETAMINES and it can produce psychological dependence. It has a high potential for abuse. Overdosage can result in restlessness, rapid respiration, confusion and hallucinations. It is supplied as Tenuate in light blue 25 mg tablets; and as Tenuate Dospan, 75 mg white capsule-shaped tablets.

Tepanil® (Riker) An anorectic that contains diethylpropion hydrochloride and is used for weight control. Tolerance can develop and because it is chemically and pharmacologically similar to AMPHETAMINES it can produce psychological dependence and social dysfunction. It has a high potential for abuse. Overdosage can result in restlessness, rapid respiration, confusion and hallucinations. It is supplied as Tepanil in 25 mg white tablets; and as Tepanil Ten-tab, 75 mg white tablets.

terpin hydrate A turpentine derivative and non-narcotic antitussive found in Terpin Hydrate & Codeine Elixir® (McKesson), Tussagesic Tablets and Suspension® (Dorsey), and Tussaminic Tablets® (Dorsey).

testing, drug See DRUG TESTING.

tetanus An acute infectious disease, commonly known as "lockjaw," which is caused by the bacillus *Clostridium tetani* found in the soil and in animal feces. It is usually transmitted through open wounds directly into the bloodstream, often by contaminated nails, knives or hypodermic needles. Tetanus is painful because of muscle spasms and often fatal. Among addicts who regularly inject drugs the chances of contracting the disease are well above average and the prognosis for recovery is less than average because of the frequency of injection, carelessness about the sterility of instruments and the general poor health of the user.

tetrahydrocannabinol (delta-9-tetrahydrocannabinol) A hallucinogen that is the active principle in CANNABIS. Also referred to as THC, it is found in the resin of the hemp plant. It was first produced synthetically in 1966.

Thai sticks Potent, seedless marijuana (see SINSEMILLA) that is grown in Thailand and Vietnam and is packaged and tied in bundles that resemble sticks.

THC See TETRAHYDROCANNABINOL.

thebaine A principal alkaloid of OPIUM, thebaine was isolated in 1835, three years after the isolation of codeine. Because of its toxicity, thebaine itself has no medical use. Its conversion products, however, include the narcotic antagonists NALOXONE and NALTREXONE. Some codeine is made from thebaine. A series of other compounds which have analgesic properties many times that of morphine are also conversion products of thebaine but their toxicity in humans limits their use to veterinary medicine.

therapeutic index The rates between an average effective dose of a drug and the

LD50—the lethal dose for 50% of the population.

therapeutic communities See HALFWAY HOUSE and TREATMENT.

thin layer chromatography A drug-testing process that could develop as the least expensive alternative. A single test can detect up to 40 different drugs in one urine sample. The process involves use of a glass plate covered with a thin layer of jelly-like substance known as gel. Urine is applied as a spot near one edge of the gel surface. The glass plate is then placed upright in a closed container with the edge adjacent to the spot at the bottom. The base of the container has just enough of a liquid solvent to wet that edge. By degrees, the solvent is carried up over the surface of the gel. When the solvent reaches the spot of urine, it pushes all the chemicals contained in the spot up along the surface.

According to Gilda Berger, the gel usually holds on to the different chemicals. "The greater the attraction between each individual chemical and the gel, the less it moves. The smaller the attraction, the farther up the glass it moves.

"After a period of time, the original spot is gone. Instead, there remains a series of spots called a chromatogram, going up along the surface of the gel. Each spot is made different by a different chemical that has been separated out of the spot of urine." Results of the TLC must necessarily depend on the skill and experience of the technician who reads the TLC plate. The technician uses his or her own judgment to determine which, if any, drugs are present. One of the popular commercially prepared TLC kits is Toxi-Lab, produced by Analytical Systems, Laguna Hill, California. TLC techniques are not sufficiently sensitive for testing for cocaine and frequently tests will be negative after 48 hours while EMIT testing remains sensitive for several days. (See also EMIT.)

Gilda Berger, *Drug Testing* (Franklin Watts: New York, 1987), 37–38.

Thorazine® (Smith, Kline & French) An antipsychotic brand of chlorpromazine, a phenothiazine derivative. It is used in the treatment of psychotic states. It is not known to cause dependence or withdrawal. Overdosage can result in respiratory depression and when taken with alcohol or other central nervous system depressants it can have an additive effect. It is supplied in tablets, capsules, suppositories, as a concentrate, and in vials and ampules for injection.

TM Transcendental meditation. TM is a form of meditation. When successfully practiced it produces a dissociative state, interpreted as an out-of-the-body experience. It has been claimed that TM decreases or abolishes drug abuse.

TMA (3, 4, 5-Trimethoxyphenyl-B-aminopropane) A little-known synthetic HALLUCINOGEN derived from MESCALINE. It is more potent than mescaline but less potent than LSD-25. TMA-2 and TMA-6 are also hallucinogenic substances.

tobacco See NICOTINE.

tolerance A state of acquired resistance to the effects of a drug. Tolerance develops after the repeated use of certain drugs. When it occurs a person must increase the dosage to obtain the original effects. (See also ADDICTION.)

toluene A liquid aromatic hydrocarbon that is used chiefly as a solvent and is found in numerous common household products. It has an intoxicating effect when inhaled. (See INHALANTS.)

tooth grinding Tooth grinding (bruxism) is relatively common among the general population during sleep. When it occurs during waking hours it can be an indication of chronic amphetamine or cocaine use.

topical administration See ADMINISTRATION.

toxic Poisonous. Toxicity refers to the quality of being poisonous, and toxicology is the science that deals with poisons and their effects.

toxic psychosis (See PSYCHOSIS.)

trafficking Drug trafficking is probably the most serious law enforcement problem in the United States. The top illicit income producer is cocaine—it generated an estimated $100 billion in retail sales in 1988. Marijuana generated an estimated $14 billion in sales, while sales of heroin generated over $10 billion. Other dangerous drugs, including amphetamines, methamphetamines, barbiturates, methaqualone and the hallucinogens, produced an estimated $17 to $20 billion in U.S. retail sales. In truth, no one really knows how much money the drug trade generates and the above are simply "best estimates."

Unlike heroin use, which is relatively localized in large urban areas, the use of cocaine has been spreading throughout the entire U.S. Cocaine use has risen at an alarming rate among the nation's youth. In 1988 an estimated 2,500 tons of cocaine hydrochloride were imported into the U.S. Availability is a major factor in the rise of cocaine abuse and, unfortunately, supplies are abundant. Coca cultivation is well established in COLUMBIA, PERU and BOLIVIA. Columbia now processes and distributes up to 70% of the cocaine entering the U.S. and is responsible for between 50% and 60% of the world's supply. It also furnishes 75% of the marijuana and 80% of the illicit methaqualone consumed in the U.S. Illicit drugs from Colombia usually enter through South Florida, Southern California, New York City, and Texas. The government has made an attempt to reduce trafficking from South American countries through control of coca production but it is faced with many obstacles when trying to negotiate with these countries. Frequent changes in South American governments, local populations which are heavily dependent on coca sales for their principal income, and, until recently, indifference to U.S. interests are just some of them.

In the 1980s approximately 60% of the heroin imported into this country was refined from opium cultivated in Southwest Asia (see GOLDEN CRESCENT); 25% was from Mexico; and the balance was from Southeast Asia (see GOLDEN TRIANGLE). The figure for Mexico shows a sharp drop: just four years earlier it supplied over two-thirds of the U.S. market. To a large extent the reduction is due to the Mexican government's aggressive eradication campaign against the opium poppy. The major importation center for heroin in the U.S. is New York City but recently Detroit has also become a major distribution center.

Although Mexico is still a source of marijuana, its overall share of the U.S. market has declined—from 18% in 1978 to 8% in the mid-1980s. In 1989, however, Mexico produced 4,750 metric tons of marijuana, 27.9% of the total sold in the U.S. Colombia supplied 32.5% of the marijuana imported into the U.S. in 1989; Jamaica supplied 5% in 1989. Domestic cultivation rose in 1989 to about 25% and is centered in seven primary states: California (where it is estimated that marijuana is the state's largest cash crop, worth between $1 billion and $2 billion annually), Hawaii, Oregon, Arkansas, Missouri, Kentucky and Florida.

Other illicit drugs, such as amphetamines and barbiturates, come from several sources. Colombia is responsible for about 80% of these drugs, particularly methaqualone. The balance comes from Europe and is often diverted through Mexico. In 1989 there were an estimated 1.2 million addicts in the U.S. and 23 million "recreational" users spending more on drugs than a company like General Motors earns.

(See also SMUGGLING, GOLDEN CRESCENT, GOLDEN TRIANGLE, FRENCH CONNECTION and individual countries.)

Trancopal® (Breon) A nonhypnotic antianxiety drug. It is a brand of chlormezanone and is used to improve the emotional state of a patient by quieting him without impairing his clarity of consciousness. It is supplied in 100 mg peach caplets and 200 mg green caplets.

tranquilizers Outdated term for two unrelated groups of drugs: antipsychotics and non-barbiturate sedatives. The latter group (Librium, Miltown, Valium, Xanax) are less potentially fatal than barbiturate and barbiturate-type sedatives but share all the other effects. If prescribed in low doses all sedatives are tranquilizing. In high doses all are sedating.

transportation system and drug abuse The White House Conference for a Drug Free America's Report in June 1988 stated, "Although no evidence exists to demonstrate that illicit drug use is more pervasive in transportation than in any other sector of society, the industry has an extraordinary obligation to ensure public safety and public trust. This obligation warrants that zero tolerance for drugs, on and off the job, must be the standard for the transportation industry, as it must be for private citizens who use our highways, waterways, and airways."

The conference made several recommendations pertinent to its goal of zero tolerance for drugs, including one to establish a Drug-Free Working Group composed of public and private sector experts, including operations in personnel, to address the long-range issues involving drug use and transportation.

Several programs are already in effect as private transportation companies—both labor and management—take steps to combat drug abuse and spread the antidrug message. Voluntary railroad employee-based drug prevention programs, such as "Operation Red Block" at Union Pacific and CSX Transportation, Inc., and "Operation Stop" at Burlington Northern, have initiated a wide variety of creative community activities that promote no drug use. Burns Brothers, Inc., owner of 23 truck stops west of the Mississippi River, sponsored a 300-truck convoy against drugs in 1987. The "world's largest truck convoy" crossed through seven states, showing the trucking industry's concern about illegal drug use. Operation Full Ahead, sponsored by American Steamship Co., Buffalo, New York, is a joint labor-management program to promote the health, safety and well-being of the company's employees. The program emphasizes awareness, education and prevention of illicit drug use.

The U.S. Supreme Court in 1989 upheld the constitutionality of the federal government's regulations requiring railroad crews involved in accidents to submit to prompt urinalysis and blood tests. This ruling followed the January 4, 1987, Amtrak wreck near Baltimore that killed 16 and injured 176 people. After a urine test the train's engineer later admitted to drug use and pleaded guilty to manslaughter.

While no precise statistics exist for prevalence of drug use among transportation workers in the U.S., a National Institute on Drug Abuse (NIDA) report on drug use in industry as a whole projected that as many as six million may currently be engaged in drug use. NIDA also estimated that lifetime marijuana prevalence trends for young adults in the U.S. increased from 4% in 1962 to 68% in 1979. Alcohol is still the nation's most serious drug problem in the industrial sector and affects transportation companies both large and small.

White House Conference Report for a Drug Free America, Washington, D.C.: U.S. Government Printing Office, 1988, 95–103.

Tranxene® (Abbott) A sedative hypnotic that contains chlorazepate dipotassium, a BENZODIAZEPINE, and is used for the treatment of anxiety and for physical illnesses in which anxiety is manifested. When taken with alcohol or other central nervous system depressants it can have an additive effect. Overdosage can result in varying degrees of central nervous system depression from slight sedation to coma. It is supplied as Tranxene: 3.75 mg gray and white capsules; 7.5 mg gray and maroon capsules; and 15 mg all gray capsules; Tranxene-SD: 22.5 mg tan tablets; and Tranxene-SD Half Strength: 11.25 mg blue tablets.

tranylcypromine See MONOAMINE OXIDASE (MAO) INHIBITORS. Its trade name is Parnate.

treatment Treatment for drug abuse falls into various categories, including drug-free or maintenance; residential or ambulatory; medical or non-medical; selective or non-selective; voluntary or involuntary. Treatment programs also offer virtually any combination of these methods.

Maintenance programs include ANTABUSE and METHADONE. ALCOHOLICS ANONYMOUS is a drug-free program aimed at abstinence. Residential approaches include drug-free therapeutic communities (Synanon, Daytop, Odyssey House and numerous others) as well as half-way houses and rehabilitation programs of one to four months duration. Involuntary treatment includes both medical and court authorizations that do not require the patient's consent. An addict may be compelled to start treatment, continue it, or both. Ambulatory treatment involves programs in which a patient visits a treatment facility as an outpatient at periodic intervals. DETOXIFICATION programs often handle only physical dependency and psychological dependency remains.

Psychological dependency is generally believed to be more difficult to manage than physical dependency, and for this reason treatment programs employ a variety of methods. Detoxification is usually, but not invariably, done in a hospital or other medically oriented facility. Upon discharge a continuing program of treatment should be implemented or the incidence of RELAPSE will be high. Not all treatment programs will work for all patients. Upon detoxification some patients will benefit greatly from a program such as Alcoholics Anonymous or Narcotics Anonymous; others will benefit more from individual or GROUP THERAPY. Many times inpatient rehabilitation lasting one to four months is attempted. Recently intensive day treatment has been developed as an alternative to inpatient rehab. Still others will need the encouragement of the kind of drug-free supportive atmosphere provided by long-term therapeutic communities. The length of time addicted and the severity of illness are often used to determine the level of care (treatment) offered, with the longer term, more disrupted individuals going to more supportive environments. However, little has been studied about choosing levels of care, and outcomes are only now being examined in an organized manner.

In the past treatment programs have centered around the patient who has abused the drug and fail to consider his family. Rehab programs in the latter 1980s began to involve the family; many require family members to attend a part of the addicted person's treatment for education and counseling.

By 1989, substance abuse treatment centers had proliferated into a $3 billion a year industry.

tremor A shaking or trembling usually from weakness or disease; also a feeling of uncertainty or insecurity. Most withdrawal states as well as the use of stimulants and hallucinogens induce tremors. (See also DELIRIUM TREMENS.)

trichloroethylene A hydrocarbon and volatile solvent that is an ingredient in various cleaning fluids and is sometimes inhaled for its intoxicating effects. (See also INHALANTS.)

triclofos sodium A depressant and sedative hypnotic generally used in the treatment of insomnia. It is a chloral derivative which converts to chloral hydrate in the body but lacks its bitter taste and smell. It is also less potent.

The drug reaches its peak level in one hour and has a half life of 11 hours. It may be habit-forming and dependency can develop. (See TRICLOS.)

Triclos® (Merrell-Dow) A hypnotic agent that contains TRICLOFOS SODIUM. It is a chloral derivative generally used in the treatment of insomnia. It may be habit-forming and dependency can develop. It is supplied in 750 mg capsule-shaped orange tablets.

Trimstat® (Laser) An anorectic that contains phendimetrazine and is used for weight control. Tolerance can develop and because its activity is similar to that of AMPHETAMINES it has a significant potential for abuse. It is supplied in 35 mg tan tablets.

Trimtabs® (Mayrand) An anorectic that contains phendimetrazine tartrate and is used for weight control. Tolerance can develop and because its activity is similar to AMPHETAMINES it has a significant potential for abuse. It is supplied in 35 mg tablets.

tripelennamine hydrochloride An antihistamine that has recently come into use in combination with pentazocine (Talwin) a narcotic analgesic as a substitute for heroin. "Cooked" and injected intravenously, the combination produces a "rush" described by users as equivalent to that of good quality heroin. The slang name for the injected compound is Ts and Blues; it is experiencing increasing use nationally among heroin addicts because it costs less than one-quarter the price of heroin and, unlike street heroin, its potency can be determined and controlled. There are major health risks associated with the use of Ts and Blues, including damage to the small blood vessels of the lungs, eyes and brain; seizures and convulsions; and fatality due to overdose. Talwin has significant opiate antagonist qualities and precipitates withdrawal in narcotic-dependent individuals. Other slang names include Tops and Bottoms, Teddies and Betties and Ts and Bs. (See also TALWIN.)

Jack E. Nelson et al, eds., *Guide to Drug Abuse Research Terminology,* Research Issue 26, U.S. Department of Health and Human Services, p. 97.

Tuinal® (Lilly) A sedative hypnotic that contains 150 mg each of the short- to intermediate-acting BARBITURATES secobarbital sodium and amobarbital sodium. A Schedule II drug, it is used for insomnia and as a preoperative medication. Tolerance can develop and both physical and psychological dependence can occur. It has a high potential for abuse and when taken with alcohol or other central nervous system depressants it can have an additive or potentiating effect. Overdosage can result in respiratory depression, lowered body temperature and coma. It is supplied in 50 mg, 100 mg and 300 mg capsules with a blue body and orange cap.

Synonyms: tooies, tuies, rainbows, red and blues.

Turkey The use of drugs in Turkey, particularly opium and marijuana (hashish), has long been a tradition. It has been customary for so long, in fact, that there is no particular stigma attached to the use and abuse of these drugs. Although Turkey has always been a heavy producer and consumer of opium, the use of heroin is rare. Opium is generally smoked or is used as opium gum (the final raw product) often for strictly medicinal purposes.

In 1923 the new republic, under the leadership of Ataturk (Mustafa Kemal), sought to modernize the nation and programs were initiated to end many of the old customs including the use of opium and hashish. Little was actually accomplished and at the end of World War II the abuse of opium had not only increased but there was also an increase in the smuggling of illicit drugs. Stringent legislation was passed in 1953 to deter domestic use and illegal trade, but the government was aware that it would take time to become effective; there had been considerable opposition to legislation that would change long-established customs and dramatically affect the economy and welfare of the country. In 1971 further legislation was passed that banned opium production and, despite attempts for its repeal, the law is still in effect. The economic hardships caused by the 1971 legislation have led to compensation programs but it is an enormous undertaking because most of the former poppy farms must be rehabilitated and the social and economic structure of whole provinces must be reorganized.

There are very tough penalties in Turkey for the importation, exportation or manufacture of drugs without a license. In the case of morphine, cocaine, heroin or hashish, the penalty can be life imprisonment and Turkish jails have a considerable reputation for extreme harshness and very uncomfortable conditions.

Despite the 1971 ban on the cultivation of the poppy, there is still active involvement in the illicit market. Turkey now plays a major role as a transit country, particularly for opium cultivated in Iran, Pakistan, and southwestern Asia. These opiates are smuggled westward through Bulgaria and Yugoslavia into Western Europe and/or the U.S. (see GOLDEN CRESCENT). During the days of the FRENCH CONNECTION, Turkey was a major producer of opium for the illicit market. The 1971 ban, which only allows opium production for scientific and medicinal markets, has led to an increase in trafficking of illicit opium, and Turkish nationals play an important role in both the refining and trafficking of imported opiates particularly through Germany. The U.S. Embassy, in an effort to assist the Turkish government's already vigorous narcotics laws, initiated a Protocol on Narcotics Cooperation which is designed to offer flexible and speedy commodity and training assistance to Turkish law enforcement officials.

Tussanil® (Misemer) A decongestant and antitussive that contains several ingredients, including the codeine derivative dihydrocodeinone bitartrate. It may be habit-forming and both physical and psychological dependence can occur. It is supplied as a syrup.

Tussionex® (Pennwalt) An antitussive that contains resin complexes of hydrocodone and phenyltoloxamine. It may be habit-forming. Overdosage can result in respiratory depression and convulsions. It is supplied as golden colored Tussionex Suspension; light brown tablets; and green and white capsules.

Twenty-first Amendment The amendment which repealed the Eighteenth Amendment and ended PROHIBITION. It became part of the Constitution on December 5, 1933.

tybamate A sedative hypnotic that is similar structurally and pharmacologically to meprobamate, but is possibly more effective as a muscle relaxant. Tybamate resembles MEPROBAMATE in its effects, use and abuse.

Appearance and activity in the body: Tybamate is a white crystalline powder which is soluble in alcohol and slightly soluble in water.

Absorbed rapidly in the gastrointestinal tract and distributed evenly in the body, tybamate is metabolized in the liver and excreted by the kidneys. It acts on the thalmus and limbic systems of the brain, stabilizing the emotional circuits, but does not affect the cerebral cortex. The substance, which has a half-life of three hours, crosses the placental barrier and appears in mother's milk.

Dosage: Tybamate is prescribed in oral doses of 20-35 mg per kilogram of body weight, in three or four daily doses for children aged 6-12; and in doses of 250-500 mg three or four times daily for adults. No more than 3 gm (3000 mg) should be administered per day.

Effects: Like meprobamate, tybamate temporarily reduces tension and anxiety. Mild adverse reactions such as drowsiness and confusion can usually be controlled by adjusting the dose. Other unpleasant side effects which have been reported include rash, nausea, anorexia and seizures.

Tolerance and physical and psychological dependence can occur, along with withdrawal symptoms. Barbiturates and tybamate display cross-tolerance to each other, and tybamate is potentiated by alcohol and other depressants. Overdosage can result in stupor and death.

Usage: Tybamate's medical application includes the treatment of tension, anxiety and insomnia resulting from psychoneurosis. It has a potential for abuse. (See TYBATRAN.)

Tybatran® (Robins) A sedative hypnotic that contains TYBAMATE and whose activity is similar to meprobamate. Tolerance can develop and both physical and psychological dependence can occur. It is supplied in 125 mg, 250 mg and 350 mg green capsules.

Tylenol with Codeine® (McNeil) An analgesic that contains acetaminophen and codeine phosphate. It is used for acute or chronic pain and to control cough. It may be habit-forming. Tolerance can develop, along with physical and psychological dependence. Overdosage can result in cardiorespiratory depression, circulatory collapse and coma. It is supplied in white tablets containing 7.5 mg, 15 mg, 30 mg and 60 mg of codeine.

U

under the influence of alcohol The term, when used generally, refers to being affected by alcohol and exhibiting a disturbance of function or behavior because of it. In some parts of the U.S. the condition is legally defined in terms of specific concentrations of alcohol in the blood.

United Kingdom Alcohol is acknowledged to be the most abused drug in the United Kingdom and has been for many years: in the late 19th century the government actively intervened to try to shift the drinking pattern from gin to beer. Although the abuse of other drugs is not nearly as serious as it is in the United States, it became a cause for concern in the 1920s and the government began to take preventive steps.

Drug addiction in the United Kingdom is treated as a medical rather than a criminal problem. A Ministry of Health committee in 1926 recommended that narcotic addicts (often people who had become addicted as a result of treatment for an illness) should receive narcotic prescriptions in the hope that they would gradually withdraw from the use of the drug. By 1960 the number of addicts had risen sharply and government committees undertook further studies. They reaffirmed the 1926 recommendations and established guidelines for what is now referred to as the "clinical system" or the "British system." A network of regular treatment centers was set up on both an inpatient and outpatient basis, and extremely controlled procedures were established for the prescribing of heroin, methadone and cocaine to addicts. The number of drug-prescribing doctors was also restricted and controlled, and the recording and registering of addicts was made compulsory.

In 1967 the Dangerous Drugs Act was passed. Along with providing detention powers for illegal possession, use and sale of "notifiable" drugs, it also provides for a doctor's license to be revoked if he or she overprescribes. The extent of an addict's habit has been a controversy in the clinical system. Addicts will obviously try to convince a doctor that they have a strong, heavy habit in order to obtain larger doses. However, doctors are rationed as to the amount they may prescribe and urine tests are frequently employed to ascertain the actual extent of an addict's habit. Once the existence of a habit has been ascertained, those addicted to notifiable drugs are registered with the government and prescriptions are filed with a pharmacy. The addict has to go to the pharmacy on a *daily* basis to collect his dose.

By 1971 the Misuse of Drugs Act was passed and came into full force in 1973. It modernized previous legislation and classified drugs according to the security required to prevent abuse and the penalties for illegal possession and sale. It also listed notifiable drugs as the following: heroin, methadone, cocaine, dextromoramide, diamorphine, dipipanone, hydrocodone, hydromorphone, levorphanol, morphine, opium, oxycodone, pethidine, piritramide and phenazocine.

The Misuse of Drugs Act also divided drugs into three categories according to their harmfulness. Maximum penalties for the chief types of offenses are related to the category of drugs involved. Class "A" drugs are the above mentioned notifiable drugs along with LSD; class "B" drugs include cannabis, cannabis plants, resin and liquid, amphetamines, dextroamphetamine, levamphetamine and methylamphetamine; class "C" drugs include methaqualone and other miscellaneous drugs.

Nearly 4,400 addicts were recorded as receiving notifiable drugs in the treatment of their addiction as of the end of 1982; nearly three times the number recorded at the end of 1972. The large increase of over 500 addicts (14%) between 1981 and 1982 followed a larger increase of about 1,000 (35%) between 1980 and 1981. Heroin addicts (those addicted solely to heroin or to heroin and other drugs) accounted for 76% of the new addicts in 1982, as compared to about 60% in 1973–78. From 1980–82 the second most frequent drug of addiction was dipipanone, for which the number of new addicts increased substantially from 20 in 1973 to over 300 in 1982. The number of new methadone addicts has remained fairly stable. The other most frequent drugs of addiction reported for new addicts were cocaine, dextromoramide, morphine and pethidine. Among former addicts, heroin was the most frequent drug of addiction, followed by methadone and dipipanone. As of December 31, 1982, the number of narcotic drug addicts recorded as receiving notifiable drugs in treatment of their addiction is broken down as follows: methadone, 3,117; dipipanone, 927; heroin, 126; other drugs (alone or in combination), 201.

The use of cannabis in the United Kingdom is not to be overlooked. Indeed, there were more seizures of cannabis and more persons found guilty of, or cautioned for, drug offenses related to cannabis than any other drug in 1982. Whereas the abuse of narcotics and other dangerous drugs is centered in the London area, cannabis use is far more widespread. This is a pattern that is found in countries throughout the world and is related to the availability and low cost of the drug. In the United Kingdom, as elsewhere, more attention is generally given to the abuse of "hard" drugs. There were about 10,700 seizures of cannabis *resin* in 1982, about 1,800 more than in 1981 and higher than in earlier years. However, in terms of potency the quality of the seizures was less. The number of cannabis *herbal* seizures was about the same as the numbers in 1980 and 1981 but was much higher than in earlier years. The number of cannabis *plants* was lower in 1982 than in 1980–81 but higher than in earlier years. Overall seizures of *all* controlled drugs during 1982 was about 11% more than in 1981 and twice the number in 1974 which was the first full year of operation of the Misuse of Drugs Act.

The average age of *new* addicts increased between 1973 and 1979 but did not change greatly in the period 1979–82; about 20% of new addicts were aged 30 and over in 1982 as compared to 10% in 1973. The number of new addicts aged under 20 in 1982 was particularly high, nearly double that of 1980, possibly indicating a trend. The average age of *former* addicts increased between 1973 and 1981, with about 40% being aged 30 and over. Some 70% of known addicts at the end of 1982 were males, a similar proportion to the previous four years. In the first half of the 1970s, the corresponding proportion was about 75%.

The clinical system of drug treatment in the United Kingdom has been a controversial issue since it was first established. Opponents of the system look on it as a "drugs-for-free" program and contend that it encourages drug use. This position is held by some drug treatment authorities in the United Kingdom and also by some authorities elsewhere in the world. Those who promote the system credit it with preventing the development of a black market, limiting narcotic use, reducing drug-related crime, and enabling addicts to lead more useful lives. It has been suggested that the United States adopt the system but the usual medical and governmental response is a "wait and see" attitude; although viewed as an interesting solution to the drug problem it seems that long-term positive results will have to be forthcoming before it is adopted in the U.S.

As in other countries around the world, alcohol and tobacco consumption is increasing in the United Kingdom. A "pub society" has evolved in this century and drinking in public places has become the primary form of entertainment. Since the government intervened to shift the drinking pattern from gin to beer in the late 19th century, beer has remained the most popular alcoholic beverage. Per capita consumption of beer rose 3.9% between 1972 and 1978—the fourth highest per capita increase among Western European countries. In addition, the income spent on beer (4.5% of household expenses) represented the highest proportion of any Western European nation. In 1980 the average consumption per adult was: distilled spirits, 6 pints; wine, 15 pints; and beer, 270 pints. Economic factors are responsible for some of the increase in alcohol abuse: although the cost of alcoholic beverages has risen, they have not risen as fast as other items in the economy. In 1984, U.K. beer consumption for persons 15 years and over was 139.5 liters; the U.K. ranked 10th among 32 nations surveyed. Total alcohol consumption was 9.2 liters per person 15 years and over, ranking the U.K. 24th of 32 nations surveyed.

The government estimates that 700,000 people suffer from alcohol-related problems. This estimate is broken down geographically because drinking patterns vary considerably within the United Kingdom. In Scotland and Northern Ireland there is a far higher incidence of alcohol abuse than in England and Wales. Taking into account the impact of alcoholism on family and friends, the Department of Health and Social Services estimates that in England and Wales one in 25 persons is affected by the abuse of alcohol; the figure is one in 10 in Scotland and Northern Ireland. The economic cost of alcohol abuse, including labor loss, health services, police and prison costs, were estimated to be $1.44 billion in 1979. That cost rose to more than $2 billion in 1989.

Government measures have attempted to reverse, or at least slow down, drinking trends. Legislative measures include public education, promotion of stricter laws for alcohol-related offenses, and revision of taxing and licensing laws affecting alcohol consumption. Some of these measures have met strong public opposition: the public opposes prohibitive taxes on alcoholic beverages, and the liquor industry resists efforts to restrain a trade that employs 700,000 people and exports $1.63 billion worth of goods.

The treatment of both drug and alcohol-related problems in the United Kingdom is handled mostly by volunteer organizations. Organizations dealing with alcohol-related problems are generally assisted by the Department of Health and Social Security along with substantial grants from the liquor industry. Rehabilitation programs for other drug-related problems are handled both through the Disabled Person's Resettlement Service of the Department of Employment, and by volunteer organizations that run special hostels for addicts who have completed treatment in a hospital. Both the Phoenix House in London and the Alpha House in Portsmouth are rehabilitation hostels modeled after the Phoenix House in New York City.

United States Drugs were in use in America long before Europeans came to the country. Early explorers found the Indians "drinking the smoke" of burning tobacco and took the habit home with them to Europe. Early colonists were skilled at distilling grain into alcoholic beverages and the rum trade flourished in New England early on. Although recognized as a stimulant, cocaine did not enjoy popularity in the U.S. until the late 1800s when it became an ingredient not only in many elixirs but in the original recipe for the popular soft drink Coca-Cola. (It was removed from the beverage in 1906 when the Pure Food and Drug Law was passed.) Cannabis was widely grown by Virginia colonists as a source of hemp, and in the 19th century large hemp plantations were found throughout the south. Cultivation of marijuana actually continued into the 1930s and it is estimated that at that time the commercial crop covered 10,000 acres. Although principally grown for hemp, marijuana was used medicinally and recreationally during the 18th and 19th centuries, but on a minute scale compared to today.

The use of opium was rampant during the 19th century; it was an ingredient in numerous patent medicines and was sold legally and at extremely low prices. Although most opium was imported, opium poppies were also cultivated in the U.S. The dangers of opium addiction were recognized but not acted upon until 1895 when San Francisco banned the smoking of opium and the opium dens that had proliferated in the city and which were supposedly a result of the influx of Chinese immigrants. Similar ordinances followed soon after in other cities, but nothing was done about the opium in patent medicines for many years. An often undisclosed aspect of the Civil War is the number of morphine addicts it produced. Soldiers were not only treated with morphine on the battlefields but were also sent home with a syringe and a supply of the drug. At that time morphine was not thought to be addictive if it was injected into the bloodstream and bypassed the stomach. The result of this belief was hundreds of thousands of addicts. The popularity of heroin over morphine developed in the early part of the 20th century when it was discovered that heroin was a more potent drug; it was also the drug being smuggled into the country at the time and addicts are always at the mercy of the availability factor.

The abuse of alcohol, a problem from America's early beginnings and one that continues today, was dealt with harshly in 1919 when Prohibition was enacted. Repeal came in 1933 when it was obvious that the government move was a failure. In the late 1980s, the U.S. began to change its drinking habits, and tolerance for drunkenness started to dry up. The proportion of people who drink in the U.S. peaked in the 1970s, and has declined since. In 1978, the percentage of drinkers was 71% of the population; by 1988 that figure had dropped to 63%.

During the 1940s and 1950s the abuse of other substances began to be a major concern. The use of newly developed drugs became widespread before their addictive qualities were acknowledged or made known. Sedatives mistakenly called "minor tranquilizers" were widely prescribed by doctors as a way of dealing with symptoms, and amphetamines were in widespread use as an "energizer." These patterns continue today. Cocaine, previously not used to any great extent, is now a leading drug of abuse. When it first gained notoriety it was mistakenly believed to be a drug of the affluent because of its high cost, but in fact its use had spread among many segments of the population. Heroin use has retained its popularity since the early 1900s, but the number of heroin dependent people remained fairly stable until the mid-1980s. Since then it has been on the upswing. In 1989, government estimates put the number of heroin addicts in the country at 500,000. Some 1.5 million were estimated to be occasional users. Heroin-related deaths increased 18% between 1981 and 1988, when 1,100 people died from the drug.

Aside from alcohol, tobacco and caffeine, the major drug of abuse today is marijuana. It has been estimated that 62 million people in the U.S. have used marijuana, though the actual number of users, whether regular or occasional, is impossible to pinpoint as sources of marijuana include not only imports from other countries but the vast amounts that are grown domestically. The U.S. government estimates that 25% of the marijuana used in America today is domestically cultivated; however, the number of people who grow a few dozen plants in the backyard for personal use, with no thought of selling or trafficking, could increase this estimate substantially.

Of major concern in the U.S. today is the early age at which drug users begin to experiment. Drug use even seems to be condoned by the general public; a fact substantiated by the number of HEAD SHOPS that have sprung up around the country. They not only sell such items as water pipes for smoking marijuana, but books on how to cultivate your own marijuana, and pamphlets that describe how to convert cocaine into freebase for smoking. In many states these items may not be marketed in windows or displays as drug paraphernalia.

Polydrug use has been on the increase in recent years and often with disastrous results. The SYNERGISTIC effects of certain drugs can be fatal. Alcohol, which remains one of the principal drugs of abuse in the U.S., is most often involved as a primary or secondary drug in polydrug use, and there are many users who take an "upper" in the morning and a "downer" at night.

The northeastern region of the U.S., an area that extends from Delaware to Maine, has more drug abusers than any other part of the country. An estimated 40% of the heroin addicts in the U.S. live in this region (the majority in New York City). Cocaine use since 1990, especially in the form of crack, has leveled off due to the impurity of the drug. Although for many years south Florida has been the hub of illicit drug trafficking, there has been a recent trend toward unloading drugs along the New England coastline as well as in southern California and Texas. This may be due to the fact that there has been increased surveillance by enforcement authorities in Florida, but it may also be a result of the high concentration of organized crime in the northeast and the desire by smugglers to move their products as quickly as possible to a densely populated area where the demand is known. Despite this recent trend, Florida and the southeastern region of the country is still a prime importation area simply because of its geographical relation to Central and South America, and transshipment points in the Caribbean area. The drugs most widely abused in the southeast include marijuana and cocaine.

The midwest, an area that previously served as a "customer" for drugs imported through the northeast, Florida or the West Coast, has recently developed its own distribution center: Chicago. Known for many years as the transportation capital of the U.S. (aircraft, trucking and train transportation) Chicago's central geographical location is now being exploited by drug traffickers. Drug gangs are also infiltrating Midwestern cities, such as Kansas City, Omaha, Des Moines, St. Louis and Cincinnati.

In the south central U.S. there are several trafficking problems. Air smugglers have long been operating between the region and South America, with much of the air traffic using secondary roads and private airstrips. Because of the increased enforcement in South Florida, smugglers are not turning to the Texas Gulf coast for shipment by boat. The main problem in this area, however, is the flow of drugs from Mexico into Texas by land. The primary drugs of abuse in the south central region are marijuana and cocaine, followed by methamphetamine and heroin.

The western region of the U.S., which encompasses the area from Alaska to the southern California coast, faces three distinct drug abuse problems: it is a source area, an importation point, and major distribution center. It is also the site of a majority of the country's clandestine drug labs, which are growing in number. Marijuana is the second major cash crop in California. The area is convenient for smuggling not only because of its deepwater ports and rugged shoreline but also because of Los Angeles' international airport. Geographically, California is an obvious point of entry for both southeast Asian and Mexican heroin. The state has also been prominent in the production of LSD, PCP and other dangerous drugs, many of which first gained their popularity in California.

The U.S. has the dubious distinction of being the world's leading consumer and "trend setter" for illicit drugs. This has been substantiated by the abuse patterns for LSD, which was popular during the 1960s, for crack in the 1980s, and for the use of inhalants, which was short lived (although it still continues on a small scale). As abuse of these substances became popular in the U.S., within a matter of months or a few short years their use also became popular in other countries. For more detailed figures on the number of addicts, the sources of a drug, and the various treatment and prevention methods involved, see individual drug entries. For information on how drug abuse has affected the U.S. economy, see BUSINESS and ACCIDENTS.

urine screen If a person has used a drug, either the drug itself or its metabolite will be present in the urine. Although other body fluids can be used to screen for the presence of drugs (blood, sweat, saliva, body tissue), urine testing has become the preferred procedure because specimens can be easily obtained with minimal facilities and by an unskilled technician. The process is also painless, relatively inexpensive and it can provide highly reliable results. Urine testing for drugs first came into general use as a part of methadone maintenance treatment programs. It is now routinely performed as a part of military, sports, business and penal drug screening programs as well as in drug abuse treatment programs.

The most widely used urine tests currently performed to detect the presence of drugs are: GAS CHROMATOGRAPHY (GC), RADIOIMMOASSAY (RIA), gas chromatography/mass spectometry (GC-MS) and enzyme multiplied immunoassay technique (EMIT). Two characteristics are basic to all the various urine tests—their sensitivity and their specifity. The sensitivity of a test is determined by the smallest concentration of a drug or metabolite that can be detected. The specifity of a test refers to the degree to which it can discriminate between closely related drugs, metabolites or naturally occurring substances.

The usual substances tested on a urine screen are THC (as acid metabolites) heroin (as morphine), amphetamines, cocaine, barbiturates and phencyclidine, though other compounds can also be detected. Methods for detecting LSD in urine are presently restricted to research laboratories.

The first over-the-counter urinalysis kit was marketed in early 1984 by Checkpoint Laboratories of Virginia. The kits are sold in drugstores and urine specimens are mailed to Checkpoint which screens for traces of marijuana, cocaine and other drugs.

(See DRUG TESTING.)

U.S. Olympic Committee Perhaps no organization has had more experience with preventing the use of illicit drugs by athletes than the Olympic Committee. The committee has for years worked extensively to make Olympic competition drug free through the use of testing, prevention and other education efforts. In the 1988 Summer Olympics, Canada's Ben Johnson was forced to return his gold medal after his drug test revealed steroid use. The committee has achieved widespread international cooperation on these issues. Today, more than 300 drugs are banned at the Olympic Games by the International Olympic Committee.

USP See *U.S. PHARMACOPEIA.*

U.S. Pharmacopeia (USP) Legally recognized book of standards for drugs published by the U.S. Pharmacopeia Convention, Inc. It contains standards for strength and purity and formulas for making nearly all drugs currently in use. The *USP*, first published in 1820, is revised every five years. Standards given in the *USP* were given legal status under the National Food and Drug Act of 1967.

V

Valium® (Roche) A sedative hypnotic that contains diazepam, a BENZODIAZEPINE derivative. It is used in the treatment of tension, anxiety, seizures and for alcohol withdrawal. Tolerance can develop along with physical and psychological dependence. One of the most widely prescribed drugs in the United States, it has a significant potential for abuse and when taken with alcohol or other central nervous system depressants it can have an additive effect. It is supplied in 2 mg white tablets; 5 mg yellow tablets; and 10 mg blue tablets.

Valmid® (Dista) A mild sedative hypnotic that contains ethinamate and is used when deep hypnosis is not needed. Tolerance can develop along with dependency. When taken with alcohol or other central nervous system depressants it can have an additive effect. Overdosage can result in respiratory depression. It is supplied in 500 mg capsules with a light blue opaque body and blue opaque cap.

vaporous anesthetics Liquid anesthetics that are readily vaporizable at relatively low temperatures. The two vaporous anesthetics which are sometimes abused as INHALANTS are CHLOROFORM and ETHER.

Veronal® A long-acting BARBITURATE that contained BARBITAL. First manufactured in 1903, Veronal was the first barbiturate used in medicine but is no longer available.

vinbarbital A short- to intermediate-acting BARBITURATE.

vinho de jurumena A hallucinogenic beverage made from the seeds of *Mimosa hostilis,* a plant native to Brazil. It contains an organic form of DMT, the plant's active principle.

violence See CRIME, ORGANIZED CRIME, CHILDREN OF DRUG DEPENDENT INDIVIDUALS, and SPOUSE ABUSE.

virola A tree belonging to the *Myristicaceae* family. The bark is made into a psychedelic snuff by the Yekwana Indians in Venezuela.

vitamins See NUTRITION.

volatile solvents See INHALANTS.

Volstead Act The popular name for the National Prohibition Act of 1920 which enforced the EIGHTEENTH AMENDMENT. Representative Andrew Volstead of Minnesota was its sponsor. The act provided for the enforcement of wartime prohibition, banned intoxicating beverages and contained provisions for the industrial use of alcohol.

Voranil® (USV Pharmaceutical) An anorectic that contains clortermine and is used for weight control. Tolerance can develop and because its activity is similar to that of AMPHETAMINES both physical and psychological dependence can occur. It has a significant potential for abuse. Overdosage can result in restlessness, tremors, confusion and hallucinations. It is supplied in 50 mg pale yellow tablets.

W

Washington, D.C., drug cases in This is one of the major drug-infested cities in the U.S. Disruption of the lives of the capital's inhabitants due to drug abuse and drug-related crime is enormous. A recent survey found that 56% of criminal suspects tested were using drugs at the time of arrest. The city has earned the dubious honor ''Murder Capital'' of the U.S.

After months of complaining by residents and some federal officials and law-makers, then drug czar William Bennett unveiled in mid-April 1989 an $80 million emergency plan for an assault on the city's drug-and-murder epidemic. Bennett's measures include: 82 additional federal agents to assist local police; a 500-bed detention facility to be built in the District and more beds available in a federal prison in nearby Maryland. Former Mayor Marion Barry, who was convicted in 1991 of drug possession, was snubbed by Bennett and was not invited to the press conference at which the plan was announced. Bennett said that Barry's administration ''has failed to serve its citizens.''

But the strangled inner-city drug situation is so pervasive that many District residents are not optimistic that Bennett's program will have much effect. Urbanologists say the long-term solution is to create more and better jobs for ghetto young people.

''Outline for a Skirmish,'' *Time,* April 24, 1989, 25.

water of life This term is applied to any of several distilled spirits. Originally, it was used in reference to a legendary elixir, probably not alcoholic, that would confer perpetual youth or immortality. Ponce de Leon, the Spanish explorer who discovered Florida, probably best exemplified the quest for such an elixir in his search for the Fountain of Youth. As early as Roman times, the term was associated with particularly strong drink that would produce a temporary feeling of blissful immortality. The Latin term was *aqua vitae* which was later anglicized to whiskey.

Webb-Canyon Law In 1913, after a veto by President William Howard Taft, Congress passed this law which prohibited the shipment of liquor into dry areas. The law was designed to allow dry states to exercise sovereignty over alcohol-related affairs within their borders, and gave each state the right to make its own laws concerning shipments of liquor by mail order.

weight loss and control See ANORECTICS.

Wernicke's encephalopathy A disease of the BRAIN and CENTRAL NERVOUS SYSTEM which is related to thiamine deficiency and afflicts alcoholics after a number of years of heavy drinking. Victims commonly suffer delirium, tremors, visual impairment and inability to maintain balance, as well as increased risk of heart failure. It is commonly seen in combination with Korsakoff's amnesia (syndrome) and the combined syndrome is called Wernicke-Korsakoff syndrome because both syndromes have a common etiology. If detected and treated early enough, Wernicke's encephalopathy may be reversed. (See also KORSAKOFF'S PSYCHOSIS.)

White House Conference for a Drug Free America In 1986, the Congress passed and the president signed the Anti-Drug Abuse Act of 1986 (P.L. 99–576). One requirement of that legislation (Subtitle S of Title I) was the establishment of a White House Conference for a Drug Free America. The legislation was implemented by President Ronald Regan through Executive Order No. 12595 on May 5, 1987, which added a new purpose for the conference: "To focus public attention on the importance of fostering a widespread attitude of intolerance for illegal drugs and their use throughout all segments of society."

Results of the conference were presented in a *Final Report to the President and the Congress,* signed by Lois Haight Herrington, June 1988. Herrington, a former deputy attorney general, noted that the "Conference met throughout the country in seven diverse cities. We asked questions, stimulated debate, and profited by the insight of national, state and local officials. We also heard from law enforcement, health care and research professionals, corporate and labor leaders, parents, educators, media and entertainment figures, and sports heroes. We involved both young and old whose lives are dedicated to fighting the scourge of illegal drugs as well as those who have been directly or indirectly tainted by drugs. We received the insight of our 127 distinguished Presidential Conferees."

More than 2,000 antidrug participants, over and above the president's appointees, took part in this historic conference. The point person of the Reagan administration's battle against illegal drugs, Nancy Reagan, stirred the attendees by saying, "If you're a casual drug user, you're an accomplice to murder."

Much of the discussion appeared to critics to be simply a rehashing of old ideas—military intervention, crop eradication, drug testing, increased law-enforcement efforts—but most agreed that a significant first step would be to shift the focus of the drug war from trying to control and cut off the supplies to reducing the demand.

The conference's Final Report, issued in June 1988, submitted to the president recommendations in 12 key areas relating to the overall drug problem. On one point, all the conferees seemed to agree. No single approach alone is going to reduce, let alone cure, the drug plague—none represents either a sure or quick fix.

The White House Conference for a Drug Free America, Final Report (U.S. Government Printing Office, Washington, D.C. June 1988).

"White Mare" Code name for a 17-month investigation that resulted in late February 1989 in the biggest heroin bust ever in the U.S. FBI agents and police in New York arrested some 40 people, including the international drug ring's kingpin, Kok Leung Woo, 71. Also arrested were members of the ring in more than half a dozen cities around the world—in Canada, Singapore and Hong Kong. An astonishing 820 pounds of the narcotic, with an estimated street value of nearly $1 billion, was confiscated from three houses in New York City. The code name "White Mare" was inspired by the color of the drug and the fact that heroin is often known as horse on the street.

"Riding a White Mare," *Time,* March 6, 1989, 33.

WHO See WORLD HEALTH ORGANIZATION.

wild cucumber *Exhinocystis lobata.* A vine native to the United States and a member of the melon family. There are claims that the seeds of the fruits can produce psychedelic effects.

wild fennel *Foeniculum vulgare.* Though there are claims that it can produce psychedelic effects, the plant is poisonous and can cause severe adverse reactions.

wino An alcoholic who drinks only wine. Also a person who consumes a large amount of wine because it can be obtained inexpensively and he wants to get the most alcohol for his money. Other alcoholic beverages are consumed when they are available.

withdrawal A series of symptoms that appear when a drug on which the user is physically dependent is abruptly stopped or severely reduced. Withdrawal occurs most dramatically and consistently in cases of addiction to sedatives or narcotics. The syndrome consists of symptoms that are broadly opposite to the drugs' usual effects—a kind of ''rebound'' effect.

The intensity and duration of withdrawal symptoms depends on individual susceptibility, properties of the particular drug and the degree of addiction. Generally speaking, shorter-acting substances, such as heroin, produce more rapidly developing, shorter and more severe withdrawal symptoms than longer-lasting, more slowly eliminated drugs such as methadone.

Alcohol and other sedatives: The precise mechanism of withdrawal from ALCOHOL and sedatives is not completely understood, although the syndrome is well-documented. The release from the burden of CNS depression over a sustained period of time results in CNS overactivity. This explains many of the symptoms and signs that are evoked. It is unclear how quickly dependence on alcohol develops and therefore exactly what symptoms constitute the first manifestations of withdrawal. The HANGOVER commonly experienced after a bout of heavy drinking and the slight tremulousness that can persist after several days' intoxication may be early withdrawal symptoms, but the more traumatic symptoms present themselves only after a drinker has consumed 400-500 ml (500 ml = 1 pint) of alcohol daily for about a month and a half. Abstinence after this level of consumption can produce withdrawal symptoms. The most common and mildest symptoms appear in a few hours and generally include tremulousness, weakness, sweating, nausea and vomiting, loss of appetite and abdominal cramps. More severe symptoms include cardiac dysrhythmia and hallucinations. If dependency is mild, only some of the above symptoms may appear briefly. In cases of more severe withdrawal, this first anxious shaky stage may be followed by a period of convulsive seizures, usually on the second or third day after abstinence. These RUM FITS, which occur in only a minority of cases, require medical intervention because they can develop into STATUS EPILEPTICUS.

The most dangerous form of withdrawal, dramatic and terrifying to the victim, consists of delirium tremens (the DTs), a period of intense auditory, visual and tactile hallucinations which can last three or four days. During this time the patient suffers severe agitation and disorientation, sleeps very little, and experiences fever and profuse sweating that may cause serious dehydration. His behavior usually becomes very aggressive and even self-destructive. Death from hyperthermia, peripheral vascular collapse, or self-inflicted injury can occur during this stage of withdrawal: there is a 10% mortality rate for alcoholics suffering untreated delirium tremens.

Abrupt withdrawal from alcohol, rather than gradual detoxification, usually lasts 5-7 days and results in complete recovery from physical dependence, although certainly not from psychological dependence. In rare cases, and due to uncertain causes, patients have remained in chronic psychotic states resembling schizophrenia. Gradual detoxification is much safer than abrupt cessation, although not recommended in treatment facilities, and convulsions can be avoided by the substitution of a drug that is cross-dependent with alcohol such as Librium or the early administration of an anticonvulsant, such as Dilantin, in large doses. These drugs are used when an individual is detoxified in a hospital or treatment setting.

Barbiturates, tranquilizers and other sedative hypnotics: The addictive nature of barbiturates came to the attention of German chemists soon after the development of these drugs in the early 1900s, but the withdrawal syndrome was less consistent and more puzzling than the one already known to occur with narcotics. Abrupt cessation of a regular intake of even large doses of sedative hypnotic drugs did not *always* precipitate withdrawal symptoms, so evidence supporting the risk of addiction to these depressants seemed inconclusive. The difference, in fact, between depressants and narcotics is that dependence to depressants develops only above a certain threshold of daily intake; even large amounts below this threshold will not always cause physical addiction and, therefore, withdrawal.

How quickly such dependence develops is still unclear, but the withdrawal syndrome brought about by abstinence or the sharp reduction of intake closely resembles that occurring in alcoholics. Withdrawal symptoms from depressants may occur within a few hours after the drug is stopped and are characterized by physical weakness, anxiety, nausea and vomiting, dizziness and sleeplessness. Hallucinations, delirium, delusions and convulsions may occur as long as three days to a week following withdrawal and may last for many days. Withdrawal from benzodiazepines is similar except that it may take longer to develop. The onset of withdrawal from tranquilizers with long half-lives is delayed but the withdrawal persists longer. Not all symptoms that emerge following cessation of tranquilizer use are withdrawal phenomena. Some represent emergent anxiety that was repressed by the medication. Withdrawal from barbiturates is dangerous and should be done either under the care of a physician or in a hospital setting.

Heroin and other narcotics: The duration and intensity of withdrawal symptoms from heroin and other narcotics is directly related to the quality of the drug, and the quantity and frequency of use. Because of limited finances and the poor quality of street drugs today, few addicts use more than 500 mg of morphine (125-150 mg of heroin) a day. Most addicts can afford to support only a relatively mild physical dependence and so are spared the most severe forms of opiate withdrawal.

If an addict who uses low regular intermittent doses does not receive his regular fix at the expected time (usually every six to twelve hours), symptoms resembling the flu are likely to occur: nausea, uneasiness, yawning, sweating alternating with chills, various aches and pains, tears and runny nose. Unless counteracted by a dose of heroin or a cross-tolerant drug such as methadone, these symptoms gradually intensify and broaden to include a range of symptoms showing central nervous system excitation: pupillary dilation, increased heart rate and blood pressure, twitching, spasms, gooseflesh, diarrhea, sexual arousal and insomnia or a "yen" sleep. Cardiovascular collapse is a risk. Withdrawal from a heavy chronic narcotic habit can be extremely severe and painful.

Depending on the habit, and on the quality and purity of the heroin, heroin withdrawal generally peaks in 24 to 48 hours and is usually completed within a week. Certain effects, such as increased blood pressure and heart rate, can persist during a period of "protracted abstinence" of up to six months.

Because narcotics readily cross the placental barrier, babies born of female addicts share their mothers' physical dependence and often exhibit withdrawal symptoms soon after birth.

As previously mentioned, withdrawal from methadone is more prolonged but less severe than heroine withdrawal, since methadone is a longer acting, more slowly eliminated drug. If administered during heroin withdrawal, methadone can ease the intensity of the experience. Conversely, the administration of a group of drugs known as narcotic antagonists, of which NALORPHINE is an example, can precipitate the withdrawal process (and increase its unpleasantness).

Amphetamines and other stimulants: Stimulant drugs, such as amphetamines and caffeine, are generally considered to be more psychologically than physically addictive. Nevertheless, sudden abstinence from amphetamines, cocaine and even coffee does produce symptoms in most people: headache, stomach cramps, lethargy, chronic fatigue and often severe emotional depression. Furthermore, abnormal EEG patterns which have been recorded under these circumstances have stabilized after administration of the drug in question.

Hallucinogens and cannabis: Neither hallucinogens nor cannabis are physically addictive; abstinence or abrupt cessation of intake from them will not produce distinct withdrawal symptoms.

women In the late nineteenth and early twentieth centuries, when the use of patent medicines containing opiates and alcohol resulted in large numbers of addicts throughout American society, three times as many women as men developed such addictions. The typical addict was a middle-aged, middle- to upper-class housewife. Today women of all ages, classes and ethnic groups are heavily involved in drug use and abuse—perhaps less visibly than men, but in alarming and increasing numbers. Women currently account for 60% of all drug-related emergency room visits. Their drug-taking behavior also exposes them to dangers which do not affect men, such as those imposed on the fetus during PREGNANCY.

During this century and especially the past few decades, women's consumption of alcohol and other drugs, as well as our awareness of it, has increased markedly as a result of social changes which have caused and allowed women to indulge more freely in mind-altering substances and to be more open about their use of drugs. There was a particularly noticeable increase in drug use during World War II when a large number of women joined the work force. Social changes experienced in recent years have increased the pressures which women face daily.

The stress felt by today's working women may be a contributing factor to the increase in alcohol and drug use. Today, 60% of women in the U.S. drink alcoholic beverages, the highest percentage ever. Perhaps as many as 25% of those women are heavy drinkers (3 to 5 drinks per day). Regular drinking is now common among high school girls, and the number of young female drinkers is increasing more rapidly than the number of young male drinkers. Women often feel they must work harder than their male counterparts to prove that they are competent. Many women also feel conflict about moving away from the traditional roles of wife and mother. In addition, working women who are divorced or separated often have financial difficulties and the responsibilities of child care; loneliness is also a frequent problem. Employed women are almost as likely to have drinking problems as unemployed women, whereas employed men are only about half as likely to have problems as unemployed men. When compared on a marital basis, the highest rate of alcohol-related problems is among divorced and separated women; single women are next; and married women and widows have the lowest rates.

Alcoholism is a particularly severe problem among female homosexuals. In 1970 a study found that 35% of all lesbians had severe drinking problems as compared with

28% of homosexual men and only 5% of heterosexual women. Women in minority groups, particularly black women, face oppression because of both their race and sex. Unemployment rates for black women are higher than those for either white women or black men and they are far more likely to head families subsisting below the official poverty level.

The tobacco and alcoholic beverage industries have recognized this growing market and many companies aim their advertising at women—not without results. Currently 27% of all women smoke cigarettes regularly, while the number of male smokers has dropped sharply over the last 20 years. Thirty-two percent of all adult smokers are male. There has been no similar decline for women. In 1989 a government survey showed that 1.7 million teenage girls smoke as compared to 1.6 million boys. Statistics also indicate that men are twice as successful as women in their efforts to quit smoking. A 1985 survey shows that among youths, more males (20%) than females (1%) report use of smokeless tobacco.

The estimated number of women alcoholics in the United States is over five million. Alcoholics Anonymous reports that one in three of its members is a woman and that in recent years more and more teenage girls with drinking problems have been attending meetings. Women are not only more susceptible than men to the transitory effects of alcoholic intoxication, because of their lower weight, but they are also more vulnerable to cirrhosis of the liver.

Women with alcohol problems are more likely to use prescribed drugs, particularly sedatives and it is harder to break a dual addiction than an addiction to alcohol alone. A 1983 survey of AA members showed that 40% of the women (but only 27% of the men) were addicted to drugs other than alcohol. Three percent of the respondents were under age 21, and of this group 79% suffer from dual addictions.

There are an estimated two to three million female prescription-drug addicts in the United States. Women are prescribed sedatives more than twice as often as men and consume 71% of all antidepressant medications and 80% of all legal amphetamines (often in the form of diet pills). In 1980, 26 million Valium prescriptions were written for women. Since then, however, Valium has been prescribed less and less than in previous years and is no longer among the 10 most frequently dispensed prescription drugs (due to federal regulation).

Numerous explanations for these high percentages have been postulated. Twice as many women as men are diagnosed as suffering from depression and such depression may be the result of the restricted and self-denying roles women often feel they must play. Some 67% of female problem drinkers correlate their drinking bouts with the days of the month when they are premenstrual, a time when many women experience emotional debility and depression. But the high rate of prescriptions for antidepressants seems also to be related to the fact that women are more likely than men to *express* their feelings and seek treatment from a physician but less likely to admit to or be diagnosed as being chemically dependent. In general women see doctors more often than men and just by the fact of exposure are more likely to receive prescriptions. Doctors are also more inclined to pacify women with drugs, as they often do with the ELDERLY. In the case of alcohol-related problems, doctors may prescribe pills for the symptoms instead of confronting the alcoholism.

Society's reaction to women's alcohol and other drug abuse has traditionally been more condemnatory than toward men's equally destructive habits. Although today women's drinking is taken for granted, female drunkenness is still frowned upon. Similarly, while the wives of alcoholics typically endure their husbands' problems and try to help them get treatment, men are more likely to leave their alcoholic wives in disgust. Consequently women have been more likely to suffer their addictions in secret and not to seek treatment. Until recently treatment programs specifically oriented toward helping women have been rare, but newer programs incorporating women's groups are proving successful. (See also DEPRESSION.)

Women's Sport Foundation drug use program An organization helping to lead the fight to end illicit drug use in amateur and professional athletics. The nonprofit foundation fosters competitive opportunities for girls and women and has been in the forefront of efforts to protect athletes from illicit drug use as well as the abuse of legal drugs and alcohol. Contact: Deborah Anderson, 342 Madison Avenue, Suite 728, New York, NY 10173. Telephone: (800) 227-3988 or (212) 972-9170.

wood alcohol See METHANOL.

workplace, antidrug policies and programs A new office was created in February 1987 at NIDA called the OFFICE OF WORKPLACE INITIATIVES (OWI). Its purpose is to raise awareness among labor leaders, employers and employees to drug abuse issues and to foster development of effective employee education, supervisory training and policy and development. OWI provides technical assistance to federal agencies and the private sector on the use of both drug-testing programs and Employee Assistance Programs to reduce drug abuse in the workplace.

The highest drug-using segment of the American work force is the young adult. The most recent NIDA household survey, of those in the 20 to 40-year-old population—representing those currently entering the work force—42% have used illicit drugs within the last year. Twenty-nine percent, or nearly a third of employed Americans in that age bracket, used an illicit drug in the past year and 19% reported some illicit drug use at least once in the past month.

A survey on workplace drug abuse conducted every five years since 1971 at Marquette University reports that 95% of companies surveyed report direct experience with substance abuse in 1986, up from 82% in 1981 and 50% in 1976.

Alcohol and drug abuse cost over $100 billion in lost or impaired productivity each year, according to the latest statistics. And these costs are increasing. Untold millions more dollars are lost as a result of problems often linked to substance abuse: increased on-the-job accidents and security breaches. Drug abuse, for example, cost the U.S. economy $60 billion in 1983, or nearly 30% more than the $47 billion in 1980. Lost productivity, absenteeism, and turnover costs, increased health benefit utilization, accidents, and losses stemming from impaired judgment and creativity are among the drug-related expenses in the estimate. A growing number of companies are now looking to EMPLOYEE ASSISTANCE PROGRAMS (EAPs) to help control skyrocketing health care costs. The total bill U.S. companies will pay for health benefits in 1989 is expected to exceed $500 billion, and experts say at least 10% of the cost can be linked to chemical dependency.

NIDA (National Institute of Drug Abuse) has a toll-free "helpline" to help employers achieve a drug-free workplace. The number is (800) 843-4971; it operates Monday through Friday from 9:00 A.M. to 8:00 P.M. Staff members provide consultation to employees about initiating a company policy that covers such efforts as employee education program, urine-testing programs and establishment of an existing Employee Assistance Program (EAP) to deal directly with drug-related problems of employees.

NIDA also operates a toll-free number for individuals to call with personal questions related to substance abuse (800) 662-HELP. Print information about such matters is also available from the National Clearinghouse for Alcohol and Drug Information (NCADI) by calling (301) 468-2600.

National Institute of Drug Abuse, NIDA Capsules, "Facts About Drugs in the Workplace," CAP 24, Rev. November 1987.

world drug production According to the U.S. State Department, global production of coca, marijuana, opium poppies and hashish increased sharply in 1988, partly due to political and economic instability in drug-producing countries.

Despite a directive issued by President Reagan in 1986 that made drug trafficking a national security issue, a U.S. State Department report concluded that "political and economic instability in drug-producing areas around the world have resulted in the subordination of our drug control agenda to other pressing concerns."

Cited as examples are civil strife in Burma (now Myanmar), war in Afghanistan, the death of President Muhammad Zia ul-Hag in Pakistan and the declining economy in Peru. These events, the report said, signaled possible setbacks for the U.S. in its war on drugs.

The report estimated that from 1987 to 1988, the production of coca increased 7.2% among the four coca-growing countries: Bolivia, Colombia, Peru and Ecuador. Over the same period, the global marijuana crop increased by 22%, the opium crop by 15% and the hashish crop by 11%.

Under a law passed in 1986, the president is required each year to certify by March 1 that countries where major drug trafficking occurs are "fully cooperating" in cracking down on the drug trade. There is a growing sentiment in Congress and the State Department that the law is flawed and applied selectively because it fails to take into account the complexities of relations between drug-trafficking countries and the U.S.

It is estimated that U.S. efforts to slow cocaine traffic from Peru, Bolivia and Colombia have cost American taxpayers $72 million since 1972. According to State Department Inspector General Sherman Funk, testifying before a Senate subcommittee in July 1989, coca production not only continues to increase every year, but efforts to seize illegal drugs have reduced the supply by less than 1%. Funk's report highlighted: inadequate security to protect drug agents, no contingency plans to evacuate them and useless intelligence data.

Mexico, Colombia, Bolivia, Peru, the Bahamas and Paraguay, all major drug-producing or drug-transit countries, are described by Ann B. Wrobleski, assistant secretary of state for international narcotics matters, as "close friends and allies." These countries were cited along with other not-so-friendly nations as needing to "do more" to cooperate with the United States.

The *New York Times* says that "the report in effect has become an annual admission of the inability of the United States to single-handedly fight narcotics."

Johanna Newman, "Drug War Abroad Gets Failing Grade," *USA Today*, July 28, 1989.

Elaine Scialino, "Drug Production Rising Worldwide, State Department Says," *New York Times*, March 2, 1989.

World Health Organization (WHO) A specialized agency of the United Nations. WHO has the primary responsibility for international health matters and public health. Created in 1948, WHO has the benefit of 160 countries that exchange knowledge and experience with the aim of attaining a level of health that permits nations to lead socially and economically productive lives.

World War II, drug use in By the beginning of the 1940s, large-scale illicit drug use in the U.S. had all but disappeared. Prescribed amphetamine use was increasing, however. Gilda Berger, writing about this in her book *Drug Abuse; The Impact on Society*, theorizes, "The success was not due to the various laws and treatment facilities that had been opened. Rather, World War II had cut off supply routes of drugs from Asia and Europe. As an editorial in *Time* stated in 1942, 'The war is probably the best thing that ever happened to the U.S. drug addicts.' " This statement referred to the decline of heroin use. Alcoholism was unaffected by the war.

Gilda Berger, *Drug Abuse: The Impact on Society* (Franklin Watts: New York, 1988), 19.

wormwood See ABSINTHE.

X

xylene A volatile solvent. Although the vapors of this aromatic hydrocarbon are extremely irritating to the nasal membranes, it has some potential for INHALANT abuse.

Y

yayin The sweet wine of Noah, considered by many cultures, such as the Palestinian, a divine gift. These cultures place the origins of this drug close to the origins of man himself. In Sumerian, the language of mankind's first medical text, the original "tree of life" was none other than "the vine that intoxicates."

Ronald K. Siegel, Ph.D., *Intoxication: Life in Pursuit of Artificial Paradise* (E. P. Dutton: New York, 1989), 102.

yerba mate A tea brewed from the leaves of *Ilex paraguariensis*, an evergreen shrub native to Paraguay and Brazil. It contains the stimulant CAFFEINE.

yohimbe *Corynanthe yohimbe*, a tree native to West Africa whose bark and roots are purported to be an aphrodisiac. It does produce hallucinations and mild euphoria but is also toxic in large doses. It is sold pharmacutically in the U.S. as an unproven treatment for impotence.

***yopo* beans** A hallucinogen used by the Guahibo Indians in South America. Used in some experiments wherein researchers gave mice and rats powdered *yopo* beans and found the animals staggering and constantly looking around as if they were orienting themselves to hallucinations.

Youth to Youth An international nonprofit drug prevention education organization with groups for youth in grades 6 to 8 and grades 9 through 12: college-age students act as group leaders. It conducts instructional seminars for youths and parents on forming their own drug prevention programs. A resource center provides training manuals, videos and other materials. A free quarterly newsletter is available upon request. The group holds regional and national conferences yearly. Contact: Youth to Youth, Robin Seymour, 700 Bryden Road, Columbus, OH 43215. Telephone: (614) 224-4506.

youths The adolescent is perhaps the most vulnerable individual confronting the growing social acceptance of drug use in the United States. In 1980 there were 10,000 emergency room visits related to marijuana and they primarily involved adolescents. A 1981 nationwide government survey showed that one out of 14 high school seniors smoke marijuana daily, and in some communities adolescents who have not tried marijuana may be in the minority.

In a report published by the National Institute on Drug Abuse, *Illicit Drug Use, Smoking, and Drinking by America's High School Students, College Students and Young Adults: 1975–1987*, key findings indicate that the use of many illicit drugs has declined or is declining from the peak levels of the 1970s. Despite these improvements, illicit drug use is still extremely prevalent among high school age youths and abuse figures are probably the highest to be found in any industrialized nation in the world.

The survey shows a significant drop in the use of cocaine, finding a decrease in about one-third, from 6.2% in 1986 to 4.3% in 1987, in the proportion of seniors who were "current users" of cocaine, and a decline of about one-fifth, from 12.7% to 10.3%, in seniors who had used cocaine at least once in the past year. The downturn in cocaine use was similar for college students and young adults.

Despite this, early data on "crack" suggests that it is not following the overall decline in cocaine use. Among seniors, 5.6% report having tried crack, while 4% said they used it in the past year.

In the mid to late 1970s, the survey found increasing drug use, especially marijuana use, among high school seniors. In 1978, the peak year, nearly 11% of high school seniors had used marijuana on a daily basis; in 1987, only 3.3% used the drug daily. Reported use of marijuana in the past year was 3.6%, the lowest level recorded since the survey began in 1925.

In addition, the illicit use of stimulants and sedatives continues to decline among high school seniors, college students, and young adults generally. Current use (use in the 30 days prior to being surveyed) of stimulants among high school seniors dropped from 5.5% in 1986 to 5.2% in 1987; and sedatives use declined from 2.2% to 1.7%.

Lloyd Johnston, Ph.D., the survey director, noted, "But despite these downward trends, there are still a significant number of young people involved with illicit drugs. Well over half (57%) have tried an illicit drug by the time they graduate from high school." This is down from a peak of 64% in 1982, but it still means, as Johnston says, "that our drug abuse prevention efforts are as important as they have ever been."

The use of chemicals overall has not been demonstrated to have decreased. Alcohol use, for example, showed no decrease among high school seniors in the years 1985 through 1987 and shows increases for the current decade when compared with the 1970s. Some 66% of students reported use within the past 30 days. Cigarette smoking, too, has not dropped among high school seniors since 1984, with 18.7% of them daily users upon graduation. Also, there was little change observed in the use of LSD, heroin or opiates other than heroin; and there was some evidence of a continuing gradual increase in the use of inhalants.

More specifically, regarding use of licit drugs covered in the study, nearly all high school seniors (92%) had experience with alcohol and 66% were current users. About 5% were daily drinkers and nearly 37.5% said that at least on one occasion they had drunk heavily in the past two weeks, that is, they drank five or more drinks in a row.

Cigarette smoking has not dropped among high school seniors since 1984. Nearly a fifth (18.7%) are daily smokers by the time they leave high school. (Note that these statistics do not include high school dropouts, the majority of whom smoke.) Most of these young people started to smoke by age 13.

Another survey, conducted in 1988 by the National Institute on Drug Abuse (NIDA), covering 8,814 people ages 12 and up found that among those ages 12 to 17 marijuana and hashish use in the month before dropped from 12% in 1985 to 6% in 1988. Alcohol use in that age group also dropped, from 31% to 25%, as did cigarette use, from 15% to 12%. Fifty-three percent of those ages 12 to 17 believed that trying cocaine was very risky compared with 31% in 1985. The rates for cocaine use in the month before the survey were highest among the unemployed (5%) and those ages 18 to 25 (5%). They were twice as high for males (2%) as for females (1%).

One percent of those surveyed had used crack at some time in their life; 0.5% had used it at least once in the previous year—which translates to 1 million users. Of those who had used cocaine at least once in the previous year, 31% had used crack.

Since 1977, teenage youths have consistently identified drugs as their biggest problem, according to a 1989 Gallup poll. But in 1989, more than twice as many put drugs at the top of their "biggest problem" list—60% as compared to 27% in 1977. Interestingly, in 1989, teenagers said their number two problem, after drugs, was peer pressure (11%); in 1977, problem number two was listed as "getting along with parents" (20%).

Causes of drug abuse: The use of drugs is increasing among younger children. This is particularly disturbing because studies have shown that the younger a person begins to experiment with drugs, the more likely he is to progress to heavier use and stronger drugs. There are any number of theories as to why a child first experiments with drugs: questions of status, peer pressure, pleasure, thrills, boredom, stimulation, sophistication, difficulty coping with problems, and so on. Whatever the reasons, they have much to do with adolescence in general; a time when a child is developing physically and emotionally and is caught up in an identity crisis. Adolescence is a time when people have difficulty meeting societal demands and have significant internal demands to face as well. Instant gratification and the feeling of euphoria can dampen the fear of developing independence and decision-making. However, every adolescent is a unique individual with his or her own physical and psychological problems and causes of drug use are speculative.

The 1975–1981 NIDA report suggests some factors that can contribute to drug abuse:

1. The use of illicit drugs generally begins when an individual associates with a friend or acquaintance who is a drug user. This association is followed by an opportunity to use the drug and actual use itself.

2. Continuing contact with people who use drugs will lead to an individual's experimentation. Most people do not try an illicit drug at the very first opportunity.

3. There is more likely to be drug abuse among adolescents whose mothers smoke cigarettes and/or drink moderately than among those whose mothers abstain.

4. If an older sibling uses alcohol and/or illicit drugs, there is a tendency for use and for the use of the specific drug that the older sibling uses.

5. The following factors do not appear to be related to a child's drug use: the fact that the father may use drugs, the family's socioeconomic status, the mother's current employment status, or the mother's marital status.

6. The presence of children seems to be an influence on drug use in parents in the 26–34 age group. Over 60% of married people with no children have tried marijuana and 24% are current users; by comparison, 40% of married people with children have tried marijuana but only 10% are current users.

Prevention and treatment: While the treatment of drug dependence is extremely important, the greatest hope for combating the problem lies in preventing drug use from starting in the first place, or interfering with its use during the early experimentation stage. Prevention strategies include:

1. *Information.* This includes providing accurate and objective information about all types of drugs and their effects on the body.

2. *Intervention.* This includes providing assistance and support to adolescents during critical periods of their life through counseling, the use of hotlines, etc.

3. *Education & skill development.* This includes clarifying values and improving problem-solving skills within a structured setting. Group discussions and role playing are common techniques in helping young people improve their ability to cope and make decisions.

4. *Alternatives.* This includes promoting confidence and self-reliance through new, challenging experiences in school, and providing positive alternatives to drug-taking behavior. Such alternatives include restoration projects, volunteer services in the community, and helping such causes as environment preservation.

High School Senior Drug Use: 1975–1988
Used In Past Month

Approx. N =	Class of 1975 (9400)	Class of 1976 (15400)	Class of 1977 (17100)	Class of 1978 (17800)	Class of 1979 (15500)	Class of 1980 (15900)	Class of 1981 (17500)	Class of 1982 (17700)	Class of 1983 (16300)	Class of 1984 (15900)	Class of 1985 (16000)	Class of 1986 (15200)	Class of 1987 (16300)	Class of 1988 (16300)	'87–'88 change
Marijuana/Hashish	27.1	32.2	35.4	37.1	36.5	33.7	31.6	28.5	27.0	25.2	25.7	23.4	21.0	18.0	−3.0ss
Inhalants	NA	0.9	1.3	1.5	1.7	1.4	1.5	1.5	1.7	1.9	2.2	2.5	2.8	2.6	−0.2
Inhalants Adjusted	*NA*	*NA*	*NA*	*NA*	*3.2*	*2.7*	*2.5*	*2.5*	*2.5*	*2.6*	*3.0*	*3.2*	*3.5*	*3.0*	*−0.5*
Amyl & Butyl Nitrites	NA	NA	NA	NA	2.4	1.8	1.4	1.1	1.4	1.4	1.6	1.3	1.3	0.6	−0.7s
Hallucinogens	4.7	3.4	4.1	3.9	4.0	3.7	3.7	3.4	2.8	2.6	2.5	2.5	2.5	2.2	−0.3
Hallucinogens Adjusted	*NA*	*NA*	*NA*	*NA*	*5.3*	*4.4*	*4.5*	*4.1*	*3.5*	*3.2*	*3.8*	*3.5*	*2.8*	*2.3*	*−0.5*
LSD	2.3	1.9	2.1	2.1	2.4	2.3	2.5	2.4	1.9	1.5	1.6	1.7	1.8	1.8	0.0
PCP	NA	NA	NA	NA	2.4	1.4	1.4	1.0	1.3	1.0	1.6	1.3	0.6	0.3	−0.3
Cocaine	1.9	2.0	2.9	3.9	5.7	5.2	5.8	5.0	4.9	5.8	6.7	6.2	4.3	3.4	−0.9ss
"Crack"	NA	NA	NA	NA	NA	NA	NA	NA	NA	NA	NA	NA	1.5	1.6	+0.1
Other cocaine	NA	NA	NA	NA	NA	NA	NA	NA	NA	NA	NA	NA	4.1	3.2	−0.9
Heroin	0.4	0.2	0.3	0.3	0.2	0.2	0.2	0.2	0.2	0.3	0.3	0.2	0.2	0.2	0.0
Other opiates	2.1	2.0	2.8	2.1	2.4	2.4	2.1	1.8	1.8	1.8	2.3	2.0	1.8	1.6	−0.2
Stimulants	8.5	7.7	8.8	8.7	9.9	12.1	15.8	13.7	12.4	NA	NA	NA	NA	NA	NA
Stimulants Adjusted	*NA*	*NA*	*NA*	*NA*	*NA*	*NA*	*NA*	*10.7*	*8.9*	*8.3*	*6.8*	*5.5*	*5.2*	*4.6*	*−0.6*
Sedatives	5.4	4.5	5.1	4.2	4.4	4.8	4.6	3.4	3.0	2.3	2.4	2.2	1.7	1.4	−0.3
Barbiturates	4.7	3.9	4.3	3.2	3.2	2.9	2.6	2.0	2.1	1.7	2.0	1.8	1.4	1.2	−0.2
Methaqualone	2.1	1.6	2.3	1.9	2.3	3.3	3.1	2.4	1.8	1.1	1.0	0.8	0.6	0.5	−0.1
Tranquilizers	4.1	4.0	4.6	3.4	3.7	3.1	2.7	2.4	2.5	2.1	2.1	2.1	2.0	1.5	−0.5s
Alcohol	68.2	68.3	71.2	72.1	71.8	72.0	70.7	69.7	69.4	67.2	65.9	65.3	66.4	63.9	−2.5s
Cigarettes	38.7	38.8	38.4	36.7	34.4	30.5	29.4	30.0	30.3	29.3	30.1	29.6	29.4	28.7	−0.7

Note: Level of significance of difference between the two most recent classes: s = .05, ss = .01 NA indicates data not available.

High School Senior Drug Use: 1976–1988
Daily Users

Approx. N =	Class of 1975 (9400)	Class of 1976 (15400)	Class of 1977 (17100)	Class of 1978 (17800)	Class of 1979 (15500)	Class of 1980 (15900)	Class of 1981 (17500)	Class of 1982 (17700)	Class of 1983 (16300)	Class of 1984 (15900)	Class of 1985 (16000)	Class of 1986 (15200)	Class of 1988 (16300)	'87–'88 change
Marijuana/Hashish	6.0	8.2	9.1	10.7	10.3	9.1	7.0	6.3	5.5	5.0	4.9	4.0	2.7	−0.6s
Inhalants	NA	0.0	0.0	0.1	0.0	0.1	0.1	0.1	0.1	0.1	0.2	0.2	0.2	+0.1
Inhalants Adjusted	*NA*	*NA*	*NA*	*NA*	*0.1*	*0.2*	*0.2*	*0.2*	*0.2*	*0.2*	*0.4*	*0.4*	*0.3*	*−0.1*
Amyl & Butyl Nitrites	NA	NA	NA	NA	0.0	0.1	0.1	0.0	0.2	0.1	0.3	0.5	0.1	−0.2
Hallucinogens	0.1	0.1	0.1	0.1	0.1	0.1	0.1	0.1	0.1	0.1	0.1	0.1	0.0	−0.1
Hallucinogens Adjusted	*NA*	*NA*	*NA*	*NA*	*0.2*	*0.2*	*0.1*	*0.2*	*0.2*	*0.2*	*0.3*	*0.3*	*0.0*	*−0.2s*
LSD	0.0	0.0	0.0	0.0	0.0	0.0	0.1	0.0	0.1	0.1	0.1	0.0	0.0	0.0
PCP	NA	NA	NA	NA	0.1	0.1	0.1	0.1	0.1	0.1	0.3	0.2	0.1	−0.2
Cocaine	0.1	0.1	0.1	0.1	0.2	0.2	0.3	0.2	0.2	0.2	0.4	0.4	0.2	−0.1
"Crack"	NA	NA	NA	NA	NA	NA	NA	NA	NA	NA	NA	NA	0.1	−0.1
Other cocaine	NA	NA	NA	NA	NA	NA	NA	NA	NA	NA	NA	NA	0.2	0.0
Heroin	0.1	0.0	0.0	0.0	0.0	0.0	0.0	0.0	0.1	0.0	0.0	0.0	0.0	0.0
Other opiates	0.1	0.1	0.2	0.1	0.0	0.1	0.1	0.1	0.1	0.1	0.1	0.1	0.1	0.0
Stimulants	0.5	0.4	0.5	0.5	0.6	0.7	1.2	1.1	1.1	NA	NA	NA	NA	NA
Stimulants Adjusted	*NA*	*NA*	*NA*	*NA*	*NA*	*NA*	*NA*	*0.7*	*0.8*	*0.6*	*0.4*	*0.3*	*0.3*	*0.0*
Sedatives	0.3	0.2	0.2	0.2	0.1	0.2	0.2	0.2	0.2	0.1	0.1	0.1	0.1	0.0
Barbiturates	0.1	0.1	0.2	0.1	0.0	0.1	0.1	0.1	0.1	0.0	0.1	0.1	0.0	0.0
Methaqualone	0.0	0.0	0.0	0.0	0.0	0.1	0.1	0.1	0.0	0.0	0.0	0.0	0.1	0.0
Tranquilizers	0.1	0.2	0.3	0.1	0.1	0.1	0.1	0.1	0.1	0.1	0.0	0.0	0.0	0.0
Alcohol														
Daily	5.7	5.6	6.1	5.7	6.9	6.0	6.0	5.7	5.5	4.8	5.0	4.8	4.2	−0.6
5+ drinks in a row/ last 2 weeks	36.8	37.1	39.4	40.3	41.2	41.2	41.4	40.5	40.8	38.7	36.7	36.8	34.7	−2.8s
Cigarettes														
Daily	26.9	28.8	28.8	27.5	25.4	21.3	20.3	21.1	21.2	18.7	19.5	18.7	18.1	−0.6
[illegible]	[illegible]	[illegible]	[illegible]	[illegible]	[illegible]	[illegible]	[illegible]	[illegible]	[illegible]	[illegible]	[illegible]	11.4	10.6	−0.8

Along with numerous federal and state funded programs designed to educate America's youth about the dangers of drug and alcohol abuse, the 1970s brought about a rash of newly formed parent and community organizations: FAMILIES IN ACTION (FIA); DO IT NOW FOUNDATION (DIN); etc. Parents and friends of youthful drug abusers, along with community and church leaders now seem to realize that drug education cannot be restricted to school programs. Young people also need to experience care and concern from other outlets. There are Drug Abuse Prevention Coordinators in every state, usually located with the Department of Mental Health or the Department of Health, and groups interested in organizing prevention programs are urged by the government to contact these coordinators.

Probably one of the driving forces behind the organization of parent groups stems from the feeling of helplessness parents feel when they realize their child has been experimenting with drugs. Many parents have no idea what actions to take, what questions to ask, and where to turn for help. One of the biggest conflicts parents face is the moment of truth when they actually find drugs in a child's possession. Do they talk it out? Do they simply seize and destroy? Do they institute punishments? Do they stop a child from seeing his friends? Because of the unpredictable nature of drug use among adolescents, where there are no patterns and use can simply come and go because of fads and pressures, parents are often at a loss for guidelines in handling the problem. Unfortunately, there are also parents who are simply unwilling to look at or deal with the problem; many feel self-guilt, anger and embarrassment and refuse to cooperate. This unwillingness works at cross-purposes with professionals who are trying to cope with the problem. There are other parents who simply want to turn the problem over to a counselor and expect him to deal with the issue without any cooperation on their part.

Professional counselors, particularly those working with school guidance programs, are deluged with cases and are simply too busy to cope effectively. Not only are drug problems a demand on their time, they often have no clear policy to follow and their expectations are often unrealistic. They also feel under pressure because they realize they cannot "do it alone" and many parents expect them to. Misclassification of drug use can also be a problem among counselors. Due to the demands on their time, many counselors often treat all drug use as "dependency" and do not address the causes. In addition, there seems to be a tendency among elementary school teachers to ignore drug use altogether and wait for high school teachers and counselors to take over the problem because they have had more training in dealing with the issue. Passing the buck, however, simply means that elementary school children become forgotten in the shuffle and lack objective information which could help them as they advance in school.

In the last ten years numerous organizations have been formed to combat use and abuse of drugs, probably as a result of a rise in awareness about the risks to health. Helping those who are becoming addicted to alcohol has been of particular importance. Throughout the country high school groups, such as Students Against Drunk Driving (SADD), are being organized to help their classmates. Telephone numbers are available at all times for teenagers who have had too much to drink. They call a "hot line," manned by their peers, and someone is sent to drive them home. As these groups are fairly new, there has been no evaluation of their effectiveness thus far, but the trend is encouraging.

Very little research has been done to determine the efficiency of prevention efforts. Dissemination of accurate and clear information and the use of peer group support seem to be important factors. Most "scare tactics" seem to actually increase teen interest. Education and early detection and treatment are the current areas of effort by most prevention programs.

APPENDIXES

Appendix 1 Street Language
Appendix 2 Slang Synonyms for Drugs
Appendix 3 Tables and Figures
Appendix 4 Sources of Information

APPENDIX 1
STREET LANGUAGE

A

A-bomb MARIJUANA and HEROIN mixed together and smoked.

A-head A heavy AMPHETAMINE user.

Acapulco gold An especially potent high-quality MARIJUANA grown near Acapulco, Mexico.

ace An obsolete term for a MARIJUANA cigarette.

acid A slang term for LSD-25; from d-lysergic acid diethylamide tartrate.

acid freak A person who exhibits bizarre behavior induced by the use of LSD.

acid head A person who is a habitual heavy user of LSD.

acid rock A type of rock 'n' roll music using electronic sound that was associated with the use of HALLUCINOGENS, particularly LSD. It originated in San Francisco in the 1960s.

acid test Parties held in the 1960s at which LSD was served. Guests dressed in bizarre clothing and listened to acid rock music to enhance the effects of the drug.

action A term that refers to the sales activity of drugs; "there's great action in this area."

a la canona To undergo HEROIN withdrawal without the aid of medication.

amies AMYL NITRATE.

AMT AMPHETAMINES.

amys AMYL NITRATE.

angel dust PHENCYCLIDINE. In powder form, it is mixed with another HALLUCINOGEN, usually MARIJUANA, and smoked, snorted or taken orally.

angel off The arrest of a drug PUSHER's customers either to obtain information on the pusher's activities or to try to put him out of business.

angel trumpet or **angel's trumpet** DATURA.

animal trank PHENCYCLIDINE.

anywhere A slang term for having drugs in one's possession.

Areca nut ARECOLINE.

army disease MORPHINE addiction. A Civil War term born from the frequent and indiscriminate use of morphine at that time, which caused the addiction of an estimated 400,000 soldiers. (See AMERICAN MILITARY.)

artillery Apparatus needed for the injection of a drug.

aurora borealis A slang term for THC, (tetrahydrocannabinol), the active principle in marijuana. Most THC sold illicitly is not THC but more often phencyclidine (PCP).

B

baby MARIJUANA. It is also a term for a person who uses heroin on an irregular basis.

back up The act of withdrawing blood back into the syringe after injecting part of a shot of HEROIN. It is done to prolong the initial sensation and effects of the drug.

backwards The use of tranquilizers to reverse the effects of LSD. The term is also used in reference to someone who renews a drug habit.

bad A term for drugs that are considered very good and very potent.

bad seed PEYOTE.

bad trip A frightening reaction after the use of a hallucinogenic drug, particularly LSD, which can cause a temporary or chronic psychosis.

bador Aztec term for MORNING GLORY SEEDS.

bag A measurement of HEROIN or MARIJUANA. A bag of heroin usually contains about 5 grains of diluted heroin (1–5% pure). A bag of marijuana usually contains 1/7–1/5 oz. The term is also applied to a person who is using one drug exclusively: "He's in an LSD bag."

bagman The person who handles the money in a drug transaction.

bale A pound of MARIJUANA.

balloons Drugs are sometimes packaged for sale in balloons: if a sale is interrupted by police the balloon can be swallowed and later excreted. This method of concealing drugs is also used in smuggling.

bam AMPHETAMINE.

Bambu A brand of cigarette papers used to roll MARIJUANA cigarettes.

bang A narcotics injection, or the act of injecting a narcotic.

bangers DEPRESSANTS.

bank bandit pills BARBITURATES.

banker A person who puts up the capital for a drug-buying trip (particularly in the case of MARIJUANA).

bar A solid block of MARIJUANA. The drug is mixed with honey or sugar water to hold it together in this way.

barbs BARBITURATES.

base Cocaine FREEBASE, CRACK.

baseball Street name for CRACK.

basing Using cocaine FREEBASE.

bazuko (bah-ZOO-koh) A cocaine-based drug similar to crack but even more potent and extremely addictive. A concoction of coca-leaf paste, kerosene, and ether, the powder is smoked in cigarettes. Its explosive impact earned the name—from bazooka. It is cheaper than crack and very dangerous.

B-bomb A BENZEDRINE inhaler. The wad inside, heavily impregnated with Benezedrine, was taken out and soaked in water. The Benzedrine extracted by this process was equal to approximately 25 tablets. The inhalers were removed from the market in 1949 because of this widespread abuse.

beans AMPHETAMINES, MESCALINE.

beast, the LSD.

beat Counterfeit drug. Also a term applied to cheating a person out of money.

bee The amount of MARIJUANA it would take to fill a penny matchbook.

behind acid Using LSD.

belly habit To satisfy a drug habit by taking a drug orally (particularly METHADONE).

belt The initial effect felt after taking a drug.

belted Being in a state of drug euphoria.

bender Being on a drug spree. Used particularly in the case of alcohol, as in "on a bender."

bennies BENZEDRINE.

bent Being in a state of drug euphoria, particularly from the use of HALLUCINOGENS. Originally it referred to HEROIN intoxication.

benz BENZEDRINE.

bernice COCAINE.

bernies COCAINE.

betel nut See ARECOLINE.

bhang The Indian word for MARIJUANA. It is also the name of a tea made from marijuana that is drunk in India.

big bags Bags of HEROIN.

big C COCAINE.

big chief, the MESCALINE.

big con A minor confidence game, as compared to a LONG CON.

big D, the LSD.

big H HEROIN.

big man, the The person who supplies a PUSHER with drugs.

big supplier The person who supplies a PUSHER with drugs.

bing Prison. The term is also used to refer to a drug injection.

bit Period of time served in prison. Also a person's favorite drug that he or she uses exclusively.

biz Apparatus needed for the injection of a drug.

black beauties BIPHETAMINES.

black drink A tea containing caffeine which is made from leaves of the YAUPON plant.

black gunion MARIJUANA that is highly potent, black in color and has a gummy consistency. The word *gunion* may come from the word *gungeon* (an especially potent variety of marijuana from Jamaica or Africa), and may be a variation of the Hindi word *ganga*; most of the marijuana that came into the United States during the 1940s was imported from Jamaica.

black mollies BIPHETAMINES.

black pills OPIUM in pellet form.

black rock Street name for CRACK.

black Russian HASHISH.

black stuff OPIUM.

blackbirds BIPHETAMINES.

blanco Spanish word for HEROIN.

blast To smoke MARIJUANA.

blast party A party at which MARIJUANA is smoked.

blind munchies The strong desire for food (sweets in particular) that is felt while under the influence of MARIJUANA.

block MORPHINE in the shape of a cube and usually sold by the ounce.

blockbusters BARBITURATES.

blond hash HASHISH that is lighter in color and less potent than other varieties of hashish.

blotter LSD in dried form on blotter paper which is chewed.

blow The sniffing of HEROIN or the smoking of MARIJUANA. The term is also applied when a vein is missed during a heroin injection and some of the drug is wasted. Also, a slang word for COCAINE.

blow a fill To smoke OPIUM.

blow a stick To smoke MARIJUANA.

blow your mind To feel the effects of HALLUCINOGENS. Also, to lose touch with reality and not have mental control.

blow-your-mind-roulette A dangerous party game played with a variety of pills—uppers, downers, and so on—which are mixed together in a container and drawn out at random. The drawer does not know what he or she has taken until the effects are felt.

blue acid LSD. The term comes from the color of LSD when it is seen in large amounts.

blue angels AMYTAL sodium.

blue bullets AMYTAL sodium.

blue cheer LSD.

blue devils AMYTAL sodium.

blue dolls AMYTAL sodium.

blue heavens AMYTAL sodium.

blue mist LSD.

blue morning glory seeds MORNING GLORY SEEDS sold under the trade name Heavenly Blues.

blue tips AMYTAL sodium.

blue velvet A mixture of elixir terpin hydrate, CODEINE and tripelenamine.

bluebirds AMYTAL sodium.

blues AMYTAL sodium. Also NUMORPHAN.

body drugs Narcotics, which depress the conscious state, as opposed to HALLUCINOGENS and psychedelics, which stimulate the mind.

bogart It is customary practice to pass a MARIJUANA cigarette around a group. To keep it to oneself is to bogart.

bogue Initial withdrawal symptoms from a drug.

bolsa Spanish term for HEROIN packaged in a bag.

bomb A large-size MARIJUANA cigarette. Also high-quality HEROIN that has had very little dilution.

bombed out Feeling the effects of a drug.

bomber A large-size MARIJUANA cigarette.

bombita COCAINE and AMPHETAMINES in a solution to be injected.

bong A water pipe used to smoke MARIJUANA or tobacco. The smoke bubbles through the water and eliminates some of the harshness.

bonita Lactose crystals (milk sugar), often used to dilute HEROIN. (See CUTTING.)

boogie A drug-buying expedition.

book, the The PHYSICIANS' DESK REFERENCE.

boost To shoplift: a common way for an addict to obtain money to support a habit.

boot and shoot A person who shoplifts and steals to support a drug habit.

booze fighter A person who is determined to "fight" a BOOZE habit. The term implies an ongoing, and therefore unsuccessful, battle characterized by a continuous stream of good intentions and broken resolutions.

booze hound A person who consumes excessive amounts of BOOZE and whose life is greatly influenced by, and even dedicated to, its consumption.

boss High-potency drugs, meaning the best or the strongest.

B.O.T. Balance of time. The sentence a parole violator must serve to fulfill the original sentence.

bouncing powder COCAINE.

boxed Feeling the high effects of, or being under the influence of, a drug.

boy HEROIN.

brain ticklers AMPHETAMINES. Also BARBITURATES.

brick A pressed block of MARIJUANA, OPIUM or MORPHINE. In the case of marijuana, it weighs one pound.

brick, throw a big The impulsive desire to do something violent or commit a crime.

bring down To cause someone to lose the exhilarated feelings induced by a drug.

broccoli MARIJUANA.

brody To feign sickness in front of a doctor in order to gain a prescription for a drug.

brother HEROIN.

brown HEROIN; particularly heroin from Mexico.

brown dots LSD.

brown mixture OPIUM.

brown rock HEROIN.

brown stuff OPIUM.

brown sugar HEROIN.

brownies AMPHETAMINES.

bum bend A frightening reaction after taking LSD, one that could cause temporary or chronic psychosis.

bum kicks Being anxious, worried or depressed about something.

bum trip See BUMMER.

bumblebees AMPHETAMINES.

bummer A frightening reaction after taking a drug. A bum (or bad) trip.

bundle HEROIN packaged (bundled) together in bags by a wholesaler for selling to the PUSHER who, in turn, sells them individually to addicts.

bunk habit Getting the effects of OPIUM by inhaling the fumes when others are smoking without smoking oneself.

burese COCAINE.

burn Cheating or being cheated in drug deals.

burn artist A person who uses the BURN technique.

burn out, burned out The term has three separate meanings: (1) It refers to a chronic drug dependent person who is so weary of the "hassle" of obtaining drugs (like HEROIN) that he discontinues usage. (2) Heavy MARIJUANA smokers, particularly young people, will become dull and apathetic and withdraw from their usual activities; they are called "burnouts" by their peers. (3) Some workers in the "helping professions," such as drug rehabilitation, social work and so on, become discouraged and leave their professions after years of trying to work with difficult patients. The usage has now spread to other professions.

burned One who has been cheated in a drug deal.

burning To smoke MARIJUANA.

bush MARIJUANA.

businessman's lunchtime high DMT, the effects of which last only 30 minutes to an hour.

bust A police raid. The term "busted" refers to being arrested.

button, the PEYOTE.

buy The purchase of a drug.

buzz Feeling the effects of a drug, particularly MARIJUANA, without unpleasant hallucinations.

buzz, rolling To continue feeling the pleasant BUZZ effects of drug.

C

C COCAINE.

caapi AYAHUASCA.

caballo heroin (Spanish for horse).

cabeza de angel A shrub, *Calliandra anomala,* that is dried and used by the Aztec Indians as a snuff.

ca-ca Counterfeit HEROIN.

cactus PEYOTE, MESCALINE.

California sunshine LSD.

came down To lose the effects of a drug, or to experience WITHDRAWAL SYMPTOMS.

can A measurement of drugs, particularly MARIJUANA, which is sometimes sold in 1 oz tobacco cans.

Canadian black MARIJUANA grown in Canada.

canceled stick A cigarette containing MARIJUANA.

C and H A mixture of COCAINE and HEROIN.

C and M A mixture of COCAINE and MORPHINE.

candy Drugs.

candy man A person who sells drugs.

canned sativa HASHISH.

canned stuff OPIUM that has been packaged.

carry, carrying Having drugs on one's person.

cartwheels AMPHETAMINES.

cassina YAUPON.

cat HEROIN.

CB DORIDEN.

cent In drug language a cent refers to a dollar; a nickel refers to $5; a dime refers to $10.

chalk AMPHETAMINE tablets that crumble easily.

change A prison sentence of short duration.

changes Interruptions in an addict's drug habit because drugs are not available at the time he wants them and his routine is changed.

channel A vein used for injecting HEROIN. Also a term that refers to a source of drugs.

charge The first onset of a drug's effects. The term also applies to an injection of drugs, and to a marijuana cigarette.

charged The sleepy, drowsy effects felt from an overdose of a depressant.

Charles COCAINE.

Charlie One dollar.

chaser Water, beer or any mild liquid taken after a drink of strong liquor to provide a contrast in sensations.

chasing the bag Being addicted to HEROIN. The term "bag" refers to a packet of the drug.

chasing the dragon Inhaling the fumes of HEROIN that has been mixed with BARBITURATE powder and melted over a flame. In recent years it has come to mean smoking heroin and crack together.

chicalote *Argemone mexicana,* also called the prickly poppy. There are claims that it produces a marijuana-like effect when smoked.

chicharra Puerto Rican slang for a mixture of tobacco and MARIJUANA.

chick HEROIN.

chicken powder AMPHETAMINES.

chick shit habit The occasional use of drugs.

chill To refuse to sell drugs to a person.

chillum A clay pipe for smoking GHANJA.

Chinese cure Mixing OPIUM with a tonic and gradually increasing the amount of the tonic in order to break an opium habit.

Chinese red HEROIN, particularly brown heroin from Mexico.

Chinese (China) white HEROIN that is pure white and very potent.

chip To use drugs on an irregular basis in order to avoid addiction.

chipping, chippying Using drugs irregularly and infrequently. (See CHIP.)

chiva MARIJUANA.

chlorals CHLORAL HYDRATE.

chocolate chips LSD.

chota Puerto Rican slang for a police informer, especially one who informs about drugs.

Christmas tree DEXAMYL.

chuck habit The strong desire for food experienced by a detoxified HEROIN addict.

chug-a-lug To consume an alcoholic beverage, particularly beer, without pausing to breathe between swallows. The practice is common among teenagers and college students who hold chug-a-lug contests. These contests can be extremely dangerous because aside from producing rapid intoxication, the practice can result in coma or death—especially when hard liquor is being consumed.

chur GANJA is often shaped into cakes. ''Chur'' is a term for the loose particles of ganja that fall off the cakes.

ciba DORIDEN.

clean Not using or possessing drugs. The term also applies to marijuana that has had the seeds and twigs removed.

cleaned up To stop using drugs, or to go through a detoxification program.

cloud nine Street name for CRACK.

coast To experience the drowsy, somnolent effects of HEROIN.

cohoba Hallucinogenic snuff. See PIPTADENIA.

coke COCAINE.

coke bugs Some cocaine users experience the hallucination that bugs are crawling under the skin. This can lead to excessive scratching and ulcerations.

Coke County A name facetiously given to Marin County, north of San Francisco. It is the home of many affluent families, some of whom work in ''Silicon Valley,'' south of San Francisco, where a concentration of high technology industries are located. It is rumored that cocaine is a popular social drug in Coke Country.

coke head A heavy user of COCAINE.

cold An abbreviation of the term COLD TURKEY.

cold bust Opposite of HOT BUST; the discovery that, by coincidence, an arrested person has drugs in his or her possession.

cold shot A drug deal that has gone wrong.

cold turkey The act of being taken off a drug suddenly and completely, without any preparation. Also the act of quitting a drug without the benefit of medication.

collar An arrest, or the act of arresting. Also applied to the injection of a drug, the term is used for a band which is placed on the tip of an eyedropper where it connects to a needle, ensuring a snug fit.

Colombian MARIJUANA grown in Colombia.

come (coming) down Returning to a normal state after the effects of a drug have worn off. For heroin addicts this state signals the beginning of withdrawal symptoms.

Conan Brand name street dealers use to identify their CRACK.

connect To purchase drugs, or to locate a drug dealer.

connection A person's source, or contact, for purchasing drugs.

connection dough The money used to purchase drugs from a connection.

contact A person's source, or drug dealer, for purchasing drugs.

contact habit To experience the effects of drugs vicariously when one is not addicted. The term has been applied to drug dealers.

contact high Feeling the effects of a drug—feeling high—without using it. For example, being around others who are using a drug and having their mood communicate to you.

contact lens LSD.

cook Heating heroin powder with water until it dissolves and is ready for injection.

cook up The act of cooking.

cooker The container used to cook HEROIN and water; often a bottle cap or spoon.

cool A person with carefully controlled emotions. Also one who is considered to be trustworthy.

cop The act of purchasing a drug.

cop man A drug dealer (pusher).

cop sickness Feeling withdrawal symptoms.

cope Functioning, with near-normal behavior, while under the effects of a drug.

copilot A person who stays with an LSD user in order to care for him but who is not under the influence of the drug himself.

copilots DEXEDRINE.

corrine COCAINE.

cotton HEROIN that has been mixed with water and cooked, is drawn through a small piece of cotton to filter out impurities on its way into the hypodermic.

cotton habit Using drugs irregularly to avoid addiction.

cotton shooter An addict who injects the residue left in the COTTON.

count The amount (weight or volume) of drugs involved in a purchase.

courage pills BARBITURATES.

cracking shorts Burglarizing cars to support a drug habit.

crank AMPHETAMINES.

crank bugs An hallucination that bugs are crawling under one's skin after the heavy use of AMPHETAMINES.

crap HEROIN that is highly diluted or of low quality.

crash Suddenly falling asleep after the heavy use of stimulants, or to return to a normal state when the effects of a drug have worn off. (See COME DOWN.)

crater A hole in an addict's flesh (at the site of a vein) caused by repeated injections in the same spot.

creep An addict who begs for drugs, or who does small tasks in return for drugs, instead of purchasing them himself.

crib A person's home, particularly a place where an addict injects drugs.

croaker A doctor who illegally prescribes drugs for addicts.

crossroads AMPHETAMINES.

crutch An object (a pin, tweezers, etc.) used to hold a MARIJUANA cigarette when it has been smoked so far down that it cannot be held with the fingers.

crystal AMPHETAMINES that are soluble for injection. They are so called because they are supplied in the form of white crystal (Methedrine, Desoxyn, etc.).

crystal palace A place where people gather to use AMPHETAMINES.

cube, the A sugar cube that has been impregnated with a dose of LSD. Also a slang term for MORPHINE.

cupcakes LSD.

cura HEROIN (Spanish for cure).

cure The length of time a person voluntarily stays in a U.S. Public Health Narcotics Hospital.

cut ounces To further dilute HEROIN. (See CUT.)

cyc CYCLAZOCINE.

D

dabbling The irregular use of drugs.

dagga South African CANNABIS.

deal, dealing To sell drugs, particularly NARCOTICS.

dealer A person who sells drugs, particularly narcotics.

dealer's band Drug dealers often fasten packets of HEROIN to their wrists with rubber bands in such a way that they can be flipped an sent flying in a hurry when police are seen.

death cap, death cup MUSCIMOL.

deck A folded paper containing HEROIN.

deck up The act of filling DECKS with heroin.

deeda LSD.

deprivation roll Using any drug that is available in order to get high.

destroying angels MUSCIMOL.

dexies DEXEDRINE, DEXAMYL.

dillies DILAUDID.

dime In drug language a dime refers to $10; a cent refers to $1; a nickel refers to $5.

dip and dab The irregular, occasional use of heroin.

dirty Having drugs in one's possession (opposite of CLEAN). Also a term that refers to MARIJUANA that still contains seeds, stems and twigs.

discon An abbreviation for disorderly conduct.

djamba Brazilian word for cannabis.

djoma African word for cannabis.

do To use a drug.

do right Someone who is a first-time patient at the U.S. Public Health Service (narcotics) Hospital at Lexington, Kentucky, and who is considered to have a good chance of being cured.

do up To prepare a vein for an injection of HEROIN by tying something around the arm to distend the vein.

DOA PHENCYCLIDINE (from ''dead on arrival'').

doctor A person from whom one can purchase liquor, usually at a very high price, at a time when bars and liquor stores are closed. The term is also used as a verb when more alcohol is added to someone's drink, usually without his or her knowledge.

dogie HEROIN.

dollar In drug language a dollar is $100; a dime is $10.

dollies DOLOPHINE.

dolls AMPHETAMINES, BARBITURATES.

domestic MARIJUANA that is grown in the U.S.

donana DONA ANA.

doobie A MARIJUANA cigarette.

doojee HEROIN.

dope Narcotic drugs.

dope fiend A person who uses dope.

dope run A trip made for the purpose of buying drugs.

double crosses AMPHETAMINES.

down, downer, downie An amphetamine user often takes a tranquilizer to reverse the stimulant effects of AMPHETAMINES when they becomes too intense. Also a slang term for any depressant, especially BARBITURATES.

down trip To be worried, depressed or troubled.

drag A panic reaction to a hallucinogenic drug.

dragged An hysterical panic reaction to smoking marijuana.

dream COCAINE.

dreamer MORPHINE.

dried out Detoxified from a drug.

drinker One who consumes alcohol. The term is also used to refer to a drunk or alcoholic.

dripper A medicine DROPPER that can be used for injecting heroin when a needle is attached to the tip.

drop To take (swallow) a pill.

drop it The act of concealing a drug.

druggies People who frequently experiment with a wide variety of drugs.

dry A prohibitionist who is against drinking, and against the sale of liquor. In the case of an alcoholic, it means abstinence and is the opposite of WET.

dry high MARIJUANA.

dry up Absence of drugs in an area. To stop the use of drugs.

duby MARIJUANA (See DOOBIE.)

duji HEROIN.

dust COCAINE. ANGEL DUST (usually) also.

duster Tobacco and HEROIN mixed in a cigarette.

dusting Historically referred to mixing HEROIN with MARIJUANA in a cigarette. Now usually refers to putting PCP in any drug.

dynamite A particularly potent drug, especially HEROIN or MARIJUANA. The term also refers to a mixture of COCAINE and heroin.

dyno HEROIN that is highly potent and only slightly diluted.

E

eater A person who only takes drugs orally.

eighth, an A measurement of powdered drugs. Usually COCAINE, HEROIN or AMPHETAMINES.

electric A substance containing a psychedelic drug. (See ELECTRIC KOOL-ADE.)

Electric Kool-Ade A punch mixture containing the psychedelic drug LSD-25. Popularized in literature, it was probably not much used.

elephant PHENCYCLIDINE.

embalao A Puerto Rican term for a person with a severe addiction; one who is unable to function socially and is physically debilitated.

embroidery The scars on an addict's veins caused by injecting HEROIN.

esrar A Turkish term for mixing cannnabis with tobacco in order to conceal the cannabis.

eye opener For an alcoholic, his first drink of the day; for an addict, his first narcotics shot of the day.

eye openers AMPHETAMINES.

F

f-40 SECONAL.

factory A secret place where drugs are diluted, packaged, or otherwise prepared for sale.

fake a blast To pretend to be under the effects of a drug.

fatty A fat, thick MARIJUANA cigarette.

feds Members of a federal agency, particularly federal narcotics.

feeling the habit (or monkey) coming on The beginning of withdrawal symptoms.

fiend One who uses drugs in an excessive and uncontrolled way.

finger Putting drugs in a condom then hiding it in the rectum or else swallowing and later excreting it. This is done in cases of pending arrest or for smuggling purposes.

fingers Sticks of hashish that resemble the shape of a finger.

firing the ack-ack gun Putting heroin on the tip of a cigarette and smoking it. It is a practice popular in China.

first line MORPHINE.

fish A new patient in a narcotics hospital.

fit The apparatus for injecting HEROIN.

five cent paper A paper filled with heroin that is sold for $5 and usually contains about 5 grains of diluted heroin.

five dollar bag The same as a five cent paper but the heroin is packaged in a glassine envelope.

fix The injecting of heroin or the heroin itself.

flake COCAINE.

flaky A person who is addicted to COCAINE.

flash The first euphoric effects of a drug.

flashing A term applied to sniffing glue.

flea powder HEROIN of an inferior quality.

flip out A panic reaction to a drug in which the user loses contact with reality. The term is also used for rapturous delight that is experienced in a state of trance.

floating Being under the effects of a drug.

Florida snow See FAKE COKE.

flow To enter a relaxed state and allow a drug's effects to take over.

flowers The buds on the top of the female marijuana plant where resin is exuded.

fluff Filtering cocaine and heroin through a nylon stocking during the process of CUTTING. Fluffing it can make it appear to be twice the size.

flunky One who takes foolish risks to obtain drugs or the money for drugs.

flush The initial euphoric effects felt after an injection of HEROIN.

fly COCAINE.

flying Being HIGH on a drug.

Flying Saucers A trade name for MORNING GLORY SEEDS.

fold up To stop selling drugs or to stop taking drugs.

food of the gods PSILOCYBIN.

footballs DILAUDID.

forwards AMPHETAMINES.

fours TYLENOL with CODEINE.

freak A person who prefers a particular drug, as in "LSD freak." Also, to experience hallucinations that are particularly grotesque or beautiful, or to have a panic reaction to a drug or situation.

freak out A bad, panicky reaction to a drug; or simply to take a drug.

freak up To purposely act in a bizarre manner.

freeze Refusing to sell drugs to a person.

Frisco speedball HEROIN, COCAINE and LSD mixed together.

front An advance payment for drugs.

fruit salad A game, usually played by teenagers, in which one pill is swallowed from each bottle in a medicine cabinet.

full moon A large piece of PEYOTE, usually the entire top of the cactus.

G

gammon One microgram.

ganga, ganja Marijuana grown in Jamaica.

gangster MARIJUANA.

gangster pills BARBITURATES.

gaping Yawning, which is a withdrawal symptom.

garbage HEROIN of a poor, inferior quality.

garbage head A person who will use any drug available to get high.

G.B. BARBITURATE. An abbreviation of goofball.

gee head A person addicted to paregoric.

geeze To inject HEROIN.

geronimo A mixture of barbiturates and alcohol.

get down To take a heroin injection.

get off To experience the effets of a drug. Also, to take a heroin injection.

get on To begin taking drugs.

get one's yen off To satisfy a craving, particularly for drugs.

get the habit off To relieve the beginnings of withdrawal symptoms by taking a drug.

getting on To feel the effects of MARIJUANA.

ghanja An Indian form of cannabis, midway in potency between CHARAS and marijuana.

Ghost, the LSD.

ghostbusters CRACK cocaine doused with liquid PCP and smoked.

giggle weed MARIJUANA.

gimmicks The apparatus for injecting drugs.

girl COCAINE.

globetrotter A person who searches out the best grade of heroin he can get in an area.

glow To feel the euphoric effects of a drug.

goblet of jam DAWAMESK.

God's flesh PSILOCYBIN.

God's medicine MORPHINE.

going down A situation in the process of happening (unfolding).

going high Being in a state of a continuing HIGH.

gold MARIJUANA. An abbreviation of Acapulco gold.

gold dust COCAINE.

gold duster A person who uses cocaine.

golden leaf ACAPULCO GOLD (marijuana).

goods Drugs, particularly narcotics.

good sick The nausea and vomiting that an addict sometimes experiences after an injection of HEROIN.

good stuff HEROIN that is not heavily diluted.

goofball BARBITURATES and AMPHETAMINES.

goofers BARBITURATES and AMPHETAMINES.

goofing Feeling the effects of BARBITURATES or AMPHETAMINES.

gorilla pills TUINAL.

grass MARIJUANA.

grass brownies Brownies that contain MARIJUANA.

gravy A mixture of heroin and backed-up blood (resulting from booting), which will clog a syringe. The mixture is heated, then after the blood dissolves it is injected.

greasy junky An addict who obtains drugs by doing favors and begging rather than by buying them.

green A cheap inferior grade of MARIJUANA that is grown in Mexico. It is also called Mexican green. Also, a slang term for KETAMINE HYDROCHLORIDE.

green dragons BARBITURATES.

grefa MARIJUANA.

greta MARIJUANA.

grifa MARIJUANA.

griffo MARIJUANA.

grog blossom A purple or reddish coloring of the nose often associated with excessive drinking over an extended period of time. (From GROG.)

groovers Young teenagers who take drugs for excitement and thrills.

grooving To feel the effects of a drug.

ground control COPILOT.

ground man COPILOT.

grower A person who grows MARIJUANA but does not get involved in its distribution or smuggling.

guide An experienced LSD user who stands by, or acts as a guide to someone taking the drug for the first time in case he or she has a panic reaction.

gun The needle used for injecting heroin.

gunja MARIJUANA.

gungeon MARIJUANA that is grown in Jamaica and is particularly potent.

guru GUIDE.

gutter A vein used for injecting heroin, particularly in the area inside the elbow.

H

H HEROIN.

half An abbreviation for HALF LOAD.

half load Drug pushers purchase heroin from wholesalers in half loads: 15 packages banded together.

handball Brand name that street dealers use to identify their crack.

hang tough To undergo withdrawal symptoms, after stopping the use of narcotics, without giving in to the need for the drug.

happy hour A designated time set by a public establishment (restaurant, bar, lounge), usually limited to an hour or two in the later afternoon, when drinks are often served at a reduced price.

hara, la Puerto Rican term for police.

harry HEROIN.

hash HASHISH.

Hashbury, the HAIGHT-ASHBURY.

hash oil LIQUID HASHISH.

hassle, hassling To have difficulties obtaining drugs, or any situation that is worrisome.

hawk, the LSD.

hay MARIJUANA.

haze LSD.

head A person who favors a particular drug, as in pot head.

head drugs Drugs that affect the mind, such as hallucinogens, as opposed to narcotics.

hearts AMPHETAMINES.

heat, the Police.

heaven, heaven dust COCAINE.

Heavenly Blue A trade name for MORNING GLORY SEEDS.

heavy drugs, heavy stuff HARD NARCOTICS.

heeled To have drugs in one's possession.

hemp MARIJUANA.

henry HEROIN.

her COCAINE.

herb MARIJUANA.

him HEROIN.

hit To take a drug, as in, to take a hit of marijuana from a bong.

hocus MORPHINE.

hog PHENCYCLIDINE.

hold, holding To be in possession of drugs, either for one's own use or for the purpose of selling.

homegrown MARIJUANA. The domestic variety grown in the United States.

hookah BONG.

hooked Addicted to a drug.

hop OPIUM.

hop dog, hop head A person addicted to opium.

horn SNIFF.

horror drugs Drugs containing the belladonna alkaloids ATROPINE, SCOPOLAMINE and HYOSCYAMINE.

horse HEROIN.

hot bust Opposite of COLD BUST. A police arrest made when drugs are expected to be found because of an informant's tip-off.

hot shot An injection of what the addict believes to be heroin but which is actually a substitute, such as the poison strychnine.

hubba CRACK cocaine.

hubbly bubbly BONG.

huffer A person who inhales deliriants or inhalants.

huilca YOPO.

hustler, hustling A person who engages in criminal activities to earn money for drugs.

hype A hoax.

I

ice Street name for crystalized smokable methamphetamine.

ice cream habit Using drugs infrequently and irregularly.

idiot pills BARBITURATES.

in action A pusher is "in action" when he has drugs for sale.

in paper To smuggle drugs in a postcard which has been specially slit to contain them.

in transit To be under the effects of LSD.

Indian hay MARIJUANA.

Indian hemp MARIJUANA.

instanfu African name for CANNABIS.

intsaga African name for CANNABIS.

iron cure To go through the process of withdrawal when there is no possibility of obtaining drugs.

J

jab To inject HEROIN.

jack, jacking Stealing.

jackroller A thief who usually steals from drunks. It is a SKID ROW term.

jag To be under the effects of a drug for an extended period of time.

jam COCAINE.

jammed up A person who has taken an overdose.

jane MARIJUANA.

jay, jay smoke MARIJUANA.

jelly beans AMPHETAMINES.

jerk off BOOTING.

jimson weed DATURA.

joint A MARIJUANA cigarette.

jones A term for a drug habit, particularly a heroin habit.

joy juice CHLORAL HYDRATE.

joypop To inject heroin infrequently. Someone who joypops is not addicted.

juanita Mexican term for MARIJUANA.

juice ALCOHOL.

juice head A person who is a heavy consumer of alcohol.

jungle drug AYAHUASCA.

junk Drugs, particularly heroin.

junkie A heroin addict.

K

kat KHAT.

katzenjammers DELIRIUM TREMENS.

key A kilogram.

ki KEY.

kick, kicking To break a drug addiction, as in "kicking the habit."

kickback To KICK a habit and then return to it.

kick cold turkey To KICK a drug habit and go through the withdrawal process without the help of medication.

kick Thrills.

kick sticks MARIJUANA cigarettes.

kick the habit To break drug addiction.

kief, kif African name for CANNABIS.

killer drugs Drugs of high potency that are considered good.

killer weed High potency MARIJUANA, or marijuana that is mixed with PHENCYCLIDINE.

kilo A kilogram.

kilo connection A high-level HEROIN distributor who purchases the substance from an importer, then cuts it once before selling it in kilos to the OUNCE MAN who further dilutes it.

kilter MARIJUANA.

King Kong A severe HEROIN habit that is extremely costly.

King Kong pills BARBITURATES.

kit The apparatus for injecting HEROIN.

knockout drops A mixture of ALCOHOL and CHLORAL HYDRATE that produces an additive effect; the person soon loses consciousness.

K.Y. The United States Public Health Service (narcotics) Hospital in Lexington, Kentucky.

L

lady, lady snow COCAINE.

lame A person who doesn't use drugs.

laughing gas NITROUS OXIDE.

layout The apparatus for injecting HEROIN.

lay up To purchase a large store of drugs, then just lie around using them without the HASSLE of having to continuously go out to purchase more.

L.B. One pound.

leapers AMPHETAMINES.

Lebanese HASHISH from Lebanon.

lemon, lemonade Highly diluted HEROIN, or a substitute substance sold as heroin. Also refers to QUAALUDES.

Lexington The United States Public Health Service (narcotics) Hospital in Lexington, Kentucky.

lid A measurement of weight used for MARIJUANA. Ranging from ¾ to 1 ounce, it is enough for approximately 40 marijuana cigarettes.

Lido Brand name street dealers use to identify their CRACK.

lid poppers AMPHETAMINES.

life, the A general term for all the characteristics surrounding an addict's life-style, including his environment, the lingo he speaks, his attitude toward crime and work, his sleeping and eating patterns, and so on.

lightning AMPHETAMINES.

light stuff The opposite of HARD DRUGS, the term covers nonopiate drugs.

light up To smoke MARIJUANA.

line The large, arterial vein in the arm. The term is an abbreviation of MAINLINE.

load A measurement of HEROIN; approximately 25–30 envelopes or packets banded together.

loaded To be heavily intoxicated, whether from ALCOHOL or any other drug.

loads A combination of Doriden (glutethimide), a sleeping pill, and Codeine #4 (a combinaton of 60 mg of codeine with aspirin or Tylenol). A load usually consists of one 400 mg Doriden tablet and two Codeine #4s. Sometimes two or three loads are swallowed together. Loads are used as substitutes for the diluted HEROIN sold on the street. The practice originated in southern California and spread to other parts of the country. (Also called pacs.)

loco MARIJUANA.

long con A confidence game that has required extensive planning.

love drug QUAALUDES, MDA.

ludes QUAALUDES.

M

macon West African word for CANNABIS.

maconha Brazilian word for CANNABIS.

made, make The act of purchasing a drug. Also to be recognized (usually by the police).

mahjueme HASHISH in concentrated form.

majoon, majoun, ma'jun Indian words for CANNABIS.

make it To experience the effects of a HEROIN injection.

making a croaker for a reader To feign sickness or bribe a doctor in order to gain a prescription for a drug.

man, the The term can refer to the police or to a high-level drug dealer.

M and C A mixture of four parts MORPHINE and one part COCAINE.

M and M's SECONAL.

mandrakes MANDRAX.

manicure To remove the twigs and sticks from marijuana.

Mannite Brand name of imported Italian baby laxative used as source of sugar to cut cocaine and heroin.

marshmallow reds BARBITURATES.

mary MORPHINE.

mary ann, mary jane, mary warner, mary weaver MARIJUANA.

mash allah OPIUM.

matchbox A measurement of MARIJUANA. It is about ⅕ of an ounce and will make approximately six to eight cigarettes.

medical hype To become addicted to a drug because of medical treatment.

meet A meeting between a seller and a purchaser.

mellow yellow LSD.

merc, merck, merk High-quality drugs. The term probably originated from the name of the drug manufacturer Merck, Sharp & Dohme.

mesc MESCALINE.

meth METHAMPHETAMINE, METHEDRINE.

meth freak A heavy user of METHEDRINE.

Mexican brown MARIJUANA grown in Mexico that has a higher resin content than MEXICAN GREEN. Also a slang term for brown HEROIN.

Mexican green MARIJUANA grown in Mexico that is less potent than MEXICAN BROWN. It is one of the commonest types of marijuana used in the U.S.

Mexican locoweed MARIJUANA.

Mexican mint DIVINER'S SAGE.

Mexican mud HEROIN.

Mexican mushrooms See MUSHROOMS, SACRED.

Mexican quaaludes Illicit QUAALUDES imported from Mexico, often very impure.

Mexican reds Illicit SECONAL imported from Mexico.

Mickey, Mickey Finn A mixture of ALCOHOL and CHLORAL HYDRATE that can render a person unconscious in a very short time.

microdots Drops of LSD supplied on blotter paper. They appear as very faint beige dots that darken to a brownish color when exposed to light.

Mighty Joe Young A severe HEROIN habit that is extremely costly.

mike One microgram of LSD (a usually dose is 200–500 "mikes").

mini-bennies BENZEDRINE.

mini-whites AMPHETAMINES.

Miss Emma MORPHINE.

M.J. MARIJUANA. An abbreviaton of mary jane.

mojo HARD DRUGS such as HEROIN and MORPHINE.

monkey, monkey on (my) back A person's drug dependence or habit. A baby born addicted to drugs (especially heroin) and the resulting withdrawal.

moon PEYOTE. The term also refers to a block of HASHISH.

moota, mooters, mootie MARIJUANA.

morf MORPHINE.

morph, morpho, morphy MORPHINE.

mota MARIJUANA.

mother MARIJUANA. Also a term for a drug dealer.

move To deal in MARIJUANA.

mu MARIJUANA.

mud MORPHINE.

muta, mutah MARIJUANA.

N

nail The needle, usually attached to an eye dropper, that is used for injecting heroin. (See SPIKE.)

narc, narco A police narcotics officer; also the U.S. Public Health Service (narcotics) Hospital in Lexington, Kentucky.

narghile A Turkish water pipe. (See BONG.)

nark NARC.

natch, on the From the word natural, it refers to a person's life-style when he is not taking drugs.

natch trips To take "natural" substances, such as lettuce, nutmeg or mace in an effort to achieve a HIGH.

nebbie NEMBUTAL.

needle freak An addict who is not particular about what drug he injects but gets his thrills simply from the act of injecting.

needle habit Some addicts, often referred to as "needle freaks," are not particular about what drug they inject but get their thrills simply from the act of injecting. (See ADMINISTRATION.)

needle park Sherman Square at Broadway and Amsterdam Avenue, in New York City. It was once a congregating place for addicts.

negative See BAD TRIP.

nemish, nemmies NEMBUTAL.

nickel In street language it refers to \$5, just as a dime refers to \$10.

nickel bag A package, usually of MARIJUANA or HEROIN, which is worth $5.

nimbies, nimby nembutal.

Nixon Narcotic drugs that are not very potent.

nod, nodding To feel the initial effects of a HEROIN injection—pleasurable drowsiness and peacefulness, probably so called because the head nods forward.

nose candy COCAINE.

nuggets AMPHETAMINES.

number two sale, the A police term for a second narcotics conviction.

O

O.D. Overdose.

O.D.ing Showing signs of having overdosed.

off Experiencing the intoxicating effects of a drug.

off artist A person who steals to pay for a drug habit. (Also rip-off artist.)

oil HASHISH oil.

on To use drugs: "He is on HEROIN," for example.

one and one To sniff 2 lines of drugs (one with each nostril); applies particulary to the use of COCAINE.

on the needle Addicted to HEROIN. To be using heroin intravenously.

op OPIUM.

Orange County QUAALUDES. So called because the area code for Orange County, California, is 714—the same as the code number on 300 mg Quaaludes.

orange mushrooms LSD.

oranges AMPHETAMINES.

ounce man The person in between the KILO CONNECTION and the PUSHER in the HEROIN distribution process. Heroin is diluted (or cut) once by the kilo connection; the ounce man cuts it again before selling it to the pusher.

outfit The apparatus for injecting heroin.

overcharged A semicoma state that can occur when too much of a drug is taken.

overjolt OVERDOSE.

over the hump, go To feel the full euphoric effect of a drug.

Owsley LSD. The name is taken from that of an illicit manufacturer during the 1960s.

O.Z., oz One ounce.

P

packed up HIGH.

pacs See LOAD.

pad A person's residence. At one time the term was reserved only for a room in which drugs were used.

Pall Mall and paregoric Cigarettes (any brand) that have been soaked in paregoric.

Panama Gold, Panama Red Alternative names for MARIJUANA grown in Panama, which is considered to be high quality.

panatella A large, fat MARIJUANA cigarette usually made from marijuana grown in Central or South America.

panic Anxiety resulting from an addict's shortage of drugs or his inability to buy them.

panic man A person suffering from PANIC.

papers Folded pieces of paper, or packages, containing narcotics, particularly HEROIN. Also rolling papers.

paper acid LSD applied to blotter paper and allowed to dry. (See BLOTTER.)

paracki PARALDEHYDE.

paradise COCAINE.

paraphernalia The equipment needed to inject HEROIN. Also known as the works.

partying To share a supply of HEROIN with others.

pass The act of taking possession of a drug once it has been paid for.

peace, peace pill PHENCYCLIDINE.

peaches BENZEDRINE.

peaking The period during an LSD trip when the most intense effects are experienced.

peanuts BARBITURATES.

pearls AMYL NITRITE.

pellets LSD.

people, the KILO CONNECTION.

pep pills AMPHETAMINES.

per A prescription.

peter CHLORAL HYDRATE.

peyote buttons The button-like growths on the peyote cactus.

peyotl PEYOTE.

P.G. PAREGORIC.

phennies, phenos PHENOBARBITAL.

picked up To have recently smoked MARIJUANA.

piece A measurement of diluted HEROIN. There are approximately 15 pieces in 1.1 pounds, each piece containing about 30 teaspoons, which are further diluted by the PUSHER.

pill AMPHETAMINES and BARBITURATES.

pill head A person who frequently uses AMPHETAMINES and BARBITURATES.

pin A MARIJUANA cigarette.

pinhead A thin MARIJUANA cigarette.

pink ladies BARBITURATES.

pinks SECONAL.

pinned Constricted eye pupils, characteristic of HEROIN addicts.

pipe A vein, particularly a large vein, used for injecting HEROIN. An instrument used to smoke drugs.

pit The main vein used for injecting HEROIN.

place The setting for an LSD trip.

plant A cache of drugs. Also a police practice that involves placing drugs in a suspected addict's residence, then arresting him for possession.

pod MARIJUANA.

point A needle used for injecting HEROIN.

poison COCAINE or HEROIN.

poison people Addicts who use COCAINE or HEROIN.

poke To inhale a MARIJUANA cigarette.

pop, popping To take a pill. Also a term for the subcutaneous injection of HEROIN.

popped To be arrested by the police.

poppers AMYL NITRITE in small glass vials that are broken and inhaled.

positive Feeling the efects of a stimulant.

pot MARIJUANA.

pot head A heavy user of MARIJUANA.

potlikker A beverage made by brewing MARIJUANA stems, twigs and seeds.

powder HEROIN.

P.R. PANAMA RED (marijuana).

primo High-quality drugs.

psychos Drugs that produce psychedelic effects.

puff, puffing Smoking OPIUM.

pure HEROIN that is undiluted or only slightly diluted.

purple hearts LUMINAL. DRINAMYL.

push, pushing From PUSHER, to sell drugs at the street level.

pusher A dealer who sells drugs directly to an addict; he is one step below the wholesaler in the drug distribution system.

put in writing or paper A method of smuggling drugs by putting them in a split postcard, or in the case of a liquid drug, to saturate a piece of paper.

put somebody on To introduce someone to MARIJUANA.

Q

Q's QUAALUDES.

q'at KHAT.

quacks, quads, quas QUAALUDES.

quarter In drug language, $25.

quarter bag Twenty-five dollars' worth of MARIJUANA.

quarter moon HASHISH.

quill A matchbook that is rolled or folded and used to hold a drug while it is being sniffed.

R

raggae See RASTAFARIANS.

ragweed Poor-quality MARIJUANA with a low level of potency.

rainbows TUINAL.

rainy-day woman A MARIJUANA cigarette.

rap, rapping Talking, particularly in addicts' jargon.

rat A police informer.

rat root ASARONE.

R.D. SECONAL.

reader A narcotics prescription obtained by bribery or by feigning an illness.

red PANAMA RED (marijuana).

red and blues TUINAL.

red birds, red bullets, red devils, red dolls, red lillies, reds SECONAL (from the color).

red chicken Chinese HEROIN.

red dirt marijuana MARIJUANA that grows wild.

red rock Chinese HEROIN.

reefer MARIJUANA.

rig Apparatus for injecting HEROIN.

righteous A good-quality drug with high potency.

righteous bush MARIJUANA.

rip off To steal.

rip-off artist Thief.

ripped To be highly intoxicated by a drug.

rippers AMPHETAMINES.

roach A MARIJUANA cigarette when it has burned down too far to be held with the fingers (at which point it looks like a cockroach).

roach clip An instrument (pin, tweezers, etc.) used to hold a ROACH.

roach holder See ROACH CLIP.

roach pick See ROACH CLIP.

rock COCAINE, HEROIN.

roll The intoxicating effect of a HIGH.

root A MARIJUANA cigarette.

rope MARIJUANA.

roses BENZEDRINE.

Rovanne Serpico Brand name street dealers use to identify their crack.

royal blue LSD.

run A period of heavy use of a particular drug, or a period of addiction.

rush The initial euphoric effects felt after a HEROIN or AMPHETAMINE injection.

S

sacrament LSD.

salt shot An injection of a saline solution; a home remedy for a HEROIN addict who is unconscious from an overdose.

sassfras A MARIJUANA cigarette made from low potency marijuana grown in the United States.

satch Paper that has been saturated with a drug for smuggling purposes.

sativa MARIJUANA.

scag HEROIN.

scars Scars from the frequent injection of narcotics. They appear as black and blue spots and are caused by collapsed veins.

scene The social pattern of drug use; as in "the drug scene around here is very open."

schmack Originally applied to HEROIN and COCAINE, the term has now been extended to include all drugs.

schmeck Yiddish term for HEROIN that is sniffed.

schmecker A heavy user of SCHMECK (heroin).

schoolboy CODEINE. COCAINE.

scoop To sniff HEROIN or COCAINE using a folded matchbook. See QUILL.

score To buy a drug.

scratch, scratching A drug addict. The term probably comes from an addict's compulsion to scratch himself.

script A prescription for a narcotic; an abbreviation of the word prescription.

script writer A doctor who illegally sells prescriptions for pain killers, stimulants, and depressants for recreational use, sometimes operating under the cover of a "diet" or "stress" clinic.

scrubwoman's kick To inhale the fumes of naphtha, an ingredient used in cleaning preparations that can produce a mild intoxicating high.

seccies, seccy SECONAL.

seggy, seggies SECONAL.

set A particular locality frequented by addicts and drug sellers.

set up See PLANT.

seventeen-fifty-one The number of the New York State statute concerning the possession of drugs with intent to sell.

seventeen-forty-seven B The number of the New York State statute concerning possession of barbiturates.

seven-fourteens QUAALUDES.

shit HEROIN.

shlook To inhale a MARIJUANA cigarette.

shooting gallery A location where addicts inject drugs. Also, the withdrawal ward in a narcotics hospital.

shooting gravy BOOTING.

shoot up To inject a drug, particularly HEROIN.

short A car.

short con A minor confidence game; the opposite of LONG CON.

short count, short go When a drug dealer (PUSHER) receives a lesser amount of a drug from a wholesaler than he has contracted for. Generally to sell less than the agreed amount.

short piece A measurement of a drug, particularly HEROIN, that has been highly diluted.

shove See PUSH.

shroom MUSHROOMS, SACRED.

sick To experience the beginning of withdrawal symptoms.

sixteenth A measurement of HEROIN or COCAINE; 1/16 of an ounce.

sizzle To have drugs on one's person.

skid bag A bag of HEROIN that is highly diluted.

skin The paper used for making MARIJUANA cigarettes.

skin pop Injecting a drug subcutaneously.

sleepers, sleeping pills BARBITURATES.

sleepwalker A person addicted to HEROIN.

smack HEROIN.

smashed Being HIGH on a drug.

smoke MARIJUANA, as in "he was using smoke."

snappers AMYL NITRITE in glass vials.

snop MARIJUANA.

snow COCAINE.

snow lights Flickering bright lights at the periphery of the visual fields that are seen after COCAINE and AMPHETAMINES have been used are called snow lights. They are probably not hallucinations, but may represent the overstimulation of the optic tracts by stimulants.

soapers, soaps SOPOR.

sobering pill L-DOPA.

softballs Drugs that fall into the DEPRESSANT category (tranquilizers, sedatives, hypnotics, etc.)

soft drugs Drugs that are non-narcotic (AMPHETAMINES, BARBITURATES, MARIJUANA, etc.).

soles HASHISH.

source, the KILO CONNECTION.

spaced, spaced out To be under the influence of a mind-altering drug such as LSD.

space basing CRACK doused with liquid PCP and smoked; also called ghostbusters.

sparkle plenties AMPHETAMINES.

speed AMPHETAMINES, particularly METHEDRINE.

speedball A mixture of HEROIN and COCAINE, or heroin and AMPHETAMINE, which is injected.

speed freak A heavy user of AMPHETAMINES.

spike The needle used for injecting a drug. See NAIL.

splash AMPHETAMINES.

spliff A Jamaican term for a thick fat MARIJUANA cigarette. (See RASTAFARIANS.)

split To leave or break away from a person, a place or a drug.

spoon A measurement of HEROIN (1/16 of an ounce), or cocaine (1/4 of a teaspoon).

square A regular tobacco cigarette.

S.S. An abbreviation for suspended sentence.

star dust COCAINE.

stash A cache of hidden drugs.

steamboat To smoke a MARIJUANA cigarette that has been inserted in a toilet paper roll. The person puts his mouth over one end of the roll and his hand over the other, and the smoke is trapped inside.

stepped on Diluted.

stick A MARIJUANA cigarette.

sticks The waste (sticks, twigs) that is left after MARIJUANA has been CLEANED.

stoned Being HIGH on a drug.

stool To cooperate with or give information to the police.

STP DOM. (Probably from the brand name motor oil additive that promises increased power.)

straight A person who doesn't use drugs. Also a term for a regular cigarette.

straighten out To prevent the beginnings of withdrawal symptoms by taking more drugs.

strawberry fields LSD.

street, on the To be a drug user.

strung, strung out An addict's panic feeling when he is unable to obtain drugs. The term is also applied to a severe habit, or to an addict's physical appearance because of a severe habit.

stuff A general term for all drugs.

stumblers BARBITURATES.

sugar LSD.

sugar weed MARIJUANA that has been soaked in a mixture of sugar and water—a process known as "curing." This is done to add bulk and increase the weight to increase sale price.

sunshine LSD.

Supercaine See FAKE COKE.

supergrass PHENCYCLIDINE. In the 1960s it was also a brand name of catnip that was sold as marijuana.

superwhite Brand name street dealers use to identify their CRACK.

sweet flag ASARONE.

sweet lucy MARIJUANA.

swingman A low-level drug dealer. PUSHER.

system, the A term used to describe an addict's TOLERANCE.

T

tabs LSD capsules or tablets.

take off To begin feeling the effects of a drug.

take-off artist Addicts who obtain their money for drugs by robbing. Also called RIP-OFF ARTISTS.

taken off Robbed, ripped off.

taking care of business Obtaining money for drugs by robbing or other means.

taking on a number The act of smoking MARIJUANA.

tall HIGH on a drug.

tank A cell or jail where drunks are kept while they sober up (from "drunk tank"). The term is also used to refer to a drunk, and to the act of drinking as in "tank up on booze."

tapita A Spanish word for "little cap." It refers to the small bottle cap addicts use to cook heroin.

tapping the bag PUSHERS often take a small amount of heroin out of the bags they sell and so shortchange addicts. The practice is particularly common when the pusher is also an addict.

tar Gum OPIUM.

taste A small amount of a drug.

tea MARIJUANA. Also a term used for psychedelics that are brewed and made into a beverage.

tea bag To smoke MARIJUANA.

tea head A heavy user of MARIJUANA.

tea pad A place where MARIJUANA users gather to smoke.

tecata HEROIN.

teetotal, teetotaler Total abstinence from ALCOHOL, or one who totally abstains. From "tee-total," a local British intensive for "total."

tens AMPHETAMINES; tablets of 10 mg.

ten cent pistol A bag of what an addict thinks is HEROIN but which actually contains a poisonous substance.

Texas tea MARIJUANA.

thing HEROIN.

third eye A psychedelic effect described by HALLUCINOGEN users. It is the feeling of having an inward look into the mind.

thirty-three-oh-five A felony under New York State statutes: the possession of narcotics but in a smaller amount than would be presumed to be possessed for selling.

throwing rocks To commit serious, violent crimes in order to obtain money for drugs.

thrusters AMPHETAMINES.

thumb A large fat MARIJUANA cigarette.

ticket, the LSD.

tie The tourniquet a heroin addict uses to distend a vein when injecting intravenously.

tie off, tie up To use a TIE.

tight A person who is intoxicated by ALCOHOL.

tighten up To give drugs to a person.

tin See CAN.

tingle The initial effects felt after a HEROIN injection.

TJ Tijuana, Mexico. The town has long been known as a place where drugs can be easily purchased.

toak, toke To smoke a MARIJUANA cigarette. The term refers to both smoking the whole cigarette and just taking a puff.

toke pipes Pipes used to smoke MARIJUANA.

toke up To light a MARIJUANA cigarette.

tooies TUINAL.

tools Apparatus used for injecting HEROIN.

toot To snort or sniff COCAINE, as in "Let's have a toot." Also a slang named for cocaine, as in "Do you have any toot?" (See also FAKE COKE.)

tootsies TUINAL.

topi PEYOTE.

torn up Feeling the effects of a drug.

torpedo A mixture of ALCOHOL and CHLORAL HYDRATE.

torture chamber A jail where it is impossible to obtain drugs.

tossed A police search for drugs.

toss out To feign an illness in order to obtain a prescription for drugs.

toy A needle used to inject HEROIN.

tracked up Covered by scars from the frequent injection of drugs.

tracks Black and blue needle scars caused by the frequent injection of drugs. Collapsed veins are also referred to as tracks.

train arrived The successful smuggling of drugs, particularly into a prison.

trap A place where a cache of drugs is hidden.

travel agent A dealer (PUSHER) who sells LSD.

trees TUINAL.

trick An illegal way of obtaining money for drugs. Probably from the word used by prostitutes for performing sexual favors.

trip The act of taking a HALLUCINOGEN, particularly LSD; or the effects of its ingestion.

tripsville San Francisco, which was the site of extensive LSD use in the late 1960s.

truck drivers AMPHETAMINES.

Ts and blues (Ts and Bs) An injected combination of Talwin (pentazocine, a narcotic agonist-antagonist) and pyribenzamine (tripelenamine, an antihistamine). It is a popular substitute for heroin. The "T" refers to Talwin and the "blues" refers to the color of the pyribenzamine tablet. Apparently, the antihistamine enhances the action of the narcotic or diminishes some of its side effects.

tuies TUINAL.

turnabouts AMPHETAMINES.

turn on To take a drug, to encourage another to take a drug, or to feel the effects of a drug.

turned out To begin to use drugs.

turp TERPIN HYDRATE with CODEINE.

twenty-five LSD-25.

twist MARIJUANA.

twisted Feeling the effects of a drug. Also a term for feeling the initial effects of withdrawal.

tying up Using a tourniquet to distend a vein in preparation for an injection.

U

U.C. A federal narcotics undercover agent.

Ultracaine See FAKE COKE.

uncle A federal narcotics agent.

up To feel the effects of a stimulant drug, particularly AMPHETAMINES. Also a term for amphetamines themselves.

up and down the lines An expression that refers to the TRACKS or collapsed veins on an addict's arm.

upper, uppies, ups AMPHETAMINES.

uptight Feeling tense, anxious and sometimes hostile.

user A person who uses drugs.

using Using drugs.

V

vendedor Spanish word for a drug PUSHER.

violated To be arrested for violation of parole.

vipe MARIJUANA.

viper A person who uses VIPE (marijuana).

vitamin Q QUAALUDES.

volunteer A person who commits himself for treatment at the U.S. Public Health Service (narcotics) Hospital in Lexington, Kentucky.

voyager A person who is feeling the effects of LSD.

W

wagon, on the A term that refers to a temporary period of abstinence from alcoholic beverages. It was probably first used by American soldiers during the 1800s and referred to the water wagon that was taken on extended trips. Presumably the soldiers had no access to liquor during these periods.

wake up An addict's first injection of the day.

wake ups AMPHETAMINES.

wallbangers METHAQUALONE. The term is of British origin and is based on abuse of the English drug MANDRAX, which contains methaqualone.

waste To use, as in "I wasted the marijuana." Also to kill.

wasted To lose consciousness from drug intoxication. To be very intoxicated.

water AMPHETAMINES, particularly methamphetamine.

watering out To go through withdrawal without the help of medication.

wedges LSD.

weed MARIJUANA.

weeding out To smoke WEED (marijuana).

weed marijuana MARIJUANA that grows wild and is not particularly potent.

weekend habit The infrequent and irregular use of a drug, particularly just on weekends.

weekend warrior A person who uses drugs infrequently and irregularly, particularly just on weekends.

weight A measurement of drugs, especially diluted HEROIN. The term can also apply to a supply or large quantity of a drug.

whacked A drug, especially HEROIN, that has been diluted.

wheat MARIJUANA.

whiskey nose See GROG BLOSSOM.

white cloud Brand name street dealers use to identify their CRACK.

white crosses AMPHETAMINES.

white lady COCAINE. HEROIN.

white light A sensation experienced by STP users.

white lightning LSD. Also a term for unaged corn whisky. (See MOONSHINE.)

white stuff HEROIN.

white tornado CRACK.

whites BENZEDRINE.

wig A person's mind.

wig out To "lose your mind (wig)," while using a hallucinogenic drug. A loss of mental control and a state of altered consciousness.

wild geronimo A mixture of ALCOHOL and BARBITURATES.

winder An addict who volunteers for treatment at a narcotics hospital and can consequently leave at any time.

window pane LSD.

wingding, throw a A person who tries to obtain a narcotics prescription by faking WITHDRAWAL symptoms.

wings A person's first experience MAINLINING heroin.

wiped out Acute drug intoxication.

wired A person who is feeling the high effects of AMPHETAMINES. The term also applies to a HEROIN addict.

working A person who is trying to obtain money for drugs in an illegal manner.

works The apparatus for injecting drugs, particularly heroin. Usually included are such items as a homemade syringe, a tourniquet (belt, rubber hose, string), and a candle and spoon for "cooking" the injected solution.

wrap An inconspicuous covering for a package when smuggling drugs.

Y

yage, yaje AYAHUASCA.

yakee A psychedelic snuff made from the bark of the VIROLA tree by the Yekwana Indians of Venezuela.

yaupon A stimulant tea with mild alcoholic effects. Made from shrubs of the genus *Ilex,* it was popular among early settlers in the United States, particularly in the southeastern region. It is known to have unpleasant adverse reactions such as vomiting.

yellow LSD.

yellow bullets, yellow dolls, yellow jackets, yellows NEMBUTAL, which is supplied in 30 mg and 100 mg yellow capsules.

yen A CRAVING.

yenning To experience the beginning of WITHDRAWAL symptoms.

yerba Spanish word for MARIJUANA.

yopo See PIPTADENIA.

Z

Zacatecas purple A potent MARIJUANA grown in the central Mexican state of Zacatecas.

zap, zapped To overpower or defeat a person with violence. Originally a science fiction term.

Zigzag A brand of cigarette paper used to smoke MARIJUANA.

ZNA A mixture of MSG (monosodium glutamate) and dill weed. When smoked it is purported to produce psychedelic effects but the oil of dill weed can produce severe adverse reactions.

zonked Acutely intoxicated by a drug.

zunked To have a strong addiction to narcotics.

APPENDIX 2
SLANG SYNONYMS FOR DRUGS

AMPHETAMINES
"A"
AMT
bam
beans
bennies
black beauties
brain ticklers
brownies
bumblebees
cartwheels
chalk
chicken powder
crank
Christmas trees
crossroads
cross tops
crystal
dexies
diet pills
dolls
double cross
eye openers
fives
footballs
forwards
hearts
jam
jellybeans
leapers
lid poppers
lightning
meth
pep pills
purple hearts
rippers
sparkle plenties
sparklers
speed
splash
sweets
tens
thrusters
truck drivers
turnabouts
uppers
uppie
ups
wake-ups
water
white crosses

AMYL NITRITE
amies
amys
blue angels
bluebirds
blue bullets
blue devils
blue dolls
blue heavens
blues
blue tips
pearls
poppers
snappers

BARBITURATES
barbs
beans
black beauties
block busters
blue angels
brain ticklers
candy
courage pills
dolls
downers
downs
G.B.
goofballs
goofers
gorilla pills
green dragons
King Kong pills
nebbies
nimbies
phennies
phenos
pink ladies
purple hearts
rainbows
reds
seccy
seggie
sleepers
yellow bullets
yellow jackets
yellows

BENZEDRINE
bennies
benz
peaches
roses
whites

BIPHETAMINES
black beauties
blackbirds

CHLORAL HYDRATE
chlorals
joy juice
knockout drops
mickey
Mickey Finn
peter

COCAINE
bernice
bernies
big C.
blow
bombita
bouncing powder
burese
"C"
charles
charlie
coke
corrine
dream
dust
flake
fly
girl
gold dust
heaven
heaven dust
her
incentive
jay
joy powder
lady
lady snow
nose candy
nose powder
paradise
poison
powder
rock
snow
star dust
sugar
white
white lady
white powder
white stuff

CRACK COCAINE
base
baseball
black rock
cloud nine
Conan
freebase
gravel
handball
Lido
rock
Rovanne Serpico
snow
space base
super white
toke
white cloud
white tornado

DATURA
angel trumpet
jimson weed

DEXAMYL
Christmas trees
dexies

DEXEDRINE
copilots
dexies

DMT
businessman's lunchtime high

HASHISH
black hash
black Russian
blond hash
canned sativa
hash
Lebanese
mahjuema

HEROIN
big bag
big H
blanco
bomb
boy
brother
brown
brown rocks
brown sugar
caballo
cat
chick
Chinese red
Chinese white
chiva
crap
dogie
doojee
dope
duji
dust
eighth
flea powder
garbage
good stuff
"H"
hard stuff
harry
H-caps
henry
him
horse
hombre
jones
joy powder
junk
Mexican mud
mojo
muzzle
pack
P-Funk
poison
powder
pure
red chicken
red rock
rock
scag
schmeck
shit
smack
stuff

tecata
thing
white boy
white junk
white stuff

LIQUOR

booze
brew
juice
spirits

LSD

acid
barrels
beast
Big D
blotter
blue acid
blue cheer
blue heaven
blue mist
brown dots
California sunshine
cap
chocolate chips
contact lens
cubes
cupcakes
"D"
deeda
domes
dots
electric Kool-Aid
flash
ghost
hawk
haze
"L"
lysergide
mellow yellows
microdots
orange cubes
paper acid
peace
pearly gates
pellets
pink owsley
purple haze
sacrament
strawberries
strawberry fields
sugar
sugar cubes
sunshine
tabs
ticket
twenty-five
wedges
white lightning
window pane
yellow

MARIJUANA

Acapulco gold
ace
African black
aunt mary
baby
bale
black gunion
bomb
boo
brick
broccoli
bush
Canadian black
charge
Colombian
doobie
dope
dry high
fatty
fingers
flowers
gage
ganga
gauge
giggleweed
grass
green
grefa
greta
grifa
grillo
grunt
hay
hemp
herb
homegrown
Indian hay
Indian hemp
"J"
jane
jay smoke
joint
joy stick
juanita
kick sticks
kif
killer
killer weed
kilter
loco
mary
maryann
maryjane
mary warner
mary weaver
meserole, messerole
Mexican brown
Mexican green
Mexican locoweed
M.J.
mooca
moota
mooters
mootie
mota
mother
mu
muggles
muta
number
Panama gold
Panama red
panatella
pin
poke
pot
ragweed
rainy day woman
red dirt
reefer

roach
root
rope
sassfras
smoke
snop
stick
sweet lucy
tea
Texas tea
twist
weed
wheat
yerba
Zacatecas purple

MESCALINE
beans
big chief
buttons
cactus
cactus buttons
mesc
mescal
moon
topi

MORPHINE
big M
birdie powder
dreamer
emm
first line
God's medicine
gunk
hocus
"M"
mary
miss emma
miss morph
morph
moocah
morpho
morphy
school boy
white stuff

MUSCIMOL
death cap
death cups
destroying angels

NEMBUTAL
nebbies
nemmies
nemish
nimby
yellow bullets
yellow dolls
yellow jackets
yellow mollies
yellows

OPIUM
black pills
black stuff
brown stuff
canned stuff
hop
mash Allah
O
op
tar

PEYOTE
bad seed
big chief
buttons
cactus
"P"
peyotl
topi

PHENCYCLIDINE
angel dust
animal trank
aurora borealis
DOA
dust
elephant
hog
PCP
peace
peace pill
rocket fuel
supergrass
tic tac

PSILOCYBIN/PSILOCIN
magic mushrooms
mushrooms
sacred mushrooms
shrooms

APPENDIX 3
TABLES AND FIGURES

CONTENTS

Drug Control Laws

Reported Patterns of Drug Use Among High School Students, College Students and Young Adults

Estimated Growth of Illicit Drug Production

Violations of Drug Laws

Population Estimates

Miscellaneous

Table 1. Key Acts, Committee Recommendations and Supreme Court Rulings on Drug Control 1903–1989

1. *American Pharmaceutical Association ad hoc Committee on the Acquirement of the Drug Habit (1903)*
   The committee recommended:
   1. Severe penalties for illegal drug sales.
   2. Strong state enforcement of laws.
   3. Elimination of *all* opium importation.
   4. Heroin prescriptions to be issued only by a physician and to be unrefillable.
2. *Pure Food and Drug Act (1906)*
   There was one noteworthy provision in this act:
   1. Patent medicines traded in interstate commerce required labeling of any narcotic content.
3. *Harrison Act (1914)*
   This act had several significant provisions:
   1. Records were to be kept of drugs received by addicts from physicians.
   2. Revenue stamps were required on packages containing more than the permitted amount of opiates, and records of transactions involving retail sales of opiates were to be kept. Severe penalties were imposed for violation of these provisions.
   3. Registration with Internal Revenue Collector of agents involved in opiate manufacture, sale, or transportation was to be made.
4. *Webb et al. v. United States (1919)*
   Supreme Court Ruling: Outlawed addiction maintenance.
   Behran v. United States (1922)
   Supreme Court Ruling: Outlawed *any* prescription of narcotics for addicts.
5. *Narcotic Drug Import and Export Act (1922)*
   By this act, severe penalties (fine of not more than $5,000 and ten years in prison) were instituted for a narcotics conviction.

6. *Linder v. United States 268 U.S. 5 (1925)*
   Supreme Court Ruling: Physician could prescribe narcotics in moderate dosage to relieve withdrawal symptoms.
7. *Uniform Narcotic Act (1932)*
   This act was designed to coordinate federal and local record keeping of drug transactions.
8. *Narcotics Drug Control Act (1956)*
   This act imposed severe penalties for drug-related offenses.

Offense	*Penalty*
Possession, 1st	2 to 10 years
Possession, 2nd	5 to 10 years (mandatory sentence)*
Selling, 1st	5 to 10 years (mandatory sentence)*
Possession, 3rd	10 to 40 years (mandatory sentence)*
Selling, 2nd	10 to 40 years (mandatory sentence)* or possibly death sentence if seller is over the age of 18 and if the sale is to a minor.

9. *American Medical Association and American Bar Association Joint Committee on Narcotic Drugs (1958)*
   The Committee recommended experimental outpatient treatment for addicts; less provision for severe penalties.
10. *Robinson v. United States 370 U.S. 660 (1962)*
    Supreme Court Ruling: Addiction should not be punished by imprisonment, except in those cases where civil commitment for treatment is refused.
11. *Comprehensive Drug Abuse Prevention and Control Act (1970) (Controlled Substances Act)*
    1. Superseded all other federal narcotic laws.
    2. Bureau of Narcotics and Dangerous Drugs (BNDD) was given enforcement powers over drugs controlled by the act.
    3. Penalties based on drug classification, whether it is a first or subsequent offense, and type of involvement (that is, possession, sale, manufacture).
    4. Severe penalties for anyone convicted of sale of narcotics to a minor.
    5. Leniency for first offender.
12. The basic provisions of the Controlled Substances Act of 1970 were strengthened—through additional enforcement powers granted to various federal agencies, more and stiffer penalties based on drug classification, etc.—by the Congress in 1984 and reinforced with the Anti-Drug Abuse Act of 1986.
13. The Anti-Drug Abuse Act of 1988 declared that it would be the policy of the U.S. government to "create a Drug-Free America by 1995." It also called for establishment of an Office of National Drug Control Policy and presidential appointment of a director of that office who would devise and submit to the Congress a 1989 National Drug Control Strategy for congressional consideration and action. President Bush sent his National Drug Control Strategy to the speaker of the House of Representatives and the president pro tem of the Senate on September 5, 1989.
14. In April 1989, the U.S. Supreme Court upheld by a 7-to-2 vote the constitutionality of federal regulations that require railroad crews involved in accidents to submit to prompt urinalysis and blood tests. The justices also upheld, 5 to 4, urine tests for U.S. Customs Service employees seeking drug enforcement posts. A 1986 executive order by then President Reagan authorizes drug testing throughout the federal government.

---

*Mitigating circumstances cannot be taken into account by the court.

SOURCE: Robert J. Wicks and Jerome J. Platt, *Drug Abuse: A Criminal Justice Primer* (Beverly Hills, California: Glencoe Press, 1977), pp. 108–109. Adapted. Reprinted by permission.

HIGHLIGHTS FROM THE FISCAL YEAR 1989 STATE ALCOHOL AND DRUG ABUSE PROFILE (SADAP) DATA COLLECTION EFFORT EXECUTIVE SUMMARY

The State Alcohol and Drug Abuse Agencies voluntarily submit a broad spectrum of fiscal, client and other service data on an annual basis to the National Association of State Alcohol and Drug Abuse Directors, Inc. (NASADAD). These data are submitted via the State Alcohol and Drug Abuse Profile (SADAP) data collection effort. With financial support from the National Institute on Alcohol Abuse and Alcoholism (NIAAA) and the National Institute on Drug Abuse (NIDA), NASADAD staff have prepared a detailed analysis of these data. The findings for Fiscal Year (FY) 1989 as reported by the States and analyzed by NASADAD follow.

The financial and client *data* provided by the State Alcohol and Drug Abuse Agencies *apply to only those units and programs "which received at least some funds administered by the State Alcohol/Drug Agency."* Forty-nine States, the District of Columbia, Guam and Puerto Rico participated in the FY 1989 State Alcohol and Drug Abuse Profile (SADAP).

Highlights from the FY 1989 SADAP study indicate that:

- Expenditures for alcohol and drug abuse treatment and prevention services totaled over $2.4 billion.
- Of the total expenditures, States provided $1.1 billion or 47.1 percent, while Federal sources provided $644.5 million or 26.7 percent, county or local sources contributed $191.8 million or 7.9 percent and other sources (e.g., private health insurance, court fines, client fees or assessments for treatment imposed on intoxicated drivers) contributed $440.1 million or 18.2 percent.
- Approximately 76.9 percent of the total monies were expended for treatment services; 14.6 percent for prevention services; and 8.6 percent for other activities (e.g., training, research, administration).
- A total 7,150 alcohol and/or drug treatment units received funds administered by the State Alcohol and Drug Abuse Agencies in FY 1989. Of the total units, 1,449 were identified as alcohol units, 1,240 as drug units and 4,461 were identified as combined alcohol/drug treatment units.
- The total alcohol and other drug client treatment admissions reported by 48 States, the District of Columbia, Guam and Puerto Rico were over 1.8 million; alcohol client admissions were 77.5 percent male; 32 percent between the ages of 25–34; and 69.7 percent White, 17.2 percent Black and 6.4 percent Hispanic.
- A total of 48 States, the District of Columbia, Guam and Puerto Rico reported total drug client admissions of 605,914. 65.7 percent were male; 20.4 percent under the age of 21; 52.6 percent White; 28.4 percent Black; and 10.2 percent Hispanic.

- Cocaine was identified in overall reporting as the leading primary illicit drug of abuse as in FY 1988. Previously, heroin had been the leading primary illicit drug of abuse.
- For the fourth time, States were asked to provide estimates relating to intravenous (IV) drug abuse. Estimates of the number of IV drug abuser client treatment admissions by a total of 50 respondents ranged from a high of 35,297 in California to a low of 26 in South Dakota and 2 in Guam. The total number of IV drug abuser client admissions identified was 186,805.
- A total of 41 respondents provided data on the total number of IV drug abusers in their State. The highest estimates of IV drug abusers were provided by New York (260,000), California (222,000) and Texas (188,000). The total number of IV drug abusers estimated by all 41 respondents was 1,482,347.
- In response to a request for the top three policy issues, States identified a need for new or expanded treatment services; a need for prevention and treatment services to special populations, such as persons with AIDS and HIV disease, indigent, homeless, dually diagnosed, women and criminal justice clients; a need for administration and staffing; a need for funding and resource allocation; and, a need for prevention and treatment services for youth.
- Narrative responses received from the 52 State and Territorial Agencies confirmed that there were major needs in the areas of prevention and treatment for which adequate resources were not available. States identified many needs to meet the requirements of special populations, such as youth, women, dually-diagnosed clients, persons with HIV disease and AIDS, minorities, the homeless and the elderly.
- Significant changes in services that occurred during FY 1989 and were reported by the States related primarily to required new services for AIDS and IV drug user populations; client and drug use trends; changes in availability of financial resources for services; and changes in youth, prevention and treatment services.

EXECUTIVE SUMMARY

In September of 1987, the National Institute on Alcohol Abuse and Alcoholism (NIAAA), with support from the National Institute on Drug Abuse (NIDA), entered into a second three year contractual relationship with the National Association of State Alcohol and Drug Abuse Directors, Inc. (NASADAD) to ensure the continued availability and analysis of data from the States. The contract provides support for the analysis of information on alcohol and drug abuse funding and services. This cooperative Federal-State effort responds to Congressional mandates and ensures that the Institutes and the Alcohol, Drug Abuse and Mental Health Administration (ADAMHA) have the information necessary to exercise a strong national leadership role in cooperation with States with regard to alcohol and drug abuse program needs and services.

Under the State Alcohol and Drug Abuse Profile (SADAP) contract relevant data is collected from all of the States and Territories. With the cooperation of both Federal and State officials, the SADAP data collection format and process have been continually refined and improved over the past six years.

This report presents and analyzes the results of the State Alcohol and Drug Abuse Profile (SADAP) data for the States' 1989 Fiscal Year (FY). Forty-nine States, the District of Columbia, Guam and Puerto Rico cooperated and contributed information on resources, services and needs related to alcohol and drug abuse problems within the States and Territories. The remaining information is categorized into the following eight areas: funding levels and sources; client admission characteristics; intravenous (IV) drug abuse; State model product availability; top policy issues; major unmet needs; significant changes in treatment and/or prevention services; and responses to special questions.

Funding Levels and Sources The total reported expenditures within 49 States, the District of Columbia, Guam and Puerto Rico for alcohol and drug services in those programs receiving at least some State administered funds during the State's 1989 Fiscal Year (FY) were over $2.4 billion. As illustrated in Figure 1, this total includes more than $1 billion (41.8 percent) from State Alcohol and Drug Agency sources, $128.6 million (5.3 percent) from other State agency sources, $474.7 million (19.7 percent) from the Alcohol and Drug Abuse Block Grant, $169.9 million (7.0 percent) from other Federal government sources, $191.8 million (7.9 percent) from county or local agency sources, and $440.1 million (18.2 percent) from other sources (e.g., reimbursements from private health insurance, client fees, court fines or assessments for treatment imposed on intoxicated drivers).

It should be emphasized that the data provided do not include information on those programs that did not receive any funding from the State Alcohol and Drug Agencies in FY 1989. These programs would include most, if not all, private for-profit programs; some private not-for-private programs, some county and local government programs; and most Federal government programs such as the Veterans' Administration. Therefore, the overall fiscal data contained in this report are conservative in nature, and, to some degree, under-

FIGURE 1. Expenditures for State Supported Alcohol and Drug Abuse Services by Funding Source for Fiscal Year 1989

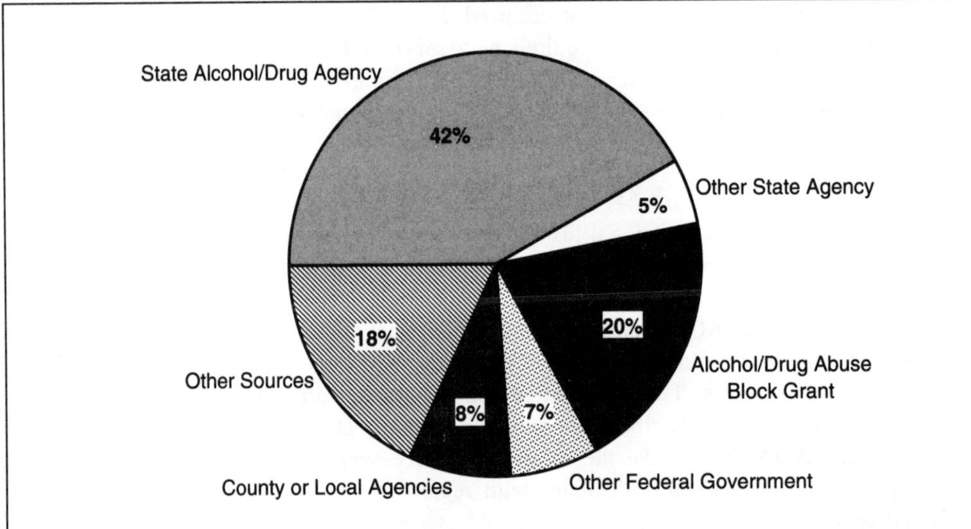

Total alcohol and drug expenditures for FY 1989 were $2,414,171,837

NOTE: The "Other Sources" category includes funding from sources such as client fees, court fines and reimbursements from private health insurance.
Source: *State Alcohol and Drug Abuse Profile, FY 1989;* data are included for "only those programs that received at least some funds administered by the State Alcohol/Drug Agency during the State's Fiscal Year 1989."

FIGURE 2. Expenditures for State Supported Alcohol and Drug Abuse Services by Type of Program Activity for Fiscal Year 1989

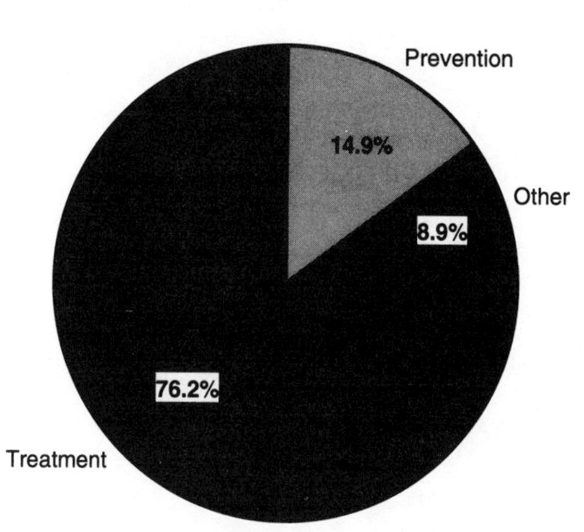

Total alcohol and drug expenditures for FY 1989 were $2,414,171,837

NOTE: The "Other" category includes expenditures for program activities such as administration, research and training.
Source: *State Alcohol and Drug Abuse Profile, FY 1989;* data are included for "only those programs that received at least some funds administered by the State Alcohol/Drug Agency during the State's Fiscal Year 1989."

estimate funding expenditures by other departments of State and Federal government and by private, non-State Agency supported alcohol and drug abuse treatment and prevention programs.

Although the specific levels of fiscal support contributed by different sources vary considerably among the States, the single largest source of funding during FY 1989 for alcohol and drug services was State monies. In 36 States and Territories, State Alcohol and Drug Agency monies constituted the largest source of funding, while in two States and in the District of Columbia, other State revenues were the largest source of support. The Alcohol and Drug Abuse Block Grant from the Federal Government was the largest revenue source in nine States. Among the remaining States, other Federal Government monies constituted the largest source of funds in one State and in one Territory and other sources (e.g., private health insurance) constituted the largest revenue source in two States.

Approximately 76.9 percent of the funds were expended for treatment services, 14.6 percent for prevention services, and 8.6 percent for other activities (e.g., training, research, administration) (See Figure 2).

Comparisons of financial expenditures reported by the States in this year's SADAP with data collected for FYs 1985, 1986, 1987 and 1988 are provided (See Figure 3). Although some other revenue sources have experienced larger percentage increases due to their smaller base, the bar graph data shown in Figure 3 clearly demonstrate that State Alcohol and Drug Agency funds have been and continue to be the largest revenue source for alcohol and drug

Figure 3. Comparison of Expenditures for State Supported Alcohol and Drug Abuse Services by Funding Source for Fiscal Years 1985, 1986, 1987, 1988 and 1989

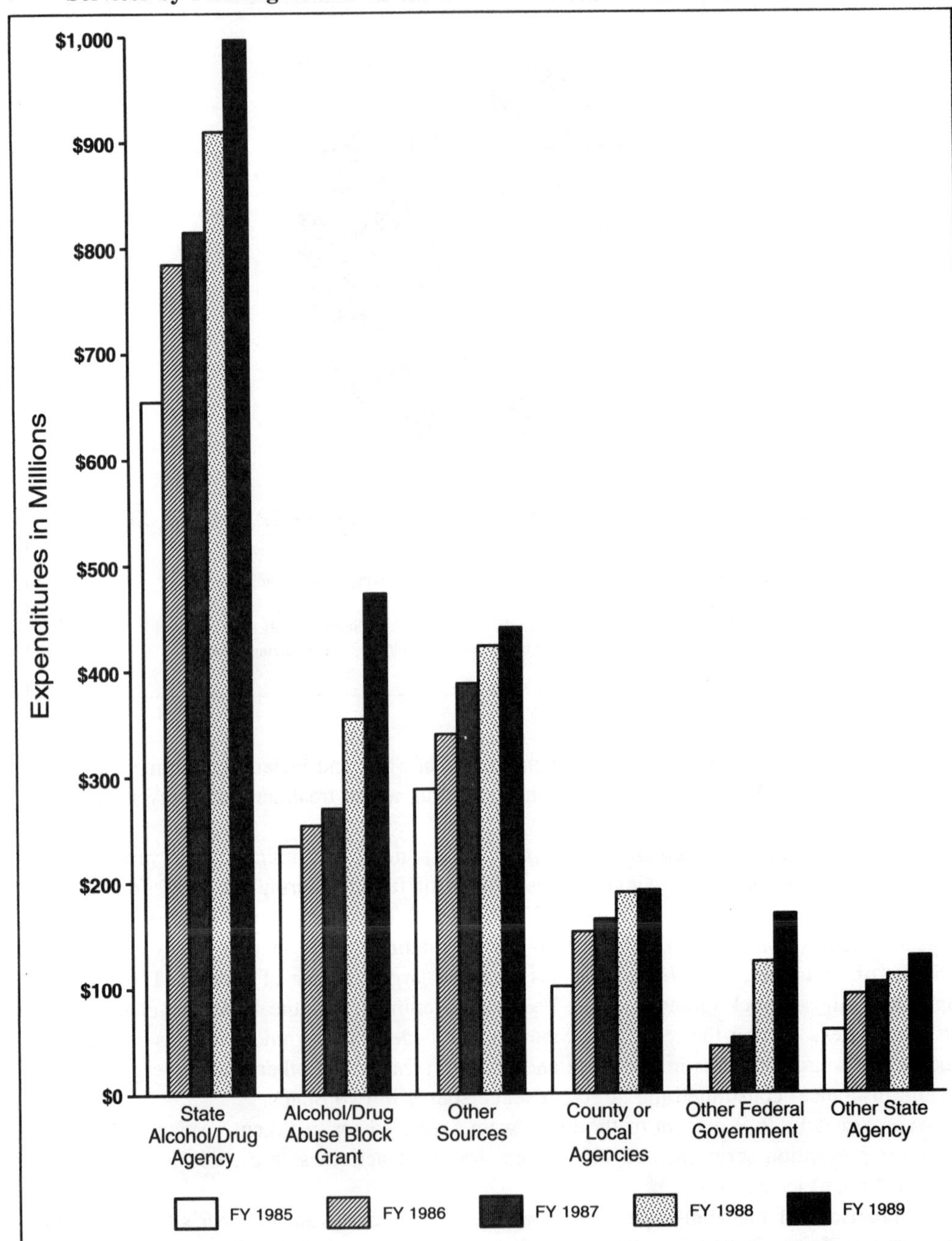

NOTE: Some of the apparent increases in expenditures may be related to an improvement in the States' ability to collect and provide data from different funding sources.

NOTE: The "Other" category includes expenditures for program activities such as administration, research and training.

SOURCE: *State Alcohol and Drug Abuse Profile, FY 1989;* data are included for "only those programs that received at least some funds administered by the State Alcohol/Drug Agency during the State's Fiscal Year 1989."

prevention services. Comparisons with data collected in earlier FYs (before 1985) are not appropriate. Such comparisons would be misleading since there were changes instituted in the specific wording of questions related to States' fiscal resources (e.g., a change from "allocations" to "expenditures").

The State Agencies identified a total of 7,150 alcohol and/or drug treatment units to which they provided at least some funding in FY 1989. In terms of treatment orientation, 4,461 of the units provided combined alcohol/drug treatment services, while 1,449 (20.3 percent) focused on alcoholism services and 1,240 (17.3 percent) concentrated on drug dependency services.

Table 2. State-by-State List of the Marijuana Laws

ALABAMA[M]
Possession:
≤1 kilo for personal use: 0-1; $2,000
≤1 kilo otherwise: 1-10; $2,000
Cultivation/Delivery/Sale:
>2.2 lb.-100 lb.: 3; $25,000
≥100 lb.-500 lb.: 5; $50,000
≥500 lb.-1,000 lb.: 15; $200,000
≥1,000 lb.: life without parole

ALASKA
Possession:
<1 oz.: $100
≥1 oz.-5 lb.: 0-90 days; $1,000
≥.5 lb.-1 lb.: 0-1; $5,000
≥1 lb.: 0-5; $50,000
Cultivation/Delivery/Sale:
≥.5 oz.-1 oz.: 0-1; $5,000
≥1 oz.: 0-5; $50,000

ARIZONA[M]
Possession:
<1 lb.: 0-1½; $750-$150,000
≥1 lb.-8 lb.: 0-2.5; $750-$150,000
≥8 lb.: 0-5; $750-$150,000
Possession for Sale:
<1 lb.: 0-5; $750-$150,000
≥1 lb.-8 lb.: 0-10; $750-$150,000
≥8 lb.: 2.5-10; $750-$150,000
Cultivation:
<1 lb.; 0-2.5; $750-$150,000
≥1 lb.-8 lb.: 0-10; $750-$150,000
≥8 lb.: 2.5-10; $750-$150,000
Sell/Transfer/Transport:
<1 lb.: 0-10; $750-$150,000
≥1 lb.-8 lb.: 0-14; $750-$150,000
≥8 lb.: 3.5-14; $750-$150,000

ARKANSAS[C,M]
Possession:
≤1 oz.: Class A misdemeanor
≥1 oz.: Rebuttable presumption of possession with intent to deliver
Cultivation/Delivery/Sale:
1 oz.-10 lbs.: 4-10; $25,000
10-100 lbs.: 5-20; $15,000-$50,000
≥100 lbs.: 6-30; $15,000-$100,000

CALIFORNIA[D,M]
Possession:
≤28.5 g.: $100.
>28.5 g.: 0-6 mos.; $500
Possession for Sale:
16 mos.-3; $20,000
Cultivation:
Any amount: 1-10; $20,000
Delivery/Sale:
Any amount: 2-4; $20,000

COLORADO[D,M]
Possession:
≤1 oz.: 15 days; $100.
>1 oz.-<8 ozs.: 0-2; $5,000.
≥8 ozs.: 1-4; $1,000-$100,000.
Cultivation/Delivery/Sale:
Any amount: 2-8; $2,000-$500,000.

CONNECTICUT[M]
Possession:
<4 ozs.: 0-1; $1,000
≥4 ozs.: 0-5; $2,000
Cultivation/Delivery/Sale:
Any amount: 0-7; $25,000

DELAWARE[C]
Possession:
Any amount: 0-1; $3,000
Cultivation/Delivery/Sale:
≤5 lb.: 0-5; $1,000-$10,000
>5 lb.-100 lb.: 3; $25,000
≥100 lb.-500 lb.: 5; $50,000
≥500 lb.: 15; $100,000

DISTRICT OF COLUMBIA[C]
Possession:
Any amount: 0-1; $1,000
Cultivation/Delivery/Sale:
Any amount: 0-1; $10,000

FLORIDA[C,M]
Possession:
≤20 g.: 0-1; $1,000
Cultivation/Delivery/Sale:
≤100 lb.: Check
>100 lb.-2,000 lb.: 3; $25,000
≥2,000 lb.-10,000 lb.: 5; $50,000
≥10,000 lb.: 15; $200,000

Table 2 (*continued*). State-by-State List of the Marijuana Laws

GEORGIA[C,M]
Possession:
<1 oz.: 0-1; $1,000
≥1 oz.-50 lb.: 1-10; $1,000
Cultivation/Delivery/Sale:
≥50 lb.-2,000 lb.: 5; $100,000
≥2,000 lb.-10,000 lb.: 7; $250,000
≥10,000 lb.: 15; $1,000,000

HAWAII[C]
Possession:
<1 oz.: 0-30 days; $1,000
≥1 oz.-1 lb.: 0-1; $2,000
≥1 lb.-2 lb.: 0-5; $5,000
≥2 lb.-25 lb.: 0-10; $25,000
≥25 lb.: 0-20; $50,000
Cultivation/Delivery/Sale:
<1 oz.: 0-1; $2,000
≥1 oz.-1 lb.: 0-5; $10,000
≥1 lb.-5 lb.: 0-10; $25,000
≥5 lb.: 0-20; $50,000

IDAHO[C]
Possession:
≤3 ozs.: 0-1; $1,000
>3 ozs.: 0-5; $10,000
Cultivation/Delivery/Sale:
Any amount: 0-5; $15,000

ILLINOIS[C,M]
Possession:
<2.5 g.: 0-30 days; $500
≥2.5 g.-10 g.: 6 mos.; $500
≥10 g.-30 g.: 1; $1,000
≥30 g.-500 g.: 1-3; $10,000
≥500 g.: 2-5; $10,000
Cultivation:
0-5 plants: 0-1; $1,000
5-20 plants: 1-3; $10,000
20-50 plants: 2-5; $10,000
>50 plants: 3-7; $100,000
Sale/Delivery:
<2.5 g.: 6 mos.; $500
≥2.5 g.-10 g.: 1; $1,000
≤10 g.-30 g.: 1-3; $10,000
≥30 g.-500 g.: 2-5; $50,000
<500 g.: 3-7; $100,000

INDIANA[C]
Possession:
≤30 g.: 0-1; $5,000
>30 g.: 1.5; $10,000
Cultivation/Delivery/Sale:
≤30 g.: 0-1; $5,000
>30 g.-10 lb.: 1.5; $10,000
≥10 lb.: 4; $10,000

IOWA[C,M]
Possession:
<50 kg.: 0-6 mos.; $1,000
≥50 kg.: See penalties below
Cultivation/Delivery/Sale:
<50 kg.: 0-5; $5,000
≥50 kg.-100 kg.: 0-10; $5,000
≥100 kg.-1,00 kg.: 0-25; $100,000
>1,000 kg.: 0-50; $1,000,000

KANSAS[C]
Possession:
Any amount: 0-1; $2,500
Cultivation:
≤50 plants: 3-30; $300,000
>50 plants: 5-life; $300,000
Delivery/Sale:
≤1500 g.: 3-20; $300,000
>1500 g.: 5-life; $300,000

KENTUCKY
Possession:
<8 ozs.: 0-90 days; $200
≥8 ozs.: 0-1; $500
Cultivation/Delivery/Sale:
<8 ozs.: 0-1; $500
≥8 ozs.-5 lbs.: 1-5; $10,000

LOUISIANA[M]
Possession:
<60 lb.: 0-6 mos.; $500
≥60 lb.: See penalties below
Cultivation/Delivery/Sale:
60-2,000 lb.: 5-15; $50,000
≥2,000-10,000 lb.: 10-40; $200,000
≥10,000 lb.: 25-40; $500,000

MAINE[D,M]
Possession:
<1.25 oz.: $200-$400
Furnishings:
>1.25 oz.-2 lbs.: 0-1; $1,000
Cultivation:
≥100 plants-500 plants: 3-5; $10,000
≥500 plants: 5-10; $25,000
Delivery/Sale:
≥2 lb.-20 lb.: 3-5; $10,000
≥20 lb.: 5-10; $25,000

MARYLAND[C]
Possession:
Any amount: 0-1; $1,000
Cultivation/Delivery/Sale:
<50 lb.: 0-5; $15,000
≥50 lb.: 5-life; $25,000

MASSACHUSETTS[C]
Possession:
Any amount: 0-6 mos.; $500
Cultivation/Delivery/Sale:
<50 lb.: 0-2; $5,000
≥50 lb.-100 lb.: 2.5-15; $10,000
≥100 lb.-2,000 lb.: 3-15; $25,000
≥2,000 lb.-10,000 lb.: 5-15; $50,000
≥10,000 lb.: 10-15; $200,000

MICHIGAN[C,M]
Use:
0-90 days; $100
Possession:
Any amount: 0-1; $1,000
Cultivation/Delivery/Sale:
Any amount: 0-4; $2,000

MINNESOTA[D,M]
Possession:
<2 kg.: Drug education; $200
≥2 kg.-10 kg.: 0-5; $10,000
≥10 kg.-50 kg.: 0-20; $250,000
≥50 kg.-100 kg.: 0-25; $500,000
≥100 kg.: 0-30; $1,000,000
Cultivation/Delivery/Sale:
≥2 kg.-5 kg.: 0-5; $10,000
≥5 kg.-25 kg.: 0-20; $250,000
≥25 kg.-50 kg.: 0-25; $500,000
≥50 kg.: 0-30; $1,000,000

MISSISSIPPI[D]
Possession:
≤1 oz.: $100-$250
>1 oz.-1 kg.: 0-1; $1,000
≥1 kg.: See below
Cultivation/Delivery/Sale:
≤1 oz.: 0-3; $3,000
>1 oz.-1 kg.: 0-20; $30,000
≥1 kg.: 0-30; $1,000-$1,000,000

MISSOURI
Possession:
≤35 g.: 0-1; $1,000
>35 g.: 0-5; $1,000
Cultivation/Delivery/Sale:
≤5 g.: 0-7; $5,000
>5 g.: 5-15; $5,000

MONTANA[M]
Possession:
≤60 g.: 0-6 mos.; $100-$500
>60 g.: 0-20; $50,000
Cultivation/Delivery/Sale:
Any amount: 1-life; $50,000

NEBRASKA[D]
Use:
3 mos; $500
Possession:
<1 oz.: $100
>1 oz.-1 lb.: 0-7 days; $500
≥1 lb.: 0-5; $10,000
Cultivation/Delivery/Sale:
Same as above

NEVADA[M]
Use:
1-6; $5,000
Possession:
Any amount: 1-6; $5,000
Cultivation/Delivery/Sale:
<100 lb.: 1-15; $5,000
≥100 lb.-2,000 lb.: 3-20; $25,000
≥2,000 lb.-10,000 lb.: 5-20; $50,000
≥10,000 lb.: 15-life; $200,000

NEW HAMPSHIRE[M]
Possession:
Any amount: 0-1; $1,000
Cultivation/Delivery/Sale:
<1 oz.: 0-3; $25,000
≥1 oz.-5 lb.: 0-7; $100,000
≥5 lb.: 0-20; $300,000

NEW JERSEY[C,M]
Possession:
≤25 g.: 0-6 mos.; $1,000
>25 g.: 0-5; $5,000
Cultivation/Delivery/Sale:
Any amount: 0-5; $15,000

NEW MEXICO[M]
Possession:
≤1 oz.: 0-15 days; $50-$100
>1 oz.-8 oz.: 0-1; $100-$1,000
Cultivation/Delivery/Sale:
≤100 lb.: 0-18 mos.; $5,000
>100 lb.: 0-3; $5,000

NEW YORK[D,M]
Possession:
≤25 g.: $100
>25 g.-2 oz.: 0-3 mos.; $500
>2 ozs.-8 oz.: 0-1; $1,000
>8 ozs.-1 lb.: 0-4; $5,000
>1 lb.-10 lb.: 0-7; $5,000
>10 lb.: 0-15; $5,000
Cultivation/Delivery/Sale:
≤25 g.: 0-1; $1,000
>25 g.-4 oz.: 0-4; $5,000
>4 ozs.-1 lb.: 0-7; $5,000
>1 lb.: 0-15; $5,000

NORTH CAROLINA[D,M]
Possession:
<.5 oz.: 0-30 days; $100
≥.5 oz.-1.5 oz.: 0-2; $2,000
>1.5 oz.-50 lb.: 0-5; $5,000
>50 lb.: See below
Cultivation/Delivery/Sale:
>50 lb.-100 lb.: 5-10; $5,000
≥100 lb.-2,000 lb.: 7-15; $25,000
≥2,000 lb.-10,000 lb.: 14-20; $50,000
≥10,000 lb.: 35-40; $200,00

NORTH DAKOTA[C]
Possession:
<.5 oz.: Class B misdemeanor (Check)
≥.5 oz.-1 oz.: 0-1; $1,000
≥1 oz.: 0-5 yrs; $5,000
Cultivation/Delivery/Sale:
<100 lb.: 0-10; $10,000
≥100 lb.: 0-20; $10,000

OHIO[D,M]
Possession:
<100 g.: $100
Delivery/Sale:
<100 g.: $100
Cultivation:
Any amount: 1.5-5; $2,500

OKLAHOMA[M]
Possession:
Any amount: 0-1; $500
Cultivation:
2-life; $50,000
Delivery/Sale:
2-life; $20,000
≥25 lb.-1,000 lb.: 5-life; $100,000
≥1,000 lb.: 5-life; $500,000

Table 2 (*continued*). State-by-State List of the Marijuana Laws

OREGON[D,M]
Possession:
<1 oz.: $500-$1,000
≥1 oz.: 0-10 yrs.: $100,000
Cultivation/Delivery/Sale:
Any amount: 0-10; $100,000

PENNSYLVANIA
Possession:
≤30 g.: 0-30 days; $500
≥30 g.: 0-1; $5,000
Cultivation/Delivery/Sale:
Any amount: 0-15; $250,000

RHODE ISLAND[M]
Possession:
Any amount: 0-1; $500
Cultivation/Delivery/Sale:
Any amount: 0-30; $100,000

SOUTH CAROLINA[M]
Possession:
<1 oz.: 0-30 days; $100-$200
Cultivation/Delivery/Sale:
<10 lb.: 0-5; $5,000
≥10 lb.-100 lb.: 25; $10,000
≥100 lb.-2,000 lb.: 25; $25,000
≥2,000 lb.-10,000 lb.: 25; $50,000
≥10,000 lb.: 25; $200,000

SOUTH DAKOTA
Possession:
≤1 oz.: 0-30 days; $100
>1 oz.-5 lb.: 0-1; $1,000
≥.5 lb.-<1 lb.: 0-2; $2,000
≥1 lb.-≤10 lb.: 0-5; $5,000
>10 lb.: 0-10; $10,000
Cultivation/Delivery/Sale:
≤1 oz.: 15 days-1; $1,000
>1 oz.-.5 lb.: 30 days-2; $2,000
≥.5 lb.-<1 lb.: 30 days-5; $5,000
≥1 lb.: 30 days-10; $10,000

TENNESSEE[C,M]
Possession:
≤.5 oz.: 0-1; $2,500
Cultivation/Delivery/Sale:
>.5 oz.-10 lbs.: 1-5; $3,000
≥10 lb.-70 lb.: 4-10; $10,000
≥70 lb.: 8-12; $200,000

TEXAS[M]
Possession:
≤2 oz.: 0-6 mos.; $1,000
>2 oz.-4 oz.: 0-1; $2,000
>4 oz.-5 lb.: 2-10; $10,000
>5 lb.-50 lb.: 2-20; $10,000
>50 lb.: See below
Cultivation/Delivery/Sale:
≤.25 oz.: 0-1; $2,000
>.25 oz.-4 oz.: 2-10; $10,000
>4 oz.-5 lb.: 2-20; $10,000
>5 lb.-50 lb.: 5-99; $10,000
>50 lb.-200 lb.: 5-99; $50,000
>200 lb.-2,000 lb.: 10-life; $100,000
>2,000 lb.: 15-99; $250,000

UTAH
Possession:
<1 oz.: 0-6 mos.; $1,000.
≥1 oz.-16 oz.: 0-1; $2,500.
≥16 oz.-100 lb.: 0-5; $5,000.
Cultivation/Delivery/Sale:
Any amount: 0-5; $10,000

VERMONT[C,M]
Possession:
<2 oz.: 0-6 mos.; $500
Deliver/Sale:
≤2 oz.-1 lb.: 0-3; $10,000
1 lb.-10 lb.: 0-5; $100,000
≥10 lb.: 0-15; $500,000
Cultivation:
>3-10 plants: 0-3; $10,000
>10-25 plants: 0-5; $100,000
>25 plants: 0-15; $500,000

VIRGINIA[C,M]
Possession:
<5 lb.: 0-30 days; $500
≥5 lb.: 1-10; $1,000
Delivery/Sale:
≤.5 oz.: 0-2; $10,000
.5 oz.-5 lb.: 0-5; $100,000
>5 lb.: 0-15; $500,000
Cultivation:
Any amount: 5-30; $10,000

WASHINGTON[M]
Possession:
<40 g.: 0-90 days; $1,000
≥40 g.: 0-5; $10,000
Cultivation/Delivery/Sale:
Any amount: 0-5; $10,000

WEST VIRGINIA[C,M]
Possession:
<15 g.: automatic conditional discharge; $1,000
>15 g.: 1-5; $15,000
Cultivation/Delivery/Sale:
Any amount: 1-15; $25,000

WISCONSIN[C,M]
Possession:
Any amount: 0-6 mos.; $1,000
Cultivation/Delivery/Sale:
≤500 g.: 0-3; $25,000
>500 g.-2,500 g.: 3 mos.-5 yr.; $50,00
>2,500 g.: 1-10; $100,000

WYOMING
Use:
0-6 mos.; $750
Possession:
Any amount: 0-6 mos.; $750
Cultivation
Any amount: 0-6 mos.; $1,000
Delivery/Sale:
Any amount: 0-10; $10,000

FEDERAL
Possession:
Any amount: 0-1; $2,500
Cultivation/Delivery/Sale:
$<$100 kg.: 0-20; $1 million
$\geq$100 kg.: 5-40; $2 million
$\geq$1000 kg.: 10-life; $4 million

NOTES

-This chart contains the penalties for first offense possession, cultivation, sale and delivery of marijuana. Most states have increased penalties for subsequent offenses.
-Many states also have enhanced penalties for involving minors and offenses within a certain distance of schools, parks, and other public recreational areas.
-Any amount for possession generally means for personal use. Possession of large amounts of marijuana will, in most cases, lead to charges of possession with intent to distribute (same as sale).
-Units of weight vary from state to state. For comparative purposes: One ounce = 28.35 grams; one pound = 453.59 grams; and one kilogram = 2.2 pounds.
-Except where otherwise indicated, sentences are in years.
-Except where otherwise indicated, fines are maximum amount.
C: State allows for the conditional release or alternative/diversion sentencing of first-time possession offenders.
D: States where marijuana is decriminalized to some degree.
M: State has enacted legislation recognizing the medical use of marijuana for certain ailments such as glaucoma, nausea associated with chemotherapy and AIDS treatment, and some spascticity and neurological disorders.

SOURCE: National Organizaiton for the Reform of Marijuana Laws.

Table 3. Expenditures for State Supported Alcohol and Other Drug Abuse Services by State and by Funding Source for Fiscal Year 1989

State	State Alcohol/ Drug Agency	Other State Agency	Alcohol/ Drug Abuse Block Grant	Other Federal Government	County or Local Agencies	Other Sources	Grand Total	
Alabama	2,565,194	N/A	6,434,653	48,916	N/A	2,592	9,051,355	
Alaska	14,843,300	869,900	2,542,300	5,014,500	3,182,400	1,907,000	28,359,400	
Arizona	11,373,259	N/A	6,904,090	0	N/A	9,322,810	27,600,159	A
Arkansas	1,694,802	1,397,927	3,928,804	974,321	583,334	0	8,579,188	
California	80,896,000	1,257,000	91,738,000	35,631,000	37,899,091	84,868,692	332,289,783	
Colorado	11,626,746	1,006,902	7,612,029	1,166,905	4,601,705	5,185,559	31,199,846	
Connecticut	39,650,694	0	7,339,332	3,100,147	0	17,918,525	68,008,698	
Delaware	3,084,606	17,389	1,469,756	136,000	N/A	8,086	4,715,837	
District of Col	130,825	27,219,188	2,815,850	1,957,501	0	1,544,539	33,667,903	
Florida	42,822,607	318,180	21,816,736	790,490	21,916,004	0	87,664,017	
Georgia	28,713,600	0	9,600,765	1,526,017	861,038	3,792,519	44,493,939	
Guam	N/A	N/A	31,830	50,400	N/A	N/A	82,230	
Hawaii	2,371,061	185,556	1,258,880	105,674	27,000	1,020,191	4,968,362	
Idaho	1,756,016	3,500	1,550,793	283,773	0	0	3,594,082	
Illinois	55,078,572	436,832	18,360,282	2,856,388	N/A	N/A	76,732,074	
Indiana	3,290,085	11,637,469	6,126,039	4,696,747	1,815,082	3,179,374	30,744,796	
Iowa	8,381,395	1,670,654	3,984,816	393,592	2,153,642	3,470,548	20,054,647	
Kansas	5,269,003	431,460	3,399,516	372,000	1,831,112	3,499,261	14,802,352	
Kentucky	5,306,551	2,669,159	4,893,895	736,718	1,429,304	0	15,035,627	
Louisiana	4,583,191	0	6,457,593	0	0	495,319	11,536,103	
Maine	6,293,644	1,385,517	2,409,862	N/A	N/A	N/A	10,089,023	
Maryland	34,332,900	0	7,023,700	749,500	4,632,000	10,730,000	57,468,100	
Massachusetts	45,174,839	0	13,470,640	960,528	0	0	59,606,007	
Michigan	28,980,537	0	21,824,793	3,164,136	10,007,302	19,887,668	83,864,436	
Minnesota	28,279,200	0	10,484,455	2,500,000	10,215,700	0	51,479,355	
Mississippi	2,326,624	615,352	3,426,500	2,414,486	N/A	N/A	8,782,962	
Missouri	10,577,694	N/A	8,508,262	1,174,207	N/A	N/A	20,260,163	
Montana	521,872	2,132,699	1,455,727	1,173,613	1,233,016	7,415,102	13,932,029	
Nebraska	4,633,268	0	2,877,579	78,504	579,225	861,464	9,030,040	
Nevada	2,336,689	0	2,674,915	303,545	59,937	2,874,169	8,249,255	B

Table 3 (*continued*). Expenditures for State Supported Alcohol and Other Drug Abuse Services by State and by Funding Source for Fiscal Year 1989

State	State Alcohol/ Drug Agency	Other State Agency	Alcohol/ Drug Abuse Block Grant	Other Federal Government	County or Local Agencies	Other Sources	Grand Total	
New Hampshire	2,566,048	0	1,679,478	20,335	0	167,878	4,433,739	
New Jersey	29,925,000	1,154,000	12,037,000	7,219,000	2,801,000	6,442,000	59,578,000	
New Mexico	12,439,853	0	1,819,289	927,686	0	0	15,186,828	
New York	242,359,672	10,830,143	53,429,794	11,634,079	37,615,433	184,649,111	540,518,232	ACD
North Carolina	27,388,261	0	4,336,710	5,829,885	0	0	37,554,856	
North Dakota	728,749	N/A	2,335,672	199,756	0	N/A	3,264,177	
Ohio	16,411,196	702,775	10,205,388	1,751,225	1,732,240	15,598,983	46,401,807	
Oklahoma	12,061,123	0	4,626,006	861,465	N/A	N/A	17,548,594	
Oregon	7,200,426	34,360,080	6,048,322	28,086,849	5,131,311	0	80,826,988	
Pennsylvania	31,830,434	8,578,612	19,365,770	956,791	8,816,672	19,898,249	89,446,528	
Puerto Rico	17,431,833	655,266	6,996,017	2,293,904	N/A	3,284,000	30,661,020	F
Rhode Island	11,501,052	0	1,860,240	719,388	0	0	14,080,680	GH
South Carolina	8,964,889	4,715,222	4,071,568	2,252,350	4,360,378	7,750,112	32,114,519	
South Dakota	461,113	417,220	1,276,876	230,741	674,684	1,251,148	4,311,782	
Tennessee	8,641,320	1,486,767	5,731,092	1,609,649	6,343,705	3,032,814	26,845,347	
Texas	4,516,055	0	22,047,859	3,852,523	0	0	30,416,437	
Utah	5,790,060	614,190	3,529,137	223,231	2,837,805	3,063,762	16,058,105	
Vermont	2,785,063	440,000	3,310,334	184,796	N/A	N/A	4,720,193	I
Virginia	19,374,877	N/A	8,203,821	N/A	11,811,086	6,163,147	45,552,931	
Washington	39,130,000	0	7,920,000	1,270,000	0	0	48,320,000	
West Virginia	2,780,685	312,963	3,474,741	0	147,555	921,785	7,637,729	
Wisconsin	17,916,600	11,084,377	9,949,600	27,375,600	6,500,820	9,924,500	82,751,497	
Wyoming	N/A	N/A	N/A	N/A	N/A	N/A	N/A	
TOTALS	**1,009,099,083**	**128,606,299**	**474,677,106**	**169,858,861**	**191,799,581**	**440,130,907**	**2,414,171,837**	
PERCENT OF TOTAL	**41.8%**	**5.3%**	**19.7%**	**7.0%**	**7.9%**	**18.2%**	**100.0%**	

A = Figures represent allocated funds rather than expenditures.
B = County or Local Agencies category includes required matching funds.
C = Other State Agency category includes methadone registry, capital construction, and Medicaid MIS suballocation from Dept. of Social Services
D = Other Federal Government category includes the Federal Crime Control and Safe Street Act, Western New York Prevention Project through th Division of Criminal Justice Services, Community Youth Activity Grant, Developmental Disabilities Planning Council Grant, Drug Use For casting Program Grant, States Helping States Grant, Uniform Alcohol and Drug Abuse Data Collection System Grant, and Intensive Supervisic Project Grant fund by Div. of Criminal Justice Services from an NIJ grant. Also includes $10,000,000 Federal waiting list reduction gra money.
E = Other Sources category includes Medicaid, client fees, etc.
F = Other Sources category includes donations to private programs which offer prevention and treatment services.
G = Figures represent an estimate of expenditures.
H = State Alcohol/Drug Agency category includes appropriation and statistical accounts.
I = Other State category includes alcohol and drug funds which are generated from fees charged by the State A/D Agency and which are part of th appropriation of the State A/D Agency.

N/A = Information not available.

CAUTIONARY NOTE: In a number of States complete information is not available on all funding sources for State supported programs. In mo instances where such information is not presented the amount of such funding, if any, is probably minimal. However, since in some instances su funding may be substantial, the percents presented at the bottom of this table should be used only as gross estimates of the overall levels of fundir from various sources. It is likely that the "Other State," "Other Federal," "County or Local" and "Other Sources" categories actually contribu more monies and higher percents than the figures shown.

SOURCE: *State Alcohol and Drug Abuse Profile, FY 1989;* data are included for "only those programs which received at least some funds admini tered by the State Alcohol/Drug Agency during the State's Fiscal Year 1989."

Table 4. Expenditures for State Supported Alcohol and Other Drug Abuse Services by State and by Type of Program Activity for Fiscal Year 1989

	Type of Program Activity			
State	**Treatment**	**Prevention**	**Other**	**Total**
Alabama	7,897,635	850,820	302,900	9,051,355
Alaska	21,442,400	4,502,700	2,414,300	28,359,400
Arizona	25,451,346	1,660,711	488,102	27,600,159 A
Arkansas	7,409,820	676,779	492,589	8,579,188
California	227,670,642	64,325,228	40,293,913	332,289,783
Colorado	23,866,811	5,587,384	1,745,651	31,199,846
Connecticut	56,609,363	4,277,942	7,121,393	68,008,698
Delaware	3,929,745	541,583	244,509	4,715,837
District of Col	28,220,306	3,011,117	2,436,480	33,667,903
Florida	79,724,238	7,716,747	223,032	87,664,017
Georgia	40,586,002	1,407,609	2,500,328	44,493,939
Guam	49,338	16,446	16,446	82,230
Hawaii	3,945,258	713,173	309,931	4,968,362
Idaho	2,906,064	427,201	260,817	3,594,082
Illinois	60,452,156	8,651,408	7,628,510	76,732,074
Indiana	27,162,216	2,619,173	936,407	30,744,796
Iowa	15,680,325	3,724,978	649,344	20,054,647
Kansas	11,948,723	1,756,154	1,097,475	14,802,352
Kentucky	11,536,974	2,576,342	922,311	15,035,627
Louisiana	9,508,694	1,223,164	804,164	11,536,103
Maine	7,090,939	2,050,051	948,033	10,089,023
Maryland	49,349,000	4,909,200	3,209,900	57,468,100
Massachusetts	50,351,136	4,863,076	4,391,795	59,606,007
Michigan	59,807,172	15,199,787	8,857,477	83,864,436
Minnesota	45,912,600	459,840	5,106,915	51,479,355
Mississippi	6,607,990	685,300	1,489,672	8,782,962
Missouri	17,388,780	1,486,323	1,385,060	20,260,163
Montana	12,252,545	1,239,473	440,011	13,932,029
Nebraska	7,690,631	956,051	383,358	9,030,040
Nevada	6,846,247	754,299	648,709	8,249,255
New Hampshire	2,989,183	669,789	774,767	4,433,739
New Jersey	43,312,000	9,523,000	6,743,000	59,578,000
New Mexico	13,665,704	1,257,503	263,621	15,186,828
New York	405,872,041	81,565,468	53,080,723	540,518,232 A
North Carolina	33,624,204	2,426,924	1,503,728	37,554,856
North Dakota	2,731,072	444,784	88,321	3,264,177
Ohio	35,362,510	6,665,698	4,373,599	46,401,807
Oklahoma	15,601,009	1,299,682	647,903	17,548,594

Table 4 (*continued*). Expenditures for State Supported Alcohol and Other Drug Abuse Services by State and by Type of Program Activity for Fiscal Year 1989

Oregon	47,045,861	29,058,989	4,722,138	80,826,988
Pennsylvania	65,443,971	15,372,433	8,630,124	89,446,528
Puerto Rico	19,022,581	4,649,426	6,989,013	30,661,020
Rhode Island	10,896,494	2,802,134	382,052	14,080,680
South Carolina	20,322,085	9,492,388	2,300,046	32,114,519
South Dakota	3,789,630	356,224	165,928	4,311,782
Tennessee	18,002,396	5,530,614	3,312,337	26,845,347
Texas	18,902,286	7,628,759	3,885,392	30,416,437
Utah	12,181,561	3,158,888	717,736	16,058,185
Vermont	3,214,729	827,015	678,449	4,720,193
Virginia	40,977,984	4,574,947	0	45,552,931
Washington	45,750,000	850,000	1,720,000	48,320,000
West Virginia	6,112,110	900,420	625,199	7,637,729
Wisconsin	61,399,338	13,498,414	7,853,745	82,751,497
Wyoming	N/A	N/A	N/A	N/A
TOTALS	**1,855,513,845**	**351,423,639**	**207,234,353**	**2,414,171,837**
PERCENT OF TOTAL	**76.9%**	**14.6%**	**8.6%**	**100.0%**

A = Figures represent allocated funds rather than expenditures.

N/A = Information not available.

NOTE: "Other" category includes other activities beyond treatment or prevention services, e.g., training, research and administration.

SOURCE: *State Alcohol and Drug Abuse Profile, FY 1989;* data are included for "only those programs which received at least some funds administered by the State Alcohol/Drug Agency during the State's Fiscal Year 1989."

Table 5. Expenditures for State Supported Alcohol and Other Drug Abuse Services by State for Fiscal Years 1985, 1986, 1987, 1988 and 1989

	Total Alcohol and Drug Abuse Service Expenditures					1985 to 1989
State	**FY 1985**	**FY 1986**	**FY 1987**	**FY 1988**	**FY 1989**	**Change**
Alabama	5,915,793	6,628,533	7,303,100	9,999,051	9,051,355	53.0%
Alaska	19,511,863	18,866,700	21,528,100	25,198,047	28,359,400	45.3%
Arizona	20,218,120	21,273,146	22,377,637	23,881,542	27,600,159	36.5%
Arkansas	5,403,542	5,770,019	6,654,927	8,029,382	8,579,188	58.8%
California	201,933,720	211,861,000	221,072,000	261,474,670	332,289,783	64.6%
Colorado	16,219,222	24,498,392	25,446,218	27,518,339	31,199,846	92.4%
Connecticut	27,087,735	36,290,844	40,466,215	57,951,823	68,008,698	151.1%
Delaware	3,756,902	3,496,879	4,006,730	4,521,439	4,715,837	25.5%
District of Col	18,897,677	23,756,425	26,579,185	30,771,287	33,667,903	78.2%
Florida	42,891,735	62,217,740	74,781,721	75,132,664	87,664,017	104.4%
Georgia	23,797,742	29,029,176	32,145,874	39,319,963	44,493,939	87.0%
Hawaii	3,673,124	4,533,022	4,349,258	5,109,783	4,968,362	35.3%

State	Total Alcohol and Drug Abuse Service Expenditures					1985 to 1989 Change
	FY 1985	FY 1986	FY 1987	FY 1988	FY 1989	
Idaho	2,822,875	2,878,325	2,405,900	3,548,345	3,594,082	27.3%
Illinois	47,356,816	61,155,276	65,509,900	68,056,000	76,732,074	62.0%
Indiana	17,683,691	21,893,125	21,310,966	22,105,345	30,744,796	73.9%
Iowa	12,281,053	14,938,060	14,637,903	17,684,279	20,054,647	63.3%
Kansas	8,402,000	9,951,855	11,868,600	14,118,882	14,802,352	76.2%
Kentucky	7,900,941	9,497,100	10,371,525	14,321,677	15,035,627	90.3%
Louisiana	12,814,939	14,840,614	11,339,400	12,233,154	11,536,103	−10.0%
Maine	8,632,814	6,398,023	7,310,944	9,317,983	10,089,023	16.9%
Maryland	28,149,997	40,803,832	42,365,613	47,539,942	57,468,100	104.1%
Massachusetts	35,934,301	34,588,516	48,910,423	50,520,000	59,606,007	65.9%
Michigan	65,545,875	77,031,584	80,857,857	81,401,541	83,864,436	27.9%
Minnesota	5,009,800	5,327,587	5,378,812	46,052,625	51,479,355	927.6%
Mississippi	6,826,300	6,094,081	5,527,359	6,433,410	8,782,962	28.7%
Missouri	11,402,338	13,389,238	16,375,024	16,947,288	20,260,163	77.7%
Montana	8,060,073	9,175,393	9,863,356	12,386,601	13,932,029	72.9%
Nebraska	6,183,667	6,836,388	7,618,509	8,656,129	9,030,040	46.0%
Nevada	6,552,090	5,548,531	5,999,831	7,594,946	8,249,255	25.9%
New Hampshire	2,335,190	2,251,114	2,406,233	3,067,060	4,433,739	89.9%
New Jersey	22,307,000	44,058,000	38,658,000	45,311,570	59,578,000	167.1%
New York	309,368,481	370,369,815	450,522,342	504,208,790	540,518,232	74.7%
North Carolina	29,179,850	28,753,576	34,850,619	40,165,453	37,554,856	28.7%
North Dakota	1,777,000	2,827,269	2,795,597	2,538,860	3,264,177	83.7%
Ohio	35,960,797	68,441,833	36,761,949	63,772,225	46,401,807	29.0%
Oklahoma	5,923,068	10,984,639	11,581,816	9,510,058	17,548,594	196.3%
Oregon	10,915,230	11,324,766	40,171,578	60,600,918	80,826,988	640.5%
Pennsylvania	65,712,000	69,570,000	74,213,581	86,250,353	89,446,528	36.1%
Puerto Rico	17,503,724	17,956,398	21,423,297	24,499,713	30,661,020	75.2%
Rhode Island	7,292,084	7,496,722	9,332,346	11,295,332	14,080,680	93.1%
South Carolina	12,512,296	20,356,999	24,075,988	29,468,452	32,114,519	156.7%
South Dakota	4,015,716	3,479,520	3,976,883	4,114,909	4,311,782	7.4%
Tennessee	10,100,800	14,194,276	19,852,378	21,044,649	26,845,347	165.8%
Texas	20,433,115	14,389,108	14,527,476	24,784,644	30,416,437	48.9%
Utah	12,929,062	15,377,966	17,117,638	16,485,593	16,058,185	24.2%
Vermont	3,778,941	4,957,943	5,441,463	4,419,773	4,720,193	24.9%
Virginia	27,027,873	29,490,704	31,539,019	36,699,439	45,552,931	68.5%
Washington	21,666,028	22,288,236	24,711,601	36,563,998	48,320,000	123.0%
West Virginia	7,447,581	6,851,015	7,800,503	8,509,016	7,637,729	2.6%
Wisconsin	52,724,554	67,863,733	65,971,112	70,765,312	82,751,497	57.0%
TOTALS	**1,361,777,135**	**1,621,853,036**	**1,792,094,306**	**2,111,903,154**	**2,398,902,779**	**76.2%**

N/A = Information not available.

NOTE: The FY 1989 totals for this table differ from Tables 3 and 4 because data in this Table are only depicted for those State and Territorial Agencies that reported all four years (ie., data for Guam, New Mexico, Virgin Islands, and Wyoming are thus not included). In addition, for a number of States the increases in expenditures shown include not only actual increases in monies, but also improved and more complete reporting of expenditure information over time.

SOURCE: *State Alcohol and Drug Abuse Profile, FY 1989*, data are included for "only those programs which received at least some funds administered by the State Alcohol/Drug Agency during the State's Fiscal Year 1989."

Table 6. Comparison of Expenditures for Alcohol and Other Drug Abuse Services by Funding Source for Fiscal Years 1985, 1986, 1987, 1988 and 1989

Funding Source	FY 1985	1985–1986 Change	FY 1986	1986–1987 Change	FY 1987	1987–1988 Change	FY 1988	1988–1989 Change	FY 1989	1985 to 1989 Change
State alcohol/ drug agency	654,430,812	12.8%	738,498,313	10.3%	814,604,015	11.7%	909,875,851	9.5%	996,659,230	52.3%
Other state agency	58,916,203	57.8%	92,950,375	11.5%	103,603,708	7.4%	111,294,111	15.6%	128,606,299	118.3%
Alcohol/drug abuse block grant	235,051,006	8.1%	254,130,628	6.3%	270,186,698	31.2%	354,597,948	33.3%	472,825,987	101.2%
Other federal government	24,313,096	80.7%	43,932,752	17.8%	51,766,318	139.2%	123,848,528	36.4%	168,880,775	594.6%
County or local agencies	100,983,237	51.1%	152,578,725	7.8%	164,547,873	15.2%	189,586,170	1.2%	191,799,581	89.9%
Other sources	288,082,781	17.9%	339,762,243	14.0%	387,385,694	9.1%	422,700,546	4.1%	440,130,907	52.8%
Grand total	1,361,777,135	19.1%	1,621,853,036	10.5%	1,792,094,306	17.8%	2,111,903,154	13.6%	2,398,902,779	76.2%

NOTE: The FY 1989 totals for these tables differ from Tables 3 and 4 because data in this table are only depicted for those State and Territorial Agencies that reported all four years (ie., data from Guam, New Mexico, Virgin Islands and Wyoming are thus not included). In addition, for a number of States the increases in expenditures shown include not only actual increases in monies, but also improved and more complete reporting of expenditure information over time.

SOURCE: *State Alcohol and Drug Abuse Profile, FY 1989;* data are included for "only those programs which received at least some funds administered by the State Alcohol/Drug Agency during the State's Fiscal Year 1989."

Table 7. Comparison of Expenditures for Alcohol and Other Drug Abuse Services by Type of Program Activity for Fiscal Years 1985, 1986, 1987, 1988 and 1989

Type of Activity	FY 1985	1985–1986 Change	FY 1986	1986–1987 Change	FY 1987	1987–1988 Change	FY 1988	1988–1989 Change	FY 1989	1985 to 1989 Change
Treatment	1,017,605,931	16.6%	1,186,940,131	13.2%	1,344,060,626	21.6%	1,634,935,457	12.7%	1,841,798,803	81.0%
Prevention	154,254,660	20.6%	186,016,989	19.6%	222,471,046	39.3%	309,859,328	13.0%	350,149,690	127.0%
Other**	189,916,544	31.1%	248,895,916	−9.4%	225,562,634	−25.9%	167,108,369	23.8%	206,954,286	9.0%
Grand total	1,361,777,135	19.1%	1,621,853,036	10.5%	1,792,094,306	17.8%	2,111,903,154	13.6%	2,398,902,779	76.2%

** "Other" Type of Activity category includes activities beyond treatment or prevention services, e.g., training, research and administration.

NOTE: The FY 1989 totals for these tables differ from Tables 3 and 4 because data in this table are only depicted for those State and Territorial Agencies that reported all four years (ie., data from Guam, New Mexico, Virgin Islands, and Wyoming are thus not included). In addition, for a number of States the increases in expenditures shown include not only actual increases in monies, but also improved and more complete reporting of expenditure information over time.

SOURCE: *State Alcohol and Drug Abuse Profile, FY 1989;* data are included for "only those programs which received at least some funds administered by the State Alcohol/Drug Agency during the State's Fiscal Year 1989."

Table 8. Number of Alcohol and/or Drug Treatment Units Which Received Funds Administered by the State Alcohol/Drug Agency for Fiscal Year 1989

State	Alcohol Treatment Units	Drug Treatment Units	Combined Alcohol/Drug Treatment Units	Total Alcohol/Drug Treatment Units
Alabama	0	0	47	47
Alaska	0	2	39	41
Arizona	17	12	115	144
Arkansas	2	5	40	47
California	635	322	N/A	957
Colorado	51	4	44	99
Connecticut	26	63	37	126
Delaware	4	2	10	16
District of Col	4	7	15	26
Florida	N/A	N/A	90	90
Georgia	0	0	41	41
Guam	0	0	1	1
Hawaii	0	1	19	20
Idaho	0	0	45	45
Illinois	0	0	295	295 A
Indiana	0	0	65	65
Iowa	0	0	31	31
Kansas	2	1	48	51
Kentucky	0	1	132	133
Louisiana	0	0	54	54
Maine	0	0	39	39
Maryland	0	14	125	139
Massachusetts	0	0	248	248
Michigan	1	0	259	260
Minnesota	0	10	233	243
Mississippi	7	1	53	61
Missouri	5	4	66	75
Montana	1	3	26	30
Nebraska	0	0	121	121
Nevada	9	1	19	29
New Hampshire	0	0	34	34
New Jersey	140	70	20	230
New Mexico	21	8	18	47
New York (A)	362	0	8	370 B
New York (D)	0	477	N/A	477
North Carolina	0	0	154	154
North Dakota	0	0	8	8
Ohio	63	111	84	258
Oklahoma	0	1	60	61
Oregon	32	4	90	126
Pennsylvania	14	11	298	323
Puerto Rico	12	65	77	154
Rhode Island	8	4	28	40
South Carolina	2	0	38	40
South Dakota	0	0	28	28
Tennessee	0	0	55	55
Texas	0	0	74	74
Utah	11	0	54	65
Vermont	0	0	26	26
Virginia	10	17	212	239 C

State	Alcohol Treatment Units	Drug Treatment Units	Combined Alcohol/Drug Treatment Units	Total Alcohol/Drug Treatment Units
Washington	10	17	97	124
West Virginia	0	0	60	60
Wisconsin	0	2	581	583
Wyoming	N/A	N/A	N/A	N/A
TOTALS	**1,449**	**1,240**	**4,461**	**7,150**
PERCENT OF TOTAL	**20.3%**	**17.3%**	**62.4%**	**100.0%**

A = Combined alcohol/drug treatment units represent non-hospital sites.
B = Combined alcohol/drug treatment units represent residential facilities for chemically dependent youths.
C = Source of information: FY 1989 CSB Data Survey Report 1989.
N/A = Information not available.

SOURCE: *State Alcohol and Drug Abuse Profile, FY 1989;* data are included for "only those programs which received at least some funds administered by the State Alcohol/Drug Agency during the State's Fiscal Year 1989."

Table 9. Estimate of Percent of Total Alcohol and/or Drug Treatment Units in Each State That Received Any Funds Administered by the State Alcohol/Drug Agency for Fiscal Year 1989

State	Estimate of Percent of Total Treatment Units Funded by State Agency	State	Estimate of Percent of Total Treatment Units Funded by State Agency
Alabama	65	Montana	75
Alaska	68	Nebraska	83
Arizona	70	Nevada	33
Arkansas	77	New Hampshire	31
California	60	New Jersey	50
Colorado	32	New Mexico	85
Connecticut	53	New York (A)	66
Delaware	50	New York (D)	77
District of Col	33	North Carolina	70
Florida	49	North Dakota	30
Georgia	N/A	Ohio	70
Guam	100	Oklahoma	58
Hawaii	75	Oregon	85
Idaho	65	Pennsylvania	53
Illinois	77	Puerto Rico	50
Indiana	23	Rhode Island	96
Iowa	54	South Carolina	60
Kansas	29	South Dakota	90
Kentucky	52	Tennessee	60
Louisiana	33	Texas	26
Maine	58	Utah	58
Maryland	53	Vermont	98
Massachusetts	85	Virginia	90
Michigan	38	Washington	34
Minnesota	95	West Virginia	93
Mississippi	75	Wisconsin	95
Missouri	46	Wyoming	N/A

A = Alcohol Agency in New York State.
D = Drug Agency in New York State.
N/A = Information not available.

SOURCE: *State Alcohol and Drug Abuse Profile, FY 1989.*

Table 10. Number of Alcohol and Other Drug Client Treatment Admissions by Type of Environment, Type of Care, and State for Fiscal Year 1989

	Detoxification, 24 Hour/Day Care						Rehabilitation/Residential									
	Hospital Inpatient			Free-Standing Residential			Hospital (Other than Detox)			Short-Term (30 Days or Less)			Long-Term (Over 30 Days)			
State	Alcohol	Other Drug	Total	Alcohol	Other Drug	Total	Alcohol	Other Drug	Total	Alcohol	Other Drug	Total	Alcohol	Other Drug	Total	
Alabama	N/A	N/A	N/A	305	436	741	N/A	N/A	N/A	964	946	1,910	712	410	1,122	
Alaska	140	29	169	1,471	319	1,790	0	0	0	1,477	320	1,797	316	69	385	
Arizona	9	11	20	2,600	280	2,880	0	0	0	1,440	259	1,699	1,313	803	2,116	
Arkansas	0	0	0	1,130	346	1,476	0	0	0	0	0	0	3,332	1,486	4,818	
California	0	0	0	46,830	1,545	48,375	0	0	0	23,294	7,642	30,936	0	0	0	A
Colorado	0	0	0	37,923	0	37,923	0	0	0	1,739	79	1,815	1,413	311	1,724	
Connecticut	3,977	1,303	5,280	5,283	144	5,427	790	0	790	1,501	141	1,642	1,218	772	1,990	
Delaware	0	0	0	2,262	1,135	3,397	0	0	0	436	0	436	12	68	80	
District of Col	0	390	390	2,949	586	3,535	0	0	0	566	0	566	253	563	816	
Florida	N/A	4,482	4,482	17,234	464	17,698	N/A	0	0	N/A	0	0	20,106	7,598	27,704	BC
Georgia	6,466	1,866	8,332	7,154	5,396	12,550	0	0	0	0	0	0	1,256	1,894	3,150	
Guam	4	0	4	N/A	N/A	N/A	N/A	N/A	N/A	N/A	N/A	N/A	N/A	N/A	N/A	
Hawaii	0	0	0	798	114	912	0	0	0	63	43	106	289	339	628	
Idaho	5	1	6	851	274	1,125	0	0	0	486	222	708	0	0	0	D
Illinois	N/A	N/A	N/A	19,316	12,408	31,724	N/A	N/A	N/A	4,113	3,106	7,219	1,425	1,955	3,380	
Indiana	0	0	0	3,737	1,917	5,654	0	0	0	1,399	1,144	2,543	1,301	1,065	2,366	
Iowa	0	0	0	160	76	236	0	0	0	780	527	1,307	248	165	413	
Kansas	0	0	0	2,087	1,167	3,254	65	23	88	992	685	1,677	435	294	729	
Kentucky	N/A	N/A	N/A	N/A	N/A	3,689	N/A	N/A	N/A	N/A	N/A	3,080	N/A	N/A	240	
Louisiana	0	0	0	743	1,266	2,009	0	0	0	785	948	1,733	303	280	583	
Maine	0	0	0	1,124	848	1,972	0	0	0	617	195	812	1,957	618	2,575	
Maryland	0	0	0	1,894	0	1,894	0	0	0	3,107	273	3,380	1,078	884	1,962	
Massachusetts	0	0	0	23,439	8,549	31,988			0	4,207	819	5,026	6,619	5,462	12,081	E
Michigan	0	0	0	3,326	2,954	6,280	0	0	0	2,629	2,039	4,668	2,397	3,732	6,129	
Minnesota	0	0	0	41,489	0	41,489	3,480	3,737	7,217	927	1,076	2,003	1,260	2,423	3,683	
Mississippi	0	0	0	0	0	0	91	662	753	3,313	734	4,047	930	156	1,086	
Missouri	0	0	0	12,489	1,439	13,928	0	0	0	5,315	3,208	8,523	0	0	0	
Montana	1,731	143	1,874	72	6	78	1,852	341	2,193	624	349	973	146	34	180	
Nebraska	6	1	7	11,896	236	12,132	28	52	80	563	193	756	848	430	1,278	
Nevada	0	0	0	6,859	238	7,097	0	0	0	562	274	836	233	938	1,171	

New Hampshire	85	10	95	2,008	223	2,231	0	0	0	315	117	432	146	77	223	
New Jersey	7,074	216	7,290	5,834	0	5,834	612	0	612	4,598	0	4,598	462	1,737	2,199	
New Mexico			0	2,930	84	3,014			0	2,829	N/A	2,829	380	16	396	F
New York	38,574	471	39,045	26,747	202	26,949	0	0	0	18,383	0	18,383	2,282	9,019	11,301	GH
North Carolina	0	0	0	9,066	262	9,328	0	0	0	2,256	0	2,256	327	380	707	
North Dakota	0	0	0	0	0	0	0	0	0	0	0	0	0	0	0	
Ohio	0	0	0	4,262	0	4,262	0	0	0	1,454	1,829	3,283	1,274	0	1,274	
Oklahoma	0	0	0	907	454	1,361	0	0	0	1,986	390	2,376	29	0	29	I
Oregon	0	0	0	4,860	1,199	6,059	0	0	0	1,157	443	1,600	1,352	541	1,893	
Pennsylvania	4,201	6,753	10,954	4,300	3,769	8,069	354	1,242	1,596	5,270	5,646	10,916	N/A	N/A	N/A	A
Puerto Rico	713	0	713	0	4,012	4,012	167	0	167	0	1,501	1,501	135	558	693	
Rhode Island	2,914	523	3,437	1,893	114	2,007	0	0	0	2,659	1,195	3,854	583	165	748	
South Carolina	0	0	0	3,543	1,949	5,492	0	0	0	2,418	738	3,156	279	143	422	
South Dakota	0	0	0	654	542	1,196	0	0	0	845	726	1,571	213	201	414	
Tennessee	60	32	92	1,542	1,585	3,127	204	145	349	668	728	1,396	667	712	1,379	
Texas	941	510	1,451	3,257	2,715	5,972	5,827	9	5,836			0	2,127	4,484	6,611	
Utah	30	0	30	5,497	260	5,757	0	0	0	N/A	N/A	N/A	2,363	678	3,041	
Vermont	0	0	0	196	234	430	0	0	0	393	433	826	N/A	N/A	N/A	
Virginia			0	4,854	2,614	7,468	106	57	163			0	2,514	1,354	3,868	JKL
Washington	N/A	N/A	N/A	N/A	N/A	N/A	N/A	N/A	N/A	N/A	N/A	N/A	N/A	N/A	N/A	
West Virginia	5	12	17	730	95	825	92	93	185	1,639	274	1,913	265	42	307	
Wisconsin	3,894	1,196	5,090	0	0	0	0	0	0	13,495	4,146	17,641	5,401	1,659	7,060	
Wyoming	N/A	N/A	N/A	N/A	N/A	N/A	N/A	N/A	N/A	N/A	N/A	N/A	N/A	N/A	N/A	
TOTALS	**70,829**	**17,949**	**88,778**	**338,501**	**62,456**	**404,646**	**13,668**	**6,361**	**20,029**	**122,264**	**43,388**	**168,732**	**70,199**	**54,515**	**124,954**	

A = Rehabilitation/Residential Short-term includes short and long term residential clients.
B = Detoxification Freestanding Residential alcohol includes hospital inpatient.
C = Rehabilitation/Residential Long-term alcohol includes short term and hospital (other than detoxification).
D = Total represents duplicate counts; a certain percentage of admissions enter more than one treatment modality.
E = Total does not include 2,850 collateral admissions.
F = The 757 clients listed in New Mexico's Not Reported category represent those clients admitted to more than one service category.
G = Alcohol client information based on actual calendar year 1988 data.
H = Ambulatory Methadone does not include 2,751 admissions to non-funded methadone programs.
I = Total Not Reported includes 67 Short-Term Rehabilitation/Residential clients and 710 Ambulatory/Outpatient clients. 1,093 clients were treated in "other service categories." These clients cannot be identified by alcohol or other drugs.
J = Detoxification Free-Standing Residential Alcohol & Other Drug includes Hospital Inpatient.
K = Rehabilitation/Residential Long Term includes Short Term admissions.
L = Ambulatory Outpatient includes Methadone and Detoxification (Non-Methadone)

N/A = Information not available.

SOURCE: *State Alcohol and Drug Abuse Profile, FY 1989;* data are included for "only those programs which received at least some funds administered by the State Alcohol/Drug Agency during the State's Fiscal Year (FY) 1989."

Table 10. (*continued*) Number of Alcohol and Other Drug Client Treatment Admissions by Type of Environment, Type of Care, and State for Fiscal Year 1989

	Outpatient			Ambulatory Methadone			Detoxification (non-methadone)			Not Reported by Treatment Modality			Total				
State	Alcohol	Other Drug	Total	Alcohol	Other Drug	Total	Alcohol	Other Drug	Total	Alcohol	Other Drug	Total	Alcohol	Other Drug	Not Reported	Total	
Alabama	5,318	3,113	8,431	0	474	474	9	2	11	0	0	0	7,308	5,381	0	12,689	
Alaska	5,556	978	6,534	0	148	148	0	0	0	0	0	0	8,960	1,863	0	10,823	
Arizona	13,096	4,000	17,096	0	1,811	1,811	0	361	361	0	0	0	18,458	7,525	0	25,983	
Arkansas	3,050	1,768	4,818	0	0	0	0	0	0	0	0	0	7,512	3,600	0	11,112	
California	39,438	26,552	65,990	0	27,577	27,577	0	662	662	0	0	0	109,562	63,978	0	173,540	A
Colorado	13,371	3,476	16,847	N/A	736	736	N/A	N/A	0	0	0	0	54,446	4,602	0	59,048	
Connecticut	4,540	4,186	8,726	2	1,903	1,905	0	0	0	0	0	0	17,311	8,449	0	25,760	
Delaware	676	562	1,238	0	112	112	0	0	0	0	0	0	3,386	1,877	0	5,263	
District of Col	1,859	1,894	3,753	0	2,804	2,804	0	0	0	0	0	0	5,627	6,237	0	11,864	
Florida	9,766	11,830	21,596	0	906	906	10,340	113	10,453	0	0	0	57,446	25,393	0	82,839	BC
Georgia	16,430	14,499	30,929	0	388	388	0	0	0	0	0	0	31,306	24,043	0	55,349	
Guam	67	7	74	N/A	N/A	0	0	0	0	0	0	0	71	7	0	78	
Hawaii	1,132	1,161	2,293	0	369	369	0	0	0	0	0	0	2,282	2,026	0	4,308	
Idaho	3,380	1,728	5,108	0	0	0	0	0	0	0	0	0	4,722	2,225	0	6,947	D
Illinois	23,592	12,418	36,010	62	2,284	2,346	N/A	N/A	0	0	0	0	48,508	32,171	0	80,679	
Indiana	5,499	2,522	8,021	0	200	200	0	0	0	0	0	0	11,936	6,848	0	18,784	
Iowa	17,308	3,766	21,074	3	96	99	12	6	18	0	0	0	18,511	4,636	0	23,147	
Kansas	6,715	1,813	8,528	N/A	N/A	0	0	0	0	0	0	0	10,294	3,982	0	14,276	
Kentucky	N/A	N/A	0	N/A	N/A	0	N/A	N/A	0	0	0	0	N/A	N/A	22,355	22,355	
Louisiana	4,078	4,915	8,893	0	0	0	0	0	0	0	0	0	5,909	7,309	0	13,218	
Maine	10,264	3,334	13,598	0	0	0	0	0	0	0	0	0	13,962	4,995	0	18,957	
Maryland	12,093	12,426	24,519	0	4,251	4,251	0	0	0	0	0	0	18,172	17,834	0	36,006	
Massachusetts	27,374	16,627	44,001	36	3,332	3,368	0	0	0	0	0	0	61,675	34,789	0	96,464	E
Michigan	27,048	14,615	41,663	0	1,264	1,264	9	40	49	0	0	0	35,409	24,644	0	60,053	
Minnesota	5,909	3,291	9,200	0	273	273	0	0	0	0	0	0	53,065	10,800	0	63,865	

Mississippi	3,280	2,228	5,508	0	0	0	0	0	0	0	0	0	7,614	3,780	0	11,394	
Missouri	7,774	4,341	12,115	0	391	391	0	0	0	0	0	0	25,578	9,379	0	34,957	
Montana	3,805	1,276	5,081	0	0	0	0	0	0	0	0	0	8,230	2,149	0	10,379	
Nebraska	9,601	1,568	11,169	0	81	81	0	0	0	0	0	0	22,942	2,561	0	25,503	
Nevada	797	498	1,295	0	200	200	0	0	0	0	0	0	8,451	2,149	0	10,599	
New Hampshire	2,503	704	3,207	0	0	0	0	0	0	0	0	0	5,057	1,131	0	6,188	
New Jersey	11,078	5,385	16,463	0	6,318	6,318	0	0	0	0	0	0	29,658	13,656	0	43,314	
New Mexico	7,132	2,930	10,062	0	462	462	40	34	74	0	0	0	13,311	3,526	(757)	16,080	F
New York	75,320	62,196	137,516	0	14,016	14,016	0	0	0	0	0	0	161,306	85,904	0	247,210	GH
North Carolina	14,053	3,630	17,683	0	734	734	74	13	87	0	0	0	25,776	5,019	0	30,795	
North Dakota	1,975	650	2,625	0	0	0	0	0	0	0	0	0	1,975	650	0	2,625	
Ohio	10,012	19,456	29,468	0	N/A	0	0	N/A	0	0	0	0	17,002	21,285	0	38,287	
Oklahoma	5,825	3,325	9,150	155	104	259	0	0	0	0	0	0	8,902	4,273	1,870	15,045	I
Oregon	23,505	6,205	29,170	0	667	667	0	0	0	0	0	0	30,874	9,055	0	39,929	
Pennsylvania	19,074	13,356	32,430	0	1,725	1,725	0	15	15	3	2	5	33,202	32,508	0	65,710	A
Puerto Rico	5,649	2,590	8,239	0	318	318	0	205	205	0	0	0	6,664	9,184	0	15,848	
Rhode Island	2,025	2,052	4,077	0	548	548	0	0	0	0	0	0	10,074	4,597	0	14,671	
South Carolina	20,786	5,036	25,822	0	116	116	0	0	0	0	0	0	27,026	7,982	0	35,008	
South Dakota	2,510	2,281	4,791	0	0	0	0	0	0	0	0	0	4,222	3,750	0	7,972	
Tennessee	3,933	2,968	6,901	0	49	49	0	0	0	1,229	1,303	2,532	8,303	7,522	0	15,825	
Texas	3,768	7,100	10,868			0	5	275	280	0	0	0	15,925	15,093	0	31,018	
Utah	4,606	1,830	6,436	N/A	309	309	116	7	123	0	0	0	12,612	3,084	0	15,696	
Vermont	2,643	1,623	4,266	0	0	0	0	0	0	0	0	0	3,232	2,290	0	5,522	
Virginia	28,540	15,370	43,910			0			0	0	0	0	36,014	19,395	0	55,409	JKL
Washington	N/A	N/A	N/A	N/A	N/A	N/A	N/A	N/A	N/A	N/A	N/A	N/A	N/A	N/A	N/A	N/A	
West Virginia	9,058	1,203	10,261	0	0	0	0	0	0	0	0	0	11,789	1,719	0	13,508	
Wisconsin	51,355	15,497	66,852	0	278	278	8	3	11	0	0	0	74,154	22,780	0	96,934	
Wyoming	N/A	N/A	N/A	N/A	N/A	N/A	N/A	N/A	N/A	N/A	N/A	N/A	N/A	N/A	N/A	N/A	
TOTALS	**588,166**	**336,679**	**924,845**	**258**	**75,244**	**75,502**	**10,613**	**1,736**	**12,349**	**1,232**	**1,305**	**2,537**	**1,215,731**	**599,634**	**23,468**	**1,838,833**	

Table 11. Number of Alcohol Client Treatment Admissions by Sex and State for Fiscal Year 1989

	Sex			
State	Male	Female	Not Reported	Total
Alabama	5,463	1,845	0	7,308
Alaska	6,577	2,383	0	8,960
Arizona	13,646	4,812	0	18,458
Arkansas	6,334	1,178	0	7,512
California	84,910	24,652	0	109,562
Colorado	44,876	9,570	0	54,446
Connecticut	10,488	2,007	4,816	17,311
Delaware	2,817	569	0	3,386
District of Col	4,898	729	0	5,627
Florida	44,670	12,776	0	57,446
Georgia	25,433	5,873	0	31,306
Guam	56	15	0	71
Hawaii	1,691	591	0	2,282
Idaho	3,657	1,065	0	4,722
Illinois	36,864	10,853	791	48,508
Indiana	9,071	2,865	0	11,936
Iowa	14,284	4,227	0	18,511
Kansas	8,466	1,828	0	10,294
Kentucky	10,587	2,680	2,977	16,244
Louisiana	4,540	1,369	0	5,909
Maine	10,445	3,517	0	13,962
Maryland	14,469	3,703	0	18,172
Massachusetts	51,685	9,990	0	61,675
Michigan	27,291	8,118	0	35,409
Minnesota	43,730	8,921	414	53,065
Mississippi	6,407	1,207	0	7,614
Missouri	20,657	4,921	0	25,578
Montana	4,763	3,467	0	8,230
Nebraska	18,705	4,237	0	22,942
Nevada	7,012	1,439	0	8,451
New Hampshire	3,783	1,274	0	5,057
New Jersey	22,469	7,189	0	29,658
New Mexico	10,159	2,832	3	12,994
New York	117,688	43,618	0	161,306 A
North Carolina	20,892	4,875	9	25,776
North Dakota	1,412	563	0	1,975
Ohio	12,938	4,064	0	17,002
Oklahoma	7,963	2,200	0	10,163
Oregon	23,896	6,978	0	30,874
Pennsylvania	26,535	6,667	0	33,202

State	Sex			Total
	Male	Female	Not Reported	
Puerto Rico	6,331	333	0	6,664
Rhode Island	6,836	3,238	0	10,074
South Carolina	21,892	4,258	876	27,026
South Dakota	2,956	1,266	0	4,222
Tennessee	6,516	1,787	0	8,303
Texas	11,839	4,086	0	15,925
Utah	10,842	1,770	0	12,612
Vermont	2,469	763	0	3,232
Virginia	28,091	7,923	0	36,014
Washington	N/A	N/A	0	N/A
West Virginia	10,019	1,770	0	11,789
Wisconsin	55,789	18,365	0	74,154
Wyoming	N/A	N/A	0	N/A
TOTALS	**955,807**	**267,226**	**9,886**	**1,232,919**
PERCENT OF TOTAL	**77.5%**	**21.7%**	**.8%**	**100.0%**

A = All client admissions data are estimated.
N/A = Information not available.

SOURCE: *State Alcohol and Drug Abuse Profile, FY 1989;* data are included for "only those programs which received some funds administered by the State Alcohol Agency during Fiscal Year 1989."

Table 12. Number of Alcohol Client Treatment Admissions by Age and State for Fiscal Year 1989

State	Under Age 18	18 to 20	21 to 24	25 to 34	35 to 44	45 to 54	55 to 64	Age 65 and Over	Not Reported	Total	
Alabama	139	374	640	2,707	1,896	828	370	119	235	7,308	
Alaska	581	564	1,006	3,182	2,162	870	484	111	0	8,960	
Arizona	942	849	1,705	6,527	4,878	2,258	921	378	0	18,458	
Arkansas	N/A	N/A	N/A	N/A	N/A	N/A	N/A	N/A	7,512	7,512	
California	2,519	3,506	9,532	40,429	33,307	13,257	5,478	1,534	0	109,562	
Colorado	1,325	2,690	5,079	19,636	14,574	6,759	3,281	1,102	0	54,446	
Connecticut	192	544	1,896	4,523	3,007	1,696	637	0	4,816	17,311	A
Delaware	9	113	261	1,347	909	424	190	133	0	3,386	
District of Col	22	225	506	2,173	1,463	844	338	56	0	5,627	
Florida	2,223	3,567	4,757	18,611	16,583	7,499	3,246	960	0	57,446	
Georgia	372	906	2,303	10,282	8,734	5,401	2,590	718	0	31,306	
Guam	5	2	10	24	26	2	2	0	0	71	
Hawaii	481	46	215	616	474	305	97	17	31	2,282	
Idaho	862	240	579	1,514	933	391	159	44	0	4,722	
Illinois	N/A	N/A	N/A	N/A	N/A	N/A	N/A	N/A	48,508	48,508	
Indiana	562	957	1,754	4,470	2,645	1,022	395	131	0	11,936	
Iowa	1,329	2,170	2,837	6,608	3,271	1,244	567	211	274	18,511	
Kansas	455	835	1,513	4,138	2,061	765	359	163	5	10,294	
Kentucky	706	863	1,439	4,552	2,698	1,344	601	166	3,875	16,244	
Louisiana	185	314	609	2,396	1,522	625	204	54	0	5,909	
Maine	438	243	2,156	5,512	1,770	1,309	353	177	2,004	13,962	
Maryland	1,467	1,149	2,398	7,216	3,705	1,392	639	202	4	18,172	
Massachusetts	1,451	3,126	7,466	22,679	15,010	7,208	3,457	1,278	0	61,675	
Michigan	2,705	2,306	4,433	13,924	7,363	2,936	1,109	345	288	35,409	
Minnesota	1,872	2,601	4,121	16,615	14,198	7,440	3,933	1,871	414	53,065	
Mississippi	168	492	1,055	3,228	1,640	683	268	80	0	7,614	
Missouri	955	1,192	2,668	9,561	6,054	3,137	1,690	317	4	25,578	
Montana	753	608	893	1,167	3,061	982	529	237	0	8,230	
Nebraska	1,389	1,747	2,402	7,030	5,352	2,847	1,685	490	0	22,942	
Nevada	N/A	N/A	N/A	N/A	N/A	N/A	N/A	N/A	8,451	8,451	

New Hampshire	128	366	622	2,140	1,107	415	164	58	57	5,057	
New Jersey	2,214	1,852	3,720	11,946	6,330	2,268	944	342	42	29,658	
New Mexico	1,203	912	1,656	4,469	2,758	1,258	507	228	3	12,994	
New York	8,065	4,838	17,744	43,553	41,940	22,583	19,357	3,226	0	161,306	B
North Carolina	600	1,186	2,686	9,902	6,168	3,227	1,475	523	9	25,776	
North Dakota	58	141	240	793	412	184	109	37	1	1,975	
Ohio	961	1,079	1,878	7,382	3,690	1,362	478	172	0	17,002	
Oklahoma	516	674	1,100	3,681	2,367	1,196	492	137	0	10,163	
Oregon	2,110	2,052	3,560	10,806	6,766	2,791	2,338	451	0	30,874	
Pennsylvania	1,921	1,984	3,743	12,651	7,470	3,441	1,547	445	0	33,202	
Puerto Rico	N/A	N/A	N/A	N/A	N/A	N/A	N/A	N/A	6,664	6,664	
Rhode Island	158	171	408	1,026	690	118	27	10	7,466	10,074	
South Carolina	1,236	1,363	2,611	9,317	6,805	3,528	1,534	632	0	27,026	
South Dakota	588	460	502	1,324	782	334	154	78	0	4,222	
Tennessee	611	558	967	3,426	1,769	685	230	57	0	8,303	
Texas	508	486	995	3,766	2,448	1,209	558	125	5,830	15,925	
Utah	703	722	1,241	4,028	3,342	1,560	824	180	12	12,612	
Vermont	208	236	371	1,146	725	388	122	36	0	3,232	
Virginia	2,161	1,802	3,638	12,641	6,735	4,646	2,486	540	1,365	36,014	
Washington	N/A	N/A	N/A	N/A	N/A	N/A	N/A	N/A	N/A	N/A	
West Virginia	768	858	1,795	3,795	2,497	1,394	510	172	0	11,789	
Wisconsin	2,661	5,161	10,231	26,442	16,167	7,636	3,967	1,889	0	74,154	
Wyoming	N/A	N/A	N/A	N/A	N/A	N/A	N/A	N/A	N/A	N/A	
TOTALS	**51,485**	**59,130**	**123,941**	**394,901**	**280,264**	**133,691**	**71,405**	**20,232**	**97,870**	**1,232,919**	
PERCENT OF TOTAL	**4.2%**	**4.8%**	**10.1%**	**32.0%**	**22.7%**	**10.8%**	**5.8%**	**1.6%**	**7.9%**	**100.0%**	

A number of the States that have the N/A designation collect age related information but not according to the specific age categories shown above.

A = Age 21 to 24 category includes Age 21 to 25, Age 25 to 34 category includes Age 26 to 35, Age 35 to 44 category includes Age 36 to 45, Age 45 to 54 category includes Age 46 to 59, Age 55 to 64 category is eliminated, and Age 65 and Over category includes Age 60 and Over.

B = All client admissions data are estimated.

N/A = Information not available.

SOURCE: *State Alcohol and Drug Abuse Profile, FY 1989;* data are included for "only those programs which received some funds administered by the State Alcohol Agency during Fiscal Year 1989."

Table 13. Number of Alcohol Client Treatment Admissions by Age, by Sex, and by State for Fiscal Year 1989

	Under Age 18				18 to 20				21 to 24				25 to 34				35 to 44			
State	Male	Female	NR	Total	Male	Female	NR	Total	Male	Female	NR	Total	Male	Female	NR	Total	Male	Female	NR	Total
Alabama	90	49		139	302	72		374	488	152		640	2,034	673		2,707	1,385	511		1,896
Alaska	424	157		581	412	152		564	738	268		1,006	2,336	846		3,182	1,587	575		2,162
Arizona	492	450		942	630	219		849	1,303	402		1,705	4,810	1,717		6,527	3,666	1,212		4,878
Arkansas	N/A	N/A		N/A	N/A	N/A		N/A	N/A	N/A		N/A	N/A	N/A		N/A	N/A	N/A		N/A
California	1,423	1,096		2,519	2,520	986		3,506	7,122	2,410		9,532	30,349	10,080		40,429	26,514	6,793		33,307
Colorado	942	383		1,325	2,154	536		2,690	4,084	995		5,079	15,617	4,019		19,636	12,296	2,278		14,574
Connecticut	125	67		192	447	97		544	1,537	359		1,896	3,763	760		4,523	2,597	410		3,007
Delaware	9	0		9	87	26		113	207	54		261	1,104	243		1,347	766	143		909
District of Col	19	3		22	196	29		225	441	65		506	1,891	282		1,273	1,273	190		1,463
Florida	N/A	N/A	2,223	2,223	N/A	N/A	3,567	3,567	N/A	N/A	4,757	4,757	N/A	N/A	18,611	18,611	N/A	N/A	16,583	16,583
Georgia	282	90		372	750	156		906	1,890	413		2,303	7,991	2,291		10,282	7,203	1,531		8,734
Guam	4	1		5	1	1		2	8	2		10	19	5		24	21	5		26
Hawaii	263	218		481	20	26		46	158	57		215	490	126		616	387	87		474
Idaho	N/A	N/A	862	862	N/A	N/A	240	240	N/A	N/A	579	579	N/A	N/A	1,514	1,514	N/A	N/A	933	933
Illinois	N/A	N/A		N/A	N/A	N/A		N/A	N/A	N/A		N/A	N/A	N/A		N/A	N/A	N/A		N/A A
Indiana	N/A	N/A	562	562	N/A	N/A	957	957	N/A	N/A	1,754	1,754	N/A	N/A	4,470	4,470	N/A	N/A	2,645	2,645
Iowa	744	585		1,329	1,629	541		2,170	2,344	493		2,837	5,282	1,326		6,608	2,498	773		3,271
Kansas	307	148		455	709	126		835	1,254	259		1,513	3,368	770		4,138	1,716	345		2,061
Kentucky	484	222		706	713	150		863	1,187	252		1,439	3,649	903		4,552	2,179	519		2,698
Louisiana	105	80		185	214	100		314	490	119		609	1,855	541		2,396	1,192	330		1,522
Maine	314	124		438	195	48		243	1,473	683		2,156	4,352	1,160		5,512	1,367	403		1,770
Maryland	1,107	360		1,467	930	219		1,149	1,877	521		2,398	5,642	1,574		7,216	2,999	706		3,705
Massachusetts	949	502		1,451	2,573	553		3,126	6,174	1,292		7,466	18,752	3,927		22,679	12,838	2,172		15,010
Michigan	1,707	998		2,705	1,848	458		2,306	3,529	904		4,433	10,752	3,172		13,924	5,735	1,628		7,363
Minnesota	1,271	601		1,872	2,047	554		2,601	3,271	850		4,121	13,486	3,129		16,615	12,080	2,118		14,198

Mississippi	126	42		168	413	79		492	940	115		1,055	2,710	518		3,228	1,360	280		1,640	
Missouri	534	421		955	924	268		1,192	2,107	561		2,668	7,519	2,042		9,561	5,040	1,014		6,054	
Montana	374	379		753	393	215		608	556	337		893	680	487		1,167	1,725	1,336		3,061	
Nebraska	855	534		1,389	1,308	439		1,747	1,847	555		2,402	5,647	1,383		7,030	4,588	764		5,352	
Nevada	N/A	N/A		N/A	N/A	N/A		N/A	N/A	N/A		N/A	N/A	N/A		N/A	N/A	N/A		N/A	
New Hampshire	78	50		128	256	110		366	445	177		622	1,628	512		2,140	839	268		1,107	
New Jersey	1,524	690		2,214	1,464	388		1,852	2,648	1,072		3,720	8,900	3,046		11,946	5,048	1,282		6,330	
New Mexico	833	370		1,203	726	186		912	1,343	313		1,656	3,502	967		4,469	2,160	598		2,758	
New York	4,920	3,145		8,065	3,532	1,306		4,838	12,953	4,791		17,744	32,665	10,888		43,553	30,291	11,649		41,940	B
North Carolina	438	162		600	939	247		1,186	2,055	631		2,686	7,790	2,112		9,902	5,189	979		6,168	
North Dakota	30	28		58	81	60		141	177	63		240	563	230		793	300	112		412	
Ohio	731	230		961	821	258		1,079	1,429	449		1,878	5,618	1,764		7,382	2,808	882		3,690	
Oklahoma	351	165		516	520	154		674	893	207		1,100	2,822	859		3,681	1,863	504		2,367	
Oregon	N/A	N/A	2,110	2,110	N/A	N/A	2,052	2,052	N/A	N/A	3,560	3,560	N/A	N/A	10,806	10,806	N/A	N/A	6,766	6,766	
Pennsylvania	1,292	629		1,921	1,594	390		1,984	3,009	734		3,743	10,008	2,643		12,651	6,120	1,350		7,470	
Puerto Rico	N/A	N/A		N/A	N/A	N/A		N/A	N/A	N/A		N/A	N/A	N/A		N/A	N/A	N/A		N/A	
Rhode Island	91	67		158	130	41		171	288	120		408	720	306		1,026	496	194		690	
South Carolina	916	310	10	1,236	1,145	166	52	1,363	2,155	383	73	2,611	7,453	1,534	330	9,317	5,452	1,026	327	6,805	
South Dakota	412	176		588	322	138		460	351	151		502	927	397		1,324	547	235		782	
Tennessee	450	161		611	446	112		558	759	208		967	2,679	747		3,426	1,388	381		1,769	
Texas	378	130		508	385	101		486	807	188		995	3,095	671		3,766	2,050	398		2,448	
Utah	452	251		703	607	115		722	1,053	188		1,241	3,422	606		4,028	2,970	372		3,342	
Vermont	144	64		208	191	45		236	291	80		371	898	248		1,146	552	173		725	
Virginia	1,405	756		2,161	1,369	433		1,802	2,809	829		3,638	9,868	2,773		12,641	5,438	1,297		6,735	
Washington	N/A	N/A		N/A	N/A	N/A		N/A	N/A	N/A		N/A	N/A	N/A		N/A	N/A	N/A		N/A	
West Virginia	525	243		768	676	182		858	1,482	313		1,795	3,278	517		3,795	2,192	305		2,497	
Wisconsin	1,509	1,152		2,661	3,758	1,403		5,161	7,942	2,289		10,231	20,031	6,411		26,442	12,149	4,018		16,167	
Wyoming	N/A	N/A		N/A	N/A	N/A		N/A	N/A	N/A		N/A	N/A	N/A		N/A	N/A	N/A		N/A	
TOTALS	**29,429**	**16,289**	**5,767**	**51,485**	**40,377**	**11,885**	**6,868**	**59,130**	**87,914**	**25,304**	**10,723**	**123,941**	**279,965**	**79,205**	**35,731**	**394,901**	**200,864**	**52,146**	**27,254**	**280,264**	

See footnotes at the bottom of next page.

SOURCE: *State Alcohol and Drug Abuse Profile, FY 1989;* data are included for "only those programs which received at least some fund administered by the State Alcohol/Drug Agency during the State's Fiscal Year (FY) 1989."

Table 13. (*continued*) Number of Alcohol Client Treatment Admissions by Age, by Sex, and by State for Fiscal Year 1989

	45 to 54				55 to 64				65 and Over				Not Reported				Totals			
State	**Male**	**Female**	**NR**	**Total**	**Male**	**Female**	**NR**	**Total**	**Male**	**Female**	**NR**	**Total**	**Male**	**Female**	**NR**	**Total**	**Male**	**Female**	**NR**	**Total**
Alabama	625	203		828	282	88		370	95	24		119	162	73		235	5,463	1,845	0	7,308
Alaska	639	231		870	355	129		484	86	25		111	0	0		0	6,577	2,383	0	8,960
Arizona	1,687	571		2,258	748	173		921	310	68		378	0	0		0	13,646	4,812	0	18,458
Arkansas	N/A	N/A		0	N/A	N/A		0	N/A	N/A		0	6,334	1,178		7,512	6,334	1,178	0	7,512
California	10,956	2,301		13,257	4,711	767		5,478	1,315	219		1,534	0	0		0	84,910	24,652	0	109,562
Colorado	5,879	880		6,759	2,917	364		3,281	987	115		1,102	0	0		0	44,876	9,570	0	54,446
Connecticut	1,473	223		1,696	546	91		637	0			0	N/A	N/A	4,816	4,816	10,488	2,007	4,816	17,311
Delaware	366	58		424	154	36		190	124	9		133	0	0		0	2,817	569	0	3,386
District of Col	735	109		844	294	44		338	49	7		56	0	0		0	4,898	729	0	5,627
Florida	N/A	N/A	7,499	7,499	N/A	N/A	3,246	3,246	N/A	N/A	960	960				0	44,670	12,776	0	57,446
Georgia	4,542	859		5,401	2,165	425		2,590	610	108		718				0	25,433	5,873	0	31,306
Guam	1	1		2	2	0		2	0	0		0	0	0		0	56	15	0	71
Hawaii	258	47		305	78	19		97	15	2		17	22	9		31	1,691	591	0	2,282
Idaho	N/A	N/A	391	391	N/A	N/A	159	159	N/A	N/A	44	44				0	3,657	1,065	0	4,722
Illinois	N/A	N/A		N/A	N/A	N/A		N/A	N/A	N/A		N/A	36,864	10,853	791	48,508	36,864	10,853	791	48,508
Indiana	N/A	N/A	1,022	1,022	N/A	N/A	395	395	N/A	N/A	131	131				0	9,071	2,865	0	11,936
Iowa	957	287		1,244	462	105		567	177	34		211	191	83		274	14,284	4,227	0	18,511
Kansas	632	133		765	321	38		359	155	8		163	4	1		5	8,466	1,828	0	10,294
Kentucky	1,109	235		1,344	523	78		601	125	41		166	618	280	2,977	3,875	10,587	2,680	2,977	16,244
Louisiana	482	143		625	160	44		204	42	12		54	0	0		0	4,540	1,369	0	5,909
Maine	1,023	286		1,309	274	79		353	134	43		177	1,313	691		2,004	10,445	3,517	0	13,962
Maryland	1,171	221		1,392	561	78		639	179	23		202	3	1		4	14,469	3,703	0	18,172
Massachusetts	6,235	973		7,208	3,027	430		3,457	1,137	141		1,278				0	51,685	9,990	0	61,675
Michigan	2,332	604		2,936	895	214		1,109	271	74		345	222	66		288	27,291	8,118	0	35,409
Minnesota	6,526	914		7,440	3,433	500		3,933	1,616	255		1,871	N/A	N/A	414	414	43,730	8,921	414	53,065
Mississippi	559	124		683	230	38		268	69	11		80	0	0		0	6,407	1,207	0	7,614
Missouri	2,703	434		3,137	1,533	157		1,690	293	24		317	4	0		4	20,657	4,921	0	25,578
Montana	578	404		982	311	218		529	146	91		237	0	0		0	4,763	3,467	0	8,230

Nebraska	2,442	405		2,847	1,575	110		1,685	443	47		490	0	0		0	18,705	4,237	0	22,942
Nevada	N/A	N/A		0	N/A	N/A		0	N/A	N/A		0	7,012	1,439		8,451	7,012	1,439	0	8,451
New Hampshire	314	101		415	135	29		164	43	15		58	45	12		57	3,783	1,274	0	5,057
New Jersey	1,835	433		2,268	772	172		944	244	98		342	34	8		42	22,469	7,189	0	29,658
New Mexico	981	277		1,258	423	84		507	191	37		228	N/A	N/A	3	3	10,159	2,832	3	12,994
New York	16,486	6,097		22,583	14,131	5,226		19,357	2,710	516		3,226	0	0		0	117,688	43,618	0	161,306 A
North Carolina	2,793	434		3,227	1,264	211		1,475	424	99		523	0	0	9	9	20,892	4,875	9	25,776
North Dakota	149	35		184	82	27		109	29	8		37	1	0		1	1,412	563	0	1,975
Ohio	1,036	326		1,362	364	114		478	131	41		172				0	12,938	4,064	0	17,002
Oklahoma	973	223		1,196	425	67		492	116	21		137				0	7,963	2,200	0	10,163
Oregon	N/A	N/A	2,791	2,791	N/A	N/A	2,338	2,338	N/A	N/A	451	451				0	23,896	6,978	0	30,874
Pennsylvania	2,849	592		3,441	1,300	247		1,547	363	82		445	0	0		0	26,535	6,667	0	33,202
Puerto Rico	N/A	N/A		N/A	N/A	N/A		N/A	N/A	N/A		N/A	6,331	333		6,664	6,331	333	0	6,664
Rhode Island	88	30		118	15	12		27	6	4		10	5,002	2,464		7,466	6,836	3,238	0	10,074
South Carolina	2,930	542	56	3,528	1,306	200	28	1,534	535	97	0	632	0	0		0	21,892	4,258	876	27,026
South Dakota	234	100		334	108	46		154	55	23		78	0	0		0	2,956	1,266	0	4,222
Tennessee	563	122		685	189	41		230	42	15		57				0	6,516	1,787	0	8,303
Texas	1,036	173		1,209	483	75		558	109	16		125	3,496	2,334		5,830	11,839	4,086	0	15,925
Utah	1,416	144		1,560	756	68		824	158	22		180	8	4		12	10,842	1,770	0	12,612
Vermont	285	103		388	83	39		122	25	11		36	0	0		0	2,469	763	0	3,232
Virginia	3,709	937		4,646	2,017	469		2,486	432	108		540	1,044	321		1,365	28,091	7,923	0	36,014
Washington	N/A	N/A		N/A	N/A	N/A		0	N/A	N/A		0	N/A	N/A		N/A	N/A	N/A	0	N/A
West Virginia	1,267	127		1,394	454	56		510	145	27		172	0	0		0	10,019	1,770	0	11,789
Wisconsin	5,704	1,932		7,636	3,190	777		3,967	1,506	383		1,889				0	55,789	18,365	0	74,154
Wyoming	N/A	N/A		N/A	N/A	N/A		N/A	N/A	N/A		N/A	N/A	N/A		N/A	N/A	N/A	0	N/A
TOTALS	**98,558**	**23,374**	**11,759**	**133,691**	**53,054**	**12,185**	**6,166**	**71,405**	**15,642**	**3,004**	**1,586**	**20,232**	**68,710**	**20,150**	**9,010**	**97,870**	**955,807**	**267,226**	**9,886**	**1,232,919**

Note: A number of the States that have the N/A designation collect age-related information but not according to the specific age categories shown above.

A = Alcohol client admissions data are estimated.

N/A = Information not available.
NR = Not Reported.

SOURCE: *State Alcohol and Drug Abuse Profile, FY 1989;* data are included for "only those programs which received at least some funds administered by the State Alcohol/Drug Agency during the State's Fiscal Year 1989."

Table 14. Number of Alcohol Client Treatment Admissions by Race/Ethnicity and State for Fiscal Year 1989

State	White, Not of Hispanic Origin	Black, Not of Hispanic Origin	Hispanic	Asian or Pacific Islander	Native American	Other	Not Reported	Total	
Alabama	5,255	1,785	N/A	N/A	N/A	33	235	7,308	
Alaska	3,855	123	98	24	4,467	248	145	8,960	
Arizona	11,417	869	3,136	84	2,952	0	0	18,458	
Arkansas	5,835	1,605	N/A	N/A	N/A	72	0	7,512	
California	70,556	24,542	10,847	549	2,082	986	0	109,562	
Colorado	33,389	3,562	13,398	N/A	2,658	160	1,279	54,446	
Connecticut	8,955	2,661	832	N/A	N/A	46	4,817	17,311	
Delaware	2,449	874	63	N/A	N/A	N/A	N/A	3,386	
District of Col	393	5,002	112	46	17	57	0	5,627	
Florida	44,614	9,278	3,308	74	172	0	0	57,446	
Georgia	21,863	9,290	79	18	19	37		31,306	
Guam	18	0	1	51	0	1	0	71	
Hawaii	1,101	48	71	731	214	59	58	2,282	
Idaho	4,008	34	406	8	232	34	0	4,722	
Illinois	28,926	16,366	2,499	102	97	124	394	48,508	
Indiana	9,586	2,151	154	6	14	25	0	11,936	
Iowa	17,270	500	259	30	221	31	200	18,511	
Kansas	8,235	1,030	592	25	350	18	44	10,294	
Kentucky	11,880	1,118	N/A	N/A	N/A	50	3,196	16,244	A
Louisiana	3,766	2,031	87	8	17	0	0	5,909	
Maine	13,100	21	N/A	20	412	129	280	13,962	
Maryland	11,665	6,336	N/A	N/A	N/A	171	0	18,172	B
Massachusetts	53,997	4,469	2,287	125	438	359	0	61,675	
Michigan	29,048	4,428	938	30	781	74	110	35,409	
Minnesota	36,188	3,492	1,200	67	11,368	93	657	53,065	
Mississippi	4,366	3,224	0	0	24	0	0	7,614	
Missouri	17,811	7,291	254	11	211	0	0	25,578	
Montana	6,833	14	114	7	1,239	23	0	8,230	
Nebraska	16,842	1,185	872	23	3,916	41	63	22,942	
Nevada	6,498	1,079	356	7	419	92	0	8,451	
New Hampshire	4,425	46	21	4	12	44	505	5,057	
New Jersey	16,854	10,140	2,414	0	76	88	86	29,658	
New Mexico	3,483	200	4,941	15	4,355	0	0	12,994	
New York	100,638	42,243	13,248	N/A	923	4,254	0	161,306	
North Carolina	15,929	9,289	75	N/A	363	70	50	25,776	
North Dakota	1,705	2	7	4	237	3	17	1,975	
Ohio	12,701	4,046	187	34	34	0	0	17,002	
Oklahoma	7,820	906	218	11	1,208	0	0	10,163	
Oregon	26,227	855	1,673	149	1,970	0	0	30,874	
Pennsylvania	26,312	6,108	694	37	N/A	51	0	33,202	
Puerto Rico	0	0	6,664	0	0	0	0	6,664	
Rhode Island	2,134	241	154	6	16	57	7,466	10,074	
South Carolina	19,075	7,808	86	24	33	0	0	27,026	
South Dakota	3,061	34	0	0	1,093	34	0	4,222	
Tennessee	6,783	1,479	24	3	5	8	1	8,303	
Texas	5,873	1,257	2,827	9	133	0	5,826	15,925	
Utah	8,970	228	1,379	76	1,858	24	77	12,612	

State	White, Not of Hispanic Origin	Black, Not of Hispanic Origin	Hispanic	Asian or Pacific Islander	Native American	Other	Not Reported	Total
Vermont	3,232	N/A	N/A	N/A	N/A	N/A	N/A	3,232
Virginia	25,210	8,644	685	72	72	649	682	36,014
Washington	N/A	N/A	N/A	N/A	N/A	N/A	N/A	N/A
West Virginia	10,742	1,033	10	2	2	0	0	11,789
Wisconsin	68,488	2,499	1,103	349	1,715	0	0	74,154
Wyoming	N/A	N/A	N/A	N/A	N/A	N/A	N/A	N/A
TOTALS	**859,381**	**211,466**	**78,373**	**2,841**	**46,425**	**8,245**	**26,188**	**1,232,919**
PERCENT OF TOTAL	**69.7%**	**17.2%**	**6.4%**	**.2%**	**3.8%**	**.7%**	**2.1%**	**100.0%**

A = "Other" category includes "Hispanic", "Asian or Pacific Islander", and "Native American" admissions.
B = All non-White, non-Black categories are grouped in the "Other" category.

N/A = Information not available.

SOURCE: *State Alcohol and Drug Abuse Profile, FY 1989;* data are included for "only those programs which received some funds administered by the State Alcohol Drug Agency during the State's Fiscal Year 1989."

Table 15. Number of Drug Client Treatment Admissions by Sex and State for Fiscal Year 1989

	Sex			
State	**Male**	**Female**	**Not Reported**	**Total**
Alabama	3,405	1,976	0	5,381
Alaska	1,253	610	0	1,863
Arizona	4,606	2,919	0	7,525
Arkansas	2,513	1,087	0	3,600
California	37,835	26,143	0	63,978
Colorado	3,083	1,519	0	4,602
Connecticut	5,235	1,713	1,501	8,449
Delaware	1,341	536	0	1,877
District of Col	4,303	1,934	0	6,237
Florida	17,939	7,454	0	25,393
Georgia	17,106	6,937	0	24,043
Guam	5	2	0	7
Hawaii	1,302	724	0	2,026
Idaho	1,409	816	0	2,225
Illinois	24,453	7,201	517	32,171
Indiana	5,204	1,644	0	6,848
Iowa	3,241	1,395	0	4,636
Kansas	2,976	1,006	0	3,982
Kentucky	3,519	1,472	1,120	6,111
Louisiana	5,327	1,982	0	7,309

Table 15. (*continued*) Number of Drug Client Treatment Admissions by Sex and State for Fiscal Year 1989

State	Sex			Total
	Male	Female	Not Reported	
Maine	3,633	1,362	0	4,995
Maryland	13,495	4,339	0	17,834
Massachusetts	24,075	10,714	0	34,789
Michigan	15,276	9,368	0	24,644
Minnesota	7,795	3,005	0	10,800
Mississippi	2,564	1,216	0	3,780
Missouri	6,982	2,397	0	9,379
Montana	1,489	660	0	2,149
Nebraska	1,573	988	0	2,561
Nevada	1,289	859	0	2,148
New Hampshire	747	384	0	1,131
New Jersey	9,298	4,358	0	13,656
New Mexico	2,073	1,013	0	3,086
New York	50,390	35,514	0	85,904
North Carolina	3,548	1,470	1	5,019
North Dakota	429	221	0	650
Ohio	13,634	7,628	23	21,285
Oklahoma	2,987	1,895	0	4,882
Oregon	5,397	3,658	0	9,055
Pennsylvania	22,292	10,216	0	32,508
Puerto Rico	N/A	N/A	9,184	9,184
Rhode Island	2,981	1,616	0	4,597
South Carolina	5,752	2,230	0	7,982
South Dakota	2,624	1,126	0	3,750
Tennessee	5,332	2,190	0	7,522
Texas	10,826	4,267	0	15,093
Utah	2,105	979	0	3,084
Vermont	1,632	658	0	2,290
Virginia	12,956	6,439	0	19,395
Washington	N/A	N/A	0	N/A
West Virginia	1,206	513	0	1,719
Wisconsin	17,453	5,327	0	22,780
Wyoming	N/A	N/A	0	N/A
TOTALS	**397,888**	**195,680**	**12,346**	**605,914**
PERCENT OF TOTAL	**65.7%**	**32.3%**	**2.0%**	**100.0%**

N/A = Information not available.

SOURCE: *State Alcohol and Drug Abuse Profile, FY 1989;* data are included for "only those programs which received some funds administered by the State Alcohol/Drug Agency during the State's Fiscal Year 1989."

Table 16. Number of Drug Client Treatment Admissions by Age and State for Fiscal Year 1989

te	Under Age 18	18 to 20	21 to 24	25 to 34	35 to 44	45 to 54	55 to 64	Age 65 and Over	Not Reported	Total	
bama	215	422	648	2,481	1,005	179	74	85	272	5,381	
ska	318	172	307	659	342	36	22	7	0	1,863	
zona	1,065	511	924	2,979	1,634	308	76	28	0	7,525	
ansas	N/A	N/A	N/A	N/A	N/A	N/A	N/A	N/A	3,600	3,600	
fornia	3,997	3,768	8,089	27,969	16,204	3,131	715	105	0	63,978	
orado	614	358	517	1,916	947	202	34	14	0	4,602	
necticut	263	656	1,478	3,274	1,151	110	16	0	1,501	8,449	A
aware	11	159	323	988	355	39	2	0	0	1,877	
rict of Col	80	374	748	2,370	1,559	935	125	46	0	6,237	
ida	3,086	2,252	3,907	11,625	3,809	545	135	34	0	25,393	
rgia	588	1,863	4,439	12,863	3,727	436	92	35	0	24,043	
m	2	1	0	1	2	1	0	0	0	7	
vaii	534	120	238	564	357	119	30	9	55	2,026	
o	621	165	272	705	290	95	58	19	0	2,225	
ois	N/A	N/A	N/A	N/A	N/A	N/A	N/A	N/A	32,171	32,171	
ana	322	549	1,006	2,565	1,517	586	228	75	0	6,848	
a	461	619	818	1,931	625	65	20	6	91	4,636	
sas	248	472	774	1,908	497	49	15	19	0	3,982	
tucky	562	582	746	1,959	708	153	55	18	1,328	6,111	
siana	682	685	1,347	3,607	816	137	35	N/A	0	7,309	
ne	203	109	885	1,780	634	240	97	80	967	4,995	
yland	1,854	1,584	3,044	7,715	3,019	502	95	18	3	17,834	
sachusetts	2,277	2,555	5,715	16,325	6,582	980	261	94	0	34,789	
higan	2,616	1,592	3,234	11,111	4,686	795	229	76	305	24,644	
nesota	958	1,289	1,830	4,822	1,592	217	46	44	2	10,800	
sissippi	124	342	678	1,914	522	122	57	21	0	3,780	
souri	510	1,028	1,789	4,547	1,324	138	34	3	6	9,379	
tana	363	293	425	415	596	33	18	6	0	2,149	
raska	412	328	358	976	346	91	35	15	0	2,561	
ada	N/A	N/A	N/A	N/A	N/A	N/A	N/A	N/A	2,148	2,148	
Hampshire	140	132	198	448	172	22	5	7	7	1,131	
Jersey	854	950	1,884	6,367	3,161	375	54	11	0	13,656	
Mexico	811	194	294	1,005	550	169	36	27	0	3,086	
York	34,366	7,347	8,362	23,160	10,472	1,728	340	64	65	85,904	
h Carolina	557	515	703	2,246	840	124	25	8	1	5,019	
h Dakota	40	62	93	325	102	18	6	4	0	650	
)	3,988	2,172	2,895	6,743	3,964	1,070	315	109	29	21,285	
ahoma	351	511	815	2,356	694	106	30	19	0	4,882	
gon	1,698	689	1,304	3,655	1,316	239	145	9	0	9,055	
sylvania	2,080	2,565	4,961	15,663	6,205	810	169	55	0	32,508	
to Rico	1,087	1,884	1,484	3,291	655	479	0	0	304	9,184	
de Island	361	264	564	1,425	750	18	14	6	1,195	4,597	
h Carolina	799	614	1,174	3,827	1,245	203	53	67	0	7,982	
h Dakota	522	409	446	1,176	694	297	137	69	0	3,750	
nessee	800	696	1,221	3,554	1,028	177	33	13	0	7,522	
as	910	1,378	2,552	6,990	2,714	441	81	19	8	15,093	
	459	284	439	1,246	477	100	43	35	1	3,084	
mont	212	241	441	1,002	303	73	15	3	0	2,290	
inia	1,766	1,572	2,599	8,243	3,259	1,222	408	97	229	19,395	
hington	N/A	N/A	N/A	N/A	N/A	N/A	N/A	N/A	N/A	N/A	
Virginia	364	238	286	505	220	84	14	8	0	1,719	
consin	1,052	1,771	3,310	10,142	4,339	1,324	593	249	0	22,780	
ming	N/A	N/A	N/A	N/A	N/A	N/A	N/A	N/A	N/A	N/A	
TALS	**76,203**	**47,336**	**80,564**	**233,338**	**98,006**	**19,323**	**5,120**	**1,736**	**44,288**	**605,914**	
RCENT OF TAL	**12.6%**	**7.8%**	**13.3%**	**38.5%**	**16.2%**	**3.2%**	**.8%**	**.3%**	**7.3%**	**100.0%**	

ımber of the States which have the N/A designation collect age related information but not in these specific categories.

Age 21 to 24 category includes Age 21 to 25, Age 25 to 34 category includes Age 26 to 35, Age 35 to 44 category includes Age 36 to 45, Age 45 to 54 category includes Age 46 to 59, Age 55 to 64 category is eliminated and Age 65 and Over category includes Age 60 and Over.

= Information not available.

JRCE: *State Alcohol and Drug Abuse Profile, FY 1989;* data are included for "only those programs which received some funds administered by the Alcohol/Drug Agency during the State's Fiscal Year 1989."

Table 17. Number of Drug Client Treatment Admissions by Age, by Sex, and by State for Fiscal Year 1989

	Under Age 18				18 to 20				21 to 24				25 to 34				35 to 44			
State	Male	Female	NR	Total	Male	Female	NR	Total	Male	Female	NR	Total	Male	Female	NR	Total	Male	Female	NR	Total
Alabama	122	93		215	312	110		422	469	179		648	1,556	925		2,481	629	376		1,005
Alaska	194	124		318	116	56		172	207	100		307	444	215		659	230	112		342
Arizona	648	417		1,065	399	112		511	558	366		924	1,706	1,273		2,979	1,033	601		1,634
Arkansas	N/A	N/A		N/A	N/A	N/A		N/A	N/A	N/A		N/A	N/A	N/A		N/A	N/A	N/A		N/A
California	2,743	1,254		3,997	2,371	1,397		3,768	4,137	3,952		8,089	14,746	13,223		27,969	10,799	5,405		16,204
Colorado	435	179		614	274	84		358	345	172		517	1,193	723		1,916	669	278		947
Connecticut	202	61		263	557	99		656	1,080	398		1,478	2,392	882		3,274	906	245		1,151 A
Delaware	11	0		11	105	54		159	239	84		323	689	299		988	269	86		355
District of Col	55	25		80	258	116		374	516	232		748	1,635	735		2,370	1,076	483		1,559
Florida	2,180	906		3,086	1,591	661		2,252	2,760	1,147		3,907	8,213	3,412		11,625	2,691	1,118		3,809
Georgia	417	171		588	1,386	477		1,863	3,140	1,299		4,439	8,952	3,911		12,863	2,826	901		3,727
Guam	2	0		2	1	0		1	0	0		0	0	1		1	2	0		2
Hawaii	323	211		534	74	46		120	137	101		238	346	218		564	258	99		357
Idaho	N/A	N/A	621	621	N/A	N/A	165	165	N/A	N/A	272	272	N/A	N/A	705	705	N/A	N/A	290	290
Illinois	N/A	N/A		N/A	N/A	N/A		N/A	N/A	N/A		N/A	N/A	N/A		N/A	N/A	N/A		N/A
Indiana	N/A	N/A	322	322	N/A	N/A	549	549	N/A	N/A	1,006	1,006	N/A	N/A	2,565	2,565	N/A	N/A	1,517	1,517
Iowa	319	142		461	476	143		619	618	200		818	1,272	659		1,931	445	180		625
Kansas	189	59		248	375	97		472	572	202		774	1,401	507		1,908	380	117		497
Kentucky	409	153		562	441	141		582	571	175		746	1,313	646		1,959	494	214		708
Louisiana	561	121		682	499	186		685	978	369		1,347	2,520	1,087		3,607	646	170		816
Maine	148	55		203	88	21		109	612	273		885	1,383	397		1,780	482	152		634
Maryland	1,282	572		1,854	1,328	256		1,584	2,448	596		3,044	5,633	2,082		7,715	2,309	710		3,019
Massachusetts	1,445	832		2,277	1,865	690		2,555	3,750	1,965		5,715	11,072	5,253		16,325	14,996	1,586		6,582
Michigan	1,611	1,005		2,616	1,141	451		1,592	2,018	1,216		3,234	6,858	4,,253		11,111	2,944	1,742		4,686
Minnesota	633	325		958	952	337		1,289	1,321	509		1,830	3,469	1,353		4,822	1,218	374		1,592
Mississippi	89	35		124	248	94		342	452	226		678	1,258	656		1,914	381	141		522
Missouri	367	143		510	804	224		1,028	1,338	451		1,789	3,332	1,215		4,547	1,004	320		1,324

Montana	245	118		363	228	65		293	309	116		425	277	138		415	399	197		596
Nebraska	292	120		412	222	106		328	216	142		358	608	368		976	175	171		346
Nevada	N/A	N/A		N/A	N/A	N/A		N/A	N/A	N/A		N/A	N/A	N/A		N/A	N/A	N/A		N/A
New Hampshire	83	57		140	90	42		132	139	59		198	307	141		448	105	67		172
New Jersey	697	157		854	729	221		950	1,269	615		1,884	3,982	2,385		6,367	2,286	875		3,161
New Mexico	557	254		811	143	51		194	214	80		294	642	363		1,005	361	189		550
New York	16,761	17,605		34,366	4,371	2,976		7,347	5,236	3,126		8,362	14,762	8,398		23,160	7,609	2,863		10,472
North Carolina	434	123		557	404	111		515	482	221		703	1,486	760		2,246	625	215		840
North Dakota	25	15		40	36	26		62	68	25		93	222	103		325	69	33		102
Ohio	2,671	1,317		3,988	1,379	793		2,172	1,838	1,057		2,895	4,284	2,459		6,743	2,522	1,442		3,964
Oklahoma	241	110		351	341	170		511	510	305		815	1,388	968		2,356	432	262		694
Oregon	N/A	N/A	1,698	1,698	N/A	N/A	689	689	N/A	N/A	1,304	1,304	N/A	N/A	3,655	3,655	N/A	N/A	1,316	1,316
Pennsylvania	1,504	576		2,080	1,832	733		2,565	3,179	1,782		4,961	10,255	5,408		15,663	4,730	1,475		6,205
Puerto Rico	N/A	N/A	1,087	1,087	N/A	N/A	1,884	1,884	N/A	N/A	1,484	1,484	N/A	N/A	3,291	3,291	N/A	N/A	655	655
Rhode Island	229	132		361	197	67		264	352	212		564	895	530		1,425	492	258		750
South Carolina	598	201		799	470	144		614	854	320		1,174	2,707	1,120		3,827	923	322		1,245
South Dakota	365	157		522	286	123		409	312	134		446	823	353		1,176	486	208		694
Tennessee	580	220		800	547	149		696	892	329		1,221	2,473	1,081		3,554	712	316		1,028
Texas	727	183		910	1,014	364		1,378	1,794	758		2,552	4,770	2,220		6,990	2,074	640		2,714
Utah	326	133		459	224	60		284	311	128		439	814	432		1,246	315	162		477
Vermont	150	62		212	152	89		241	326	115		441	727	275		1,002	223	80		303
Virginia	1,261	505		1,766	1,145	427		1,572	1,668	931		2,599	5,353	2,890		8,243	2,192	1,067		3,259
Washington	N/A	N/A		N/A	N/A	N/A		N/A	N/A	N/A		N/A	N/A	N/A		N/A	N/A	N/A		N/A
West Virginia	256	108		364	180	58		238	195	91		286	352	153		505	160	60		220
Wisconsin	783	269		1,052	1,419	352		1,771	2,422	888		3,310	7,597	2,545		10,142	13,439	900		4,339
Wyoming	N/A	N/A		N/A	N/A	N/A		N/A	N/A	N/A		N/A	N/A	N/A		N/A	N/A	N/A		N/A
TOTALS	**43,170**	**29,305**	**3,728**	**76,203**	**31,070**	**12,979**	**3,287**	**47,336**	**50,852**	**25,646**	**4,066**	**80,564**	**146,107**	**77,015**	**10,216**	**233,338**	**67,016**	**27,212**	**3,778**	**98,006**

See footnotes at the bottom of next page.

SOURCE: *State Alcohol and Drug Abuse Profile, FY 1989;* data are included for "only those programs which received at least some funds administered by the State Alcohol/Drug Agency during the State's Fiscal Year (FY) 1989."

Table 17. (*continued*) Number of Drug Client Treatment Admissions by Age, by Sex, and by State for Fiscal Year 1989

State	45 to 54				55 to 64				65 and Over				Not Reported				Totals			
	Male	Female	NR	Total	Male	Female	NR	Total	Male	Female	NR	Total	Male	Female	NR	Total	Male	Female	NR	Total
Alabama	87	92		179	32	42		74	26	59		85	172	100		272	3,405	1,976	0	5,381
Alaska	33	3		36	22	0		22	7	0		7				0	1,253	610	0	1,863
Arizona	199	109		308	51	25		76	12	16		28	0	0		0	4,606	2,919	0	7,525
Arkansas	N/A	N/A		N/A	N/A	N/A		N/A	N/A	N/A		N/A	2,513	1,087		3,600	2,513	1,087	0	3,600
California	2,406	725		3,131	554	161		715	79	26		105	0	0		0	37,835	26,143	0	63,978
Colorado	139	63		202	19	15		34	9	5		14	0	0		0	3,083	1,519	0	4,602
Connecticut	85	25		110	13	3		16				0	N/A	N/A	1,501	1,501	5,235	1,713	1,501	8,449 A
Delaware	26	13		39	2	0		2	0	0		0	0	0		0	1,341	536	0	1,877
District of Col	645	290		935	86	39		125	32	14		46				0	4,303	1,934	0	6,237
Florida	385	160		545	95	40		135	24	10		34	0	0		0	17,939	7,454	0	25,393
Georgia	317	119		436	55	37		92	13	22		35				0	17,106	6,937	0	24,043
Guam	0	1		1	0	0		0	0	0		0	0	0		0	5	2	0	7
Hawaii	88	31		119	25	5		30	9	0		9	42	13		55	1,302	724	0	2,026
Idaho	N/A	N/A	95	95	N/A	N/A	58	58	N/A	N/A	19	19				0	1,409	816	0	2,225
Illinois	N/A	N/A		N/A	N/A	N/A		N/A	N/A	N/A		N/A	24,453	7,201	517	32,171	24,453	7,201	517	32,171
Indiana	N/A	N/A	586	586	N/A	N/A	228	228	N/A	N/A	75	75	N/A	N/A	0	0	5,204	1,644	0	6,848
Iowa	39	26		65	7	13		20	2	4		6	63	28		91	3,241	1,395	0	4,636
Kansas	34	15		49	8	7		15	17	2		19	0	0		0	2,976	1,006	0	3,982
Kentucky	98	55		153	33	22		55	9	9		18	151	57	1,120	1,320	3,519	1,472	1,120	6,111
Louisiana	104	33		137	19	16		35	N/A	N/A		0	0	0		0	5,327	1,982	0	7,309
Maine	170	70		240	62	35		97	60	20		80	628	339		967	3,633	1,362	0	4,995
Maryland	402	100		502	76	19		95	15	3		18	2	1		3	13,495	4,339	0	17,834
Massachusetts	710	270		980	184	77		261	53	41		94				0	24,075	10,714	0	34,789
Michigan	396	399		795	100	129		229	22	54		76	186	119		305	15,276	9,368	0	24,644
Minnesota	152	65		217	26	20		46	22	22		44	2	0		2	7,795	3,005	414	10,800
Mississippi	74	48		122	46	11		57	16	5		21	0	0		0	2,564	1,216	0	3,780
Missouri	109	29		138	19	15		34	3	0		3	6	0		6	6,982	2,397	0	9,379
Montana	18	15		33	11	7		18	2	4		6	0	0		0	1,489	660	0	2,149

Nebraska	39	52		91	16	19		35	5	10		15	0	0		0	1,573	988	0	2,561
Nevada	N/A	N/A		N/A	N/A	N/A		N/A	N/A	N/A		N/A	1,289	859		2,148	1,289	859	0	2,148
New Hampshire	13	9		22	4	1		5	0	7		7	6	1		7	747	384	0	1,131
New Jersey	285	90		375	42	12		54	8	3		11				0	9,298	4,358	0	13,656
New Mexico	114	55		169	22	14		36	20	7		27				0	2,073	1,013	0	3,086
New York	1,328	400		1,728	239	101		340	47	17		64	37	28		65	50,390	35,514	0	85,904
North Carolina	97	27		124	13	12		25	7	1		8	N/A	N/A	1	1	3,548	1,470	1	5,019
North Dakota	7	11		18	1	5		6	1	3		4	0	0		0	429	221	0	650
Ohio	678	392		1,070	195	120		315	65	44		109	2	4	23	29	13,634	7,628	23	21,285
Oklahoma	61	45		106	10	20		30	4	15		19				0	2,987	1,895	0	4,882
Oregon	N/A	N/A	239	239	N/A	N/A	145	145	N/A	N/A	9	9	N/A	N/A	0	0	5,397	3,658	0	9,055
Pennsylvania	639	171		810	125	44		169	28	27		55				0	22,292	10,216	0	32,508
Puerto Rico	N/A	N/A	479	479	N/A	N/A		0	N/A	N/A		0	N/A	N/A	304	304	N/A	N/A	9,184	9,184
Rhode Island	7	11		18	5	9		14	3	3		6	801	394		1,195	2,981	1,616	0	4,597
South Carolina	127	76		203	28	25		53	45	22		67	0	0		0	5,752	2,230	0	7,982
South Dakota	208	89		297	96	41		137	48	21		69	0	0		0	2,624	1,126	0	3,750
Tennessee	105	72		177	16	17		33	7	6		13	0	0		0	5,332	2,190	0	7,522
Texas	368	73		441	68	13		81	11	8		19	0	8		8	10,826	4,267	0	15,093
Utah	57	43		100	33	10		43	25	10		35	0	1		1	2,105	979	0	3,084
Vermont	42	31		73	11	4		15	1	2		3	0	0		0	1,632	658	0	2,290
Virginia	834	388		1,222	291	117		408	58	39		97	154	75		229	12,956	6,439	0	19,395
Washington	N/A	N/A		N/A	N/A	N/A		N/A	N/A	N/A		N/A	N/A	N/A		N/A	N/A	N/A	0	N/A
West Virginia	53	31		84	6	8		14	4	4		8	0	0		0	1,206	513	0	1,719
Wisconsin	1,080	244		1,324	504	89		593	209	40		249	0	0		0	17,453	5,327	0	22,780
Wyoming	N/A	N/A		N/A	N/A	N/A		N/A	N/A	N/A		N/A	N/A	N/A		N/A	N/A	N/A	0	N/A
TOTALS	**12,858**	**5,066**	**1,399**	**19,323**	**3,270**	**1,419**	**431**	**5,120**	**1,028**	**605**	**103**	**1,736**	**30,507**	**10,315**	**3,466**	**44,288**	**397,869**	**195,680**	**12,346**	**605,914**

A number of the States which have the N/A designation collect age related information but not in these specific categories.

A = Age 21 to 24 category includes Age 21 to 25, Age 25 to 34 category includes Age 26 to 35, Age 35 to 44 category includes Age 36 to 45, Age 45 to 54 category includes Age 46 to 59, Age 55 to 64 category is eliminated and Age 65 and Over category includes Age 60 and Over.

N/A = Information not available.
NR = Not Reported.

SOURCE: *State Alcohol and Drug Abuse Profile, FY 1989;* data are included for "only those programs which received at least some funds administered by the State Alcohol/Drug Agency during the State's Fiscal Year (FY) 1989."

Table 18. Number of Drug Client Treatment Admissions by Race/Ethnicity and State for Fiscal Year 1989

State	White, Not of Hispanic Origin	Black, Not of Hispanic Origin	His-panic	Asian or Pacific Islander	Native American	Other	Not Reported	Total
Alabama	3,185	1,912	N/A	N/A	N/A	12	272	5,381
Alaska	1,163	218	39	6	415	12	10	1,863
Arizona	4,721	599	1,812	36	357	0	0	7,525
Arkansas	2,227	1,348	N/A	N/A	N/A	25	N/A	3,600
California	33,520	11,094	17,444	1,315	584	0	21	63,978
Colorado	2,946	598	966	N/A	46	46	0	4,602
Connecticut	3,447	2,069	1,404	N/A	N/A	29	1,500	8,449
Delaware	797	1,029	51	N/A	N/A	N/A	N/A	1,877
District of Col	498	5,593	124	8	14	0	0	6,237
Florida	13,781	9,128	2,382	36	66	0	0	25,393
Georgia	9,950	13,992	48	13	8	32	0	24,043
Guam	3	0	0	4	0	0	0	7
Hawaii	657	43	58	925	190	58	95	2,026
Idaho	2,042	14	104	7	38	20	0	2,225
Illinois	19,188	10,856	1,657	67	65	82	256	32,171
Indiana	5,500	1,234	88	4	8	14	0	6,848
Iowa	3,967	439	59	14	54	11	92	4,636
Kansas	2,673	1,106	106	4	72	14	7	3,982
Kentucky	4,128	819	N/A	N/A	N/A	29	1,135	6,111 A
Louisiana	3,800	3,391	108	5	5	0	0	7,309
Maine	4,710	10	N/A	12	119	50	94	4,995
Maryland	8,294	9,379	N/A	N/A	N/A	161	0	17,834 B
Massachusetts	22,985	7,493	3,745	72	175	319	0	34,789
Michigan	13,831	10,001	418	26	186	82	100	24,644
Minnesota	8,149	1,512	124	19	938	55	3	10,800
Mississippi	1,982	1,796	0	0	2	0	0	3,780
Missouri	5,928	3,354	55	17	25	0	0	9,379
Montana	1,832	15	30	3	263	6	0	2,149
Nebraska	2,101	293	68	5	80	7	7	2,561
Nevada	1,612	362	133	14	3	24	0	2,148
New Hampshire	1,022	24	14	0	3	35	33	1,131
New Jersey	5,960	5,800	1,867	19	10	0	0	13,656
New Mexico	1,095	96	1,313	2	580	0	0	3,086
New York	21,006	17,798	10,394	70	89	423	36,124	85,904
North Carolina	2,944	1,943	12	N/A	97	19	4	5,019
North Dakota	576	3	2	2	63	1	3	650
Ohio	13,775	6,427	317	16	53	99	598	21,285
Oklahoma	3,323	1,170	98	4	287	0	0	4,882
Oregon	7,710	772	287	40	246	0	0	9,055
Pennsylvania	14,865	15,809	1,768	44	N/A	22	0	32,508
Puerto Rico	0	0	9,184	0	0	0	0	9,184
Rhode Island	2,790	379	147	5	12	69	1,195	4,597

State	White, Not of Hispanic Origin	Black, Not of Hispanic Origin	His-panic	Asian or Pacific Islander	Native American	Other	Not Reported	Total
South Carolina	4,337	3,615	21	3	6	0	0	7,982
South Dakota	2,719	30	0	0	971	30	0	3,750
Tennessee	5,613	1,869	13	5	6	14	2	7,522
Texas	6,505	4,462	4,052	19	49	0	6	15,093
Utah	2,559	149	279	22	48	6	21	3,084
Vermont	2,290	N/A	N/A	N/A	N/A	N/A	N/A	2,290
Virginia	10,898	7,708	223	25	31	58	452	19,395
Washington	N/A	N/A	N/A	N/A	N/A	N/A	N/A	N/A
West Virginia	1,468	250	1	0	0	0	0	1,719
Wisconsin	17,450	4,214	535	114	467	0	0	22,780
Wyoming	N/A	N/A	N/A	N/A	N/A	N/A	N/A	N/A
TOTALS	**318,522**	**172,215**	**61,550**	**3,002**	**6,731**	**1,864**	**42,030**	**605,914**
PERCENT OF TOTAL	**52.6%**	**28.4%**	**10.2%**	**.5%**	**1.1%**	**.3%**	**6.9%**	**100.0%**

A = "Other" category includes "Hispanic," "Asian or Pacific Islander," and "Native American" admissions.
B = All non-White, non-Black categories are grouped in the "Other" category.

N/A = Information not available.

SOURCE: *State Alcohol and Drug Abuse Profile, FY 1989;* data are included for "only those programs which received some funds administered by the State Alcohol/Drug Agency during Fiscal Year 1989."

Table 19. Number of Drug Client Treatment Admissions in State Supported Facilities by Primary Drug of Abuse and State for Fiscal Year 1989

State	Heroin	Non-RX Methadone	Other Opiates/ Synthetics	Barbi-turates	Tran-quil-izers	Other Sedatives/ Hypnotics	Amphet-amines	Cocaine
Alabama	N/A	N/A	559	N/A	N/A	131	33	2,113 A
Alaska	125	3	49	3	9	6	23	911
Arizona	2,141	23	230	55	97	64	420	1,914
Arkansas	64	1	160	33	37	89	370	1,589
California	33,207	69	797	82	194	61	6,645	14,926
Colorado	428	18	133	5	60	14	189	1,261
Connecticut	2,968	23	100	9	15	5	24	2,808
Delaware	206	8	13	1	4	3	16	1,373
District of Col	3,802	N/A	N/A	N/A	N/A	0	N/A	1,996
Florida	1,046	0	542	78	89	98	149	17,468
Georgia	841	N/A	N/A	82	142	N/A	336	14,974
Guam	2	0	0	0	1	0	0	1
Hawaii	398	8	66	17	23	14	486	389
Idaho	42	13	31	10	15	8	176	421
Illinois	3,934	N/A	N/A	N/A	N/A	700	N/A	16,566 B
Indiana	306	N/A	305	703	N/A	N/A	701	1,540 C
Iowa	278	3	93	46	46	46	417	1,484

Table 19. (*continued*) Number of Drug Client Treatment Admissions in State Supported Facilities by Primary Drug of Abuse and State for Fiscal Year 1989

State	Heroin	Non-RX Methadone	Other Opiates/ Synthetics	Barbi- turates	Tran- quil- izers	Other Sedatives/ Hypnotics	Amphet- amines	Cocaine
Kansas	N/A	N/A	244	N/A	24	48	667	1,361
Kentucky	75	25	427	105	309	186	131	1,174
Louisiana	81	3	161	36	80	53	128	3,379
Maine	N/A	N/A	N/A	N/A	N/A	N/A	N/A	N/A
Maryland	5,293	49	181	28	55	23	95	5,259 D
Massachusetts	17,777	0	548	189	412	N/A	58	11,209 E
Michigan	2,505	59	521	38	152	45	264	12,369
Minnesota	297	0	439	0	0	560	947	4,227
Mississippi	18	0	126	77	27	47	52	1,645
Missouri	714	14	330	77	88	54	622	3,611
Montana	47	N/A	87	47	54	N/A	271	489
Nebraska	110	10	53	20	40	39	209	623
Nevada	329	4	23	7	7	5	234	556
New Hampshire	60	1	4	2	27	0	20	507
New Jersey	7,457	62	126	117	51	73	204	4,148
New Mexico	191	1	9	5	11	11	66	168
New York	17,984	294	315	133	303	102	188	19,529
North Carolina	N/A	N/A	N/A	N/A	N/A	N/A	N/A	N/A
North Dakota	N/A	N/A	20	27	N/A	N/A	42	46
Ohio	482	9	523	136	214	191	208	3,555
Oklahoma	238	8	132	60	79	60	713	1,562 F
Oregon	1,574	11	184	11	38	24	2,176	2,035
Pennsylvania	6,190	N/A	N/A	198	N/A	N/A	902	20,407 G
Puerto Rico	2,556	0	0	0	0	0	0	2,012
Rhode Island	1,167	70	119	19	78	26	26	1,208
South Carolina	662	26	136	88	166	68	86	4,101
South Dakota	5	0	24	32	42	28	161	313
Tennessee	38	5	452	32	132	169	75	2,100 H
Texas	3,378	33	223	51	79	64	1,973	6,199
Utah	420	12	160	59	66	33	192	888
Vermont	45	5	N/A	17	35	21	36	746
Virginia	2,522	97	660	117	369	214	311	7,894
Washington	N/A	N/A	N/A	N/A	N/A	N/A	N/A	N/A
West Virginia	13	1	138	82	133	70	44	507
Wisconsin	2,711	113	3,304	341	1,277	364	1,573	5,308
Wyoming	N/A	N/A	N/A	N/A	N/A	N/A	N/A	N/A
TOTALS	**124,727**	**1,081**	**12,747**	**3,275**	**5,080**	**3,817**	**22,659**	**210,869**

See footnotes at bottom of next page.

N/A = Information not available.

SOURCE: *State Alcohol and Drug Abuse Profile, FY 1989;* data are included for "only those programs which received some funds administered by the State Alcohol/Drug Agency during the State's Fiscal Year (FY) 1989."

Table 19. (*continued*) Number of Drug Client Treatment Admissions in State Supported Facilities by Primary Drug of Abuse and State for Fiscal Year 1989

State	Marijuana/ Hashish	PCP	Other Hallucin- ogens	Inhalants	Over-the- Counter	Other	Not Reported	Total
Alabama	642	N/A	24	11	N/A	1,212	656	5,381 A
Alaska	702	0	19	12	0	1	0	1,863
Arizona	1,880	17	69	100	14	501	0	7,525
Arkansas	1,157	0	4	27	0	69	0	3,600
California	4,578	1,925	189	39	35	1,231	0	63,978
Colorado	1,855	0	60	46	18	515	0	4,602
Connecticut	936	0	40	4	0	12	1,505	8,449
Delaware	181	34	5	1	3	21	8	1,877
District of Col	30	390	0	0	N/A	N/A	19	6,237
Florida	5,637	8	90	36	9	143	0	25,393
Georgia	1,555	3,720	N/A	N/A	N/A	612	1,781	24,043
Guam	2	0	0	1	0	0	0	7
Hawaii	520	0	5	22	5	0	73	2,026
Idaho	742	2	23	19	6	631	86	2,225
Illinois	5,289	N/A	421	N/A	N/A	2,380	2,881	32,171 B
Indiana	2,594	133	363	N/A	N/A	203	0	6,848 C
Iowa	2,040	3	93	8	6	46	27	4,636
Kansas	1,570	N/A	45	N/A	N/A	23	0	3,982
Kentucky	2,354	14	68	48	0	0	1,195	6,111
Louisiana	1,246	25	43	22	4	37	2,011	7,309
Maine	N/A	N/A	N/A	N/A	N/A	N/A	4,995	4,995
Maryland	3,534	1,466	81	57	15	1,698	0	17,834 D
Massachusetts	3,614	N/A	191	N/A	N/A	791	0	34,789 E
Michigan	4,156	30	79	44	14	3,657	711	24,644
Minnesota	3,687	0	316	105	0	222	0	10,800
Mississippi	692	1	36	23	8	610	418	3,780
Missouri	3,417	186	69	66	14	117	0	9,379
Montana	1,032	14	59	32	N/A	17	0	2,149
Nebraska	935	0	33	30	14	445	0	2,561
Nevada	529	8	8	4	1	8	425	2,148
New Hampshire	415	1	21	0	0	36	37	1,131
New Jersey	883	80	53	7	14	381	0	13,656
New Mexico	591	4	11	44	6	401	1,567	3,086
New York	6,419	158	151	21	57	38,022	2,228	85,904
North Carolina	N/A	N/A	N/A	N/A	N/A	N/A	5,019	5,019
North Dakota	416	N/A	1	N/A	N/A	98	N/A	650
Ohio	3,566	11	70	94	72	199	11,955	21,285
Oklahoma	1,055	45	26	121	11	669	103	4,882 F
Oregon	2,614	9	64	15	4	296	0	9,055
Pennsylvania	3,676	N/A	N/A	N/A	N/A	1,135	0	32,508 G
Puerto Rico	3,329	0	0	48	0	810	429	9,184
Rhode Island	593	5	67	10	14	0	1,195	4,597
South Carolina	1,960	1	40	79	27	175	367	7,982

Table 19. (*continued*) Number of Drug Client Treatment Admissions in State Supported Facilities by Primary Drug of Abuse and State for Fiscal Year 1989

State	Marijuana/ Hashish	PCP	Other Hallucin-ogens	Inhalants	Over-the-Counter	Other	Not Reported	Total
South Dakota	782	5	23	75	0	2,250	10	3,750
Tennessee	1,308	3	30	55	4	2,650	469	7,522
Texas	2,675	2	71	259	7	33	46	15,093
Utah	938	5	42	92	9	66	102	3,084
Vermont	756	N/A	48	3	23	112	443	2,290
Virginia	4,209	582	291	136	59	1,934	0	19,395
Washington	N/A	N/A	N/A	N/A	N/A	N/A	N/A	N/A
West Virginia	554	13	29	73	13	49	0	1,719
Wisconsin	6,605	341	616	113	113	0	1	22,780
Wyoming	N/A	N/A	N/A	N/A	N/A	N/A	N/A	N/A
TOTALS	**100,450**	**9,241**	**4,087**	**2,002**	**599**	**64,518**	**40,762**	**605,914**

A = Alabama's "Other" drug category includes mixed or polydrug abuse where a single primary drug of abuse is not specified.
B = Illinois' "Heroin" drug category includes all narcotics, the "Other Sedatives/Hypnotics" category includes all sedatives and hypnotics, and the "Other Hallucinogens" category includes all hallucinogens.
C = Indiana's "Barbiturates" drug category includes tranquilizers and the "Other" category includes inhalants.
D = Maryland's "Other" drug category includes 1,364 clients with primary alcohol problems and 313 collaterals with no alcohol or drug abuse problems themselves.
E = Massachusetts' "Other Sedatives and Hypnotics" category includes Barbiturates, and "Other Hallucinogens" category includes PCP.
F = Oklahoma's "Other" drug category includes alcohol.
G = Pennsylvania's "Heroin" category is primarily heroin users but includes some "Non-Rx Methodone" users and some "Other Opiates and Synthetics" users.
H = Tennessee's "Other" drug category includes 2,573 drug treatment admissions where alcohol is the primary drug of abuse.

N/A = Information not available.

SOURCE: *State Alcohol and Drug Abuse Profile, FY 1989;* data are included for "only those programs which received at least some funds administered by the State Alcohol/Drug Agency" during the State's Fiscal Year (FY) 1989."

Table 20. Estimates of Intravenous (IV) Drug Abuser Client Treatment Admissions to State Funded and Non-State Funded Programs and Estimates of Total IV Drug Abusers by State for Fiscal Year 1989

State	Number of Admissions in *State Funded* Programs Who Were IV Drug Abusers	Basis of Estimate	Number of Admissions in *Non-State Funded* Programs Who Were IV Drugs Abusers	Basis of Estimate	Estimated Total Number IV Drug Abusers in State
Alabama	500	G	40	G	N/A
Alaska	584	G/IND	288	G	4,410
Arizona	2,648	G	N/A		5,313
Arkansas	783	IND	24	G	7,830
California	35,297	IND	36,388	IND	222,000 A
Colorado	2,431	IND	N/A		12,000
Connecticut	4,866	G/IND	N/A		35,000
Delaware	1,358	G	N/A		13,000
District of Col	2,804	G	N/A		16,000
Florida	11,911	G	3,522	G	67,192
Georgia	5,000	G/IND	N/A		N/A
Guam	2	IND	N/A		200
Hawaii	593	IND	N/A		1,200
Idaho	759	IND	N/A		2,896
Illinois	5,986	IND	645 B	IND	100,000

State	Number of Admissions in *State Funded* Programs Who Were IV Drug Abusers	Basis of Estimate	Number of Admissions in *Non-State Funded* Programs Who Were IV Drugs Abusers	Basis of Estimate	Estimated Total Number IV Drug Abusers in State
Indiana	2,863	G	5,135	G	28,220
Iowa	1,389	IND	1,000	G	14,883
Kansas	1,829	IND	2,341	IND	N/A
Kentucky	853	IND	N/A		5,000
Louisiana	3,100	IND	N/A		N/A
Maine	3,379	IND C	N/A	N/A	950
Maryland	7,741	IND	1,739	IND	45,000
Massachusetts	13,001	IND	2,000	G	40,000
Michigan	3,100	IND	N/A		50,000
Minnesota	1,300	IND	1,300	IND	4,500
Mississippi	N/A	G	N/A		N/A
Missouri	3,781	IND	N/A		22,000
Montana	963	IND	N/A		2,500
Nebraska	223	G	N/A		800
Nevada	700	G	400	G	5,000
New Hampshire	242	IND	630	G	9,000
New Jersey	5,782	IND	316	IND	40,000
New Mexico	672	G	N/A		N/A
New York	14,875	IND	2,600	IND	260,000
North Carolina	2,000	G	N/A		N/A
North Dakota	26	G	26	G	100
Ohio	4,000	IND	N/A		N/A
Oklahoma	1,900	G	800	G	14,000
Oregon	2,622	IND	N/A		26,220 D
Pennsylvania	9,731	IND	N/A		88,000
Puerto Rico	2,707	IND	1,054	IND	5,093
Rhode Island	2,016	G	N/A		10,080
South Carolina	1,500	G	N/A		N/A
South Dakota	183	IND	47	IND	1,530
Tennessee	1,688	IND	676	G	N/A
Texas	7,858	IND	N/A		188,000
Utah	671	G/IND	N/A		N/A
Vermont	700	IND	N/A		3,900 E
Virginia	1,933	G/IND	N/A		19,330
Washington	N/A		N/A		25,000
West Virginia	176	G	N/A		200
Wisconsin	5,779	G	125	G	21,000
Wyoming	N/A		N/A		N/A
TOTALS	**186,805**		**61,096**		**1,482,347**

A = California's 36,388 IV drug abuse admissions into non-State funded programs represent methadone clients only.
B = Non-State funded admissions figures represent non-hospital based services only.
C = Based on information obtained from new client information system recently implemented for FY 1989.
C = Information does not include drug detox clients.
D = Figures based on admit data collected on over 40% of client admits.

N/A = Information not available.

G = Guesstimate of number of admissions who were IV drug abusers.
IND = Individual client data were used to determine numbers of admissions who were IV drug abusers.

SOURCE: *State Alcohol and Drug Abuse Profile, FY 1989;* data are included for "only those programs which received at least some funds administered by the State Alcohol/Drug Agency during the State's Fiscal Year (FY) 1989."

Table 21. Sample Sizes and Response Rates

	Class of 1975	Class of 1976	Class of 1977	Class of 1978	Class of 1979
Number public schools	111	108	108	111	111
Number private schools	14	15	16	20	20
Total number schools	125	123	124	131	131
Total number students	15,791	16,678	18,436	18,924	16,662
Student response rate	78%	77%	79%	83%	82%

	Class of 1980	Class of 1981	Class of 1982	Class of 1983	Class of 1984	Class of 1985	Class of 1986	Class of 1987
Number public schools	107	109	116	112	117	115	113	117
Number private schools	20	19	21	22	17	17	16	18
Total number schools	127	128	137	134	134	132	129	135
Total number students	16,524	18,267	18,348	16,947	16,499	16,502	15,713	16,843
Student response rate	82%	81%	83%	84%	83%	84%	83%	84%

SOURCE: DHHS Publication No. (ADM) 89-1602, 1986. *Illicit Drug Use, Smoking and Drinking by America's High School Students, College Students, and Young Adults,* 1985–1987.

Table 22. Lifetime Prevalence (Percent Ever Used) of Eighteen Types of Drugs: Observed Estimates and 95% Confidence Limits, Class of 1987

(Approx. N = 16,300)

	Lower Limit	Observed Estimate	Upper Limit
Marijuana/Hashish	48.1	50.2	52.3
Inhalants[a]	15.9	17.0	18.2
Inhalants Adjusted[b]	*17.3*	*18.6*	*20.0*
Amyl & Butyl Nitrites[c]	3.8	4.7	5.8
Hallucinogens	9.2	10.3	11.5
Hallucinogens Adjusted[d]	*9.6*	*10.6*	*11.6*
LSD	7.4	8.4	9.5
PCP[c]	2.3	3.0	4.0
Cocaine	13.9	15.2	16.6
"Crack"[g]	5.0	5.6	6.3
Other cocaine[c]	12.5	14.0	15.7
Heroin	0.9	1.2	1.5
Other opiates[e]	8.5	9.2	10.0
Stimulants Adjusted[e,f]	*20.1*	*21.6*	*23.1*
Sedatives[e]	7.7	8.7	9.8
Barbiturates[e]	6.5	7.4	8.4
Methaqualone[e]	3.3	4.0	4.8
Tranquilizers[e]	9.8	10.9	12.1

	Lower Limit	Observed Estimate	Upper Limit
Alcohol	90.7	92.2	93.5
Cigarettes	65.5	67.2	68.9

[a]Data based on four questionnaire forms. N is four-fifths of N indicated.
[b]Adjusted for underreporting of amyl and butyl nitrites. See text for details.
[c]Data based on a single questionnaire form. N is one-fifth of N indicated.
[d]Adjusted for underreporting of PCP. See text for details.
[e]Only drug use which was not under a doctor's orders is included here.
[f]Based on the data from the revised question, which attempts to exclude the inappropriate reporting of non-prescription stimulants.
[g]Data based on two questionnaire forms. N is two-fifths of N indicated.

SOURCE: 1987 National High School Senior Drug Abuse Survey "Monitoring the Future Survey" University of Michigan Institute for Social Research.

Table 23. Lifetime Prevalence (Percent Ever Used) and Recency of Use of Eighteen Types of Drugs, Class of 1987

(Approx. N = 16,300)

	Ever Used	Past Month	Past Year, Not Past Month	Not Past Year	Never Used
Marijuana/Hashish	50.2	21.0	15.3	13.9	49.8
Inhalants[a]	17.0	2.8	4.1	10.1	83.0
Inhalants Adjusted[b]	*18.6*	*3.5*	*4.6*	*10.5*	*81.4*
Amyl & Butyl Nitrites[c]	4.7	1.3	1.3	2.1	95.3
Hallucinogens	10.3	2.5	3.9	3.9	89.7
Hallucinogens Adjusted[d]	*10.6*	*2.8*	*3.9*	*3.9*	*89.4*
LSD	8.4	1.8	3.4	3.2	91.6
PCP[c]	3.0	0.6	0.7	1.7	97.0
Cocaine	15.2	4.3	6.0	4.9	84.8
"Crack"[h]	5.6	1.5	2.5	1.6	94.4
Other cocaine[c]	14.0	4.1	5.7	4.2	86.0
Heroin	1.2	0.2	0.3	0.7	98.8
Other opiates[e]	9.2	1.8	3.5	3.9	90.8
Stimulants Adjusted[e,f]	*21.6*	*5.2*	*7.0*	*9.4*	*78.4*
Sedatives[e]	8.7	1.7	2.4	4.6	91.3
Barbiturates[e]	7.4	1.4	2.2	3.8	92.6
Methaqualone[e]	4.0	0.6	0.9	2.5	96.0
Tranquilizers[e]	10.9	2.0	3.5	5.4	89.1
Alcohol	92.2	66.4	19.3	6.5	7.8
Cigarettes	67.2	29.4	(37.8)[g]		32.8

[a]Data based on four questionnaire forms. N is four-fifths of N indicated.
[b]Adjusted for underreporting of amyl and butyl nitrites. See text for details.
[c]Data based on a single questionnaire form. N is one-fifth of N indicated.
[d]Adjusted for underreporting of PCP. See text for details.
[e]Only drug use which was not under a doctor's orders is included here.
[f]Based on the data from the revised question, which attempts to exclude the inappropriate reporting of non-prescription stimulants.
[g]The combined total for the two columns is shown because the question asked did not discriminate between the two answer categories.
[h]Data based on two questionnaire forms. N is two-fifths of N indicated.

Figure 4. Prevalence and Recency of Use Thirteen types of drugs, class of 1988

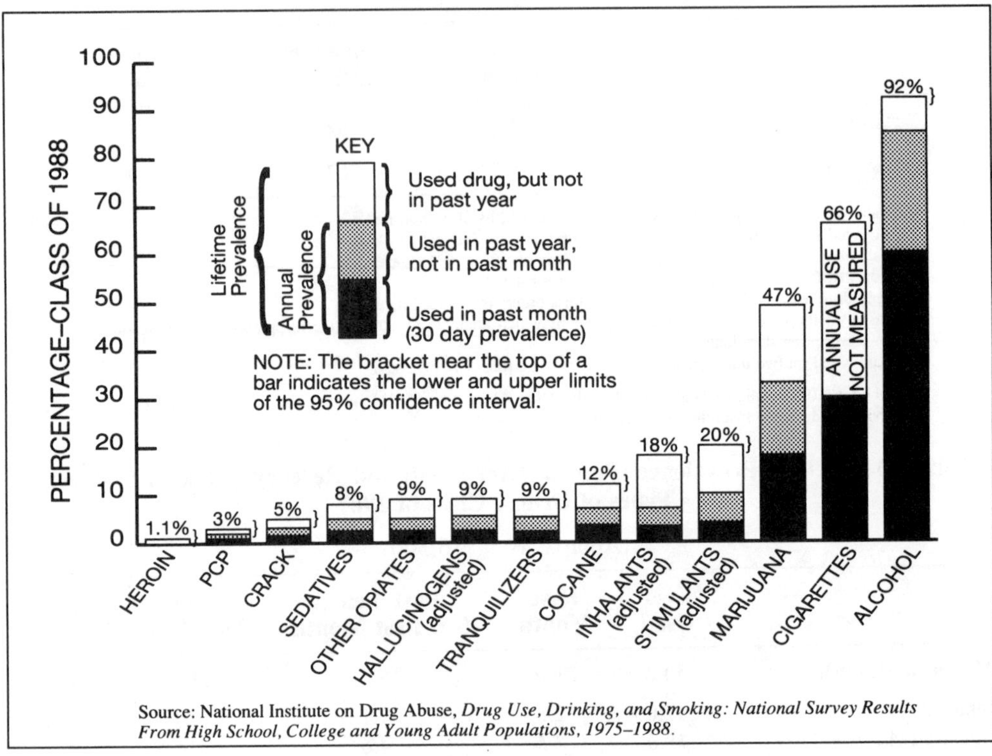

Source: National Institute on Drug Abuse, *Drug Use, Drinking, and Smoking: National Survey Results From High School, College and Young Adult Populations, 1975–1988.*

Figure 5. Thirty-Day Prevalence of Daily Use Thirteen Types of Drugs, Class of 1988

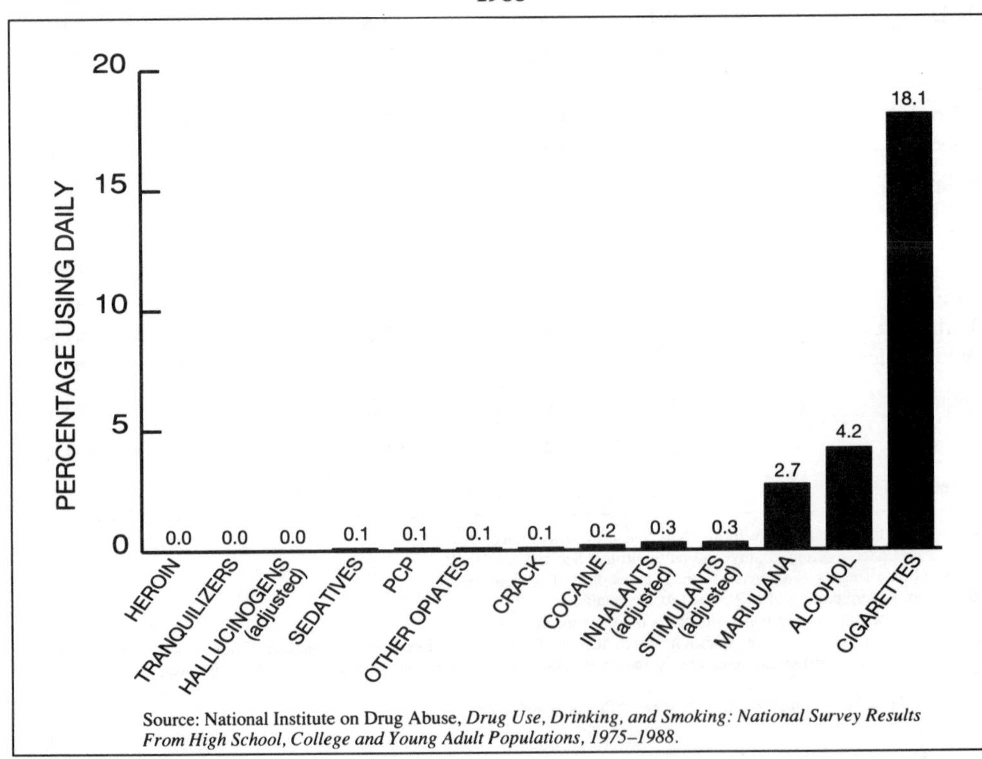

Source: National Institute on Drug Abuse, *Drug Use, Drinking, and Smoking: National Survey Results From High School, College and Young Adult Populations, 1975–1988.*

Figure 6. Noncontinuation Rates: Percent of Seniors Who Used Drug Once or More in Lifetime but Did Not Use in Past Year

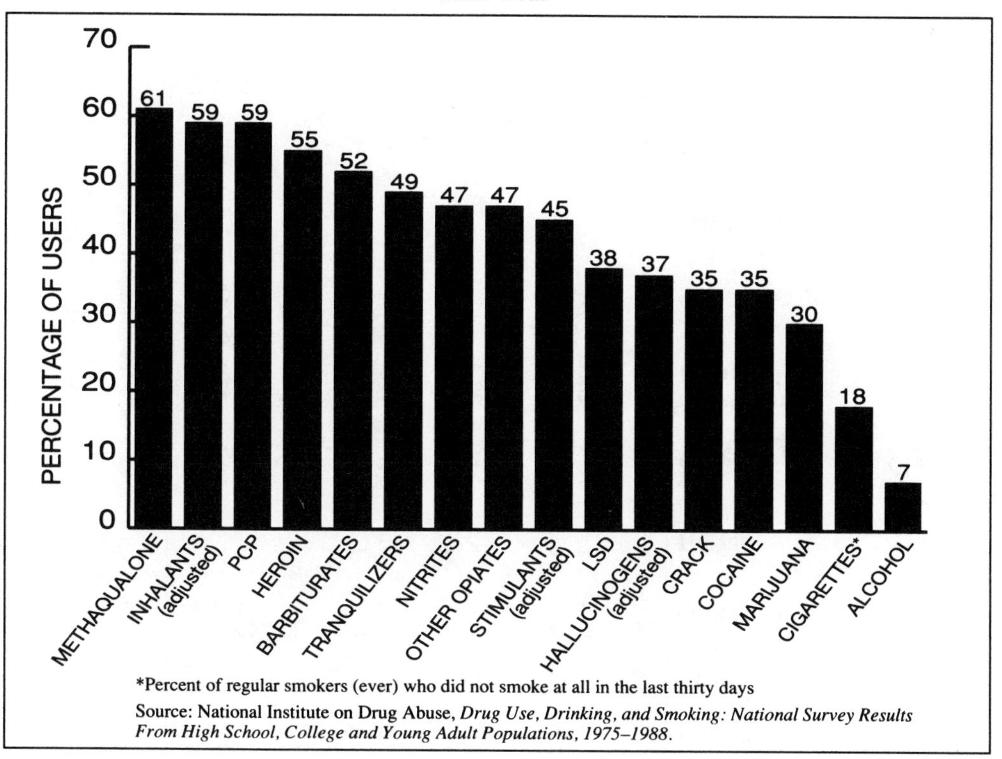

*Percent of regular smokers (ever) who did not smoke at all in the last thirty days

Source: National Institute on Drug Abuse, *Drug Use, Drinking, and Smoking: National Survey Results From High School, College and Young Adult Populations, 1975–1988.*

Table 24. Lifetime Prevalence of Use of Eighteen Types of Drugs by Subgroups, Class of 1987 (Entries are percentages)

	Marijuana	Inhalants[a]	Amyl/Butyl Nitrites	Hallucinogens[a]	LSD	PCP	Cocaine[b]	"Crack"[b]	Other Cocaine[b]	Heroin	Other Opiates	Stimulants[c] (adjusted)	Sedatives	Barbiturates	Methaqualone	Tranquilizers	Alcohol	Cigarettes
All Seniors	50.2	17.0	4.7	10.3	8.4	3.0	15.2	5.6	14.0	1.2	9.2	21.6	8.7	7.4	4.0	10.9	92.2	67.2
Sex:																		
Male	52.0	20.1	6.2	11.3	9.7	3.8	16.5	6.7	15.4	1.6	10.1	20.1	9.3	7.9	4.7	10.5	92.4	65.1
Female	48.0	14.2	3.5	8.9	6.8	2.3	13.6	4.2	12.0	0.8	8.3	22.9	8.0	6.7	3.3	11.0	92.2	68.9
College Plans:																		
None or under 4 yrs	57.0	19.6	5.8	13.1	11.3	4.9	18.4	7.9	14.8	1.5	10.9	28.1	11.2	9.7	5.1	13.1	93.2	74.9
Complete 4 yrs	46.4	15.9	4.3	8.5	6.6	2.0	13.2	3.8	11.9	1.0	8.3	18.4	7.4	6.2	3.4	9.9	92.1	63.0
Region:																		
Northeast	55.7	16.6	5.7	12.6	8.6	3.6	18.5	5.9	17.1	1.2	10.0	19.3	9.7	7.8	5.0	12.4	94.0	70.1
North Central	50.1	17.9	4.2	9.6	8.0	3.0	11.1	4.8	10.9	1.3	8.5	22.9	7.8	6.8	3.4	8.9	93.6	68.0
South	43.6	15.4	3.8	8.3	7.2	2.2	11.3	4.1	9.3	1.2	8.1	20.7	9.0	7.5	4.1	11.7	89.5	64.4
West	55.1	19.2	6.1	11.9	10.7	3.9	23.7	8.9	22.9	1.1	11.0	23.8	8.5	7.4	3.8	10.5	92.8	67.7
Population Density:																		
Large SMSA	53.2	16.3	4.8	13.0	8.9	3.8	18.0	6.7	17.1	1.1	9.1	20.5	8.5	6.9	4.0	11.2	92.1	66.4
Other SMSA	52.0	17.0	4.0	10.0	9.0	2.5	15.7	5.3	13.8	1.3	9.6	22.1	9.0	7.5	4.5	11.1	92.7	66.9
Non-SMSA	43.5	17.9	6.0	8.0	6.8	3.2	11.3	4.9	11.2	1.2	8.5	21.8	8.3	7.4	3.3	10.1	91.3	68.7

[a] Unadjusted for known underreporting of certain drugs. See text for details.
[b] Cocaine data based on five questionnaire forms, "crack" data based on two questionnaire forms, and other cocaine data based on one questionnaire form.
[c] Based on the data from the revised question, which attempts to exclude the inappropriate reporting of non-prescription stimulants.

Table 25. Trends in Lifetime Prevalence of Eighteen Types of Drugs

	Percent Ever Used													
	Class of 1975	Class of 1976	Class of 1977	Class of 1978	Class of 1979	Class of 1980	Class of 1981	Class of 1982	Class of 1983	Class of 1984	Class of 1985	Class of 1986	Class of 1987	'86–'87 Change
Approx. N =	**(9400)**	**(15400)**	**(17100)**	**(17800)**	**(15500)**	**(15900)**	**(17500)**	**(17700)**	**(16300)**	**(15900)**	**(16000)**	**(15200)**	**(16300)**	
Marijuana/Hashish	47.3	52.8	56.4	59.2	60.4	60.3	59.5	58.7	57.0	54.9	54.2	50.9	50.2	−0.7
Inhalants[a]	NA	10.3	11.1	12.0	12.7	11.9	12.3	12.8	13.6	14.4	15.4	15.9	17.0	+1.1
Inhalants Adjusted[b]	*NA*	*NA*	*NA*	*NA*	*18.2*	*17.3*	*17.2*	*17.7*	*18.2*	*18.0*	*18.1*	*20.1*	*18.6*	*−1.5*
Amyl & Butyl Nitrites[c,h]	NA	NA	NA	NA	11.1	11.1	10.1	9.8	8.4	8.1	7.9	8.6	4.7	−3.9sss
Hallucinogens	16.3	15.1	13.9	14.3	14.1	13.3	13.3	12.5	11.9	10.7	10.3	9.7	10.3	+0.6
Hallucinogens Adjusted[d]	*NA*	*NA*	*NA*	*NA*	*17.7*	*15.6*	*15.3*	*14.3*	*13.6*	*12.3*	*12.1*	*11.9*	*10.6*	*−1.3s*
LSD	11.3	11.0	9.8	9.7	9.5	9.3	9.8	9.6	8.9	8.0	7.5	7.2	8.4	+1.2*s*
PCP[c,h]	NA	NA	NA	NA	12.8	9.6	7.8	6.0	5.6	5.0	4.9	4.8	3.0	−1.8ss
Cocaine	9.0	9.7	10.8	12.9	15.4	15.7	16.5	16.0	16.2	16.1	17.3	16.9	15.2	−1.7s
"Crack"[g]	NA	NA	NA	NA	NA	NA	NA	NA	NA	NA	NA	NA	5.6	NA
Other cocaine[c]	NA	NA	NA	NA	NA	NA	NA	NA	NA	NA	NA	NA	14.0	NA
Heroin	2.2	1.8	1.8	1.6	1.1	1.1	1.1	1.2	1.2	1.3	1.2	1.1	1.2	+0.1
Other opiates[e]	9.0	9.6	10.3	9.9	10.1	9.8	10.1	9.6	9.4	9.7	10.2	9.0	9.2	+0.2
Stimulants[e]	22.3	22.6	23.0	22.9	24.2	26.4	32.2	35.6	35.4	NA	NA	NA	NA	NA
Stimulants Adjusted[e,f]	*NA*	*NA*	*NA*	*NA*	*NA*	*NA*	*NA*	*27.9*	*26.9*	*27.9*	*26.2*	*23.4*	*21.6*	*−1.8s*
Sedatives[e]	18.2	17.7	17.4	16.0	14.6	14.9	16.0	15.2	14.4	13.3	11.8	10.4	8.7	−1.7ss
Barbiturates[e]	16.9	16.2	15.6	13.7	11.8	11.0	11.3	10.3	9.9	9.9	9.2	8.4	7.4	−1.0
Methaqualone[e]	8.1	7.8	8.5	7.9	8.3	9.5	10.6	10.7	10.1	8.3	6.7	5.2	4.0	−1.2ss
Tranquilizers[e]	17.0	16.8	18.0	17.0	16.3	15.2	14.7	14.0	13.3	12.4	11.9	10.9	10.9	0.0
Alcohol	90.4	91.9	92.5	93.1	93.0	93.2	92.6	92.8	92.6	92.6	92.2	91.3	92.2	+0.9
Cigarettes	73.6	75.4	75.7	75.3	74.0	71.0	71.0	70.1	70.6	69.7	68.8	67.6	67.2	−0.4

NOTES: Level of significance of difference between the two most recent classes: s = .05, ss = .01, sss = .001. NA indicates data not available.

[a]Data based on four questionnaire forms. N is four-fifths of N indicated.
[b]Adjusted for underreporting of amyl and butyl nitrites. See text for details.
[c]Data based on a single questionnaire form. N is one-fifth of N indicated.
[d]Adjusted for underreporting of PCP. See text for details.
[e]Only drug use which was not under a doctor's orders is included here.
[f]Based on the data from the revised question, which attempts to exclude the inappropriate reporting of non-prescription stimulants.
[g]Data based on two questionnaire forms. N is two-fifths of N indicated.
[h]Question text changed slightly in 1987.

Table 26. Trends in Annual Prevalence of Eighteen Types of Drugs

	Percent Who Used in Last Twelve Months													
	Class of 1975	Class of 1976	Class of 1977	Class of 1978	Class of 1979	Class of 1980	Class of 1981	Class of 1982	Class of 1983	Class of 1984	Class of 1985	Class of 1986	Class of 1987	'86–'87 Change
Approx. N =	**(9400)**	**(15400)**	**(17100)**	**(17800)**	**(15500)**	**(15900)**	**(17500)**	**(17700)**	**(16300)**	**(15900)**	**(16000)**	**(15200)**	**(16300)**	
Marijuana/Hashish	40.0	44.5	47.6	50.2	50.8	48.8	46.1	44.3	42.3	40.0	40.6	38.8	36.3	−2.5s
Inhalants[a]	NA	3.0	3.7	4.1	5.4	4.6	4.1	4.5	4.3	5.1	5.7	6.1	6.9	+0.8
Inhalants Adjusted[b]	*NA*	*NA*	*NA*	*NA*	*8.9*	*7.9*	*6.1*	*6.6*	*6.2*	*7.2*	*7.5*	*8.9*	*8.1*	*−0.8*
Amyl & Butyl Nitrites[c,h]	NA	NA	NA	NA	6.5	5.7	3.7	3.6	3.6	4.0	4.0	4.7	2.6	−2.1sss
Hallucinogens	11.2	9.4	8.8	9.6	9.9	9.3	9.0	8.1	7.3	6.5	6.3	6.0	6.4	+0.4
Hallucinogens Adjusted[d]	*NA*	*NA*	*NA*	*NA*	*11.8*	*10.4*	*10.1*	*9.0*	*8.3*	*7.3*	*7.6*	*7.6*	*6.7*	*−0.9*
LSD	7.2	6.4	5.5	6.3	6.6	6.5	6.5	6.1	5.4	4.7	4.4	4.5	5.2	+0.7
PCP[c,h]	NA	NA	NA	NA	7.0	4.4	3.2	2.2	2.6	2.3	2.9	2.4	1.3	−1.1ss
Cocaine	5.6	6.0	7.2	9.0	12.0	12.3	12.4	11.5	11.4	11.6	13.1	12.7	10.3	−2.4sss
"Crack"[g]	NA	NA	NA	NA	NA	NA	NA	NA	NA	NA	NA	4.1	4.0	−0.1
Other cocaine[c]	NA	NA	NA	NA	NA	NA	NA	NA	NA	NA	NA	NA	9.8	NA
Heroin	1.0	0.8	0.8	0.8	0.5	0.5	0.5	0.6	0.6	0.5	0.6	0.5	0.5	0.0
Other opiates[e]	5.7	5.7	6.4	6.0	6.2	6.3	5.9	5.3	5.1	5.2	5.9	5.2	5.3	+0.1
Stimulants[e]	16.2	15.8	16.3	17.1	18.3	20.8	26.0	26.1	24.6	NA	NA	NA	NA	NA
Stimulants Adjusted[e,f]	*NA*	*NA*	*NA*	*NA*	*NA*	*NA*	*NA*	*20.3*	*17.9*	*17.7*	*15.8*	*13.4*	*12.2*	*−1.2*
Sedatives[e]	11.7	10.7	10.8	9.9	9.9	10.3	10.5	9.1	7.9	6.6	5.8	5.2	4.1	−1.1ss
Barbiturates[e]	10.7	9.6	9.3	8.1	7.5	6.8	6.6	5.5	5.2	4.9	4.6	4.2	3.6	−0.6
Methaqualone[e]	5.1	4.7	5.2	4.9	5.9	7.2	7.6	6.8	5.4	3.8	2.8	2.1	1.5	−0.6s
Tranquilizers[e]	10.6	10.3	10.8	9.9	9.6	8.7	8.0	7.0	6.9	6.1	6.1	5.8	5.5	−0.3
Alcohol	84.8	85.7	87.0	87.7	88.1	87.9	87.0	86.8	87.3	86.0	85.6	84.5	85.7	+1.2
Cigarettes	NA	NA	NA	NA	NA	NA	NA	NA	NA	NA	NA	NA	NA	NA

NOTES: Level of significance of difference between the two most recent classes: s = .05, ss = .01, sss = .001. NA indicates data not available.

[a]Data based on four questionnaire forms. N is four-fifths of N indicated.
[b]Adjusted for underreporting of amyl and butyl nitrites. See text for details.
[c]Data based on a single questionnaire form. N is one-fifth of N indicated.
[d]Adjusted for underreporting of PCP. See text for details.
[e]Only drug use which was not under a doctor's orders is included here.
[f]Based on the data from the revised question, which attempts to exclude the inappropriate reporting of non-prescription stimulants.
[g]Data based on a single questionnaire form in 1986 (N is one-fifth of N indicated), and on two questionnaire forms in 1987 (N is two-fifths of N indicated).
[h]Question text changed slightly in 1987.

Percent Who Used Daily in Last Thirty Days

	Class of 1975	Class of 1976	Class of 1977	Class of 1978	Class of 1979	Class of 1980	Class of 1981	Class of 1982	Class of 1983	Class of 1984	Class of 1985	Class of 1986	Class of 1987	'86–'87 Change[g]
Approx. N =	**(9400)**	**(15400)**	**(17100)**	**(17800)**	**(15500)**	**(15900)**	**(17500)**	**(17700)**	**(16300)**	**(15900)**	**(16000)**	**(15200)**	**(16300)**	
Marijuana/Hashish	6.0	8.2	9.1	10.7	10.3	9.1	7.0	6.3	5.5	5.0	4.9	4.0	3.3	−0.7s
Inhalants[a]	NA	0.0	0.0	0.1	0.0	0.1	0.1	0.1	0.1	0.1	0.2	0.2	0.1	−0.1
Inhalants Adjusted[b]	*NA*	*NA*	*NA*	*NA*	*0.1*	*0.2*	*0.2*	*0.2*	*0.2*	*0.2*	*0.4*	*0.4*	*0.4*	*0.0*
Amyl & Butyl Nitrites[c,i]	NA	NA	NA	NA	0.0	0.1	0.1	0.0	0.2	0.1	0.3	0.5	0.3	−0.2
Hallucinogens	0.1	0.1	0.1	0.1	0.1	0.1	0.1	0.1	0.1	0.1	0.1	0.1	0.1	0.0
Hallucinogens Adjusted[d]	*NA*	*NA*	*NA*	*NA*	*0.2*	*0.2*	*0.1*	*0.2*	*0.2*	*0.2*	*0.3*	*0.3*	*0.2*	*0.0*[g]
LSD	0.0	0.0	0.0	0.0	0.0	0.0	0.1	0.0	0.1	0.1	0.1	0.0	0.1	0.0[g]
PCP[c,i]	NA	NA	NA	NA	0.1	0.1	0.1	0.1	0.1	0.1	0.3	0.2	0.3	+0.1
Cocaine	0.1	0.1	0.1	0.1	0.2	0.2	0.3	0.2	0.2	0.2	0.4	0.4	0.3	−0.2[g]
"Crack"[h]	NA	NA	NA	NA	NA	NA	NA	NA	NA	NA	NA	NA	0.2	NA
Other cocaine[c]	NA	NA	NA	NA	NA	NA	NA	NA	NA	NA	NA	NA	0.2	NA
Heroin	0.1	0.0	0.0	0.0	0.0	0.0	0.0	0.0	0.1	0.0	0.0	0.0	0.0	0.0
Other opiates[e]	0.1	0.1	0.2	0.1	0.0	0.1	0.1	0.1	0.1	0.1	0.1	0.1	0.1	0.0
Stimulants[e]	0.5	0.4	0.5	0.5	0.6	0.7	1.2	1.1	1.1	NA	NA	NA	NA	NA
Stimulants Adjusted[e,f]	*NA*	*NA*	*NA*	*NA*	*NA*	*NA*	*NA*	*0.7*	*0.8*	*0.6*	*0.4*	*0.3*	*0.3*	*0.0*
Sedatives[e]	0.3	0.2	0.2	0.2	0.1	0.2	0.2	0.2	0.2	0.1	0.1	0.1	0.1	0.0
Barbiturates[e]	0.1	0.1	0.2	0.1	0.0	0.1	0.1	0.1	0.1	0.0	0.1	0.1	0.1	0.0
Methaqualone[e]	0.0	0.0	0.0	0.0	0.0	0.1	0.1	0.1	0.0	0.0	0.0	0.0	0.0	0.0
Tranquilizers[e]	0.1	0.2	0.3	0.1	0.1	0.1	0.1	0.1	0.1	0.1	0.0	0.0	0.1	0.0[g]
Alcohol														
Daily	5.7	5.6	6.1	5.7	6.9	6.0	6.0	5.7	5.5	4.8	5.0	4.8	4.8	0.0
5+ drinks in a row/ last 2 weeks	36.8	37.1	39.4	40.3	41.2	41.2	41.4	40.5	40.8	38.7	36.7	36.8	37.5	+0.7
Cigarettes														
Daily	26.9	28.8	28.8	27.5	25.4	21.3	20.3	21.1	21.2	18.7	19.5	18.7	18.7	0.0
Half-pack or more per day	17.9	19.2	19.4	18.8	16.5	14.3	13.5	14.2	13.8	12.3	12.5	11.4	11.4	0.0

NOTES: Level of significance of difference between the two most recent classes: s = .05, ss = .01, sss = .001. NA indicates data not available.

[a]Data based on four questionnaire forms. N is four-fifths of N indicated.
[b]Adjusted for underreporting of amyl and butyl nitrites. See text for details.
[c]Data based on a single questionnaire form. N is one-fifth of N indicated.
[d]Adjusted for underreporting of PCP. See text for details.
[e]Only drug use which was not under a doctor's orders is included here.
[f]Based on the data from the revised question, which attempts to exclude the inappropriate reporting of non-prescription stimulants.
[g]Any apparent inconsistency between the change estimate and the prevalence estimates for the two most recent classes is due to rounding error.
[h]Data based on two questionnaire forms. N is two-fifths of N indicated.
[i]Question text changed slightly in 1987.

Figure 7. Trends in Thirty-Day Prevalence of an Illicit Drug Use Index—All Seniors

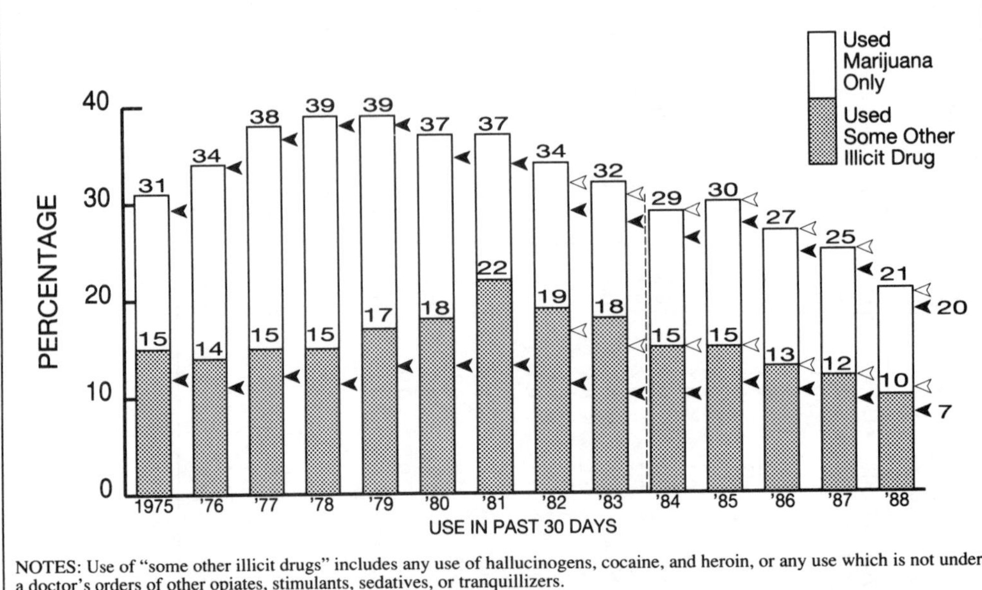

NOTES: Use of "some other illicit drugs" includes any use of hallucinogens, cocaine, and heroin, or any use which is not under a doctor's orders of other opiates, stimulants, sedatives, or tranquillizers.
◀ indicates the percentage which results if all stimulants are excluded from the definition of "illicit drugs."
◁ shows the percentage which results if only non–prescription stimulants are excluded.
The dashed vertical line indicates that after 1983 the shaded and open bars are defined by using the amphetamine questions which were revised to exclude non-prescription stimulants from the definition of "illicit drugs."
Source: National Institute on Drug Abuse, *Drug Use, Drinking, and Smoking: National Survey Results From High School, College and Young Adult Populations, 1975–1988.*

Figure 8. Trends in Lifetime Prevalence of an Illicit Drug Use Index—All Seniors

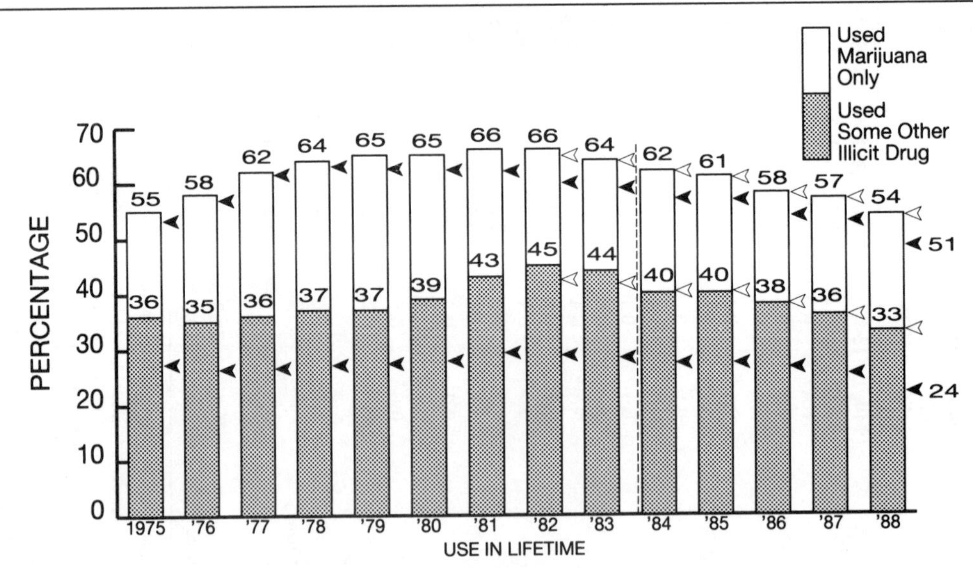

NOTES: Use of "some other illicit drugs" includes any use of hallucinogens, cocaine, and heroin, or any use which is not under a doctor's orders of other opiates, stimulants, sedatives, or tranquillizers.
◀ indicates the percentage which results if all stimulants are excluded from the definition of "illicit drugs."
◁ shows the percentage which results if only non–prescription stimulants are excluded.
The dashed vertical line indicates that after 1983 the shaded and open bars are defined by using the amphetamine questions which were revised to exclude non-prescription stimulants from the definition of "illicit drugs."
Source: National Institute on Drug Abuse, *Drug Use, Drinking, and Smoking: National Survey Results From High School, College and Young Adult Populations, 1975–1988.*

Figure 9. Estimated Coca Leaf Production in Three Andean Countries, 1985–88

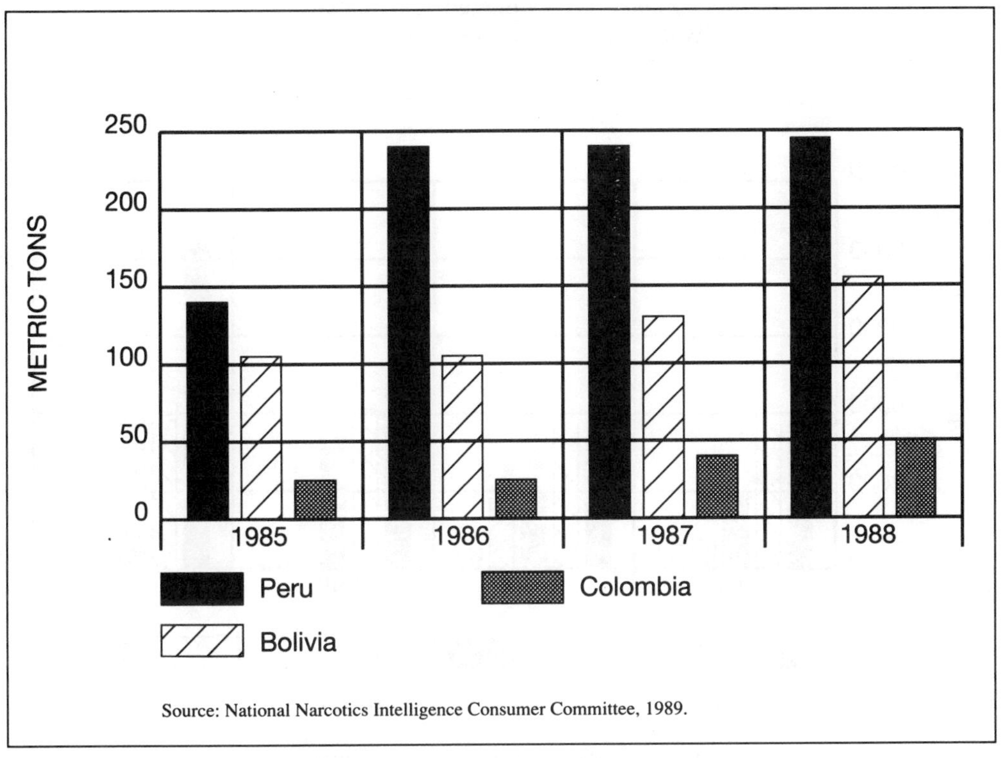

Source: National Narcotics Intelligence Consumer Committee, 1989.

Figure 10. Estimated Opium Production in Six Countries, 1985–88

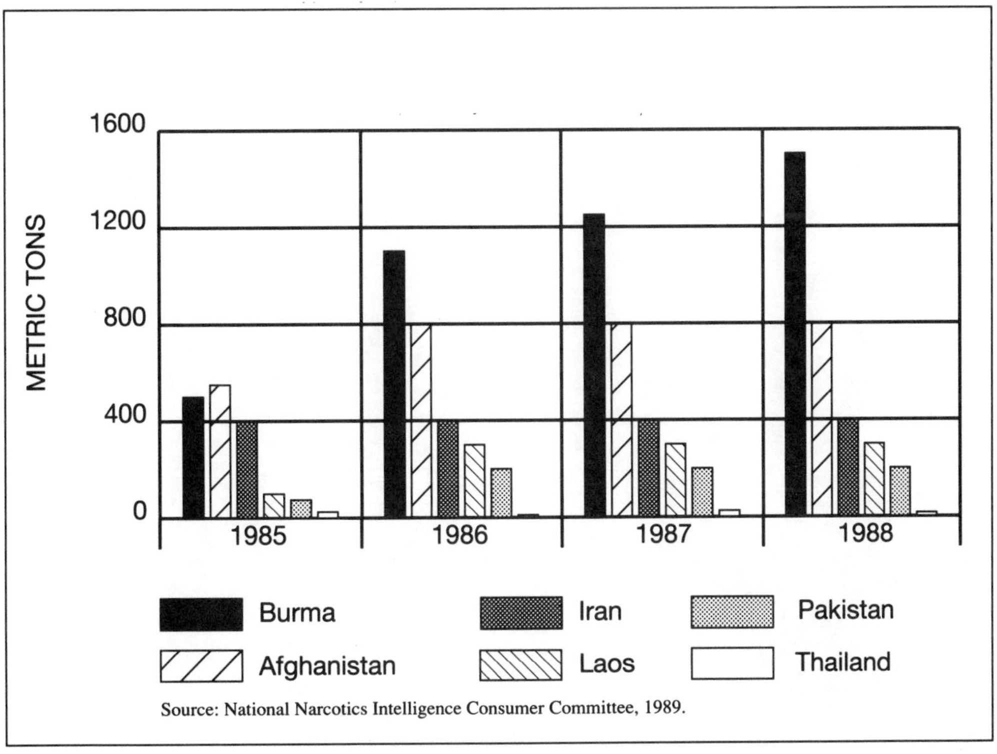

Source: National Narcotics Intelligence Consumer Committee, 1989.

Figure 11. Estimated Marijuana Production in Five Countries, 1985–88

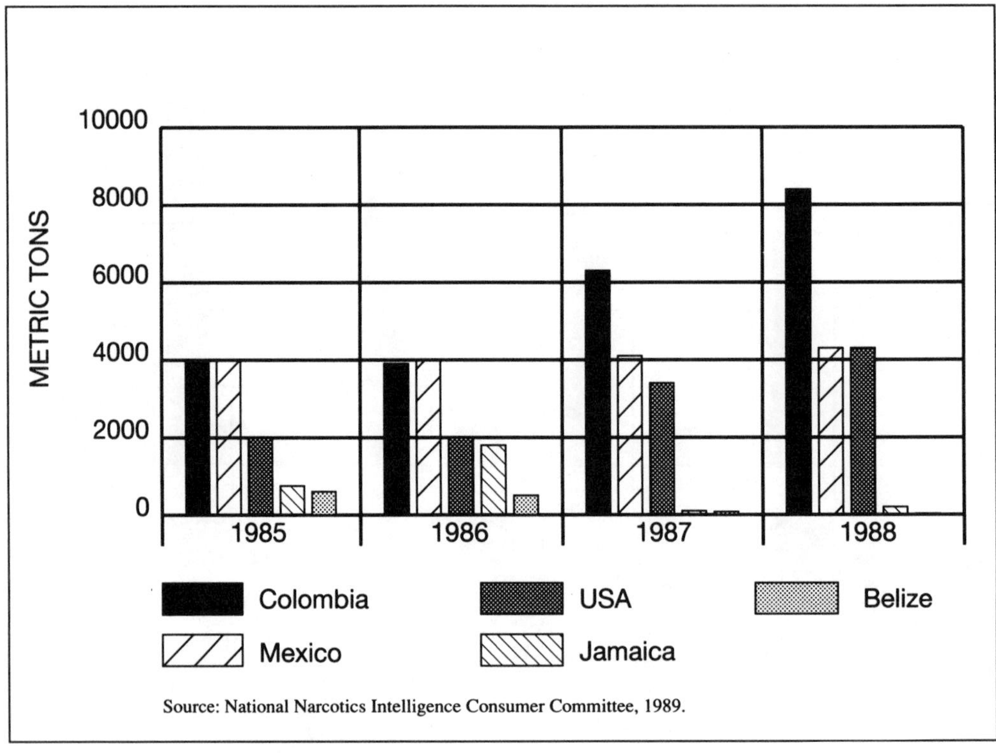

Source: National Narcotics Intelligence Consumer Committee, 1989.

Table 28. Federal Trafficking Penalties

<table>
<tr><th rowspan="2">CSA</th><th colspan="2">PENALTY</th><th rowspan="2">Quantity</th><th rowspan="2">DRUG</th><th rowspan="2">Quantity</th><th colspan="2">PENALTY</th></tr>
<tr><th>2nd Offense</th><th>1st Offense</th><th>1st Offense</th><th>2nd Offense</th></tr>
<tr><td rowspan="8">I

and

II</td><td rowspan="8">Not less than 10 years. Not more than life.

If death or serious injury, not less than life.

Fine of not more than $4 million individual, $10 million other than individual.</td><td rowspan="8">Not less than 5 years. Not more than 40 years.

If death or serious injury, not less than 20 years. Not more than life.

Fine of not more than $2 million individual, $5 million other than individual.</td><td>10–99 gm or 100–999 gm mixture</td><td>METHAMPHETAMINE</td><td>100 gm or more or 1 kg[1] or more mixture</td><td rowspan="8">Not less than 10 years. Not more than life.

If death or serious injury, not less than 20 years. Not more than life.

Fine of not more than $4 million individual, $10 million other than individual.</td><td rowspan="8">Not less than 20 years. Not more than life.

If death or serious injury, not less than life.

Fine of not more than $8 million individual, $20 million other than individual.</td></tr>
<tr><td>100–999 gm mixture</td><td>HEROIN</td><td>1 kg or more mixture</td></tr>
<tr><td>500–4,999 gm mixture</td><td>COCAINE</td><td>5 kg or more mixture</td></tr>
<tr><td>5–49 gm mixture</td><td>COCAINE BASE</td><td>50 gm or more mixture</td></tr>
<tr><td>10–99 gm or 100–999 gm mixture</td><td>PCP</td><td>100 gm or more or 1 kg or more mixture</td></tr>
<tr><td>1–10 gm mixture</td><td>LSD</td><td>10 gm or more mixture</td></tr>
<tr><td>40–399 gm mixture</td><td>FENTANYL</td><td>400 gm or more mixture</td></tr>
<tr><td>10–99 gm mixture</td><td>FENTANYL ANALOGUE</td><td>100 gm or more mixture</td></tr>
</table>

	Drug	Quantity	First Offense	Second Offense
	Others*	Any	Not more than 20 years. If death or serious injury, not less than 20 years, not more than life. Fine $1 million individual, $5 million not individual.	Not more than 30 years. If death or serious injury, life. Fine $2 million individual, $10 million not individual.
III	All	Any	Not more than 5 years. Fine not more than $250,000 individual, $1 million not individual.	Not more than 10 years. Fine not more than $500,000 individual, $2 million not individual.
IV	All	Any	Not more than 3 years. Fine not more than $250,000 individual, $1 million not individual.	Not more than 6 years. Fine not more than $500,000 individual, $2 million not individual.
V	All	Any	Not more than 1 year. Fine not more than $100,000 individual, $250,000 not individual.	Not more than 2 years. Fine not more than $200,000 individual, $500,000 not individual.

*Does not include marijuana, hashish, or hashish oil. (See separate chart.)

NOTE: CSA is the Controlled Substances Act.

SOURCE: U.S. Department of Justice, Drug Enforcement Administration, 1988.

[1] Law as originally enacted states 100 gm. Congress requested to make technical correction to 1 kg.

Table 29. Federal Trafficking Penalties—Marijuana

Quantity	Description	First Offense	Second Offense
1,000 kg or more or 1,000 or more plants	Marijuana Mixture containing detectable quantity*	Not less than 10 years, not more than life. If death or serious injury, not less than 20 years, not more than life. Fine not more than $4 million individual, $10 million other than individual.	Not less than 20 years, not more than life. If death or serious injury, not less than life. Fine not more than $8 million individual, $20 million other than individual.
100 kg to 1,000 kg or 100 to 999 plants	Marijuana Mixture containing detectable quantity*	Not less than 5 years, not more than 40 years. If death or serious injury, not less than 20 years, not more than life. Fine not more than $2 million individual, $5 million other than individual.	Not less than 10 years, not more than life. If death or serious injury, not less than life. Fine not more than $4 million individual, $10 million other than individual.
50 to 100 kg	Marijuana	Not more than 20 years. If death or serious injury, not less than 20 years, not more than life. Fine $1 million individual, $5 million other than individual.	Not more than 30 years. If death or serious injury, life. Fine $2 million individual, $10 million other than individual.
10 to 100 kg	Hashish		
1 to 100 kg	Hashish Oil		
50 to 99 plants	Marijuana		
Less than 50 kg	Marijuana	Not more than 5 years Fine not more than $250,000, $1 million other than individual.	Not more than 10 years. Fine $500,000 individual, $2 million other than individual.
Less than 10 kg	Hashish		
Less than 1 kg	Hashish Oil		

*Includes hashish and hash oil (Marijuana is a Schedule I controlled substance.)

SOURCE: U.S. Department of Justice, Drug Enforcement Administration, 1988.

Table 30. Regulatory Requirements

Controlled Substances	Schedule I	Schedule II	Schedule III	Schedule IV	Schedule V
REGISTRATION	required	required	required	required	required
RECORDKEEPING	separate	separate	readily retrievable	readily retrievable	readily retrievable
DISTRIBUTION RESTRICTIONS	order forms	order forms	records required	records required	records required
DISPENSING LIMITS	research use only	Rx: written; no refills	Rx: written or oral; refills *Note 1*	Rx: written or oral; refills *Note 1*	OTC (Rx drugs limited to M.D.'s order)
MANUFACTURING Security	vault/sale	vault/safe	secure storage area	secure storage area	secure storage area
MANUFACTURING Quotas	yes	yes	NO but some drugs limited by Schedule II	NO but some drugs limited by Schedule II	NO but some drugs limited by Schedule II
IMPORT/EXPORT Narcotic	permit	permit	permit	permit	permit to import; declaration to export
IMPORT/EXPORT Non-Narcotic	permit	permit	*Note 2*	declaration	declaration
REPORTS TO DEA by Manufacturer/Distributor Narcotic	yes	yes	yes	manufacturer only	manufacturer only
REPORTS TO DEA by Manufacturer/Distributor Non-Narcotic	yes	yes	*Note 3*	*Note 3*	no

Note 1: With Medical authorization, refills up to 5 in 6 months
Note 2: Permit for some drugs, declaration for others
Note 3: Manufacturer reports required for specific drugs

SOURCE: U.S. Department of Justice, Drug Enforcement Administration, 1988.

Table 31. Domestic Statistical Summary

	FY 1981	FY 1982	FY 1983	FY 1984	FY 1985	FY 1986	FY 1987	FY 1988	FY 1981–88 % Change
Total arrests	13,266	12,166	12,981	13,118	15,709	18,681	21,869	23,972	80.7%
Case Class I and II	6,491	6,376	6,828	7,458	9,443	12,928	14,691	17,026	162.3%
Violater Class I and II	2,318	2,121	2,498	2,848	4,051	5,990	6,862	8,195	253.5%
Total convictions	5,515	5,861	9,844	10,668	10,403	11,994	12,427	13,485	144.5%
Case Class I and II	2,519	2,944	4,820	5,579	6,155	7,494	8,376	9,020	258.1%
Violator Class I and II	1,002	1,189	1,845	2,193	2,549	3,432	4,148	4,729	372.0%
Drug removal									
Heroin (kgs)	204.5	234.0	313.8	354.2	439.9	388.6	382.4	793.9	288.2%
Cocaine (kgs)	1,937.8	5,587.0	8,434.0	10,985.2	24,654.9	27,500.1	37,404.8	55,896.9	2,784.6%
Cannabis (kgs)	1,149,462.8	1,081,491.4	887,751.5	1,289,406.8	860,840.2	715,923.6	649,489.3	532,014.3	−53.7%
Dangerous drugs (du)	86,947,651	32,178,326	21,300,310	13,292,517	38,531,643	34,774,658	33,788,528	103,132,890	18.6%
Clandestine lab seizures	184	225	226	312	425	509	682	810	340.2%
Asset seizures (in millions)					$246.3	$400.0	$509.0	$655.0	
Asset forfeitures (in millions)	FY 1981–84 either not available or not comparable to later years.				$59.1	$69.0	$152.4	$197.8	
Average no. of special agents on board*	1,460	1,396	1,502	1,732	1,780	1,865	1,950	2,120	45.2%
Total arrests per agent	9.1	8.7	8.6	7.6	8.8	10.0	11.2	11.3	24.4%

*Does not include Special Agents assigned to Intelligence Positions.

NOTE: Headquarters data are not included in any figures.

SOURCE: U.S. Department of Justice, Drug Enforcement Administration, 1989.

Table 32. Population Estimates of Lifetime and Current Drug Use, 1988

The following are estimates of the number of people 12 years of age and older who report they have used drugs nonmedically. Drugs used under a physician's care are not included. The estimates were developed from the 1988 National Household Survey on Drug Abuse.

	12–17 yrs. (pop. 20,250,000)				18–25 yrs. (pop. 29,688,000)				26+ years** (pop. 148,409,000)				Total*** (pop. 198,347,000)			
	%	Ever Used	%	Current User	%	Ever Used	%	Current User	%	Ever Used	%	Current User	%	Ever Used	%	Current User
Marijuana & Hashish	17	3,516,000	6	1,296,000	56	16,741,000	16	4,594,000	31	45,491,000	4	5,727,000	33	65,748,000	6	11,616,000
Hallucinogens	3	704,000	1	168,000	14	4,093,000	2	569,000	7	9,810,000	*	*	7	14,607,000	*	*
Inhalants	9	1,774,000	2	410,000	12	3,707,000	2	514,000	4	5,781,000	*	*	6	11,262,000	1	1,223,000
Cocaine	3	683,000	1	225,000	20	5,858,000	5	1,323,000	10	14,631,000	1	1,375,000	11	21,171,000	2	2,923,000
Crack	1	188,000	*	*	3	1,000,000	1	249,000	*	*	*	*	1	2,483,000	*	484,000
Heroin	1	118,000	*	*	*	*	*	*	1	1,686,000	*	*	1	1,907,000	*	*
Stimulants	4	852,000	1	245,000	11	3,366,000	2	718,000	7	9,850,000	1	791,000	7	14,068,000	1	1,755,000
Sedatives	2	475,000	1	123,000	6	1,633,000	1	265,000	3	4,867,000	*	*	4	6,975,000	*	*
Tranquilizers	2	413,000	*	*	8	2,319,000	1	307,000	5	6,750,000	1	822,000	5	9,482,000	1	1,174,000
Analgesics	4	840,000	1	182,000	9	2,798,000	1	440,000	5	6,619,000	*	*	5	10,257,000	1	1,151,000
Alcohol	50	10,161,000	25	5,097,000	90	26,807,000	65	19,392,000	89	131,530,000	55	81,356,000	85	168,498,000	53	105,845,000
Cigarettes	42	8,564,000	12	2,389,000	75	22,251,000	35	10,447,000	80	118,191,000	30	44,284,000	75	149,005,000	29	57,121,000
Smokeless Tobacco	15	3,021,000	4	722,000	24	6,971,000	6	1,855,000	13	19,475,000	3	4,497,000	15	29,467,000	4	7,073,000

*Amounts of less than .5% are not listed.

"Ever Used": used at least once in a person's lifetime.
"Current User": used at least once in the 30 days prior to the survey.

SOURCE: National Institute on Drug Abuse, August 1989.

Figure 12. Any Lifetime Experience with Illicit Drug Use*—1988

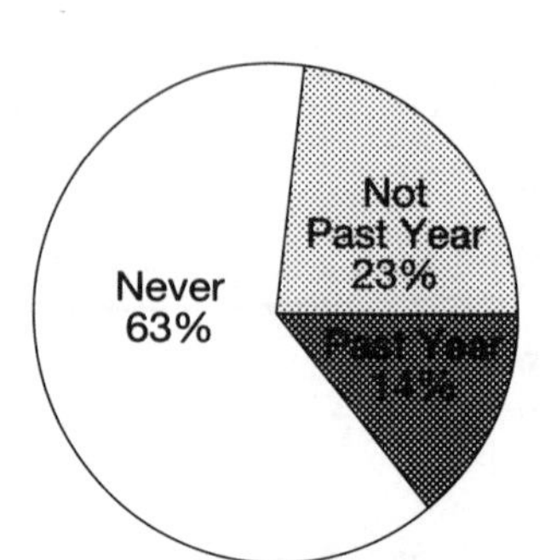

Household Population 12 and Older

	Youth 12–17	Young Adults 18–25	Adults 26–34	Adults 35 and Older
Never	75	41	36	77
Past Year	17	32	23	6
Not Past Year	8	27	41	17

*Includes marijuana, hallucinogens, inhalants, cocaine, or prescription–type psychotherapeutic drugs (stimulants, sedatives, tranquilizers, and analgesics) for nonmedical purposes.

Source: National Institute on Drug Abuse, National Household Survey on Drug Abuse, 1988.

Figure 13. Marijuana Trends in Past Month Use by Age Group

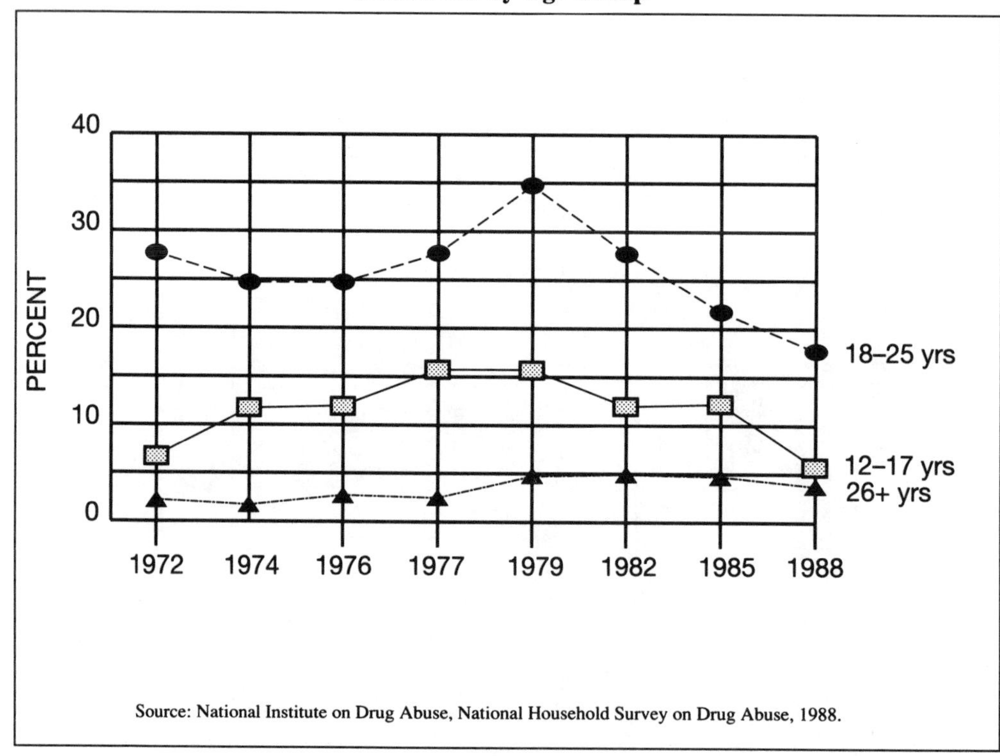

Source: National Institute on Drug Abuse, National Household Survey on Drug Abuse, 1988.

Figure 14. Cocaine Trends in Past Month Use by Age Group

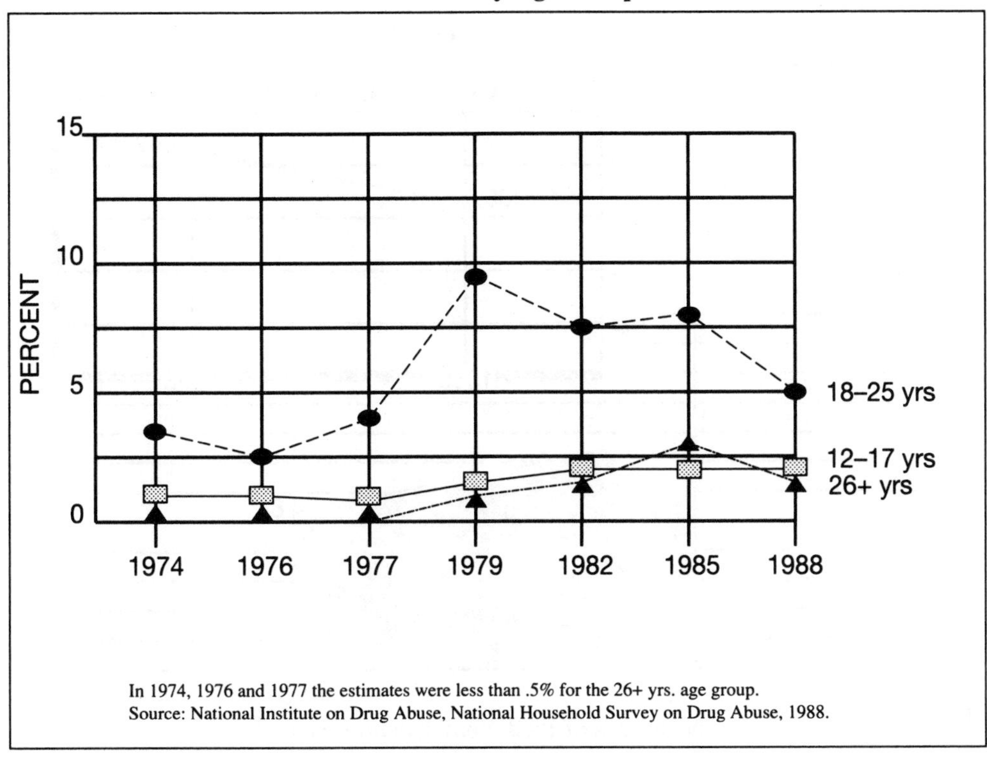

In 1974, 1976 and 1977 the estimates were less than .5% for the 26+ yrs. age group.
Source: National Institute on Drug Abuse, National Household Survey on Drug Abuse, 1988.

Figure 15. Annual Use of Illicit Drugs (in Millions)

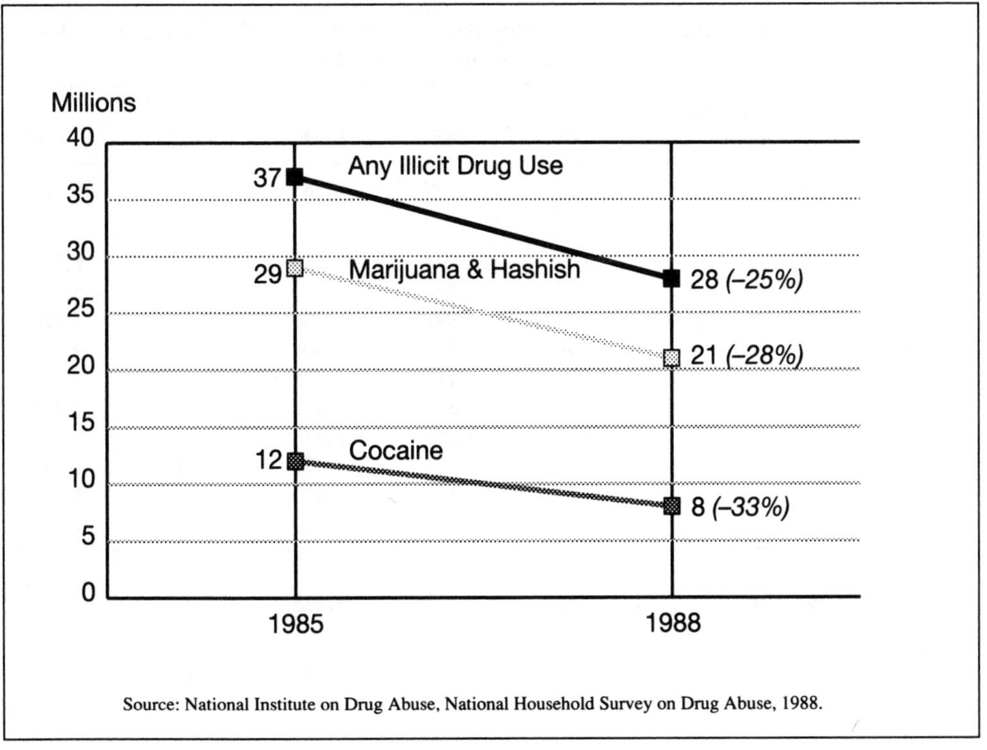

Source: National Institute on Drug Abuse, National Household Survey on Drug Abuse, 1988.

Figure 16.

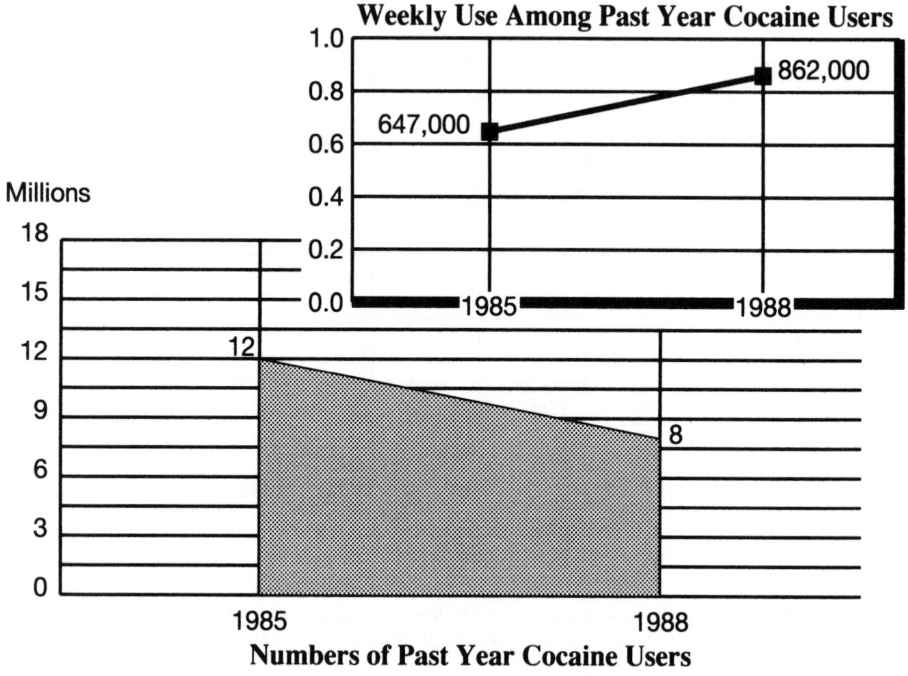

Weekly Use Among Past Year Cocaine Users

1.0
0.8
0.6
0.4
0.2
0.0
647,000
862,000
1985
1988

Millions
18
15
12
9
6
3
0
12
8
1985
1988

Numbers of Past Year Cocaine Users

Source: National Institute on Drug Abuse, National Household Survey on Drug Abuse, 1988.

Table 33. Trends in Hospital Emergency Rooms (ER) and Medical Examiner (ME) Mentions of Cocaine—1984–1988

Total DAWN System and Metropolitan Areas	1984	1985	1986	1987	1988
Total ER Mentions*	8,831	11,099	20,383	34,661	46,020
of which:					
New York	2,643	2,944	4,515	6,486	6,540
Washington, D.C.	522	793	1,350	3,182	5,211
Detroit	600	992	2,596	4,633	4,422
Philadelphia	399	570	1,306	2,670	4,156
Chicago	521	714	1,635	2,817	3,907
New Orleans	477	501	442	1,907	3,221
Los Angeles	1,006	1,606	2,339	2,248	2,988
Baltimore	148	221	498	962	1,341
Dallas	77	157	480	985	1,381
Seattle	238	246	434	839	1,321
Total ME Mentions* (excludes New York)	628	717	1,223	1,724	1,589**
of which:					
Philadelphia	21	36	72	173	254
Los Angeles	176	151	378	447	198

Total DAWN System and Metropolitan Areas	1984	1985	1986	1987	1988
San Francisco	67	63	86	152	155
Washington, D.C.	57	61	92	179	124
Miami	90	70	124	47	91
Detroit	14	41	107	159	83
Boston	14	51	74	56	83
Newark	47	53	46	160	81

*Based on consistently-reporting ERs with at least 90 percent reporting in the first 12 months, the second 12 months, and the last 36 months. The metropolitan areas listed represent those which make up 76 percent of ER and 67 percent of ME mentions in calendar year 1988.

**Provisional data due to lag in reporting.

SOURCE: NIDA, Drug Abuse Warning Network (DAWN) March 1989 data file.

Table 34. Trends in Hospital Emergency Rooms (ER) By Number of Mentions of Smoking or Injecting Cocaine—1984–1988

Total DAWN System and Metropolitan Areas	1984	1985	1986	1987	1988
Total ER Cocaine Mentions*	8,831	11,099	20,383	34,661	46,020
Number Smoking Cocaine	549	1,166	4,400	10,698	15,306
By Selected Metro Area:					
New York	99	140	1,252	2,681	2,846
Detroit	51	159	948	2,419	2,522
Washington, D.C.	12	29	219	1,132	2,191
New Orleans	11	12	25	466	1,459
Los Angeles	243	561	746	726	1,048
Philadelphia	13	31	171	623	1,013
Chicago	33	70	276	717	883
Number Injecting Cocaine	3,717	4,210	6,041	9,754	12,461
By Selected Metro Area:					
Philadelphia	167	226	443	921	1,485
New York	1,102	1,148	1,170	1,471	1,416
Baltimore	92	113	281	605	1,283
New Orleans	304	324	202	988	1,238
Chicago	186	246	521	918	1,224
Los Angeles	193	280	515	615	833
Washington, D.C.	234	330	395	674	684

*Based on consistently-reporting ERs with at least 90 percent reporting in the first 12 months, the second 12 months, and the last 36 months.

SOURCE: NIDA, Drug Abuse Warning Network (DAWN) March 1989 data file.

Table 35. Controlled Substances—Uses & Effects

Drugs/ CSA Schedules		Trade or Other Names	Medical Uses	Dependence: Physical	Dependence: Psychological	Tolerance	Duration (Hours)	Usual Methods of Administration	Possible Effects	Effects of Overdose	Withdrawal Syndrome
NARCOTICS											
Opium	II III V	Dover's Powder, Paregoric, Parepectolin	Analgesic, antidiarrheal	High	High	Yes	3–6	Oral, smoked	Euphoria, drowsiness, respiratory depression, constricted pupils, nausea	Slow and shallow breathing, clammy skin, convulsions, coma, possible death	Watery eyes, runny nose, yawning, loss of appetite, irritability, tremors, panic, cramps, nausea, chills and sweating
Morphine	II III	Morphine, MS-Contin, Roxanol, Roxanol-SR	Analgesic, antitussive	High	High	Yes	3–6	Oral, smoked, injected			
Codeine	II III V	Tylenol w/Codeine, Empirin w/Codeine, Robitussan A-C, Fiorinal w/Codeine	Analgesic, antitussive	Moderate	Moderate	Yes	3–6	Oral, injected			
Heroin	I	Diacetylmorphine, Horse, Smack	None	High	High	Yes	3–6	Injected, sniffed, smoke			
Hydromorphone	II	Dilaudid	Analgesic	High	High	Yes	3–6	Oral, injected			
Meperidine (Pethidine)	II	Demerol, Mepergan	Analgesic	High	High	Yes	3–6	Oral, injected			
Methadone	II	Dolophine, Methadone, Methadose	Analgesic	High	High–Low	Yes	12–24	Oral, injected			
Other Narcotics	I II III IV V	Numorphan, Percodan, Percocet, Tylox, Tussionex, Fentanyl, Darvon, Lomotil, Talwin[2]	Analgesic, antidiarrheal, antitussive	High–Low	High–Low	Yes	Variable	Oral, injected			
DEPRESSANTS											
Chloral Hydrate	IV	Noctec	Hypnotic	Moderate	Moderate	Yes	5–8	Oral	Slurred speech, disorientation, drunken behavior without odor of alcohol	Shallow respiration, clammy skin, dilated pupils, weak and rapid pulse, coma, possible death	Anxiety, insomnia, tremors, delirium, convulsions, possible death
Barbiturates	II III IV	Amytal, Butisol, Fiorinal, Lotusate, Nembutal, Seconal, Tuinal, Phenobarbital	Anasthetic, anticonvulsant, sedative, hypnotic, veterinary euthanasia agent	High–Mod.	High–Mod.	Yes	1–16	Oral			

Benzodiazepines	IV	Ativan, Dalmane, Diazepam, Librium, Xanax, Serax, Valium, Tranxene, Verstram, Versed, Halcion, Paxipam, Restoril	Antianxiety, anticonvulsant, sedative, hypnotic	Low	Low	Yes	4–8	Oral			
Methaqualone	I	Quaalude, 711's, lemons	Sedative, hypnotic	High	High	Yes	4–8	Oral			
Glutethimide	III	Doriden	Sedative, hypnotic	High	Moderate	Yes	4–8	Oral			
Other Depressants	III IV	Equanil, Miltown, Noludar, Placidyl, Valmid	Antianxiety, sedative, hypnotic	Moderate	Moderate	Yes	4–8	Oral			
STIMULANTS											
Cocaine[1]	II	Coke, Flake, Snow, Crack	Local anesthetic	Possible	High	Yes	1–2	Sniffed, smoked, injected	Increased alertness, excitation, euphoria, increased pulse rate & blood pressure, insomnia, loss of appetite	Agitation, increase in body temperature, hallucinations, convulsions, possible death	Apathy, long periods of sleep, irritability, depression, disorientation
Amphetamines	II	Biphetamine, Delcobese, Desoxyn, Dexedrine, Obetrol	Attention deficit disorders, narcolepsy, weight control	Possible	High	Yes	2–4	Oral, injected			
Phenmetrazine	II	Preludin	Weight control	Possible	High	Yes	2–4	Oral, injected			
Methylphenidate	II	Ritalin	Attention deficit disorder, narcolepsy	Possible	Moderate	Yes	2–4	Oral, injected			
Other Stimulants	III IV	Adipex, Cylert, Didrex, Ionamin, Melfiat, Plegine, Sanorex, Tenuate, Tepanil, Prelu-2	Weight control	Possible	High	Yes	2–4	Oral, injected			
HALLUCINOGENS											
LSD	I	Acid, Microdot	None	None	Unknown	Yes	8–12	Oral	Illusions and hallucinations, poor perception of time and distance	Longer, more intense "trip" episodes, psychosis, possible death	Withdrawal syndrome not reported
Mescaline and Peyote	I	Mexc, Buttons, Cactus	None	None	Unknown	Yes	8–12	Oral			
Amphetamine Variants	I	2,5-DMA, PMA, STP, MDA, MDMA, TMA, DOM, DOB	None	Unknown	Unknown	Yes	Variable	Oral, injected			

Table 35. (*continued*) Controlled Substances—Uses & Effects

Drugs/ CSA Schedules		Trade or Other Names	Medical Uses	Dependence: Physical	Dependence: Psychological	Tolerance	Duration (Hours)	Usual Methods of Administration	Possible Effects	Effects of Overdose	Withdrawal Syndrome
HALLUCINOGENS											
Phencyclidine	II	PCP, Angel Dust, Hog	None	Unknown	High	Yes	Days	Smoked, oral, injected			
Phencyclidine Analogues	I	PCE, PCPy, TCP	None	Unknown	High	Yes	Days	Smoked, oral, injected			
Other Hallucinogens	I	Bufotenine, Ibogaine, DMT, DET, Psilocybin, Psilocyn	None	None	Unknown	Possible	Variable	Smoked, oral, injected, sniffed			
CANNABIS											
Marijuana	I	Pot, Acapulco Gold, Grass, Reefer, Sinsemilla, Thai Sticks	None	Unknown	Moderate	Yes	2–4	Smoked, oral	Euphoria, relaxed inhibitions, increased appetite, disoriented behavior	Fatique, paranoia, possible psychosis	Insomnia, hyperactivity, and decreased appetite occasionally reported
Tetrahydrocannabinol	I II	THC, Marinol	Cancer chemotherapy antinauseant	Unknown	Moderate	Yes	2–4	Smoked, oral			
Hashish	I	Hash	None	Unknown	Moderate	Yes	2–4	Smoked, oral			
Hashish Oil	I	Hash Oil	None	Unknown	Moderate	Yes	2–4	Smoked, oral			

[1] Designated a narcotic under the CSA.
[2] Not designated a narcotic under the CSA.

Table 36. Approximate Equivalents*

LIQUID	
1000 milliliters or 1 liter	= 1 quart
500 milliliters or 0.5 liter	= 1 pint
250 milliliters or 0.25 liter	= ½ pint or 8 fluid ounces
30 milliliters	= 1 fluid ounce
15 milliliters	= 4 fluid drams or ½ fluid ounce
4 milliliters	= 1 fluid dram
1 milliliters	= 15 minims
0.6 milliliters	= 10 minims
0.2 milliliters	= 3 minims
0.06 milliliters	= 1 minim
0.3 milliliters	= ½ minim
WEIGHT	
1 kilogram	= 2.2 pounds (avoirdupois)
30 grams	= 1 ounce
4 grams	= 1 dram
1 gram	= ¼ dram or 15 grains
0.75 gram	= 12 grains
0.6 gram	= 10 grains
0.5 gram	= 7½ grains
0.4 gram	= 6 grains
0.3 gram	= 5 grains
0.25 gram	= 4 grains
0.2 gram	= 3 grains
0.15 gram	= 2½ grains
0.12 gram	= 2 grains
0.1 gram	= 1½ grains
75 milligrams	= 1¼ grains
60 milligrams	= 1 grain
50 milligrams	= ¾ grain
30 milligrams	= ½ grain
25 milligrams	= ⅜ grain
20 milligrams	= ⅓ grain
15 milligrams	= ¼ grain
10 milligrams	= ⅛ grain
8 milligrams	= ⅛ grain
6 milligrams	= 1/10 grain
4 milligrams	= 1/15 grain
3 milligrams	= 1/20 grain
2 milligrams	= 1/30 grain
1.5 milligram	= 1/40 grain
1.0 milligram	= 1/80 grain
0.8 milligram	= 1/80 grain
0.6 milligram	= 1/100 grain
0.5 milligram	= 1/120 grain
0.4 milligram	= 1/150 grain
0.3 milligram	= 1/200 grain
0.25 milligram	= 1/250 grain
0.2 milligram	= 1/300 grain
0.15 milligram	= 1/400 grain
0.12 milligram	= 1/500 grain
0.1 milligram	= 1/600 grain
0.05 milligram	= 1/1200 grain

*From the *United States Pharmacopeia*, XVI.

APPENDIX 4
SOURCES OF INFORMATION

This section contains selected major sources of information on alcohol and drug abuse, including some organizations which provide treatment. Further information in treatment programs is usually available from national or local government agencies. In addition it was not possible to provide information sources for every foreign country, since many countries failed to or chose not to supply such information despite repeated requests.

CONTENTS

UNITED STATES

NATIONAL ASSOCIATIONS, INSTITUTES, ORGANIZATIONS AND GOVERNMENT AGENCIES

A.A. World Services, Inc.
P.O. Box 459
Grand Central Station
New York, New York 10163-1100

Action
Drug Prevention Program
806 Connecticut Avenue, N.W.
Washington, D.C. 20525

Adult Children of Alcoholics
P.O. Box 3216
Torrance, California 90505
Tel: (213) 534-1815

AFL-CIO
Community Service Programs
815 Sixteenth Street, N.W., Suite 603
Washington, D.C. 20006-4189
Tel: (202) 637-5189

Al-Anon Family Group Headquarters
P.O. Box 862
Midtown Station
New York, New York 10018-0862
Tel: (212) 302-7240

Alcohol and Drug Problems Association of North America
1101 Fifteenth Street, N.W., #204
Washington, D.C. 20005

Alcohol, Drug Abuse and Mental Health Administration
Department of Health and Human Services
5600 Fishers Lane, Room 6C15
Rockville, Maryland 20857
Tel: (301) 443-4797

Alcohol Epidemiologic Data System (AEDS)
c/o CSR, Incorporated
1400 I Street, N.W., Suite 600
Washington, D.C. 20005
Tel: (202) 842-7600

Alcohol Health and Research World
c/o CSR, Incorporated
1400 I Street, N.W., Suite 600
Washington, D.C. 20005
Tel: (202): 842-7600

Alcoholics Anonymous
General Service Office
468 Park Avenue South
New York, New York 10016

Alcohol-Narcotics Education Council, Inc. of Virginia Churches
3202 West Cary Street
Richmond, Virginia 23221

Almaca (Association of Labor-Management Administrators and Consultants on Alcoholism)
1800 North Kent Street, Suite 907
Arlington, Virginia 22209

American Association Against Addiction
1668 Bush Street
San Francisco, California 94109
Tel: (415) 775-0165

American Association of Critical Care Nurses
101 Columbia
Aliso Viejo California 92656-1458
Tel: (714) 362-2000

American Correction Association
4321 Hartwick Road
College Park, Maryland 20740

American Council for Drug Education (ACDE)
204 Monroe Street, Suite 110
Rockville, Maryland 20850
Tel: (301) 294-0600

American Council on Alcohol Problems
119 Constitution Avenue, N.E.
Washington, D.C. 20002

American Council on Marijuana and Other Psychoactive Drugs
6193 Executive Boulevard
Rockville, Maryland 20852

American Institute of Family Relations
5287 Sunset Boulevard
Los Angeles, California 90027

American Medical Association
Department of Health Education
535 N. Dearborn Street
Chicago, Illinois 60610

American Nurses Association
2420 Pershing Road
Kansas City, Missouri 64108
Tel: (816) 474-5720

Americans for Democratic Action
Counsumer Affairs Committee
3005 Audubon Terrace, N.W.
Washington, D.C. 20008

American Society of Addiction Medicine
5225 Wisconsin Avenue, N.W.
Washington, D.C. 10015
Tel: (202) 244-8948

Association for Advancement of Health Education
1201 16th Street, N.W.
Washington, D.C. 20036

Association for Medical Education and Research in Substance Abuse (AMERSA)
Center for Alcohol and Addiction Studies
Box G, Brown University
Providence, RI 02912

Association of Halfway House Alcoholism Programs of North America
786 East 7th Street
St. Paul, Minnesota 55106

B'nai B'rith C.V.S.
1640 Rhode Island Avenue, N.W.
Washington, D.C. 20036

Center for Multicultural Awareness
2924 Columbia Pike
Arlington, Virginia 22204

Center for the Study of Drug Policy
530 Eighth Street, S.E.
Washington, D.C. 20003
Tel: (202) 547-3708
Center for the Study of Responsive Law
P.O. Box 19367
Washington, D.C. 20036

Center of Alcohol Studies
Rutgers, The State University of New Jersey
P.O. Box 969
Piscataway, New Jersey 08854

Chemical Awareness Training Institute
16042 N. 36th Street, Suite B1
Phoenix, Arizona 85032
Tel: (602) 863-9671

Chemical People Institute
1 Allegheny Square, Suite 720
Pittsburgh, Pennsylvania 15212
Tel: (412) 391-0900

Children Are People Support Groups, Inc.
2489 Rice Street, Suite 275
St. Paul, Minnesota 55113
Tel: (612) 490-9257

Children of Alcoholics Foundation
555 Madison Avenue, 4th Floor
New York, New York 10022
Tel: (212) 754-0656

Cocanon Family Groups
P.O. Box 64742-66
Los Angeles, California 90064

Commission for the Advancement of Public Interest Organization
1875 Connecticut Avenue, N.W.
Washington, D.C. 20009

Committee on Problems of Drug Dependence
4105 Dunnel Lane
Kensington, Maryland 20795

Committees of Correspondence
57 Conant Street, Room 113
Danvers, Massachusetts 01923
Tel: (508) 774-2641

Comp Care Publications
2415 Annapolis Lane
Minneapolis, Minnesota 55441
Tel: (612) 559-4800

Consumer Federation of America
1314 14th Street, N.W.
Washington, D.C. 20005

COSSMHO
1030 15th Street, N.W., Suite 1053
Washington, D.C. 20005
Tel: (202) 371-2100

Data Centers and Clearinghouse for Drugs and Crime
1600 Research Boulevard
Rockville, Maryland 20850

DAYTOP
54 West 40th Street
New York, New York 10018
Tel: (212) 354-6000
(oldest and largest drug abuse therapeutic program in U.S.)

Department of Housing and Urban Development (HUD)
Drug-Free Program
451 7th Street, S.W., Room 10214
Washington, D.C. 20202
Tel: (202) 708-1422

Do It Now Foundation
P.O. Box 5115
Phoenix, Arizona 85010
Tel: (602) 257-0797

Drug-Anon
P.O. Box 473
Ansonia Station
New York, N.Y. 10023
Tel: (212) 484-9095

Drug Enforcement Administration
1405 I Street, N.W.
Washington, D.C. 20537

ETOH, Alcohol & Alcohol Problems Science Database
1400 I Street N.W., Suite 600
Washington, D.C. 2000-I
Tel: (202) 842-7600

Families Anonymous, Inc.
P.O. Box 528
Van Nuys, California 91408
Tel: (818) 989-7841

Families in Action (FIA)
2296 Henderson Mill Road, Suite 204
Atlanta, Georgia 30345
Tel: (404) 934-6364

Family Life Publications
Box 427
Saluda, North Carolina 28773

Federal Trade Commission
Bureau of Consumer Protection
Division of Professional Service
6th Street & Pennyslvania Avenue, N.W.
Washington, D.C. 20580

Food and Drug Administration (FDA)
Consumer Inquiries HFI-10
5600 Fishers Lane
Rockville, Maryland 20857

Hazelden Foundation, Inc.
Pleasant Valley Road
Box 176
Center City, Minnesota 55012-0176

Health Communications, Inc.
3201 S.W. 15th Street
Deerfield Beach, Florida 33442
Tel: (305) 360-0909

House Select Committee on Narcotics
Abuse & Control
3287 House Office Building–Annex 2
2nd and D Streets, S.W.
Washington, D.C. 20515

Independent Community Consultants, Inc.
Design and Planning Assistance Center
120 Yale, S.E.
Albuquerque, New Mexico 87109

Indian Alcoholism Counseling and
Recovery House Program
375 South 300 W.
Salt Lake City, Utah 84101
Tel: (801) 328-8515

Indian Health Service (IHS)
Alcohol and Substance Program
5600 Fishers Lane, Room 38
Rockville, Maryland 20857
Tel: (301) 443-4297

Institute on Black Chemical Abuse
2616 Nicollet Avenue S.
Minneapolis, Minnesota 55408
Tel: (612) 871-7878

Institute on Pluralism and Group Identity
165 East 56th Street
New York, New York 10022

Johnson Institute
7151 Metro Boulevard, Suite 250
Minneapolis, Minnesota 55439-2122
Tel: (612) 944-0511

Mental Health Material Center
30 East 29th Street
New York, New York 10016

Mothers Against Drunk Driving (MADD)
National Office
669 Airport Freeway, Suite 310
Hurst, Texas 76053
Tel: (817) 595-0192

The Myrin Institute
521 Park Avenue
New York, New York 10021

Narcotics Anonymous
P.O. Box 9999
Van Nuys, California 91409
Tel: (818) 780-3951

Narcotics Education
6830 Laurel Avenue, N.W.
Washington, D.C. 20012
Tel: (202) 723-4774

Narcotics Educational Foundation of
America
5055 Sunset Boulevard
Los Angeles, California 90027
Tel: (213) 663-5171
National Anti-Drug Coalition
304 West 58th Street, 5th Floor
New York, New York 10019
Tel: (212) 247-8820

National Asian Pacific American Families
Against Substance Abuse
6303 Friendship Court
Bethesda, Maryland 20817
Tel: (301) 530-0945

National Association for Children of
Alcoholics
31582 Coast Highway, Suite B

South Laguna, California 92677
Tel: (714) 499-3889

National Association for City Drug and Alcohol Coordination
House Officers Building, Suite 711
818 Harrison Avenue
Boston, Massachusetts 02118
Tel: (617) 424-4757

National Association of Addiction Treatment Providers
25201 Paseo de Alicia, #100
Laguna Hills, California 92653
Tel: (714) 837-3038
(Information source on intensive alcoholism rehab centers)

National Association of Broadcasters (NAB) Abuse Programs
1771 N Street, N.W.
Washington, D.C. 20036
Tel: (202) 429-5447

National Association of Social Workers (NASW)
7981 Eastern Avenue
Silver Spring, Maryland 20910
Tel: (301) 565-0333

National Association of State Alcohol and Drug Abuse Directors
918 F Street, N.W., Suite 400
Washington, D.C. 20004
Tel: (202) 783-6868

National Association on Drug Abuse Problems
355 Lexington Avenue
New York, New York 10017
Tel: (212) 986-1170

National Basketball Association (NBA)
Drug Policy and Abuse Program
15 Columbus Circle
New York, New York 10023
Tel: (212) 541-6608

National Center for Health Statistics (NCHS)
6525 Belcrest Road Rm. 1064
Hyattsville, Maryland 20782
Tel: (301) 436-8500

National Center for Voluntary Action
1785 Massachusetts, N.W.
Washington, D.C. 20036

National Clearinghouse for Alcohol Information
P.O. Box 2345
Rockville, Maryland 20852

National Clearinghouse for Drug Abuse Information
Department of Health and Human Services
5600 Fishers Lane, Room 10A53
P.O. Box 2345
Rockville, Maryland 20857
Tel: (301) 443-6500

National Collegiate Athletic Association (NCAA)
Drug Program
6201 College Blvd.
Overland Park, Kansas 66211-2422
Tel: (913) 339-1906

National Committee for the Prevention of Alcoholism and Drug Dependency
6830 Laurel Street, N.W.
Washington, D.C. 20012

National Council on Alcoholism
12 West 21st Street, 7th Floor
New York, New York 10010

National Council on Alcoholism, Inc.
1424 16th Street, N.W.
Washington, D.C. 20036

National Council on Crime and Delinquency
Continental Plaza
422 Hackensack Avenue
Hackensack, New Jersey 07601

National Crime Prevention Council (NCPC)
1700 K St., N.W., 2nd floor
Washington, D.C. 20006
Tel: (202) 466-6272

National Family Council Against Drug Abuse
40 Westminister Drive
Pearl River, New York 10965
Tel: (914) 735-9250

National Federation of Parents for Drug Free Youth
8730 Georgia Avenue, Suite 200
Silver Spring, Maryland 20910
Tel: (301) 585-5437

National Foundation—March of Dimes
Public Health Education Department
Box 2000
White Plains, New York 10602

National Hispanic Family Against Drugs
1511 K Street, N.W.
Washington, D.C. 20005
Tel: (202) 393-5136

National Institute on Alcohol Abuse and Alcoholism
Department of Health and Human Services
P.O. Box 2345
5600 Fishers Lane
Rockville, Maryland 20857
Tel: (301) 468-2600

National Institute on Drug Abuse
Division of Research
Department of Health and Human Services
5600 Fishers Lane
Rockville, Maryland 20857

National Nurses Society on Addictions (NNSA)
5700 Old Orchard Road
Skokie, Illinois 60077
Tel: (708) 966-5010

National Organization for the Reform of Marijuana Laws (NORML)
2035 P Street, N.W., Suite 401
Washington, D.C. 20036

National Self-Help Clearinghouse
Graduate School and University Center—CUNY
33 West 42nd Street—Room 620-N
New York, New York 10036

Navy Drug and Alcohol Abuse Treatment Program
Navy Drug and Alcohol Abuse Prevention Control Division
Naval Military Personnel Command (NMPC-63)
Washington, D.C. 20370
Tel: (202) 694-8008

New York City Affiliate, Inc.
National Council on Alcoholism
133 East 62nd Street
New York, New York 10021

North Conway Institute
14 Beacon Street
Boston, Massachusetts 02108

Nurses Society on Addictions, Committee on Impaired Nurses
1020 Sunset Drive
Lawrence, Kansas 66044
Tel: (913) 254-3652

Odyssey Institute
656 Avenue of the Americas
New York, New York 10010
Tel: (212) 691-8510

Office for Substance Abuse Prevention
P.O. Box 2345
Rockville, Maryland 20852
Tel: (301) 468-2600

Office of National Drug Control Policy
Executive Office of the President
Washington, D.C. 20500

Office of Workplace Initiatives (OWI)
c/o NIDA-OWI
5600 Fishers Lane
Rockville, Maryland 20857
Tel: (301) 443-6245

Parent Resources and Information on Drug Education
Georgia State University
University Plaza
Atlanta, Georgia 30303
Tel: (404) 658-2548

Pew Charitable Trusts
3 Parkway
Philadelphia, Pennsylvannia 19102-1305
Tel: (215) 568-3330

Pharmaceutical Manufacturers Association
Consumer Services
115 15th Street, N.W.
Washington, D.C. 20005

Phoenix House Foundation
164 West 74th Street
New York, New York 10023
Tel: (212) 595-5810

Pil-Anon Family Program
P.O. Box 120
Gracie Square Station
New York, New York 10028
Tel: (212) 744-2020

Pills Anonymous
P.O. Box 473
Ansonia Station
New York, New York 10023
Tel: (212) 375-8872

Potsmokers Anonymous
316 East 3rd Street
New York, New York 10009
Tel: (212) 254-1777

Project Cork Institute
Dartmouth Medical School
Hanover, New Hampshire 03756
Tel: (603) 643-9273

The Proprietary Association
1700 Pennsylvania Avenue, N.W.
Washington, D.C. 20006

Public Affairs Pamphlets
381 Park Avenue South
New York, New York 10016

Public Citizen, Inc.
Health Research Group
2000 P Street, N.W.
Washington, D.C. 20036

RADAR Network Support
c/o National Clearinghouse for Alcohol and Drug Information (NCADI)
P.O. Box 2345
Rockville, Maryland 20852
Tel: (301) 468-2600

RID, Remove Intoxicated Drivers
P.O. Box 520
Schnectady, New York 12301
Tel: (518) 393-4357

SADD, Students Against Drunk Driving
P.O. Box 800
200 Pleasant St.
Marlborough, Massachusetts 01752
Tel: (508) 481-3568

SANE (Substance Abuse Narcotics Education Program)
c/o Los Angeles County Sheriff's Department, SANE Unit
11515 S. Colima Road—Building D111
Whittier, California 90604
Tel: (213) 946-7263

SPECDA (New York City School Program to Educate and Control Drug Abuse)
c/o New York City Police Department
One Police Plaza, Room 200
New York, New York 10038
Tel: (212) 374-5112

Sports Drug Awareness Program
Demand Reduction Section, Office of Congressional and Public Affairs, Drug Enforcement Administration (DEA)
1405 I Street, N.W.
Washington, D.C. 20537
Tel: (202) 786-4096

Substance Abuse Treatment Programs and National Cocaine Hotline
19 Prospect Street
Fair Oaks Hospital
Summit, New Jersey 07901
Tel: (201) 522-700 (business)
Cocaine Hotline: 1-800-COCAINE

Synanon Church
P.O. Box 786
6055 Marshall-Petaluma Road
Marshall, California 94940
Tel: (415) 663-8111

TARGET, National Federation of State High School Associations
11724 NW Plaza Circle
Kansas City, MO 64195
Tel: (816) 464-5400

Toughlove
P.O. Box 1069
Doylestown, Pennsylvania 18901
Tel: (215) 348-7090

U.S Department of Education Drug-Free Schools and Communities
400 Maryland Avenue, S.W.
Washington, D.C. 20202-4101
Tel: (202) 401-1576

U.S. Department of Health and Human Services
Office of Education
Alcohol and Drug Education Program
400 Maryland Avenue, S.W.
Washington, D.C. 20202

Valium Anonymous
P.O. Box 404
Altoona, Iowa 50009
Tel: (515) 967-6781

Women for Sobriety
P.O. Box 618
Quakertown, Pennsylvania 18951
Tel: (215) 536-8026

Women's Sport Foundation Drug Use Program
342 Madison Avenue, Suite 728
New York, NY 10173
Tel: (212) 972-9170 or (800) 227-3988 (out of the city)

Youth to Youth
700 Bryden Road
Columbus, OH 43215
Tel: (614) 224-4506

''Zero Tolerance'' Program
c/o U.S. Attorney's Office
U.S. Court House, Room SN19
940 Front Street
San Diego, California 92189
Tel: (619) 557-5690

STATE DRUG ABUSE PREVENTION AND TREATMENT COORDINATORS

Alabama

Commissioner
Department of Mental Health and Mental Retardation
200 Interstate Park Drive
P.O. Box 3710
Montgomery, Alabama 36109-0710
Tel: (205) 271-9209

Alaska

Coordinator
Office of Alcoholism and Drug Abuse
Department of Health and Social Services
P.O. Box H
Juneau, Alaska 99811-0607
Tel: (907) 586-6201

Arizona
Manager
Drug Abuse Section
Department of Health Services
Division of Behavioral Health Services
411 North 24th St.
Phoenix, Arizona 85008
Tel: (602) 220-6478

Arkansas
Director
Office on Alcohol and Drug Abuse Prevention
400 Donaghey Plaza, N.
P.O. Box 1437
Little Rock, Arkansas 72203-1437
Tel: (501) 371-2603

California
Director
Department of Alcohol and Drug Programs
700 K St.
Sacramento, California 95814
Tel: (916) 322-6690

Colorado
Director
Alcohol and Drug Abuse Division
Department of Health
4210 East 11th Ave.
Denver, Colorado 80220
Tel: (303) 331-8201

Connecticut
Executive Director
Connecticut Alcohol and Drug Abuse Commission
999 Asylum Avenue
Third Floor
Hartford, Connecticut 06105
Tel: (203) 566-4145

Delaware
Chief
Bureau of Alcoholism and Drug Abuse
1901 North DuPont Highway
Newcastle, Delaware 19720
Tel: (302) 421-6101

District of Columbia
Chief
Health Planning and Development
1660 L Street, N.W.
Suite 1117
Washington, D.C. 20036
Tel: (202) 673-7481

Florida
Director
Drug Abuse Program
1317 Winewood Blvd.
Building 6, Room 182
Tallahassee, Florida 32399-0700
Tel: (904) 488-0900

Georgia
Director
Alcohol and Drug Section
Division of Mental Health, Mental Retardation and Substance Abuse
Department of Human Resources
Suite 319
878 Peach Tree St. N.E.
Atlanta, Georgia 30309
Tel: (404) 894-4785

Hawaii
Branch Chief
Alcohol and Drug Abuse Branch
Department of Health
P.O. Box 3378
Honolulu, Hawaii 96801
Tel: (808) 548-4280

Idaho
Director
Bureau of Substance Abuse
Department of Health and Welfare
450 West State Street
Boise, Idaho 83720
Tel: (208) 334-5935

Illinois
Director
Department of Alcoholism and Substance Abuse
Suite 5-600
100 W. Randolph St.
Chicago, Illinois 60601
Tel: (312) 917-3840

Indiana
Director
Division of Addiction Services
Department of Mental Health
117 East Washington St.
Indianapolis, Indiana 46204
Tel: (317) 232-7816

Iowa
Director
Iowa Division of Substance Abuse and Health Promotion
320 E. 12th Street
Des Moines, Iowa 50319
Tel: (515) 281-3641

Kansas
Commissioner
Alcohol and Drug Abuse Services
300 SW Oakley 2nd Flr
Biddle Building
Topeka, Kansas 66606-1861
Tel: (913) 296-3925

Kentucky
Manager
Division of Substance Abuse
275 East Main Street
Frankfort, Kentucky 40621
Tel: (502) 564-2880

Louisiana
Director
Department of Health and Hospitals
Office of Prevention and Recovery from Alcohol and Drug Abuse
Baton Rouge Area Substance Abuse Clinic
134 N 19th St
Baton Rouge, Louisiana 70806
Tel: (504) 342-6685

Maine
Director
Office of Alcoholism and Drug Abuse Prevention
State House Station 11
Augusta, Maine 04333
Tel: (207) 289-2781

Maryland
Director
Alcohol and Drug Abuse Administration
201 W. Preston St.
Baltimore, Maryland 21201
Tel: (301) 225-6910

Massachusetts
Director
Division of Alcoholism and Drug Rehabilitation
150 Tremont St.
6th Floor
Boston, Massachusetts 02111
Tel: (617) 727-8617

Michigan
Director
Office of Substance Abuse Services
Department of Public Health
2150 Apollo Dr.
P.O. 30206
Lansing, Michigan 48909
Tel: (517) 335-8810

Minnesota
Director
Chemical Dependency Program Division
Department of Human Services
444 Layfayette Rd.
St. Paul, Minnesota 51555
Tel: (612) 296-4610

Mississippi
Director
Division of Alcohol and Drug Abuse

Department of Mental Health
1500 Woolfolk Building
Jackson, Mississippi 39201
Tel: (601) 359-1288

Missouri

Director
Division of Alcohol and Drug Abuse
Department of Mental Health
1706 E. Elm
P.O. Box 687
Jefferson City, Missouri 65102
Tel: (314) 751-4942

Montana

Administrator
Alcohol and Drug Abuse Director
Department of Institutions
1539 11th Ave.
Helena, Montana 59620
Tel: (406) 444-3904

Nebraska

Director
Division of Alcoholism and Drug Abuse
Department of Public Institutions
P.O. Box 94728
Lincoln, Nebraska 68509
Tel: (402) 471-2851

Nevada

Chief
Bureau of Alcohol and Drug Abuse
Department of Human Resources
Room 500
505 East King St.
Carson City, Nevada 89710
Tel: (702) 885-4790

New Hampshire

Director
Office of Alcohol and Drug Abuse Prevention
State Office Pk. So.
105 Pleasant St.
Concord, New Hampshire 03301
Tel: (603) 271-6108

New Jersey

Director
Division of Alcohol and Drug Abuse Addiction Services
129 E. Hanovor St.
Department of Health
CN 362
Trenton, New Jersey 08625
Tel: (609) 292-5760

New Mexico

Chief
Substance Abuse Bureau
Behavioral Health Services Division
P.O. Box 26110
Santa Fe, New Mexico 87502
Tel: (505) 827-2601

New York

Assistant Director
Division of Substance Abuse Services
Executive Park South
Box 8200
Albany, New York 12203
Tel: (518) 457-7629

North Carolina

Deputy Director
Alcohol and Drug Abuse Services
Division of Mental Health, Developmental Disabilities and Substance Abuse Services
325 North Salisbury St.
Raleigh, North Carolina 27603
Tel: (919) 733-4670

North Dakota

Director
Division of Alcoholism and Drug Abuse
Department of Human Services
1839 E. Capitol Ave.
Bismarck, North Dakota 58501-2152
Tel: (701) 224-2769

Ohio

Chief
Department of Alcohol & Drug Addiction Services

2 Nationwide Pl.
280 North High
12 Floor
Columbus, Ohio 43215
Tel: (614) 466-7893

Oklahoma

Director
Alcohol and Drug Programs
Department of Mental Health
P.O. Box 53277, Capitol Station
1200 N. East 13th
Oklahoma City, Oklahoma 73152-3277
Tel: (405) 271-7474

Oregon

Associate Administrator
State Alcohol and Drug Programs Office
1178 Chemeketa, NE Salem, Rm 102
Salem, Oregon 97310
Tel: (503) 378-2163

Pennsylvania

Deputy Secretary
Drug and Alcohol Programs
Department of Health
Room 809
Health & Welfare Building
P.O. Box 90
Harrisburg, Pennsylvania 17108
Tel: (717) 787-9857

Rhode Island

Assistant Director
Department of Mental Health, Mental Retardation and Hospitals
Division of Substance Abuse
Substance Abuse Administration Building
P.O. Box 20363
Cranston, Rhode Island 02920
Tel: (401) 464-2091

South Carolina

Director
South Carolina Commission on Alcohol and Drug Abuse
Suite 300
3700 Forest Dr.
Columbia, South Carolina 29204
Tel: (803) 734-9520

South Dakota

Director
Division of Alcohol and Drug Abuse
Department of Human Services
Kneip Building
700 Governor's Dr.
Pierre, South Dakota 57501
Tel: (605) 773-3123

Tennessee

Assistant Commissioner
Alcohol and Drug Abuse Services
Department of Mental Health and Mental Retardation
Doctor's Building
4th Floor
706 Church St.
Nashville, Tennessee 37243-0675
Tel: (615) 741-1921

Texas

Director
Texas Commission an Alcohol and Drug Abuse
Prevention Department
1720 Brazos, Suite 403
Austin, Texas 78701
Tel: (512) 463-5510

Utah

Director
Division of Substance Abuse
120 North 200 West, 4th Floor
P.O. Box 45500
Salt Lake City, Utah 84145-0500
Tel: (801) 538-3939

Vermont

Director
Office of Alcohol and Drug Abuse Programs

103 South Main St.
Waterbury, Vermont 05676
Tel: (802) 241-2170

Virginia

Assistant Commissioner
Department of Mental Health, Mental Retardation and Substance Abuse
109 Governor St. (ZIP 23214)
P.O. Box 1797 (ZIP 23219)
Richmond, Virginia
Tel: (804) 786-3906

Washington

Director
Bureau of Alcoholism and Substance Abuse
Department of Social and Health Services
Mail Stop 21W
Olympia, Washington 98504
Tel: (206) 753-5866

West Virginia

Director
Division of Alcohol and Drug Abuse
State Capitol Complex
Bld. 3 Rom 402
Charleston, West Virginia 25305
Tel: (304) 348-2276

Wisconsin

Director
Bureau of Alcohol and Other Drug Abuse
1 West Wilson St.
P.O. Box 7851
Madison, Wisconsin 53707
Tel: (608) 266-2717

Wyoming

Director
Alcohol and Drug Abuse Programs
451 Hathaway Building
Cheyenne, Wyoming 82002-0710
Tel: (307) 777-6945

DRUG ENFORCEMENT ADMINISTRATION DIVISION OFFICES

Atlanta Field Division

Richard B. Russell Federal Building
75 Spring St. S.W., Room 740
Atlanta, Georgia 30303
Tel: (404) 331-4401

Boston Field Division

Rm. G-64 JFK Federal Building
Boston, Massachusetts 02203
Tel: (617) 565-2800

Chicago Field Division

500 Dirksen Federal Building
219 S. Dearborn St.
Chicago, Illinois 60604
Tel: (312) 353-7875

Dallas Field Division

1880 Regal Row
Dallas, Texas 75235
Tel: (214) 767-7151

Denver Field Division

721 19th St., Room 316 (ZIP 80201)
P.O. Box 1860 (ZIP 80202)
Denver, Colorado
Tel: (303) 844-3951

Detroit Field Division

357 Federal Building
231 West Lafayette
Detroit, Michigan 48226
Tel: (313) 226-7290

Houston Field Division

333 West Loop North
Suite 300
Houston, Texas 77024
Tel: (713) 681-1771

Los Angeles Field Division

Suite 800
350 South Figueroa St.

Los Angeles, California 90071
Tel: (213) 894-2650

Miami Field Division
8400 N.W. 53rd St.
Miami, Florida 33166
Tel: (305) 591-4870

Newark Field Division
970 Broad St.
806 Federal Office Building
Newark, New Jersey 07102
Tel: (201) 645-6060

New Orleans Division
1661 Canal St.
Suite 2200
New Orleans, Louisiana 70112
Tel: (504) 589-3894

New York Field Division
555 W. 57th St.
Suite 1900
New York, New York 10019
Tel: (212) 399-5151

Philadelphia Field Division
10224 William J. Green Federal Building
600 Arch St.
Philadelphia, Pennsylvania 19106
Tel: (215) 597-9530

Phoenix Field Division
One North First St.
Suite 201
Phoenix, Arizona 85004
Tel: (602) 261-4866

San Diego Field Division
402 W. 35th St.
National City, California 92050
Tel: (619) 585-4200

San Francisco Field Division
Room 12215
450 Golden Gate Ave.
P.O. Box 36035
San Francisco, California 94102
Tel: (415) 556-6771

Seattle Field Division
Suite 301
220 West Mercer
Seattle, Washington 98119
Tel: (206) 442-5443

St. Louis Field Division
7911 Forsythe Blvd.
Suite 500
United Missouri Bank Bldg.
St. Louis, Missouri 63105
Tel: (314) 425-3241

Washington Field Division
Room 2558
400 Sixth St., S.W.
Washington, D.C. 20024
Tel: (202) 724-7834

CANADA

PROVINCIAL AND TERRITORIAL AGENCIES

Alberta
Alberta Alcoholism and Drug Abuse Commission
10909 Jasper Avenue
Edmonton, Alberta T5J 3M9
Tel: (403) 427-4275

British Columbia
The Alcohol and Drug Commission of British Columbia
805 West Broadway, 8th Floor

Vancouver, British Columbia V5Y 1P9
Tel: (604) 731-9121

Manitoba

Alcoholism Foundation of Manitoba
1580 Dublin Avenue
Winnipeg, Manitoba R3E OL4

Alcohol and Drug Programs Division of Inter-Regional Operations
Department of Health and Social Development
139 Tuxedo Boulevard, Building 21, Box 17
Winnipeg, Manitoba

New Brunswick

Alcoholism and Drug Dependency Commission
103 Church Street
P.O. Box 6000
Fredericton, New Brunswick E3B 5H1
Tel: (506) 453-2136

Alcoholism Program
Department of Health
P.O. Box 6000
348 King Street
Fredericton, New Brunswick

Newfoundland

Department of Health
Confederation Building
St. John's, Newfoundland A1C 5T7
Tel: (709) 737-2300

Alcohol and Drug Addiction Foundation of Newfoundland
3 Blackmarsh Road
St. John's, Newfoundland A1E 1S2
Tel: (709) 579-4041

Nova Scotia

Nova Scotia Commission on Drug Dependency
5668 South Street
Halifax, Nova Scotia B3J 1A6
Tel: (902) 424-4270

Ontario

Ministry of Health
9th Floor, Hepburn Block
Queen's Park
Toronto, Ontario M7A 1S2
Tel: (416) 965-5167

Alcoholism and Drug Addiction Foundation
33 Russell Street
Toronto, Ontario M5S 2S1

Drug Advisory Bureau
Department of National Health and Welfare
Tunney's Pasture
Ottawa, Ontario

Prince Edward Island

Addiction Foundation of Prince Edward Island
Box 37
Charlottetown, Prince Edward Island C1A 7K2
Tel: (902) 892-4265

Quebec

Department of Social Affairs
Information Centre on Alcoholism and Other Addictions
1075 Chemin Ste. Foy
Quebec, P.Q. G1S 2M1
Tel: (418) 643-9621

Saskatchewan

Alcoholism Commission of Saskatchewan
3475 Albert Street
Regina, Saskatchewan S4S 6X6
Tel: (306) 565-4085

The Canadian Foundation of Alcohol and Drug Dependence
602 Main Street
Noosomin, Saskatchewan

Northwest Territories

Alcohol and Drug Program
Department of Social Services
Goverment of the Northwest Territories
Yellowknife, N.W.T. X1A 2L9
Tel: (403) 873-7155

Alcohol and Drug Coordinating Council
Box 1769
Yellowknife, N.W.T. X0E 1H0
Tel: (403) 873-7155

Yukon

Alcohol and Drug Services
Box 2703
Whitehorse, Y.T. Y1A 2C6
Tel: (403) 667-5777

INTERNATIONAL AND FOREIGN AGENCIES AND ORGANIZATIONS

SPECIALIZED AGENCIES OF THE UNITED NATIONS

International Labour Office (ILO)
4, rue de Morillon
CH-1218 Grand Saconnex, Switzerland

Pan American Health Organization
Regional Office of the WHO
525 Twenty-third Street, N.W.
Washington, D.C.

United Nations
Division of Narcotic Drugs (DND)
P.O. Box 500
A-1400 Vienna, Austria

United Nations Educational, Scientific and Cultural Organization (UNESCO)
7, place de Fontenoy
F-7500 Paris, France

United Nations Social Defence Research Institute
Via Giulia 52
I-00186 Rome, Italy

World Health Organization (WHO)
Regional Office for the Western Pacific
P.O. Box 2932
12115 Manila, Philippines

World Health Organization (WHO)
Regional Office for Europe
Scherfigsvej, 8
DK-2100 Copenhagen, Denmark

World Health Organization (WHO)
20, avenue Appia
CH-1211 Geneva, Switzerland

OTHER INTERNATIONAL ORGANIZATIONS

Centre for Social Development and Humanitarian Affairs (CSDHA)
P.O. Box 500
A-1400 Vienna, Austria

Customs Cooperation Council
40, rue Washington
B-1050 Brussels, Belgium

International Commission for the Prevention of Alcoholism
6830 Laurel Street, N.W.
Washington, D.C. 20012

International Council of Volunteer Agencies
17, avenue de la Paix
CH-1202 Geneva, Switzerland

International Criminal Police Organization (ICPO/Interpol)

26, rue Armengaud
F-9200 Saint Cloud, France

International Federation of the Temperance Blue Cross Societies
52, rue de Florissant
CH-1206 Geneva, Switzerland

International Narcotics Control Board (INCB)
P.O. Box 500
A-1400 Vienna, Austria

International Council on Social Welfare
Berggasse None A-1090
Vienna, Austria

REGIONAL INTERGOVERNMENTAL ORGANIZATIONS

Pan-Arab Anti-Nacrotics Bureau
Pan-Arab Organization for Social Defence Against Crime
P.O. Box 17225
Amman, Jordan

Pompidou Group
Council of Europe
Strasbourg, France

South American Agreement
Combate de los Pozos 2133
1245 Buenos Aires, Argentina

Colombo Plan Bureau
12 Melbourne Avenue
Colombo, Sri Lanka

NON-GOVERNMENTAL ORGANIZATIONS

International Council on Alcohol and Addictions
Case Postale 140
CH-1001 Lausanne, Switzerland

International Union for Child Welfare
1, rue de Varembi
CH-1211 Geneva, Switzerland

INSTITUTES IN DIFFERENT COUNTRIES OR AREAS

Argentina

Comision Nacional de Toxicomanias y Narcoticos
Ministerio de Bienestar Social de la Nacion
Defensa 120, piso 1
Buenos Aires, Argentina

Centro Nacional de Reeducacion Social
Combate de los Pozos 2133
Buenos Aires, Argentina

Australia

Alcohol and Drug Addicts Treatment Board
1st Floor,3/161 Greenhill Road
Parkside, South Australia 5063

Alcohol and Drug Services
Mental Health Division
Health Commission of Victoria
Enterprise House
555 Collins Street
Melbourne, Victoria 3000
Australia

Australian Council of Social Services, Inc.
149 Castlereagh Street
Sydney, New South Wales 2000
Australia

Australian Foundation on Alcoholism and Drug Dependence
2nd Floor, T and G Building
London Circuit
Canberra City, A.C.T. 2601
Australia

Department of Health
Alcohol and Drug Dependence Service
"BIALA"

279 Roma Street
Brisbane, Queensland 4000
Australia

Department of Health
Drug Information Centre
Box 3944 V, G.P.O.
Sydney, New South Wales 2001
Australia

Department of Health Services
Public Buildings
Davey Street
Hobart, Tasmania 7000
Australia

National Drug Information Service
Commonwealth
Department of Health
P.O. Box 100
Wooden, A.C.T. 2606
Australia

Western Australia Alcohol and Drug
Authority
Greenchurch House
25 Richardson Street
West Perth, Western Australia 6005

Austria
Republik Oesterreich
Bundeministerium fuer Gesundheit und
Umweltschutz
Stubenring 1
1010 Wein, Austria

Belgium
Comite National pour l'Etude et al
Prevention de l'Alcoolisme et des
Autres Toxicomanies
Ministère de Santé Publique
Cabinet du Ministre
Rue Joseph II 30
Brussels 1040, Belgium

Brazil
Instituto Oscar Freire
Caixa Postal 22215
Sao Paulo, Brazil

Bulgaria
Centre de nevroligie, psychiatrie et
neurochirurgie
Secteur pour la lutte contre l'alcoholisme et
les narcomanies
Sofia 62, Bulgaria

Colombia
Coordinador de la Oficina de Control y
Prevencion del Alcoholismo y las
Drogas Heroicas
Calle 13, No. 9-33
Oficina 605-606
Apartado Aereo 13891
Bogota, Colombia

Seccion de Control de Drogas
Laboratories y Farmacias del Servicio
Seccional de Salud del Risaralda
Pereira, Colombia

Denmark
Commission on Drug Abuse in Youth
Sundhedsstyrelsen
Store Kongensgade 1
Copenhagen K, Denmark

Husset
Readhusstrade 13
1466 Copenhagen K, Denmark

Egypt
Ministry of Health
People's Assembly Street
Lazoglie
Cairo, Egypt

Finland
The Finnish Foundation for Alcohol
Studies
Kalevankatu 12
SF-00100 Helsinki 10, Finland

France
Association Regionale Contre la
Toxicomanie chez les Jeunes

39, boulevard Carnot
Toulouse, France

Centre DIDRO
9, rue Pauly
F-75014 Paris, France

Comité de Lutte contre l'Aggression de la Drogue et Aide aux Jeunes Drogues
31, rue Dieude
Marseilles, France

Club Social
"Drug Information"
4, rue Edith Cavell
Rennes, France

Haut Comité d'Etude et d'Information sur l'Alcoolisme
27, rue Oudinot
75700 Paris, France

Germany

Deutsche Hauptstelle gegen die Suchtoefahren
Westring 2 4700
Hamm, West Germany

Hygiene Museum
GDR 8010 Dresden
Julius—Fucik—Allee
German Democratic Republic

Ministerium fuer Gesundheitswesen der DDR
Hauptabt. Int. Beziehg
GDR 1020 Berlin
Rathausstrasse
German Democratic Republic

Hong Kong

Caritas Lok Heep Club
P.O. Box K2089
Kowloon, Hong Kong

The Society for the Aid and Rehabilitation of Drug Addicts
290–296 Tak Wah Building
Hennessy Road
Hong Kong

Hungary

Alkolizmus Elleni Orszagos Bizottsag
Budapest, V., Arany Janos v. 31
1051
Hungary

Egeszsegugyi Miniszterium
Budapest, V., Akademia v. 10
1055
Hungary

Iceland

Liquor Prevention Council
Eiriksgata 5
101 Reykjavik
Iceland

India

Indian Council on Medical Research
Ansari Nagar
P.O. Box 4508
New Delhi 110029
India

Iraq

Drug Combating Bureau Directorate
General of Police
Operation Branch
Baghdad, Iraq

Ireland

The Economic and Social Research Institute
4 Burlington Road
Dublin 4, Republic of Ireland

Eastern Health Board Day Centre
9 Usher's Island
Dublin S, Republic of Ireland

Public Relations Unit
Department of Health
Custom House

Room 36A
Dublin 1, Republic of Ireland

The Drug Treatment and Advisory Centre
Jervis Street Hospital
Dublin 1, Republic of Ireland

Israel

Department of Alcoholism Treatment Services
Ministry of Labour and Social Affairs
10 Yad Harutzim Street, Talpiot
P.O. Box 1260
Jerusalem 9100, Israel

Italy

Ministero della Sanita
D.G. Servizi Medicina Sociale
Viale della Civilta' Romana (EUR)
00144 Roma, Italy

Stampa Alternative
Casella Postale 741
Roma, Italy

Jamaica

The Permanent Secretary
Ministry of Health
10 Caledonia Avenue
Kingston 5, Jamaica W.I.

Japan

Mental Health Division
Public Health Bureau
Ministry of Health and Welfare
1-2-3 Kasumigaseki
Chiyoda-ku, Tokyo, Japan

Luxembourg

Centre de Santé Mentale
30, Ave. Marie Therese
Luxembourg

Service Multidisciplinaire de la Lutte contre la Toxicomanie
Ministère de la Santé Publique
1, rue Aug. Lumière
Luxembourg

Malaysia

Central Narcotics Bureau
P.O. Box 85
Petaling Jaya, Selangor
Malaysia

Mexico

Centro Mexicano de Estudios en Farmacodependencia (CEMEF)
Insurgentes Sur 1991-B, piso 7
Mexico 20, D.F.

Censejo Nacional de Saud Mental
Secretaria de Salubridad y Asistencia
Reforma y Lieja
Mexico 5, D.F.

Centros de Integracion Juvenil, A.C.
Jose Ma. Olloqui 48
Mexico 12, D.F.

Instituto Mexicano de Psiquiatria
Antiguo Camino a Xochimilco 101
Mexico 22, D.F.

Netherlands

Information and Education Department
Medisch Consultatie Bureau voor Alcoholisme
Jellinek Kliniek
Keizersgracht 674
Amsterdam, Holland

New Zealand

National Society on Alcoholism and Drug Dependence New Zealand (Inc.)
Box 1642
Wellington, New Zealand

Philippines

Dangerous Drugs Board
P.O. Box 3862
Manila, Philippines

The Narcotics Foundation of the Philippines
P.O. Box 3849
Manila, Philippines

Prevent and Rehabilitate Drug Abusers
PREDA Foundations, Inc.
Olongapo, Luzon, Philippines

Poland

Research Center on Alcoholism
Department of Information on Alcoholism and Drug Addiction
UL. Narbutta 54
02-541 Warsaw, Poland

Spoteczny Komitet Przeciwalkoholowy
(Committee to Fight Alcoholism)
Ul. Kopernika 36.40
00-328 Warsaw, Poland

South Africa

Department of Health, Welfare and Pensions
Private Bag X88
Pretoria 0001
Republic of South Africa

South African National Council on Alcoholism and Drug Dependence
Indian Branch
W.O. 1997 Indian Information Office
84 C.N.R. House
22 Cross Street
Durban, South Africa

Sweden

Centralforbundet for Alkohol
Karlavagen 117
Box 27302
10254 Stockholm, Sweden

Drug Dependence Bureau (SN4)
National Board of Health and Welfare
Stockholm, Sweden

Alkohol och Narkotika
Centralforbundet for Alkohol-och narkotikanpplysning
Fach 102 50
Stockholm, Sweden

Switzerland

Drop-In
Rheingasse 23
4058 Basel, Switzerland

Institut Suisse de Prevention de L'Alcoolisme et Autres Toxicomanies
Case Postale 1063
CH-1001 Lausanne, Switzerland

Institut Suisse de Prophylaxie de L'Alcoolisme
ISPA, Case Postale 203
1000 Lausanne 13, Switzerland

International Council on Alcohol and Addictions
Case Postale 140
1001 Lausanne, Switzerland

Office Federal de la Santé Publique
Coordination et Information en Matière de Drogues
Bollwerk 27
CH-3001 Bern, Switzerland

Schweizerische Fachstelle fuer Alkoholprobleme
Avenue Ruchonnet 14
CH-1003 Lausanne, Switzerland

Thailand

Central Bureau of Narcotics
Parusakawan Palace
Bangkok, Thailand

United Kingdom

Alcoholics Anonymous
11 Redcliffe Gardens
London SW10, England

Association for the Prevention of Addiction (APA)
32–33 Long Acre
London WC2, England

Drug Information Centre
Pharmacy Department
City Hospital
Huckmall Road
Nottingham, England

Government Advisory Committee on Alcoholism
Department of Health and Social Security Alexander Fleming House
Elephant and Castle
London SE1, England

Health Education Council
78 New Oxford Street
London WC1A 1AH, England

Institute of Psychiatry
Addiction Research Unit
DeCrespigny Park
London SE5, England

Institute for the Study of Drug Dependence
Kingsbury House
3 Blackburn Road
London NW6 1XA, England

Mental Health
c/o National Association for Mental Health
39 Queen Anne Street
London W1, England

Medical Council on Alcoholism
3 Grosvenor Crescent
London SW1, England

Narcotics Anonymous
37 Albert Square
London SW8, England

Release
1 Elgin Avenue
London W9, England

The Society for the Study of Addiction to Alcohol and Other Drugs
Tooting Bec Hospital
London SW17, England

Venezuela

Division de Higiene Mental
Ministerio de Sanidad
Edifico Sur, Picso 8
Centro Simon Bolivar
Caracas 1010, Venezuela

Comision contra el Uso Indebido de las Drogas
Fiscalia General de la Republica
Despacho del Fiscal
General de la Republica
Ministerio Publico
Caracas, Venezuela

Yugoslavia

Institute for Study and Prevention of Alcoholism and Drug Dependence
Clinical Hospital ''Mladen Stojanovic''
Zagreb, Yugoslavia

Institute of Mental Health
Palmoticeva 37
Belgrade, Yugoslavia

Institute on Alcoholism and Drug Dependence
Gornjacka 21
Belgrade, Yugoslavia

MAJOR ENGLISH-LANGUAGE JOURNALS, NEWSPAPERS AND PERIODICALS

Addictive Behaviors: An International Journal
Pergamon Press, Inc.
Fairview Park
Elmsford, New York 10523

Alcohol: An International Biomedical Journal
Center for Alcohol Studies
University of North Carolina Medical School
Chapel Hill, North Carolina 22514

Alcohol and Alcoholism: International Journal of the Medical Council on Alcoholism
University of Nebraska Medical Center
4101 Woolworth Avenue
Omaha, Nebraska 68105

Alcohol Health and Research World
P.O. Box 2345
Rockville, Maryland 20852

Alcoholism & Addiction
P.O. Box 31329
Seattle, Washington 98103

Alcoholism and Drug Abuse Week
P.O. Box 3357
Wayland Square
Providence, Rhode Island 02906-0357

The Alcoholism Report
1511 K Street, N.W.
Suite 708
Washington, D.C. 20005

Alcoholism: The National Magazine
P.O. Box C19051
Queen Anne Station
Seattle, Washington 98109

American Journal of Drug and Alcohol Abuse
Marcel Dekker, Inc.
P.O. Box 11305, Church Street Station
New York, New York 10249

American Journal of Epidemiology
Johns Hopkins University
School of Hygiene and Public Health
615 North Wolfe Street
Baltimore, Maryland 21205

American Journal of Obstetrics and Gynecology
C. V. Mosby Co.
11830 Westline Industrial Drive
St. Louis, Missouri 63141

American Journal of Pharmacy and the Sciences Supporting Public Health
Philadelphia College of Pharmacy and Science
43rd Street and Kingsessing Mall
Philadelphia, Pennsylvania 19104

American Journal of Psychiatry
American Psychiatric Association
1700 18th Street, N.W.
Washington, D.C. 20009

American Journal of Psychology
University of Illinois Press
Urbana, Illinois 61801

American Journal of Public Health
American Public Health Association
1015 18th Street, N.W.
Washington, D.C. 20036

American Journal of Sociology
University of Chicago Press

5801 South Ellis Avenue
Chicago, Illinois 60637

Annals of Internal Medicine
American College of Physicians
4200 Pine Street
Philadelphia, Pennsylvania 19104

Annals of the New York Academy of Sciences
The New York Academy of Sciences
2 East 63rd Street
New York, New York 10021

Archives of General Psychiatry
American Medical Association
535 North Dearborn Street
Chicago, Illinois 60610

Australian Alcohol Drug Review
Royal Prince Alfred Hospital
Missenden Road
Camperdown N.S.W. 2050 Australia

British Journal of Addiction
Addiction Research Unit
Institute of Psychiatry
DeCrespigny Park
London SE5 8AF

British Journal on Alcohol and Alcoholism
3 Grosvenor Crescent
London SW1X 7EE, England

British Journal of Criminology
Sweet and Maxwell Stevens Journals
11 New Fetter Lane
London EC4 P4EE, England

British Journal of Psychiatry
Headley Bros. Ltd.
Ashford, Kent TN24 8HH, England

British Medical Journal
British Medical Association
B.M.A. House, Tavistock Square
London WC1, England

Canadian Medical Association Journal
Canadian Medical Association
Box 8650
Ottawa K1G 068, Ontario, Canada

Clinical Pharmacology and Therapeutics
C.V. Mosby Co.
11830 Westline Industrial Drive
St. Louis, Missouri 63141

Clinical Toxicology
Marcel Dekker Journals
270 Madison Avenue
New York, New York 10016

Contemporary Drug Problems
Federal Legal Publications, Inc.
157 Chamber Street
New York, New York 10007

Crime and Delinquency
National Council on Crime and Delinquency
411 Continental Plaza
Hackensack, New Jersey 07601

Criminology
Sage Publications, Inc.
275 South Beverly Drive
Beverly Hills, California 90212

Digest of Alcoholism Theory and Application (DATA)
10700 Olson Memorial Highway
Minneapolis, Minnesota 55441

Diseases of the Nervous System
Physicians Postgraduate Press
Box 38293
Memphis, Tennessee 38138

Drug Abuse and Alcoholism Newsletter
Vista Hill Foundation
3420 Camino del Rio North, Suite 100
San Diego, California 92108

Drug and Alcohol Dependence
Elsevier Sequoia S.A.

Box 851
CH-1001 Lausanne 1, Switzerland

Drug Forum
Baywood Publishing Co., Inc.
120 Marine Street
Farmingdale, New York 11735

Drugs and Society: A Journal of Contemporary Issues
Center for Alcohol and Addiction Studies
University of Alaska
3211 Providence Drive
Anchorage, Alaska 99508

European Journal of Clinical Pharmacology
Springer-Verlag
175 Fifth Avenue
New York, New York 10010

Federal Probation
Administrative Office of the U.S. Courts
Supreme Court Building
Washington, D.C. 20544

Focus on Family and Chemical Dependency
U.S. Journal of Drug and Alcohol Dependence, Inc.
1721 Blount Road, Suite 1
Pompano Beach, Florida 33069

The Forum
1 Park Avenue
New York, New York 10016

The Globe—An International Magazine on Alcohol and Drug Problems
Oxelbarsgrand 21
S-16240 Vällingby, Sweden

The Grapevine
The Alcoholics Anonymous Grapevine, Inc.
468 Park Avenue South
New York, New York 10016

Human Pathology
Saunders Co.
West Washington Square
Philadelphia, Pennsylvania 19105

International Journal of the Addictions
Marcel Dekker Journals
270 Madison Avenue
New York, New York 10016

Japanese Journal of Alcohol Studies and Drug Dependence
Japanese Medical Society
c/o Department of Pharmacology of Kyoto Prefectural
University of Medicine
Kawaramachi—Hirokoii, Kamikyu-Ku,
Kyoto, 602 Japan

John Marshall Journal of Practice and Procedure
John Marshall Law School
315 South Plymouth Court
Chicago, Illinois 60604

The Journal
Addiction Research Foundation
33 Russell Street
Toronto, Ontario M5S 2S1, Canada

Journal of Abnormal Psychology
American Psychological Association
1200 17th Street, N.W.
Washington, D.C. 20036

Journal of Altered States of Consciousness
Baywood Publishing Co., Inc.
43 Central Drive
Farmingdale, New York 11735

Journal of the American Medical Association
535 North Dearborn Street
Chicago, Illinois 60610

Journal of Clinical Psychology
Clinical Psychology Publishing Co., Inc.

4 Conant Square
Brandon, Vermont 05733

Journal of Consulting and Clinical Psychology
American Psychological Association
1200 17th Street, N.W.
Washington, D.C. 20036

Journal of Criminal Law and Criminology
Williams and Wilkins Co.
428 East Preston Street
Baltimore, Maryland 21202

Journal of Drug Education
Baywood Publishing Co., Inc.
120 Marine Street
Farmingdale, New York 11735

Journal of Drug Issues
Box 4021
Tallahassee, Florida 32315-4021

Journal of Forensic Sciences
American Society for Testing and Material
1916 Race Street
Philadelphia, Pennsylvania 19103

Journal of General Psychology
Journal Press
2 Commercial Street
Provincetown, Massachusetts 02657

Journal of Health and Social Behavior
American Sociological Association
1722 North Street, N.W.
Washington, D.C. 20036

Journal of Nervous and Mental Diseases
Williams and Wilkins Co.
428 East Preston Street
Baltimore, Maryland 21202

Journal of Personality
Duke University Press
6697 College Station
Durham, North Carolina 27708

Journal of Personality and Social Psychology
American Psychological Association
1200 17th Street, N.W.
Washington, D.C. 20036

Journal of Pharmacy and Pharmacology
Pharmaceutical Society of Great Britain
1 Lambeth High Street
London SE1 7JN, England

Journal of Pharmacology and Experimental Therapeutics
Williams and Wilkins Co.
428 East Preston Street
Baltimore, Maryland 21202

Journal of Psychoactive Drugs
409 Clayton Street
San Francisco, California 94117

Journal Psychology
Journal Press
2 Commercial Street
Provincetown, Massachusetts 02657

Journal of Social Psychology
Journal Press
2 Commercial Street
Provincetown, Massachusetts 02657

Journal of Studies on Alcohol
Alcohol and Drug Abuse Research Center, McLean Hospital
Harvard Medical School
115 Mill Street
Balmont, Massachusetts 02178

Journal on Alcohol and Drug Education
1120 East Oakland
P.O. Box 10212
Lansing, Michigan 48901

New England Journal of Medicine
Massachusetts Medical Society
10 Shattuck Street
Boston, Massachusetts 02115

New York State Journal of Medicine
Medical Society of the State of New York
420 Lakeville Road
Lake Success, New York 11040

Problemy Alkohollzmu
Lwowska 5,00-600
Warszawa, Poland

Psychiatry
William Alanson White Psychiatric Foundation, Inc.
1610 New Hampshire Avenue, N.W.
Washington, D.C. 20009

Psychological Reports
Box 9229
Missoula, Montana 59801

Psychology
Box 6495, Station C
Savannah, Georgia 31405

Psychopharmacology
Springer-Verlag
174 Fifth Avenue
New York, New York 10010

Research Communications in Substances of Abuse
P.O. Box 966
Westbury, New York 11590

Social Problems
Society for the Study of Social Problems
114 Rockwell Hall
State University College
Buffalo, New York 14222

Sociological Quarterly
Midwest Sociological Society
Department of Sociology
Southern Illinois University
Carbondale, Illinois 62901

Suchigsfahren
Westring 2, Postfach 1369
4700 Hamm, Germany

U.S. Journal of Drug and Alcohol Dependence
2119-A Hollywood Boulevard
Hollywood, Florida 33020

BIBLIOGRAPHY

Aafen, Brent. *Marijuana*. Center City, Minn.: Hazelden Foundation, 1980.

Abel, Ernest L. *Marijuana: The First Twelve Thousand Years*. New York: Plenum Publishing Corp., 1980.

Abramson, H. A., ed. *The Use of LSD in Psychotherapy and Alcoholism*. Indianapolis: Bobbs-Merrill Co. Inc., 1967.

Ackerman, Robert J. *Children of Alcoholics*. Hollywood, Fla.: Health Communications, 1978.

Ackoff, R. L.; Gupta, S.; and Minas, J. S. *Scientific Method: Optimizing Applied Research Decisions*. New York: John Wiley and Sons, 1969.

Addiction Research Foundation. *Alcohol, Drugs and Traffic Safety*. Toronto, 1976.

———. *The Forgotten Children*. Toronto, 1969.

———. *R.I.D.E.—A Driving-While-Impaired Countermeasure Program*. Toronto, 1979.

Akins, Carl, and Beschner, George. *Ethnography: A Research Tool for Policymakers in the Drug and Alcohol Fields*. Rockville, Md.: National Institute on Drug Abuse, 1980.

Alcoholics Anonymous World Services. *Alcoholics Anonymous*. New York, 1965.

———. *Alcoholics Anonymous Comes of Age: A Brief History of A.A.* New York, 1957.

———. *Twelve Steps and Twelve Traditions*. New York, 1952.

Alexander, M. *The Sexual Paradise of LSD*. North Hollywood, Calif.: Brandon House, 1967.

Alexander, Tom. *The Drug Takers*. New York: Time Inc., 1965.

Allen, Lloyd V., Jr. *Drug Abuse: What Can We Do?* Ventura, Calif.: Regal Press, 1981.

Alpert, R., and Cohen, S. *LSD*. New York: New American Library, 1967.

American Medical Association. "Dependence on Cannibis (Marijuana)." *Journal of the American Medical Association*, 201:368–371, 1967.

———. *Manual on Alcoholism*. Chicago, 1977.

———. "Marijuana and Society." *Journal of the American Medical Association*, 204:1181–1182, 1968.

American Pharmaceutical Association. *Handbook of Nonprescription Drugs*. Sixth edition. Washington, D.C., 1979.

Anders, Rebecca. *A Look at Drug Abuse*. Minneapolis: Lerner Publications, Co., 1977.

Anderson, J. R., and Bower, G. H. *Human Associative Memory*. Washington, D.C.: Winston and Sons, 1973.

Andolfi, M. *Family Therapy: An Interactional Approach*. New York: Plenum Press, 1979.

Andrews, G., and Vinkenoog, S., eds. *The Book of Grass: An Anthology of Indian Hemp*. New York: Grove Press, 1967.

Andrews, George, and Solomon, David, eds. *The Coca Leaf and Cocaine Papers*. New York: Harcourt, Brace, Jovanovich, 1975.

Angmann and Associates. *Health Insurance Coverage of Alcoholism Benefits: Results of a National Survey and Implications for California.* San Francisco: California State Senate Committee on Health and Welfare, n.d.

Anon. "Cocaine Smuggled in Water Skis." *Washington Post.* August 26, 1974.

Anon. "Cocaine: Middle Class High." *Time Magazine,* July 6, 1981.

Anon. *Legal Highs, A Concise Encyclopedia of Legal Herbs and Chemicals with Psychoactive Properties.* New York: High Times Press, 1973.

Anon. "Private Violence: Child Abuse, Wife Beating, Rape." *Time Magazine,* September 5, 1983.

Anon. "The Cocaine Scene." *Newsweek Magazine,* May 30, 1977.

Ansbacher, H., and Ansbacher, R. *The Individual Psychology of Alfred Adler.* New York: Basic Books, 1946.

Armor, David J.; Polich, J. Michael; and Stambul, Harriet B. *Alcoholism and Treatment.* New York: John Wiley and Sons, 1978.

Arndt, J. R., and Blockstein, W. L. *Problems in Drug Abuse.* Madison, Wis.: University of Wisconsin, 1970.

Ashbrook, Debra L., and Solley, Linda C. *Women & Heroin Abuse: A Survey of Sexism in Drug Abuse Administration.* Palo Alto, Calif.: R & E Research Associates, 1979.

Ashley, R. *Cocaine: Its History, Uses and Effects.* New York: St. Martin's Press, 1975.

Asimov, I. *The Human Brain: Its Capacities and Functions.* Boston: Houghton Mifflin, 1964.

Augsburger, David. *So What? Everybody's Doing It!* Chicago: Moody Press, 1969.

Australian Foundation on Alcoholism and Drug Dependence. *National Alcohol and Drug Dependence Multidisciplinary Institute, August 27 to September 1, 1978.* Canberra, 1978.

Ausubel, David P. *Drug Addiction: Physiological, Psychological and Sociological Aspects.* New York: Random House, 1958.

———. *What Every Well-Informed Person Should Know About Drug Addiction.* Chicago: Nelson-Hall Publishers, 1980.

Avogaro, P.; Sirtori, C. R.; and Tremoli, E. *Metabolic Effects of Alcohol.* New York: Elsevier, 1979.

Bacon, M., and Jones, M. B. *Teen-age Drinking.* New York: Crowell, 1968.

Bacon, Selden D. *Understanding Alcoholism.* Philadelphia: American Academy of Political and Social Science, 1958.

Bahr, Howard M. *Skid Row: An Introduction to Disaffiliation.* New York: Oxford University Press, 1973.

Bailey, C. B.; Ginter, D. J.; and Woodlock, B. K. *Handbook for Alcoholism Counselors.* Cleveland: Alcoholism Services of Cleveland, 1978.

Bandura, Albert. *Principles of Behavior Modification.* New York: Holt, Rinehart and Winston, 1969.

Barber, Bernard. *Drugs and Society.* Beverly Hills, Calif.: Russell Sage, 1967.

Barnes, G. M.; Abel, E. L.; and Ernst, C. A. S. *Alcohol and the Elderly: A Comprehensive Bibliography.* Westport, Conn.: Greenwood Press, 1980.

Barnes, T., and Price, S. *Interaction of Alcohol and Other Drugs—Supplement.* Toronto: Addiction Research Foundation, 1973.

Barr, H. L., and Cohen, A. *The Problem-Drinking Drug Addict.* Washington, D.C.: National Institute on Drug Abuse, 1979.

Bauman, Carl. E. *Predicting Adolescent Drug Use.* New York: Praeger Publishers, 1980.

Beauchamp, Dan E. *Beyond Alcoholism: Alcohol and Public Health Policy*. Philadelphia: Temple University Press, 1980.

Becker, Howard S. *Outsiders: Studies in the Sociology of Deviance*. San Francisco: Jossey-Bass, 1969.

Beckman, Harry. *Dilemmas in Drug Therapy*. W. B. Saunders Co., 1967.

———. *Pharmacology: the Nature, Action and Use of Drugs*. Philadelphia: W. B. Saunders Co., 1961.

Beenel, Barbara Cottman. *Parents Who Help Their Children Overcome Drugs*. Chicago: Contemporary Books; Los Angeles: Lowell House, 1989.

Begleiter, H. *Biological Effects of Alcohol*. New York: Plenum Publishing Corp., 1980.

Bejerot, Nils. *Addiction and Society*. Springfield, Ill.: Charles C. Thomas, 1970.

Bell, Judith, and Billington, D. Rex. *Annotated Bibliography of Health Education Research Completed in Britain from 1948–1978*. Edinburgh: Scottish Health Education Unit, 1980.

Bemko, Jane. *Substance Abuse Book Review Index 1980*. Toronto: Addiction Research Foundation, 1981.

Benjamin, Fred. B. *Alcohol, Drugs, and Traffic Safety: Where Do We Go From Here?* Springfield, Ill.: Charles C. Thomas, 1980.

Bennett, James C., and Demos, George D. *Drug Abuse and What We Can Do About It*. Springfield, Ill.: Charles C. Thomas, 1979.

Benson, W. M., and Schiele, B. C. *Tranquilizing and Anti-depressive Drugs*. Springfield, Ill.: Charles C. Thomas, 1962.

Berger, Gilda. *Drug Abuse: The Impact on Society,* New York: Franklin Watts, 1988.

———. *Drug Testing,* New York: Franklin Watts, 1987.

———. *Crack*. New York: Franklin Watts, 1987.

Bergin, A. E., and Strupp, H. H. *Changing Frontiers in the Science of Psychotherapy*. Chicago: Aldine Atherton, 1972.

Berkow, Robert ed. *The Merck Manual of Diagnosis and Therapy*. Rahway, N.J.: Merck Sharp and Dohme Research Laboratories, 1977.

Berman, A. *Analysis of Drugs of Abuse*. Philadelphia: Heyden and Son, Inc., 1977.

Bermandt, Gordon, et al. *Psychology and the Law*. Lexington, Mass: Lexington Books, 1976.

Birdwood, George. *The Willing Victim*. New York: International Publications Service, 1969.

Birnbaum, Isabel M., and Parker, Elizabeth S. *Alcohol and Human Memory*. Hillsdale, N.J.: Lawrence Erlbaum Associates, 1977; dist. John Wiley and Sons.

Bishop, M. G. *The Discovery of Love: A Psychedelic Experience with LSD-25*. New York: Dodd, Mead & Co., 1963.

Blachly, Paul H., ed. *Drug Data and Debate*. Springfield, Ill.: Charles C. Thomas, 1973.

Black, P., ed. *Drugs and the Brain*. Baltimore: Johns Hopkins Press, 1969.

Blakeslee, Alton. *What You Should Know about Drugs and Narcotics*. New York: Associated Press, 1969.

Blane, H. T. *The Personality of the Alcoholic: Guises of Dependency*. New York: Harper and Row, 1968.

———. and Chafetz, M. E. *Youth, Alcohol, and Social Policy*. New York: Plenum Publishing Corp., 1979.

Blocker, Jack S., Jr. *Alcohol, Reform and Society: The Liquor Issue in Social Context*. Westport, Conn.: Greenwood Press, 1979.

Blombert, R. D.; Preusser, D. F.; Hale, A.; and Ulmer, R. G. *A Comparison of Alcohol Involvement in Pedestrians and Pedestrian Casualties*. Springfield, Va: National Technical Information Service, 1979.

Bloomquist, Edward R. *Marijuana, the Second Trip*. Beverly Hills, Calif.: Glencoe Press, 1971.

Blum, R. H. *The Dream Sellers*. San Francisco: Jossey-Bass, 1972.

———. and Associates. *The Utopiates: Uses and Users of LSD*. New York: Atherton Press, 1964.

———. et al. *Society and Drugs*. San Francisco: Jossey-Bass, 1969.

———. et al. *Students and Drugs: Drugs II*. San Francisco: Jossey-Bass, 1969.

Blume, Sheila B. *Fetal Alcohol Syndrome: Task Force Report to the Governor*. Albany: New York State Division of Alcoholism and Alcohol Abuse, 1979.

Bonnie, Richard J, and Whitebread, Charles H. *Marihuana Conviction: A History of Marihuana Prohibition in the United States*. Charlottesville, Va.: University Press of Virginia, 1974.

———. *Marijuana Use and Criminal Sanctions: Essays on the Theory and Practice of Law Reform*. Charlottesville, Va.: Michie/Bobbs-Merrill Law Publishing, 1980.

Bourne, Peter G. *Methadone: Benefits and Shortcomings*. Washington, D.C.: Drug Abuse Council, 1975.

———. ed. *Acute Drug Abuse Emergencies: A Treatment Manual*. New York: Academic Press, 1976.

———. ed. *Addiction*. New York: Academic Press, 1974.

Bowen, Haskell, and Landin, Les. *About Drugs*. Belmont, Calif.: Pitman Publishers, 1971.

Bowker, Lee H. *Drug Use Among American Women, Old & Young: Sexual Oppression & Other Themes*. Palo Alto, Calif.: R & E Research Associates, 1977.

Braden, William. *The Private Sea: LSD and the Search for God*. Chicago: Quadrangle Books, 1967.

Braude, M. C., and Szara, S., eds. *Pharmacology of Marijuana*. New York: Raven Press, 1976.

Brecher, Edward M. and the Editors of Consumer Reports. *Licit & Illicit Drugs*. Boston: Little, Brown and Company, 1972.

Brill, L., and Liberman, L. *Authority and Addiction*. Boston: Little, Brown and Company, 1969.

———. and Winick, Charles. *The Yearbook of Substance Use and Abuse*. Vol. II. New York: Human Sciences Press, 1980.

———. et al. *The Treatment of Substance Abusers*. New York: Free Press, 1981.

Brisolara, Ashton. *The Alcoholic Employee: A Handbook of Useful Guidelines*. New York: Human Sciences Press, 1979.

British Royal College of Psychiatrists. *Alcohol and Alcoholism*. Report of a Special Committee of the Royal College of Psychiatrists. London: Tavistock Publications, 1979.

Brody, Jane. *Jane Brody's Nutrition Book*. New York: W. W. Norton & Company, Inc., 1981.

Bronetto, J. *Alcohol Price, Alcohol Consumption and Death by Liver Cirrhosis*. Toronto: Addiction Research Foundation, 1960–63.

Brook, Robert, and Whitehead, Paul. *Drug-free Therapeutic Community*. New York: Human Sciences Press, 1980.

Brooks, Cathleen. *The Secret Everyone Knows*. San Diego, Calif. Joan B. Kroc Foundation, 1981.

Brown, B. B. *New Mind, New Body.* New York: Harper & Row, 1974.

Bugenthal, J. F. *The Search for Authenticity.* New York: Holt, Rinehart & Winston, 1965.

Bullington, Bruce. *Heroin Use in the Barrio.* Lexington, Mass.: Lexington Books, 1977.

Burack, Richard, and Fox, Fred J. *The Handbook of Prescription Drugs.* New York: Ballantine Books, 1975.

Bureau of Narcotics and Dangerous Drugs. *Glossary of Terms in the Drug Culture.* Washington, D.C.: U.S. Department of Justice, 1970.

Burger, Alfred E. *Drugs Affecting the Central Nervous System.* New York: Marcel Dekker Inc., 1968.

Burns, John. *Answer to Addiction.* Blauvelt, N.Y.: Multimedia Publishing Corp., 1980.

Burroughs, William. *Naked Lunch.* New York: Grove Press, 1966.

Burt, Marvin R. *Drug Abuse: Its Natural History and the Effectiveness of Current Treatments.* Cambridge, Mass.: Schenkman Publishing Co. Inc., 1979.

Bush, Patricia J. *Drugs, Alcohol & Sex.* New York: Richard Marek, 1980.

Busse, S., et al. *Disulfiram in the Treatment of Alcoholism: An Annotated Bibliography.* Toronto: Addiction Research Foundation, 1978.

Butters, Nelson, and Cermak, Laird S. *Alcoholic Korsakoff's Syndrome: An Information-Processing Approach to Amnesia.* New York: Academic Press, 1980.

Buys, Donna, and Saltman, Jules. *The Unseen Alcoholics—The Elderly.* Pamphlet No. 602. New York: Public Affairs Pamphlets, 1982.

Byck, Robert ed. *Cocaine Papers by Sigmund Freud.* New York: Stonehill Publishing Co., 1972.

Byrd, P. D., ed. *Medical Readings on Drug Abuse.* Reading, Mass.: Addison-Wesley, 1970.

Cahalan, Donald; Cisin, I. H.; and Crossley, H. M. *American Drinking Practices.* New Haven: College and University Press, 1969.

———. *American Drinking Practices: A National Survey of Behavior and Attitudes.* Monograph No. 6. New Brunswick, N. J.: Rutgers Center of Alcohol Studies, 1969.

———. *Implications of American Drinking Practices and Attitudes for Prevention and Treatment of Alcoholism.* Berkeley: Social Research Group, School of Public Health, University of California, n.d.

Cahn, S. *The Treatment of Alcoholics: An Evaluation Study.* New York: Oxford University Press, 1970.

Caldwell, William V. *LSD Psychotherapy.* New York: Grove Press, 1968.

Callaway, E., et al. *Neuropsychological Studies of Alcohol: Final Report.* Springfield, Va.: National Information Service, 1978.

Canada Commission of Inquiry into the Non-medical Use of Drugs (The Le Dain Commission). *Cannabis, A Report of the Commission . . .* Ottawa: Information Canada, 1972.

———. *Final Report of the Commission . . .* Ottawa: Information Canada, 1973.

———. *Interim Report of the Commission . . .* Ottawa: Information Canada, 1970.

———. *Treatment, A Report of the Commission . . .* Ottawa: Information Canada, 1972.

Candlin, A. H. S. *Psychochemical Warfare.* New Rochelle, N.Y.: Arlington House, 1973.

Caplovitz, David. *The Working Addict.* White Plains, N.Y.: M. E. Sharpe, 1976.

Carey, J. T. *The College Drug Scene.* Englewood Cliffs, N.J.: Prentice-Hall, 1963.

Carney, Richard E., ed. *Risk-Taking Behavior: Concepts, Methods, and Applications to Smoking and Drug Abuse.* Springfield, Ill.: Charles C. Thomas, 1971.

Carone, Pasquale A., and Kreinsky, Leonard W. *Drug Abuse in Industry.* Springfield, Ill.: Charles C. Thomas, 1973.

———. et al. *Addictive Disorder Update: Alcoholism, Drug Abuse, Gambling.* New York: Human Sciences Press, 1981.

Carriel, D. *So Fair a House: The Story of Synanon.* Englewood Cliffs, N.J.: Prentice-Hall, 1963.

Carroll, C. *Drugs In Modern Society.* New York: William C. Brown, 1985.

Cashman, John. *The LSD Story.* Greenwich, Conn.: Fawcett Publications, 1966.

Castenada, C. *Journey to Ixthlan: The Lessons of Don Juan.* New York: Simon and Schuster, 1972.

Chafetz, M. E. *Liquor: The Servant of Man.* Boston: Little, Brown and Company, 1965.

———. *Why Drinking Can Be Good for You.* New York: Stein and Day, 1976.

———., and Demone, H. W. *Alcoholism and Society.* New York: Oxford University Press, 1962.

———. Blane, Howard T.; and Hill, Marjorie J. *Frontiers of Alcoholism.* New York: Science House, 1970.

Chambers, Carl D., and Brill, Leon, eds. *Methadone Experiences and Issues.* New York: Human Sciences Press, 1973.

———. and Heckman, Richard D. *Employee Drug Abuse: A Manager's Guide for Action.* Boston: CBI Publishing Co. Inc., 1972.

Chapin, W. *Wasted: The Story of My Son's Drug Addiction.* New York; McGraw-Hill, 1972.

Chasen, Dave. *The Gourmet Cokebook, A Complete Guide to Cocaine.* New York: White Mountain Press, 1972.

Chein, I., et al. *The Road to H.* New York: Basic Books, 1964.

Chesler, Phyllis. *Women and Madness.* New York: Doubleday, 1972.

Chiles, John. *Teenage Depression and Suicide.* New York: Chelsea House, 1986.

Chopra, G. S., and Chopra, I. C. *Drug Addiction with Special Reference to India.* New York: International Publications Service, 1965.

Clark, P. M. S., and Kricka, L. J. *Medical Consequences of Alcohol Abuse.* New York: Halsted Press, and John Wiley and Sons, 1980.

Clarke, Frank H., ed. *How Modern Medicines Are Developed.* Mount Kisco, N.Y.: Futura Publications, 1977.

Clarke, Robert C. *Marijuana Botony.* Berkeley, Calif.: And/Or Press, 1981.

Clouet, D. H., ed. *Narcotic Drugs: Biochemical Pharmacology.* New York: Plenum Publishing Corp., 1971.

Cohen, Charles P., et al. *Psychotherapy and Drug Addiction: Diagnosis and Treatment.* New York: Irvington Publishers, Inc., 1974.

Cohen, Sidney, ed. *Drug Abuse and Alcoholism.* New York: The Haworth Press, 1981.

———. *The Beyond Within: The LSD Story.* New York: Atheneum, 1967.

———. *The Drug Dilemma.* New York: McGraw-Hill, 1975.

———. *The Substance Abuse Problems.* New York: The Haworth Press, 1981.

Coleman, James S. *The Adolescent Society.* New York: Free Press, 1961.

Coleman, Richard. *Is Your Prescription Killing You?* Port Washington, N.Y.: Ashley Books, Inc., 1981.

Coles, Robert. *The Grass Pipe.* Boston: Little, Brown and Company, 1969.

Collins, James J., Jr. *Drinking and Crime: Perspectives on the Relationships between Alcohol Consumption and Criminal Behavior.* New York: Guilford Publications, 1981.

Committee on Mental Health Services. *Drug Misuse: A Psychiatric View of a Modern Dilemma.* Volume VII. Report No. 80. Pamphlet. New York: Group for the Advancement of Psychiatry, June 1971.

Connell, P. H. *Amphetamine Psychosis.* London: Chapman and Hall, 1958.

Coombs, Robert, et al., eds. *Socialization in Drug Abuse.* Cambridge, Mass.: Schenkman Co. Inc., 1976.

Cooper, M. L.; Schawar, T. G.; and Smith, L. S. *Alcohol, Drugs and Road Traffic.* Cape Town: Juta and Co., 1979.

Corsini, Raymond J. *Current Psychotherapies.* 2nd ed. Itasca, Ill.: F. E. Peacock Publishers, 1979.

Cowan, Ronald, and Roth, Rodney. "The Turned On Generation: Where Will They Turn To?" *Journal of Drug Education,* 2(1):39–47, 1972.

Cox, Ann E. *Training Guidelines and Workbook for the Behavioral Management of Intoxicated and Disruptive Clients.* Toronto: Addiction Research Foundation, 1981.

Craig, Robert, and Baker, Stewart. *Drug Dependent Patients.* Springfield, Ill.: Charles C. Thomas, 1981.

Crenshaw, Mary. *The End of the Rainbow.* New York: Macmillan, 1981.

Crohn, Leslie P. *Self-Awareness, Drug Abuse and Drug Control.* New York: McGraw-Hill, 1981.

Crowley, Aleister. *Cocaine.* Reprint of the 1918 edition. San Francisco: Level Press, 1973.

———. *The Diary of a Drug Fiend.* New York: Lancer Books, 1972.

Cull, J. G., and Hardy, R. E. *Types of Drug Abusers and Their Abuse.* Springfield, Ill.: Charles C. Thomas, 1974.

Cutler, R., and Storm, T. *Drinking Practices in Three British Columbia Cities II. Student Survey.* Vancouver: Alcoholism Foundation of British Columbia, 1973.

Dahlstrom, W. G., and Welsch, G. S. *An MMPI Handbook: A Guide to Use in Clinical Practice and Research.* Minneapolis: University of Minnesota Press, 1965.

David, Kenneth, and Cowley, James. *Pastoral Care in Schools and Colleges.* London: Edward Arnold, n.d.

Dawkins, Marvin P. *Alcohol and the Black Community: Exploratory Studies of Selected Issues.* Saratoga, Calif.: Century Twenty-One, 1980.

De Leon, George, ed. *Phoenix House: Studies in a Therapeutic Community.* New York: Irvington Publishers Inc., 1974.

De Long, J. V. "The Methadone Habit." *New York Times Magazine.* March 16, 1975.

De Quincey, T. *Confessions of an English Opium Eater.* Reprint. New York: Three Sirens Press, 1932.

DeRopp, Robert S. *Drugs and the Mind.* New York: Grove Press, 1961.

———. *The Master Game.* New York: Delta Books, 1968.

Department of Health and Human Services. *The Alcohol, Drug Abuse, and Mental Health National Data Book.* Rockville, Md., 1980.

———. *National Survey on Drug Abuse: Main Findings 1982.* Rockville, Md., 1983.

Department of Health, Education, and Welfare. *Smoking and Health: A Report of the Surgeon General.* Washington, D.C.: Government Printing Office, 1979.

Diehm, A. P.; Seaborn, R. F.; and Wilson, G. C. *Alcohol in Australia: Problems and Programmes.* New York: McGraw-Hill, 1978.

Do It Now Foundation. *Alcohol, Drugs, and Safety.* Phoenix, 1975.

Dominick, John. *The Drug Bust.* New York: The Light Co., 1970.

Domino, E. F., ed. *PCP (Phencyclidine): Historical and Current Perspectives.* Ann Arbor, Mich.: NPP Books.

Drake, Bill. *The Cultivator's Handbook of Marijuana.* Berkeley, Calif.: Book People, 1970.

Drake, William Daniel, Jr. *The Connoisseur's Handbook of Marijuana.* San Francisco: Straight Arrow Books, 1971.

Drug Abuse Council. *The Facts About Drug Abuse.* New York: Free Press, 1980.
Drug Enforcement Administration. *Drugs of Abuse.* Vol. 6, No. 2 (Reprinted from Drug Enforcement). Washington, D.C., July, 1979.
———. *Drug Enforcement.* Vol. 6. No. 3. Washington, D.C. October, 1979.
———. *Marijuana.* Vol. 7, No. 1. Washington, D.C. March, 1980.
———. *Drug Enforcement.* Vol. 8, No. 1. Washington, D.C. Summer, 1981.
———. *Drug Enforcement.* Vol. 9, No. 1. Washington, D.C. Summer, 1982.
———. *Drug Enforcement.* Vol. 9, No. 2. Washington, D.C. Fall, 1982.
———. *Drug Enforcement.* Vol. 10, No. 1. Washington, D.C. Spring, 1983.
Du-Torr, B. M. *Drugs, Rituals, and Altered States of Consciousness.* Rotterdam: A. A. Balkema, 1977.
Dubos, Rene. *Man Adapting.* New Haven, Conn.: Yale University Press, 1965.
Duncan, T. L. *Understanding and Helping the Narcotic Addict.* New York: Prentice-Hall, 1965.
Dunlap, James. *Exploring Inner Space: Personal Experiences under LDS-25.* New York: Harcourt, Brace, Jovanovich, 1961.
Dunnell, Karen, and Cartwright, Ann. *Medicine Takers, Prescribers and Hoarders.* London: Routledge and Kegan Paul, 1972.
Durkheim, Emile. *Suicide.* New York: Free Press, 1962.
Dusek, Dorothy, and Girdano, Daniel. *Drugs: A Factual Account.* Reading, Mass.: Addison-Wesley Publishing Co., 1980.
Duster, T. *The Legislation of Morality: Law, Drugs, and Moral Judgment.* New York: Free Press, 1970.
Ebin, David, ed. *The Drug Experience.* New York: Grove Press, 1961.
Eddy, Paul, with Saboczl, Hugo and Walden, Sara. *The Cocaine Wars.* New York: W. W. Norton, 1988.
Edwards, Griffith, et al. *Drugs and Drug Dependence.* Lexington, Mass.: Lexington Books, 1976.
Eells, Kenneth. *Pot: Medical and Psychological Aspects of Marihuana.* Pasadena, Calif.: California Institute of Technology, 1968.
Efron, D. H., ed. *Psychotomimetic Drugs.* New York: Raven Press, 1969.
Einstein, Stanley. *Beyond Drugs.* Elmsford, N.Y.: Pergamon Press, 1974.
———. ed. *The Community's Response to Drug Use.* Elmsford, N.Y.: Pergamon Press, 1980.
———. *Drugs in Relation to the Drug User.* Elmsford, N.Y.: Pergamon Press, 1980.
———. *Use and Misuse of Drugs.* Belmont, Calif.: Wadsworth Publishing Co., 1970.
Eldridge, William Butler, *Narcotics and the Law.* New York: New York University Press, 1962.
Elgin, Kathleen, and Osterritter, John F. *The Ups and Downs of Drugs.* New York: Alfred A. Knopf, 1972.
Ellinwood, E. H., and Cohen, S. *Current Concepts on Amphetamine Abuse.* Washington, D.C.: Government Printing Office, 1972.
Ellis, Albert. *Reason and Emotion in Psychotherapy.* New York: Lyle Stuart, 1962.
Endore, G. *Synanon.* Garden City, N.Y.: Doubleday, 1967.
Engel, Madeline, H. *The Drug Scene: A Sociological Perspective.* Rochelle Park, N.J.: Hayden Book Co., Inc., 1974.
Englemann, Larry. *Intemperance: The Lost War against Liquor.* New York: Free Press, 1979.

Engs, Ruth C. *Responsible Drug and Alcohol Use*. New York: Macmillan, 1979.

Epstein, Samuel, and Lederberg, Joshua, eds. *Drugs of Abuse: Their Genetic and Other Chronic Nonpsychiatric Hazards*. Cambridge, Mass.: The MIT Press, 1971.

Eriksson, K.; Sinclair, J. D.; and Kiianmaa, K. *Animal Models of Alcohol Research*. New York: Academic Press, 1980.

Etons, Ursula. *Angel Dusted: A Family's Nightmare*. New York: Macmillan, 1981.

Evans, Glen, and Farberow, Norman. *The Encyclopedia of Suicide*. New York, Facts On File, 1988.

Faber, Stuart J., et al. *Angel Dust: What Everyone Should Know About PCP*. Los Angeles: Lega Books, 1979.

Falco, Mathea. *Methaqualone: A Study of Drug Control*. Washington, D.C.: Drug Abuse Council, 1975.

Farrere, Claude. *Black Opium*. San Francisco: And/Or Press, 1974.

Feit, Marvin D. *Management and Administration of Drug and Alcohol Programs*. Springfield, Ill.: Charles C. Thomas, 1979.

Fenichel, Otto. *The Psychoanalytic Theory of Neurosis*. New York: W. W. Norton and Co., 1945.

Fiddle, S. *Portraits from a Shooting Gallery*. New York: Harper and Row, 1967.

Fieve, Ronald R. *Moodswing*. Rev. ed. New York: Bantam, 1989.

Fisher, Richard B., and Christie, George A. *A Dictionary of Drugs: The Medicines You Use*. New York: Schocken Books, 1976.

Follmann, Joseph F., Jr. *Helping the Troubled Employee*. New York: Amacom, 1978.

Ford Foundation. *Dealing with Drug Abuse*. New York: Praeger Publishers, 1972.

Forney, Thomas, and Hughes, Frances. *Combined Effects of Alcohol and Other Drugs*. Springfield, Ill.: Charles C. Thomas, 1968.

Fort, Joel. *The Addicted Society: Pleasure-Seeking and Punishment Revisited*. New York: Grove Press, 1981.

———. *The Pleasure Seekers: The Drug Crisis, Youth and Society*. New York: Grove Press, 1970.

Fox, Ruth. *The Alcoholic Spouse*. New York: National Council on Alcoholism, 1956.

Frank, Jerome D. *Persuasion and Healing*. Baltimore, Md.: Johns Hopkins Press, 1961.

Frank, Mel, and Rosenthal, Ed. *Marijuana Grower's Guide*. San Francisco: And/Or Press, 1974.

Frazier, J. *Marijuana Farmers: Hemp Cults and Cultures*. Indian Mill, W.V.: Solar Age Press, 1973.

Freedman, M., and Kaplan, H. I. *Comprehensive Textbook of Psychiatry*. Baltimore: Williams and Wilkins, 1967.

Freidson, Eliot. *Profession of Medicine*. New York: Dodd, Mead, 1970.

French, Scott. *The Complete Guide to the Street Drug Game*. Secaucus, N.J.: Lyle Stuart, Inc., 1980.

Freund, E. Edith. *Drugs! Why?* New York: Carlton Press, 1980.

Fuqua, Paul. *Drug Abuse: Investigation and Control*. New York: McGraw-Hill, 1977.

Gage, Freddie. *Everything You Always Wanted to Know About Dope*. Houston: Pulpit Productions, 1971.

Galanter, Marc. *Alcohol and Drug Abuse in Medical Education*. Rockville, Md.: National Institute on Drug Abuse, 1980.

Gannon, Frank. *Drugs: What They Are, How They Look, What They Do*. New York: Warner Books, 1972.

Garattini, S.; Mussini, E.; and Randall, L. O. *The Benzodiazepines.* New York: Raven Press, 1973.

Geller, Allen, and Boas, Maxwell. *The Drug Beat: A Complete Survey of the History, Distribution, Uses and Abuses of Marijuana, LSD and the Amphetamines.* Chicago: Contemporary Books, 1969.

Gibbins, Robert J., et al. *Research Advances in Alcohol and Drug Problems, Vol. 1.* New York: John Wiley and Sons, 1974.

———. et al. *Research Advances in Alcohol and Drug Problems, Vol. 2.* New York: John Wiley and Sons, 1975.

———. et al. *Research Advances in Alcohol and Drug Problems, Vol. 3.* New York: John Wiley and Sons, 1976.

Gillette, Paul J., ed. *The U.S. Government's Directory of Prescription Drugs and Over-the-Counter Drugs.* New York: Award Books, 1971.

Girdano, Dorothy Dusek, and Girdano, Daniel. *Drugs—A Factual Account.* Reading, Mass.: Addison-Wesley Publishing Company, 1973.

Glasser, William. *The Identity Society.* New York: Harper and Row, 1975.

Glatt, M. M. *Drug Scene in Great Britain.* Baltimore: Williams and Wilkins, 1968.

Goldstein, Paul J. *Prostitution and Drugs.* Lexington, Mass.: Lexington Books, 1979.

Goode, Erich. *Drugs in American Society.* New York: Alfred A. Knopf, 1972.

———. *The Drug Phenomena: Social Aspects of Drug Taking.* Indianapolis: Bobbs-Merrill Co. Inc., 1973.

———. ed. *Marihuana.* New York: Atherton Press, 1969.

Goodman, Donald. *Is Alcoholism Hereditary?* Oxford, New York and London: Oxford University Press, 1976.

Goodman, L. S., and Gilman, A. Z., eds. *The Pharmacological Basis of Therapeutics.* New York: Macmillan, 1975.

Goodman, William. *Only Dopes Use Drugs.* Grand Rapids, Mich.: Baker Book House, 1979.

Goodwin, Donald W., and Erickson, Carlton K. *Alcoholism and Affective Disorders: Clinical, Genetic, and Biochemical Studies.* New York: SP Medical and Scientific Books, 1979.

Gordon, Barbara. *I'm Dancing As Fast As I Can.* New York: Bantam Books, 1980.

Goshen, Charles E. *Drinks, Drugs and Do-Gooders.* New York: Free Press, 1973.

Gottheil, Edward A., et al. *Matching Patient Needs and Treatment Methods in Alcoholism and Drug Abuse.* Springfield, Ill.: Charles C. Thomas, 1981.

———. and Alterman, Arthur I. *Addiction Research and Treatment: Converging Trends.* London: Pergamon Publishing Co., 1979.

———. McLellan, A. Thomas; and Druley, Keith A. *Substance Abuse and Psychiatric Illness: Proceedings of the Second Annual Coatsville-Jefferson Conference on Addiction, 1978.* New York: Pergamon Press, 1980.

Gottlieb, A. *The Pleasures of Cocaine.* San Francisco: And/Or Press, 1976.

Gould, Leroy, et al. *Connections: Notes from the Heroin World.* New Haven, Conn.: Yale University Press, 1974.

Graedon, Joe. *The People's Pharmacy.* New York: Avon Books, 1977.

———. *The People's Pharmacy-Two.* New York: Avon Books, 1980.

Grassroots: A Comprehensive Alcohol and Drug Information Service. Hollywood, Calif.: The U.S. Journal, 1981–83.

Gray, Nancy. *Chemical Use and Abuse and the Female Reproductive System.* Phoenix: Do It Now Foundation, 1976.

Greer, Germaine. *The Female Eunuch.* New York: McGraw-Hill, 1971.

Griffin, J. P., and D'Arcy, P. F. *A Manual of Adverse Drug Interactions.* Chicago: Year Book Medical Publications, Inc., 1980.

Grifith, J. Winter. *Drug Information for Patients.* Philadelphia: W. B. Saunders, 1978.

Grinspoon, Lester. *Marijuana Reconsidered.* Cambridge, Mass.: Harvard University Press, 1971.

———. and Bakalar, J. B. *Cocaine: A Drug and Its Social Evolution.* New York: Basic Books, 1976.

———. and Hedblom, Peter. *The Speed Culture: Amphetamine Use and Abuse in America.* Cambridge, Mass.: Harvard University Press, 1975.

Groves, W. E.; Rossi, P. H.; and Grafstein, D. *Study of Life Styles and Campus Communities: Preliminary Report.* Baltimore: Johns Hopkins University, 1970.

Grupp, Stanley. *Marijuana.* Columbus, Ohio: Charles E. Merrill Publishing Co., 1971.

Gugliotta, Guy and Leen, Jeff. *Kings of Cocaine: Inside the Medellin Cartel.* New York: Simon & Schuster, 1984.

Guthrie, D. *A History of Medicine.* London: Nelson and Sons, 1945.

Haberman, Paul W., and Baden, Michael M. *Alcohol, Other Drugs and Violent Death.* New York: Oxford University Press, 1978.

Halper, Sibyl Cline. *The Heroin Trade: From Poppies to Peoria.* Washington, D.C.: Drug Abuse Council, 1977.

Hardy, Richard E., and Cull, John G. *Drug Dependence and Rehabilitation Approaches.* Springfield, Ill.: Charles C. Thomas, 1973.

———. and Cull, John G., eds. *Drug Language and Lore.* Springfield, Ill.: Charles C. Thomas, 1975.

Harms, E. *Drug Addiction in Youth.* Elmsford, N.Y.: Pergamon Press, 1965.

Hayes, Bill, and Hoffer, William. *Midnight Express.* New York: Popular Library, Inc., 1978.

Hawley, Richard A. *Drugs and Society: Responding to an Epidemic.* New York: Walker & Co., 1988.

———. *The Purpose of Pleasure.* Wellesley, Mass.: Independent School Press, 1989.

Heath, Dwight B., and Cooper, A. M. *Alcohol Use and World Cultures: A Comprehensive Bibliography of Anthropological Sources.* Toronto: Addiction Research Foundation, 1981.

Heffern, Richard. *Secrets of the Mind-Altering Plants of Mexico.* New York: Pyramid Books, 1975.

Helmer, John. *Drugs and Minority Oppression.* New York: The Continuum Publishing Corp., 1975.

Hendin, Herbert. *Age of Sensation.* New York: McGraw-Hill, 1977.

High Times Magazine Editors. *The High Times Encyclopedia of Recreational Drugs.* New York: Stonehill Publishing Co., 1978.

Hill, N., ed. *Marijuana: Teenage Killer.* New York: Popular Library, 1971.

Hoffer, A., and Osmond, H. *The Hallucinogens.* New York: Academic Press, 1967.

Hofmann, Frederick G. *A Handbook on Drug and Alcohol Abuse: The Biomedical Aspects.* New York: Oxford University Press, 1975.

Hogins, Burl, and Bryant, Gerald, Jr. *Drugs and Dissent.* New York: Macmillan, 1970.

Hollander, C., ed. *Background Papers on Student Drug Involvement.* Washington, D.C.: U.S. National Student Association, 1967.

Hollister, L. E. *Chemical Psychosis: LSD and Related Drugs.* Springfield, Ill.: Charles C. Thomas, 1967.

Houser, Norman W. *Drugs: Facts on Their Use and Abuse.* New York: Lothrop, Lee & Shepard Books, a division of William Morrow & Co. Inc., 1969.

Huelke, D. F., and David, R. A. *Pedestrian Fatalities.* Ann Arbor: Highway Safety Research Institute, University of Michigan, 1969.

Hunt, W. A., ed. *Learning Mechanisms in Smoking.* Chicago: Aldine Press, 1970.

Huxley, Aldous. *The Doors of Perception.* New York: Harper & Row, 1954.

Hyde, Margaret O. *Mind Drugs.* New York: McGraw-Hill, 1974.

Ianni, F. A. *Black Mafia: Ethnic Succession in Organized Crime.* New York: Simon and Schuster, 1974.

Idestrom, Carl-Magnus, ed. *Alcohol and Brain Research.* Copenhagen: Munksgaard, 1980.

Inciardi, James A., ed. *The Drugs-Crime Connection.* Beverly Hills, Calif.: Sage Publications, Inc., 1981.

———. *The War on Drugs.* Palo Alto, Calif.: Mayfield, 1986.

Indian Hemp Drugs Commission. *Report of the . . . Commission, 1893–94.* Reprinted as *Marijuana: The Report of the . . . Commission, 1893–94.* Introduction and Glossary by John Kaplan. Silver Springs, Md.: Jefferson, 1969.

Institute of Medicine, Division of Health Promotion and Disease Prevention. *Alcoholism, Alcohol Abuse and Related Problems: Opportunities for Research.* Washington, D.C.: Academy Press, 1980.

Isabell, Harris. "Clinical Research on Addiction in the United States." In *Narcotic Drug Addiction Problems,* edited by Robert B. Livingston. Bethesda, Md.: National Institute of Mental Health, 1958.

Iverson, S., and Iversen, L. *Behavioral Pharmacology.* New York: Oxford University Press, 1975.

Jacobson, Richard, and Zinberg, Norman E. *The Social Basis of Drug Abuse Prevention.* Washington, D.C.: Drug Abuse Council, 1975.

Jaffe, Jerome, et al. *Addictions: Issues and Answers.* New York: Harper & Row, 1979.

James, John D., et al. *A Guide to Drug Interaction.* New York: McGraw-Hill, 1978.

Jeffee, Saul. *Narcotics—An American Plan.* New York: Paul S. Eriksson, Inc., 1972.

Jellinek, E. M. *Government Programs on Alcoholism: A Review of the Activities in Some Foreign Countries.* Ottawa: Department of National Health and Welfare, 1963.

———. *The Alcoholism Complex.* New York: Christopher D. Smithers Foundation, 1960.

———. *The Disease Concept of Alcoholism.* New Haven, Conn.: Hillhouse Press, 1960.

Jessor, Richard, et al. *Society, Personality, and Deviant Behavior.* New York: Holt, Rinehart and Winston, 1968.

Johnson, B. D. *Marihuana Users and Drug Subcultures.* New York: John Wiley and Sons, 1973.

Joint Commission on Accreditation of Hospitals. *Consolidated Standards for Child, Adolescent, and Adult Psychiatric Alcoholism and Drug Abuse Programs.* Chicago, 1979.

Joint Committee of the American Bar Association and the American Medical Association on Narcotic Drugs. *Drug Addiction: Crime or Disease?* Introduction by Alfred R. Lindesmith. Bloomington, Ind.: Indiana University Press, 1971.

Jones, E. *The Life and Work of Sigmund Freud.* Vol. 1. New York: Basic Books, 1961.

Jones, Hardin, and Jones, Helen. *Sensual Drugs.* New York: Cambridge University Press, 1979.

Jones, Helen C., and Lovinger, Paul W. *The Marijuana Question.* New York: Dodd, Mead & Co., 1985.

Jones, Kenneth L., et al. *Drugs and Alcohol.* New York: Harper and Row, 1978.

Josephson, Eric, and Carroll, Eleanor E., eds. *Drug Use: Epidemiological and Sociological Approaches.* New York: John Wiley and Sons, 1974.

Judson, H. F. *Heroin Addiction in Britain: What Americans Can Learn from the English Experience.* New York: Harcourt, Brace, Jovanovitch, 1974.

Julien, Robert M. *A Primer of Drug Action.* San Francisco: W. H. Freeman and Co., 1981.

Kalant, Harold, and Kalant, Oriana Josseau. *Drugs, Society and Personal Choice.* Don Mills, Ontario: General Publishing, 1971.

Kalant, Oriana Josseau. *Alcohol and Drug Problems in Women.* Vol. 5. New York: Plenum Publishing Corp., 1980.

Kalant, P. J. *The Amphetamines: Toxicity and Addiction.* Toronto: University of Toronto Press, 1966.

Kalent, L. *Mushrooms, Molds, and Miracles.* New York: John Day, 1965.

Kaplan, John. *Marijuana: The New Prohibition.* New York: World Press, 1970.

———. *The Hardest Drug: Heroin and Public Policy.* Chicago: University of Chicago Press, 1983.

Kaplan, Eugene H., and Wieder, Herbert. *Drugs Don't Take People, People Take Drugs.* Secaucus, N.J.: Lyle Stuart, 1974.

Kastl, Albert J., and Kastl, Lena. *Journey Back: Escaping the Drug Trap.* Chicago: Nelson-Hall Publishers, 1975.

Kaufman, Edward, and Kaufman, Pauline N. *Family Therapy of Drug and Alcohol Abuse.* New York: Gardner Press, 1979.

Kavaler, L. *The Amphetamines.* Springfield, Ill.: Charles C. Thomas, 1966.

Keller, Mark; McCormick, Mairi; and Efron, Vera. *A Dictionary of Words About Alcohol.* New Brunswick, N.J.: Rutgers Center of Alcohol Studies, 1982.

Keniston, Kenneth. *Youth and Dissent: The Rise of a New Opposition.* New York. Harcourt, Brace, Jovanovich, 1971.

Kerlinger, Frederick N. *Foundations of Behavioral Research.* New York: Holt, Rinehart and Winston, 1964.

Keup, Wolfram, ed. *Drug Abuse: Current Concepts and Research.* Springfield, Ill.: Charles C. Thomas, 1972.

Kiloh, L. G., and Bell, D. S., eds. *Alcoholism and Drug Dependency.* London: Butterworth, 1969.

King, Rufus. *The Drug Hang-up: America's Fifty Year Folly.* Springfield, Ill.: Charles C. Thomas, 1974.

Kirkland, Gelsey, and Lawrence, Gregory. *Dancing On My Grave.* New York: Doubleday, 1986.

Kissin, Benjamin, and Begleiter, Henri, eds. *The Biology of Alcoholism, Vol. 1, Biochemistry.* New York: Plenum Press, 1972.

———. and Begleiter, Henri, eds. *The Biology of Alcoholism, Vol. 2, Physiology and Behavior.* New York: Plenum Press, 1972.

———. and Begleiter, Henri, eds. *The Biology of Alcoholism, Vol. 3, Clinical Pathology.* New York: Plenum Press, 1974.

———. and Begleiter, Henri, eds. *The Biology of Alcoholism, Vol. 4, Social Aspects of Alcoholism*. New York: Plenum Press, 1976.

———. and Begleiter, Henri, eds. *The Biology of Alcoholism, Vol. 5, Treatment and Rehabilitation of the Chronic Alcoholic*. New York: Plenum Press, 1977.

Kleps, Arthur J. *The Boo Hoo Bible*. New Mexico: Toad Books, 1971.

Kline, Nathan S.; Alexander, Stuart F.; and Chamberlain, Ampero. *Psychotropic Drugs: A Manual for Emergency Management of Overdosage*. Oradell, N.J.: Medical Economics Company, 1974.

Kluver, H. *Mescal and Mechanics of Hallucination*. Chicago: University of Chicago Press, 1966.

Knapp Commission. *The Knapp Commission Report on Police Corruption*. New York: G. Braziller, 1973.

Kolb, Lawrence. *Drug Addiction: A Medical Problem*. Springfield, Ill.: Charles C. Thomas, 1962.

Krasnegor, N. A. *Behavioral Analysis and Treatment of Substance Abuse*. Washington, D.C.: National Institute on Drug Abuse, 1979.

Kron, Yves J. *Mainline to Nowhere: The Making of a Heroin Addict*. New York: Pantheon, 1965.

Kropp, Paul. *Dope Deal*. St. Paul, Minn.: EMC Corp., 1981.

Krusich, Walter S. *Drugs: It Can't Happen to Me!* Denver, Col.: Accent Books, 1979.

Laing, R. D. *The Divided Self*. Harmondsworth, England: Penguin, 1965.

Lall, Bernard, and Lall, Geeta. *Marijuana—Friend or Foe?* Washington, D.C.: Review and Herald Publishing Association, 1979.

Larkin, E. J. *The Treatment of Alcoholism: Theory, Practice, and Evaluation*. Ontario: Addiction Research Foundation, 1974.

Laurie, Peter. *Drugs: Medical, Psychological and Social Facts*. Harmondsworth, England: Penguin, 1967.

Leary, T.; Metzner, R.; and Alpert, R. *The Psychedelic Experience*. New Hyde Park, N.Y.: University Books, 1964.

Leary, Timothy. *High Priest*. Cleveland, N.Y.: World Publishing Company, 1968.

Lee, David. *Cocaine Consumer's Handbook*. Berkeley, Calif.: And/Or Press, 1976.

Leech, K., and Jordan, Brenda. *Drugs for Young People: Their Use and Misuse*. Elmsford, N.Y.: Pergamon Press, 1968.

Leech, Kenneth. *Youthquake: The Growth of a Counter Culture Through Two Decades*. Totowa, N.J.: Littlefield, Adams and Co., 1977.

Leiberman, M. A., and Borman, L. D. *Self-Help Groups for Coping with Crises: Origins, Members, Processes, and Impact*. San Francisco: Jossey-Bass, 1979.

Leonard, Henry L., et al. *Mystification and Drug Misuse*. San Francisco: Jossey-Bass, 1971.

Lewin, Louis. *Phantastica: Narcotic and Stimulating Drugs*. Trans. by P. H. A. Wirth. London: Routledge & Kegan Paul, 1964.

Lewis, Arthur J., ed. *Modern Drug Encyclopedia and Therapeutic Index: A Compendium*. New York: Yorke Medical Books, 1981.

Lewis, B. *The Sexual Power of Marijuana: An Intimate Report on 208 Adult Middle-Class Users*. New York: Wyden, 1970.

Li, T. K.; Schenker, S.; and Lumeng, L. *Alcohol and Nutrition: Proceedings of a Workshop, September 26–27, 1977, Indianapolis, Indiana*. Washington, D.C.: Government Printing Office, 1979.

Lieberman, Florence, et al. *Before Addiction: How to Help Youth.* New York: Human Sciences Press, 1973.

Linder, Ronald L. *PCP: The Devil's Dust.* Belmont, Calif.: Wadsworth Publishing Co., 1981.

Lindesmith, A. R. *Addiction and Opiates.* Chicago: Aldine Publishing Co., 1965.

———. *The Addict and the Law.* New York: Random House, 1965.

Lingeman, Richard R. *Drugs from A to Z.* New York: McGraw-Hill, 1974.

Linkletter, Art, and Gallup, George. *My Child on Drugs? Youth and the Drug Culture.* Cincinnati, Ohio: Standard Publishing Co., 1981.

Liska, Ken. *Drugs and the Human Body.* New York: Macmillan, 1981.

Lockhart, D. L. *The Swinging Door: An Evaluation of Services to and Needs of Street People in Downtown Salinas.* Salinas, Calif.: Sun Street Centers, Community Alcoholism Programs, 1979.

Loftus, Elizabeth. *Memory.* Reading, Mass.: Addison-Wesley Publishing Company, 1980.

Long, James W. *The Essential Guide to Prescription Drugs: What You Need to Know for Safe Drug Use.* New York: Harper and Row, 1980.

Long, Robert Emmet, ed. *AIDS.* New York: Wilson, 1987.

———. *Drugs and American Society.* New York: Wilson, 1986.

Lotter, J. M. *Social Problems in the RSA.* Pretoria: Institute for Sociological, Demographic and Criminological Research, South African Human Sciences Research Council, 1979.

Louria, D. B. *Overcoming Drugs.* New York: McGraw-Hill, 1971.

———. *The Drug Scene.* New York: McGraw-Hill, 1968.

———. *Nightmare Drugs.* New York: Simon & Schuster, 1966.

Lowinson, Joyce H., and Ruiz, Pedro. *Substance Abuse: Clinical Problems and Perspectives.* Easton, Md.: Williams and Wilkins Co., 1981.

Ludwig, Arnold M. *Understanding the Alcoholic's Mind.* New York: Oxford, 1988.

Luks, Allan and Barbato, Joseph. *You Are What You Drink.* New York: Villard, 1989.

MacLennan, Anne. *Women: Their Use of Alcohol and Other Legal Drugs.* Toronto: Addiction Research Foundation, 1976.

MacLeod, Anne. *Growing Up in America.* Rockville, Md.: National Institute on Drug Abuse, 1978.

Madden, J. S. *Guide to Alcohol and Drug Dependence.* Bristol, England: J. Wright and Sons, 1979.

———. Walker, Robin; and Kenyon, W. H. *Aspects of Alcohol and Drug Dependence.* Kent, England: Pitman Medical Limited, 1980.

Madison, Arnold. *Drugs and You.* New York: Pocket Books, 1972.

Majchrowicz, Edward, and Noble, Ernest P. *Biochemistry and Pharmacology of Ethanol.* 2 vols. New York and London: Plenum Publishing Corp., 1979.

Malcolm X. *Autobiography.* New York: Grove Press, 1965.

Malcolm, A. I. *The Craving for the High.* New York: Simon & Schuster, 1975.

Malcolm, Andrew I. *The Pursuit of Intoxication.* New York: Pocket Books, 1971.

Malzberg, Benjamin. *The Alcoholic Psychosis.* New Haven: Yale Center of Alcohol Studies, 1960.

Mann, George A. *Recovery of Reality: Overcoming Chemical Dependency.* New York: Harper and Row, 1979.

Mann, Marty. *New Primer on Alcoholism.* New York: Holt, Rinehart and Winston, 1963.

———. *Primer on Alcoholism.* New York: Holt, Rinehart and Winston, 1958.

Manning, Peter K. *The Narc's Game: Organizational and Informational Limits on Drug Law Reinforcement*. Cambridge, Mass.: The MIT Press, 1980.

Margolis, Jack S. *Complete Book of Recreational Drugs*. Los Angeles: Price/Stern/Sloan, 1978.

———. and Clorfene, Richard. *A Child's Garden of Grass*. Los Angeles: Cliff House Books, a division of Price/Stern/Sloan, 1976.

Marin, P., and Cohen, A. Y. *Understanding Drug Use*. New York: Harper and Row, 1971.

Markham, J. M. "What's All This Talk of Heroin Maintenance?" *New York Times Magazine*, July 2, 1972.

Marr, John S. *The Good Drug and the Bad Drug*. New York: M. Evans and Company, Inc., 1970.

Marriott, Alice, and Rachlin, Carol K. *Peyote*. New York: New American Library, 1972.

Maslow, Abraham H. *Religions, Values, and Peak Experiences*. New York: The Viking Press, 1970.

Mason, David, and Dyller, Fran. *Pharmaceutical Dictionary & Reference for Prescription Drugs*. New York: Playboy Paperback, 1982.

Masters, W. R., and Houston, J. *The Varieties of Psychedelic Experience*. New York: Dell Publishing, 1966.

Maurer, David W., and Vogel, Victor H. *Narcotics and Narcotic Addiction*. Springfield, Ill.: Charles C. Thomas, 1973.

McClelland, David C. *The Achieving Society*. Princeton: Van Nostrand, 1961.

———. Davis, William N.; Kalin, Rudolf; and Wanner, Eric. *The Drinking Man*. New York: Free Press, 1972.

McCord, William, and McCord, Joan. *Origins of Alcoholism*. Stanford, Calif.: Stanford University Press, 1960.

McCoy, A. M. *The Politics of Heroin in Southeast Asia*. New York: Harper and Row, 1972.

McLennan, Ross J. *Booze, Bucks, Bamboozle and You!* Oklahoma City: Sane Press, 1978.

Mechoulam, R., ed. *Marijuana: Chemistry, Pharmacology, Metabolism, and Clinical Effects*. New York: Academic Press, 1973.

Meehan, Bob. *Beyond the Yellow Brick Road*. New York: Contemporary Books, 1984.

Mello, Nancy K. *Advances in Substance Abuse: Behavioral and Biological Research*. Greenwich, Conn.: JAI Press, 1980.

Meltzoff, Julian, and Kornreich, Melvin. *Research in Psychotherapy*. New York: Atherton Press, 1970.

Mendelson, Wallace B. *The Use and Misuse of Sleeping Pills: A Clinical Guide to Treatment*. New York: Plenum Publishing Corp., 1980.

Menditto, Joseph. *Drugs of Addiction and Non-Addiction: Their Use and Abuse*. Troy, N.Y.: Whitson Publishing Co., 1970.

Messick, Hank. *Of Grass and Snow*. Englewood Cliffs, N.J.; Prentice-Hall, 1979.

Meyer, N. *The Seven Per Cent Solution*. New York: Ballantine Books, 1976.

Miller, L. L., ed. *Marijuana: Effects on Human Behavior*. New York: Academic Press, 1974.

Miller, William R. *The Addictive Behaviors: Treatment of Alcoholism, Drug Abuse, Smoking and Obesity*. Elmsford, N.Y.: Pergamon Press, 1980.

Mishara, Brian L., and Kastenbaum, Robert. *Alcohol and Old Age. New York:* Grune and Stratton, 1980.

Mitchell, Alexander. *Drugs—The Parents' Dilemma*. Westport, Conn.: Technomic Publishing Co., Inc., 1972.

Modell, Walter. *Drugs in Current Use and New Drugs.* New York: Springer Publishing Co., 1981.

Moller, Richard. *Marijuana: Your Legal Rights.* Reading, Mass.: Addison-Wesley Publishing Co., 1981.

Moore, Mark H. *Buy and Bust.* Lexington, Mass.: Lexington Books, 1977.

Morgan, H. Wayne, ed. *Yesterday's Addicts: American Society and Drug Abuse.* Norman, Okla.: University of Oklahoma Press, 1980.

———. *Drugs in America: A Social History 1800–1980.* Syracuse, New York: Syracuse University Press, 1981.

Mortimer, W. Golden. *History of Coca, The Divine Plant of the Incas.* San Francisco: And/Or Press, 1974.

Moskowitz, Herbert, ed. *Drugs and Driving.* Elmsford, N.Y.: Pergamon Press, 1976.

Menicolli, A. *Drug Trafficking: A North-South Perspective.* Ottawa: North-South Institute, 1983.

Musto, D. *The American Disease: Origins of Narcotic Control.* New Haven: Yale University Press, 1973. Expanded ed. New York: Oxford University Press, 1989.

Musto, D. F. "A Study of Cocaine: Sherlock Holmes and Sigmund Freud." *Journal of American Medical Association,* 1968, 204(1):27–32.

Myer, R. E., and Mirin, S. M., eds. *The Heroin Stimulus: Implications for a Theory of Addiction.* New York: Plenum Publishing Corp., 1979.

Nahas, G. G. *Marihuana: Deceptive Weed.* New York: Raven Press, 1973.

National Anti-Drug Coalition. *What Every Parent Should Know About Drugs.* New York: New Benjamin Franklin House, 1981.

National Clergy Conference on Alcoholism. *The Blue Book, Vol XXXI. Proceedings of the 31st National Clergy Conference on Alcoholism, Omaha, Nebraska, May 22–26, 1979,* n.d.

National Commission on Marihuana and Drug Abuse. *Drug Use in America: Problem in Perspective,* 4 vols. Washington, D.C.: Government Printing Office, 1973.

National Council on Alcoholism. *The Rights of Alcoholics and Their Families.* New York, 1976.

National Institute of Mental Health. *Peanuts and Tea: A Selected Glossary of Terms Used by Drug Addicts.* Lexington, Ky.: the Institute, 1972.

National Institute on Alcohol Abuse and Alcoholism. *Alcohol and Health.* First Special Report to the U.S. Congress from the Secretary of Health, Education and Welfare. Washington, D.C.: Government Printing Office, 1971.

———. *Alcohol and Health: New Knowledge.* Second Special Report to the U.S. Congress from the Secretary of Health, Education and Welfare. Washington, D.C.: Government Printing Office, 1978.

———. *Alcohol and Health.* Third Special Report to the U.S. Congress from the Secretary of Health, Education and Welfare. Washington, D.C.: Government Printing Office, 1978.

National Institute on Drug Abuse. *Research Monograph Series:* Willette, Robert, ed. *Narcotic Antagonists: The Search for Long-acting Preparations;* Williams, Jay R. *Effects of Labeling the "Drug Abuser": An Inquiry;* Willette, Robert, ed. *Drugs and Driving;* Blaine, Jack D., and Julius, Demetrios A., eds. *Psychodynamics of Drug Dependence;* Petersen, Robert C., and Stillman, Richard C., eds. *Cocaine: 1977;* Sharp, Charles Wm., and Brehm, Mary Lee, eds. *Review of Inhalants: Euphoria to Dysfunction;* Rittenhouse, Joan Dunne, ed. *The Epidemiology of Heroin and other Narcotics;* Jarvik, Murray E., et al., eds. *Research on Smoking Behavior;* Petersen, Robert C., eds. *The International*

Challenge of Drug Abuse; Petersen, Robert C., and Stillman, Richard C., eds. *Phencyclidine (PCP) Abuse: An Appraisal;* Gottschalk, Louis A., et al. *Drug Abuse Deaths in Nine Cities: A Survey Report;* Petersen, Robert D. *Marijuana Research Findings: 1980.* Washington, D.C.: Government Printing Office; Nelson, Jack E., eds. *Guide to Drug Abuse Research Technology.* Washington, D.C.: Government Printing Office, 1982.

Nellis, Muriel. *The Female Fix.* New York: Penguin, 1981.

Nicholi, Armand M., Jr. *The Harvard Guide to Modern Psychiatry.* Cambridge, Mass.: Harvard University Press, 1979.

Nimble, J. B. *The Construction and Operation of Clandestine Drug Laboratories.* Port Town, Washington: Loompanics, 1986.

Non-Medical Use of Drugs Directorate. *Core Knowledge in the Drug Field.* Edited by Lorne A. Phillips, G. Rosee Ramsey, Leonard Blumenthal, and Patrick Crawshaw. Ottawa, Canada: National Health and Welfare, 1978.

Norback, Judith. *The Alcohol and Drug Abuse Yearbook/Directory 1979–80.* New York: Van Nostrand Reinhold Co., 1979.

Nowlis, Helen. *Drugs on the College Campus.* New York: Anchor Books, 1969.

———. *Drugs Demystified.* Paris: UNESCO, 1980.

Null, Gary, and Null, Steven. *How to Get Rid of the Poisons in Your Body.* New York: Arco Publishing Co., 1977.

O'Brien, Robert, and Chafetz, Morris. *The Encyclopedia of Alcoholism.* New York: Facts On File, 1982.

O'Donnell, John A., and Ball, John C., eds. *Narcotic Addiction.* New York: Harper and Row, 1966.

Olive, G. *Drug—Action Modification—Comparative Pharmacology.* Oxford, England: Pergamon Publishing Corp., 1979.

Osol, Arthur, and Pratt, Robertson, eds. *The United States Dispensatory.* Philadelphia: J. B. Lippincott Company, 1973.

Patterson, H. Robert, et al. *Falconer's Current Drug Handbook: 1980–1982.* Philadelphia: W. B. Saunders Co., 1980.

Patterson, H. Robert; Gustafson, Edward A.; and Sheridan, Eleanor. Current Drug Handbook 1982–1984. Philadelphia: W. B. Saunders Co., 1982.

Pattison, E. Mansell, and Kaufman, eds. *Encyclopedic Handbook of Alcoholism.* New York: Gardner Press, Inc., 1982.

———. Sobell, Mark B.; and Sobell, Linda Carter. *Emerging Concepts of Alcohol Dependence.* New York: Springer, 1977.

Pearl, Raymond. *Alcohol and Longevity.* New York: Alfred A. Knopf, 1926.

Peele, Stanton. *Love and Addiction.* New York: Signet, 1976.

———. *The Addiction Experience.* Center City, Minn.: Hazelden Foundation, 1980.

Perry, Samuel W. *The Simon and Schuster Pocket Encylopedia of Prescription and Nonprescription Drugs,* New York: Simon and Schuster, 1982.

Peterson, David M., et al. *Drugs and the Elderly: Social and Pharmacological Issues.* Springfield, Ill.: Charles C. Thomas, 1979.

Phillips, Joel L., and Wynne, Ronald D. *Cocaine: The Mystique and the Reality.* New York: Avon Books, 1980.

Phillipson, R. B. *Modern Trends in Drug Dependence and Alcoholism.* Woburn, Mass.: Butterworth Publications, Inc. 1970.

Physician's Desk Reference, 36th edition. Oradell, N.J.: Medical Economics Company, 1982.

Pittman, David Joshua. *World Health Organization Committee of Experts in Alcoholism.* New York: Harper and Row, 1967.

———. and Gordon, C. W. *Revolving Door. A Study of the Chronic Police Case Inebriate.* Glencoe, Ill.: Free Press, 1958.

Polacsek, E., et al. *Interaction of Alcohol and Other Drugs.* Toronto: Addiction Research Foundation, 1972.

Polich, J. Michael, and Armor, David J. *The Course of Alcoholism: Four Years after Treatment.* Santa Monica: Rand Corp., 1980.

Polson, Beth. *Not My Kid.* New York: Arbor House, 1984.

Pope, Harrison, Jr. *Voices from the Drug Culture.* Boston: Beacon Press, 1971.

Popham, R. E., ed. *Alcohol and Alcoholism.* Toronto: University of Toronto Press, 1970.

Powell, David J. *Clinical Supervision, Skills for Substance Abuse Counselors: Manual.* New York: Human Sciences Press, 1980.

Pradhan, S. N., and Dutta, S. N. *Drug Abuse: Clinical and Basic Aspects.* St. Louis, Mo.: Mosby, 1977.

Pratt, Arthur. *How to Help and Understand the Alcoholic or Drug Addict.* Louisville: Love Street Books, 1980.

Prattenberg, J. F. X. Carroll, and Bolognese, C. *Treating Mixed Psychiatric-Drug Addicted and Alcoholic Patients.* Eagleville, Pa.: Eagleville hospital and Rehabilitation Center, 1979.

Puharich, A. *The Sacred Mushroom.* Garden City, N.Y.: Doubleday, 1959.

Rachman, S., and Teasdale, J. *Aversion Therapy and Behavior Disorders.* London: Routledge and Kegan Paul, 1969.

Rankin, J. G., ed. *Alcohol, Drugs and Brain Damage.* Toronto: Alcoholism and Drug Addiction Research Foundation of Ontario, 1975.

Richard, J.; Whitehead III, Bonnie and Charles. *The Marihuana Convictions: A History of Marihuana Prohibition in the United States.* Charlottesville: University of Virginia Press, 1974.

Richter, Derek. *Addiction and Brain Damage.* Baltimore: University Park Press, 1980.

Richter, Ralph W., ed. *Medical Aspects of Drug Abuse.* Hagerstown, Md.: Harper and Row, 1975.

Riesman, David. *The Lonely Crowd.* New Haven, Conn.: Yale University Press, 1950.

Robins, L. N. *The Vietnam Drug User Returns.* U.S. Executive Office of the President, Special Action Office for Drug Abuse Prevention. Special Action Office Monograph, Series A, No. 2. Washington, D.C.: Government Printing Office, 1974.

Rock, Paul, ed. *Drugs and Politics.* New Brunswick, N.J.: Transaction Books, 1977.

Rodman, Morton J., and Dipalma, Joseph R. *More Readings in Drug Therapy.* Oradell, N.J.: Medical Economics Company, 1972.

Roe, Daphne. *Alcohol and the Diet.* Westport, Conn.: AVI Press, 1981.

Roffman, R. A., and Sapil, E. "Marijuana in Vietnam." *Technical Report for the Surgeon-General.* Department of the Army, 1969.

Roffman, Roger. *Marijuana as Medicine.* Austin, Tex.: Madrona Press Inc., 1981.

Rorabaugh, W. J. *The Alcoholic Republic: An American Tradition.* New York: Oxford University Press, 1979.

Roseman, Bernard. *LSD: The Age of Mind.* Hollywood, Calif.: Wilshire Book Co., 1966.

———. *The Peyote Story.* Hollywood, Calif.: Wilshire Book Co., 1966.

Rosenbaum, Marsha. *Women on Heroin.* New Brunswick, N.J.: Rutgers University Press, 1981.

Rosenbaum, Max. *Drug Abuse and Drug Addiction.* New York: Gordon and Breach, Science Publishers, Inc., 1973.

Rosenthal, M. S. *Drugs, Parents, and Children.* Boston: Houghton Mifflin, 1972.

Rosevear, John. *Pot, A Handbook of Marijuana.* New Hyde Park, N.Y.: University Books, 1967.

Rossi, Peter H.; Freeman, Howard E.; and Wright, Sonia R. *Evaluation: A Systematic Approach.* Beverly Hills: Sage Publications, 1979.

Rubenstein, Morton K. *A Doctor's Guide to Non-Prescription Drugs.* New York: Signet, 1977.

Russel G. K. *Marihuana Today: A Compilation of Medical Findings for the Layman.* Elmsford, N.Y.: Pergamon Press, 1979.

Russo, J., ed. *Amphetamine Abuse.* Springfield, Ill.: Charles C. Thomas, 1968.

Rutman, L., ed. *Drugs: Use and Abuse.* Winnipeg: University of Winnipeg Press, 1969.

Sabbag, R. *Snowblind: A Brief Career in the Cocaine Trade.* New York: Avon Books, 1978.

Saltman, Jules. *Marijuana and Your Child.* New York: Grosset and Dunlap, 1970.

Sanders, Ed. *Coming Down.* New York: The United International Copyright Representatives, Ltd., 1966.

Satinder, Paul K. *Drug Use: Criminal, Sick or Cultural?* Rosalyn Heights, N.Y.: Libra Books, 1980.

Schaef, Anna Wilson. *When Society Becomes an Addict.* New York: Harper & Row, 1987.

Schecter, A. et al., eds. *Drug Abuse: Modern Trends, Issues and Perspectives.* New York: Marcel Dekker, Inc., 1978.

———. ed. *Drug Dependence and Alcoholism, Vol. 1, Biomedical Issues.* New York: Plenum Publishing Corp., 1980.

———. ed. *Drug Dependence and Alcoholism, Vol. 2, Social and Behavioral Issues.* New York: Plenum Press, 1980.

Scher, Jordan M. *Drug Abuse in Industry: Growing Corporate Dilemma.* Springfield, Ill.: Charles C. Thomas, 1981.

Scherer, Roy B. *Identity Crisis: ''Lookalike'' Drugs & ''Peashooters''—Identifying Over-the-Counter Drugs.* Richmond, Va.: ADAPTS, 1981.

Schaffer, Dick. *Choice & Consequences: What to Do When a Teenager Uses Alcohol/Drugs.* Minneapolis, Minn.: Johnson Institute Books, 1987.

Schmidt, J. E. *Narcotics: Lingo and Lore.* Springfield, Ill.: Charles C. Thomas, 1959.

Schuckit, M. A. *Drug and Alcohol Abuse: A Clinical Guide to Diagnosis and Treatment.* New York: Plenum Medical Book Co., 1979.

Schulberg, A.; Sheldon, A.; and Baker, F. *Program Evaluation in the Health Fields.* New York: Behavioral Publications, 1969.

Schur, Edwin M. *Narcotic Addiction in Britain and America.* Bloomington: Indiana University Press, 1962.

Schwarzrock, Shirley, and Wrenn, C. Gilbert. *Facts and Fantasies About Drugs.* Circle Pines, Minn.: American Guidance Service, 1970.

———. and Wrenn, C. Gilbert. *The Mind Benders.* Circle Pines, Minn.: American Guidance Service, 1971.

Seymour, Richard R. *Drug Free,* New York: Facts On File, 1987.

Shafer, Raymond P., ed. *Marihuana, A Signal of Misunderstanding: The Official Report of the National Commission on Marihuana and Drug Abuse.* New York: New American Library, 1972.

Shain, Martin, et al. *Influence, Choice and Drugs: Toward a Systematic Approach to the Prevention of Substance Abuse.* Lexington, Mass.: Lexington Books, 1977.

Sharples, Anthony. *The Scorpion's Tail.* New York: Taplinger Publishing Co. Inc., 1976.

Shedd, Charlie W. *Is Your Family Turned On? Coping with the Drug Culture.* Waco, Tex.: Word Books, 1971.

Siegel, Ronald K. *Intoxication: Life in Pursuit of Artificial Paradise.* New York: E. P. Dutton, 1989.

Silverman, Harold L., and Simon, Gilbert I. *The Pill Book.* New York: Bantam Books, 1979.

Silverman, Milton, et al. *Pills and the Public Purse.* Berkeley, Calif.: University of California Press, 1981.

Silverstein, Alvin, and Silverstein, Virginia B. *Alcoholism.* Philadelphia: J. B. Lippincott Co., 1975.

Simmons, J. L. *Marihuana: Myths and Realities.* North Hollywood, Calif. Brandon House, 1967.

Simmons, Luis R., and Said, Abdul A., eds. *Drugs, Politics and Diplomacy: The International Connection.* Beverly Hills, Calif.: Sage Publications, Inc., 1974.

Smart, R. E. *LSD in the Treatment of Alcoholism.* Toronto: University of Toronto Press, 1968.

Smart, Reginald G. *The New Drinkers: Teenage Use and Abuse of Alcohol.* 2nd ed. Toronto: Addiction Research Foundation, 1980.

———. et al. *Lysergic Acid Diethylamide (LSD) in the Treatment of Alcoholism: An Investigation of Its Effects on Drinking Behavior, Personality Structure and Social Functioning.* Toronto: University of Toronto Press, 1967.

Smith, David E. *The New Social Drug.* Englewood Cliffs, N.J.: Prentice-Hall, 1970.

———. and Gay, G. R. *It's So Good, Don't Even Try It Once: Heroin in Perspective.* Englewood Cliffs, N.J.: Prentice-Hall, 1972.

———., and Wesson, Donald R. *Uppers and Downers.* Englewood Cliffs, N.J.: Prentice-Hall, 1973.

Snyder, S. *Madness and the Brain.* New York: McGraw-Hill, 1974.

Sobel, Robert. *They Satisfy: The Cigarette in American Life.* Garden City, N.Y.: Doubleday, 1975.

Sobell, Linda Carter; Sobell, Mark B.; and War, Elliott. *Evaluating Alcohol and Drug Abuse Treatment Effectiveness.* New York: Pergamon Press, 1980.

Social Service Publications. *Narcotics and Drug Abuse, A to Z.* Queens Village, N.Y.: Croner Publications, Inc., 1982.

Sokoloff, Boris. *The Permissive Society.* New Rochelle, N.Y.: Arlington House, 1971.

Solomon, D., ed. *LSD: The Consciousness-Expanding Drug.* New York: G. P. Putnam, 1964.

———. ed. *The Marihuana Papers.* Indianapolis: Bobbs-Merrill Company, Inc., 1966.

Souter, John. *The Pleasure Seller.* Wheaton, Ill.: Tyndale Publishers, 1979.

Srimson, G. V. *Heroin and Behavior.* New York: John Wiley and Sons, 1973.

Stafford, P. G., and Golightly, B. H. *LSD: The Problem-Solving Psychedelic.* New York: Universal Publishing, 1967.

Starks, Michael. *Cocaine Fiends and Reefer Madness: An Illustrated History of Drugs in the Movies.* East Brunswick, N.J.: Cornwall Books, 1981.

———. *Marijuana Potency.* Berkeley, Calif.: And/Or Press, 1977.

Stearn, Jess. *The Seekers.* New York: Doubleday, 1969.

Stefanis, C.; Dornbush, R.; and Fink, M., eds. *Hashish—Studies of Long-term Use.* New York: Raven Press, 1977.

Steinmetz, E. F. *Kava-Kava, Famous Drug Plant of the South Sea Islands*. New York; High Times Press, 1973.

Stevenson, G. H. *Drug Addiction in British Columbia*. Vancouver: University of British Columbia, 1956.

Stewart, George R. *American Ways of Life*. New York: Doubleday and Co., 1954.

Strack, Jay. *Drugs and Drinking*. Nashville, Tenn.: Sceptre Books, 1979.

Stone, Nanette; Fromme, Marlene; and Kegan, Daniel. *Cocaine,* New York: Crown, 1984.

Storti, Ed, and Keller, Janet, *Crisis Intervention: Acting Against Addiction:* New York: Crown, 1988.

Stwertka, Eve, and Stwertka, Albert. *Marijuana*. New York: Franklin Watts, Inc., 1979.

Sumach, Alexander. *Growing Your Own Stone*. Toronto: Yellow Ford Truck, 1973.

Summers, Marcia, et al. *Our Chemical Culture: Drug Use and Misuse*. Nashville, Tenn.: Nelson Thomas Inc., 1981.

Szasz, Thomas. *Ceremonial Chemistry: The Ritual Persecution of Drugs, Addicts, and Pushers.* Garden City, N.Y.: Anchor Press, 1974.

Talland, George A. *Deranged Memory*. New York: Academic Press, 1965.

———. and Waugh, N.C., eds. *The Pathology of Memory*. New York, Academic Press, 1969

Task Force Report. *Narcotics, Marijuana and Dangerous Drugs: Findings and Recommendations*. The President's Commission on Law Enforcement and Administration of Justice. Washington, D.C.: Government Printing Office, 1967.

Taylor, Norman. *Narcotics, Nature's Dangerous Gifts*. New York: Dell Publishing Company, 1966.

Tec, Nechame. *The Grass Is Green in Suburbia: A Sociological Study of Adolescent Usage of Illicit Drugs*. New York: Libra Books, 1974.

Tenin, Peter. *Taking Your Medicine: Drug Regulation in the United States*. Cambridge, Mass.: Harvard University Press, 1980.

Tessler, Diane Jane. *Drugs, Kids, and Schools: Practical Strategies for Educators and Other Concerned Adults*. Rockville, Md.: National Institute on Drug Abuse, 1980.

The Mayor's Committee on Marihuana. *The Marihuana Problem in the City of New York.* New York: The Ronald Press Company, 1972.

The National Narcotics Intelligence Consumers Committee. *The Supply of Drugs to the U.S. Illicit Market From Foreign and Domestic Sources in 1980 (With Projections Through 1984)*. Washington, D.C.: Drug Enforcement Administration, 1982.

Thompson, J. *Alcohol and Drug Research in Saskatchewan, 1970–78: Subject, Index and Abstracts*. Regina: Saskatchewan Alcoholism Commission, 1978.

Tinklenberg, J. R. *Marihuana and Health Hazards*. New York: Academic Press, 1975.

Tolstoy, Leo. *Why Do Men Stupify Themselves?* Blauvelt, N.Y.: Multimedia Publishing Corp., 1978.

Towery, O. B.; Seidenberg, G. R.; and Santoro, V. *Quality Assurance for Alcohol, Drug Abuse, and Mental Health Services: An Annotated Bibliography*. Rockville, Md.: U.S. Alcohol, Drug Abuse, and Mental Health Administration, 1979.

Towns, Charles B. *Habits That Handicap: The Menace of Opium, Alcohol and Tobacco, and the Remedy*. Reprint of 1915 edition. New York: Arno Press, 1981.

Treadway, David C. *Before It's Too Late: Working with Substance Abuse in the Family.* New York: W. W. Norton, 1989.

Trebach, Arnold. *The Great Drug War*. New York: Macmillan, 1987.

Trice, Harrison M. *Alcoholism in America.* New York: McGraw-Hill, 1966.

———. *Alcoholism in Industry—Modern Procedures.* New York: Christopher D. Smithers Foundation, 1962.

Truax, Lyle H. *Judge's Guide for Alcohol Offenders.* New York: National Council on Alcoholism, 1972.

Tuell, Jim. *The Drug Scene.* Dallas: Tane Press, 1972.

Turner, W. W., ed. *Drugs and Poisons.* Rochester, N.Y.: Aqueduct Books, 1965.

U.S. Department of Health and Human Services. *Research Issues Series:* 1. *Drugs and Employment;* 2. *Drugs and Sex;* 3. *Drugs and Attitude Change;* 4. *Drugs and Family; Peer Influence;* 5. *Drugs and Pregnancy;* 6. *Drugs and Death;* 7. *Drugs and Addict Lifestyles;* 8. *A Cocaine Bibliography;* 9. *Drug Themes in Science Fiction;* 10. *Drug Themes in Fiction;* 11. *Predicting Adolescent Drug Abuse;* 12. *Drug Abuse Instrument Handbook;* 13. *Data Analysis Strategies and Designs for Substance Abuse Research;* 14. *Drugs and Personality;* 15. *Cocaine—Summaries of Psychosocial Research;* 16. *The Lifestyles of Nine American Cocaine Users—Summary;* 17. *Drugs and Crime;* 18. *Drugs Users and the Criminal Justice System;* 19. *Drugs and Psychopathology;* 20. *Drug Users and Driving Behaviors;* 21. *Drugs and Minorities;* 22. *Research Issues Update, 1978;* 23. *International Drug Use;* 24. *Perspectives on the History of Psychoactive Substance Use;* 25. *Use and Abuse of Amphetamine and its Substitutes;* 26. *Guide to Drug Abuse Research Terminology;* 27. *Guide to the Drug Research Literature;* 28. *Assessing Marijuana Consequences: Selected Questionnaire Items;* 29. *Drugs and the Family. Washington, D.C.: Government Printing Office.*

U.S. Department of Justice, Drug Enforcement Administration. *Drugs of Abuse.* Washington, D.C.: Government Printing Office, 1988.

Uhr, L., ed. *Drugs and Behavior.* New York: Wiley, 1960.

Usdin, Earl, and Efron, Daniel H. *Psychotropic Drugs and Related Compounds.* Rockville, Md.: Department of Health, Education and Welfare, 1972.

Vischi, T. R., et al. *The Alcohol, Drug Abuse, and Mental Health National Date Book.* Washington, D.C.: U.S. Alcohol, Drug Abuse and Mental Health Administration, 1980.

Vuylsteek, K. *Health Education: Smoking, Alcoholism, Drugs.* Albany: World Health Organization Publications Centre, 1979.

Waddell, Jack O., and Everett, Michael W. *Drinking Behavior among Southwestern Indians: An Anthropological Perspective.* Tucson: University of Arizona Press, 1980.

———. and Watson, O. Michael. *The American Indian in Urban Society.* Boston: Little, Brown and Company, 1971.

Wakefield, D. *The Addict.* New York: Fawcett Books, 1969.

Walker, Lenore E. *The Battered Woman.* New York: Harper and Row, 1979.

Wallace, Bill C. *Education and the Drug Scene.* Lincoln, Neb.: Cliff's Notes, 1974.

Walton, R. P. *Marihuana: America's New Drug Problem.* Philadelphia: J. B. Lippincott Co., 1938.

Washton, Arnold M. *Cocaine Addiction: Treatment, Recovery and Relapse Prevention.* New York: W. W. Norton, 1989.

Wasson, R. G. *Soma: Divine Mushroom of Immortality.* New York: Harcourt, Brace, Jovanovich, 1971.

Way, Walter L. *The Drug Scene: Help or Hang-Up?* Englewood Cliffs, N.J.: Prentice-Hall, 1970.

Weil, A. *The Natural Mind.* Boston: Houghton Mifflin, 1972.

Weil, R. G., ed. *The Psychedelic Reader.* New York: University Books, 1965.

Weinswig, Melvin H. *Use and Misuse of Drugs Subject to Abuse.* Indianapolis: Pegasus Books, 1973.

Weiss, Kenneth L., and Kurland, David J. *Drug Laws and the Rights that Protect You.* New York: Simon and Schuster, 1979.

Weiss, Roger D., M.D., and Mirin, Steven M., M.D. *Cocaine: The Human Danger, The Social Costs, The Treatment Alternatives.* N.p., 1987.

Weissman, James C. *Drug Abuse: The Law and Treatment Alternatives.* Cincinnati, Ohio: Anderson Publishing Co., 1978.

———. and DuPont, Robert L., eds. *Criminal Justice and Drugs: The Unresolved Connection.* Port Washington, N.Y.; Kennikat Press, Corp., 1981.

Wesson, D. R., and Smith, D. E. *Barbiturates: Their Use, Misuse and Abuse.* Washington, D.C.: Government Printing Office, 1977.

———. and Adams, Kenneth, eds. *Polydrug Abuse: The Results of a National Collaborative Study.* New York: Academic Press, 1978.

Westermeyer, Joseph. *A Primer on Chemical Dependency.* Baltimore, Md.: Williams and Wilkins Publishers, 1978.

Westman, Wesley. *Drug Epidemic: What It Means and How to Combat It.* New York: Dial Press, 1970.

Whitlock, F. *Drugs, Morality, and the Law.* St. Lawrence, Mass.: University of Queensland Press, 1975.

Wicks, Robert J., and Platt, Jerome J. *Drug Abuse: A Criminal Justice Primer.* Beverly Hills, Calif.: Glencoe Press, 1977.

Wigder, H. Neil. *Wigder's Guide to Over-the-Counter Drugs.* Burlington, Mass.: J. P. Tarcher, 1979.

Wikler, Abraham. *Opioid Dependence—Mechanisms and Treatment.* New York: Plenum Publishing Corp., 1980.

Wilkerson, Don. *Marijuana.* Old Tappan, N.J.: Fleming H. Revell Co., 1980.

Williams, Henry S. *Drugs Against Men.* Reprint of 1935 edition. New York: Arno Press, 1981.

Williams, Melvin H. *Drugs and Athletics.* Springfield, Ill.: Charles C. Thomas, 1974.

Wilner, D. M., and Kassebaum, G. G. *Narcotics.* McGraw-Hill, 1965.

Wilson, Morrow, and Wilson, Suzanne. *Drugs in American Life.* Bronx, N.Y.: H. W. Wilson. 1975.

Windholz, Martha, ed. *The Merck Index.* Ninth edition. Rahway, N.J.: Merck Sharp and Dohme Research Laboratories, 1976.

Winek, Charles. *Everything You Wanted to Know About Drug Abuse But Were Afraid to Ask.* New York: Marcel Dekker Inc., 1974.

Winick, C., and Kinsie, P. *The Lively Commerce: Prostitution in the United States.* Chicago: Quadrangle Books, 1971.

Wisotsky, S. *Breaking the Impasse in the War on Drugs.* Westport, Conn.: Greenwood Press, 1986.

Wittenborn, J. R., ed. *Drugs and Youth.* Springfield, Ill.: Charles C. Thomas, 1969.

———. et al. *Communication and Drug Abuse: Proceedings of the Second Rutgers Symposium on Drug Abuse.* Springfield, Ill.: Charles C. Thomas, 1970.

Witters, Weldon L., and Jones-Witters, Patricia. *Drugs and Sex.* New York: Macmillan, 1974.

Wolfe, T. *The Electric Kool-Aid Acid Test.* New York: Farrar, Straus & Giroux, 1968.

Wolstenholme, G. E. W., and Knight, J., eds. *Hashish: Its Chemistry and Pharmacology.* Boston: Little, Brown and Company, 1965.

Woodley, R. *Dealer: Portrait of a Cocaine Merchant.* New York: Holt, Rinehart, and Winston, 1971.

Worick, W., and Schaller, W. *Alcohol, Tobacco and Drugs: Their Use and Abuse.* Englewood Cliffs, N.J.: Prentice-Hall, 1977.

World Health Organization Study Group. *Youth and Drugs Report.* Geneva, 1971.

World Health Organization. *Alcohol-Related Disabilities.* Geneva, 1977.

———. *Expert Committee on Mental Health, Alcoholism Subcommittee, Second Report.* World Health Organization Technical Report Series, no. 48. Geneva, 1952.

———. *Public Health Aspects of Alcohol and Drug Dependence: Report of a WHO Conference, Dubrovnik, 21–25 August 1978.* Copenhagen: WHO Regional Office for Europe, 1979.

Wrenn, C. Gilbert. *Facts and Fantasies about Drugs.* Circle Pines, Minn.: American Guidance Service, 1970.

Wurmser, Leon. *Drug Abuse: Hidden Dimension.* New York: Jason Aronson, Inc., 1978.

Yablonsky, L. *The Tunnel Back: Synanon.* New York; Macmillan, 1965.

Young, J. *The Drugtakers: The Social Meaning of Drug Use.* London: Paladin Press, 1971.

Young, James H. *American Self-Dosage Medicines: An Historical Perspective.* Lawrence, Kan.: Coronado Press, 1974.

———. *The Toadstool Millionaires.* Princeton: Princeton University Press, 1961.

Young, Lawrence A., et al. *Recreational Drugs.* New York: Macmillan, 1977.

Young, Warren R., and Hixon, Joseph R., eds. *LSD on Campus.* New York: Dell Publishing Co., Inc., 1966.

Zador, P. *Statistical Evaluation of the Effectiveness of Alcohol Safety Action Programs.* Washington, D.C.: Insurance Institute for Highway Safety, 1974.

Zeese, K. B., and Meyers, P. H. *Ronald Reagan Wars on Drugs,* Washington, D.C.: National Organization for the Reform of Marijuana Laws, 1983.

Zimmerman, S. "A Windfall in Recovered Assets," *Drug Enforcement,* 11:31–33, 1984.

Zinberg, N. E. *Drug, Set, and Setting: The Basis for Controlled Intoxicant Use.* New Haven: Yale University Press, 1984.

Zinberg, N. E., and Robertson, J. A. *Drugs and the Public.* New York: Simon and Schuster, 1972.

INDEX

Boldface type indicates main headings

A

D

E

F

G

H

I

J

K

N

Q

R

S

T

U

V

W

X

Y

Z